JESSICA STOCKHOLDER

LYNNE TILLMAN
BARRY SCHWABSKY
LYNNE COOKE
GERMANO CELANT

Φ

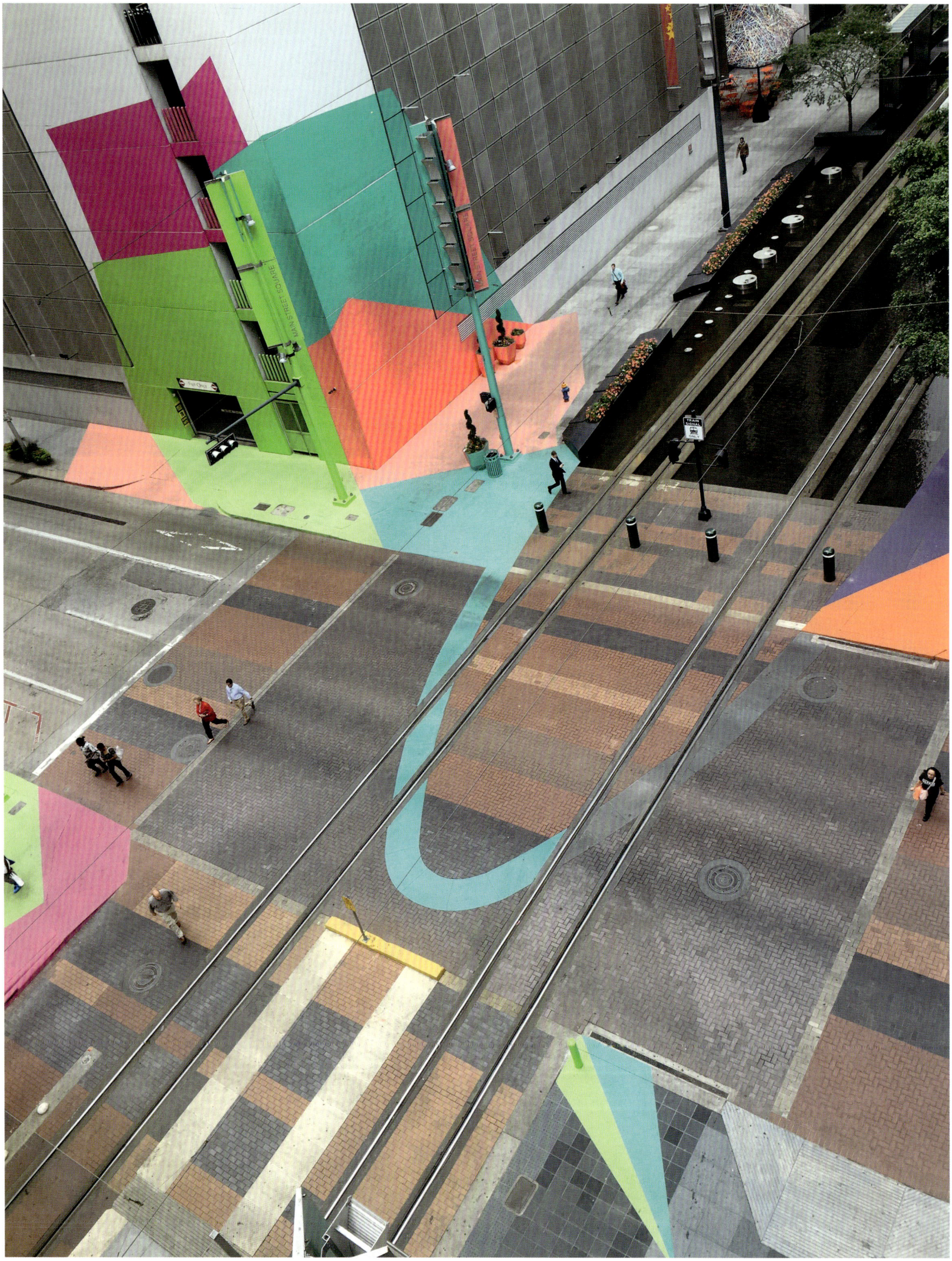
MAIN STREET SQUARE

COLOR JAM HOUSTON, 2012–16
ADHESIVE VINYL, VINYL SCRIM

INSTALLATION VIEW AT THE THE INTERSECTION OF McKINNEY AND MAIN STREETS, HOUSTON, 2016

CONTENTS

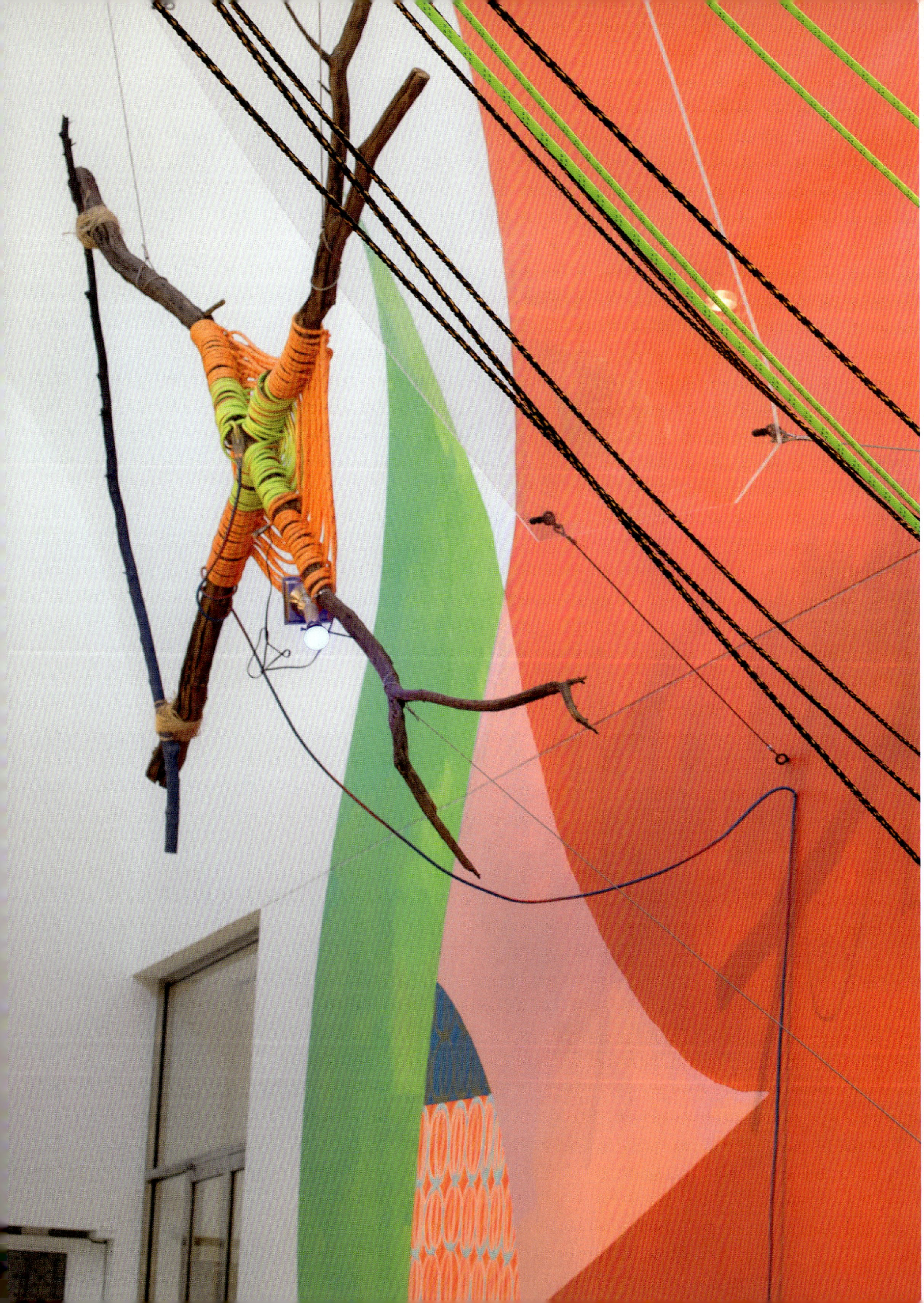

007 INTERVIEW

Lynne Tillman in conversation with Jessica Stockholder

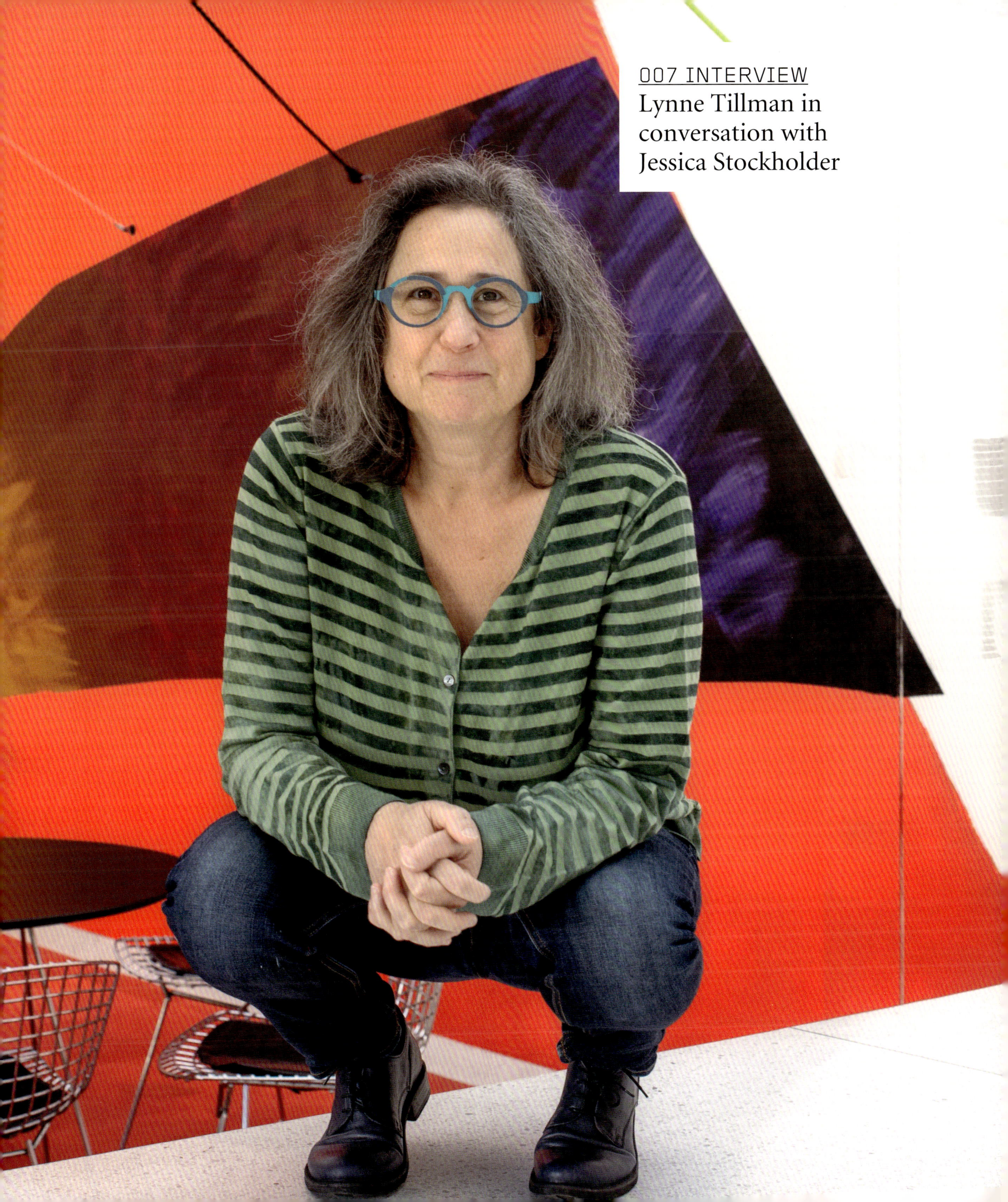

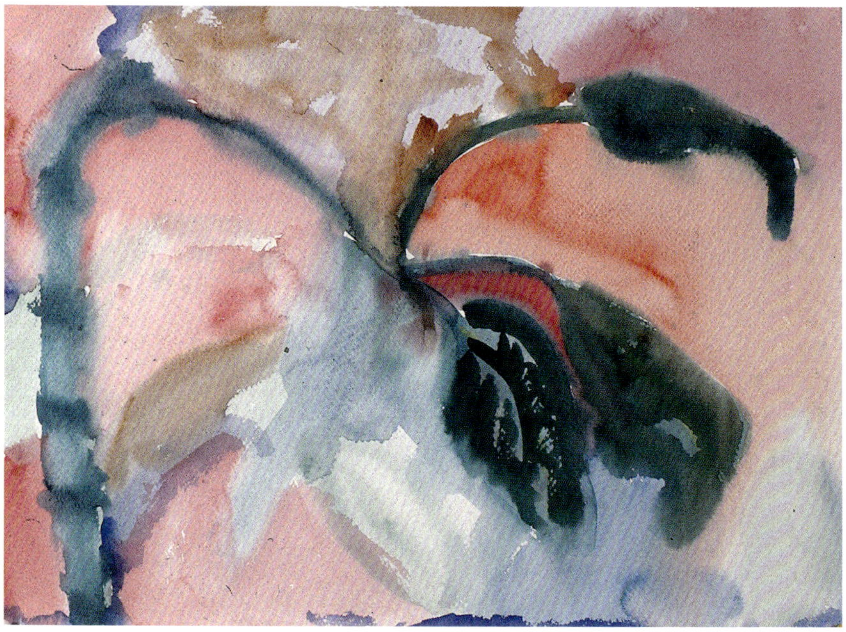

left,
1978
WATERCOLOUR ON PAPER
APPROX 56 X 33 CM

below,
1980
ACRYLIC ON CANVAS
APPROX 36 X 66 CM

previous pages,
JESSICA STOCKHOLDER,
CHICAGO, 2017

next page,
1978
ACRYLIC ON PAPER
55 X 70 CM

1979
ACRYLIC ON CANVAS
80 X 140 CM

JESSICA STOCKHOLDER: I started painting on un-stretched canvas.

LYNNE TILLMAN: *Did you paint when you were a kid?.*

STOCKHOLDER: Yes. I remember getting into a mood where I just wanted to make something. It was always a frustrating experience. I felt that I lacked facility, that I was inept.

TILLMAN: *How did you know what to measure against?*

STOCKHOLDER: My mother painted. For a while. I painted next to her. I remember making one painting that was a sort of stage with figures on it. It was an orange and black painting.

TILLMAN: *You still make stages – platforms, ramps.*

STOCKHOLDER: In a journal I have from when I was a kid, I have a dream written down about yellow newspaper. I've used a lot of yellow newspaper in my work. This is un-stretched canvas, with little bits of pieces of stuff stuck on it. Actually it's cloth, not canvas. There are different pieces of cloth stuck together, painted, then there are bits of acrylic paint – this was in 1980.

TILLMAN: *Do you have a name for it?*

STOCKHOLDER: I didn't title pieces until much later … These are made with pieces of cloth and stuff stuck together.

TILLMAN: *Did you go to art school?*

STOCKHOLDER: No, I went to university. Earlier I studied with Mowry Baden, who's a sculptor. This is a very early one – a watercolour of me.

TILLMAN: *Looks more like a wolf man or a farmer –*

STOCKHOLDER: Overalls were in style then. Here's one I like very much.

TILLMAN: *That's beautiful. Like a Matisse.*

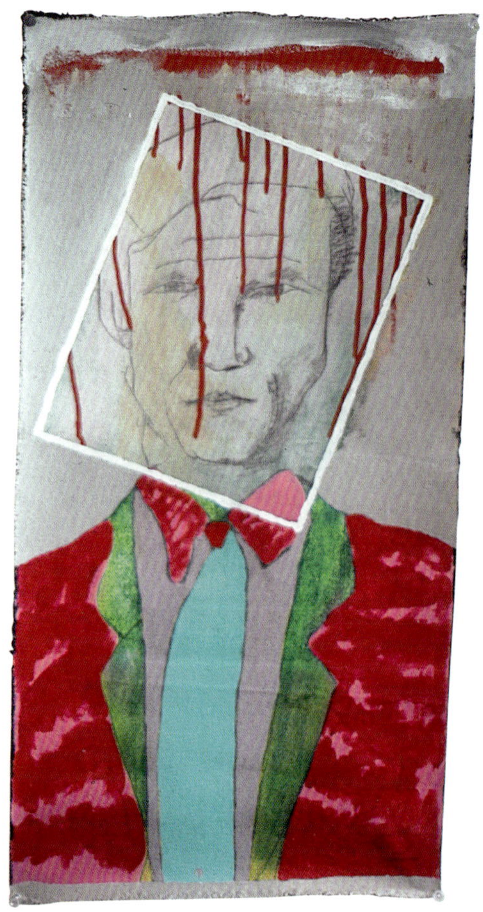

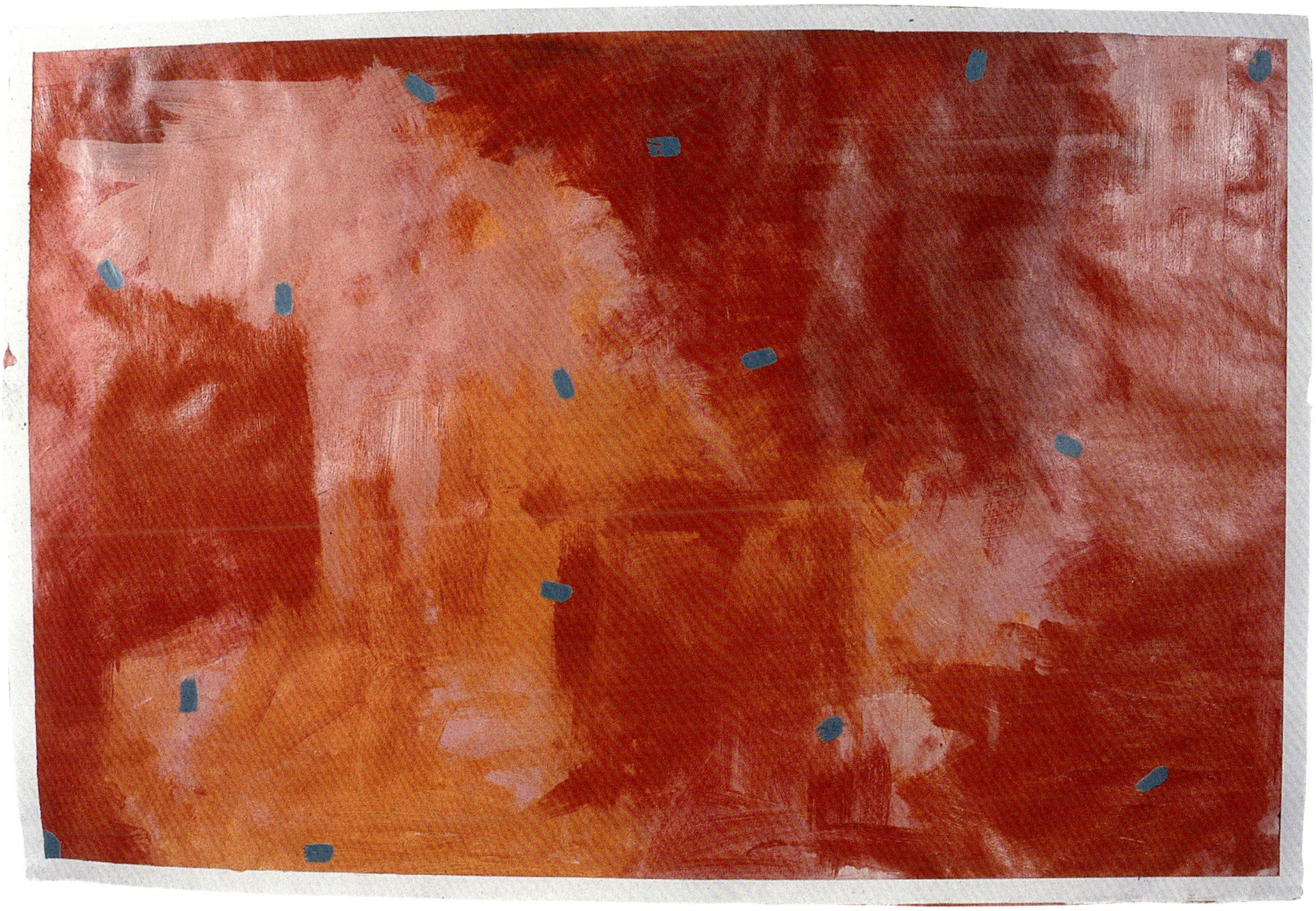

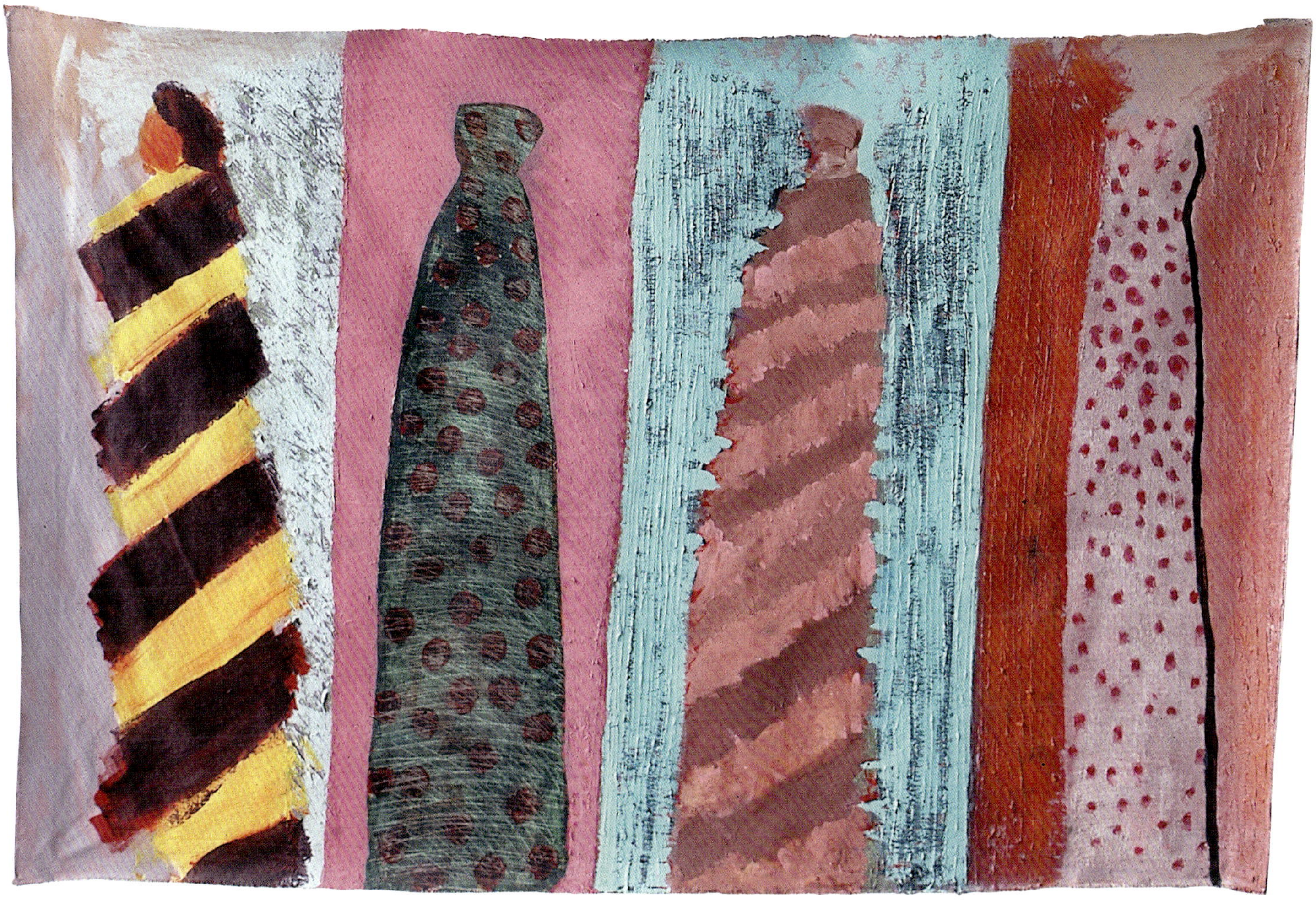

STOCKHOLDER: He's one of my favourite painters ... These are all close to square or rectangular painting.

TILLMAN: *Was this while you were studying with Baden?*

STOCKHOLDER: Yes. He's a friend of my father's. When I was fourteen, I had private lessons. He taught me to draw – line drawings of objects that became quite abstract. He taught me to appreciate the surprise of making something unexpected. He would talk about the drawing in terms of how it addressed the page. It wasn't about representing the thing that was on the table.

TILLMAN: *Most artists, writers too, recapitulate a number of different styles. It's about working with a language. You have to figure out what's already there, then see what you can do with it.*

STOCKHOLDER: Here's my Larry Poons. And this is one of the first paintings where I started to break up the pieces, so that there'd be space between the things on the wall.

TILLMAN: *How did that come to you: to begin using cloth and ...*

STOCKHOLDER: Mowry spoke about the un-stretched pieces not having integrity as objects.

TILLMAN: *Why was that?*

STOCKHOLDER: The cloth hanging on the wall was flimsy. He talked about the easel painting as a small replica of the wall it hangs on. He pointed to architecture giving meaning to the historical structure of painting. This way of thinking made a lot of sense to me. I later found similar ideas discussed by Brian O'Doherty in *The White Cube*. Though his view of painting's history is more cynical.

An un-stretched canvas hanging on the wall doesn't provide a place to take off from the material and forget it's there.

TILLMAN: *Is it a neither here nor there state?*

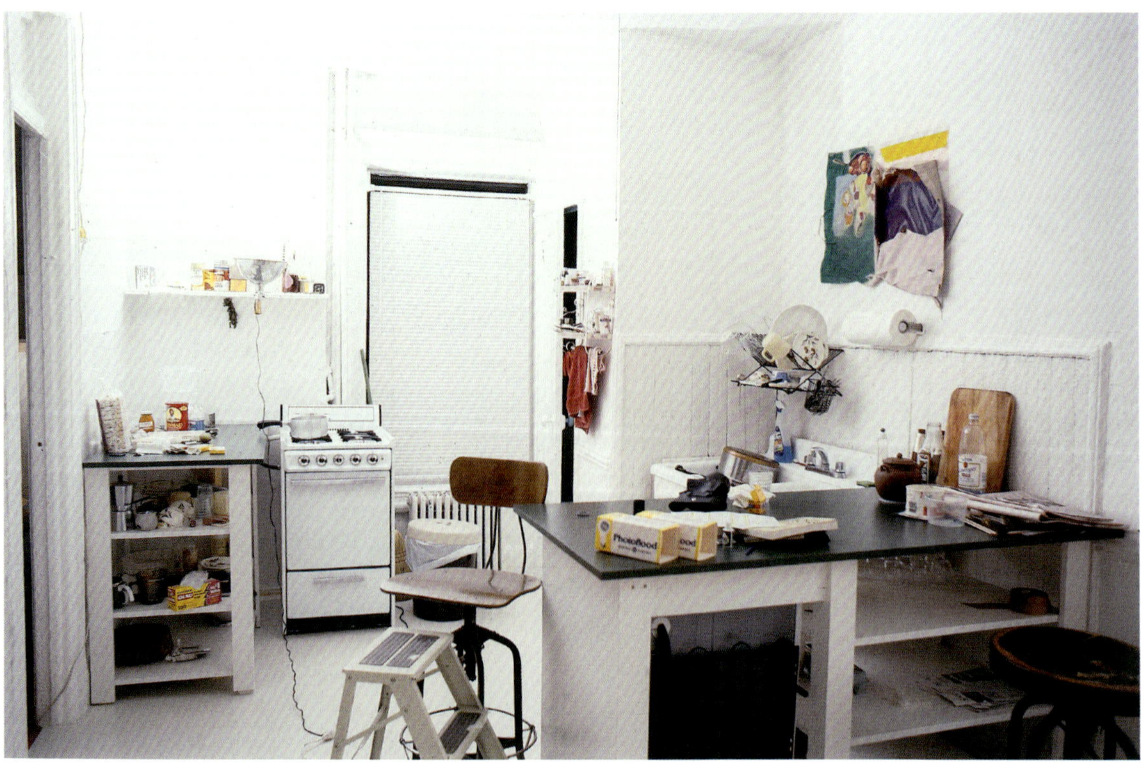

THE ARTIST'S STUDIO, NEW YORK, 1986

1986
PAPER, PINK CANVAS
HANDBAG, MAGAZINE
COLLAGED IMAGE, PAPER
MACHE, ACRYLIC PAINT, OIL
PAINT, OIL PASTEL
APPROX 51 X 71 CM

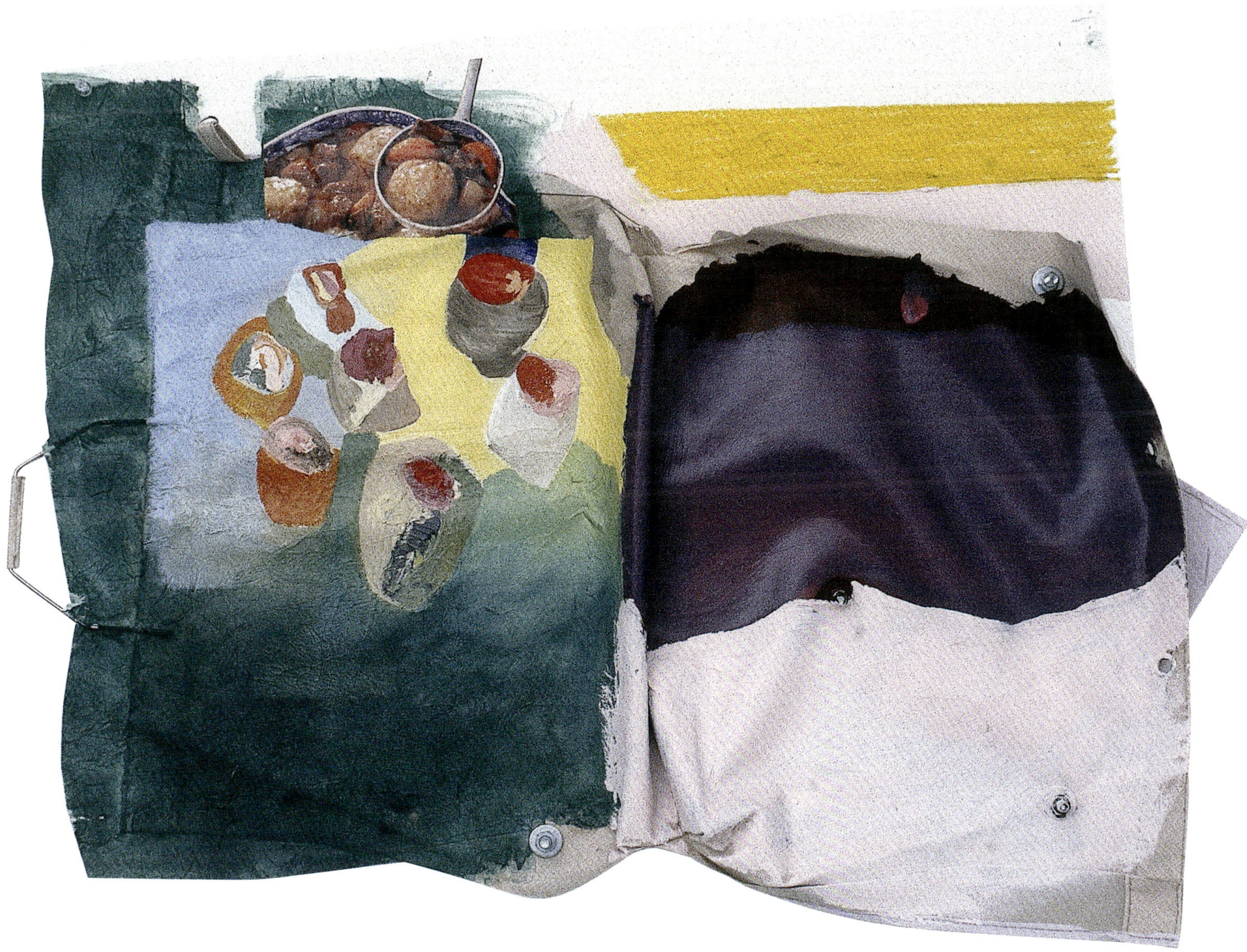

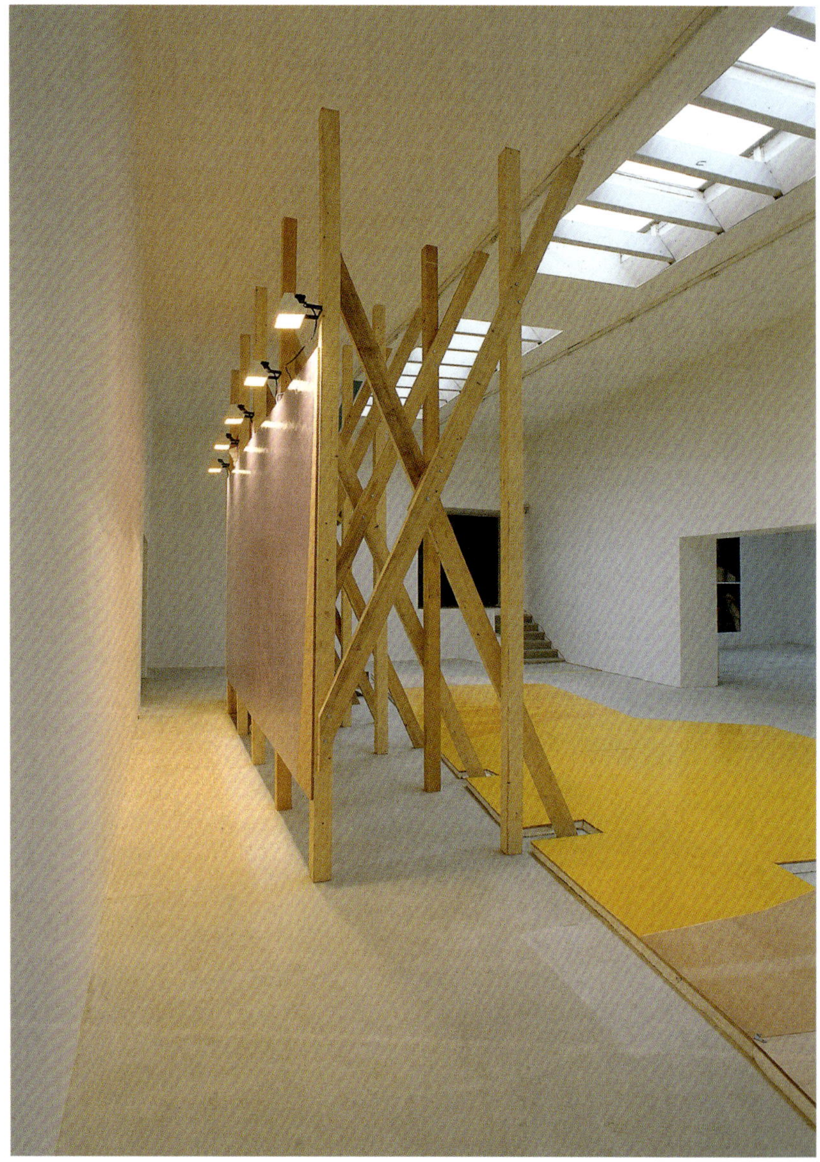

STOCKHOLDER: For me painting is wonderful because it provides a place to forget the material, even while your attention is drawn to it.

TILLMAN: *How do you mean? – forget the material –*

STOCKHOLDER: I use material as a place to make fiction, fantasy and illusion. When this happens, attention is drawn to something abstract and separate from the material – the physical paint and canvas.

TILLMAN: *Do you use a material in order to forget it?*

STOCKHOLDER: I like there to be places where the material is forgotten; but I also love to force a meeting of abstraction with material or stuff. Colour is very good at this, always very ready to assert itself as independent of material.

TILLMAN: *Particularly when its use is idiosyncratic. In* Recording Forever Pickled *(1990), in front of a kind of skeletal wall, a wooden structure, there's a wrapped armchair. What seems a coffee table is in front of the chair, but it's made of concrete. I think about the impossible living room. The space one can't talk in. The spaces or things one can't talk about. I think that piece is, again, a kind of stage, with an element of the absurd in it. And the yellow on the floor could be any other colour. One's attention is called to the yellow just as a colour. It's bright, challenging, odd.*

STOCKHOLDER: It couldn't be any other colour, because the colours are keyed to each other. There's plywood holding the crosses or Xs up. The back is painted violet, and this violet reflects onto the wall. Then the red –

TILLMAN: *The wall seems to disappear. I can't tell if there's space behind.*

STOCKHOLDER: I often use white to do that, because visually white sinks back into the wall of the gallery. When the viewer moves around to the edge of this piece, the reflected purple or violet between the wall I made and the wall of the gallery is seen as a volume of colour. The violet complements the yellow-orange on the floor. The colours are keyed to carry the eye around; they read across space. In this way the colour is very specific.

TILLMAN: *You could have set up a different set of colour combinations. But you call attention to colour by what seems to be an arbitrariness in the decision, since it's not linked to a 'natural' concern.*

STOCKHOLDER: That's right. The colour is not descriptive of something else in the world.

this and previous page,
RECORDING FOREVER PICKLED, 1990
WOOD, STYROFOAM, PAINT, HALOGEN LIGHTS, ELECTRIC CORD, CONCRETE MEBEDDED WITH PLASTIC RESIN-COATED COOKIES AND A RED BALL ON WHEELS, ONE COUCH, ONE METAL FRAMED CHAIR, ABOUT 12-CLEAR PLASTIC GARBAGE BAGS FILLED WITH LEAVES, STICKS AND TWIGS; TWO BLACK GARBAGE BAGS FILLED WITH THE SAME YELLOW GREEN DUCT TAPE
400 X 580 CM

INSTALLATION VIEW AT LE CONSORTIUM, DIJON, FRANCE, 1990

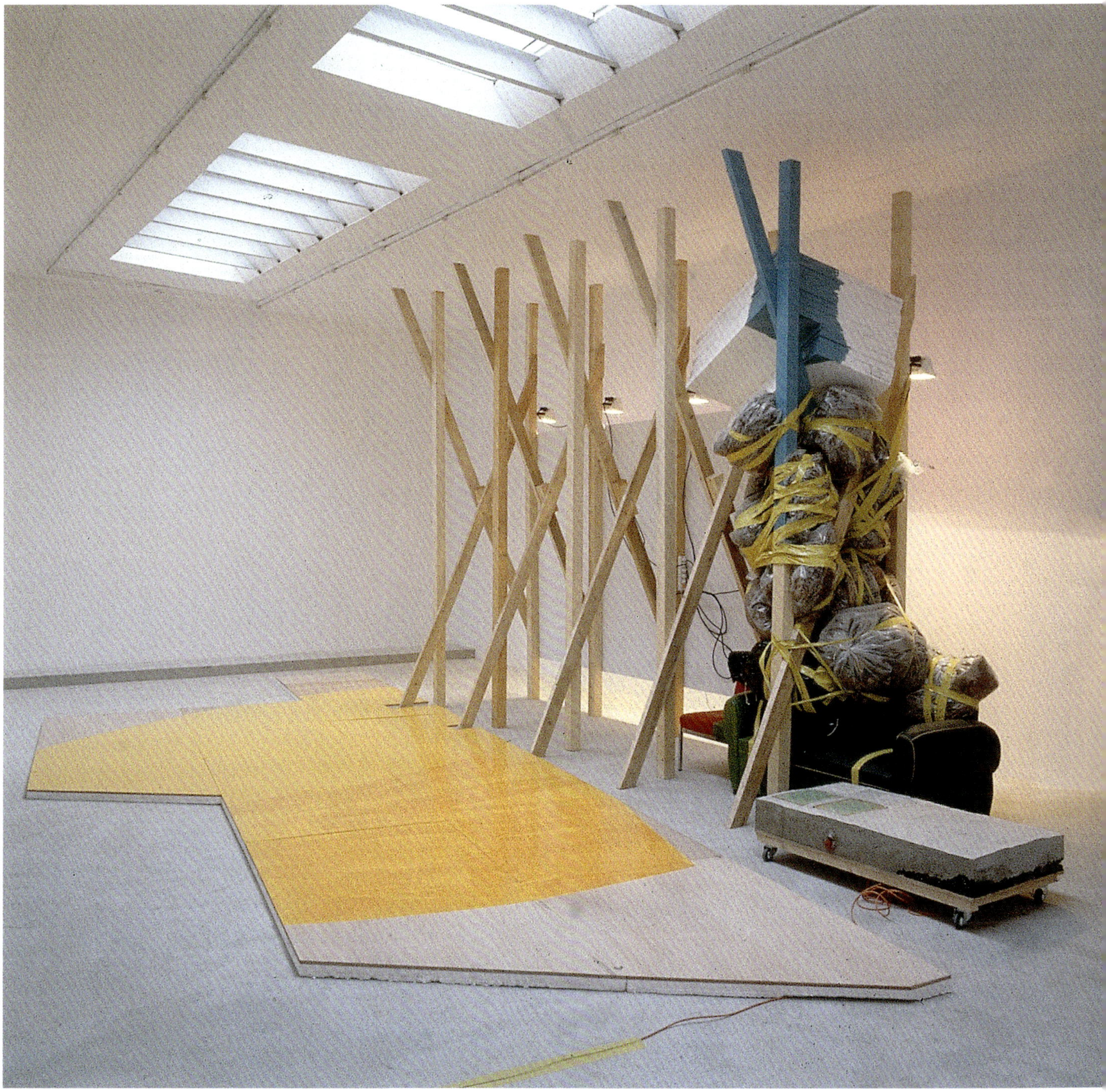

RAWHIDE HARANGUE OF ACHING INDICES AS TOLD BY LIGHT, 2005
PLASTIC BINS, CERAMIC VESSELS, LAMPS, RED BULBS, CARPETS, ACRYLIC PAINT, DROPPED CEILING, FLUORESCENT FIXTURES AND BULBS, ALUMINUM FOIL

INSTALLATION VIEW AT THE MUSEUM OF FINE ARTS, BOSTON, 2005

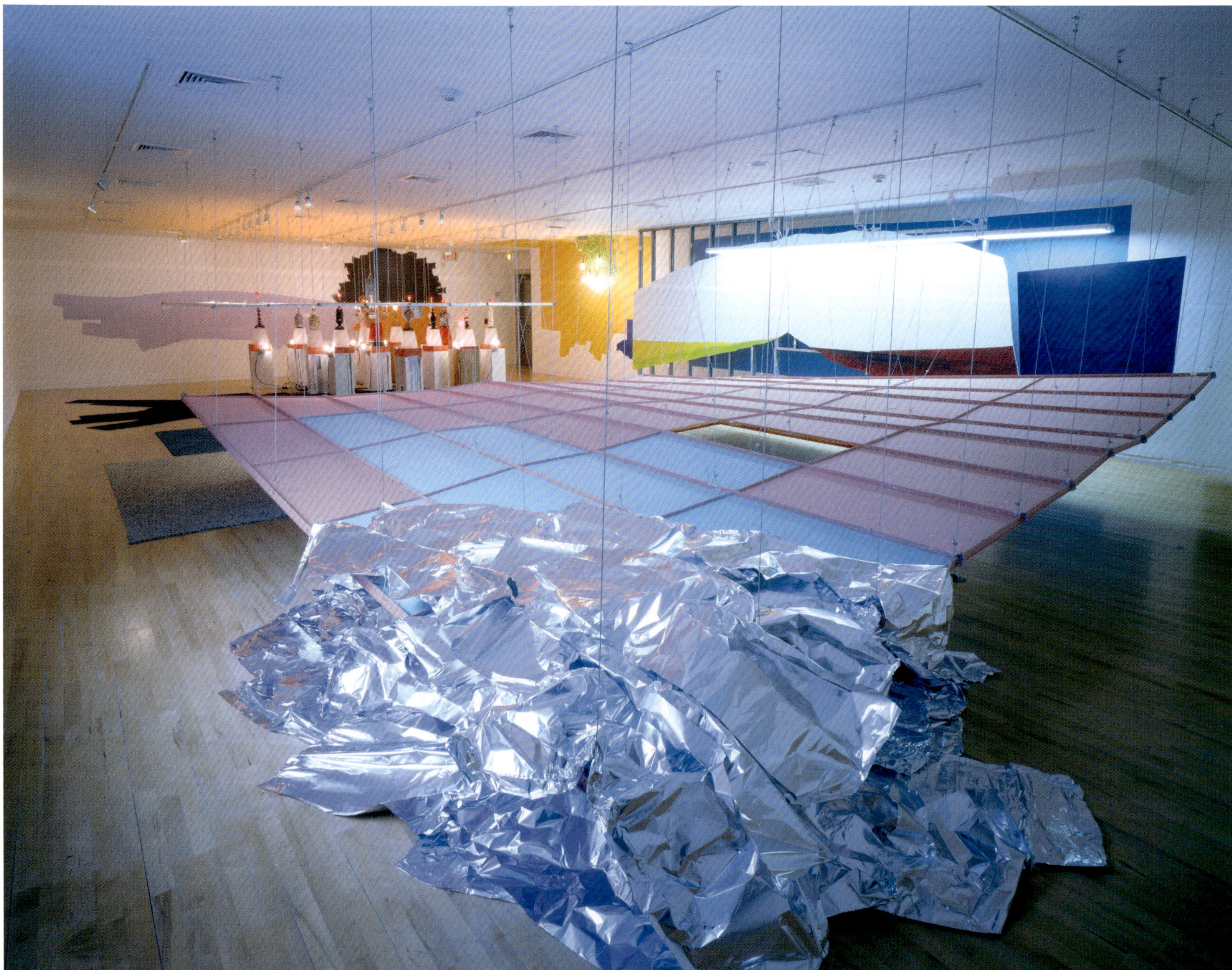

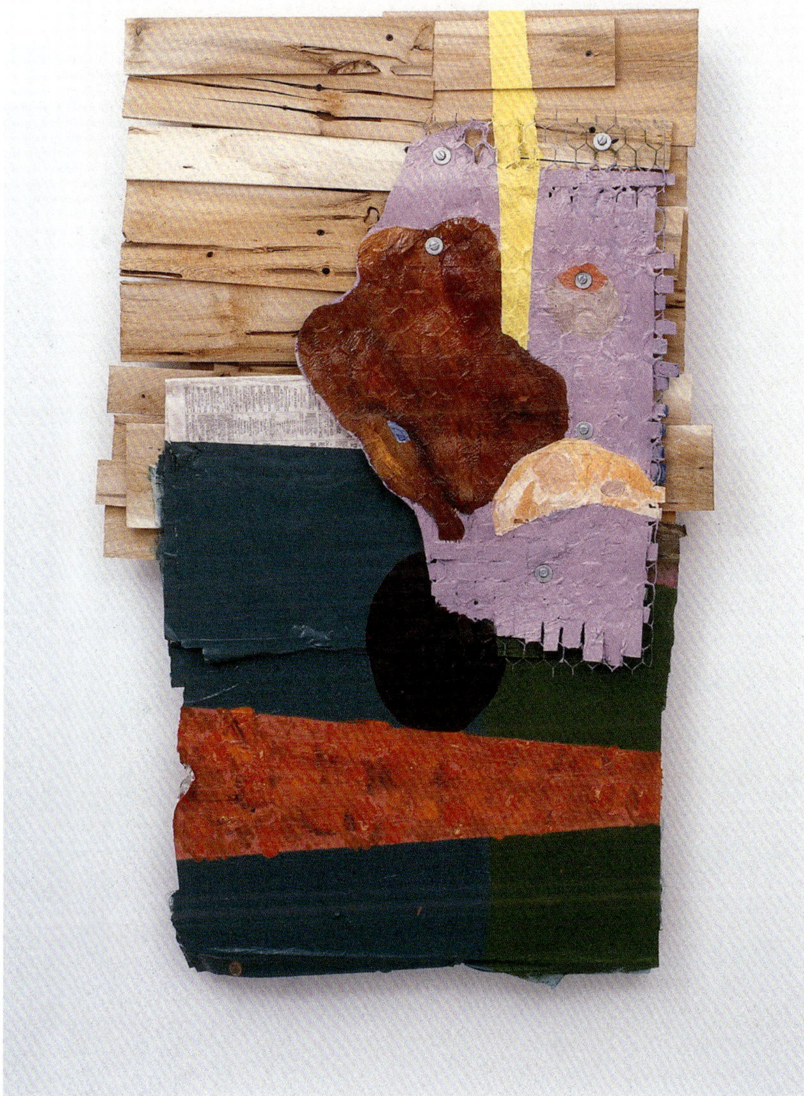

1986
WOODEN ROOF SHINGLES, CHICKEN WIRE, PAPER, NEWSPAPER, ACRYLIC PAINT, AND HARDWARE
APPROX 81 X 41 CM

TILLMAN: *It has its own life as colour. You use it idiosyncratically, calling attention to it, which is painterly …*

STOCKHOLDER: I weave the fiction that the colour makes together with what the objects are and suggest, along with a structure that I make.

TILLMAN: *You moved from painting on paper, to un-stretched canvas, then to bits of cloth, things stuck on cloth, to something that begins to fill a whole space.*

STOCKHOLDER: I can show and tell you how that happened. In this work, I found painted boards and stuck them to the wall. The little pink wiry thing comes out from the wall onto the floor, and a piece on the edge goes up through the ceiling. So, though this piece is still very rectangular and framed by the wall, it poked out a little bit, up through the ceiling and onto the floor.

TILLMAN: *When was this?*

STOCKHOLDER: 1980.

TILLMAN: *When you became more interested in the space between things, objects started coming off the wall. You became interested in the space between two objects – and the wall itself. Did you feel that you were involved in a critique of painting and a critique of the institution of the gallery?*

STOCKHOLDER: I don't think I work from a space of critique. My work isn't, in the end, a critique of anything. It's more of an exploration. I work against the kind of polarization that's implied by the word critique. I could critique the institution, and I certainly have feelings of criticism about institutions, but it's undeniable that my work depends on the institution that is art.

TILLMAN: *That's a contradiction that everybody lives with – whatever system one's in. The scientific, academic or literary community. You work within it.*

STOCKHOLDER: I have always felt uncomfortable in museums and galleries. There's a kind of a deadening in those places that I work in response to. I try to bring the work closer instead of having it all framed off and moved from me. Even so, I love what the art institution makes possible; there's a kind of intensity and it's a place where you can express anything, and explore any thing without hurting your neighbour. Art is elevated – presented as special. This makes it possible to pay close attention to very wonderful mundane things.

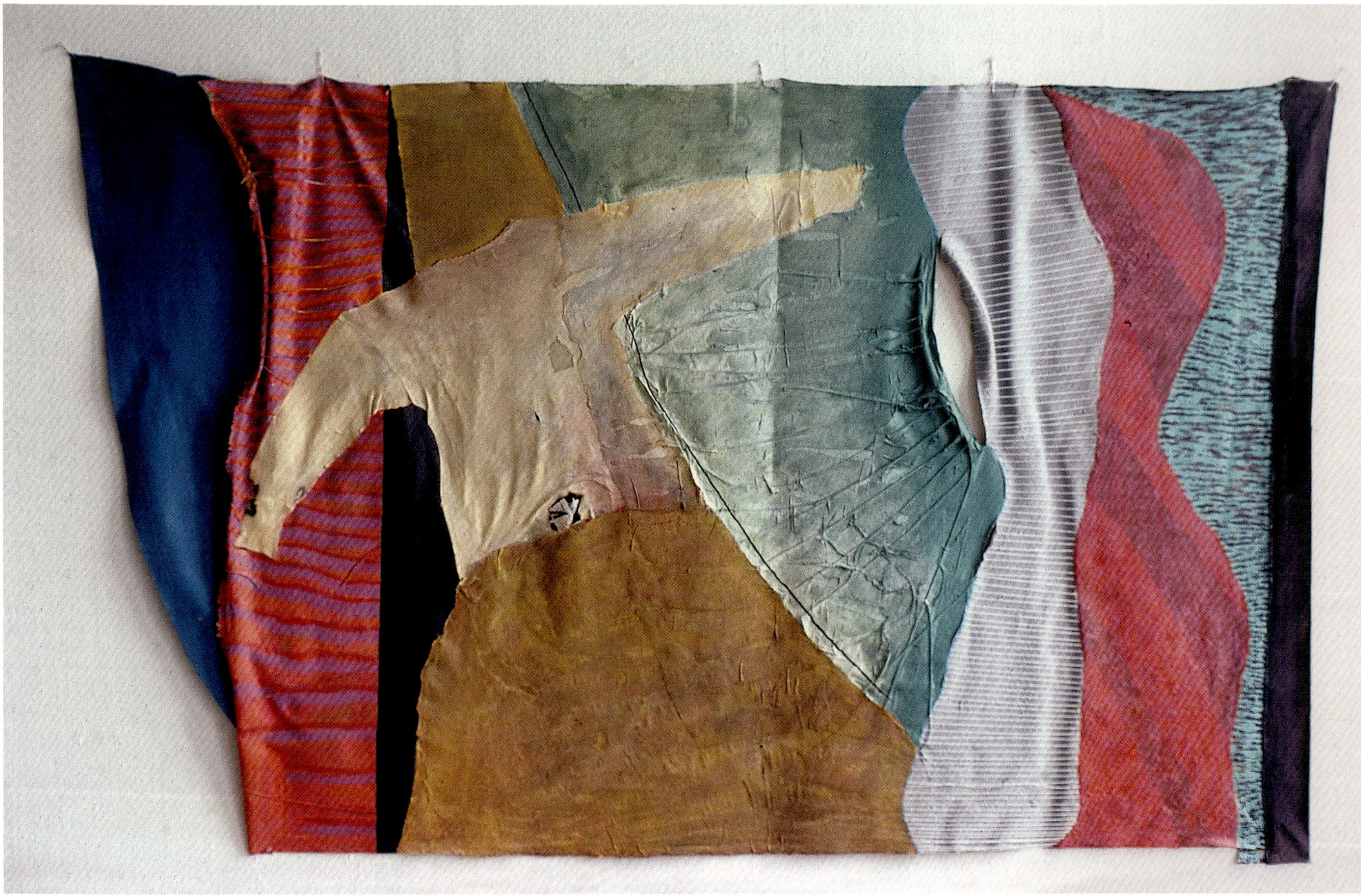

1980
CANVAS, CLOTHING, YARN, PAPER, ACRYLIC PAINT
APPROX 107 X 183 CM

TILLMAN: *Without that distinction, between art and something else –*

STOCKHOLDER: It just runs into brushing your teeth.

TILLMAN: *Warhol confounded that, problematized it. If you make a picture of a soup can, you will think about what's outside the frame of that picture, and maybe you will think differently about that ordinary can. Representing it takes it out of the realm of the so-called ordinary.*

STOCKHOLDER: I try to bring some of that specialness, or heightened quality, from art-making to the ordinary. This work was outside at the University of Victoria. The little pieces of wood are painted and hinged. There's a figurative element too. This piece never was finished; it was just arranged. I was thinking about the colour being thrown around, an idea I'm still interested in. the planes of wood were throwing colour back and forth or reading across to each other. The colours bridge the space at the speed that's much quicker than walking. So the interaction of the colour starts to feel abstract, as though it's not material. And me moving, I'm another kind of material.

TILLMAN: *The way you think about art relates to science, geometry, physics. Speed, light, volume. As a viewer, I'll use my frames of reference. The concrete wall has an object jutting out. It raises – projects – certain questions. My eye might be moving, because of the colour play, but I don't think I would be thinking that. There are different moments in it. It's arresting in terms of your process.*

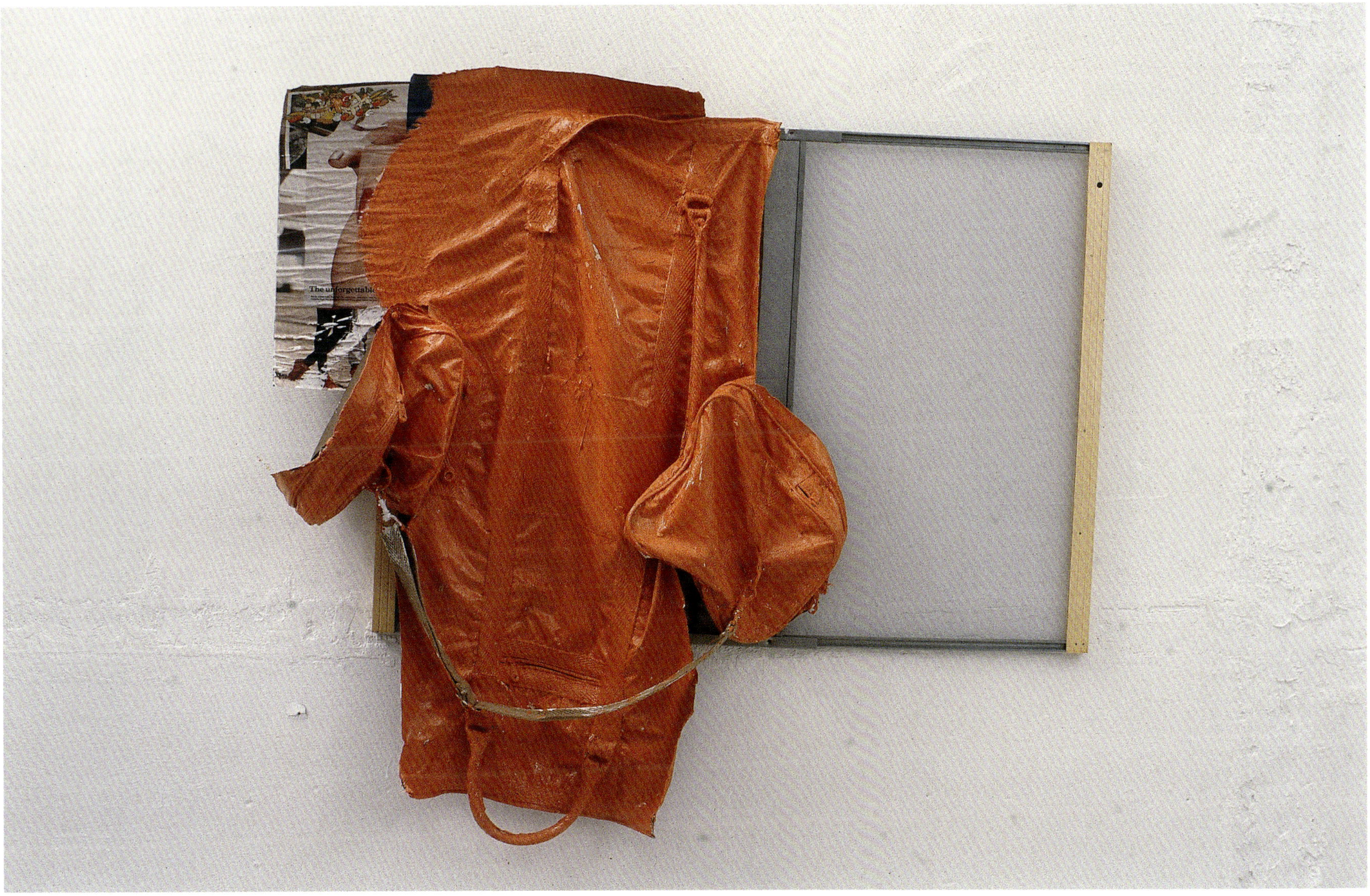

1986
WINDOW SCREEN, CANVAS
LUGGAGE, MAGAZINE IMAGE
COLLAGE, ACRYLIC PAINT
APPROX 76 X 91 CM

STOCKHOLDER: I begin in a very physical place, without a lot of words. When you were speaking about the colour in *Recording Forever Pickled* – how it doesn't refer to anything, that it is its own matter-of-fact thing. I thought, there's a kind of muteness in that. When I'm asked what my plans are for the future I look inside and find a mute feeling. There's a quiet – there are no words for what I'm going to do.

TILLMAN: *In* Recording Forever Pickled, *what would a conversation be in an impossible living room? The spaces are what one can't talk about. Using the yellow you might also be signifying something that can't be spoken about.*

STOCKHOLDER: It's interesting to consider that as a meaning of yellow. Manipulating material is a way to speak.

TILLMAN: *How did you move into installation?*

STOCKHOLDER: Installation is a very poorly defined word. The earlier work started to elbow the space of the wall. It doesn't seem like such a huge jump to dealing with the spaced of the room. In 1982 Barbara Fisher invited me to put drawings in a show at Open Space Gallery in Victoria. I didn't want to put drawings in the show.

TILLMAN: *And then she said: You can have this space to do anything you want?*

STOCKHOLDER: Yes. This was the first time I consciously addressed the space rather than just the wall. I've kept doing it. It certainly doesn't make life easy! And installation has become so prevalent a part of art-making. People don't buy it for their homes, to be cute about it. You set up a challenge for yourself. There's not much of an art market in Canada. As an art student I wasn't thinking about selling work, and I had no place to store it, so I didn't think about keeping it.

TILLMAN: *It's almost impossible for me to imagine – not keeping one's work.*

STOCKHOLDER: I keep the slides. The process is what matters to me – making the work, how one work leads to another, and how showing the work and having people look at it and talk about it feeds it.

TILLMAN: *That fits in with some of the art movements of the 1960s and 1980s which were responding to the object-orientated nature of art.*

STOCKHOLDER: It was in the air. Mowry was very much involved with thinking about how art objects function politically within an economy; this was all part of the discussion around me.

TILLMAN: *A curator says: Here are these walls. Instead you want to use the whole space. To do something that fills that space or speaks about space. Takes it up or shows some sort of relationship to it. That's intriguing not only formally, but also psychologically.*

STOCKHOLDER: It's an attempt to make things immediate.

1981
PLYWOOD, 2X4 WOOD, METAL,
CARPET, OIL PAINT
288 X 460 CM

INSTALLATION VIEW AT THE
UNIVERSITY OF VICTORIA,
BRITISH COLUMBIA, 1981

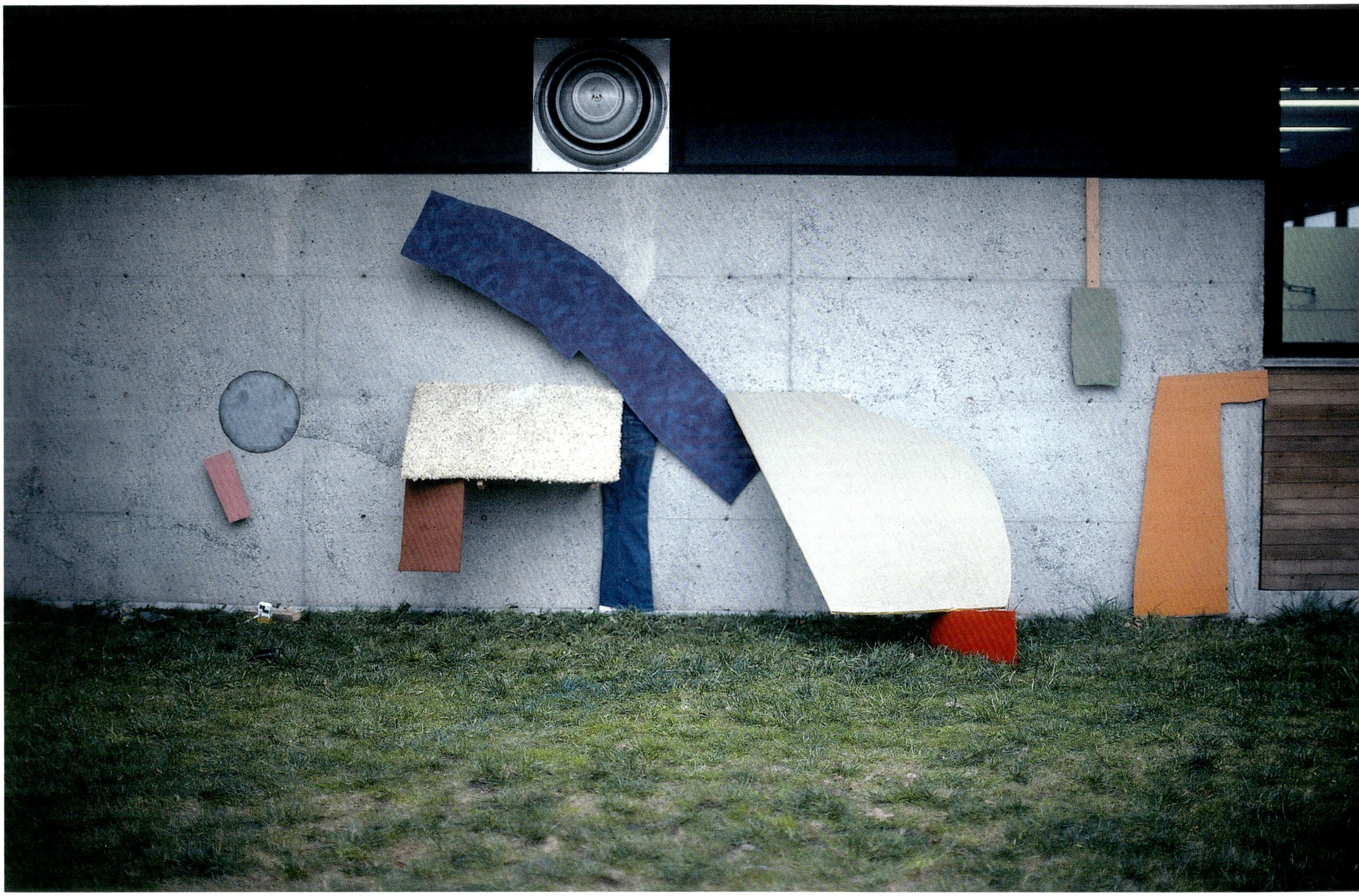

TILLMAN: *I don't know that writing functions in that immediate way. Maybe it does. But the process of reception –*

STOCKHOLDER: The way I read is probably more immediate than you would like!

TILLMAN: *Maybe the way I perceived art is less immediate than you would like. I don't think about tactility, a word that crops up about your work. Some artists want the sense that this could be something you'd want to touch. In some way I guess I don't feel myself in the world physically. Although you push that. In the piece with a ramp,* The Lion, the Witch and the Wardrobe (1985), *I understand it as something goes nowhere.*

STOCKHOLDER: How do you see that?

TILLMAN: *Usually a ramp leads somewhere. Again you take something that has a function and use it in a way that calls attention to it as other than its function – ramps take you from one place to another. Now, it does take me from one part of your art work to another. But it's in such an absurd way that it speaks to me of a certain futility – about going anywhere. I'm a pessimist, but it did confront me, made a physical impression on me. I don't know if that means 'tactility'. I think of it as this object in the room –*

STOCKHOLDER: – calling attention to itself as a thing, yes. That's what I like to do.

TILLMAN: *Your later work pushes that, off the wall. You seven make your own walls. Architecture's 'the art of science of building'. Not one or the other – both. In a sense you can take y our choice. Science and art relate to your work.*

STOCKHOLDER: I once proposed a work for the San Francisco Exploratorium, a science museum with an artist in residence program. I proposed that it was a matter of scientific interest to what degree we brought information with us that coloured our vision when faced with art. They didn't go for it. I began making art without much sense of the physical world and discovered how much it mattered to me through the process of working. It was a part of the world I was able to encounter entirely on my own terms.

TILLMAN: *It's also about making a place for itself, for oneself. In the world. If you enter a space, as you did at Open Space Gallery in 1981, and decide: no, I won't hang on the wall, I'll be this space. It's like making yourself, constructing yourself also.*

STOCKHOLDER: The work has always functioned as a place to affirm my subjectivity. That we have intense subjective response to objects is curious. It can't be denied.

TILLMAN: *The way you treat that subjectivity resorts to, employs, a certain level of abstraction to handle your own psychological needs. I don't feel, when I walk into a room of yours, that I'm dealing with Jessica Stockholder's psyche. I feel that it's all been mediated, thought through, worked through, so that your uses of colour may indeed go back to some psychological meaning to you about colour. But it informs the work and has a resonance within the work that's not specific to you.*

STOCKHOLDER: That makes perfect sense to me. I'm trying to think about why that's so, and why that happens. To turn something that's intensely personal into something that's publicly available.

TILLMAN: *It's one of the fascinations about making art, writing. In my writing I'll use 'I', and it's usually not me. Yet there is the desire to write it, or just to write, which is from oneself. You became engaged in the space between two objects. That wall – maybe the wall was you, between you and the world.*

STOCKHOLDER: When I began I experienced architecture as a kind of given. Buildings were the world. A building was as much a given as the fact that the ground is

WALL SANDWICH, 1985
UPHOLSTERED FURNITURE IN PIECES, STYROFOAM, METAL STUDS, PLASTER WITH PERLITE, METAL LATH, ACRYLIC AND OIL PAINT, LIGHT FIXTURE

INSTALLATION VIEW AT MELINDA WYATT GALLERY, NEW YORK, 1985

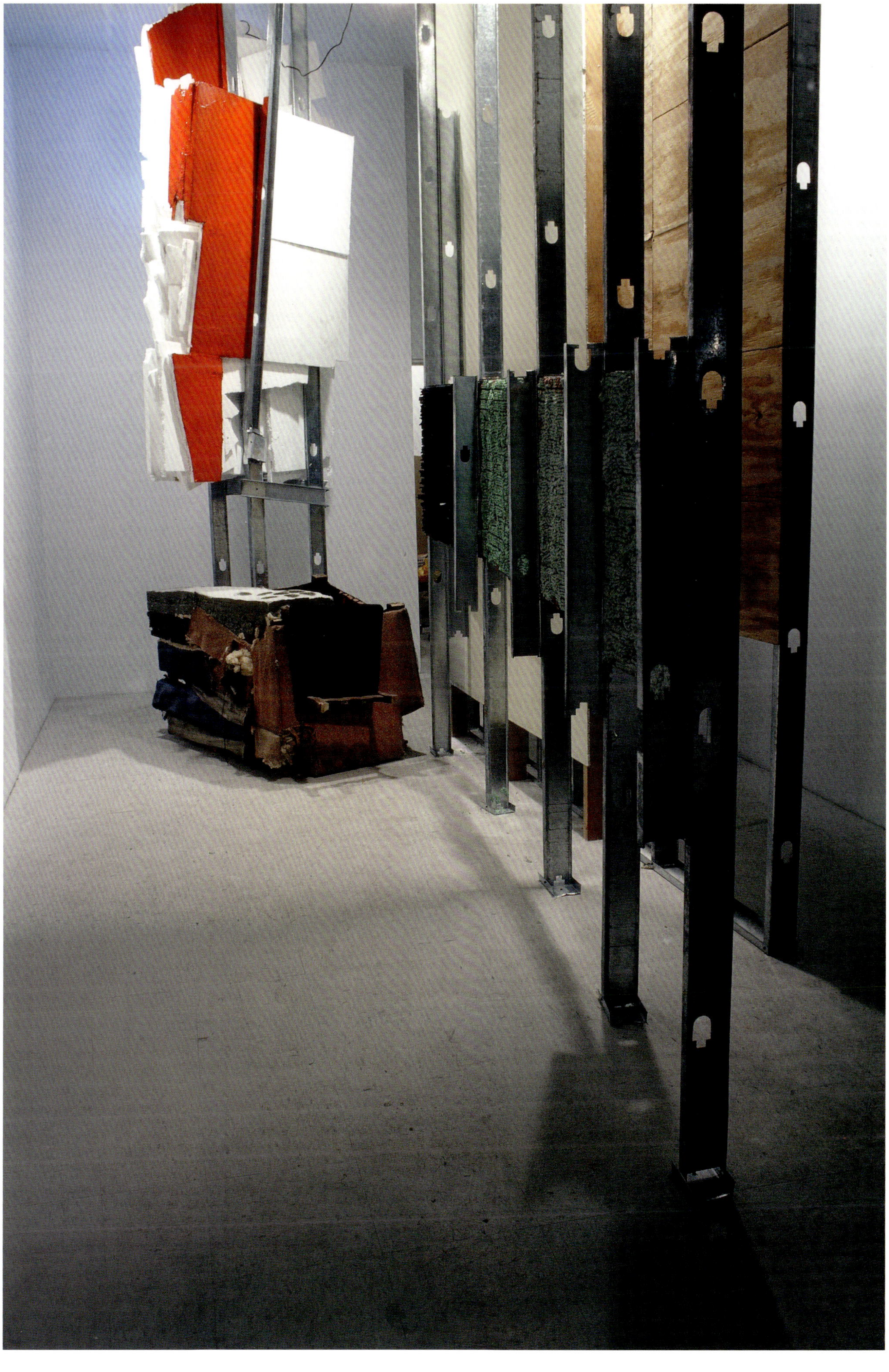

made of earth. Through my work, I've come to understand that buildings are invented by other people as was our history, civilization and society – it's all made by people, it's not a given.

TILLMAN: *Buildings don't have to look like this.*

STOCKHOLDER: Exactly. They all carry meaning. Galleries aren't neutral. They signify a kind of neutrality that we gave them.

TILLMAN: *You explode into that so-called neutral space with work that is sometimes very theatrical. In* Edge of Hot House Glass, *there's a raised platform. Had you ever done that before? Raised the floor?*

STOCKHOLDER: It's not unlike *The Lion, the Witch and the Wardrobe*. But it's not a ramp, it's a platform.

EDGE OF HOT HOUSE GLASS, 1993
SUN UMBRELLA, ACRYLIC PAINT, CONCRETE, CABLE FEATHERS, CLOTH, GROLIGHTS SUSPENDED FROM THE CEILING WITH CABLE
190 X 230 X 70 CM

INSTALLATION VIEW AT CARRE D'ART/MUSÉE D'ART CONTEMPORAIN DE NIMES, 1993

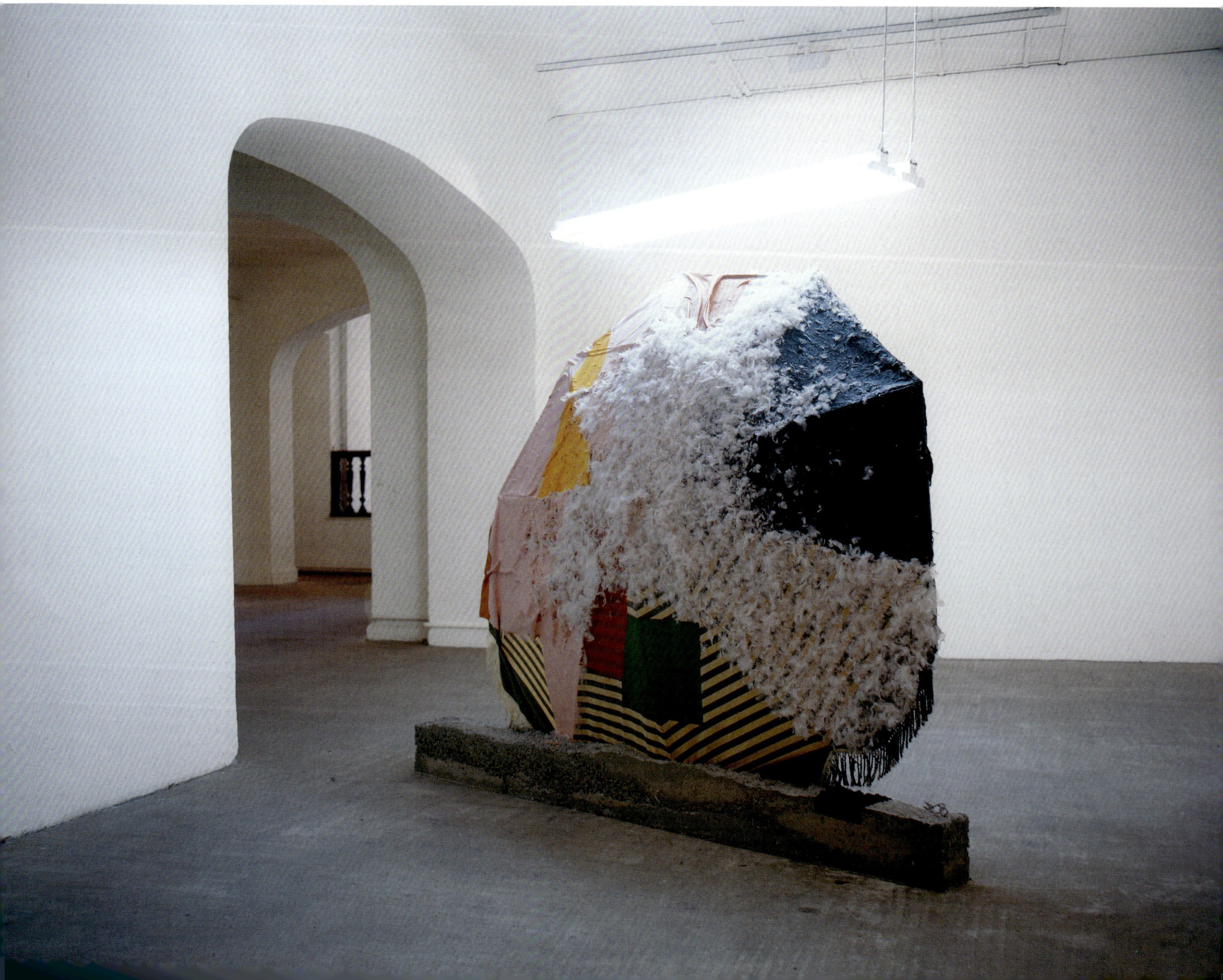

TILLMAN: *There was no entry onto that floor?*

STOCKHOLDER: No.

TILLMAN: *You literally raised the stakes on your own practice, as if saying: Here's a new floor, new ground. It's a huge piece, isn't it?*

STOCKHOLDER: It's not one of the biggest pieces I've made, but it's big – the platform's probably 20 by 20. The space was difficult – dark, almost a basement in feeling with little lighting, dark, shadowy. Generally, I don't like my work to be atmospheric. Theatrical was a bad word when I was in school.

TILLMAN: *It's hard to avoid when there's what looks like a stage or a ramp.*

STOCKHOLDER: But I like the work to be immediate. I don't like the work to be lit differently from the space you're standing in. It's not theatrical in that its audience isn't in a different space from the work. I struggle very hard to keep the work in the same place as the viewer. This particular space was hard for that reason.

TILLMAN: *Is that opposed to some notion of illusion in a way?*

STOCKHOLDER: No. It's that I want the illusion to coexist with my experience of the table next to my piece, or the staircase next to the work. I don't want there to be a divide. Many people like their experience of work to be heightened, separate from one's experience of having walked into the gallery. Gallery windows are often covered, galleries are often dark. I like the windows to be open, to have no drapes on them. I like to walk in and be aware of where I came from, to have that experience of having just entered into the gallery next to the experience of looking at the work. This space in Nîmes was hard for that reason. You didn't see the daylight that you'd just left behind.

TILLMAN: *Is that why you moved the floor up?*

STOCKHOLDER: I moved the floor up to try and counter the feeling of being sunk into this room. I contemplated having a place where the viewer could stand and not be able to move around. But I like the viewer to be able to move, so that there's choice. I like there to be pathways.

TILLMAN: *You want a continuous experience between what's art and what's so-called everyday?*

STOCKHOLDER: Fredric Jameson gave a wonderful lecture at Bard College in 1994. The lecture was outside – we were all sitting on the steps outside a building because there was a power outage; behind Jameson was a backdrop of trees and birds; the sun was slowly setting, and the moon was coming up. And he delivered his very abstract, formal, and organized lecture just as he would inside, only in this new context it was a completely other thing. The contrast between the formed, abstract thing that he was delivering, and how independent it was of wherever he was, and the birds, and his lectern being messed with while he was talking – for me that was beautiful. That this abstraction that he's in the business of making coexisted with the trees, and the birds, and these things that are so easily romantic, was beautiful.

TILLMAN: *We have all sorts of feelings about trees that have nothing to do with trees.*

STOCKHOLDER: They have to do with us.

TILLMAN: *We think about nature, place it in relation to our human lives. It has significance for us because we make it, or don't make it, significant.*

STOCKHOLDER: But I also think that it does exist separately from us, as distinct from Jameson's lecture, which doesn't. Jameson's lecture exists only in so far as he

1991
4 ELEMENTS
NO. 1: PLYWOOD COVERED WITH LINOLEUM TILES, ENAMALAC PAINT, LATEX PAINT, OIL PAINT, CLOTH, PAPIER, MACHÉ, 2 WHEELS, ALUMINIUM, METAL STRAPPING, HARDWARE
NO. 2: ESCALATOR SLEEVE BANDED TOGETHER
NO. 3: CARPETS, WOOL, ONE BOLT AND NUT
NO. 4: BLUE EXTENSION CORD, ORANGE HOOK
209 X 288 X 74 CM

INSTALLATION VIEW AT GALERIE NATHALIE OBADIA, PARIS, 1991

made it. He manufactured his lecture, which can exist next to a tree or inside a university building. In my work I manufacture something like that, like his lecture, that's very abstract and ordered, by me, and by the culture that houses me. But all that I make is meshed with, and sits on top of, stuff that is incontrovertibly there. I understand that we could talk – and philosophers do talk, ad infinitum, about whether in fact it's there if you don't see it. But I – and I imagine most people – have an experience of some things as really there, and other things as not quite there. I'm interested in how those two experiences mesh.

TILLMAN: *Your concern almost from the beginning was to deal with a structure that was already there. You didn't choose to ignore it.*

STOCKHOLDER: That's true both of the physical structure and the social structure that contains my process.

TILLMAN: *It didn't happen in a vacuum. You're not alone in that concern. The way in which you handle it has its own particularity, the way you try to encounter a space – it's fun even to use the word encounter when you use a structure like a counter. To me your work is filled with words, with metaphors, that I as a writer can immediately, and not the way you want me to, probably, translate. I'm beginning to be more aware of the physical world, of the built environment, let's say, than I was. I'm even more aware of birds. But it's taken me a long time.*

STOCKHOLDER: Me too. I start from a place that's not unlike what you're describing. Only I don't have the words. I don't trust the words.

TILLMAN: *I don't trust them exactly. I use them. I don't believe they say everything, but, obviously, I want to be working with them. Maybe I'm interested in visual material as much as I am because there may be some similar sources to making it, but it's translated into something I could never accomplish. Especially in three-dimensional forms. To be that's one of the strangest, hardest things to do.*

STOCKHOLDER: It's funny, in some ways, that's also true of me. I started on flat surfaces, with planar images. To make them three-dimensional was a challenge. I could conceptualize, and had a real facility with things on a page, graphically, but I couldn't, and still have difficulty, conceptualizing in three-dimensions. I don't begin installations knowing what they're gong to be in the space. As my work grows, part of the challenge

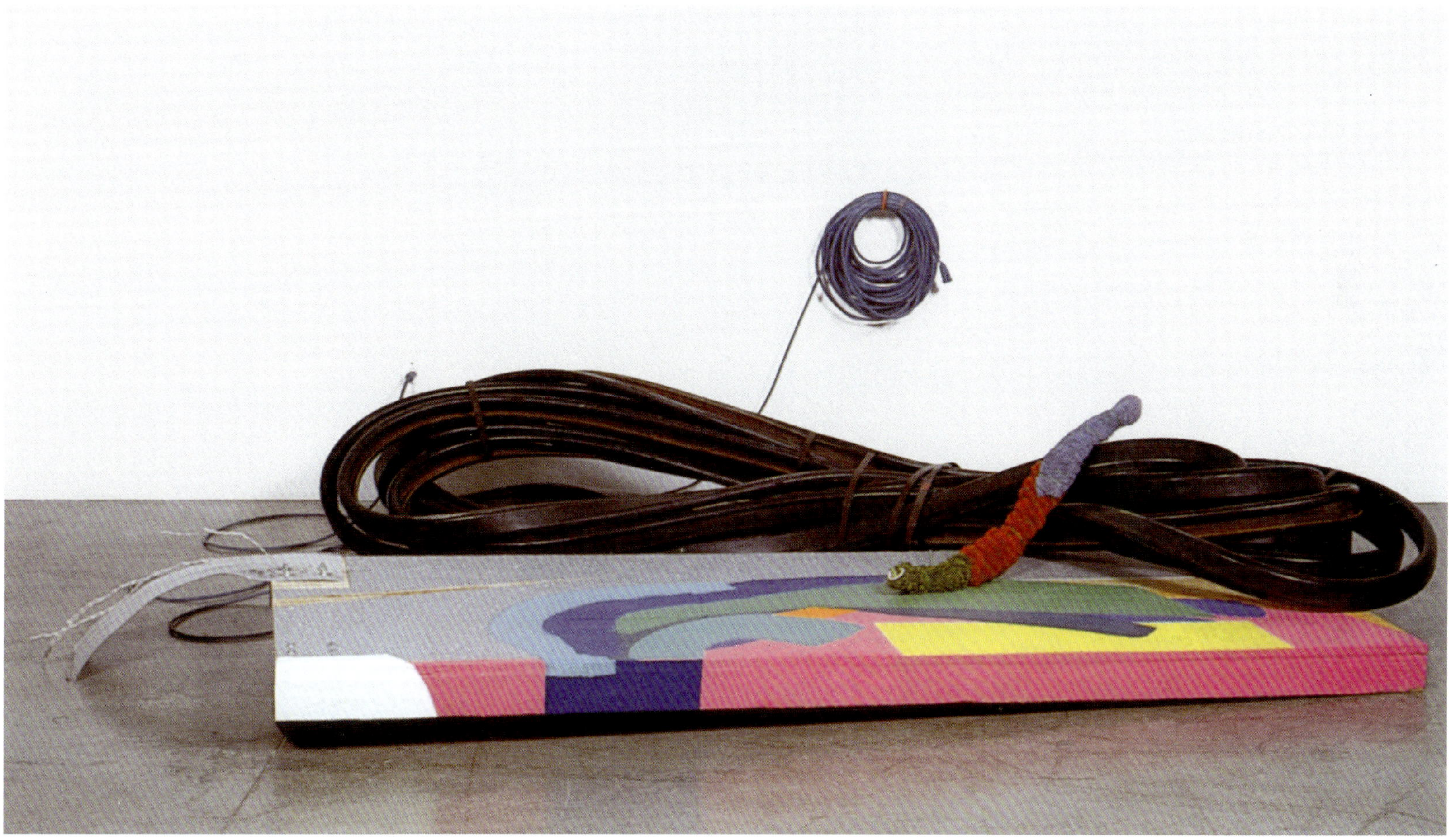

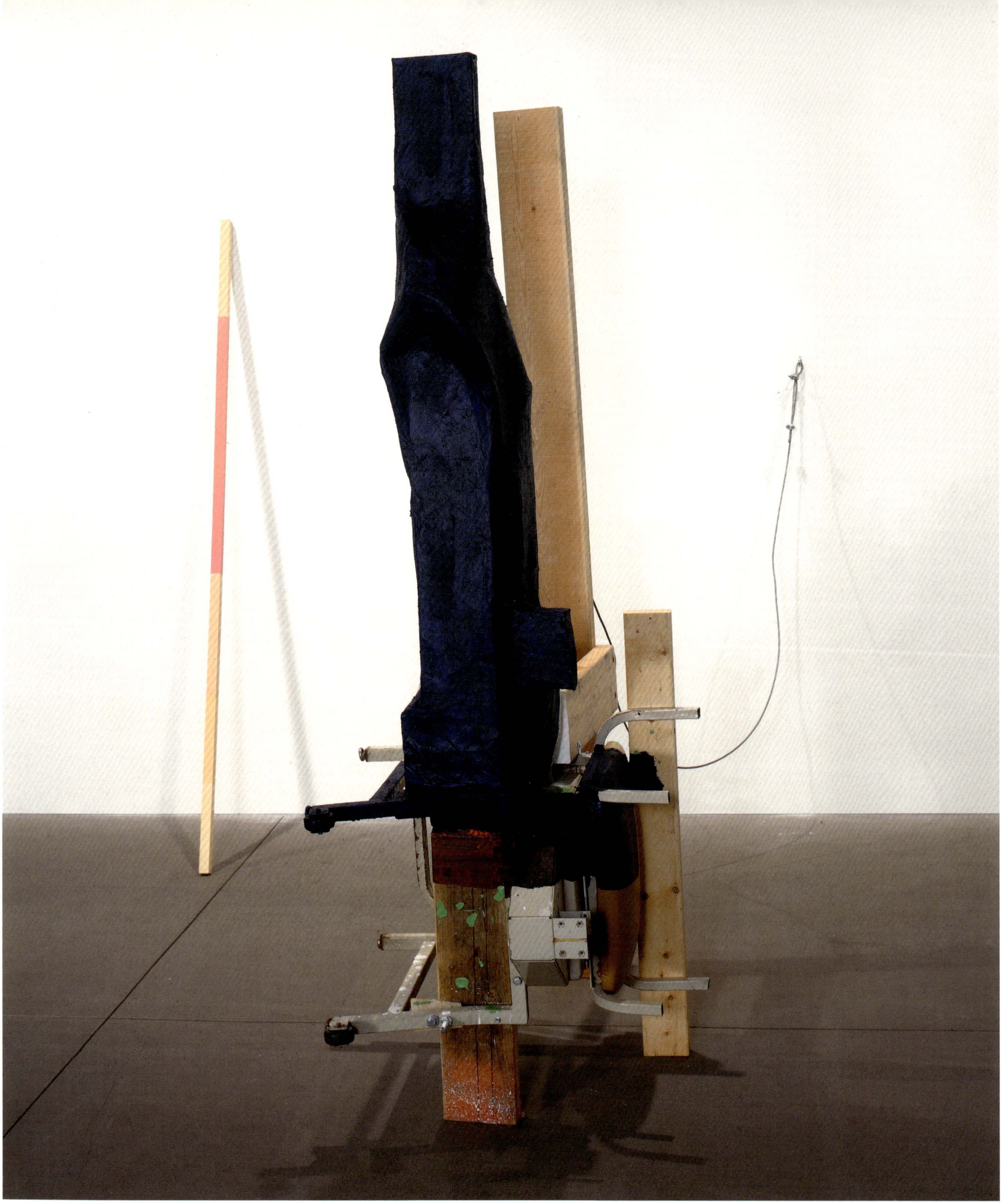

1991
2 ELEMENTS
NO. 1: WOOD, FURNITURE, PAPIER MACHÉ, NEWSPAPER, ACRYLIC PAINT, CABLE
NO. 2: WOOD AND PAINT
OVERALL: 173 X 55 X 200 CM

INSTALLATION VIEW AT CHRISTINE BURGIN GALLERY, NEW YORK, 1991

is to continue putting myself in a place where I am in the dark and required to respond immediately, where I can't predict the outcome.

TILLMAN: *Maybe that's why I find jokes in your work. One's a play on the truism that art is organized out of chaos. There's chaos in your art. There's clearly a mind at work organising, with a system, responding to the space, but it's discomforting. Your work asks: where do I look first? It's not organized so that there's a front, or a frontal perspective. You don't have a vanishing point. At least I can't find it.*

STOCKHOLDER: There isn't one.

TILLMAN: *In Western art, the vanishing point, frontality, and other devises, organize it, so as to organize vision, the world – but there's another sense of organization in your work.*

STOCKHOLDER: Part of the work is highly ordered and organized, and part of it just lays where it falls. To use a visual metaphor for this idea – objects in the place of ideas – if I use five different objects, parts of them will fit together in a very tight, formal way, and the rest will just hang out chaotically. Another way to visualize my order in chaos is to imagine a bunch of threads over-lapping in one place. Where they overlap, things are tight and ordered. But the ends fly off in a million different directions, often having nothing more to do with each other.

TILLMAN: *That's a scary way of working. There's not a contradiction but odd consequences. On the one hand you want the viewer's experience to be of the same order as the experience of walking down the stairs and going to a place. On the other hand – this may be what your experience of the world is – you make a disorderly organization. A disquieting, sometimes demented –*

STOCKHOLDER: Yes!

TILLMAN: ... *bunch of things.*

STOCKHOLDER: Yes, it's amazing that things work as well as they do. I am not interested in making work that pretends the world is not like that. But I do appreciate the work of Richard Long. He'll place a bunch of stones in a circle, or a path. He works out in the landscape. His work is very cohesive, and ordered – round things, or square things – very unified. I think his work functions as meditation.

TILLMAN: *Your art doesn't leave room for rest. It's not a resting place. In the way you were describing the Long work, one could, as in Noguchi's, imagine standing, looking, and feeling a sense of quiet.*

STOCKHOLDER: I miss that in life!

TILLMAN: *Maybe that's why he does what he does. He wants ...*

STOCKHOLDER: – to make it.

TILLMAN: *Maybe it represents what's missing in his life. Or what he thinks life –*

STOCKHOLDER: – needs.

TILLMAN: *You might want that, but insist instead: I don't find it anywhere. I don't know that I can make that, in order to say this is as it should be.*

STOCKHOLDER: Though I agree there's no quiet place in my work that compares with the quiet of Noguchi or Long, there are places in most of my pieces where you as viewer are definitely outside, looking as a quieter, static whole.

TILLMAN: *You said you allow pathways. There are exits.*

STOCKHOLDER: And points of detachment. In *Where It Happened?* (1990) and in *Mixing Food with the Bed* (1989), you enter and just at the gallery door the piece is in front of you as if it were a stage set or a painting. Then you walk through it, and it's chaotic and formally difficult to get a handle on. Having walked through and turned around, you are definitely not in that piece anymore.

TILLMAN: *How do you know for sure?*

STOCKHOLDER: *You're standing on the normal gallery floor. White walls are around you. You can, from this point of view, make a distinction between the elements of the piece and the gallery. So you have detachment.*

TILLMAN: *But then what is the shape of it? That's often what I wonder about your work: What is its shape? One walks into a space in which you've installed an art work, where the viewer's given a place somewhere in the room to feel distance from it. I don't know if it's detachment.*

STOCKHOLDER: I don't make environments that you walk into in which the space or place has been disguised. My work isn't like wallpaper. You always know there are two elements – the building and the work. But just where the building begins or ends, and where the work begins or ends, isn't clear.

TILLMAN: *There's an issue about boundaries.*

STOCKHOLDER: Absolutely.

TILLMAN: *What are the boundaries? On the other hand, you do leave some breathing room within that questionable symbiosis between thing and person or between art and so-called life.*

STOCKHOLDER: That matters to me tremendously.

TILLMAN: *In* Installation in My Father's Backyard *(1983) you hung a red mattress on the side of a barn –*

STOCKHOLDER: Garage.

TILLMAN: *Garage, sorry. The garage wall, part of it is grey and there's some blue. You've painted the grass and flowers, or shrubs, in front of that wall. It's a real mattress?*

STOCKHOLDER: It's a double or a queen-size mattress spray painted with fluorescent paint – a little bit transparent so the markings of the mattress show through. There is a blue, or purple, cupboard door that's mounted on top of the garage with a roll of chicken wire.

TILLMAN: *It's compelling and weird for many different reasons.*

STOCKHOLDER: Let's hear.

TILLMAN: *You make a mattress red which underscores sex and sexuality. Then you confound the build, the garage, with the object itself; and the ground is grass which you paint. You put something on the grass that makes it unnatural. That seems to have some reference to a family structure, to the idea that the family is considered a natural unit, though each unit is different – has its own colour. But it has a basic structure we recognize; father, mother – or lack of – and children. Then your use of the blue on the roof and door are in relation, reflecting each other; blue grass, blue do or. A door opens and shuts and could be an obstacle. Also an entrance or exit. Many meanings. Then there's wire, which is an aggressive element. If you landed on it, if it touched you it wouldn't –*

WHERE IT HAPPENED, 1990
WOOD, CONCRETE, PLASTER, STYROFOAM, CARPETS, WALLPAPER, NEWSPAPER, WIRE LATH, PAPIER MACHÉ, A YELLOW CHEST OF DRAWERS, SHEET ROCK, WHEELS, ASPHALT, ROOFING TAR, LEMONS

INSTALLATION VIEW AT AMERICAN FINE ARTS, CO., NEW YORK, 1990

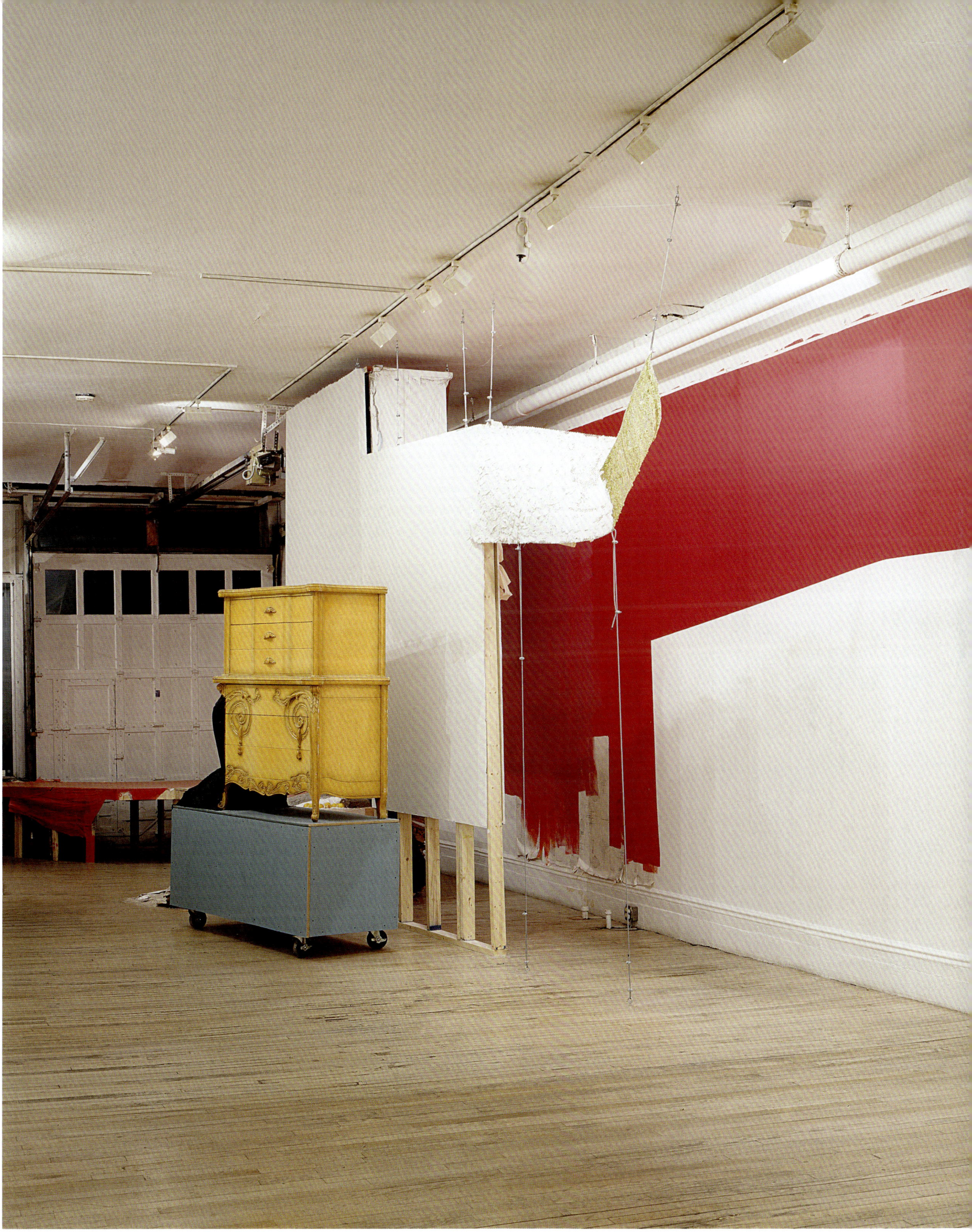

STOCKHOLDER: It would not feel good.

TILLMAN: *The piece is also deeply site-specific.*

STOCKHOLDER: I enjoy your reading, but I can't say whether I agree or disagree. The way I came to making this piece has none of that conscious information in it.

TILLMAN: *Tell me how you did it.*

STOCKHOLDER: I found this mattress in the garage and painted it red as the complement to the grass. The backyard is more or less rectangular, so it's similar in shape to the mattress and garage. The lawn is brought into a dialogue with the mattress, and with the history of painting, because paintings are rectangular too. Here I'm making a painting – only it's also a backyard. The red of the mattress called to the colour of the berries in the tree, heightening colour that's already there. I painted the grass with a hard-edged form, kind of rectangular so it has a formal relationship to the door, and to the mattress. I never know exactly why I choose materials. Your analysis makes sense, but part of my interest is to work with materials that are in some way randomly selected – to put them together so that they speak for me. I have some faith that I will be able to speak through what is at hand.

TILLMAN: *A mattress is so redolent. One couldn't go to one's father's house, take a queen-size mattress out of the garage and hand it without having some awareness that it referred to a father-daughter relationship, the Oedipal, the family.*

STOCKHOLDER: I can see why you might say that, but I don't think about that stuff when I'm working. In order to avoid having my personal history, which drives the work, making the work cliché or diminished, I don't spend a lot of time thinking about it. I think about the form that the work takes. I make sure that in the end the experience is right – that the work is active.

TILLMAN: *The formal elements are first what one's conscious of: you've used two rectangles – all of that is there. But I think what makes the work have resonance is that the formal is logged into this narrative, through its metaphors …*

STOCKHOLDER: I don't mean to say that I'm not aware of the psychological. But I don't feel as if I can control it or the narrative.

TILLMAN: *I don't think one can – not control one's being drawn to, driven to, taking up the material. Why one's driven to tackle a particular formal problem, why write it in this way – there are psychological issues involved that formal concerns don't conceal.*

STOCKHOLDER: And the formal concerns are not interesting unless they carry his other information.

TILLMAN: *In some way, for me.*

STOCKHOLDER: For me also.

TILLMAN: *It seems that you use two kinds of titles, one kind seems to refer more to narrative.*

STOCKHOLDER: Narrative is something I'm trying to find a way to talk about now, though I'm not sure 'narrative' is the right word. There is a kind of building or layering of meaning that results from the literary content of the objects I use, but the structure is not linear. There is no beginning, middle or end. My aim is to throw the next as wide as possible, even while there are focused in areas of literary meaning that develop here and there.

INSTALLATION IN MY FATHER'S BACKYARD, 1983
CUPBOARD DOOR, MATTRESS, PAINTED GRASS, CHICKEN WIRE

INSTALLATION VIEW AT PRIVATE RESIDENCE IN VANCOUVER, 1983

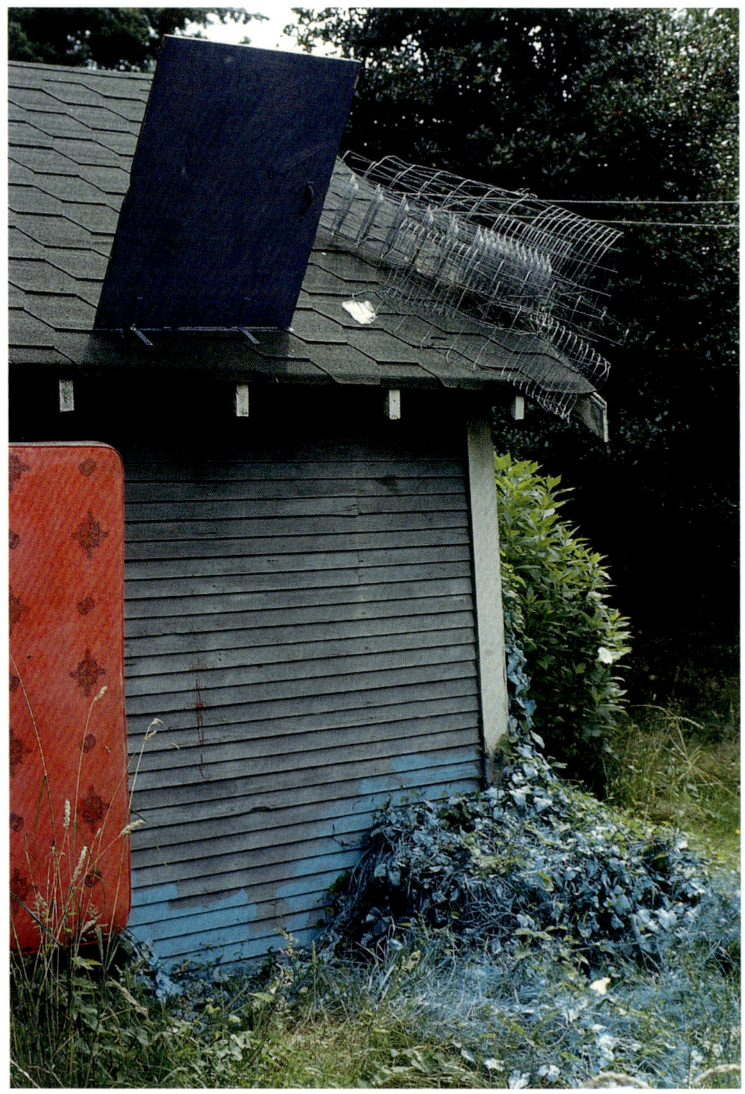

INSTALLATION IN MY FATHER'S BACKYARD, 1983
CUPBOARD DOOR, MATTRESS, PAINTED GRASS, CHICKEN WIRE

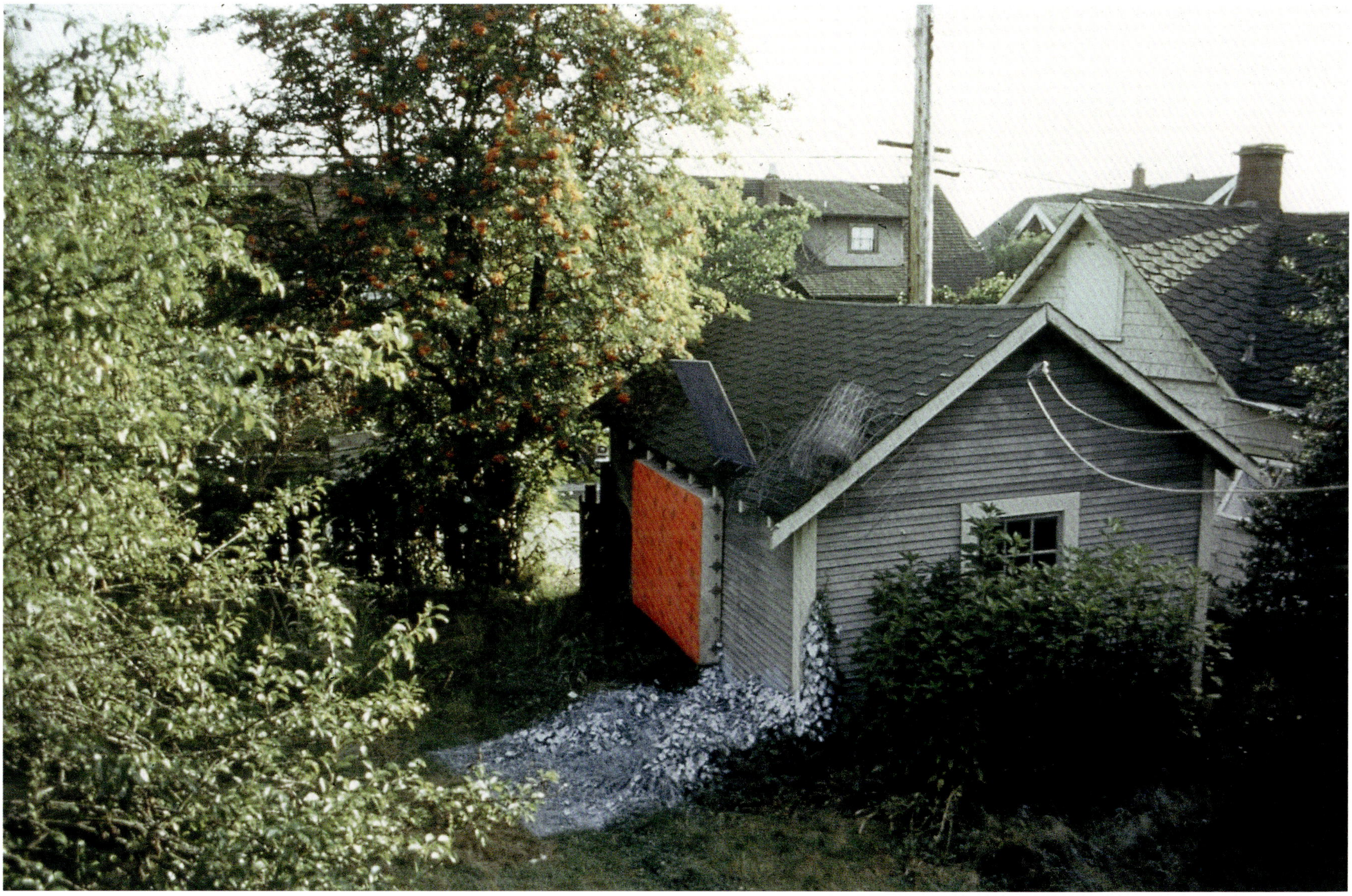

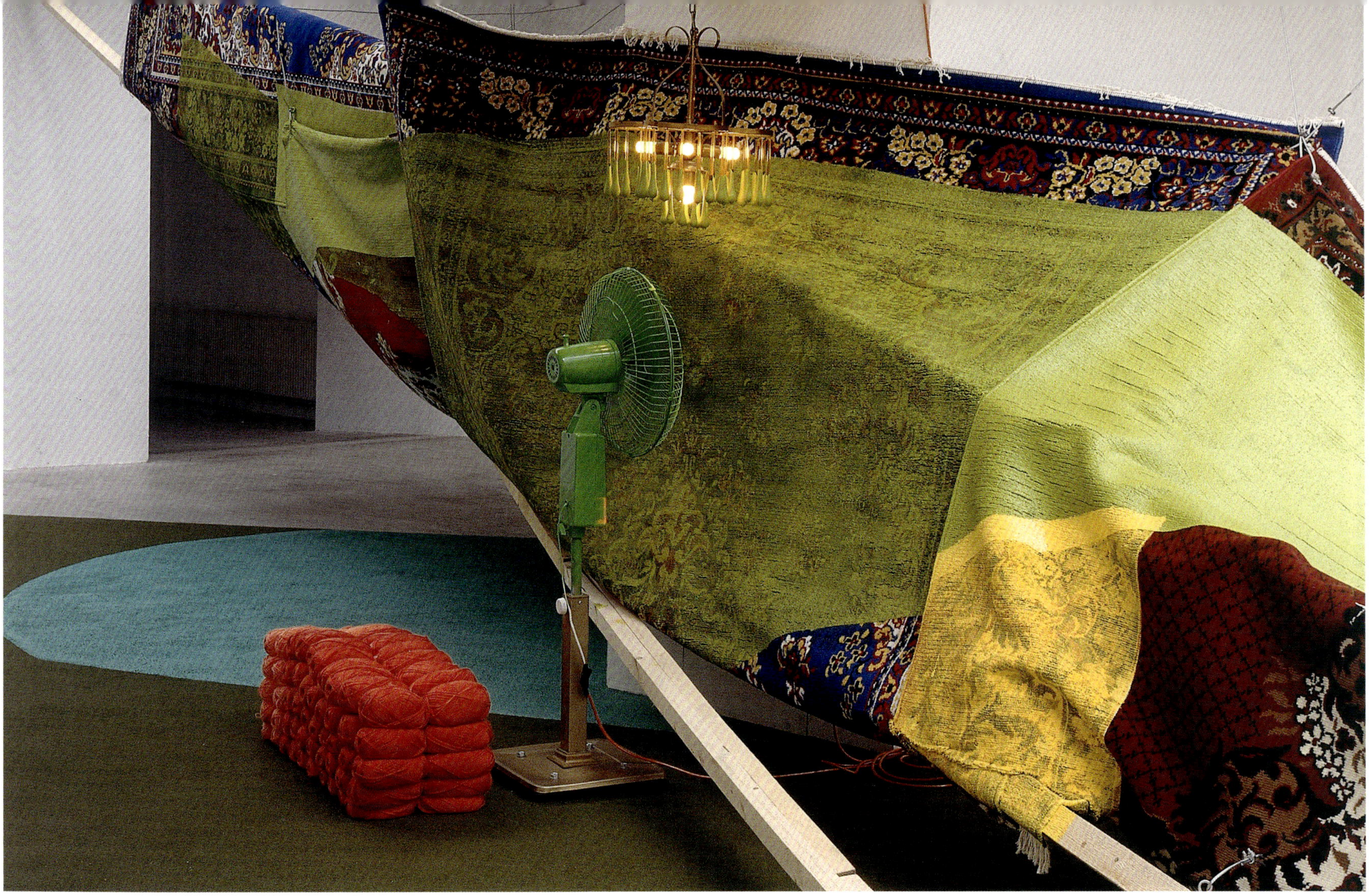

TILLMAN: *Some of your titles are long and specific about the thing itself, about naming itself. For example,* Yellow sponges, Plexiglas, small piece of furniture, newspaper maché, plastic, oil and acrylic paint, cloth, small blue light and fixture, glass on the wall, *1990. All the elements are named, yet the piece is not merely an aggregate of those elements. The pieces with the long titles are more, it seems to be, object oriented and can be taken in my standing in front of them. They seem to be more about painting, the limits and possibilities of painting.*

STOCKHOLDER: The titles consisting of a long list of objects are titles by default. My intention was to leave these pieces untitled. I always request that there be no title – and that the word 'untitled' not be used. In many cases the list of materials is used instead of a title. People just can't get their heads around the space being blank where they're used to seeing a title. But I'm not unhappy about the conversation this has given rise to. When I do use titles, I often work with the words in a way that feels parallel to the way I work with objects. I like the title to work alongside the piece rather than lead you down a path.

TILLMAN: *My interpretation's by default then, too, I guess. Some of the titles signal that the piece will be more narrative, about time and space, like* The Lion, the Witch and the Wardrobe. *That long ramp seems to be about space as well as about the time it might take to walk on it, if you were to walk on it.*

STOCKHOLDER: Even walking alongside of it, that takes time.

TILLMAN: *Even if it's immediate in feeling, it also requires duration, which is about narrative, so that if you want the viewer to be physically in that space with that piece, the viewer must be active. To go from point A to point B.*

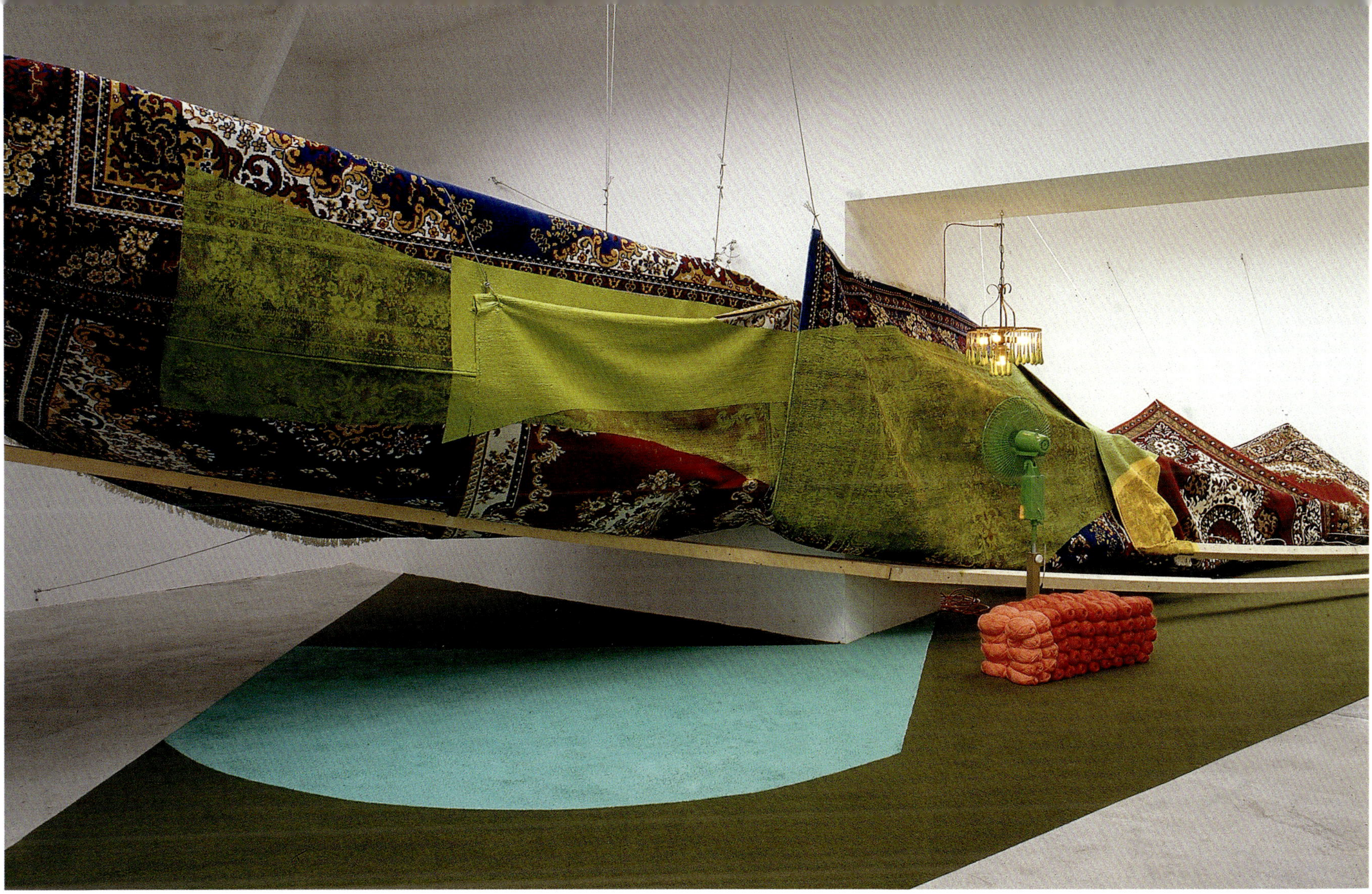

STOCKHOLDER: And in the process of going from point A to point B, there are places where the work becomes very ordered and static, as a painting is static and separate from you. In that process, the memory of one side, or one view, of the work informs the viewing of the next side. If I'm looking at something that's read, and I know the other side of it's black, my memory of the black part functions in my forming of the composition, as if that black were visible. Do you understand?

TILLMAN: *I think so. It relates to issues about narrative and psychology. If black is the memory, the unseen colour in back of the memory, it's present no matter if it's in the past or if it's visually present in the moment.*

STOCKHOLDER: That your memory is equal to what you're viewing in the present is fascinating.

TILLMAN: *It's another kind of dialectic in your work. On the one hand you want the experience to be in the present – you want the viewer to come in and have this experience. On the other hand, you're very aware that no one comes into a space without memory.*

STOCKHOLDER: How those two things merge is most exciting. It's a struggle. It's not a modern struggle; it's an ancient struggle, actually to be present for the moment and what that means. I'm sure that's part of Richard Long's struggle too.

TILLMAN: *I could imagine he might think, or someone making work that allowed for contemplation in one place might say: you are present, I am.*

STOCKHOLDER: Or he would hope to be providing the opportunity to be present.

these and previous pages,
HOUSE BEAUTIFUL, 1994
WOOD, HINGES, HARDWARE, SEVEN RUGS, BRAIDED STEEL CABLE, FAN, CHANDELIER, GREEN CARPET, 100 BALLS OF YARN GLUED TOGETHER WITH STILICONE CAULKING AND PAINT

INSTALLATION VIEW AT LE CONSORTIUM, DIJON, FRANCE, 1994

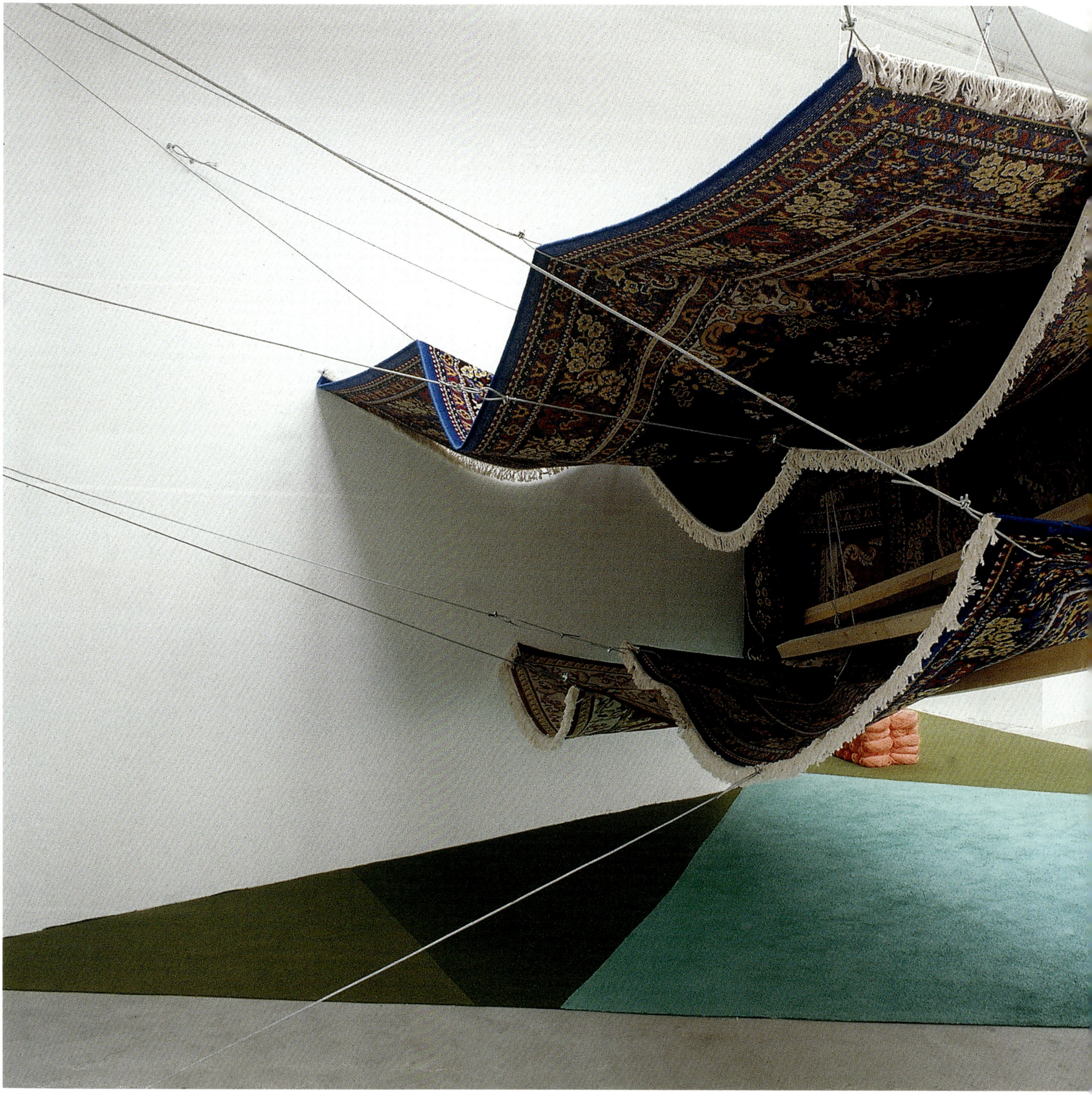

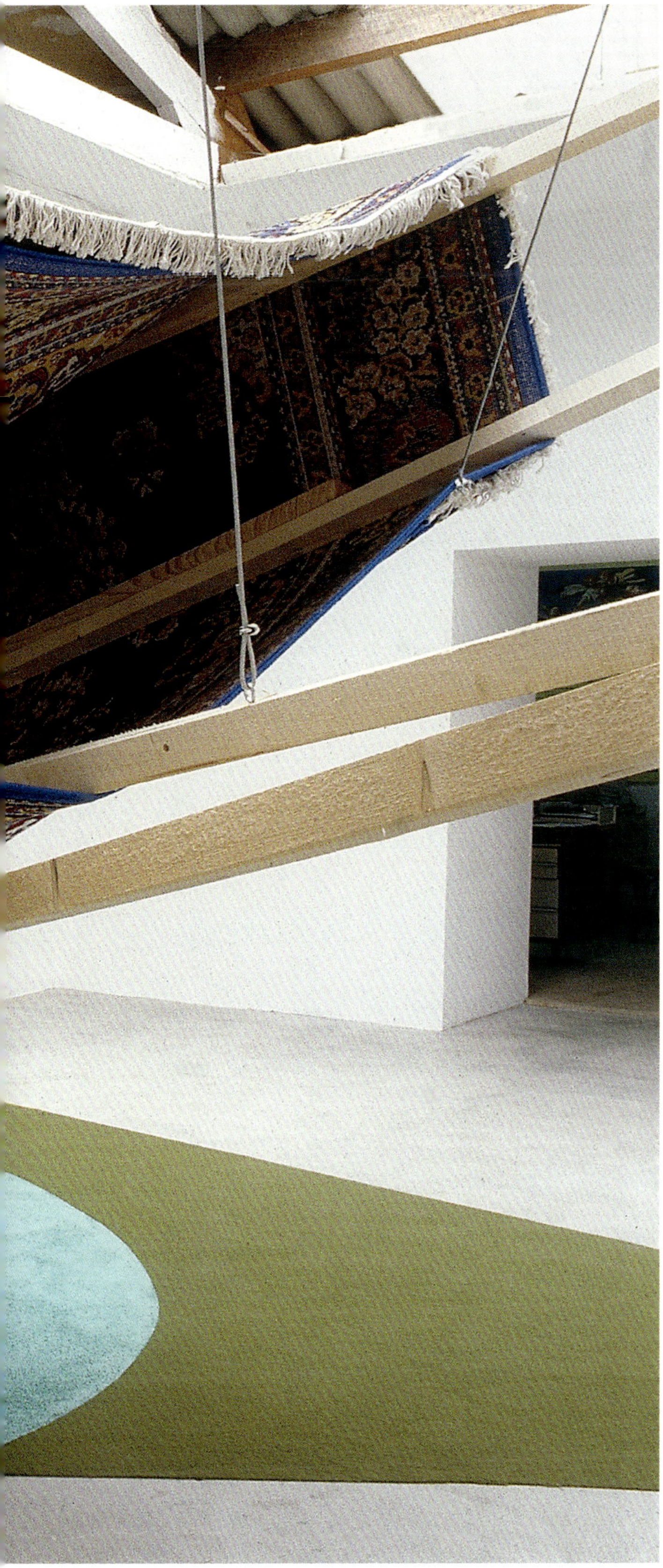

TILLMAN: *Now, what is that desire about?*

STOCKHOLDER: I think it has something to do with providing a place to experience will. If you can actually be aware of a moment and aware of yourself existing immediately, separate from, or in addition to, your history or memory, and culture, and all that makes you you, then there's room for choice.

TILLMAN: *To give one some sense of agency – that you are somehow able in that moment to recognize yourself and another object's being there. But your work doesn't make presence in the world easy. It's not about a unity or a unified presence.*

STOCKHOLDER: Well, I think it is and it isn't. But this takes us to the next stage – in the next location.

TILLMAN: *Which you're choosing.*

STOCKHOLDER: Right. (Laughs)

These photos are of a piece I made in the spring, *House Beautiful* (1994). The white is the wall of the gallery; the work spans three rooms. The carpets are stretched with cables to the walls, floor and ceiling.

TILLMAN: *You couldn't take one photograph of the piece?*

STOCKHOLDER: No.

TILLMAN: *Craig Owens once said that the history of art was the history of images of art. This piece would need at least two to represent it. I don't know immediately where the work begins or ends, or if, in the photograph, it is right side up or upside down. It returns me to the place we left, or left off, last week. Even though you use brightly coloured materials, which are often supposed to mean 'happy', you very contradictorily propose to this happiness a discomforting sense of disorientation and dislocation. You're not using the ramp in this one, but you are taking the viewer on an excursion. And there isn't a single, unified form.*

STOCKHOLDER: Spatially, this isn't one of the most difficult pieces I've made. There is a green carpet on the floor; it is similar to the ground; you can walk over it or along it. The rectangular volume of yarn is a literal volume of colour; we know that the colour goes right through; it's not like a painted surface, or an object that has been painted. The yarn is a solid volume of colour contrasted to the flat areas of colour; we know the flat areas of colour are flat skins of paint on top of the carpets but they have an illusion of volume. Colour seems to project into the air in front of it. The fan which I painted green – like this green on the carpet – blows the air filled with colour.

TILLMAN: House Beautiful *contains puns. Carpet/ground, a household fan/audience. Hanging the carpet so that it refers to background/foreground, craft, laundry. To women's work and again to a stage set. It is a Persian carpet?*

STOCKHOLDER: It is a one hundred percent polypropylene Persian carpet. I used it because it was easily available and inexpensive. I would love to use real Persian carpets.

TILLMAN: *What would be the difference for you?*

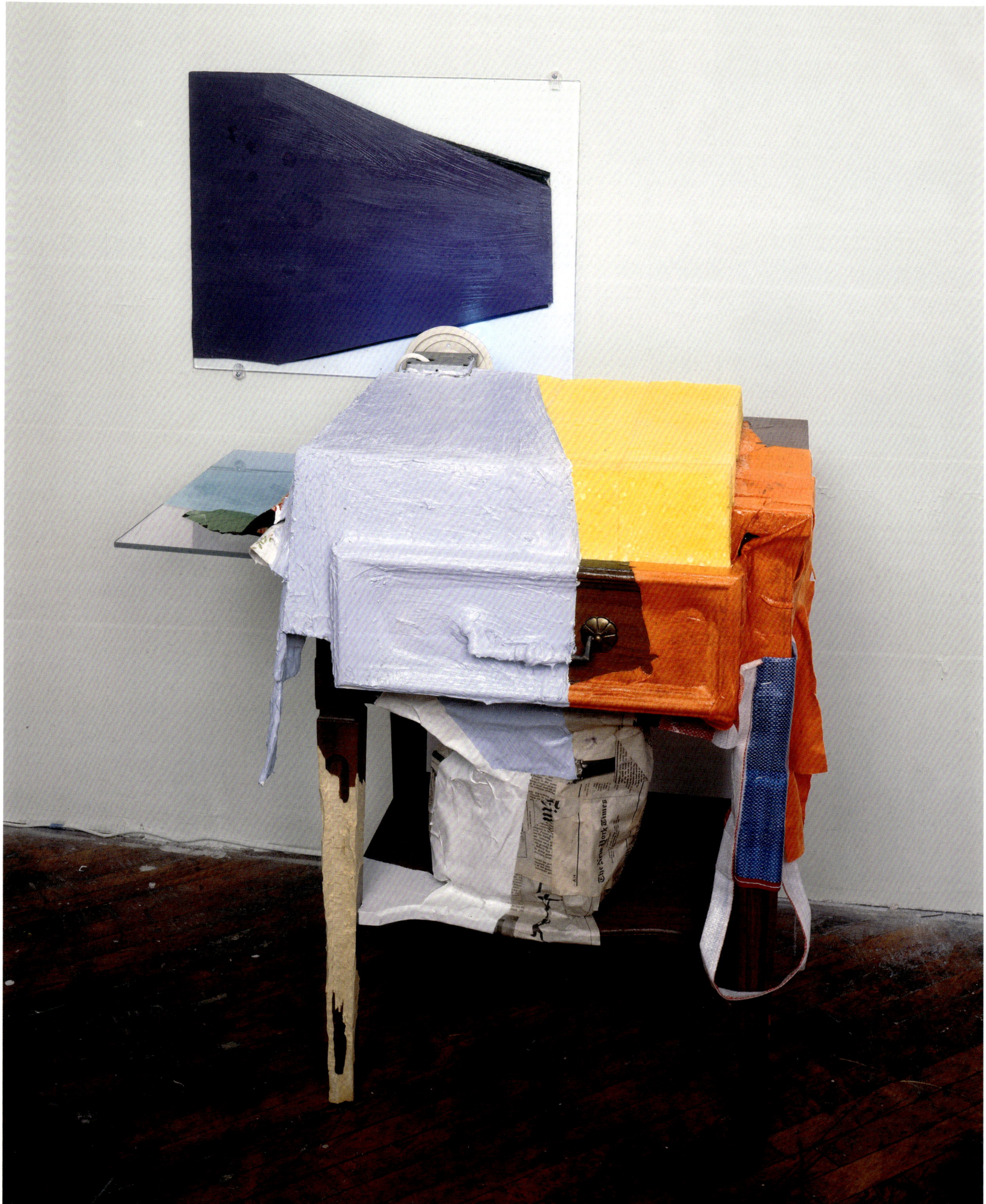
The New York Times

1990
YELLOW SPONGES, PLEXIGLAS, SMALL PIECE OF FURNITURE, NEWSPAPER MACHÉ, PLASTIC, OIL AND ACRYLIC PAINT, CLOTH, SMALL BLUE LIGHT AND FIXTURE, GLASS ON THE WALL
FURNITURE: 76 X 70 X 58 CM
GLASS: 48 X 37 CM

STOCKHOLDER: A real Persian carpet is truly a rich experience.

TILLMAN: *If it were a real Persian carpet, you'd be aware of that. You hang it now like laundry. Persian carpets are a form of art, people hang them on their walls. If you had a real Persian carpet, it would have a different valance, wouldn't it?*

STOCKHOLDER: The other day Jay [Gorney] asked me, 'If you had a lot of money, would you use expensive things instead of cheap things?' We were talking about the fact that my work isn't about junk. This is an issue because critics have often written about my work that way. It's about things – some of them are junky, some of them are new and some of them are old.

TILLMAN: *Why isn't it about junk? It's not that I thought of it as junk. Why do you think people see it that way?*

STOCKHOLDER: Because I take objects out of their normal context, and there's a dishevelled, jumbled quality to the way I use them. Things are jumbled when they are thrown out. Perhaps that's how people arrive at that.

TILLMAN: *Is it because you take everyday, ordinary material, and then don't use it in its expected way? In other words, because you make things no longer have their necessity, their function?*

STOCKHOLDER: Perhaps that combines with the fact that the way in which I put things together doesn't adhere to a standard craft. When I use wood and nails and glue, the craft doesn't match the craft that one uses making cabinets. When I sew, the craft isn't the same as when you put together a garment. The work isn't about being well crafted, but the way the thing is made is important. Ways of making are meaningful – as significant as the meaning we attach to objects.

TILLMAN: *That's different from the issue of junk. When John Chamberlain, in the 1960s, took a car and crumpled it up, was it about junk or disaster?*

STOCKHOLDER: People have discussed his work in terms of disaster and also more formally. In contract to my work, his is formally very consistent; he lays out a formal language using one material. It's easy to forget that he is using crushed cars and see his work in terms of volume and shape. In my work the formal language is much more varied and there is a question as to whether or not one should look at what the objects are. They are much more in your face than in his work. I don't think he invites you to think very much about cars.

TILLMAN: *If those carpets had been ancient Persian carpets, would you have done the same thing? Ancient Persian carpets are valuable in and of themselves.*

STOCKHOLDER: They have two kinds of value, a value in terms of the pleasure they give and a monetary value. If I were to use them instead of polypropylene we would be very aware of how I had taken away their previous value. This brings up all kinds of questions that I haven't had to deal with.

TILLMAN: *Hard questions, whether one would take something rare and ruin it – but you're not doing that.*

STOCKHOLDER: I feel curious about what you said a while back about the colours all being upbeat and happy in contrast to this structure that leaves you in a place of discomfort.

TILLMAN: *That's one of the most peculiar aspects of your work – you construct a controlled situation that recreates the discomfort of being disoriented within and by the familiar stuff of our lives.*

STOCKHOLDER: I've been reading Anthony Vidler's book on the architectural uncanny; I think that is what he would call uncanny, to take these familiar objects and make something unfamiliar with them.

TILLMAN: *'Uncanny', from unheimlich, 'unhomed by' – great word. One could also say your work is about de-familiarizing ordinary objects or feeling unfamiliar in familiar circumstances. I don't see junk in relation to your work. The word 'junket', going on a junket, comes up. Or junking certain notions about familiar objects, loosening them from the familiar grip. Many of your materials are 'traditional' women's materials; cloth, bright colours, wool. You use objects from a domestic space, couches, for example.*

STOCKHOLDER: Things from a domestic space are associated with women, that's perfectly standard but it's a little odd. Men inhabit domestic spaces too.

TILLMAN: *Too often the divide is women/domestic or private space, men/public space. Your work isn't traditional 'women's work'; but you take risks by using what some might consider benighted materials – junk to some, maybe because it's from the home. You do it in such an aggressive, peculiar, uncanny way. It's not about protecting the home or simply valorising that space. It allows the domestic other interpretations. Your use of ramps, rooms, carpets, raised floors – things spill over and out. It's not a contained or containable world. In your play with the domestic, the so-called private sphere is always either threatened by or merging with the public, and the distinctions between public and private are blurred.*

STOCKHOLDER: And between femininity and masculinity.

TILLMAN: *When one walks into* House Beautiful, *will she or he feel that the carpet is masking or covering anything?*

STOCKHOLDER: No, since what you first see as you enter the room is the structure around which the carpet is wrapped. There's nothing hidden. There are many things or actions that build on each other and inform each other, but I don't like to create mystery about what is actually there.

TILLMAN: *It seems to say that something doesn't have to be hidden or covered in order for it not be apprehended. This work is hard to apprehend; it builds, it moves, you have to walk with it, there are many elements. How do you apprehend this? It's not that you're hiding anything, not that a mystery is something hidden, but a complexity that can't be understood even when seen. The turquoise – what did you think when you were doing that? Is that paint?*

STOCKHOLDER: Yes. Why do you ask?

TILLMAN: *It's like a swimming pool. It suggests many allusions, from Narcissus, to ideas about thought, art and reflection – the green chandelier in it is a light after all – to an art reference, David Hockney's swimming pool.*

STOCKHOLDER: Hockney's pools.

TILLMAN: *The turquoise appears to be an exit, a moment of escape.*

STOCKHOLDER: It's more abstract, lighter than anything else.

TILLMAN: *Your work's often concerned with exits and entrances, giving the viewer a number of them. It's a relief here in several senses – a rectangular relief that's on the floor, a painting on the floor, a relief from the piece and its insistence to move on. One can stop at the turquoise. Would you call it a moment?*

STOCKHOLDER: A pause.

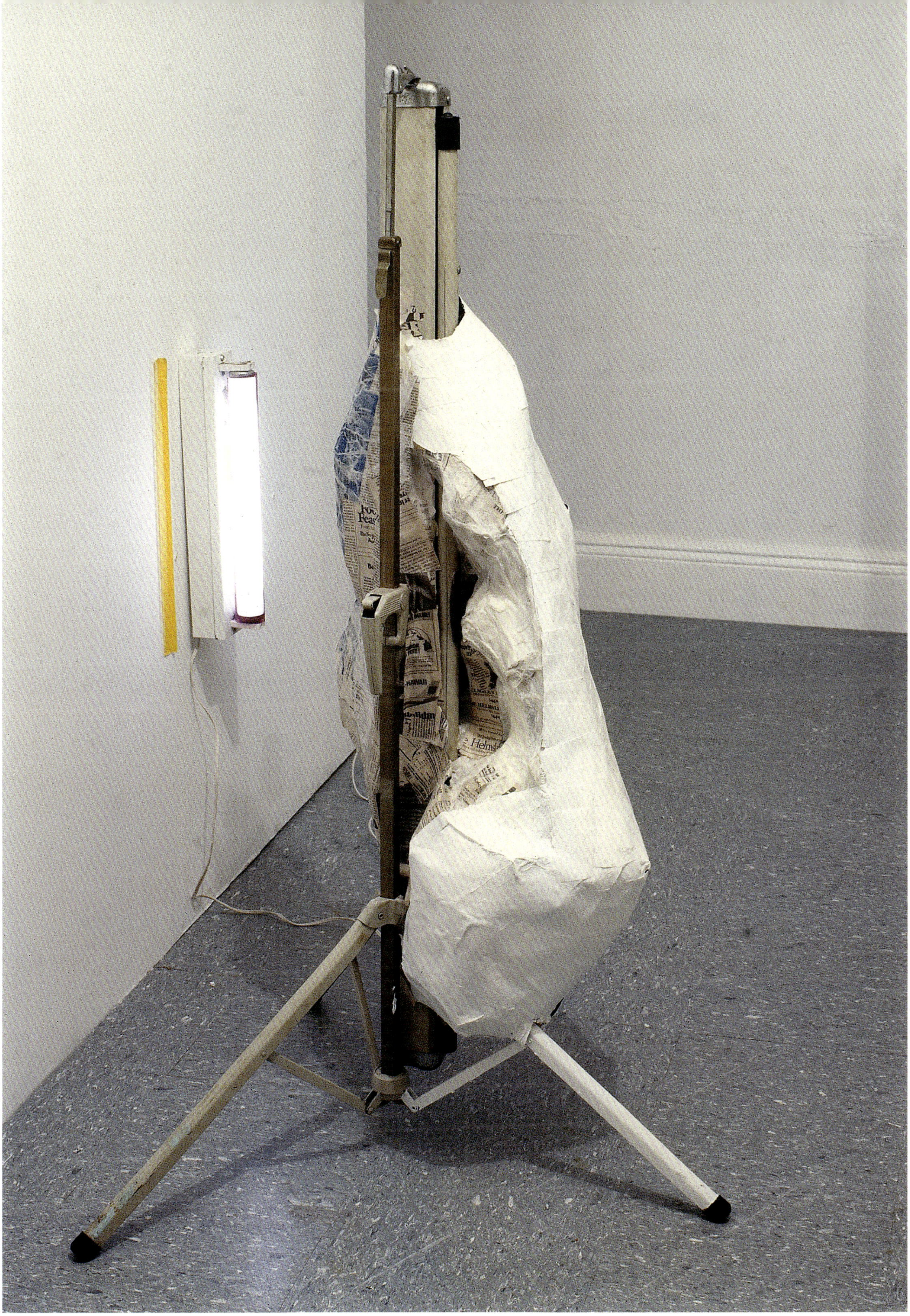

KISSING THE WALL #2, 1988
SLIDE PROJECTOR SCREEN,
NEWSPAPER, PLASTER,
OIL AND ACRYLIC PAINT,
FLUORESCENT TUBE WITH
PURPLE SLEEVE, WALLPAPER
126 X 84 X 79 CM

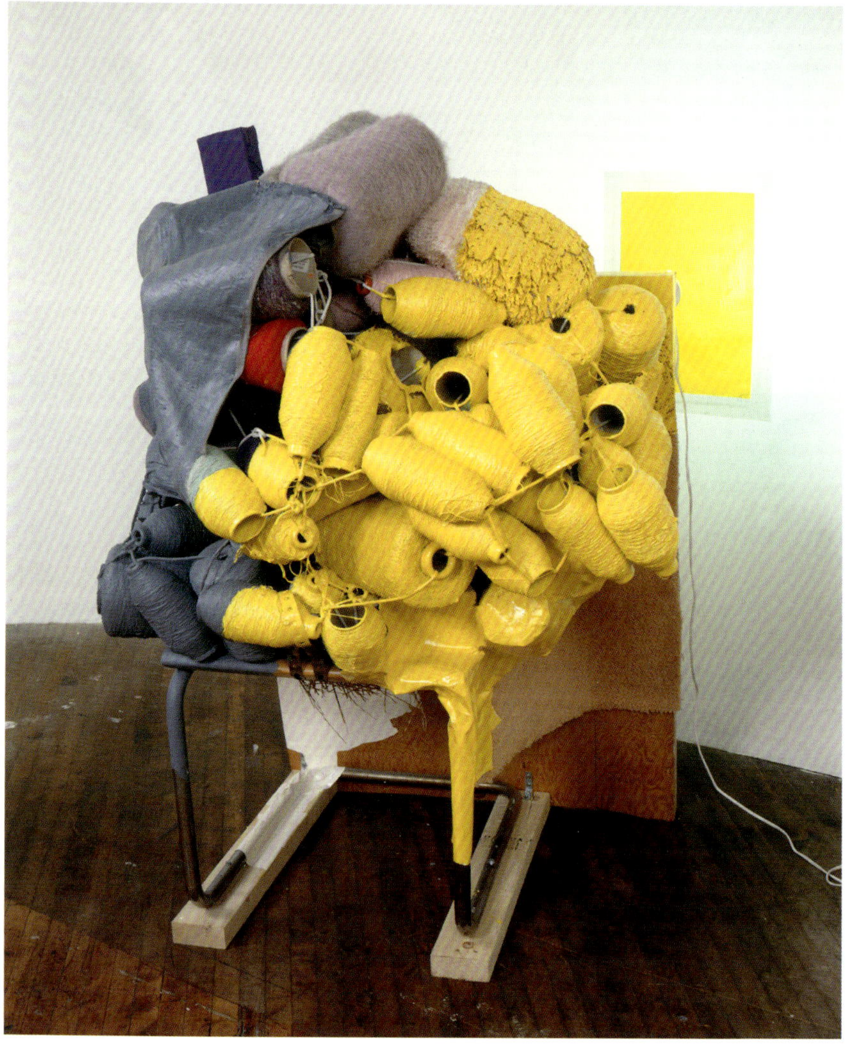

KISSING THE WALL #5, 1990
METAL STRAPPING, SPOOLS OF THREAD AND WOOD, CHAIR, OIL AND LATEX AND ACRYLIC PAINT, FLUORESCENT LIGHT, PAPER, GLUE
72 X 86 X 130 CM

TILLMAN: *A pause that refreshes. Why did you title it* House Beautiful*?*

STOCKHOLDER: *House Beautiful* is a magazine about controlling the structure and surface quality of one's environment. This work is about that too, but from a very different point of view. The materials I use here could be from a house – in a sort of turned upside-down manner. The title refers to taste and structure.

TILLMAN: *It also challenges the idea of taste.*

STOCKHOLDER: I think about taste a lot. The magazine *House Beautiful* reinforces and puffs up the notion of good taste, as if there's a right way to do it. My work opens that up to question and proposes that there is no right way to do it, that there's a lot of meaning apparent in the decisions that people make.

In 1987 I made my first piece at this furniture-life scale. It had a light pointed at the wall, so there was a circle of light on the wall, seen in relationship to the object in front of the wall. These smaller works activate the spaced between the wall and the thing in front of it, creating an event but in a more limited or proscribed way than the installations do. I titled the first six *Kissing the Wall.* Since then, almost all of the smaller pieces have had a relationship to the wall.

TILLMAN: *An immediate, probably off the wall response to it: because the green rope is tied to the wall, what comes to mind is 'the tie that binds'. A relationship, about art to the gallery wall, and an interaction between two things – tense because the green rope is taut. The green rope ties what looks like a lounge chair and a kind of picket fence, to the wall. One side of this stuffed chair is very brightly coloured, a patchwork pastiche. A crazy quilt, and it's painted. What is the material?*

KISSING THE WALL OUT OF SEQUENCE, 1989
SMALL LOW TABLE/CUPBOARD, GREEN NEWSPAPER MACHÉ, ENAMEL PAINT, ORANGE PEES, SMALL LIGHT FIXTURE ON THE WALL WITH A SMALL ORANGE LIGHT BULB
70 X 190 X 50 CM

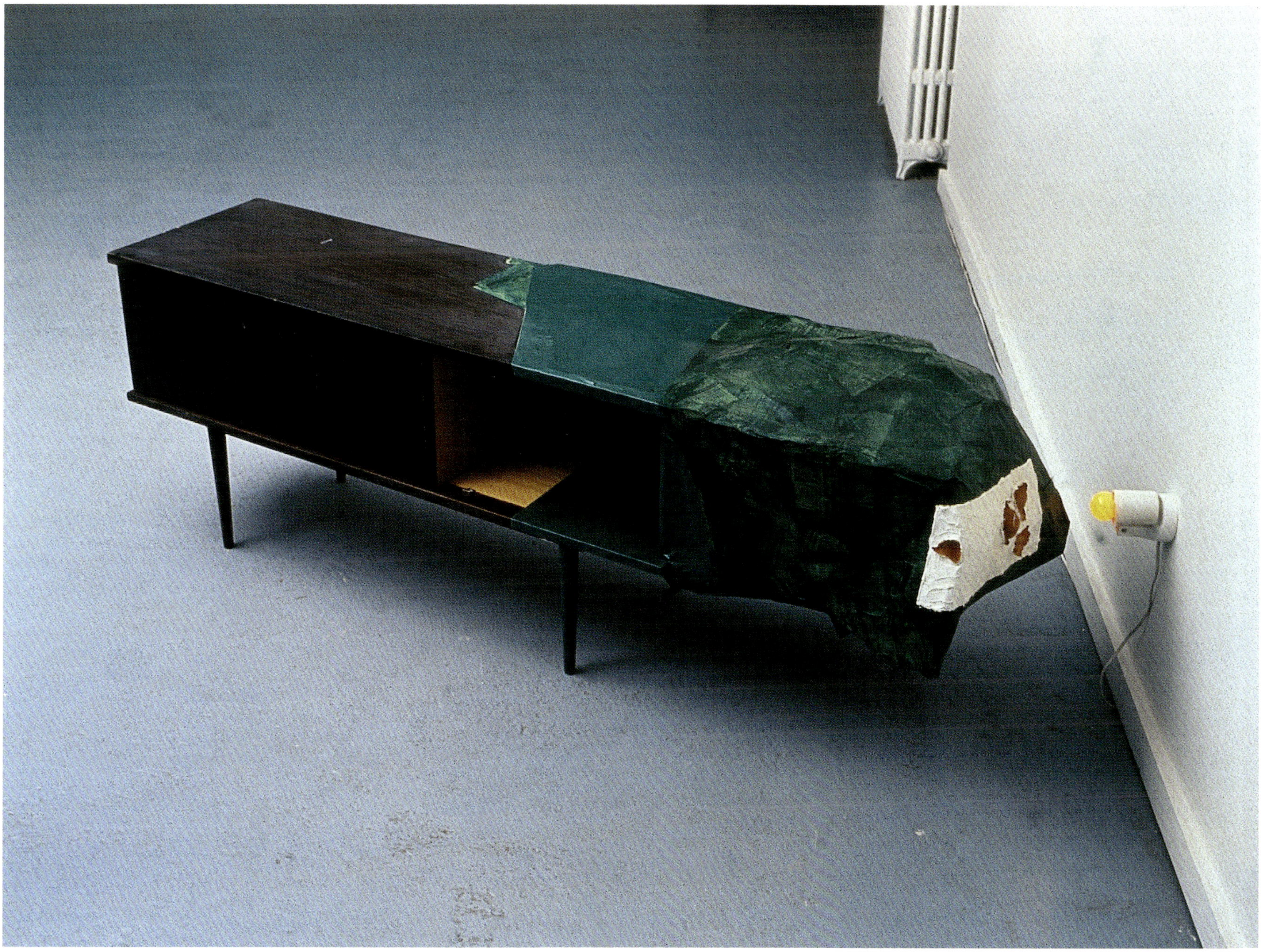

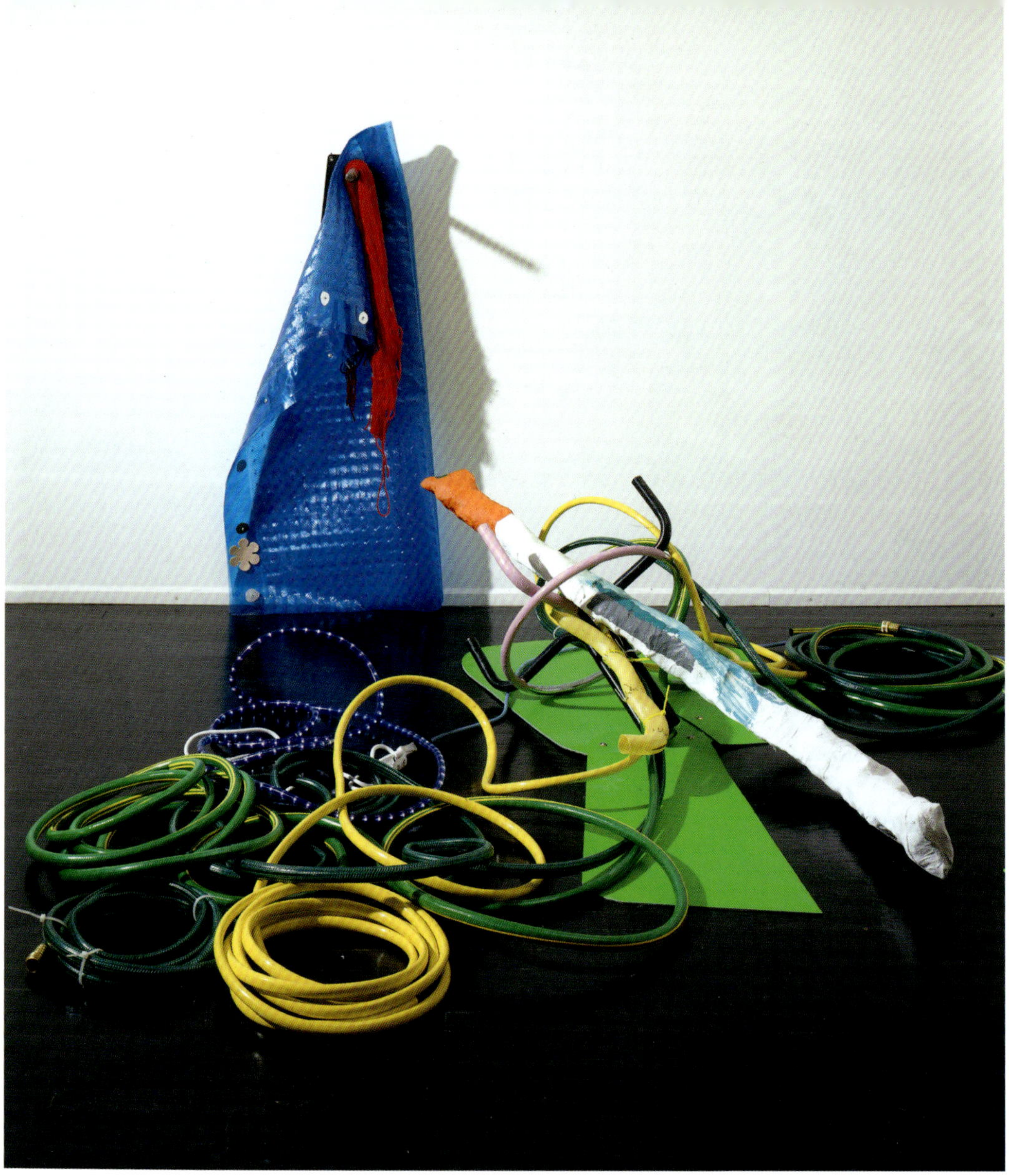

STOCKHOLDER: The red is fabric, there is a white shirt glued to the sofa with paint on top of it; there's plastic, and the rest of it is painted colour.

TILLMAN: *The couch or sectional's sort of grotesque. You've built an armature around it, indicating a fence to me. Sectional plays on 'sexual'. Your work takes 'real' things and makes a mockery of that reality. Is* Mother *the sectional/couch? Is the art/wall* Mother*? It's the green rope – I can't help thinking of ties, dependency, the umbilical cord. Then the gap between wall and chair could represent a formal relationship of art viewer to gallery wall. The strangely painted couch could stand for the spectator and the spectator's relationship to seeing paintings and drawings on a wall. One formative relationship – mother/child – leads into other relationships, like what is a viewer's relationship to a piece of art?*

STOCKHOLDER: And what is the relationship of the piece of art to context? Does a particular context support art, like an umbilical cord from the mother supports the child? What do buildings mean to us? What about independence? All of these are questions in the work.

In this smaller piece, one part is a cast concrete inflatable ball; the ball served as the form for the concrete.

previous page,
1997
METAL BRACKET, WOOL YARN, PLASTIC MAT, PLASTIC DECAL, HARDWARE, STOOL LEGS, HOSES, ELECTRICAL PLASTIC TIES, FLUORESCENT FLOOR TILE, PLASTER, CHEESE CLOTH
217 X 227 X 193 CM

1996
ACRYLIC PAINT, OIL ON GLASS, WOODEN SHINGLES, WIRE MESH, GREEN WIRE, HARDWARE, ACRYLIC YARN, THREAD, SILICONE CAULKING
180 X 122 X 74 CM

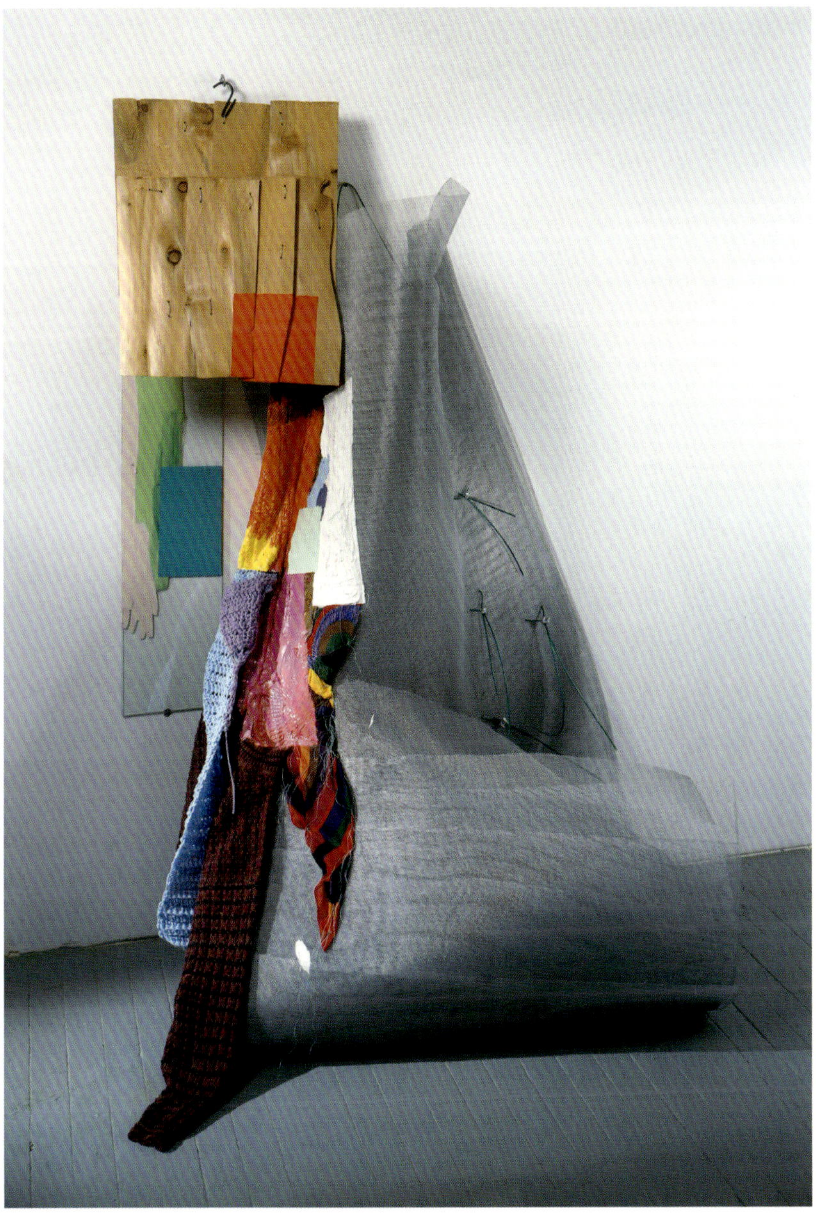

TILLMAN: *It's attached to the wall under a bird cage, but not attached to the bird cage. Birds, flight, imprisonment … Being imprisoned would be pretty weighty. But the cage is open, so again, there's an exit. It reminds me of Buñel's film* The Exterminating Angel. *The characters can't leave a room when there's nothing physical stopping them.*

STOCKHOLDER: And there is a shower curtain and a piece of flowered clothing attached to the bird cage; there is also paint, silicone caulking, and yarn.

TILLMAN: *Oranges …*

STOCKHOLDER: … apples, plums, lemons and peaches.

TILLMAN: *Because there are so many, it's like a growth.*

STOCKHOLDER: This yarn piece is very much like a growth. It's quite beautiful and sort of hideous. An accumulation of things in a cancerous sort of way.

TILLMAN: *Cancer is what I thought of immediately, a wild cell division.*

STOCKHOLDER: There's bias tape hanging down the back with a few threads and a few wires. For me that implies frivolity – it might be ribbon – and also leftovers, bits and pieces from something just finished or not quite done.

TILLMAN: *It's funny to use concrete as a 'concrete' object in the midst of this fantasy, this phantasm.*

STOCKHOLDER: Exactly, a phantasm, all these things coming together produce something quite fantastic; and then the concrete is a real heavy, simple, known quantity that weighs it down to the floor.

TILLMAN: *Some of your pieces are human scale, and some are much bigger.*

STOCKHOLDER: I love shifts in scale – shifts in point of view.

TILLMAN: *We're now looking at scenery – trees and grass, a park, a baseball diamond.*

STOCKHOLDER: I thought this would be a good place to come because it provides a vantage point that's unusual in a city. The vistas are so long here. How my relation to things changes here has something to do with my work. This place is more reminiscent of the landscape in Vancouver than any place else in NYC.

TILLMAN: *How does this intersect with your interest in architecture, and how your work is architectonic? How does your interest in landscape turn into a built environment?*

STOCKHOLDER: Architecture is a landscape we make. I often experience architecture and landscape as if they weren't make, as if they just happen to be there framing my life process. The landscape we're looking at is made. But in general, there is more about landscape that exists before us and without us than in architecture.

TILLMAN: *Most landscapes we see are built.*

STOCKHOLDER: There is a difference between the Vancouver of my childhood and this part of the world. In Vancouver there were, and there still are, more places where you can view a landscape which hasn't been manipulated by us. It has been less touched.

TILLMAN: *An idea of wilderness, something untouched by human beings. But you want to touch things, you want to move the environment around.*

STOCKHOLDER: The landscape in Vancouver provides a particular spatial experience which is wedded to my work. The way the water meets an island, or another piece of land, and forms a horizon line below the one made by the tops of the mountings meeting the sky – that particular horizon line has something to do with the kind of space that I am interested in. I'm also very interested in the difference between what we make and what is.

TILLMAN: *When you see things in terms of art, you're thinking how nature is like art. Of course, things confirm our beliefs, most of the time, since we look for that.*

STOCKHOLDER: Are you less comfortable at this angle, looking at nature instead of at art?

TILLMAN: *I have some agoraphobia, some fear of open spaces, empty, six-lane highways – not crowded cities. There's something strange about the distance between us, this long space between us, and the trees. In that space there could be an incredible amount of horrible things happening.*

STOCKHOLDER: The work you called 'raising the stakes' – *Edge of Hot House Glass* – had a second title, *The Body Repeats the Landscape*, a quotation from Jane Smiley. In that work I became aware of something that carried through my work. I saw it as a very large body. There was velvet, there were beads; but things didn't cohere. They did at moments but always threatening to come apart at the seams. It was as if you, the viewer, were very small, looking at a giant body. The body as a landscape. I think this has something to do with having been a child, very small and growing.

TILLMAN: *Some more than others – physically, mentally, emotionally.*

STOCKHOLDER: That physical experience, that shift in point of view, happens to everyone. Ina way, the landscape changes on us. Perhaps our first experience of landscape is of the big bodies holding us.

TILLMAN: *I don't know that, as a viewer. I would have thought of the landscape as a body, although I might have thought of a body of land, an island jutting into the space. I don't know if I can reverse my position. I would become the thing that a body would normally be looking at. A sort of reversal of positions.*

STOCKHOLDER: It's not that the work is a body. It's about the experience of the body as landscape. I'm interested in conveying an experience having to do with the difficulty of having things cohere – the feeling that sometimes things are too close so you can't see the edges; or things are so large that you can't see the edges – a lack of definition, or a possibility for expansion lurking in the background of everything we make.

TILLMAN: *Maybe that's from having grown up in surroundings that were majestic, the physical situation in which you lived in Vancouver. I was in Vancouver once and remember looking up suddenly, and seeing towering mountains around the city. It did draw off the city itself; it surrounded it, giving it this odd feeling of temporariness. I felt very much aware that the city was something that had been built in the middle of something that had been around much longer.*

STOCKHOLDER: Vancouver is located – there is a sense of place that's missing here in New York.

TILLMAN: *Though Manhattan is bordered on both sides by rivers. When I was a kid, it was very hard for me to understand how all the big buildings could be on a little island. Obviously rivers are flat. They're not towering over Manhattan; Manhattan towers over the rivers.*

STOCKHOLDER: New York hasn't been constructed to call attention to the rivers

1994
TWO ELEMENTS:
NO. 1: BIRD CAGE, PLASTIC SHOWER CURTAIN, CLOTHING, PLASTIC FRUIT, HINGE, BALLS OF YARN, WIRE, RIBBON
NO. 2: STRING, CONCRETE AND EYE HOOK
188 X 84 X 60 CM

and not much is made of the water front. I miss that. Growing up in Vancouver with American parents involved feeling confused about my place culturally and nationally. Perhaps the particularity of the landscape became more important for that reason.

TILLMAN: *You're very much in a place when looking at your work, it's about positioning you there. I guess that's the physical sensation of it – it's not as if you are just looking at an object which lets you think only in the abstract. You have to do both, you look and think abstractly and are aware that you are standing somewhere.*

STOCKHOLDER: It's nice to hear you say that. That's why I wanted to come here.

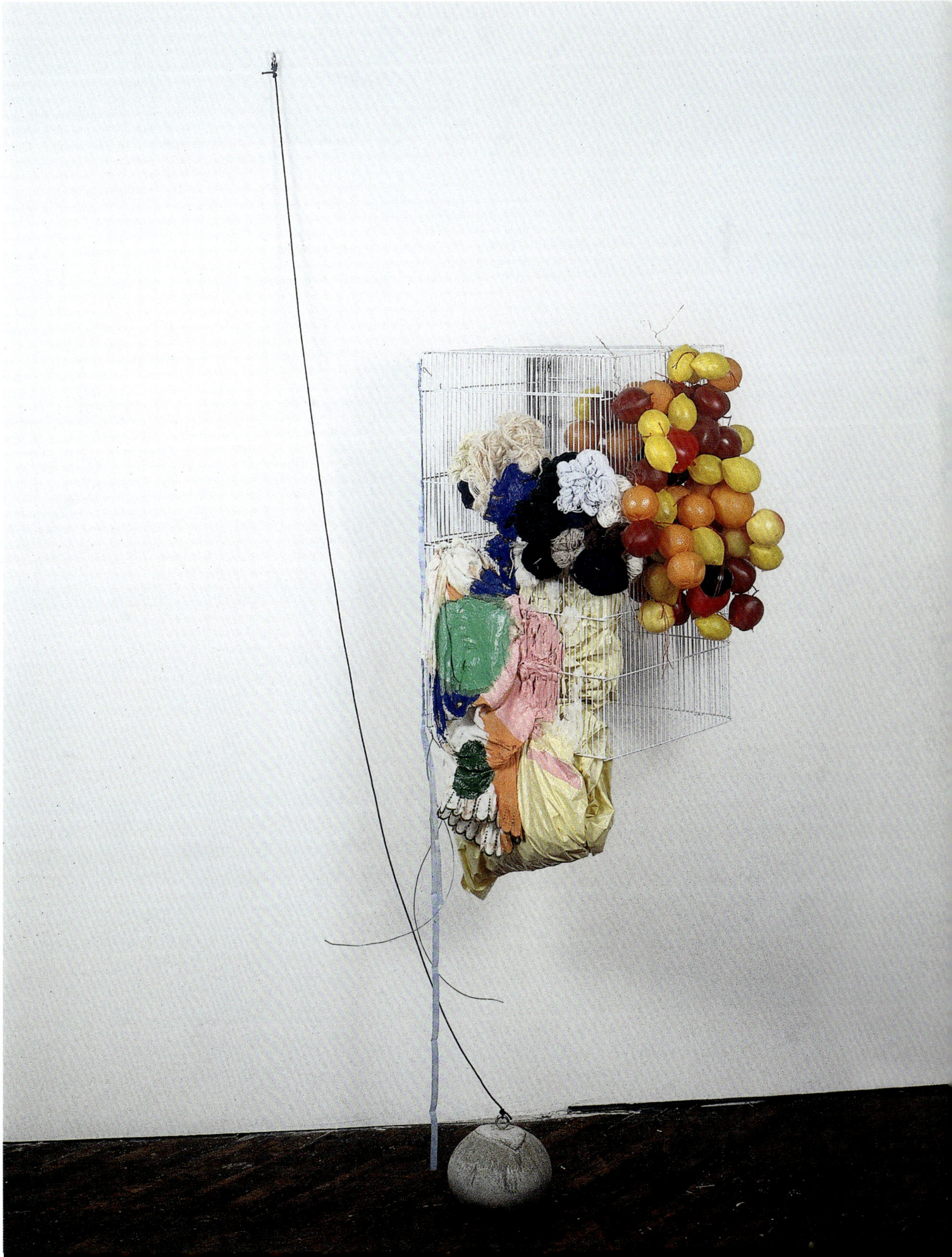

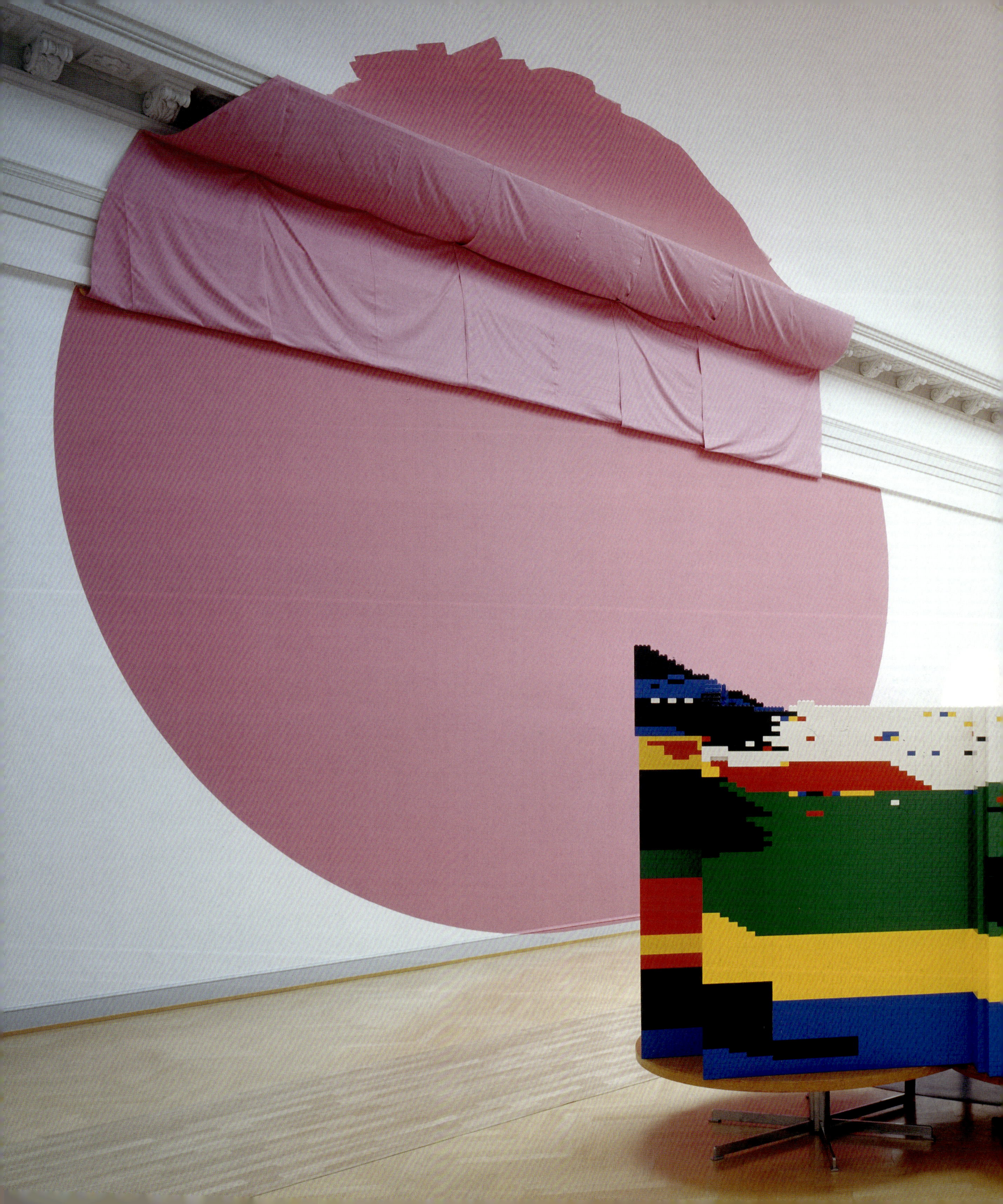

047 SURVEY

The Magic of Sobriety

Barry Schwabsky

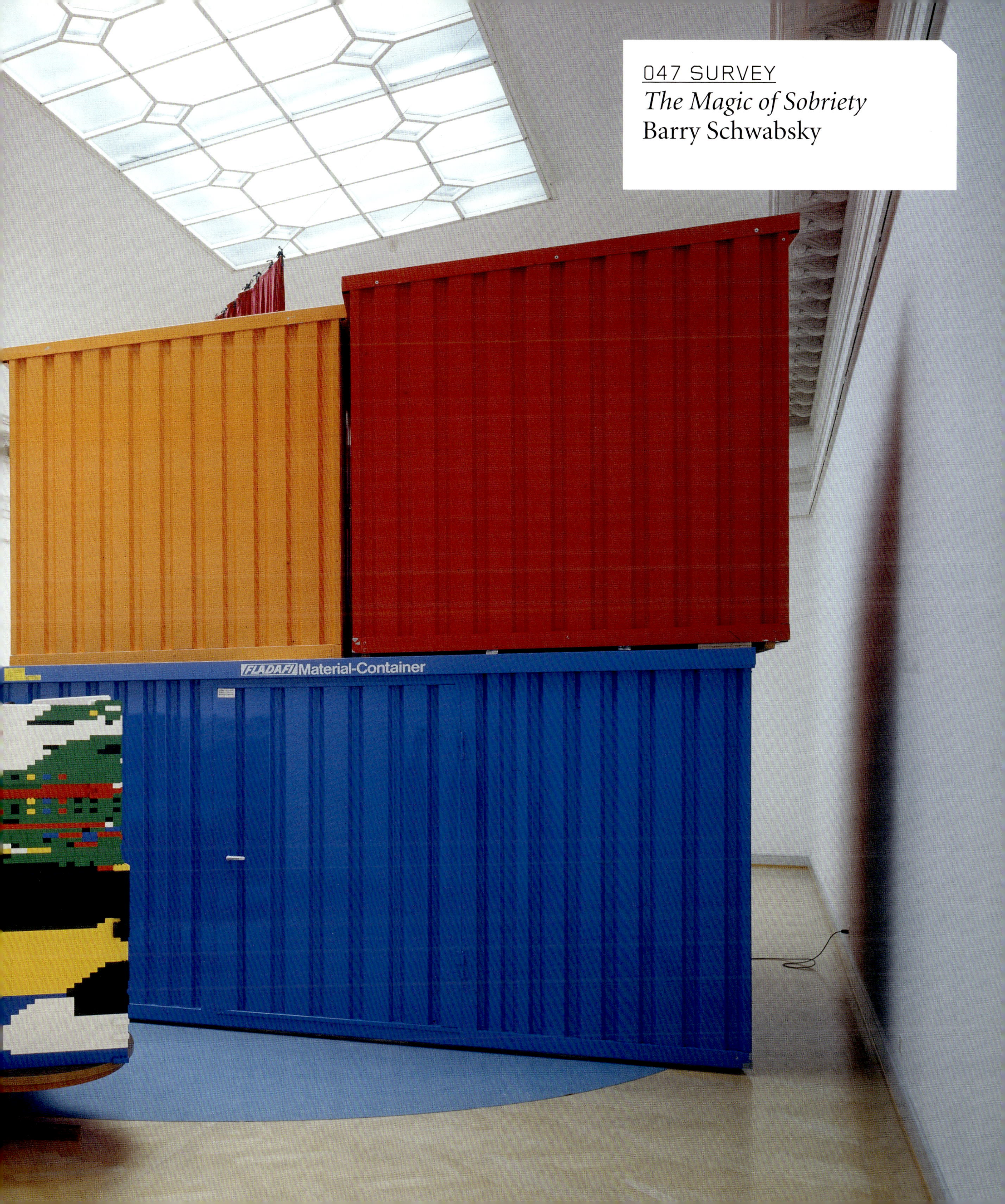

I

Although I'd like to think that art speaks for itself and that an acquaintance with the artist should not affect our view of her work, my experience tells me that's not always so. In Jessica Stockholder's case, what seemed most salient in her work before I met her was its outrageousness, its sense of fantasy and prolific inventiveness. What matters to me more now – and I'm sure I'm influenced in this by my sense of the artist as a person, of her careful presentation of self to world – is just the opposite: its orderliness, its discipline, its sense of reality. Before I saw that this work was marvellously inventive; now I know that it is also acutely observant; it is a deep attentiveness that allows for the effortlessness, the verisimilitude with which Stockholder disposes all this *stuff*, a deployment of materials that neither insists on nor denies the intentionality involved. Not that freedom and discipline, fantasy and reality are as mutually contradictory as we sometimes imagine: listen to the ecstatic dialectic between improvisation and structure in a great jazz performance. I don't now think my early sense of the effect of Stockholder's work was wrong; but it was one-sided. The artist's personal reticence and matter-of-factness harbours the secret core of fantastication and joyous subversiveness which we know from her art – but the art, in manifesting the latter, delivers in a concealed way a core of quiet fidelity to the real.

And yet as soon as I use that word – 'real' – I feel moved to quality it, compromise it even, in any case to place it within quotation marks. The 'real' that Stockholder's work addresses is in the first instances the place and time in which it finds itself, most immediately, the architectural situation of its installation. In this essay I will concentrate on Stockholder's large-scale installations, but they are not in themselves completely definitive of her art, which could be said to consist of three groups or series, whose identities rest most obviously on issues of scale but more specifically on the kind of space addressed. The installations are environmental in scale and are created in and for specific gallery or museum situations – quasi-public spaces. The more or less self-contained assemblages reflect the scale of the human individual rather than an abstract 'public' but also that of the artist's studio; these seem to function not only as relatively portable and saleable commodities but as 'essays' through which the artist can work out in a more private way with the forms and materials that concern her. Finally there are Stockholder's collages, which unfortunately I will not have occasion to discuss at all. These are even more fully self-contained than the assemblages not only because they are considerably smaller but above all because they are flat and because their supports – often rectangular or nearly rectangular sheets of glass – give them a feeling of 'framedness' that her other work, with its dishevelments and seepages, resists. These collages correspond neither to the public space of the museum nor the working space of the studio, but to the intimate scale of the average urban

FAT FORM AND HAIRY: SARDINE CAN PEELING, 1994
REFRIGERATORS, PAINT, GREEN TARP, AIRCRAFT CABLES, SWEATERS, GARBAGE CANS, PILLOWS, CONCRETE, WOOL, STYROFOAM, BUILDING MATERIALS, GREEN LIGHTS, ELECTRIC CABLE AND PLEXIGLASS

INSTALLATION VIEW AT THE HAYWARD GALLERY, LONDON, 1994

previous pages,
VORTEX IN THE PLAY OF THEATER WITH REAL PASSION, IN MEMORY OF KAY STOCKHOLDER, 2000
DUPLO, THEATER CURTAIN, WORK SITE CONTAINERS, BENCH, THEATER LIGHT, LINOLEUM, TABLES, FUR, NEWSPAPER, FABRIC, AND PAINT

INSTALLATION VIEW AT KUNSTMUSEUM ST. GALLEN, 2000

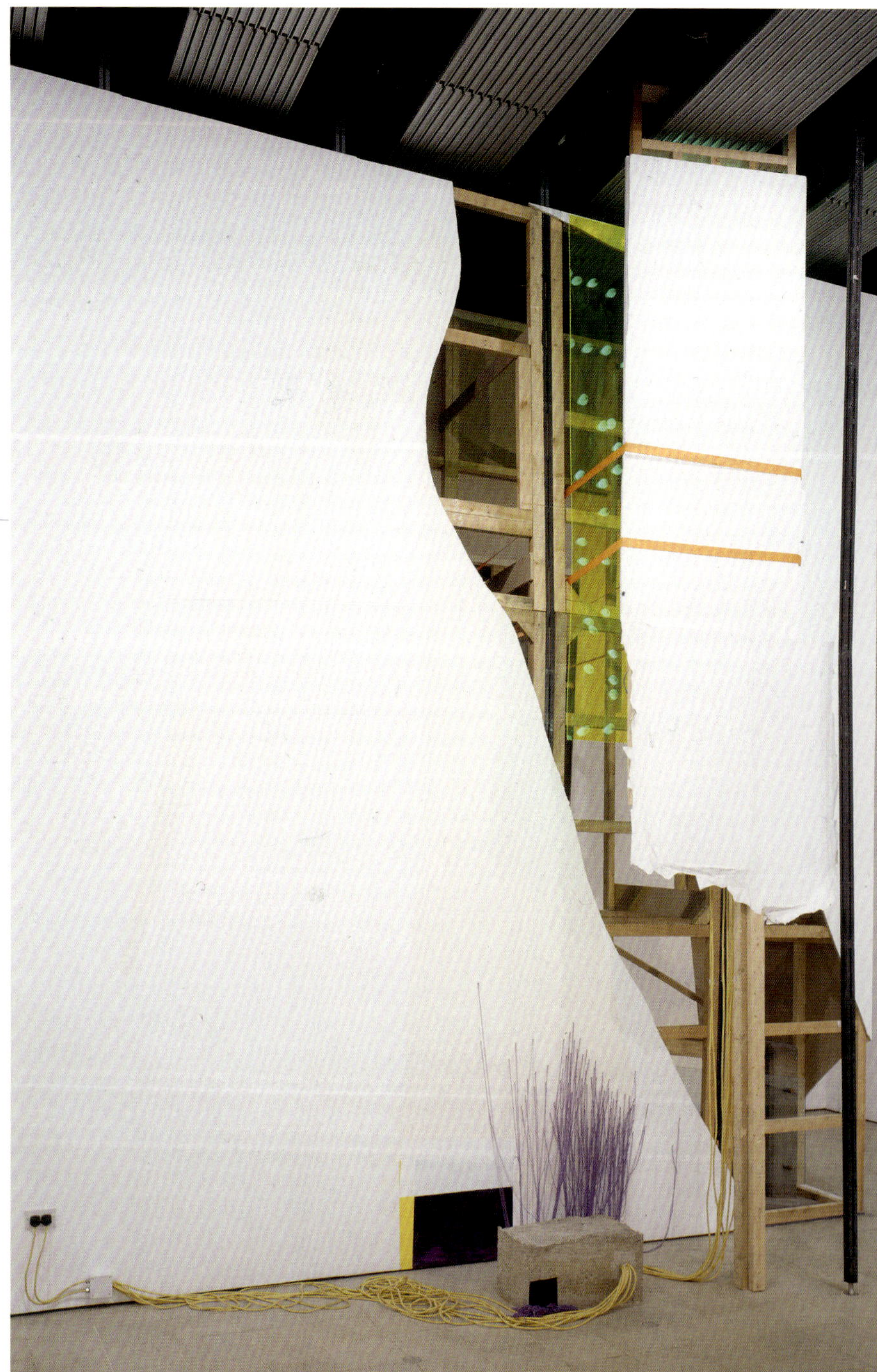

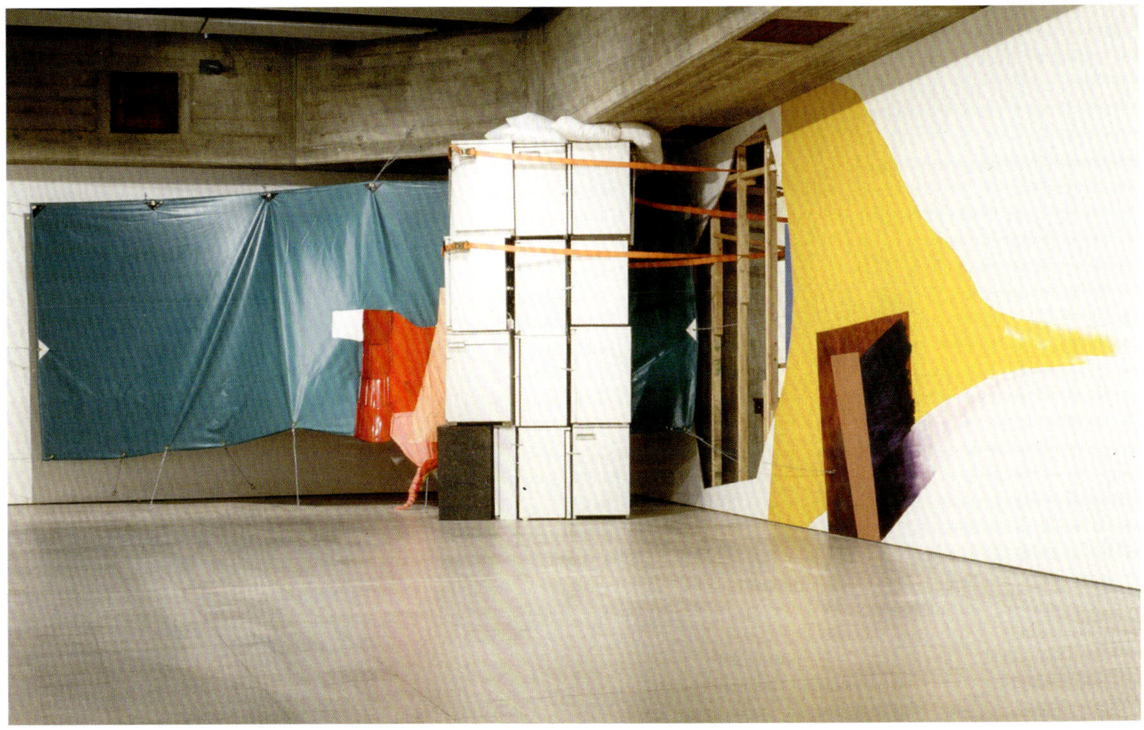

FAT FORM AND HAIRY: SARDINE CAN PEELING, 1994
REFRIGERATORS, PAINT, GREEN TARP, AIRCRAFT CABLES, SWEATERS, GARBAGE CANS, PILLOWS, CONCRETE, WOOL, STYROFOAM, BUILDING MATERIALS, GREEN LIGHTS, ELECTRIC CABLE AND PLEXIGLASS

apartment. In any case, the address of Stockholder's work to its architectural setting is relevant even with her smaller assemblages, whose specific character always derives in large part from their specific relations to the floor and particularly to the wall, despite their having been designed for no one wall or floor in particular. It's no accident that Stockholder gave to a number of these works the name *Kissing the Wall*. But the real is more than just a given. As that title implies, the real allows itself to be seduced by the work of art. It changes, reveals its unreality with respect to the supreme fictions of art.

II

Some thirty years ago the American critic Harold Rosenberg could still credibly insist that, in modern art, 'movements' were the source of 'continuity of style, ... interchanges of ideas and perception among artists rather than local "schools" such as are familiar to art historians: instead of "the Venetians" or "the Flemish School", our era presents practitioners of aesthetic "isms".'[1] Yet the intervening decades have radically changed this picture. After the emergence of Colour Field painting, Minimalism, Fluxus and Pop Art early in the 1960s and then of conceptual Art toward the end of the decade, the idea of the art movement seems to have lost its élan and to have become more of a marketing ploy than an authentic artistic phenomenon. At the same time, the idea of regionalism seems to have gained a new force – in tension with a contrasting, partly market-based internationalism. The great modernist movements tended to present themselves as universally valid, as culminating points in a total history of art. But now, when what have been called 'grand narratives' (Jean-François Lyotard) or 'final vocabularies' (Richard Rorty) have become increasingly suspect, cultural relativism and the incommensurability of local histories thereby became more attractive ideas.

So Perhaps it's not surprising that when Jessica Stockholder and I began the discussions that would form part of my raw material for this essay, one of the first things she said was, 'We should talk about Vancouver'. And yet this is not because her work is part of the 'micro-narrative' of art in Vancouver. Far from it, although the curator who casually wrote of her work as being 'so typically American' might be just as far off.[2] I think rather of a remark made by fellow-Vancouverite Jeff Wall: 'I'm A Canadian and so I'm into the magic of sobriety'.[3] One of the most salient things about Stockholder and her work is that they escape any merely local definition. Although she grew up in Vancouver, she was born in Seattle, her mother is an American citizen (as was her most important teacher in Vancouver) and she maintains dual Canadian and American citizenship. After leaving school, she lived briefly in Toronto, but quickly made her way to New York and although that has remained her base, her career as an artist has been a determinedly international one.

Still, even when escaping local definitions seems important, it is worth knowing what the escaped-from definitions actually might be. The Vancouver-based curator Jo-Anne Birnie Danzker has noted three basic

KISSING THE WALL #4, RED AND GREEN, 1988
SMALL PIECE OF FURNITURE, RED AND GREEN LIGHTS, PAINT, NEWSPAPER, STYROFOAM
H. 61 CM

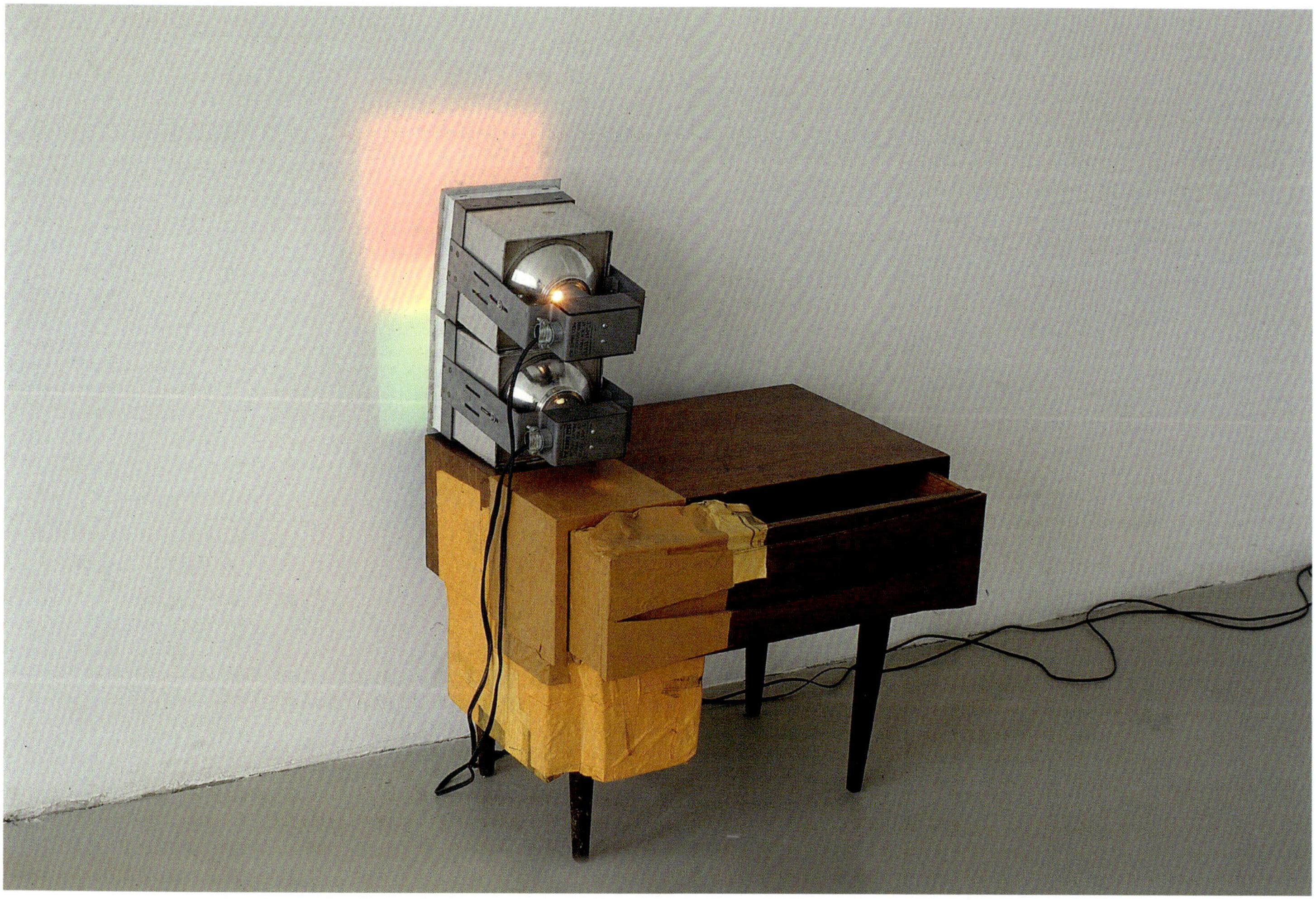

KISSING THE WALL #3, 1988
FAKE CHRISTMAS TREE, PAPIER MACHÉ, PAINT, LIGHT
H. 76 CM

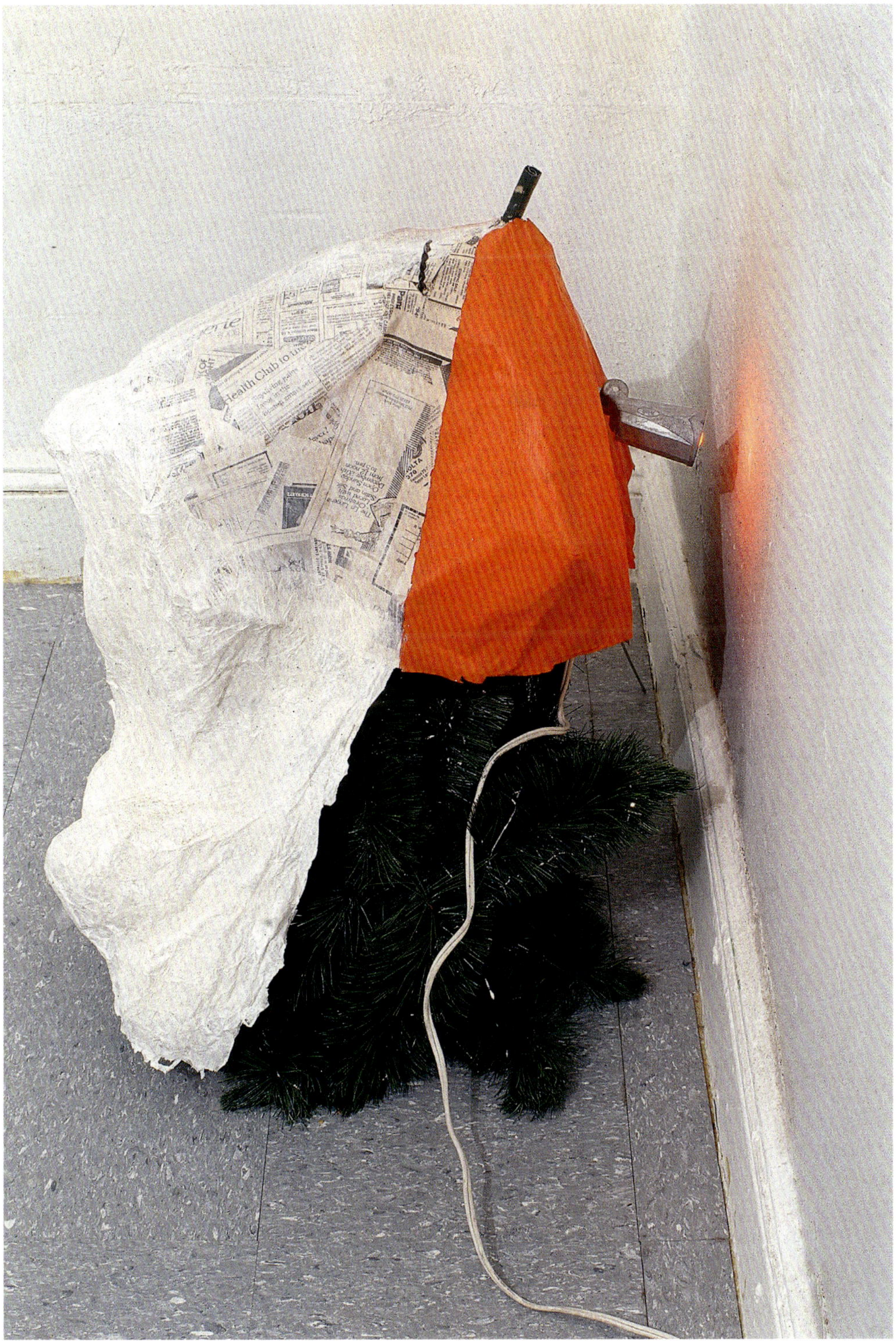

responses to their local situation among artists there in the 1970s, that is, when Stockholder was living and studying there:

- *to apply European and American painting traditions to local subject matter (the British landscape tradition, surrealism, abstract expressionism, 'naïve art', realism, New image painting);*
- *to reject traditional artistic media and utilize 'new' media such as photography, film, video, radio;*
- *to embrace a-historicism, the mass media, stereotypes, instant identities, career and lifestyles associated with 'frontier' cultures;*
- *to apply a strong historical and art-historical approach (including citation) to new media with an emphasis on rationalism, conceptualism, structuralism and ideologically rigid positions.*[4]

What is striking – aside from the fact that such approaches were hardly specific to Vancouver but rather near-universal except where there was some strongly countervailing local tradition – is how thoroughly removed Stockholder's work appears to be from any of these options. Although her work is art-historically informed, it is neither governed by any strict intellectual or ideological stance, nor does it simply re-apply a 'found' style. When asked 'Do you relate more closely to an American or a European painting tradition?', Stockholder replied,

> *I relate more to an American tradition, though probably to both. Matisse, Cézanne and the Cubists certainly are important to me. I also feel a strong affinity to Clyfford Still, Frank Stella, the New York School hard-edge painting and Minimalism, as well as Richard Serra.*[5]

That's quite a range of twentyeth century art, but overall it implies a distinct bias towards artists whose work emphasizes physicality, whether of the surface of a painting or of the artwork as three-dimensional object – and therefore, perhaps, towards a 'materialist' understanding of artistic modernity. Cubism especially should be important to Stockholder in this regard, because the Cubist *papier collé* and collage in particular are seen as initiating the tendency of modern art to admit bits of unmediated reality into art, to include real things cut out of their original contexts and granted onto the artwork rather than depicting or transcribing them by conventionally artistic means. Cézanne was the Cubists' great precursor – and that of Matisse as well – in using the application to paint to canvas to elicit

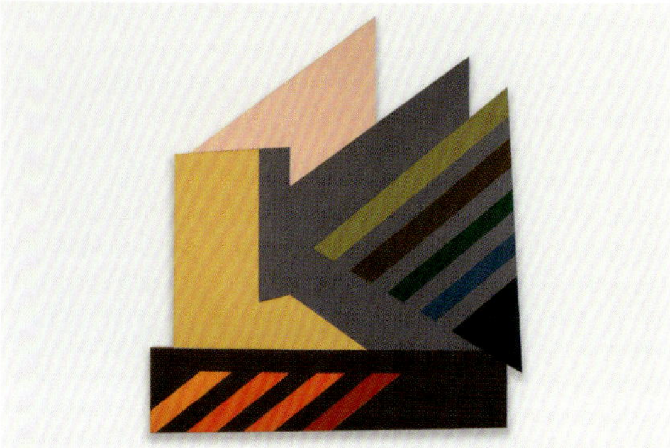

FRANK STELLA
GRODNO 1, 1973
MIXED MEDIA COLLAGE
285 X 227 CM

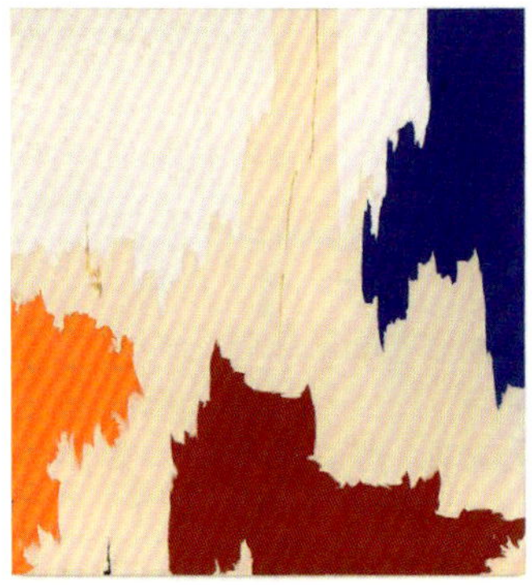

CLYFFORD STILL
PH-973, 1959
OIL ON CANVAS
292 X 267 X 3 CM

what Clement Greenberg called 'a two-dimensional, literal solidity' more than 'a representational one'.[6] By the same token, it is surprising that Stockholder does not mention any of the artists who, in the late 1950s, around the time of her birth, began re-exploring and indeed amplifying art's appropriation of everyday reality; I am thinking in particular of the American artists Jasper Johns and Robert Rauschenberg, but also of others such as the French *Nouveaux Réalistes* and the Zero group in Germany. Rauschenberg's omission may seem especially curious, not only because critics have often mentioned his work as a precedent for that of Stockholder, but also in light of Scott Watson's suggestion that for the Vancouver art scene, 'the capital of America was *not* New York, but Black Mountain and its own revisionist "post-Modernism" springs from this connection with Robert Creeley, John Cage and Charles Olson – and therefore, one would think to add, Rauschenberg.'[7] Yet there is a clue in this omission; for the art of the 1960s which Stockholder cites – Stella, hard-edge painting, Minimalism – claims a relation to the literal, the quotidian, the non-aesthetic as well, but in a less overt, less representational, one might even say more formal and less sociological way. In any case, the story to which Stockholder's work relates is mainly a New York story, but as recounted from the inquisitive yet unromanticizing viewpoint of an outsider.

III

The relation of Stockholder's work to Minimalism in particular deserves to be more fully investigated – and when I speak of Minimalism, I mean not only a set of works by a particular group of artists, but also the ideas that circulated around those works and the polemical thrust of t hose ideas in relation to others current at the time of the movement's inception. Donald Judd was not only one of the leading artists of Minimalism, but, as a frequent contributor to *Arts Magazine, Artforum, Studio International* and other publications, its principal critical spokesman as well. 'Half or more of the best

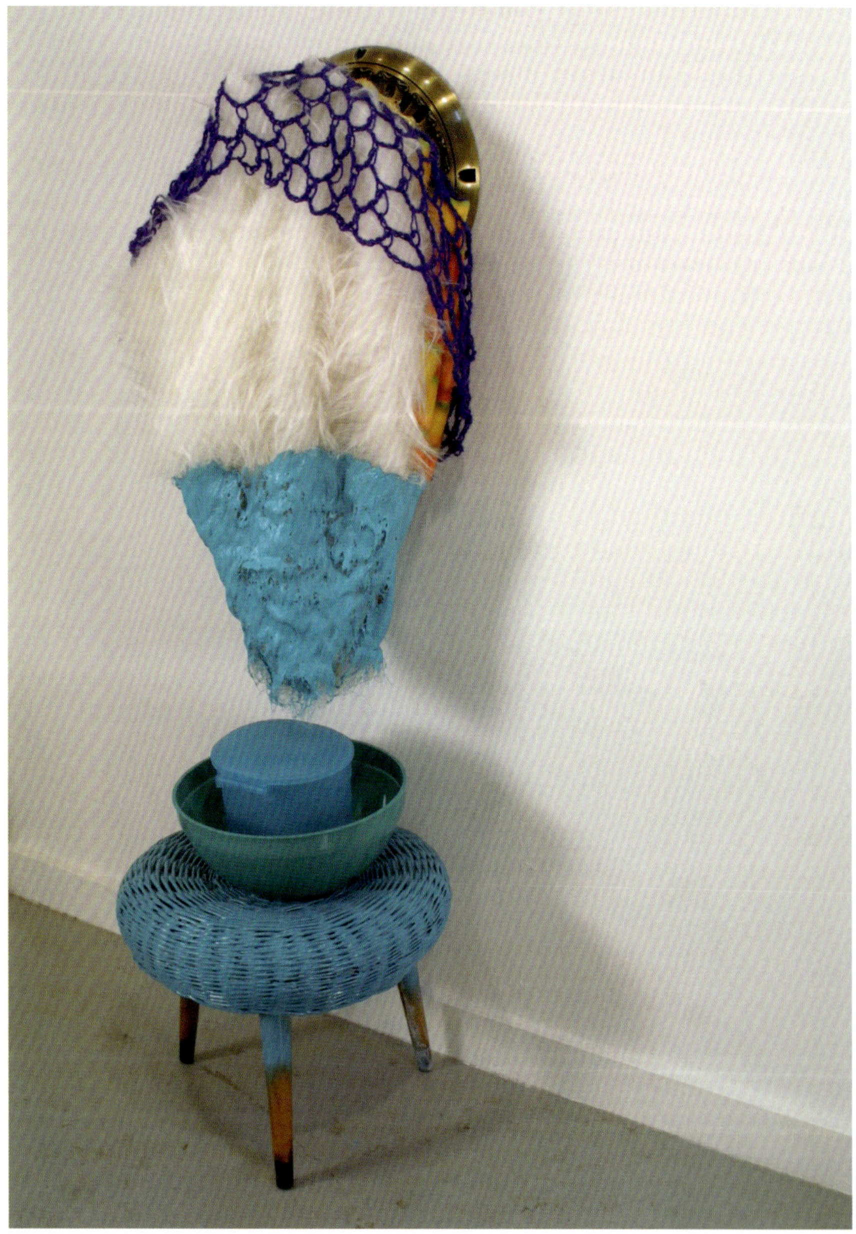

TABLE TOP SCULPTURE, 2003
FAN COLLAR, WHITE FAKE FUR, FABRIC, CROCHETED ACRYLIC YARN, BLUE PLASTIC CONTAINERS, WICKER STOOL
140 X 51 X 44 CM

INSTALLATION VIEW AT GORNEY BRAVIN + LEE, NEW YORK, 2003

1995
ACRYLIC AND OIL PAINTS, FABRIC, YARN, PLASTIC, METAL, LOG, PLASTER, PAIER MACHÉ, ROPE, NYLON DUSTER, HARDWARE
168 X 79 X 43 CM

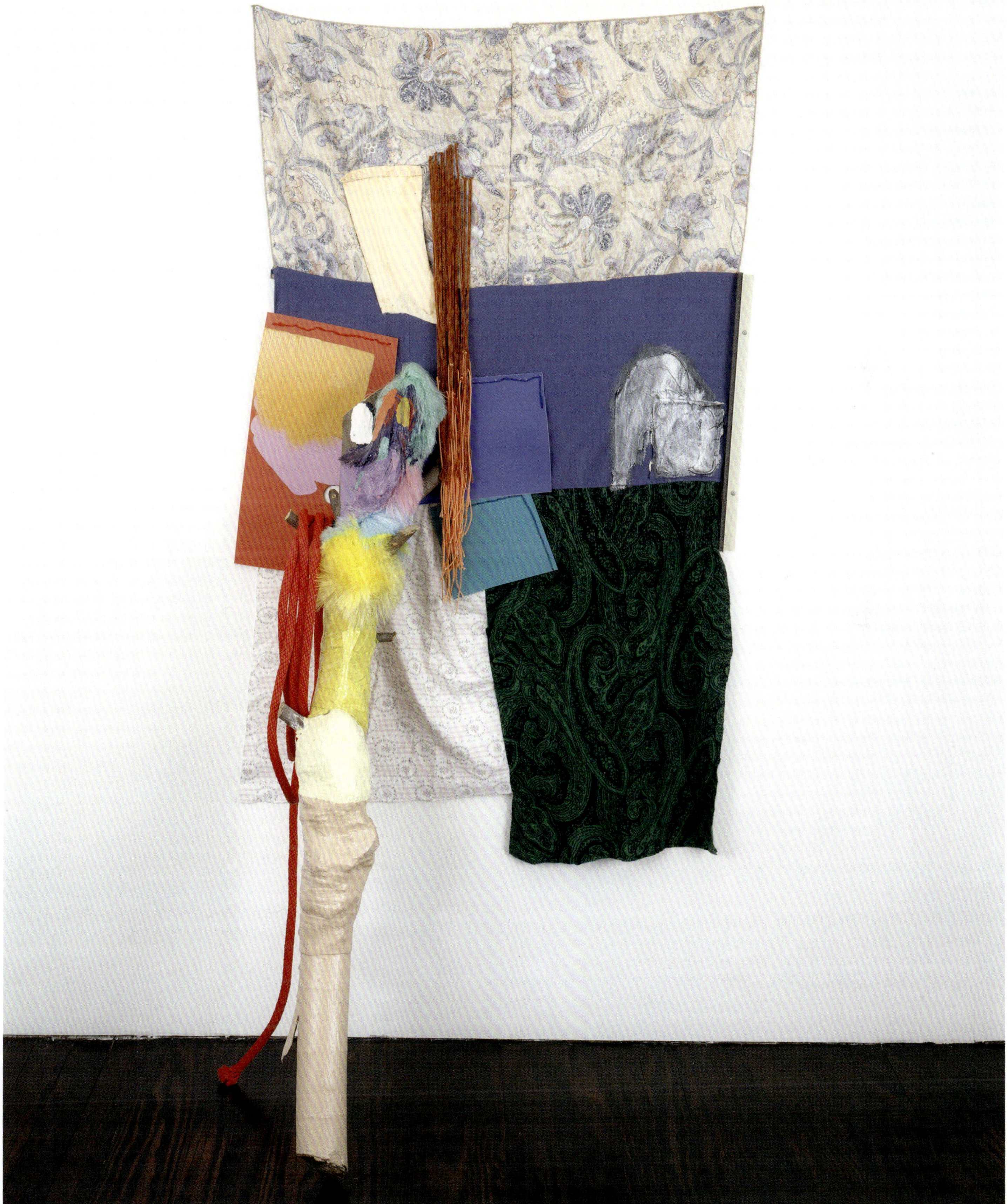

1995
ACRYLIC AND OIL PAINT, ACRYLIC YARN ON GLASS SHELF, WICKER, CHAIR, PLASTIC, TUB, LIGHT FIXTURE AND BULB, CRUSHED VELVET, PLASTIC PIGGY BANKS, CLOTH, CONCRETE, COOKIE IN RESIN, WOOD ON WHEELS
172 X 154 X 125 CM

new work', Judd declared in his 1965 manifesto 'Specific Objects', has been neither painting nor sculpture'.[8] In general, Stockholder's work appears to fit comfortably into certain aspects of the paradigm established by Judd thirty years ago: although its historical roots are more in painting than in sculpture, just as with Judd's work, it is three-dimensional; its materials are employed in a direct and sometimes aggressive fashion, without illusionism and so on. Replying to Judd, Michael Fried declared that ' concepts of quality and value ... are meaningful ... only within the individual arts' so that this art that is neither painting nor sculpture is merely 'theatre' and that 'theatre is now the negation of art'.[9] Putting aside for now the question of why one would assert that theatre negates art – the statement is odd on the face of it, since theatre is ordinarily thought of as an art form in its own right – we can see that Stockholder's art is thoroughly theatrical, in the sense that, as Fried claimed of Minimalist art, it does not claim to enclose itself in its own autonomous presence, but rather solicits the participation of the viewer or 'beholder' as a real body in real time.[10] No wonder her installations have been compared, for their makeshift, ephemeral ambience, to the funky and chaotic sets for the 'Happenings' of artists like Jim Dine, Allan Kaprow or Carolee Schneeman in the early 1960s.[11]

But there is a contradiction in Judd's text; on the one hand it asserts that 'because the nature of three dimensions isn't set, given beforehand, something credible can be made, almost anything' (an implication of almost limitless possibility emphasized by Judd's reference to a broad range of work from the Pop sculpture of Claes Oldenburg to the shaped canvases of Frank Stella, from the gruesome environments of Edward Kienholz to the light icons of Dan Flavin). On the other hand, its narrowing demand, contradicted by so much of the art Judd cited, is that the work be 'not scattered but asserted by one form', which of course was more specifically characteristic of his own work and that of the other artists who came to be called Minimalists. It would not be long, of course, before the emergence of various forms of 'post-Minimalism' – Process Art, Conceptual Art, 'Eccentric Abstraction' and Land Art – emerged from the rich context of Neo-Dada, Assemblage, Happenings, Fluxus, Pop Art and others. Among these, the Minimalist stance, with its theoretical and formal perspicuity, had arisen to take the lead in the reaction against formalist/modernist doctrine as embodies by Clement Greenberg, Michael Fried and the colour-field painting and constructed sculpture they championed.

The post-Minimalist art that began to emerge later in the 1960s was often notably 'scattered' and not 'asserted by a single form'. In contradiction to the prescriptions of Judd and, to a great extent, of Judd's ideological opponents Fried and Greenberg, this scatteredness nonetheless forwarded the injunction against composition, against the adjustment and comparison of part against part, which was the major desideratum of Minimalism. But much of the horizontal, floor-oriented sculpture of the 1970s – and again of recent years – was covertly pictorial, with the floor functioning as a surrogate for the vertical picture-plane. Stockholder's work, though painterly, is not pictorial in that sense. Her

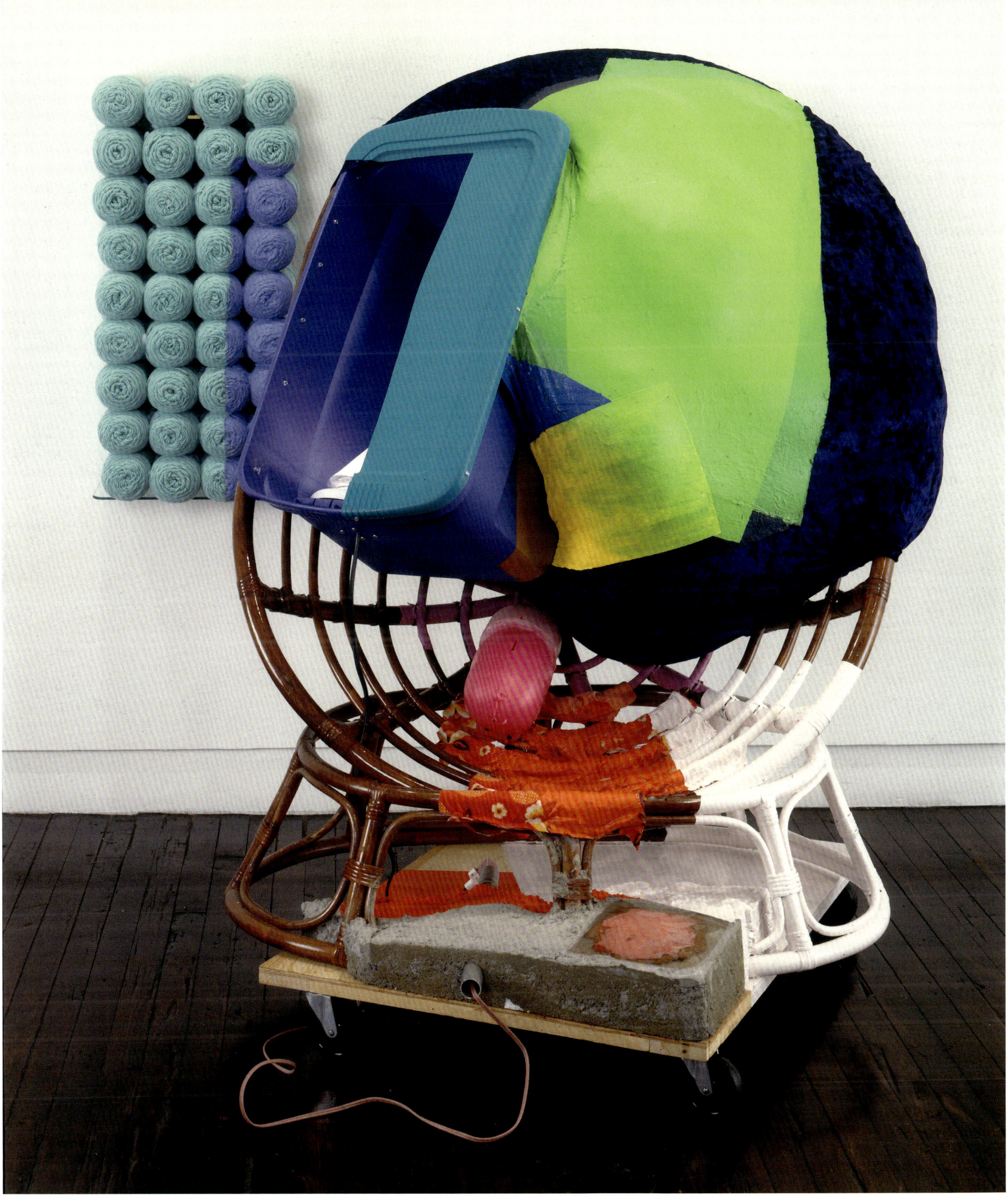

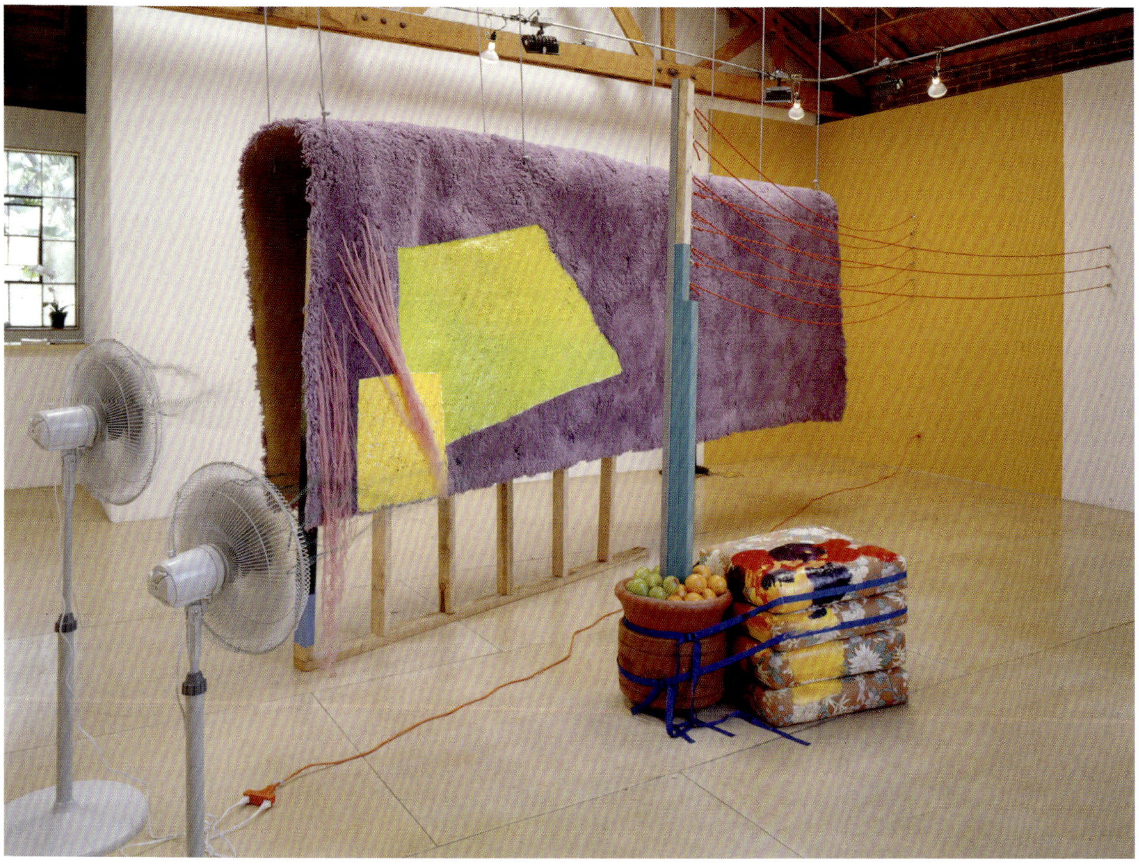

BOWTIED IN THE MIDDLE, 1996
WOOD, CARPET, LAMPS, BLUE BULBS, ORANGE BOATING ROPE, YELLOW AND ORANGE EXTENSION CORDS, PLASTIC PLANT POT, TERRACOTTA PLANT POT, CONCRETE, GALVANIZED STEEL CHANNEL, STEEL CABLE AND HARDWARE, COTTON FABRIC CUSHIONS, RIBBON, PLASTIC AND FRESH FRUIT, YARN

INSTALLATION VIEW AT TOM SOLOMON'S GARAGE, LOS ANGELES, 1996

work may have a greater affinity for another aspect of post-Minimal art – for its contentious stance towards architecture, towards its own built environment, a stance embodies most vividly and iconically in Gordon Matta-Clark's dissected houses; more understatedly in work like Mell Bochner's measurement pieces (1969-71), which, in an otherwise arbitrary gesture suggestive of dismantling or rebuilding, display the rooms they inhabit under the condition of being temporary and contingent.

In fact, the implications of Cubist collage led in two possible directions: towards a rhetoric of anti-illusionism, anti-pictorialism and therefore towards abstraction, literalism and thus Judd's Minimalism; but also towards the breaking of the 'frame' and towards a stylistic and material heterogeneity and impurity that could never rule out representation, illusion, or any sort of pictorial device whatsoever – above all to that 'art of radical juxtaposition', the Happening, to which the affinity of Stockholder's work has been acknowledged. Stockholder has resolutely chosen both directions at once. What she has retained from Happenings is the primacy of materials employed, as Susan Sontag put it, 'for their sensuous properties rather than their conventional uses'; what is eliminated is the idea of the performer and therefore, more importantly, the idea of an audience as a group of spectators bound together through their shared experience of the work in a limited span of time. And since the 'classic' stance of the Happening towards the audience was one of aggression ('In the Happening this scapegoat is the audience', writes Sontag), Stockholder's abdication of audience is equally an abdication of aggression.[12] Like the otherwise utterly different art of Cy Twombly, as analyzed by Roland Barthes, Stockholder's is an exploration of the notion of the 'Event' but since it is 'without goal, without model, without instance ... it follows that any aggression is somehow futile'.[13]

IV

Stockholder's work is always open, accessible and obvious – but only bit by bit, never all at once. As wholes, or ensembles, her installations are complex, contrary and mysterious. They depend on memory, on reconstruction. This is so in the obvious sense that Stockholder's large-scale installations are impossible to perceive inn a single synoptic glance or even, usually, to contain, in retrospect, a single synthetic image, however complex. They absolutely demand the temporal dimension of narration or discourse in order to be understood as wholes – also because they are conceived for specific exhibition spaces, constructed on site and disassembled after a few weeks or months, never to be seen again except in photographs.

Stockholder's work was initially received, to a great extent, as part of a new trend in the New York art world – as part of a reaction against the slick 'commodities' that had been favoured by such art stars of the mid-

1996
ACRYLIC PAINT, WOODE CRATES,
RED CARPET, WOOD, ROPE,
HARDWARE, SWEATER,
ACRYLIC YARN
142 X 241 X 196 CM

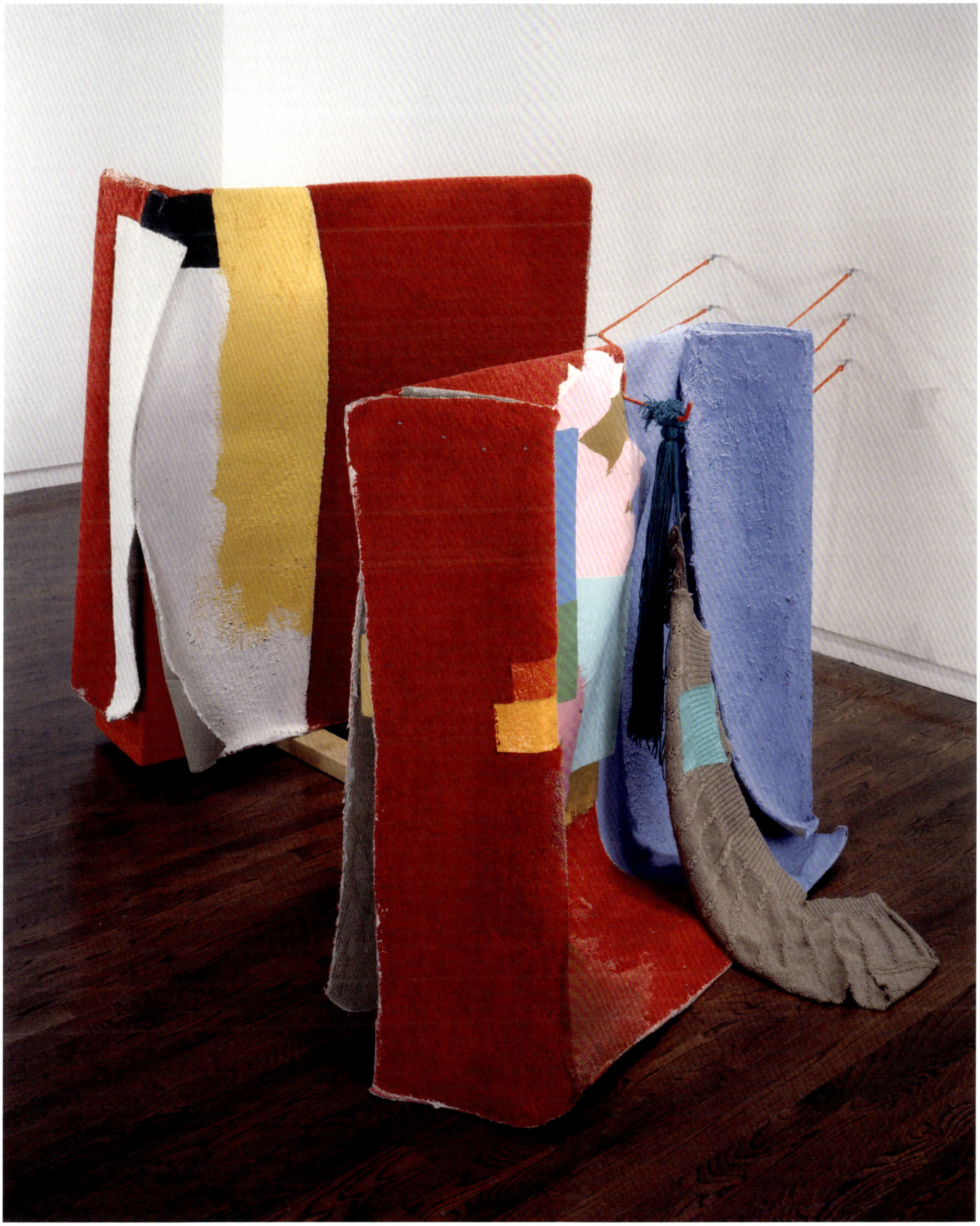

1998–99
ACRYLIC PAINT, WIRE FENCE, PLASTIC TIES, COUCH CUSHIONS, HARDWARE, UMBRELLA, BLUE STRING, BLACK AND ORANGE CORDS, BRASS LAMP BASE, PAINTED METAL GEAR, WIRE, MULTI-COLOURED PLASTIC FUNNELS
235 X 135 X 144 CM

1980s as Jeff Koons and Haim Steinbach. Such 'neo-geo' art was, in essence, a canny synthesis of the formal absoluteness of minimalist sculpture with a sensibility reminiscent of Pop Art. For all the 'criticality' certain proponents wished to claim for it, its success testified to the obviousness with which it rested on the inherited 'good will' of the canonical art movements of the 60s. Its glamour, which was often undeniable, was that of mannerist self-enclosure.

Towards the end of the 1980s, as the limitations of this art became more apparent, critics, collectors and dealers began to cast about for a plausibly contemporary art that appeared to do more than celebrate its own saleability. One solution was to look away from art whose subject was the perfectly self-contained manufactured object, for one that would engage the living, suffering body as a fragile, imperfect, fragmented construct, utterly devoid of imaginary unity – this is how the work of Robert Gober and Kiki Smith was received, for instance. A second solution was to look for a formal reversal rather than a change of subject; to look for an art of dispersions and blurred boundaries, an art open to contingency and awkwardness, one difficult to commodify. It was this desire that, towards the end of the 1980s, created an opening for Jessica Stockholder. Along with the work of Cady Noland (who showed at American Fine Art, Co., in New York) and subsequently Karen Kilimnik, Thom Merrick and others, Stockholder's work was seen to herald a renewed possibility for rawness, improvisation and the unfinished. 'Scatter art', a term that had been coined to describe some of the 'anti-form' art of the 1970s, was returned to circulation.

The conditions of art's reception never fully correspond to those of its production, but in this case the gap between the work's motives and the immediate need it mazy have appeared to fill is especially glaring. No more than in the cases of the other artists I have mentioned was Stockholder's work developed as a reaction against he commodity art of the 1980s, but in addition hers

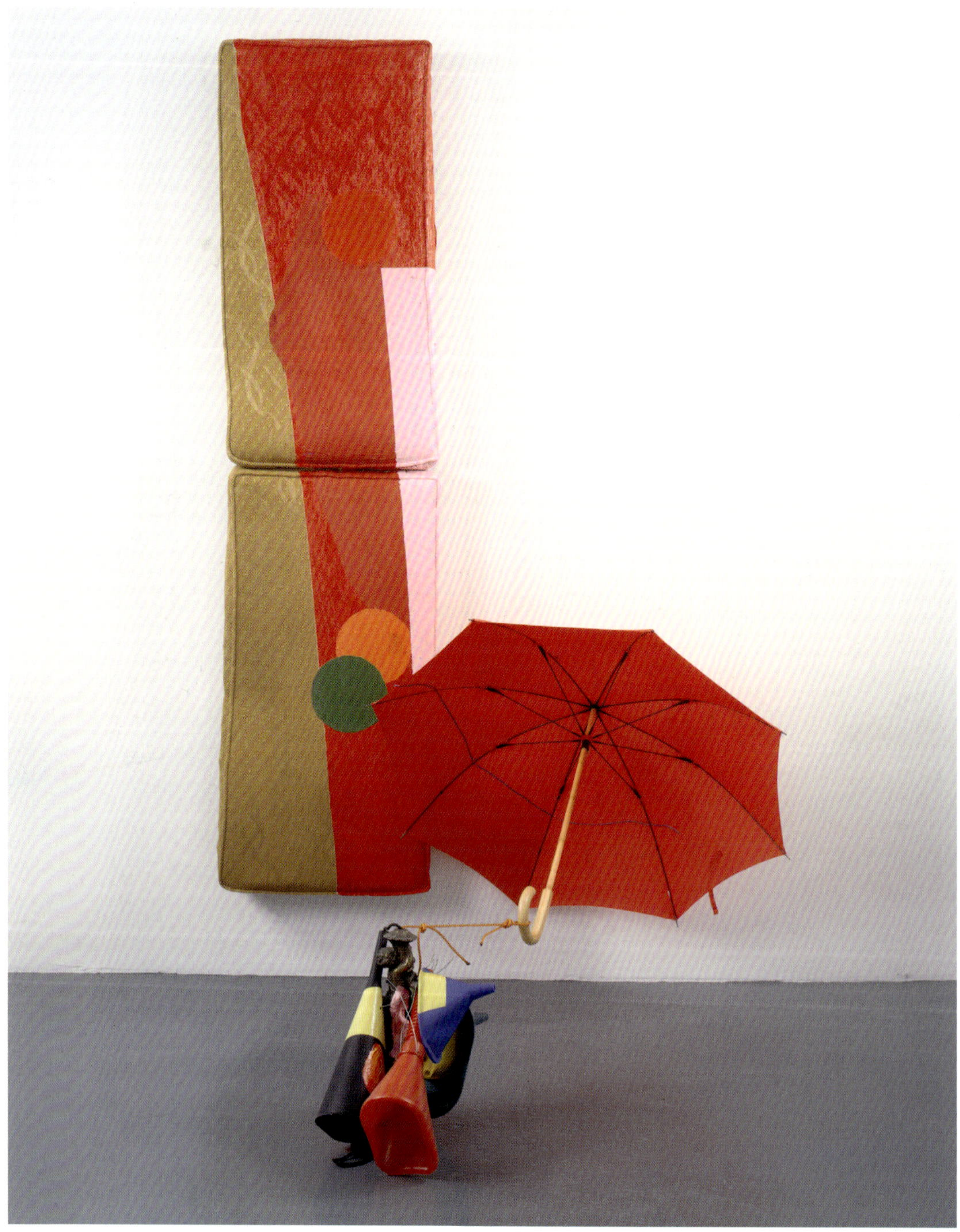

1999
BLACK METAL RACK, LINOLEUM, BRASS METAL BRACKER, ACRYLIC YARN, PAPER, PLASTIC, PHOTOS, OIL AND ACRYLIC PAINT
84 X 81 X 30 CM

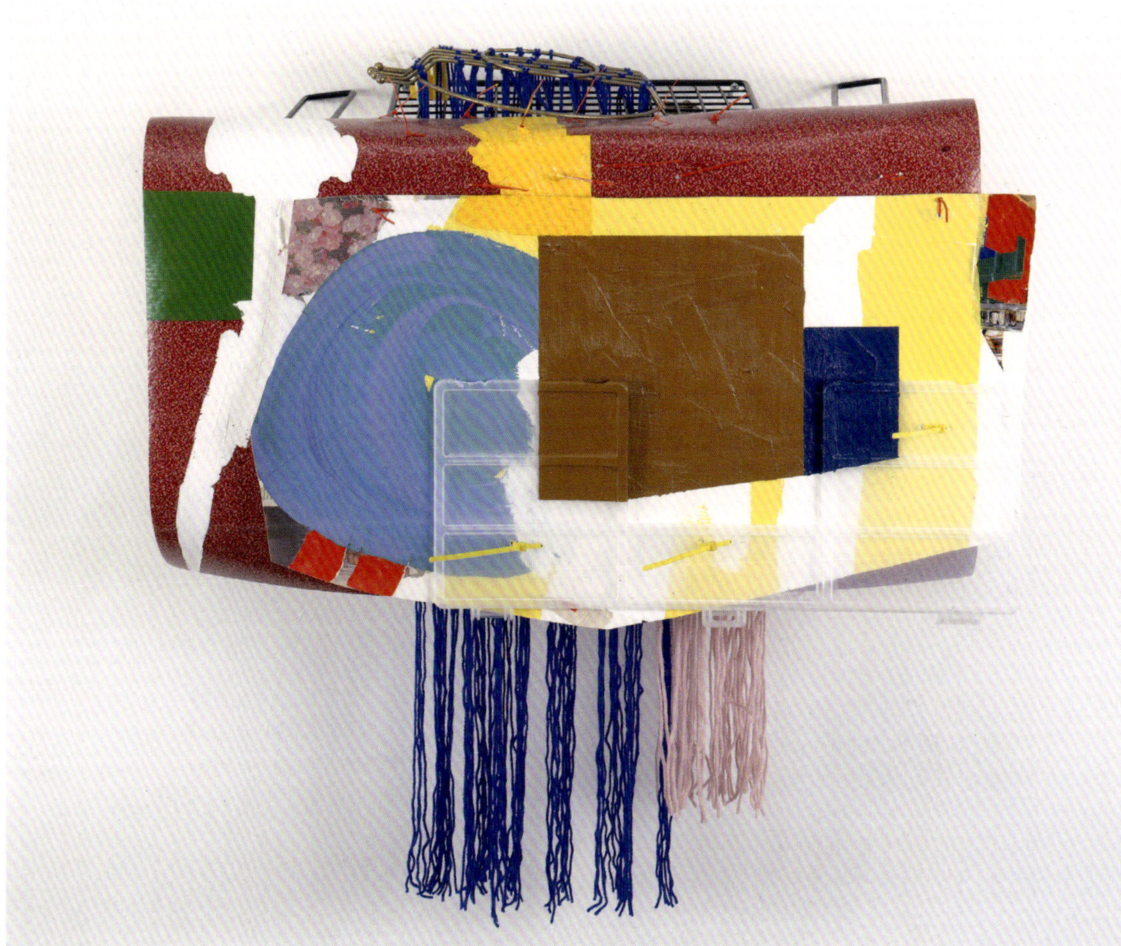

has been resolutely ambivalent about the constitutive role of 'subject matter' in a way that some critics have found disquieting. Perhaps this discrepancy accounts for the recurrent critical nervousness about Stockholder's 'formalism', a term that in the criticism of recent years has taken on connotations nearly as reproachful as in the Soviet Union forty years ago. More daring than most was the critic who recognized the formalist component of Stockholder's work as something worth polemically exaggerating, seeing precisely that as responsible for her 'decisive revisioning of a range of precidents'.[14]

In fact, the work Stockholder has produced in New York since 1985 shows unusual continuity with what she was doing as a graduate student at Yale (1983–85) and even earlier in Vancouver; for instance the installation Stockholder made in her father's backyard in 1983, which primarily consisted of a double mattress painted red and affixed to the side of his garage and a sort of blue 'shadow painted on the grass nearby. Above these, from the sloped roof of the garage, a cupboard door leans over at a right angle to the roof, while rolled chicken wire unravels at the roof's edge. The artist writes of this work that,

'It plays against the yard as other works play against architectural space. The blue grass calls to the red berries of the tree; the red mattress calls to the green grass. The play in the yard is alive and open in contrast to the dark closed interior of the garage'.[15]

Although this work is considerably simpler than installations Stockholder would be doing within a few years and while she has not since worked with open, outdoor spaces, the basic assumptions on which her art is still based today are already in place. It is an art that exists in relation to architecture; it combines quotidian domestic objects with conventionally artistic materials such as paint; it proceeds by means of a dialectical interplay of qualities that may seem to exist in simple contradiction but often end up turning each other inside out, exchanging attributes.

Furthermore, Stockholder's is an art that synthesizes or at least conjoins what might be called allegorical and abstractionist ('formalist') modes. The red-painted mattress demands to be seen as a piece of household paraphernalia with all the associations attendant on it as a familiar everyday object. The reversal of expectations brought about by its being situated outdoors rather than indoors, vertically rather than horizontally and painted the colour of blood and rubies may cause us to wonder about implications of disrupted domesticity (remember that this yard belongs to the artist's father) or 'murdered sleep' (Stockholder's parents are both literary scholars, her mother a specialist in Shakespeare, so one imagines that allusions to the Bard might come as second nature to her, part of the atmosphere of her upbringing). All this takes one far from any immediate sensate experience one may have of the work; this is what I mean by allegorical. On the other hand the mattress, in part thanks to the very same displacement from its usual context that gave rise to allegorical considerations, also becomes more visible than it might ordinarily be as an object of a certain mass and volume, that is, as a sculptural entity. Having been painted it may be seen as taking part in an arrangement of colours and textures of a sort calculated to elicit sensations sufficiently heightened as to justify the figurative language which describes the red of the mattress 'calling' to the green of the grass. The work's abstractionism consists in its mobilization of formal or phenomenological considerations which necessarily call for the bracketing out of those referential and contextual aspects which are essential to the comprehension of its allegorical dimension. What is already impressive in this early work is not simply that it calls on both of these putatively incompatible modes of comprehension, but that it calls attention to their mutual implication in the same originating displacement. It is not exactly true that 'Stockholder is simply more interested in the fundamental way meanings are generated – in how differences are perceived and read – than in revealing a specific social subtext'.[16] Rather, her work does not support our ability to make this distinction, to operate in one signifying mode (let's call it formal) without taking the other (let's call it semantic) into account. The risk this early work takes – one it does not necessarily overcome – is in its still fairly schematic development of these two modes and of their intertwining.

NIT PICKING TRUMPETS OF ICED BLUE VAGARIES, 1997
COLLING CHAMBER PARTITIONS, PLASTIC BUCKETS, WOOD, IRON WIRE, SCREWS, ROPE, ENAMEL, OIL, ACRYLIC, CARPET, BASKET, WOOL, PARTS OF A SWING, PAPIER MÂCHÉ, WEIGHT AND PIPES
381 X 855 X 670 CM

INSTALLATION VIEW AT MUSÉE DES BEAUX-ARTS DE NANTES, FRANCE, 1997

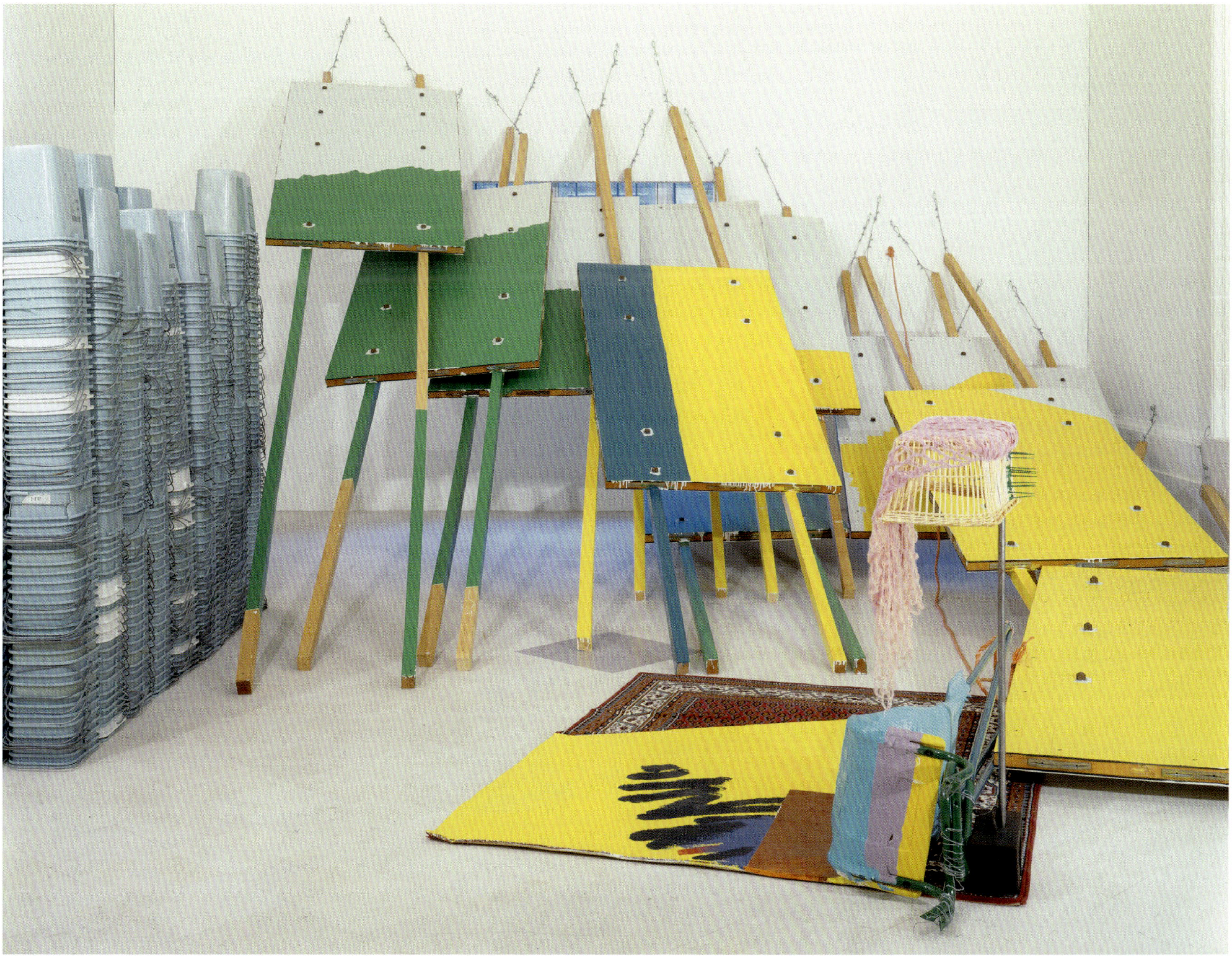

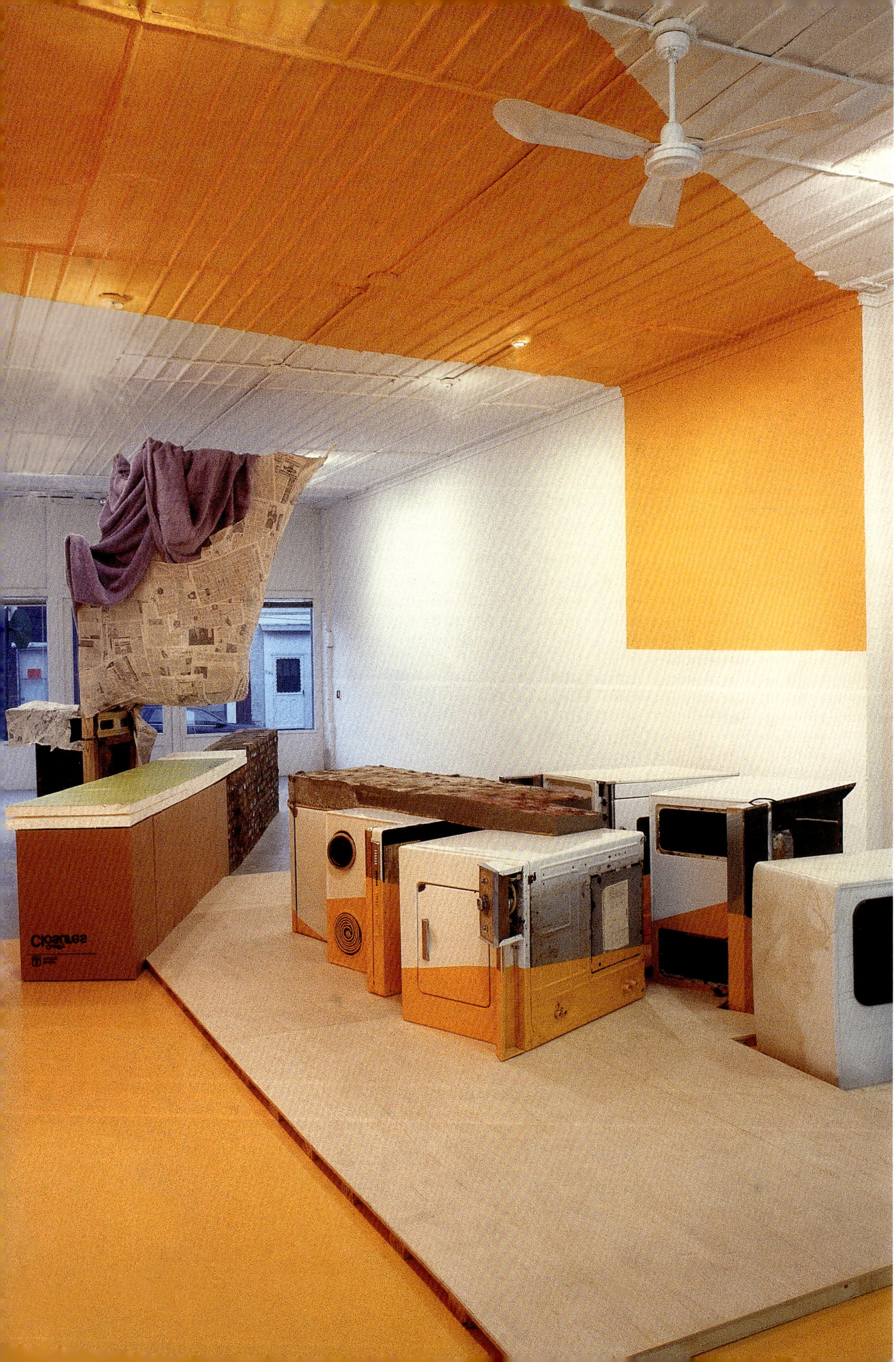

MIXING FOOD WITH THE BED, 1989
CONSTRUCTION MATERIALS,
NEWSPAPER, CLOTH,
CONCRETE, HUMAN HAIR, PAINT,
BRICKS, STOVES,
REFRIGERATORS, BATHTUB

INSTALLATION VIEW AT THE
MATTRESS FACOTRY,
PITTSBURGH, 1989

That risk is not one easily ascribed to most of Stockholder's work of the past half-dozen years. Living in New York, I have been able to see just four of Stockholder's major installations: *Making a Clean Edge* (The Institute for Contemporary Art/P.S.1 Contemporary Art Center, Long Island City, 1989), *Where it Happened* (American Fine Arts, Co., 1990), *Recording Forever Pickled Too* (Whitney Museum of American Art, 1991 – a rare example of a second chance in Stockholder's oeuvre, since this was a 're-make' of *Recording Forever Pickled*, made for Le Consortium, Dijon, 1990) and *Flower Dusted Prosies* (American Fine Arts, Co., 1992). To give some sense of what is involved in Stockholder's installations, let me describe the experience of the one I have seen most recently, relying not only on my memory but on photographs of the work. The massive constructed portions of *Flower Dusted Prosies* (the work also involved painting, as well as other materials, on some of the gallery walls), though at points quite near the wall, never actually touched it, leaving a sometimes cramped path around the heterogeneous conglomeration of stuff that occupied the space. It was a work designedly just a bit 'too large' for the space it occupied; it had the effect of crowding the viewer to the margin of the space.

In face, my use of the word 'viewer' is only accurate to the extent that it represents this figure pressed to the work's margin but never expelled. I retain this conventional usage for want of a better alternative, for it is not at all clear that the main task of the (shall we say) user of this work involves vision independently of other modes of cognition, though neither does it reject this ability. Certainly there is much to be seen here – perhaps too much. Mere viewership seems inadequate to the challenge the work presents; or perhaps it might be described as a virtual reward promised to anyone capable of negotiating the piece on levels both physical and more intellectual. I remember, at the opening, being inexorably drawn around and around the space by my desire to 'know' the work, to encompass it and feeling somehow pleasantly stymied in this desire. I told the artist, then that the piece gave me the feeling that I was always at the back of it, walking around to find a front that I eventually concluded did not exist. I am happy that she recognized this description as accurate to the extent that she subsequently described it as a piece that 'feels as if it is all back'.[17]

Entering the room, one was faced with the edge of a wall and therefore a choice of paths: left (north) or right (south). Left was more inviting, or rather right was less inviting, for two reasons: the left side of the wall was finished and painted red while the side to the right comprised exposed wood beams, so that the left was implicitly promised to be the 'face' of the piece, the right its back; and then the right path offered a particularly narrows squeeze pas the gallery receptionist's desk, whereas the path to the left was relatively spacious. So one took the left path and turned to face a bare red wall, flatly painted with little variation or evidence of the painter's hand except at its very top and bottom, near the floor and ceiling. Another such red wall jutted out at a right angle pointing towards the gallery's north wall.

Here, at last, one began to find something like an event: two bunches of red yarn hanging down in tangles skeins from small holes in the wall down to the floor and between them two rolls of green yarn. The soft red loose yarn and the soft green bundled yarn on the hard red wall suggested comparisons of similarity and difference; one might have thought as well about the difference between the wall as a façade of colour on the one hand and the yarn as coloured through and through on the other. The holes from which the red yarn poured, in any case, aroused curiosity about the other side and so one stepped around the wall to see that, like the first one, it was unfinished on the other side, nothing but wood beams supporting sheetrock. Expectation and disappointing? Not exactly, for what had one expected? Anything might have been possible, but this eventuality was the one suggested by what one already knew of the first wall. Here one found oneself in an open space between structures.

The first conspicuous thing about the second construction of *Flower Dusted Prosies* was fabric: several sheets of differently coloured or patterned material – most prominently a solid turquoise one – hanging from the ceiling. The fabric did not hang down quite as far as the floor and so through the gap one could glimpse brown cardboard – large boxes, apparently. Continuing around to the left, passing more fabric (a flowered print now), one noticed that some of this material was actually draped over a simple structure made of more wooden beams, a structure built at an angle to the stacks of cardboard boxes. But were they empty, or filled (and with what?), stashed behind or beneath all that cloth? Storage! That which is kept in reserve ... At last one began to have a thematic clue to the work.

But there was more to see. Behind the piles boxes, on a wall separating the gallery's office area from the exhibition, there was a geometrical pattern made of vinyl wall tiles. The work led into the office area, or rather called attention to the fact that this other space was there without quite leading one into it, because here the yellow and red paint applied directly to much of the gallery's south wall trailed off. (So did the newspaper pages also covering some of the lower part of this wall beneath the paint but were revealed here as the colour diminished). But nearing the receptionist's desk, the wall painting came to an end, and at the front corner of the rear structure (the one with the cloth and boxes and wooden beams) there was one more element. This had been noticeable on the walk to the back of the installation, but was in itself unimposing: a sort of column, made of large cushions of the sort that might be part of a couch, covered with newspaper (but bare at the very top) – in turn partly painted white and blue – a distinctly clumsy and awkward thing, almost distasteful or even ugly.

I have omitted many details from my account of *Flower Dusted Prosies*, for like all of Stockholder's installations, it synthesizes every degree of scale from the vast to the miniscule and no description could hope to exhaust all of them, except perhaps at the cost of exhausting both critic and reader as well. But there is one element in the work which it would be especially unfortunate to pass over in silence. I mean its title. There is a special Stockholder way of titling which is quite distinctive. Like the works themselves, the titles appear to be assemblages from different sources, distinct registers of linguistic usage: *Mixing Food with the Bed, Recording Forever Pickled, Skin Toned Garden Mapping, Growing Rock Candy Mountain Grasses in Canned Sand* ... such titles suggest absurd experiments, bizarre cuts and elisions among contradictory realms of experience. *Flower Dusted Prosies* is a phrase comparatively compact in its effect, although equally enigmatic. Most striking is the nounce word 'Prosies', presumably a portmanteau of 'prosy' and 'prosies'. The latter word already presents a certain ambiguity, since a posy is both a poetic motto or legend (originally the word was written poesy) and a bouquet or nosegay – connecting back with the first word of the title. A 'prosy', then, must be something like the opposite of a posy, a bouquet of ordinariness. And 'Flower Dusted'? If one is to make sense of the notion of flower dust, it must refer to pollen, 'the mass of microspores in a seed plant appearing usually as a fine dust', which allows the flower to reproduce but which is feared by the hay-fever sufferer as causes of his or her seasonal misery. *Flower Dusted Prosies* are the prosaic version of things otherwise poetic or flowerlike – of 'flowery' things in both senses of the word, perhaps – but whose very common-ness has become fertile or fecundated. This dense title wants to have things both ways, clearly, just as the work itself does: Stockholder is continually concerned to evoke the kinds of effects that result from the deployment of 'obvious' dualisms in such a way that these contaminate or exchange qualities with one another – the kind of effect that unveils the 'prosy' in 'poesy', for instance, or vice versa.

We have seen something of how these interchanges of qualities operate in particular works like the 1983 backyard installation and *Flower Dusted Prosies*. It would be just as instructive to follow certain recurrent dualisms from work to work to see how they are variously inflected. Since Stockholder's work refers both to painting and to sculpture, it would be interesting, for instance, to see how it figures the dualism *vision/touch*. The distinction is a venerable one and most important to the ideological battles of the art of the 1960s; thus Robert Morris called in 1966 for 'clearer distinctions between sculpture's essentially tactile nature and the optical sensibilities involved in painting'.[18]

Stockholder's work almost always involves the uses of paint, but paint is not usually the most painterly element in her work. (This has been starting to change somewhat.) She typically uses paint – whether oil, acrylic, or enamel – as a vernacular material just like any other. It tends to be laid on evenly and opaquely, as a houses painter would do it, as a material covering a surface. But this paint hardly ever succeeds in covering the surface. Either it only covers it partially, or else it sits on some material that, because of its texture or for

MIXING FOOD WITH THE BED, 1989
CONSTRUCTION MATERIALS,
NEWSPAPER, CLOTH,
CONCRETE, HUMAN HAIR, PAINT,
BRICKS, STOVES,
REFRIGERATORS, BATHTUB

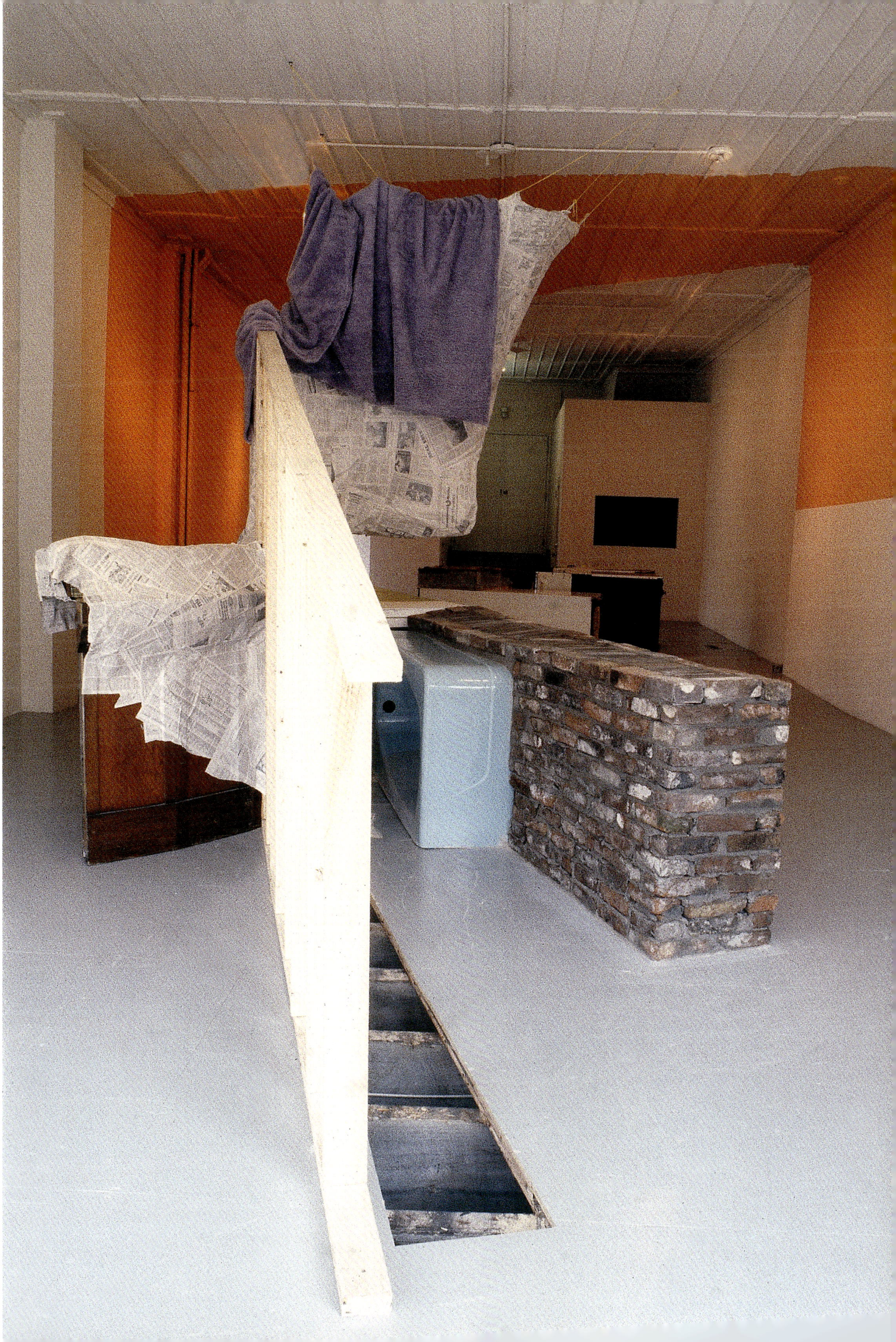

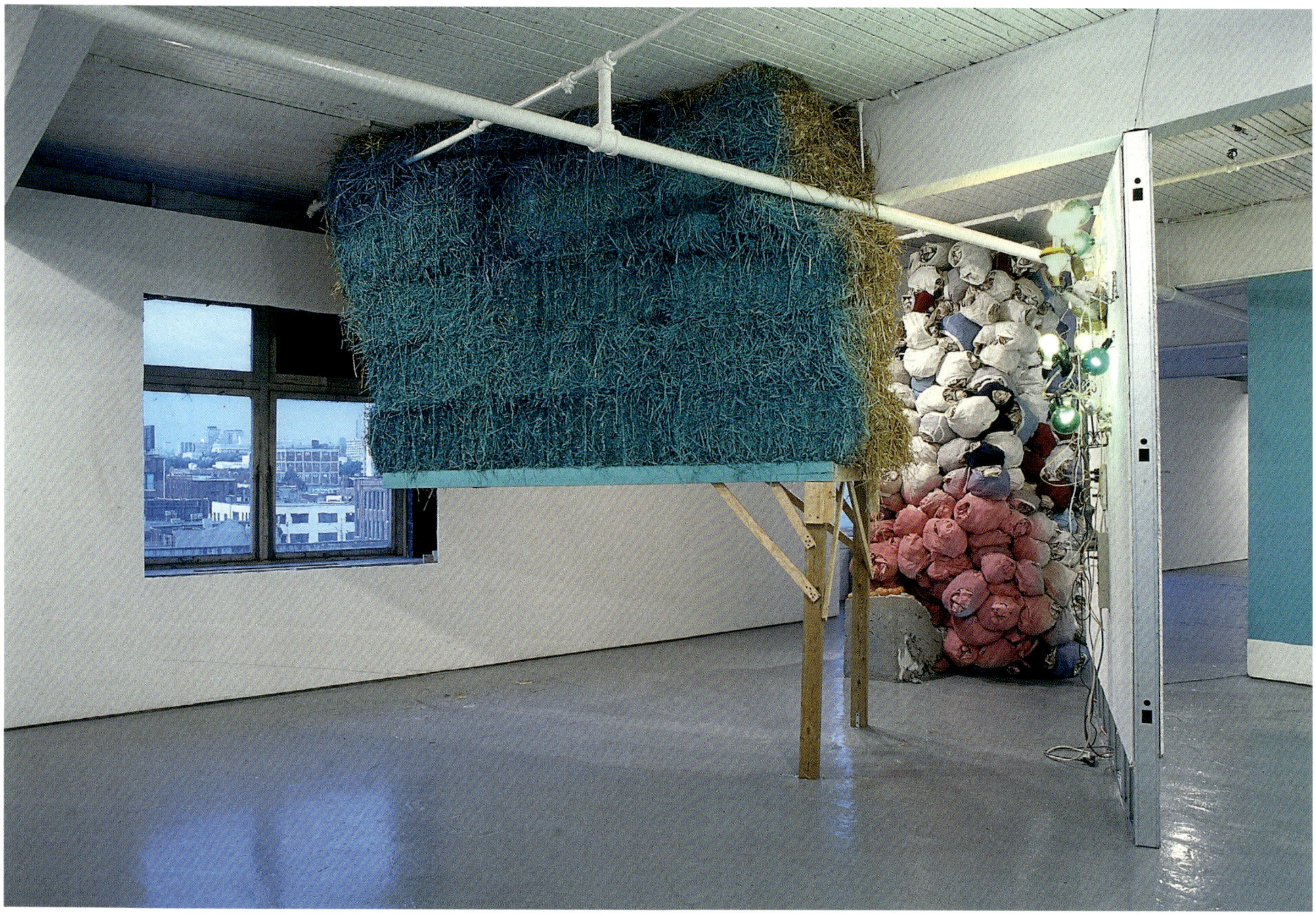

INDOOR LIGHTING FOR MY FATHER, 1988
NEWSPAPER, MEN'S AND WOMEN'S UNDERWEAR, CEMENT, STYROFOAM, ORANGES, HAY, LIGHTING
ROOM: 430 X 276 CM
CEILING: 134 CM

INSTALLATION VIEW AT MERCER UNION, TORONTO, 1988

some other reason, just isn't the sort of thing that can be covered over by a coat of paint: the suspended hay bales of *Indoor Lighting for My Father*, the grass of *Installation in My Father's Backyard*. At the same time, it can be precisely this inartistic, uninflected and vernacular employment of paint that modified an object in such a way as to subtract it from the realm of the ordinary. For instance, *Kissing the Wall #1* (1988) is among Stockholder's simpler works even by the standards of her smaller assemblages; it takes as its sub-structure a single object, a small piece of wooden domestic furniture, a night table perhaps, whose dingy white paint has been worn away in spots. What had been the front of this object – it is not the front of the artwork Stockholder has made of it – has been covered over with a large bulbous wad of newspaper. The battered, cast-off night table, its hard rectilinearity, mitigated by the restrained curves of its legs and decorative mouldings – a wan but effective compromise between functional efficiency and comfortable anthropomorphic familiarity, mediated by the demands of cheap production – has become the host for a fungal or cancerous growth. It is embodied in the unreadable newspapers representing everything that takes place outside the domestic enclosure for which the night table is a metonymy. They stand not only for the events of the public realm, but also for all that is ephemeral; yesterday's news, in comparison to the relative stability of such durable goods as furniture. Now this object is turned away from the wall at an angle, so that the face it presents to the world is not a plane but a corner, formed by the back and one side of the night table. Painted across these two planes and around onto the swell of the newspapers is a roughly rectangular zone of olive enamel. In connecting and crossing between the wooden surface and the newspaper, it simultaneously equalizes and effaces them by rendering both as mere 'grounds'. It also highlights their difference at a more profound level than that of immediate appearance. The tactile qualities of the painted area show up as completely different, despite the fact that the paint itself has not changed or been applied any differently. The paint displays what it nominally hides. An incandescent light attached to the night table's other side, the one facing the wall, sheds a circle of greenish light on the backing wall. This light turns the wall into a ground (rather than a mere background) for the object that stands before it, just as the object itself is used as a ground for the green enamel. Establishing a kind of pictorial atmosphere for the object, the light claims the space between the night table and the wall. The assemblage touches the wall, not physically, but optically.

What is tactile? What is optical? *Kissing the Wall #1* shows us that colour – whether embodied as paint or as

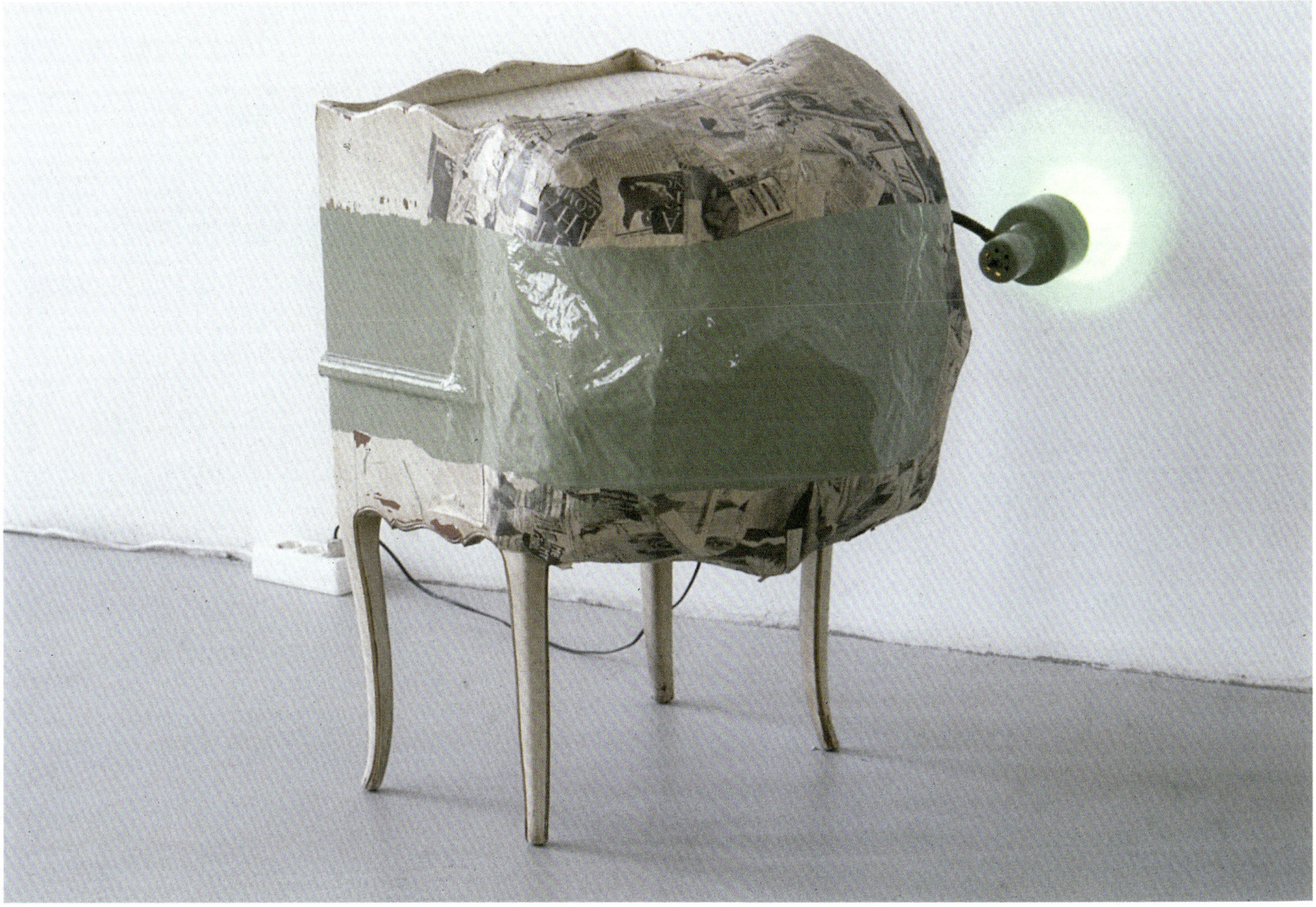

KISSING THE WALL #1, 1988
SMALL PIECE OF FURNITURE, ENAMEL, INCANDESCENT LIGHT, NEWSPAPER, GLUE
H. 76 CM

light, whether opaque or transparent – can be a tactile value more than an optical one. Likewise, Stockholder's work shows that three-dimensional objects can function optically as well as sculpturally. They may be used as elements in an essentially pictorial composition, as when an arrangement is flattened either by sheer distance, for example in *Indoor Lighting for My Father*. Or else the optically recessive and advancing properties of strongly coloured objects may be cancelled out by their actual positions in three-dimensional space. This effect also contributes to the pictorial tendency of *Indoor Lighting*, as the optically recessive turquoise of the forward hay bales balances the optically advancing red-stained underwear bundles seen behind and below it. Stockholder not only uses colour to 'flatten' objects, but she uses three-dimensionality to expand or 'swell' colour. Her use of yarn, such as we have seen in *Flower Dusted Prosies*, is one of the more common instances of this.

V

Stockholder's work is not autobiographical in any narrative sense, but it is always concerned with intimacy. *Installation in My Father's Backyard* suggests the possibility of taboo-breaking by exposing the business of the paternal bed to the eyes of the outside world. An installation made five years later, *Indoor Lighting for My Father* (Mercer Union, Toronto, 1988) insinuates the opposite. A gaze penetrating to the interior here reveals, above all, a floor-to ceiling 'column' made of 500 pairs of men's and women's cotton underwear – one area of the column, like the mattress in the 1983 installation, has been painted red – stuffed with crumpled newspaper. I wonder what the artist's father thought of a work dedicated to him that consisted most prominently of underwear? Not that she could be accused of washing the family laundry in public. But surely there is some sense of displaying that which is normally hidden here.

The recurrence of the father in Stockholder's titles may have another significance. I wonder if she doesn't consider her own commitment to art – her detour from the wholly verbal and intellectual world of her parents – to be in some way a gift from her father, for it was he who, when she was fourteen years old, hired his university colleague, the sculptor Mowry Baden, to give private drawing lessons to his daughter. And since Baden remained Stockholder's mentor for a good many crucial years thereafter, he must be a sort of father figure as well; it would be worth re-reading Stockholder's work for its commentary on his attempt to repudiate what he calls 'stand-off-and-look-at-it' art through provoking 'the self-awareness generated in the completion of a specific task' – an art of proprioception.[19]

Placed towards the rear of the first gallery space at Mercer Union, this installation was deliberately distanced and pictorialized, framed by the architecture and 'seen apart and separate' by viewers entering the gallery. But Stockholder arranged for what she calls 'a more intimate and time bound experience'[20] to become available to those proceeding to the corridor linking this space to the one behind it. Viewing the installation from there, those who thereby behold the work from its backside enjoy the closest view of the underwear and crumpled paper ('time bound' indeed, in so far as the dailies are confined by the 'unmentionables' they so unaesthetically stuff).

A subsequent installation evokes the early *Installation in My Father's Backyard* by its title: *Mixing Food with the Bed* certainly sounds like a recipe for a stained mattress – it was installed at The Mattress Factory (!), Pittsburgh, in 1989. But in this case other objects of domestic necessity are actually displayed: no bedding, despite the title, but more than enough stoves and refrigerators to prepare the food – and a bathtub to clean off in afterward. These refrigerators will appear, multiplied in number but in the guise of their doors alone, in *Skin Toned Garden Mapping* (The Renaissance Society, Chicago, 1991), where they will gather to form a sort of crazed wall. Nearly everyone has a refrigerator in our culture, but it's not the kind of object we think of as having 'personal' resonance the way a bed does. At most, the refrigerator door may be what gets in your way when you're dying to know what's to eat. Seeing a hundred of those doors, all bare, may evoke a bad dream on am empty stomach. That's one way the work may become, as Stockholder once put it, 'a site for the personal to be mixed with, compared to, or made into concrete reality'.[21]

VI

The street I live on – just a few blocks away from where Stockholder lives – is called Prospect Park West. It's the main shopping street for my little Brooklyn area and it divides, or once did, an almost exclusively Iris neighbourhood to the East from a predominantly Latino one to the West. It used to be the scene of gang wars between youths from the two communities, but that was before I moved here, back when Prospect park West was still Ninth Avenue. Sometimes since the change of name that was supposed to make the street sound more attractive and the minor improvements accompanying it, such as the pleasant brick sidewalks, the boundaries have been growing blurrier and the ethnic mix more complex. The area is more relaxed, though if the city fathers had gentrification in mind it hasn't worked and the street remains a bit rundown, many of its storefronts vacant, some of them now housing sweatshops instead.

Down this street there is a store called *Bargain Land.* It is not a grocery store, although it sells some packaged food items, not a stationery store, despite carrying a range of paper goods and school supplies, n or a hardware store, even though some of its stock would be at home there too. It fits into no particular category. Many of the products stocked there sport obscure and unfamiliar brand names; others are the products of foreign subsidiaries of national brands; Canadian Q-Tips, South American shampoo. I have bought extension cords, roach traps, manila envelopes, paper towers, hair conditioner, underwear, an ironing board cover and who knows what else there. The place is chockablock with the miscellaneous ordinaria of plebeian existence. It exists in profound syntony with the art of Jessica Stockholder, whose art materials are always liable to include such potential *Bargain Land* wares as bed sheets, yellow bug lights, tinfoil, electric wiring, mirrored tiles, plastic fruit, wine glasses, duct tape, plastic garbage bags, toilet paper, cookies, dried fruit, cardboard boxes and underwear as well as more specialized materials that must be sought elsewhere in that vast *Bargain Land* which is our demotic late-capitalist economic system: hay, refrigerators, plywood, Styrofoam, bicycles, carpet, theatre lights, sheetrock, asphalt, couches, chairs, newspaper, fresh fruit, bricks, stoves, bathtubs, steel studs, movie seats, concrete, sandstone, spandex ... Stockholder does not overtly comment on the system that makes all these things available for her use, neither in critique nor in celebration. Rather, she translates its flavour into a work of dreamlike abandon.

Something that interests me about *Bargain Land* is the relation between its inside and its outside. With a quantity of each item on hand, the shelves combine storage and display into a single function, but everything is available: you can reach out and pick up the thing you want. Nothing unusual in any of this, of course. But where things get more complicated is with the store's long, two-part display window, where it beckons to the

INSTALLATION IN MY FATHER'S BACKYARD, 1983
CUPBOARD DOOR, MATTRESS, PAINTED GRASS, CHICKEN WIRE

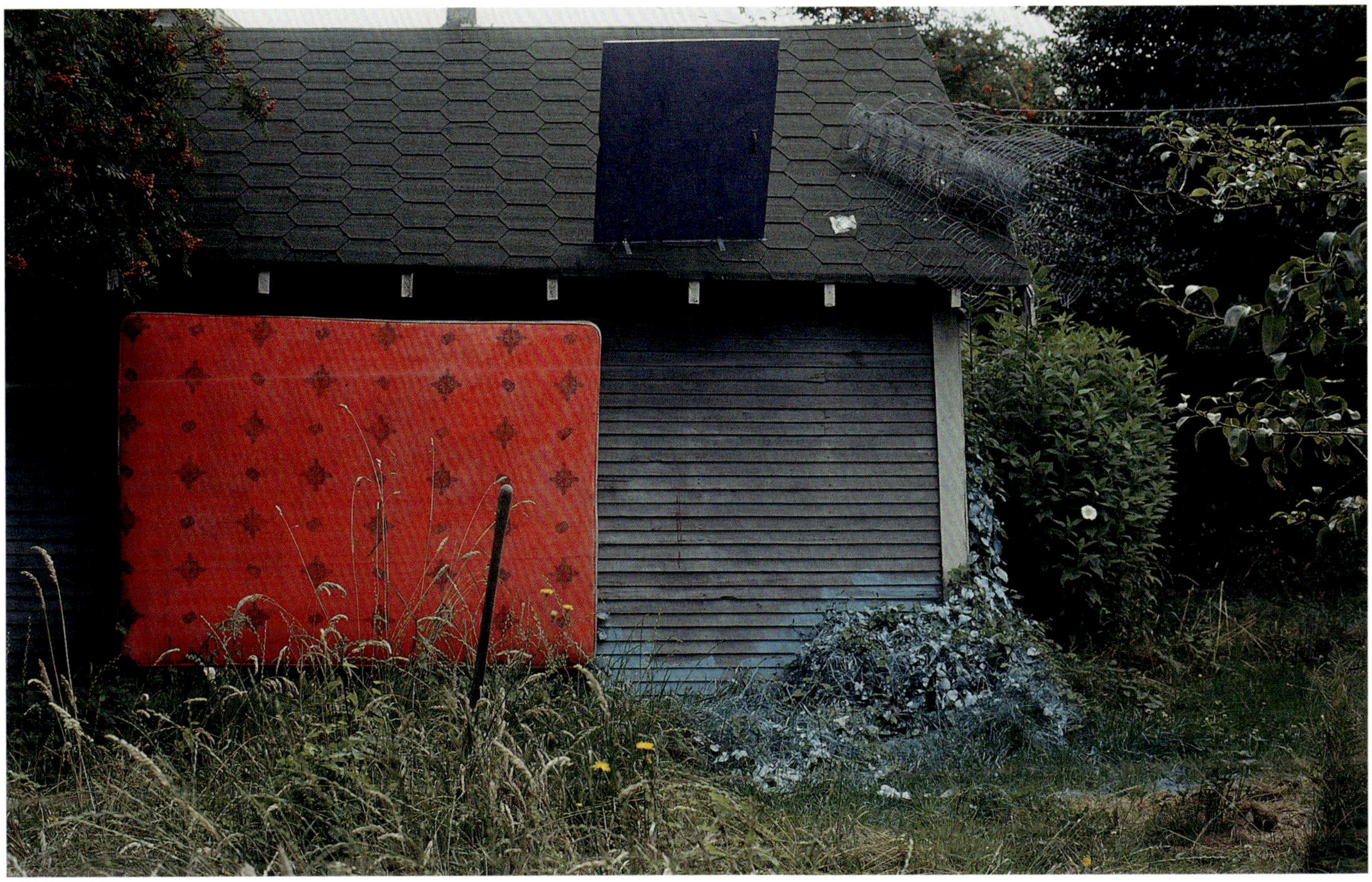

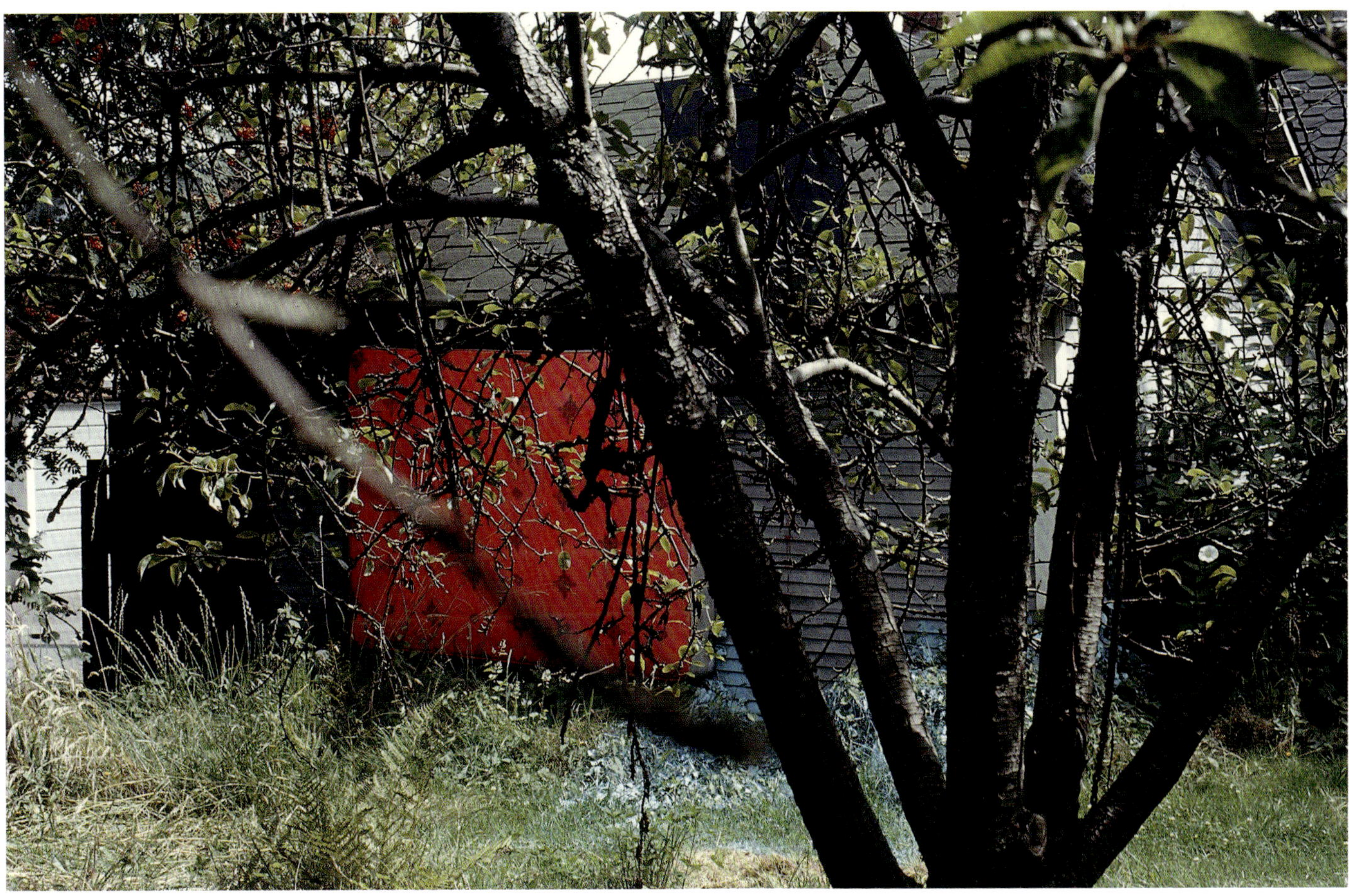

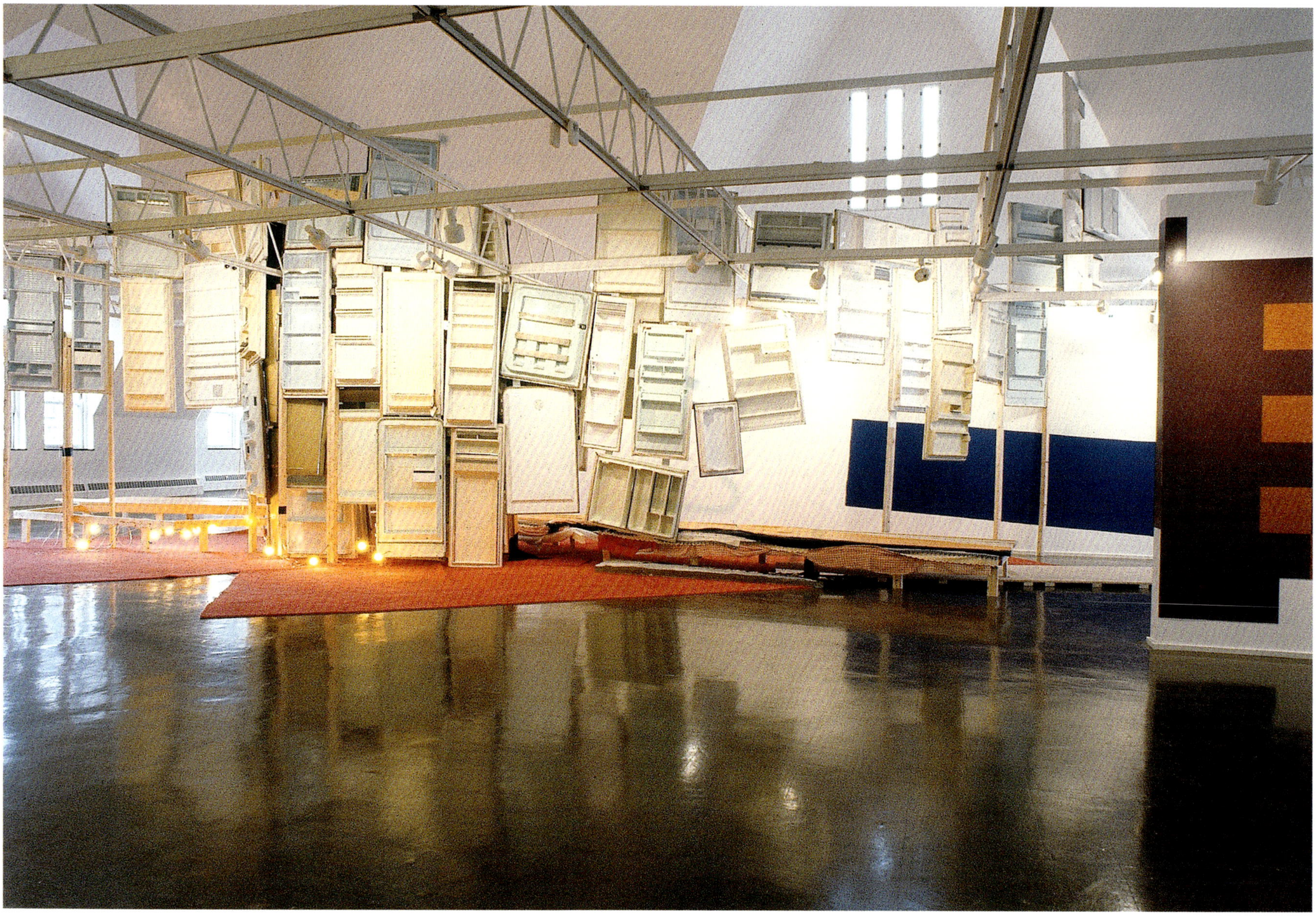

outside. The window reduces the place to a picture of itself, but to a modernist picture rather than a classical one. In the window one sees the following: the space of representation is quite shallow, with a background consisting of an overall decorative pattern or, often enough, a couple of patters that meet and clash; in front of this, a selection of items for sale in the store, not singly but in quantity, as though these were overstock items for which there is no space in the store proper or its basement storage space; and then the foreground, signs attached to the window pane. Finally, one should add that there is a projection in front of the 'picture plane', a rocking horse kiddy ride.

What is striking about this window is that it does not represent the store's contents through their spectacularization, as would be the case in a more upscale enterprise, but more through a kind of seepage. Always changing, sometimes jam-packed, sometimes nearly bare, in its random layerings and juxtapositions, its collisions of colours, patterns and textures. To see a neighbourhood storefront as 'art-like' is not to see it 'abstractly', 'formalistically', 'aesthetically' only; it is also to se it metonymically and allegorically, to see it as an 'unconscious place' (to borrow a phrase from the photographer Thomas Struth) representing processes that are going on in its immediate surroundings and in the wider world whose productions are continually being routed through it.

I have meant to photograph the window I've been talking about, but since I started writing this the display has changed again. It no longer exists except in my memory of it and perhaps never did exist except in memory; I'm no longer entirely sure that the image I've given of it here is not a conflation of several states of its development over a period of time. An artist, it is said, creates a world of her own, or her own way of looking at the world, which it becomes the viewer's privilege to enter. No doubt. And yet the power of

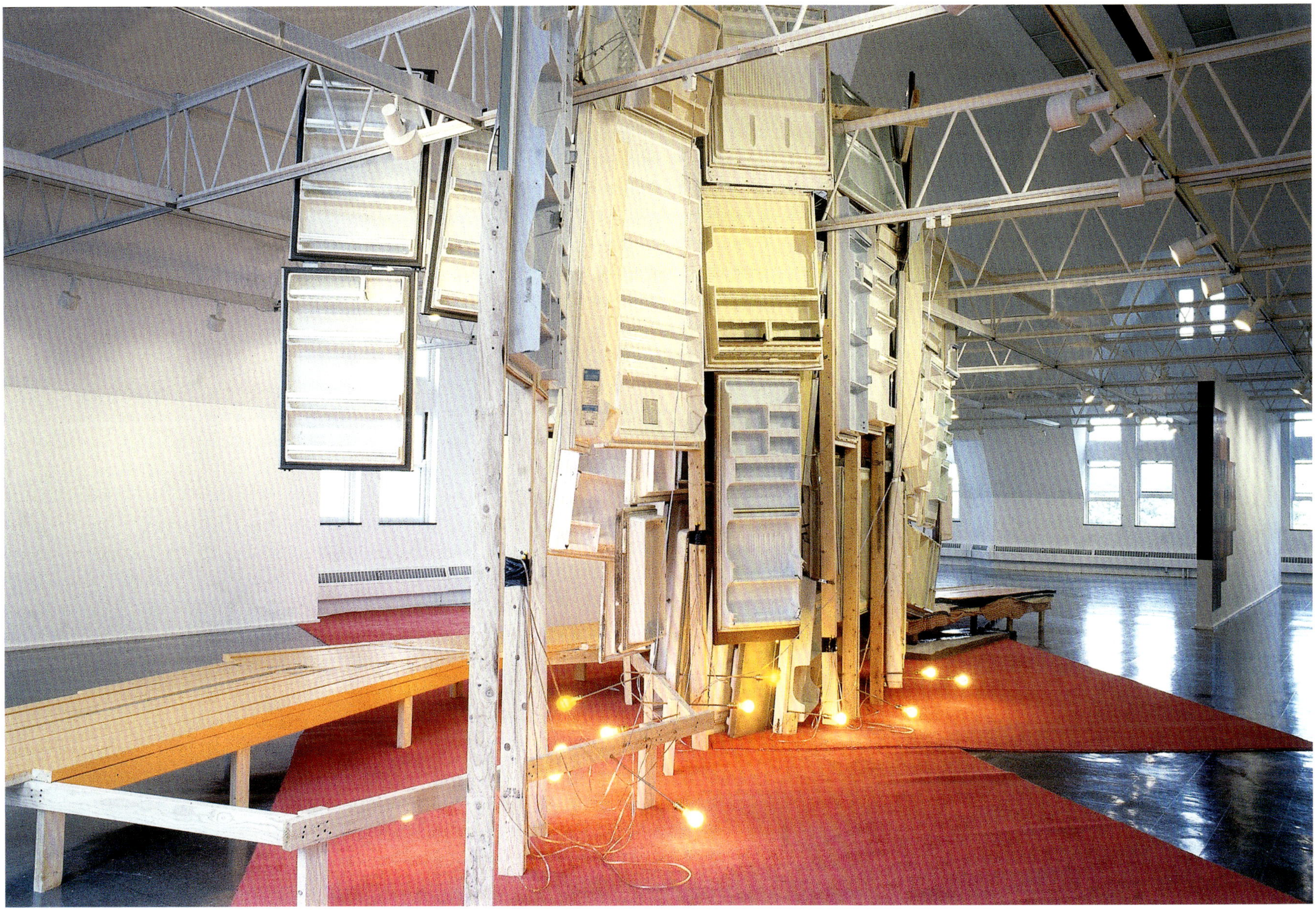

the artist is not simply that of producing an alternative reality into which we may plunge as into a pool, but of saturating the world we all share with her way of seeing it, so that it can no longer be set apart as a personal vision but as a revelation of 'things as they are', to use Wallace Stevens' phrase. I couldn't have seen *Bargain Land* as I do if I hadn't steeped myself in the art of Jessica Stockholder. At the same time I wonder whether I could make sense of her art if I wasn't immersed in a world in which places and processes like those represented by *Bargain Land* are prominent.

I spoke before of how Stockholder's work has been seen as part of a reaction against he 'Neo-Geo' and commodity-fetish art that was so prominent in the mid to late 1980s. But like that work, Stockholder's turns out to be in good measure about the commercial culture which determines so much of what we see and how we live and which provides the materials out of which her work is constructed. The difference is that their gleaming fetish objects – icons of what Fredric Jameson called the 'hysterical sublime' and its 'hallucinatory exhilaration'[22] – accepted the media masters' presumption of control (not for nothing were advertising moguls like Jay Chiat and Charles Saatchi among their prominent collectors). On the other hand Stockholder's work assumes the position from which the products of commercial culture are unspectacularly received and idiosyncratically redeployed, an oblique and decentred position that reflects Prospect Park West more than Madison Avenue. As such it is congruent with what has been recognized as a 'new rhetoric' in urbanism that abjures the 'impulse to romanticise the dystopian' found in critics like Jameson and artists like the postmodernists of the 1980s and which recognizes the 'realm of smudged boundaries … the interstices of the city, the forgotten bits between', amounting to a recovery of the periphery.[23]

I think I understand why, in beginning to talk about her art, Stockholder wanted to talk about Vancouver

this page and previous pages,
SKIN TONED GARDEN MAPPING, 1991
RED CARPET, PINT, ROOFING TAR, REFRIGERATOR DOORS, HARDWARE, YELLOW BUG LIGHTS AND FIXTURES, CLOTH, VINYL, COMPOSITION FLOOR TILES, CONCRETE, TINFOIL
ROOM: 452 SQ M

INSTALLATION VIEW AT THE RENAISSANCE SOCIETY, CHICAGO, 1991

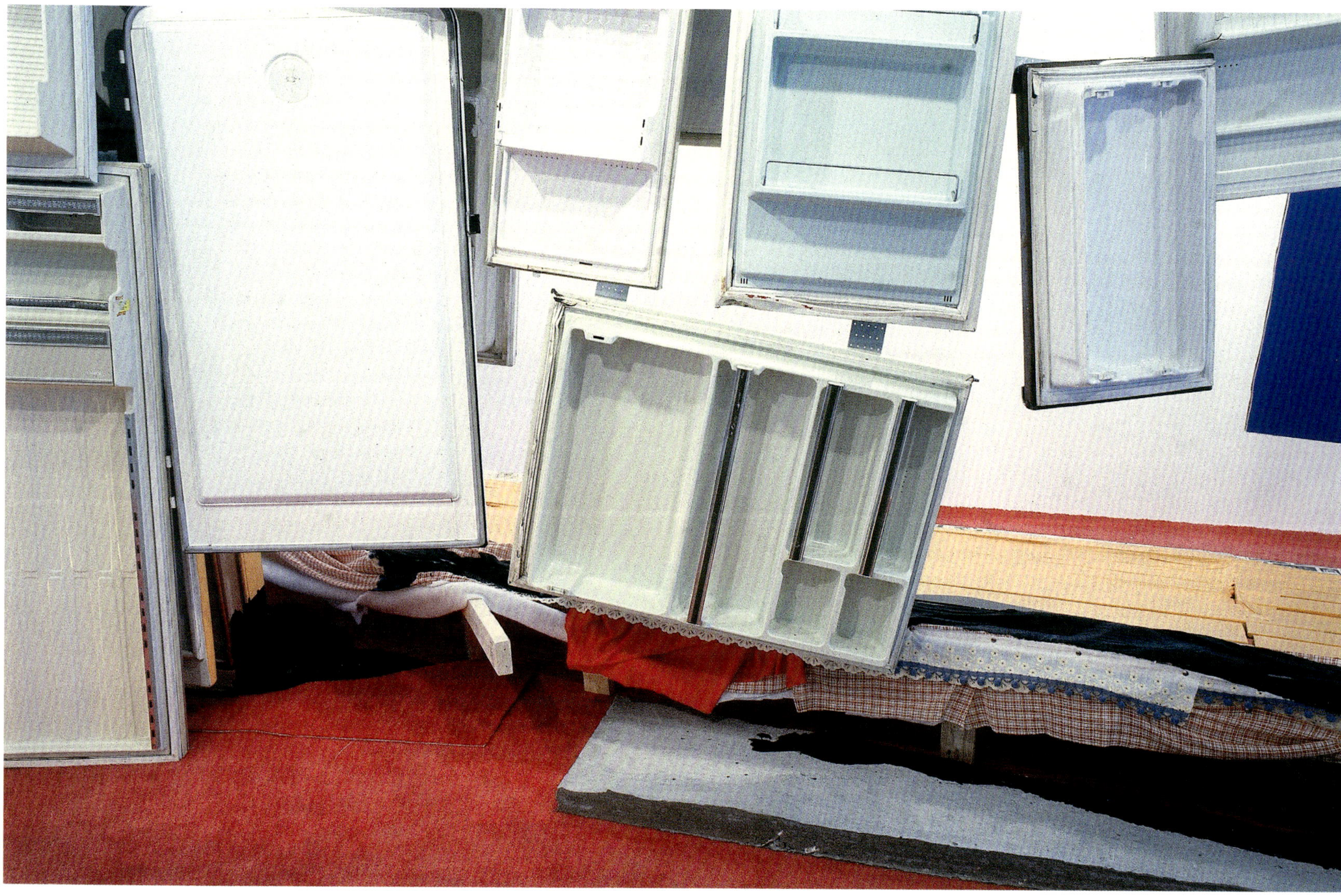

1994
TWO FANS, PINK POWER BAR, SKEINS OF ACRYLIC YARN, FLANNEL CLOTH, SILICONE CAULKING, ACRYLIC PAINT, THREAD, GLASS SHELF
163 X APPROX 25 CM

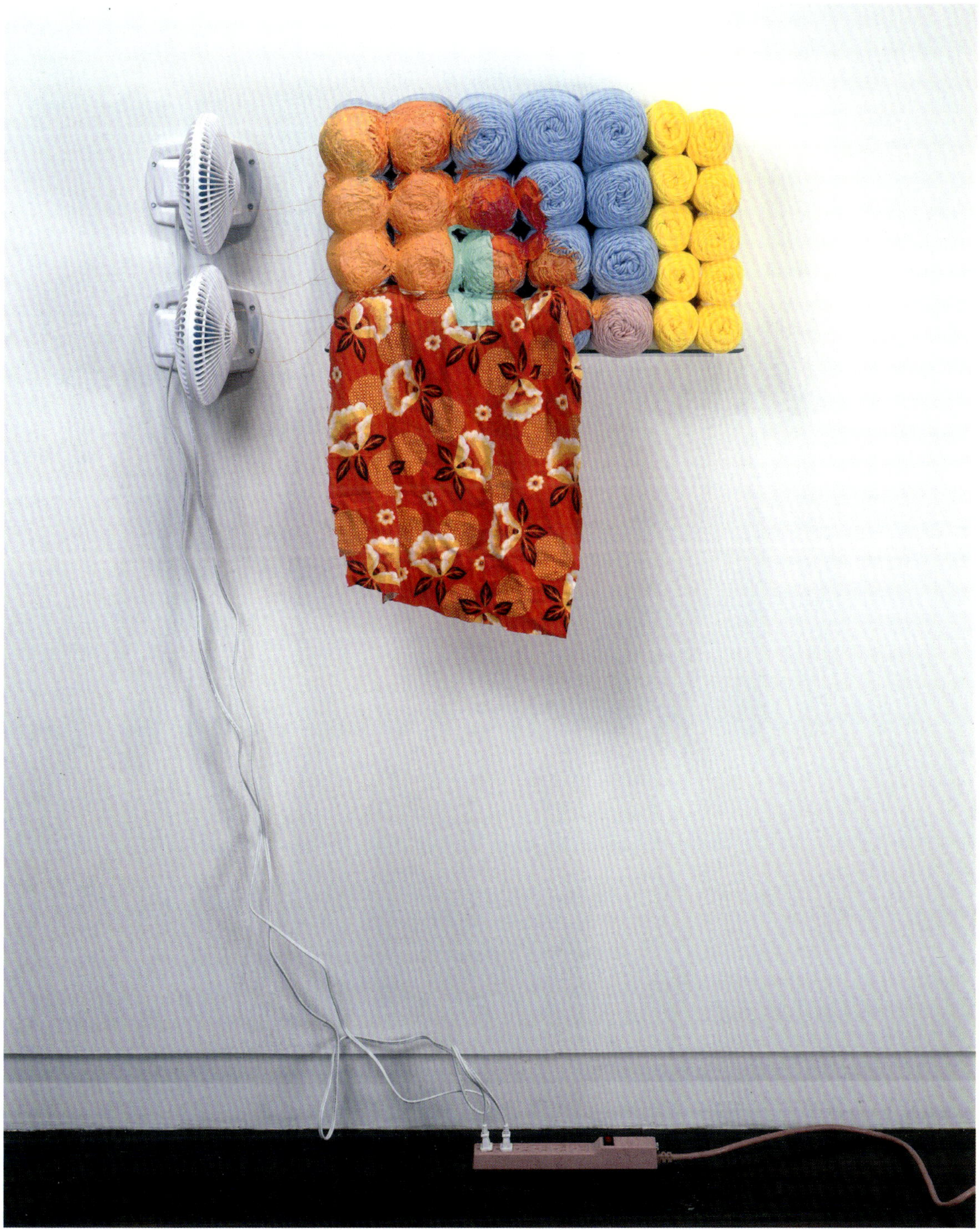

I think I know from the work of artists like Ian Wallace, Ken Lum and EFF Wall feels very familiar; peripheral cities like Vancouver and peripheral segments of great urban centres, as Brooklyn is to Manhattan, are the sites at which contradictions and shifts in changing global markets and changing global cultures are allowed to display themselves relatively unsupervised. Just as, in his classic 'Homes for America' (1966–67), Dan Graham was able to describe suburban tract housing developments in the language that had been developed for discussing Minimalist sculpture, so my description of Stockholder's installations converges on that of the contemporary urban fringe.[24]

I wanted to underline and defend the 'formalism' of Stockholder's work; and that work has led me, abruptly but not illogically, by one of the sudden changes of perspective which is one of the typical formal features of her installations, to touch on broader social forces that our stereotype of formalism would have us ignore, but which circulate incessantly through her work. As the artist herself has written, 'There is an attempt to bring the city inside the gallery, not to erase fiction, but to inform and expand it; and perhaps shed light on the city'[25]. One of her commentators puts it that 'her meditation on how we build and perpetuate visual order can lead us at least to the fringes of meaning' – which we are now in a position to translate into the urban periphery – 'where anxieties about the orders we implicitly condone enter the field of vision'.[26] A little formalism, it has been said, takes you away from everyday life, but a lot of formalism sets you right back into it. And here we are.

NEAR WEATHER WALL, 1991
WOOD, PAPIER MACHÉ, MOVIE SEATS, SMALL REFRIGERATOR DOORS, MASONRY, BLOCKS, PAINT, STYROFOAM, BED, SHEETS, PLYWOOD
ROOM: 360 X 60 CM
CEILING H: 433 CM

INSTALLATION VIEW AT WITTE DE WITH, ROTTERDAM, 1991

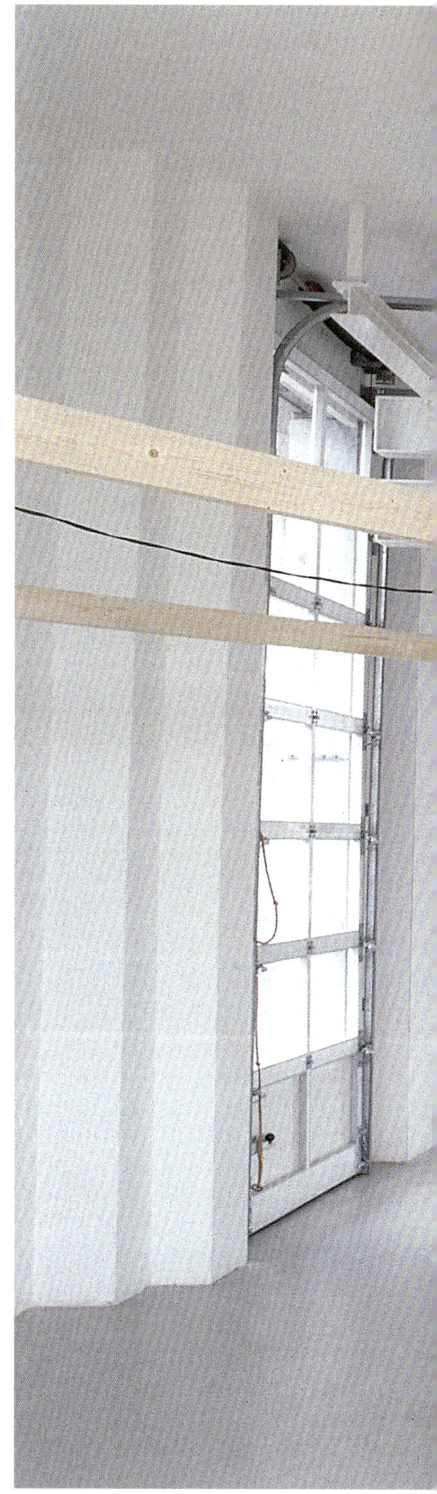

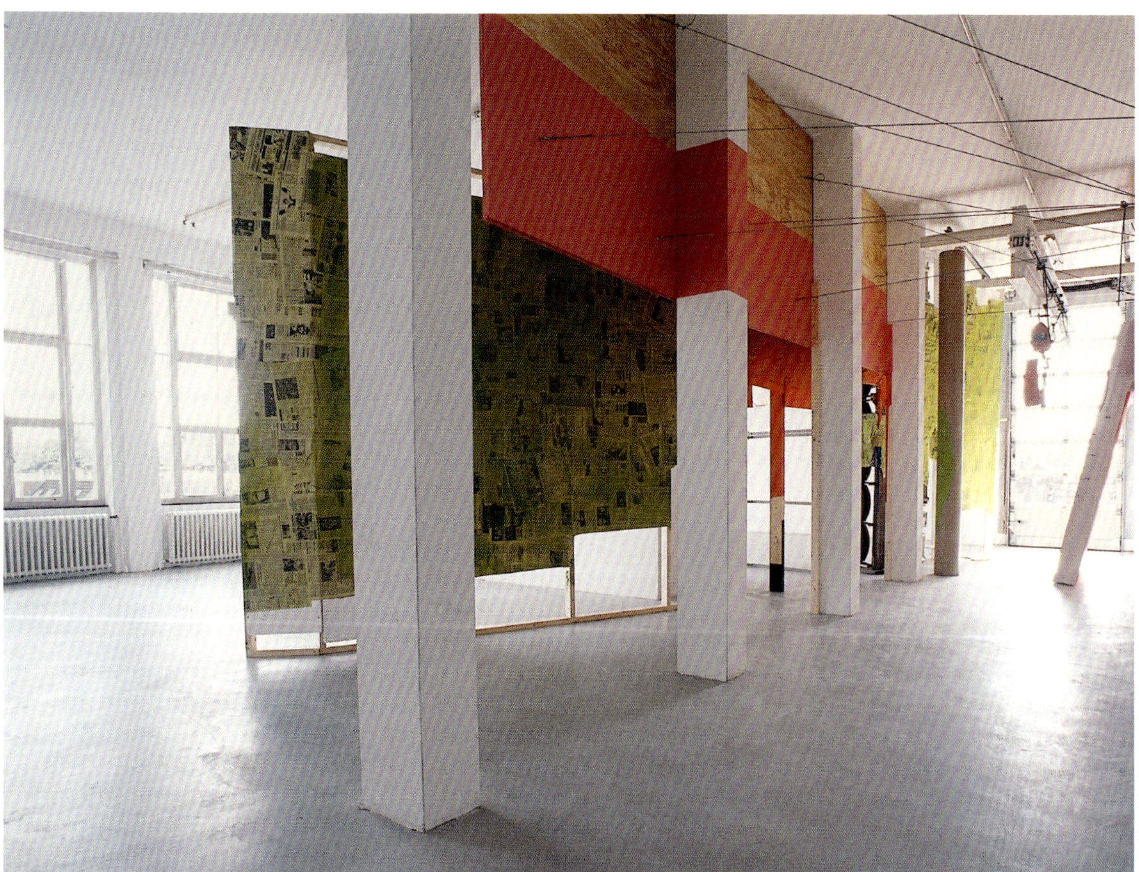

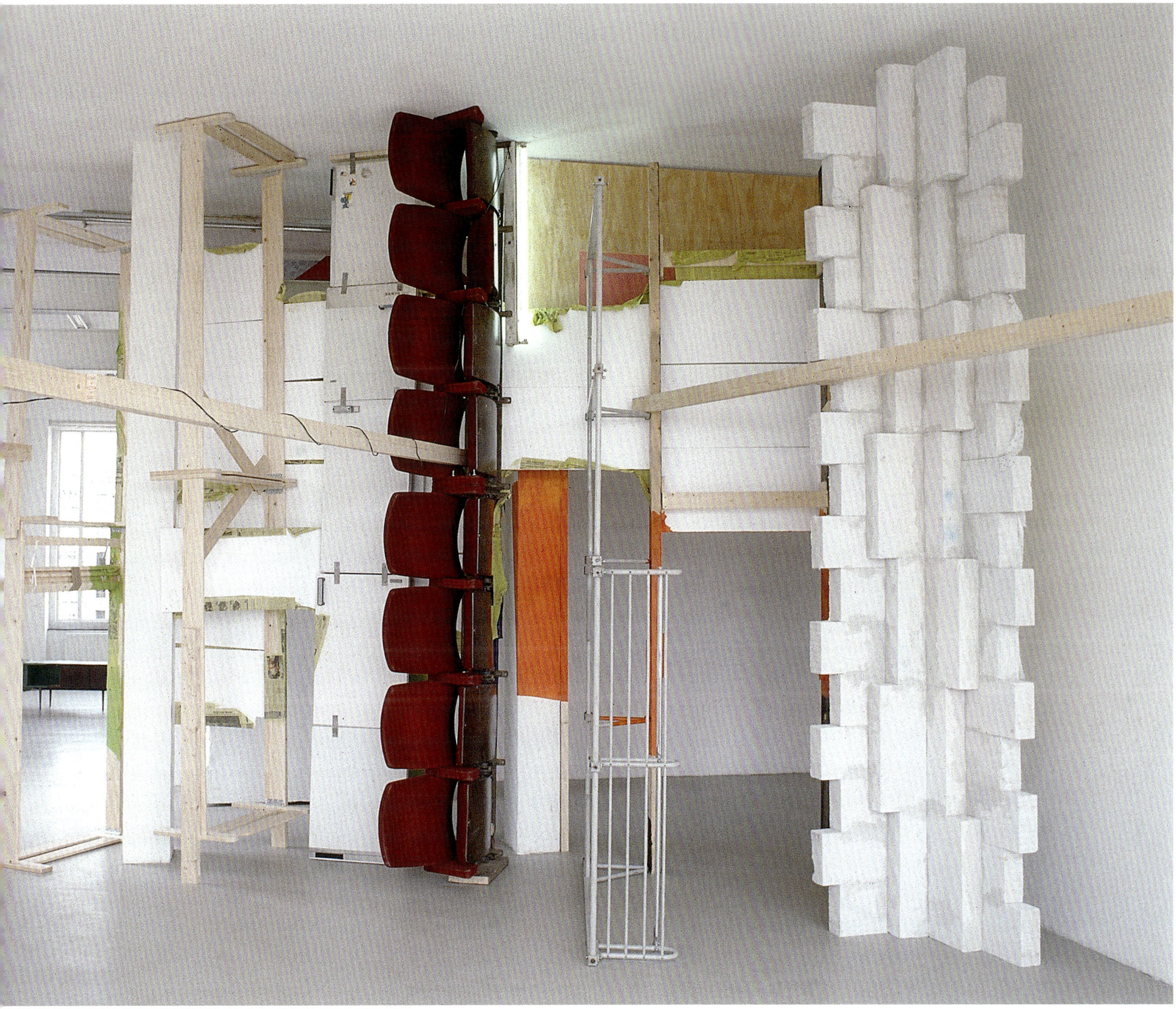

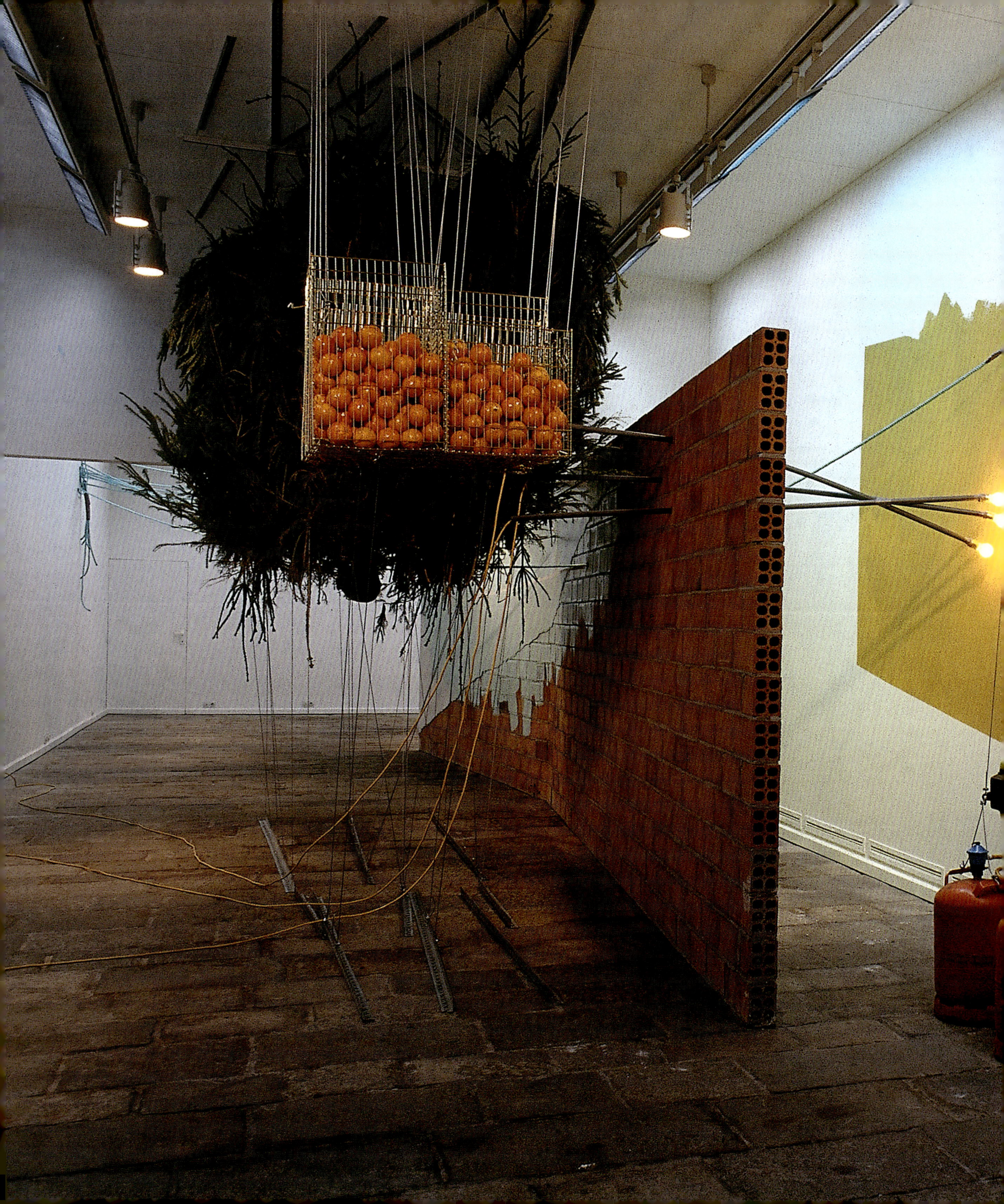

077 FOCUS

A Suite for … Three Oranges

Lynne Cooke

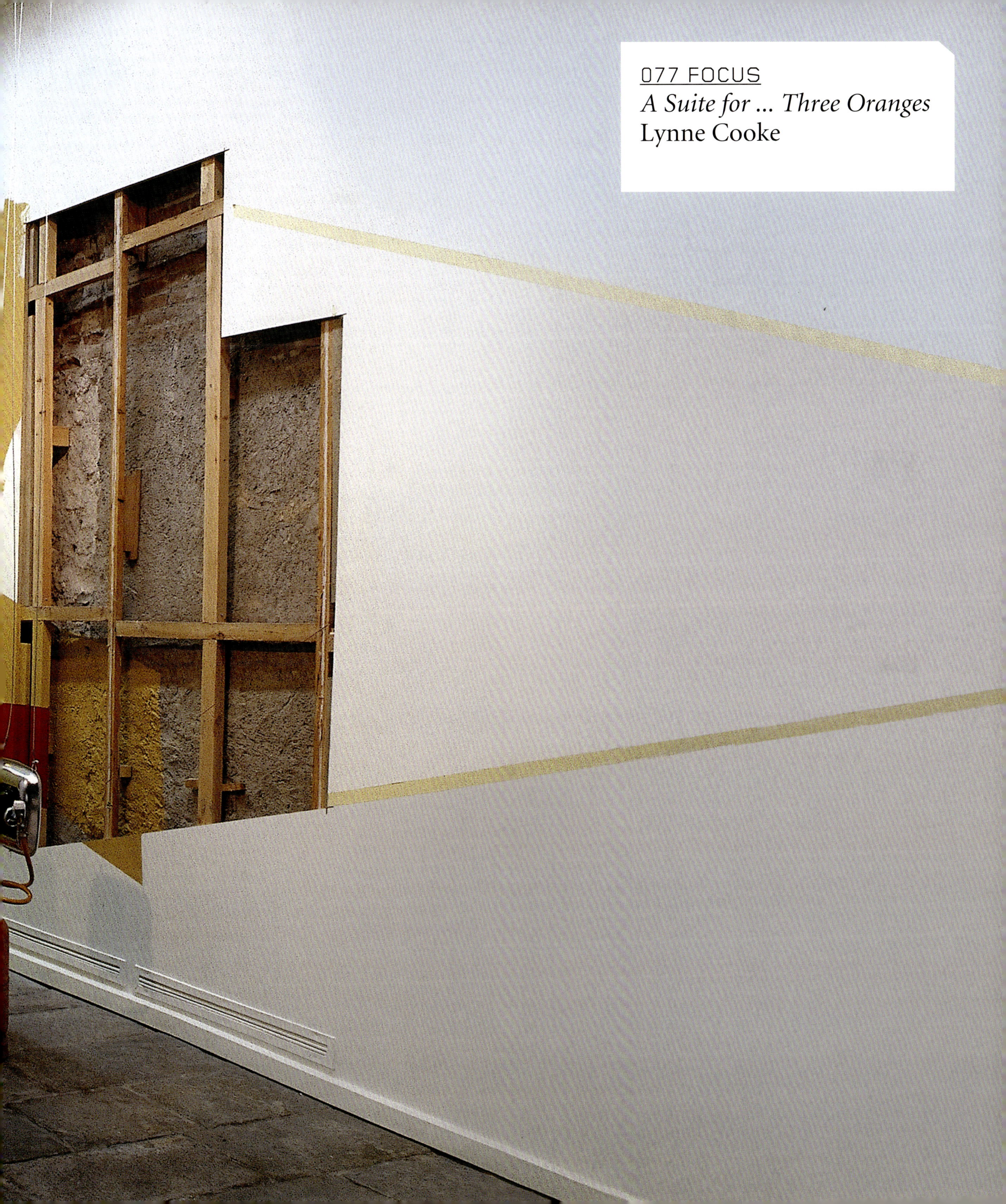

previous pages,
SWEET FOR THREE ORANGES, 1995
40 CHRISTMAS TREES, 50 KILOS OF ORANGES, 4 BIRD CAGES, BRICK WALL, AIR CRAFT, CABLE, BUTANE HEATERS, ROPE, ROOFING PAPER AND ROOFING TAR, PAINT, LIGHT BULBS AND YELLOW ELECTRIC CORD, PVC, PIPING ANGLE IRON
ROOM: 2100 X 500 CM

INSTALLATION VIEW AT FUNDACIO LA CAIXA, BARCELONA, 1995

He hangs in shades the orange bright,
Like golden lamps in a green night.
– Andrew Marvell, Bermudas[1]

I

In 'orange' several things meet, economically, succinctly. Not only does the word imply both the colour and the fruit, but in the fruit, its namesake, the colour, takes concrete and abstract form: an orange approximates to a perfect orb, a luminous sphere. That its near complement blue – a colour and a condition, but not a thing – holds little fascination for Jessica Stockholder in comparison to the lure of the reddish-yellow hue is perhaps no accident – for at the core of her art the concrete and the abstract, the material and the immaterial, the literal and the fictive insersect.[2]

At once colour accents and pure forms, a string of orange balls meanders from the perimeter of Edge of Hot House Glass, metamorphosing in the process, turning first yellow then crimson, while simultaneously growing in scale as it approaches the inner reaches of the work. Its slow arabesque and clear shapes contrast with the more unruly flat collaged elements, swathes of newspaper and painted planes, over and against which it moves. At the opposite end of the platform from this 'necklace' of giant beads four potted plants, their leaves shiny and dark, stand like sentinels marking the far boundary. The leap of the imagination required to encompass this installation, to fuse one disparate and dispersed part with another, makes possible the wedding of the orange balls – surrogate fruit – with the ornamental bushes, now read as expectantly bare. Such connections while never preordained are nonetheless encouraged in Stockholder's work and override, as Jack Bankowsky notes, the denotative sense of the individual components. Thus, he claims, Stockholder 'skips across the surface by the most improbably syntagmatic routes, dragging a nebulous cargo of dissembled meaning in her wake'.[3] The act of traversing the installation, of moving through real space inn actual time in order

SWEET FOR THREE ORANGES,
1995
40 CHRISTMAS TREES,
50 KILOS OF ORANGES, 4
BIRD CAGES, BRICK WALL,
AIR CRAFT, CABLE, BUTANE
HEATERS, ROPE, ROOFING
PAPER AND ROOFING TAR,
PAINT, LIGHT BULBS AND
YELLOW ELECTRIC CORD, PVC,
PIPING ANGLE IRON
ROOM: 2100 X 500 CM

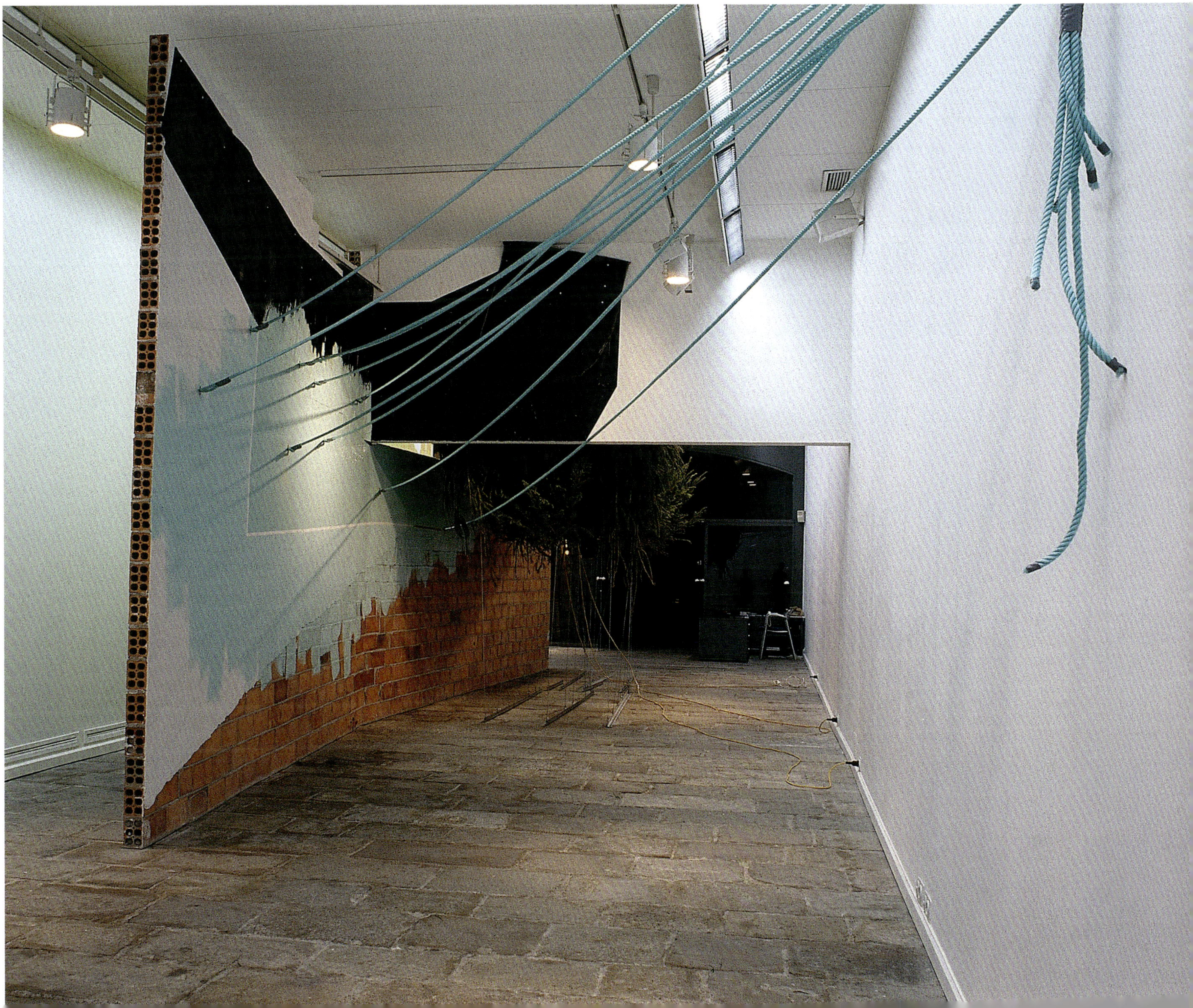

Indoor Lighting for My Father, 1988
Newspaper, men's and women's underwear, cement, Styrofoam, oranges, hay, lighting
Room: 430 x 276 cm
Ceiling: 134 cm

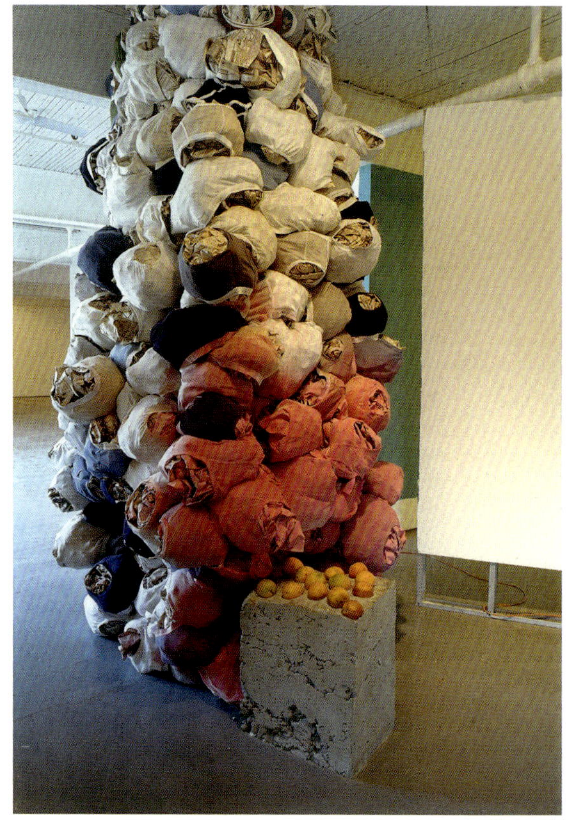

to comprehend it fully, can never be separated from the metaphorical journeys that accompany physical circumlocution. If on the one hand the balls seem to seek the plants as natural affiliates, they equally turn their support, a manufactured 'landscape', into a body. It is in part by establishing such elusive textures of connectives as this that Stockholder achieves a resolution, a resolution that far from requiring the suppression of one alternative in favour of another, conjures meanings amid the disintegration of readings. 'The various parts of my work are multivalent as are the various parts of dreams', Stockholder contends: 'At best there are many ways to put the pieces together'.[4] Given the level of abstraction and formality on which her compositions function, narrative plays no role in her art. Through emphasizing what David Pagel terms 'the incommensurability ... between that which exists in the material world and its unfixable (and not necessarily language bases) meaning', her installations become analogues for thinking processes, even for the structure of thought itself.[5]

Earlier, in 1989, in Making a Clean Edge, Stockholder had scattered a number of oranges along a shelf, juxtaposing them with several fluorescent lights loosely bundles together. 'The oranges were once fed by the daylight as is the piece now', the artist wrote in the notes accompanying this work, in which she had underlined the significance of light to the installation as much by the provision of a turquoise backdrop to the fruit (which had the effect of making them appear irradiated from within) as by the functionally redundant neon tubes. To the artist the colour accents on this occasion were less worthy of remark than the fact that the piece was 'playing to the windows, the daylight, and the tall green building across the parking lot'. 'It is impossible to see the painting that this drive-in movie screen displays while standing in the two foot space between it and the windows', she commented, adding 'but it would be more comfortable if you were in your car 30 feet away'.[6] That the ideal, if improbably, vantage point for this piece was arguably more accessible to the minds than to the bodies of most of the audience is not uncharacteristic in Stockholder's oeuvre.

Indoor Lighting for My Father, the installation that had preceded Making a Clean Edge, also incorporated oranges. This time they were embedded into the top of a block of concrete. Nearby, a clutch of green bulbs contributed not only to the overall illumination but served as a visual complement to the fruit. Among the bevy and heterogeneity of quotidian materials and artefacts included in her work over the past decade, the frequency with which citrus recurs is notable. Here, as customary in her art, a signature tension was set up between the referential capacity of the object and its more purely abstract potential.

That it is both the multivalent associations of oranges and their formal beauty and perfection that fascinates Stockholder is perhaps best demonstrated in Sweet for Three Oranges. In this installation created for the Sala Montcada in Barcelona in 1995, the fruit, in effect, finally occupied centre stage. Quartered in four cages which hung suspended from the ceiling, and framed against a stand of deep green pines, the oranges dominated the viewer's initial encounter with the work. Not just visual but tactile and, above all, olfactory senses, were immediately aroused. Compared with the tangy pine odour, the citrus introduced a heavy pungent fragrance. With their glistening skins and brilliant hue it constituted the prevailing colour accent from which all else took its cue. For orange was threaded throughout this installation in a series of mutating colour chords, ranging from the deeper tones of the bricks comprising the purpose-built free-standing wall, to the vivid accents of the gas cylinders whose fierce heat seemed to threaten to melt the patches of scarlet and yellow on the wall opposite, fusing them into yet another orange zone. Warmth, colour, odour; this succulent, sensual blend involved a world at once opulent and pleasurable, bringing to mind the fact that for centuries (in the West) citrus were prized, almost exotic, treasures, the subject of display and celebration in many a Baroque still life, and later, the staple of Christmas stockings and Yuletide festivities.

II

Suspended high above the ground the bundles firs at first appeared incongruous, displaced – an unruly, ungainly volume compared with the tightly caged fruit. Numerous linear elements further dissected the space: serpentine yellow electric cords; taut wires holding fruit and foliage in place; turquoise ropes leashing architecture to the makeshift wall that the artist had fabricated. To move along the length of this obtusely angled structure meant following the principal axis of the gallery. Yet only after reaching its end and turning back was it apparent that the key architectural feature of the otherwise generic gallery, the white cube that

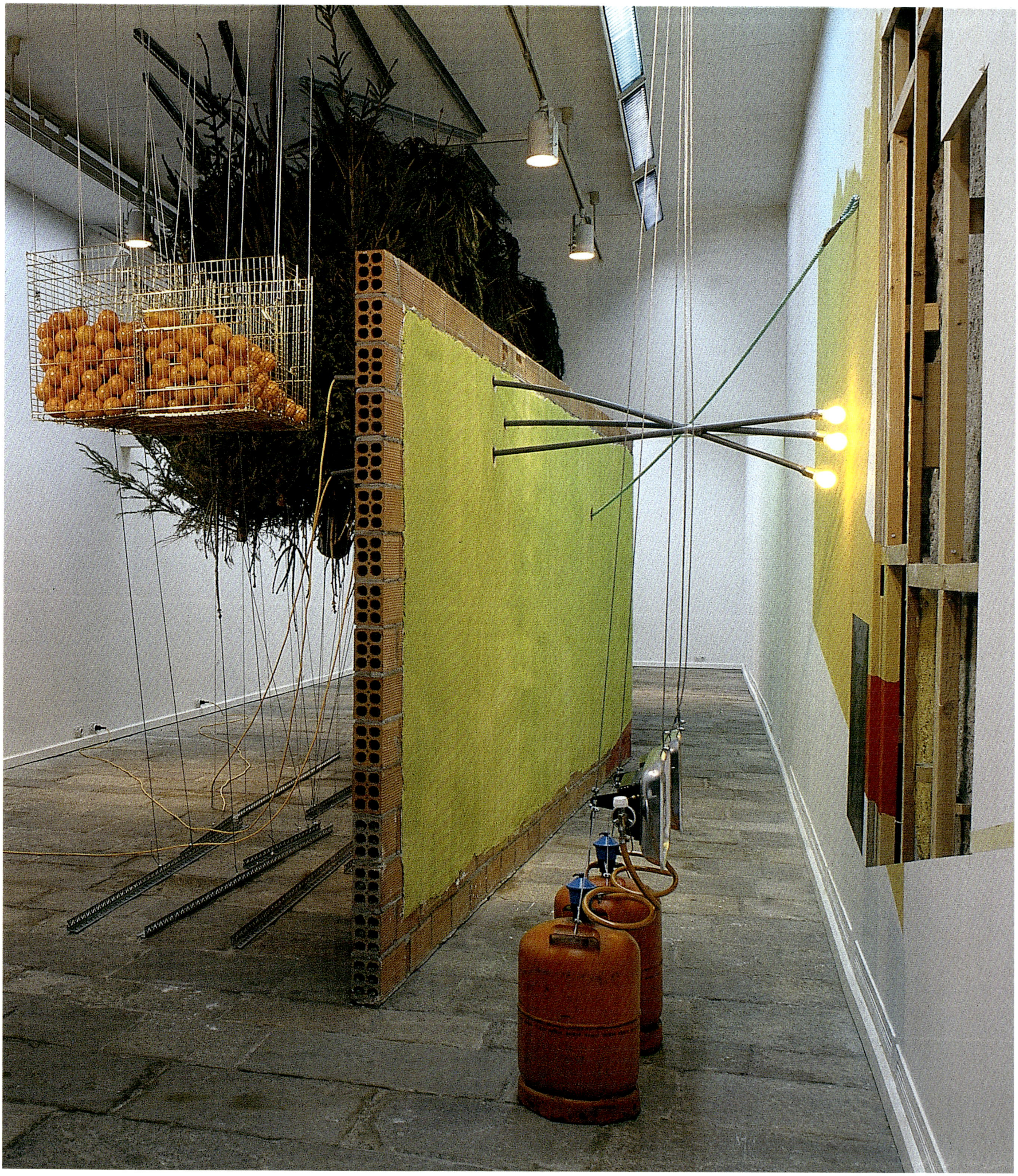

SWEET FOR THREE ORANGES, 1995
40 CHRISTMAS TREES, 50 KILOS OF ORANGES, 4 BIRD CAGES, BRICK WALL, AIR CRAFT, CABLE, BUTANE HEATERS, ROPE, ROOFING PAPER AND ROOFING TAR, PAINT, LIGHT BULBS AND YELLOW ELECTRIC CORD, PVC, PIPING ANGLE IRON
ROOM: 2100 X 500 CM

constituted the Sala Montcada, is a partition suspended from the ceiling mid-way down its length.

Stockholder's installation both denigrated and capitalized on this architectural anomaly. From the threshold of the room she concealed it visually via the introduction of the fruit and foliage, simultaneously mimicking its activation of the upper zone of the space. Somewhat contrarily, she then acknowledged its gesture of bisection, for the brick wall she introduced into the gallery bent precisely al the dividing point. Seen from the rear of the Sala Montcada this partition reasserted itself by means of a dynamic overlay of painted black shapes which melded into a similarly tones area on the top of the brick wall and which, like the adjacent cables, once again implicated the installation with its site. It was telling that from the back of the room little cold be glimpsed of the trees and nothing of the fruit, though their mingled scents, respecting no boundaries, permeated the room, overlaying memory onto immediate experience. From there is was possible to return to the entrance along the narrow corridor formed to the left of the free-standing wall, yet to do so it was necessary to step around and under several elements, negotiating boundaries and implied barriers at each stage. Navigating this carefully orchestrated choreography the viewer was constantly beckoned on by the appearance of unexpected features, coaxed forward by the introduction of novel colour accents or of new chromatic relationships in a schema that counterpointed red, yellow and orange with lime, turquoise and deep green. Offering no single overview and no encompassing vantage point, Sweet for Three Oranges memorably embodied Stockholder's proclivity for a sequence of perceptual, visceral and somatic experiences based in change, relativity and variation.

III

In Sweet for Three Oranges the mixture of materials and elements relating to building and furnishing – plaster, paint, bricks, electric cords, heating appliances, even the excavation that revealed the lath and inner structure of the wall – seemed consistent with the need to modify the architecture in order to realize a site-specific project. Yet these materials and artefacts were not employed in conventional ways: rather they playfully made reference to the notion of an in situ installation while in fact operating according to a more autonomous and abstract formal logic. The yellow lights, for example, did little to illuminate the space but functioned rather like large felt-tipped pens colouring a section of the gallery wall. Within this coherent lexicon two elements stood out as untoward: the trees and the fruit. Organic entities, they, unlike the other material components, were in a state of imminent decay, of incipient death.

In numerous explicit and implicit ways Sweet for Three Oranges invoked or explored duration: real time, as in the time taken to apprehend the work, was compared with the limited life span of the gas in the cylinders,

SWEET FOR THREE ORANGES, 1995
40 CHRISTMAS TREES, 50 KILOS OF ORANGES, 4 BIRD CAGES, BRICK WALL, AIR CRAFT, CABLE, BUTANE HEATERS, ROPE, ROOFING PAPER AND ROOFING TAR, PAINT, LIGHT BULBS AND YELLOW ELECTRIC CORD, PVC, PIPING ANGLE IRON
ROOM: 2100 X 500 CM

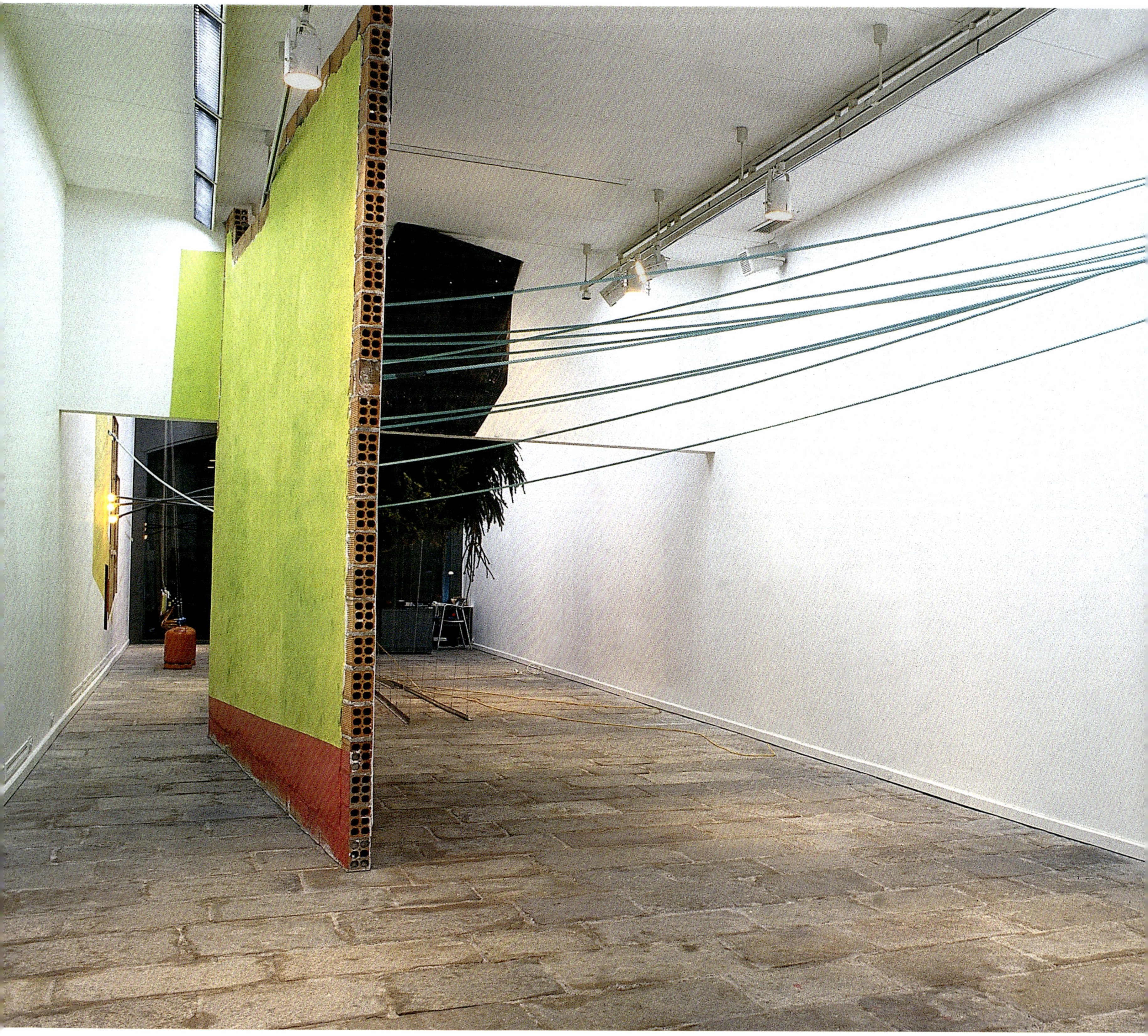

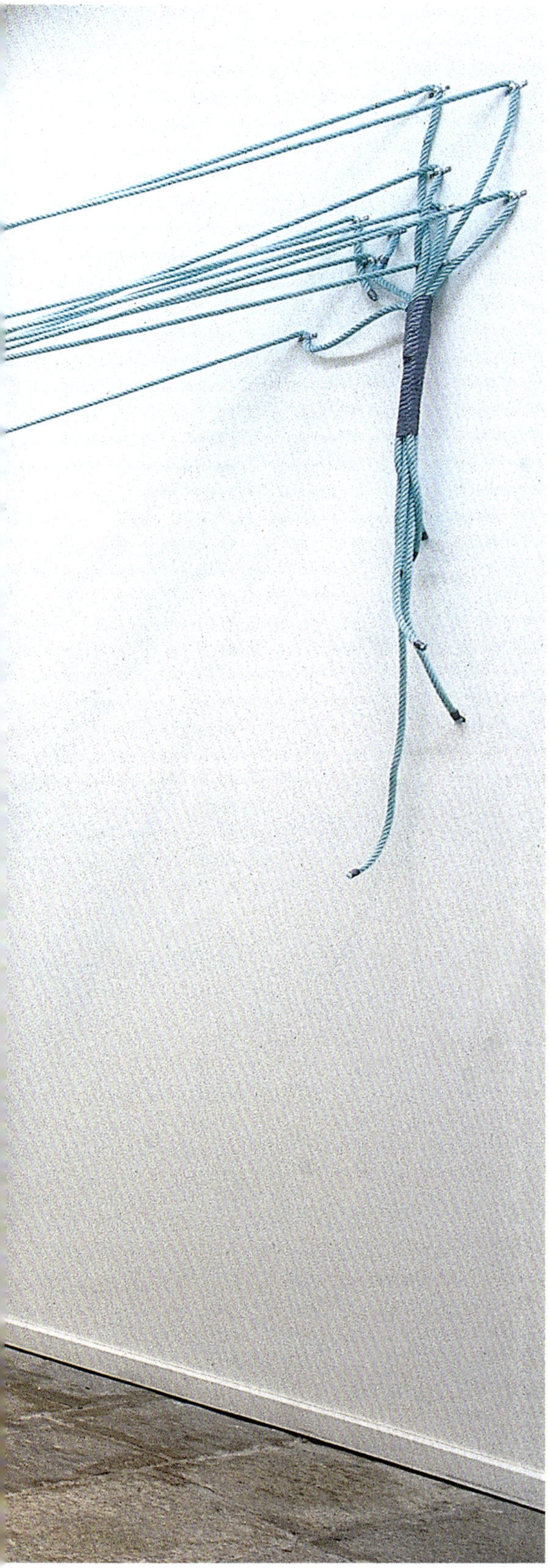

the nearly imperceptible deterioration of trees and fruit, the extended life of the light bulbs fuelled by electricity, the relative transience of the installation itself, and the unquantifiable timescales measured by memory. Taken together these temporal aspects reverberated in a singular way, serving to structure the work in the present and in recollection.

Nor was the metaphorical dimension of the temporal overlooked. The juxtaposition of trees with fruit recalls a certain moment in the annual calendar. With its particular rites and celebrations this moment functions as a cyclical index for the death of the old and the promise of the new. The first inevitably evoke rituals surrounding Christmas, rituals now practiced throughout the world irrespective of climate, and even of Christian belief (just as Christianity had previously appropriated and transmuted pagan customs). The warmth of the brilliant colour of the fruit and the warmth generated by the gas burners together synaesthetically conjured the warmth of the zones where such fruit grows, and contrasted sharply with the experience of winter, literally present outdoors and metaphorically present in Yuletide associations.[7] Georges Braque once argued that our emotions are determined less by the object itself than by the history of our mind's engagement with the object.[8] Jessica Stockholder might add that our associations and allusions are similarly generated less by the object itself than by the history of our mind's engagement with that object.

Contingent, charged, but unforced, the conjunction of firs and fruit in Sweet for Three Oranges floats or hovers as might an image in fact as, a mental projection or an imaginative construct. On one level provisional, even hypothetical, on another, it is obdurately present, concretely rooted in the space, tied and tethered to the physical fabric of the building. At once literal and fictive, it eloquently bears out the artist's claim that 'the knowledge that we have invented our world does not erase the possibility that we might believe in it'.[9] In Sweet for Three Oranges as always in Stockholder's art, it is difficult to separate the actual and experiential from the evoked and invoked, to mark, that is, the boundary between physical and mental space. 'My work often arrives in the world like an idea arrives in your mind', she contends. 'You don't quite know where it came from or when it got put together, nevertheless it's possible to take it apart and see that it has an internal logic. I'm trying', she avers, 'to get closer to thinking processes as they exist before the idea is fully formed'.[10]

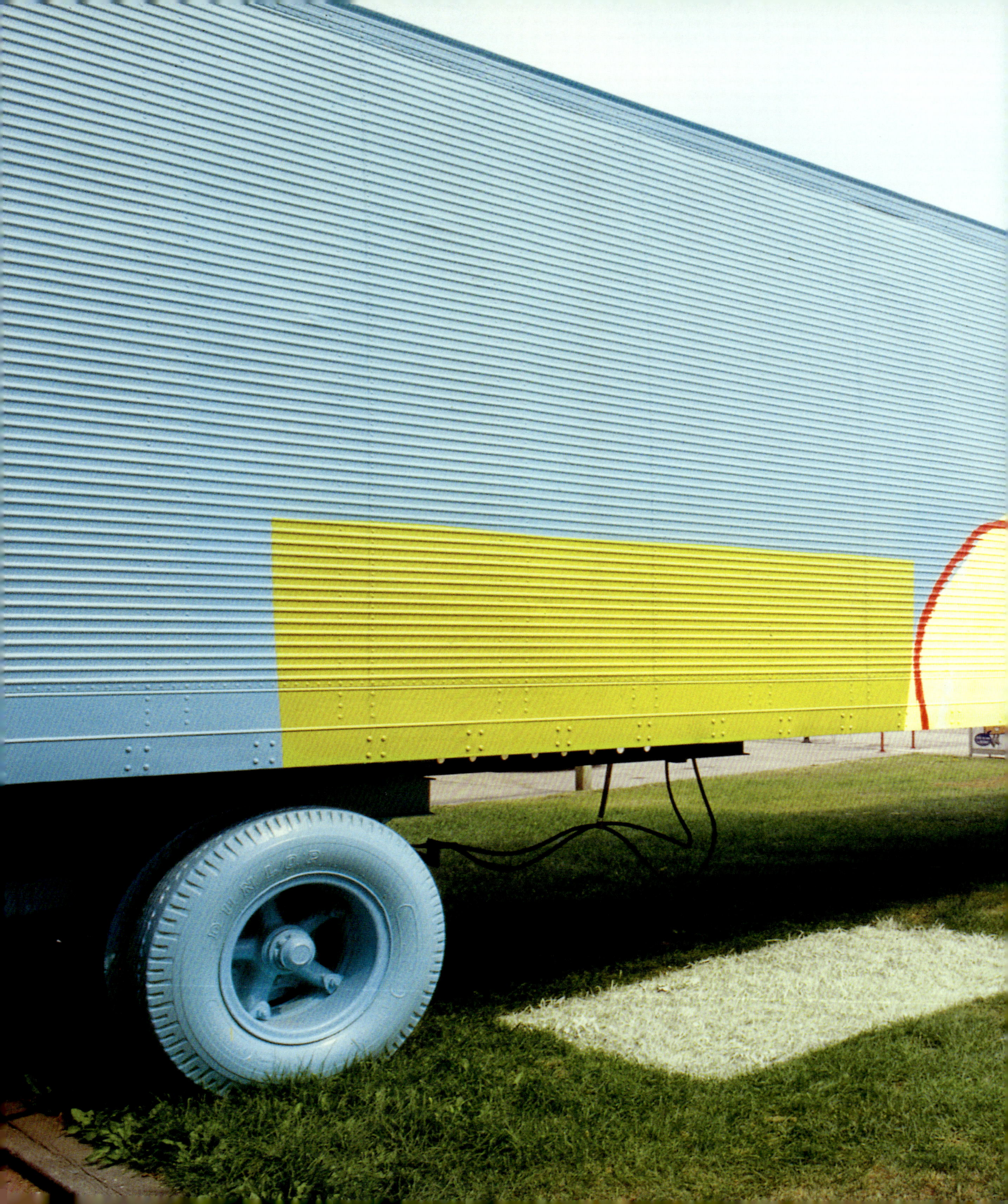
DUNLOP

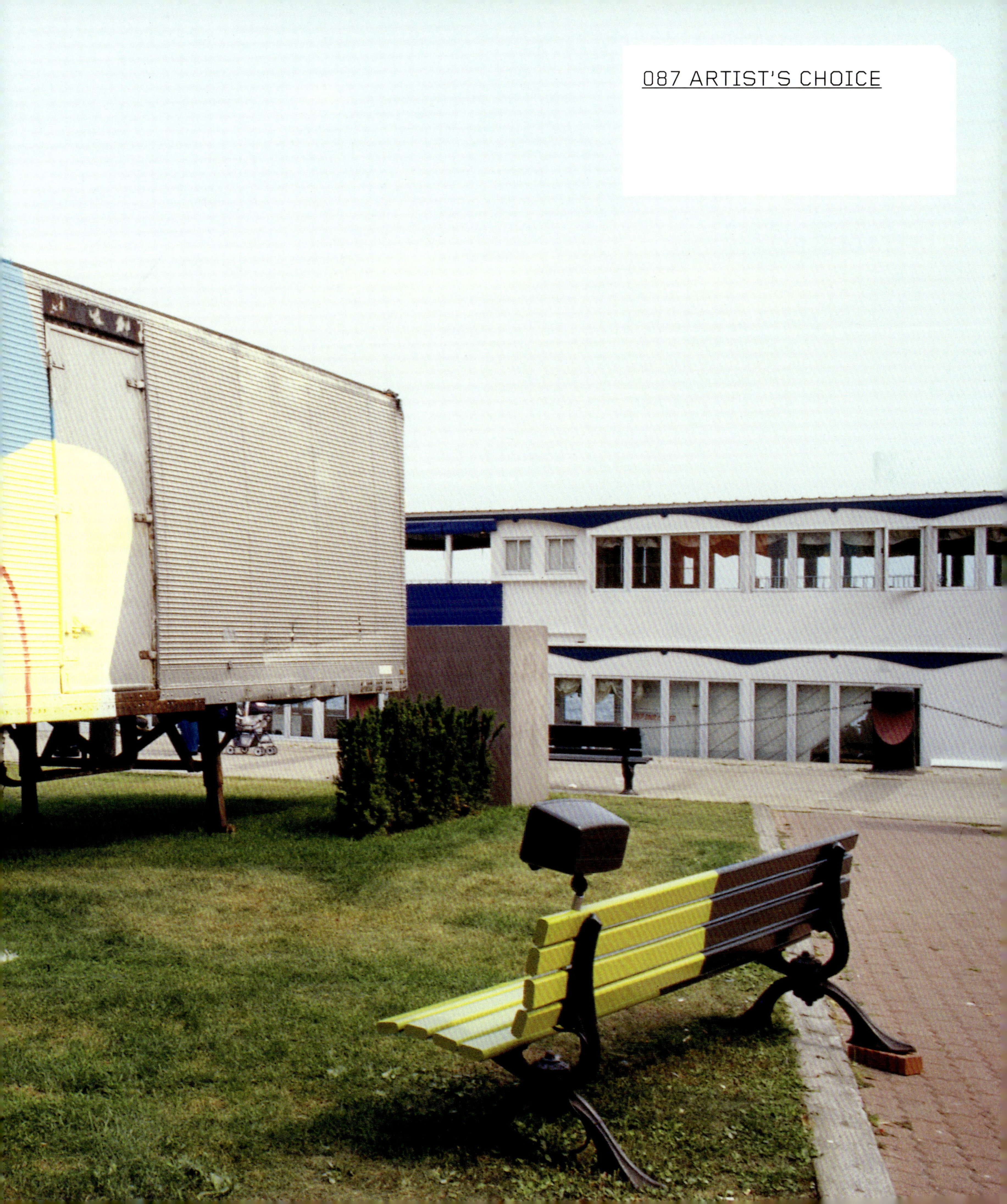

Julian Jaynes

The Origin of Consciousness in the Breakdown of the Bicameral Mind (extract), 1976

Chapter 2: Consciousness

Metaphor and Language

Let us speak of metaphor. The most fascinating property of language is its capacity to make metaphors. But what an understatement! For metaphor is not a mere extra trick of language, as it is so often slighted in the old schoolbooks on composition; it is the very constitutive ground of language. I am using metaphor here in its most general sense: the use of a term for one thing to describe another because of some kind of similarity between them or between their relations to other things. There are thus always two terms in a metaphor, the thing to be described, which I shall call the metaphrand, and the thing or relation used to elucidate it, which I shall call the metaphier. A metaphor is always a known metaphier operating on a less known metaphrand. I have coined these hybrid terms simply to echo multiplication where a multiplier operates on a multiplicand.

It is by metaphor that language grows. The common reply to the question 'what is it?' is, when the reply is difficult or the experience unique, 'well, it is like –'. In laboratory studies, both children and adults describing nonsense objects (or metaphrands) to others who cannot see them use extended metaphiers that with repetition become contracted into labels. This is the major way in which the vocabulary of language is formed. The grand and vigorous function of metaphor is the generation of new language as it is needed, as human culture becomes more and more complex.

A random glance at the etymologies of common words in a dictionary will demonstrate this assertion. Or take the naming of various fauna and flora in their Latin indicants, or even in their wonderful common English names, such as stag beetle, lady's-slipper, darning needle. Queen Anne's lace or buttercup. The human body is a particularly generative metaphier, creating previously unspeakable distinctions in a throng of areas. The *head* of an army, table, page, bed, ship, household or nail, or of stream of water; the *face* of a clock, cliff, card or crystal; the *eyes* of needles, winds, storms, targets, flowers or potatoes; the *brow* of a hill; the *cheeks* of a vice; the *teeth* of cogs or combs; the *lips* of pitchers, craters, augers; the *tongues* of shoes, board joints or railway switches; the *arm*

MADONNA AND CHILD, 1988
METAL STUDS, LAMP BASE, NEWSPAPER, ENAMEL PAINT, FLUORESCENT LIGHT, SWEATERS, STRING
124 X 56 X 51 CM

previous pages,
FIRST COUSIN ONCE REMOVED OR CINEMA OF BRUSHING SKIN, 1999
TRAILER TRUCK, HARDWARE, BENCH, PAINTED GRASS, LIGHTS, PAINT, FLOOR TILES, DROPPED CEILING, DROPPED LIGHTING TRACK, YELLOW ROPE, TABLE LAMP, WHEEL BARROW, BUILDING MATERIALS, VINYL,

INSTALLATION VIEW AT THE POWER PLANT, TORONTO, 1999

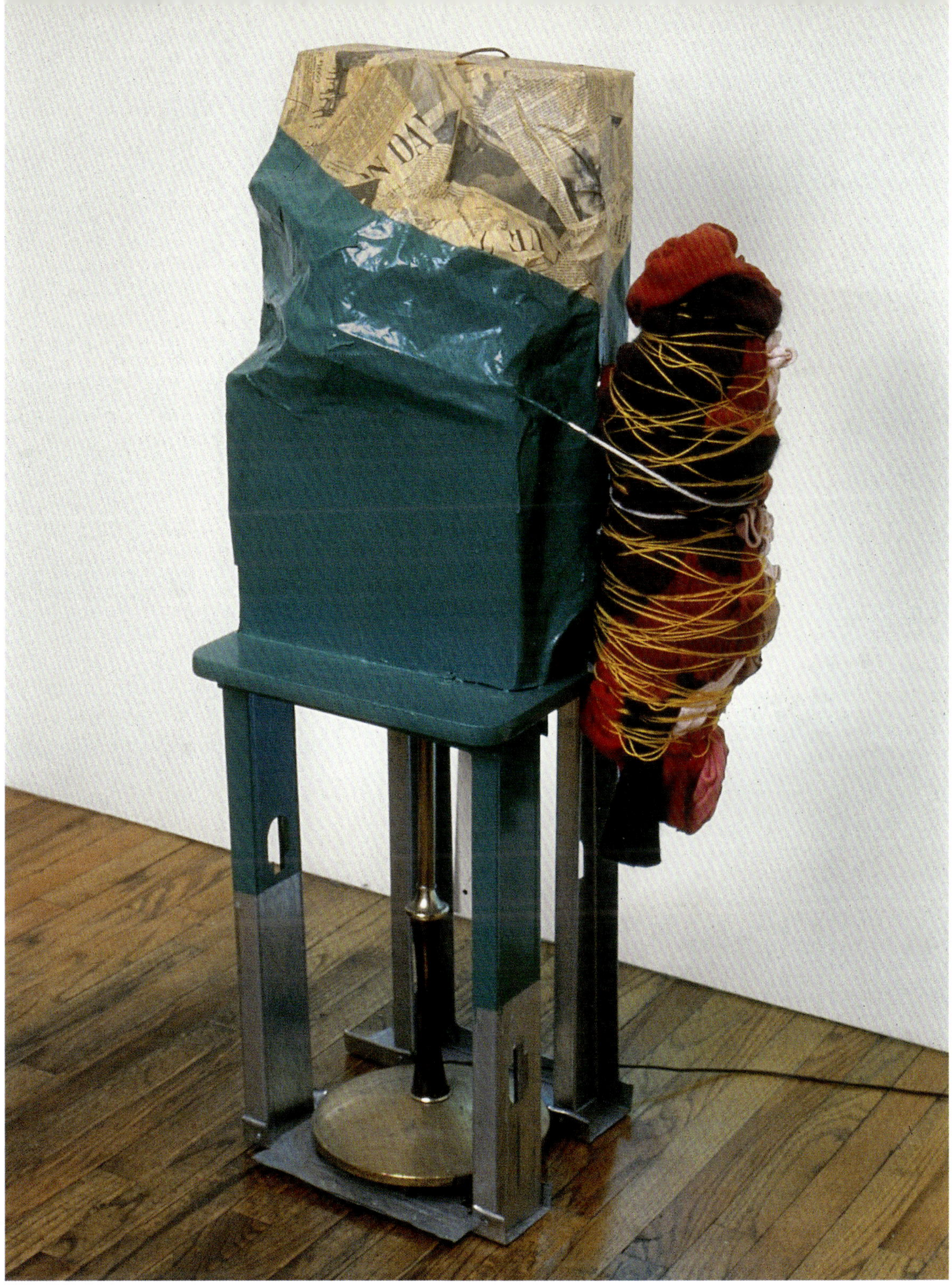

of a chair or the sea; the *leg* of a table, compass, sailor's voyage, or cricket field; and so on and on. Or the foot of this page. Or the leaf you will soon turn. All of these concrete metaphors increase enormously our powers of perception of the world about us and our understanding of it, and literally create new objects. Indeed, language is an organ of perception, not simply a means of communication.

This is language moving out synchronically (or without reference to time) into the space of the world to describe it and perceive it more and more definitely. But language also moves in another and more important way, diachronically, or through time, and behind our experiences on the basis of haptic structures in our nervous system to create

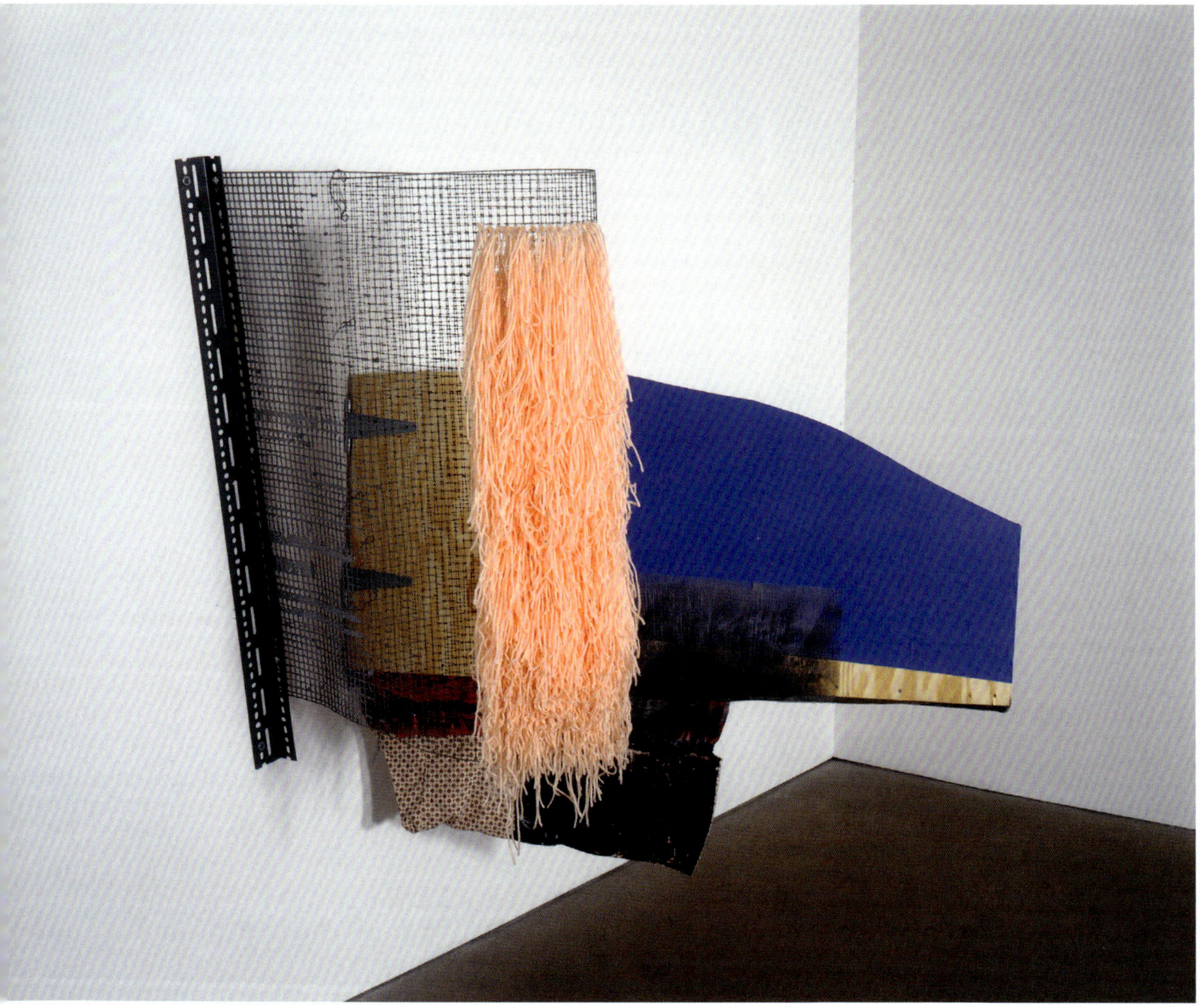

1991
TWO ELEMENTS
ELEMENT NO. 1: WIRE MESH
ACRYLIC YARD, WIRE AND
METAL BAR
101 X 74 X 31 CM
ELEMENT NO. 2: TWO PIECES
OF PLYWOOD LAMINATED
TOGETHER WITH CLOTH AND
TWO HINGES, ACRYLIC PAINT
101 X 74 X 31 CM

abstract concepts whose referents are not observables except in a metaphorical sense. And these too are generated by metaphor. This is indeed the nub (knob), heart, pith, kernel, core, marrow, etc. of my argument, which itself is a metaphor and 'seen' only with the mind's 'eye'.

In the abstractions of human relations, the skin becomes a particularly important metaphier. We get or stay 'in touch' with others who may be 'thick-' or 'thin-skinned' or perhaps 'touchy' in which case they have to be 'handles' carefully lest we 'rub' them the wrong way' we may have a 'feeling' for another person with whom we may have a 'touching' experience.

The concepts of science are all of this kind, abstract concepts generated by concrete metaphors. In physics, we have force, acceleration (to increase one's steps), inertia (originally an indolent person), impedance, resistance, fields and now charm. In physiology, the metaphier of a machine has been at the very centre of discovery. We understand the brain by metaphors to everything from batteries and telegraphy to computers and holograms. Medical practice is sometimes dictated by metaphor. In the eighteenth century, the heart in fever was like a boiling pot, and so bloodletting was prescribed to reduce its fuel. And even today, a great deal of medicine is based upon the military metaphor of defense of the body against attacks of this or that. The very concept of law in Greek derives from *nomos*, the word for the foundations of a building. To be liable, or bound in law, comes from the Latin *ligare*, meaning to bind with cord.

In early times, language and its referents climbed up from the concrete to the abstract on the steps of metaphors, even, we may say, created the abstract on the bases of metaphors.

It is not always obvious that metaphor has played this all-important function. But this is because the concrete metaphiers become hidden in phonemic change, leaving the words to exist on their own. Even such an unmetaphorical-sounding word as the verb 'to be' was generated from a metaphor. It comes from the Sanskrit *bhu*, 'to grow, or make grow' while the English forms 'am' and 'is' have evolved from the same root as the Sanskrfit *asmi*, 'to breathe'. It is something of a lovely surprise that the irregular conjugation of our most nondescript verb is thus a record of a time when man had no independent word for 'existence' and could only say that something 'grows' or that it 'breathes'. Of course we are not conscious that the concept of being is thus generated from a metaphor about growing and breathing. Abstract words are ancient coins whose concrete images in the busy give-and-take of talk have worn away with use.

Understanding as Metaphor

We are trying to understand consciousness, but what are we really trying to do when we try to understand anything? Like children trying to describe nonsense objects, so in trying to understand a thing we are trying to find a metaphor for that thing. Not just any metaphor, but one with something more familiar and easy to our attention. Understanding a thing is to arrive at a metaphor for that thing by substituting something more familiar to us. And the feeling of familiarity is the feeling of understanding.

Generations ago we would understand thunderstorms perhaps as the roaring and rumbling about in battle of superhuman gods. We would have reduced the racket that follows the streak of lightning to familiar battle sounds, for example. Similarly today, we reduce the storm to various supposed experiences with friction, sparks, vacuums, and the imagination of bulgeous banks of burly air smashing together to make the noise. None of these really exist as we picture them. Our images of these events of physics are as far from the actuality as fighting gods. Yet they act as the metaphor and they feel familiar and so we say we understand the thunderstorms.

If understanding a thing is arriving at a familiarizing metaphor for it, then we can see that there always will be a difficulty in understanding consciousness. For it should be immediately apparent that there is not and cannot be anything in our immediate experience that is like immediate experience itself. There is therefore a sense in which we shall never be able to understand consciousness in the same way that we can understand things that we are conscious of.

Most of the errors about consciousness that we have been studying have been errors of attempted metaphors. We spoke of the notion of consciousness being a copy of experience coming out of the explicit metaphor of a schoolboy's slate. But of course no one really meant consciousness copies experience; it was as if it did. And we found on analysis, of course, that it did no such thing. And even the idea behind that last phrase, that consciousness does anything at all, even that is a metaphor. It is saying that consciousness is a person behaving in physical space who does things, and this is true only if 'does' is a metaphor as well. For to do things is some kind of behaviour in a physical world by a living body. And also in what 'space' is the metaphorical 'doing' being done? (Some of the dust is beginning to settle.) This 'space' too must be a metaphor of real space. All of which is reminiscent of our discussion of the location of consciousness, also a metaphor. Consciousness is being thought of as a thing, and so like other things must have a location, which, as we saw earlier, it does not actually have in the physical sense.

The Metaphor Language of Mind

Subjective conscious mind is an analog of what is called the real world. It is built up with a vocabulary or lexical field whose terms are all metaphors or analogs of behaviour in a physical world. Its reality is of the same order as mathematics. It allows us to shortcut behavioural processes and arrive at more adequate decisions. Like mathematics, it is an operator rather than a thing or repository. And it is intimately bound up with volition and decision.

Consider the language we use to describe conscious processes. The most prominent group of words used to describe mental events are visual. We 'see' solutions to problems, the best of which may be 'brilliant', and the person 'brighter'; and 'clear-headed' as opposed to 'dull', 'fuzzy-minded', or 'obscure' solutions. These words are all metaphors and the mind-space to which they apply is a metaphor of actual space. In it we can 'approach' a problem, perhaps from some 'viewpoint', and 'grapple' with its difficulties, or seize together or 'comprehend' parts of a problem, and so on, using metaphors of behaviour to invent things to do in this metaphored mind-space.

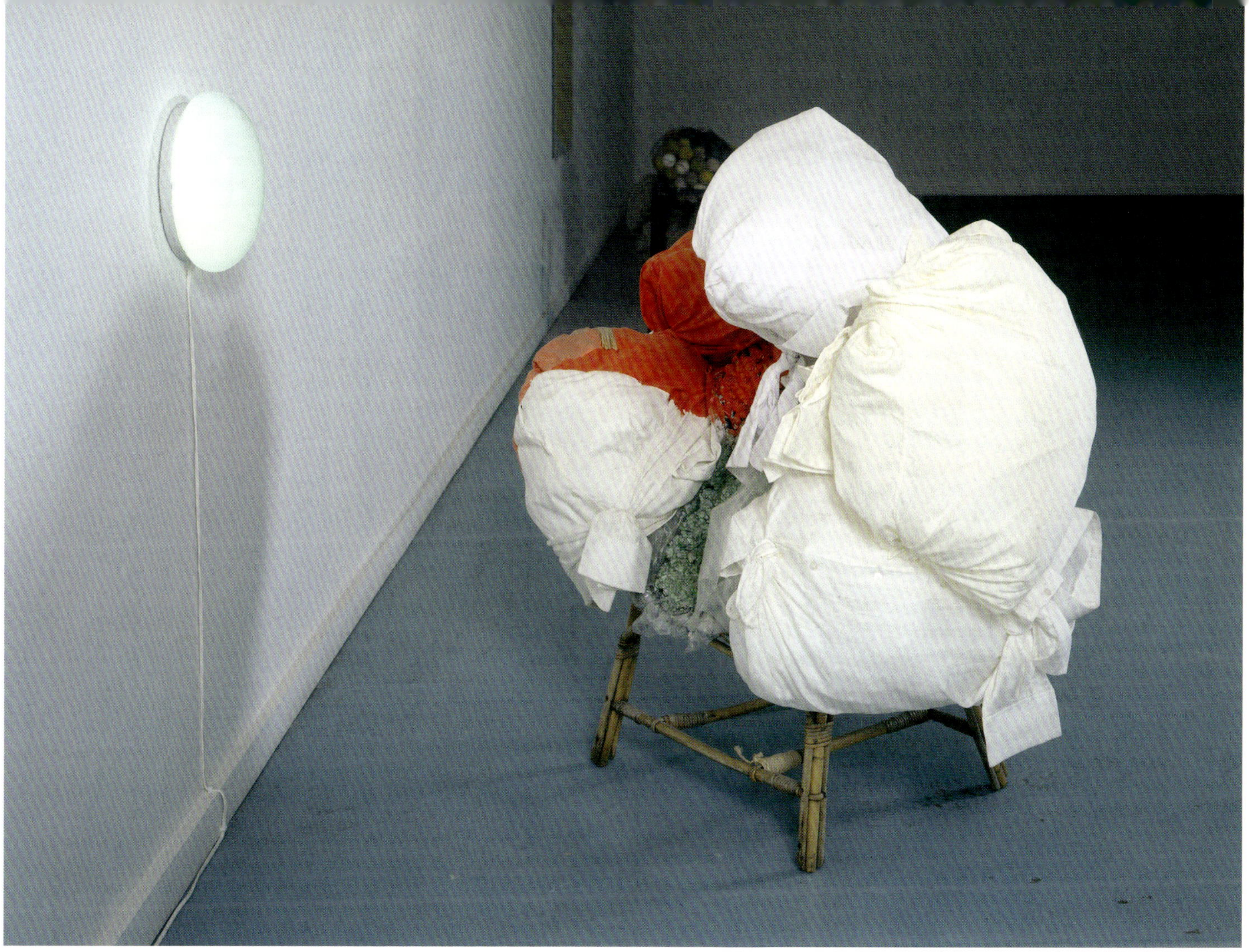

1989
WICKER CHAIR, MEN'S SHIRTS STUFFED WITH FOAM WRAPPING MATERIAL, RED OIL PAINT, PLASTER, A ROUND FLUORESCENT LIGHT FIXTURE MOUNTED ON THE WALL
H. 130 CM

And the adjectives to describe physical behaviour in real space are analogically taken over to describe mental behaviour in mind-space when we speak of our minds as being 'quick', 'slow', 'agitated' (as when we cogitate or co-agitate), 'nimble-witted', 'strong-' or 'weak-minded'. The mind-space in which these metaphorical activities go on has its own group of adjectives; we can be 'broad-minded', 'deep', 'open', or 'narrow-minded'; we can be 'occupied'; we can 'get something off our minds', 'put something out of mind', or we can 'get it', let something 'penetrate', or 'bear', 'have', keep', or 'hold' it in mind.

As with a real space, something can be at the 'back' of our mind, in its 'inner recesses', or 'beyond' our mind, or 'out' of our mind. In argument we try to 'get things through' to someone, to 'reach' their 'understanding' or find a 'common ground', or 'point out', etc., all actions in real space taken over analogically into the space of the mind.

1991
2X4S, TREE, OIL AND ACRYLIC PAINT, METAL LATH, PAPIER MACHÉ, MIRROR
230 X 206 X 77 CM

If we look more carefully at the nature of metaphor (noticing all the while the metaphorical nature of almost everything we are saying), we find (even the verb 'find'!) that it is composed of more than a metaphier and a metaphrand. There are also at the bottom of most complex metaphors various associations or attributes of the metaphier which I am going to call paraphiers. And these *paraphiers* project back into the metaphrand as what I shall call the paraphrands of the metaphrand. Jargon, yes, but absolutely necessary if we are to be crystal clear about our referents.

Some examples will show that the unravelling of metaphor into these four parts is really quite simple, as well as clarifying what otherwise we could not speak about.

Consider the metaphor that the snow blankets the ground. The metaphrand is something about the completeness and even thickness with which the ground id covered by snow. The metaphier is a blanket on a bed. But the pleasing nuances of this metaphor are in the paraphiers of the metaphier, blanket. These are something about warmth, protection, and slumber until some period of awakening. These associations of blanket then automatically become the associations or paraphrands of the original metaphrand, the way the snow covers the ground. And we thus have created by this metaphor the idea of the earth sleeping and protected by the snow cover until its awakening in spring. All that is packed into the simple use of the word 'blanket' to pertain to the way snow covers the ground.

Not all metaphors, of course, have such generative potential. In that often-cited one that a ship plows the sea, the metaphrand is the particular action of the bow of the ship through the water, and the metaphier is plowing action. The correspondence is exact. And that is the end of it.

But if I say the brook sings through the woods, the similarity of the metaphrand of the brook's bubbling and gurgling and the metaphier of (presumable) a child singing is not at all exact. It is the paraphiers of joy and dancingness becoming the paraphrands of the brook that are of interest.

Or in the many-poemed comparison of love to a rose, it is not the tenuous correspondence of metaphrand and metaphier but the paraphrands that engage us, that love lies in the sun, smells sweet, has thorns when grasped, and blooms for a season only. Or suppose I say less visually and so more profoundly something quite opposite, that my love is like a tinsmith's scoop, sunk past its gleam in the meal-bin. The immediate correspondence here of metaphrand and metaphier, of being out of casual sight, is trivial. Instead, it is the paraphrands of this metaphor which create what could not possible be there, an enduring careful shape and hidden shiningness and

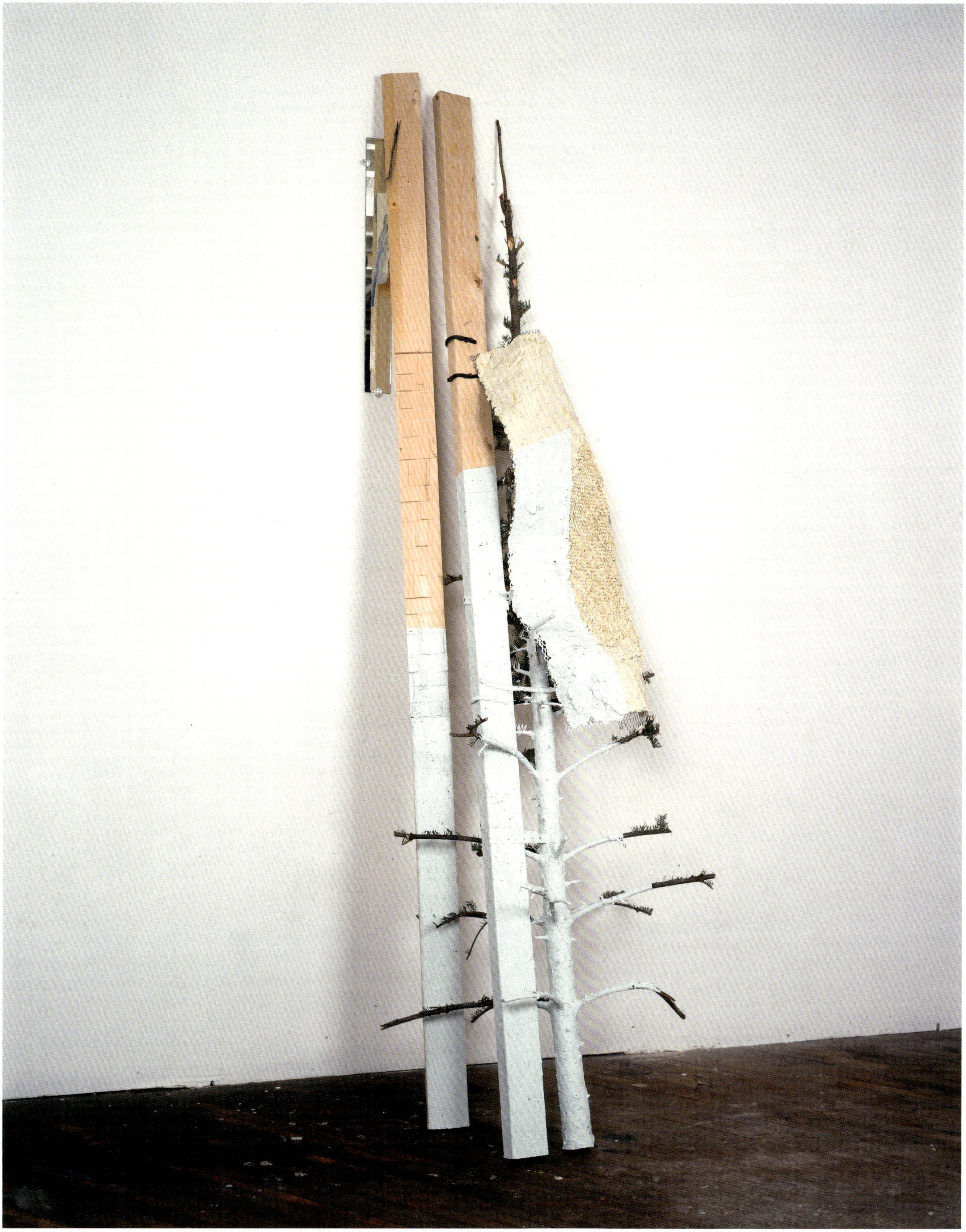

previous page and next pages,
QUIET STOPS RATTLING THIN AIR, 2002
LAMPS, LIGHT FIXTURES, FARM EQUIPMENT, CAR, WASHING MACHINE, PLASTIC COVERED CHAIR, WHITE SHEETS CLOTHING AND FABRIC, HOSE, CONCRETE, WATER, PAINT, THEATRE LIGHT

INSTALLATION VIEW AT THE BALTIC ART CENTER, VISBY, SWEDEN, 2002

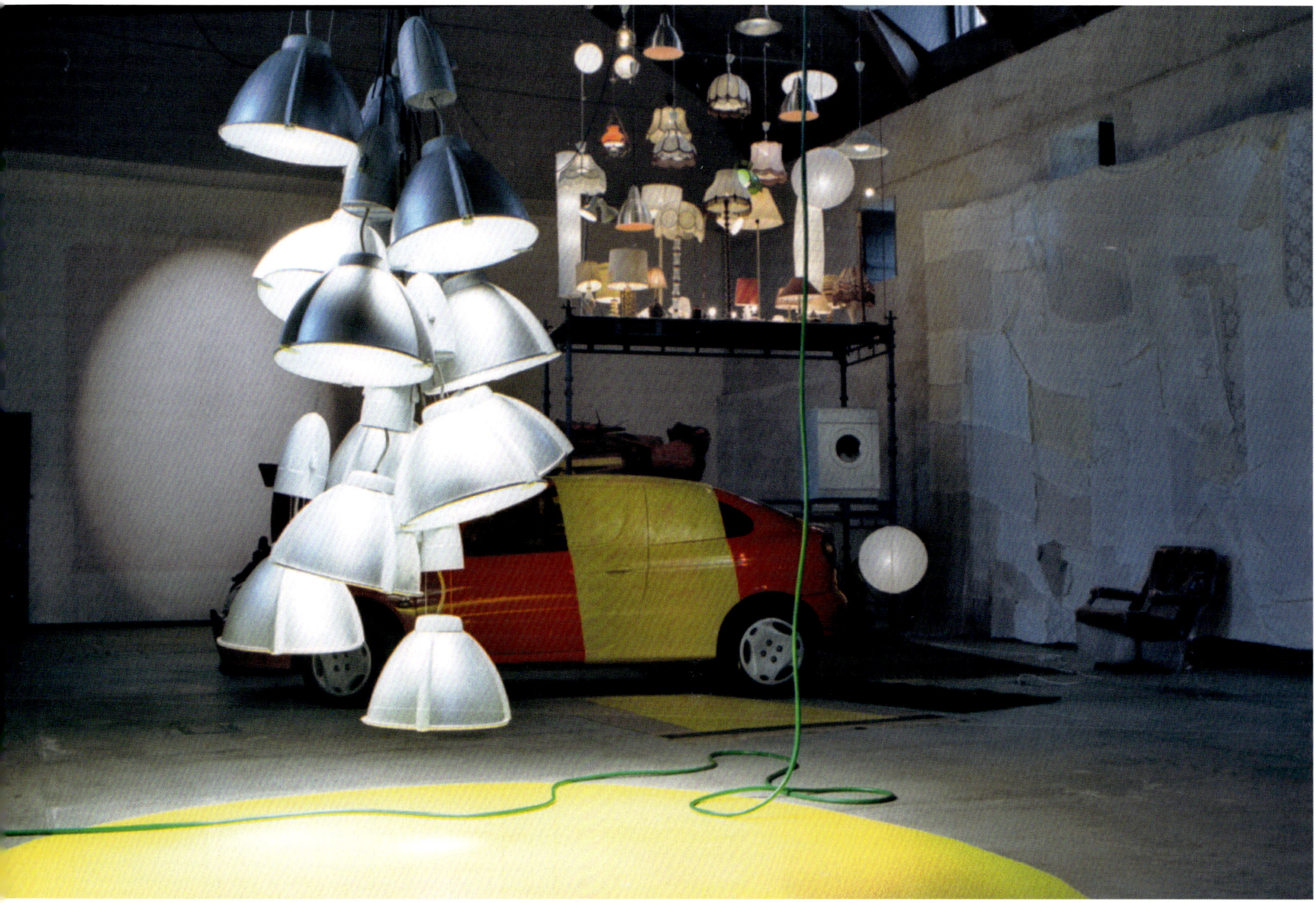

holdingness of a lasting love deep in the heavy manipulable softnesses of mounding time, the whole simulating (and so paraphranding) sexual intercourse from a male point of view. Love has not such properties except as we generate them by metaphor.

We have said that consciousness is an operation rather than a thing, a repository, or a function. It operates by way of analogy, by way of constructing an analog space with an analog 'I' that can observe that space, and move metaphorically in it. It operates on any reactivity, excerpts relevant aspects, narratizes and conciliates them together in a metaphorical space where such meanings can be manipulated like things in space. Conscious mind is a spatial analog of the world and mental acts are analogs of bodily acts. Consciousness operates only on objectively observable things. Or, to say it another way with echoes of John Locke, there is nothing in consciousness that is not an analog of something that was in behaviour first.

If consciousness is this invention of an analog world on the basis of language, paralleling the behavioural world even as the world of mathematics paralleled the world of quantities of things, what then can we say about its origin?

We have arrived at a very interesting point in our discussion, and one that is completely contradictory to all of the alternative solutions to the problem of the origin of consciousness which we discussed in the introductory chapter. For if consciousness is based on language, then it follows that it is of a much more recent origin than has heretofore been supposed. Consciousness came after language! The implications of such a position are extremely serious.

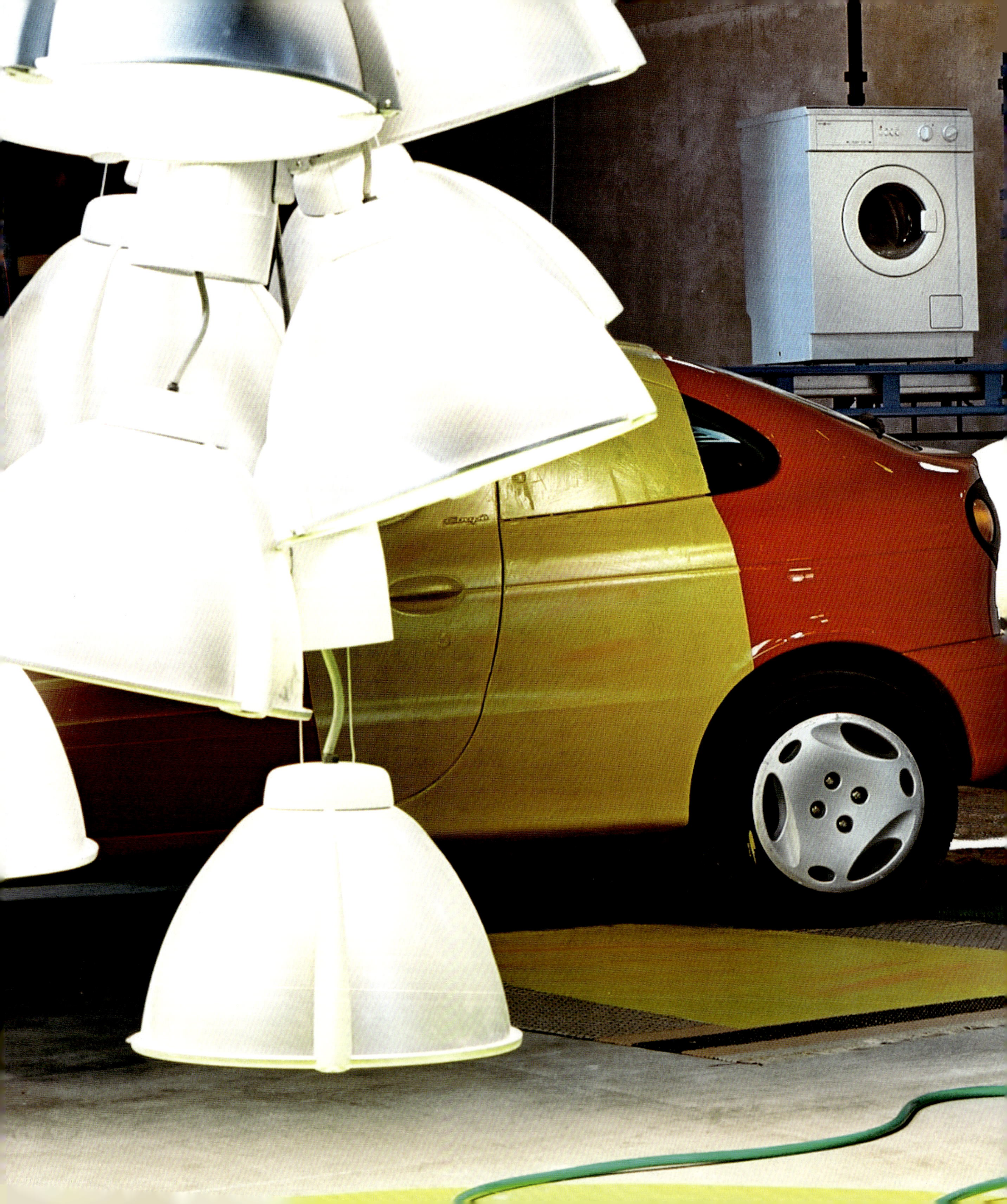

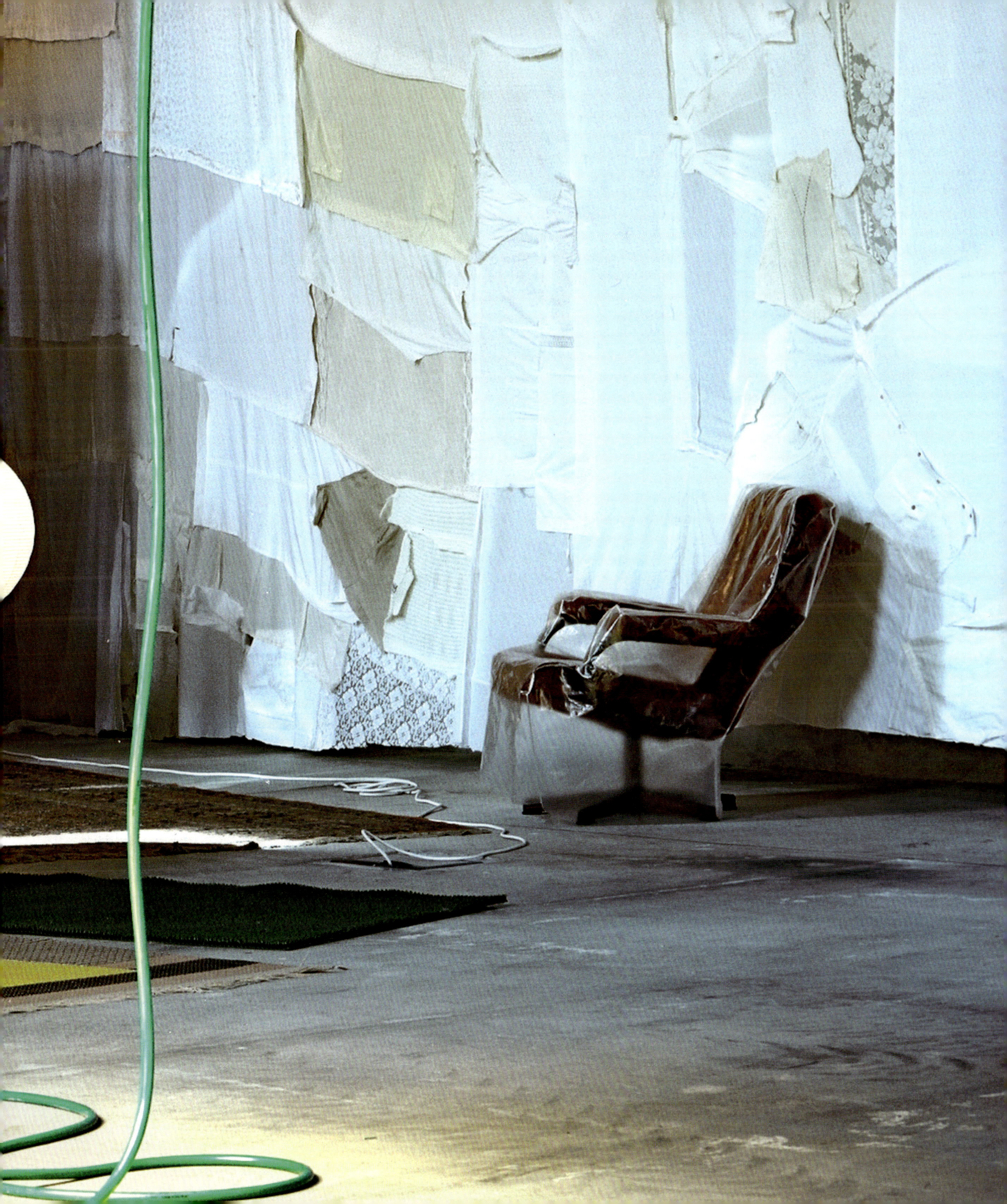

Cornelius Castoriadis

The Imaginary Institution of Society (extract), 1987

To say that the institution of society leans on the organization of the first natural stratum means that it does not reproduce or reflect this organization, is not *determined* by it in any way. Instead, society finds in it a series of conditions, supports and stimuli, stops and obstacles. To use the language of the preceding pages, society, like any automaton, defines its own universe of discourse. And to the extent that society is not simply the human species as a mere living or animal being, this universe of discourse is necessarily different from that of the animal, man. What is more, each society is an automaton of a different type, since (or in so far as) each establishes a different universe of discourse, since each institution of society establishes what, for the society in question, is and is not, what is relevant and what is not, the weight, the value, the 'translation' of what is relevant – and the 'response' that corresponds to this (...)

In the first place, for society there exist entities that correspond to no organization (whether identitary or not) of the natural stratum; to cite a few obvious examples, spirits, gods, myths and so on do *exist* for society. And what *does not exist* for society is not always, and not necessarily, pure non-being, absolute non-being, that which could never enter into the universe of discourse, even if it is only to be denies. Quite the opposite, the being of non-being, or non-being as such, always exists for society; into its universe of discourse enter entities whose being is or has to be negated, positions that must be asserted by means of explicit negations or that are presented only to be negated. The possibility of 'this does not exist' or of 'it is not like that' is always explicitly posed in the institution of society.

In the second place, for society as such there is no irrelevant information; the irrelevant exists only as a limiting case of the relevant. In other words, for society, there is no 'noise' qua noise; 'noise' always exists as something and at its limit is explicitly posed as noise or as irrelevant information. This takes us, by way of a seemingly minor route, to the very heart of the question of the social: everything that is, in one way or another, grasped or perceived by society has to *signify* something, has to be endowed with signification, and what is more, it is always already grasped in and through the possibility of signification, and it is only as a result of this possibility that it can finally be defined as devoid of signification, insignification or absurd. It is clear that the absurd can appear – even, and especially, when it is irreducible – only on the basis of the absolute requirement of signification.

LIKE WATER IF POND AS LILY, 2013–14
RESIN, CONCRETE, METAL POLES,
ARTISANAL GLASS, AND THE
ARCHITECTURE OF UCFS HOSPITAL

INSTALLATION VIEW AT UCSF
MEDICAL CENTER MISSION BAY
HOSPITAL, SAN FRANCISCO, 2013

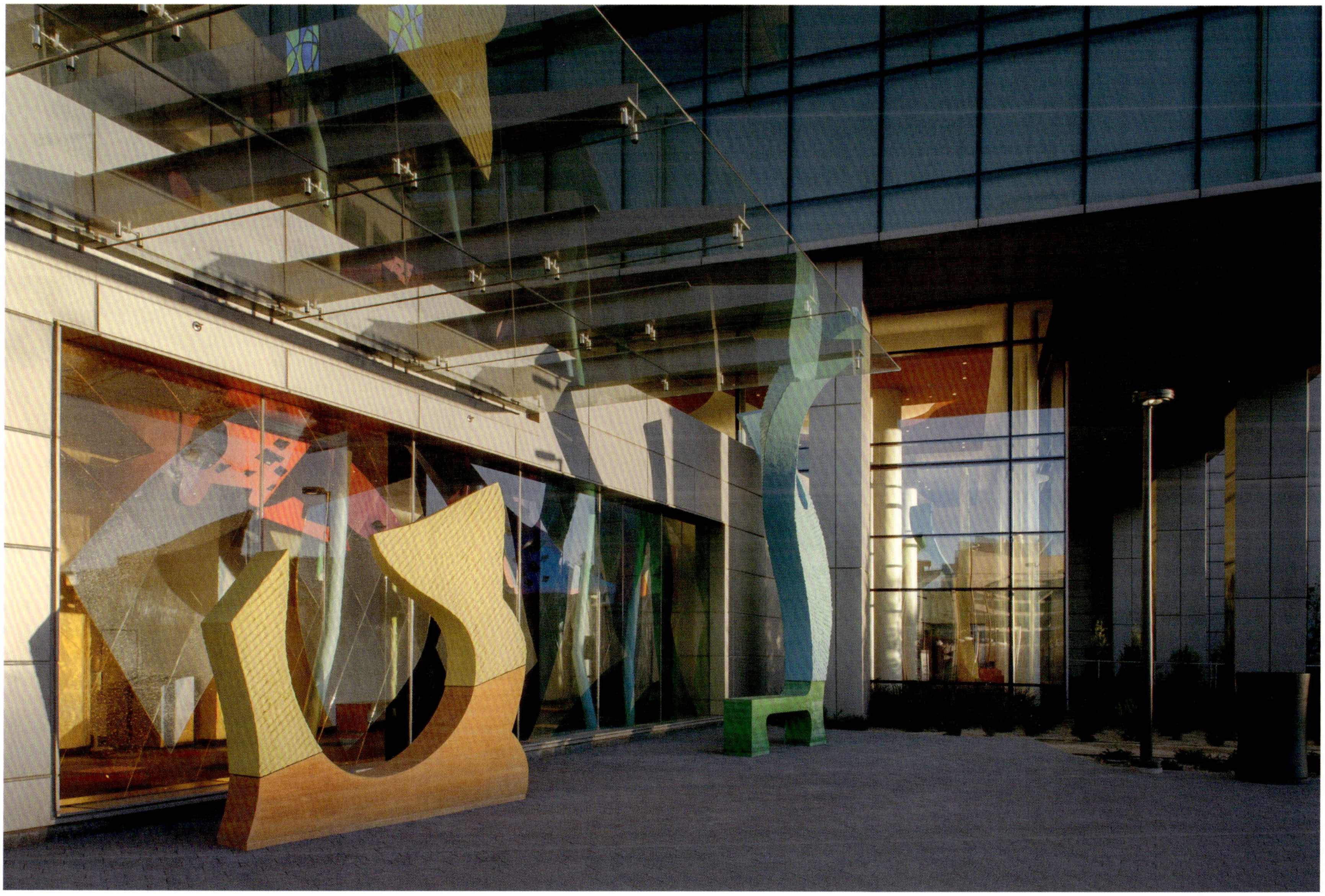

LIKE WATER IF POND AS LILY,
2013–14
RESIN, CONCRETE, METAL
POLES, ARTISANAL GLASS,
AND THE ARCHITECTURE OF
UCFS HOSPITAL

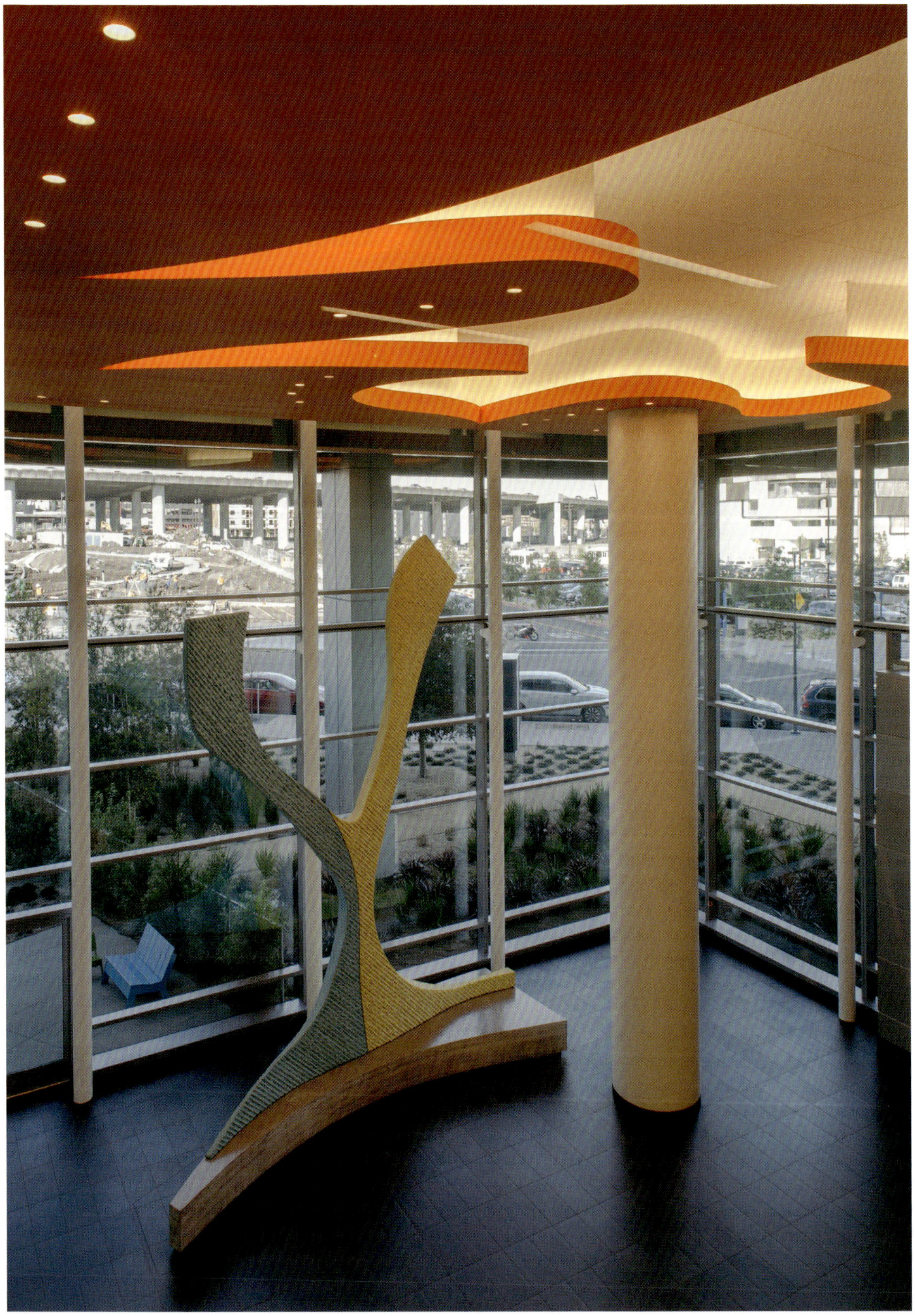

For an identitary automaton (or, for what amounts to the same thing, for a completely formalized calculus) to say that a term is means that it has a recognizable form that is determined and predetermined (it is an instance of a given *eidos*). And to say that a term 'has a meaning' (actually an abuse of language) is to say that this form determines the entry of this term into a determined and predetermined syntax of operations. (Of course, what is not or has no meaning for the automaton can act on it and, even, partly or totally destroy it.)

For a society, to say that a term is means that it signifies (is a signification, is posited as a signification, is tied to a signification). Once it *is*, it *always* has meaning, in a narrow sense indicated above, that is it can always enter into a syntax or can constitute a syntax in which to enter. The institution of society is the institution of a world of significations – which is obviously a creation as such, and a specific one in each case.

The Mode of Being of the Unconscious

The unconscious, Freud wrote, is unaware of time and of contradiction. This dizzying thought, amplified and made even more insistent by Freud's entire work, has been almost entirely neglected – when it has not been made to say the opposite of what it states, by transforming the psychical apparatus into a real machinery or by reducing it to a logical structure. The unconscious constitutes a 'place' where (identitary) time – as determined by and as itself determining an ordered succession – does not exist, where contraries do not exclude one another; more precisely, where there can be no question of contradictory terms and which, itself, is not really a place since place implies order and distinction. Of the essential stuff of the unconscious, the representation, we can say practically nothing, if we confine ourselves to our customary logic. We are already doing violence to it when, in speaking of the unconscious (and even of consciousness) we speak of representation separating it from the unconscious effect and intention, which is impossible both *de jure* and *de facto*. The unconscious exists only as an indissociably representative/affective/intentional flux. But let us suppose this separation to be effectuable and already effected, and let us halt at representation as such. How could we fail to see that it escapes the most elementary logical schemata, that it slips past them on all sides, that it can never be subjected to any of the requirements of determinacy?

Consider, for example, Freud's dream: 'My friend R is my uncle, he wears a long yellow bears … 'Does this dream form one representation or several, and *how many*? What sort of thing is it of which we cannot say, even with *respect* to …, whether it is one or many? Or consider the analysis of 'little Hans'; what is, *for* little Hans, the representation of his father, of the horse, of his phobia and the relation between them? We are fooling ourselves, in the last cases, when, carried away by the habit of interpretation, the necessity of translating the givens of the unconscious in linguistic terms and in the relations forged in and through language, we posit *the* representation of the father and its representation or 'symbolization' by the animal of the phobia as a clear and distinct relation, a simple *quid pro quo*, the positing of one thing for another thing. To be sure, if we do not return to this world of interpretation and of the translation into waking language, we would be able to say nothing at all. But the actual situation is not really similar to what we do when we speak about it – as anyone who has ever dreamed will know. What is more, you do not even have to dream to see this. Mélanie Klein's little Richard says: 'Mama *is* the fish *and* the big fish above'; he is not saying that *x* is (for) *y*, he is saying that *y* is at once *x* and *y* (…)

The Leaning of Society on Nature

How are we to understand the leaning of the first natural stratum on the ensemblizable dimension? Men and women live in society; they can be unambiguously classified (biologically) as male and female. They give birth to boys and girls who are, always and everywhere, incapable of surviving unless they are cared for by adults for a rather long period of time. All of this results neither from the legislation of transcendental consciousness nor from the institution of society. The ensembles of males and females,

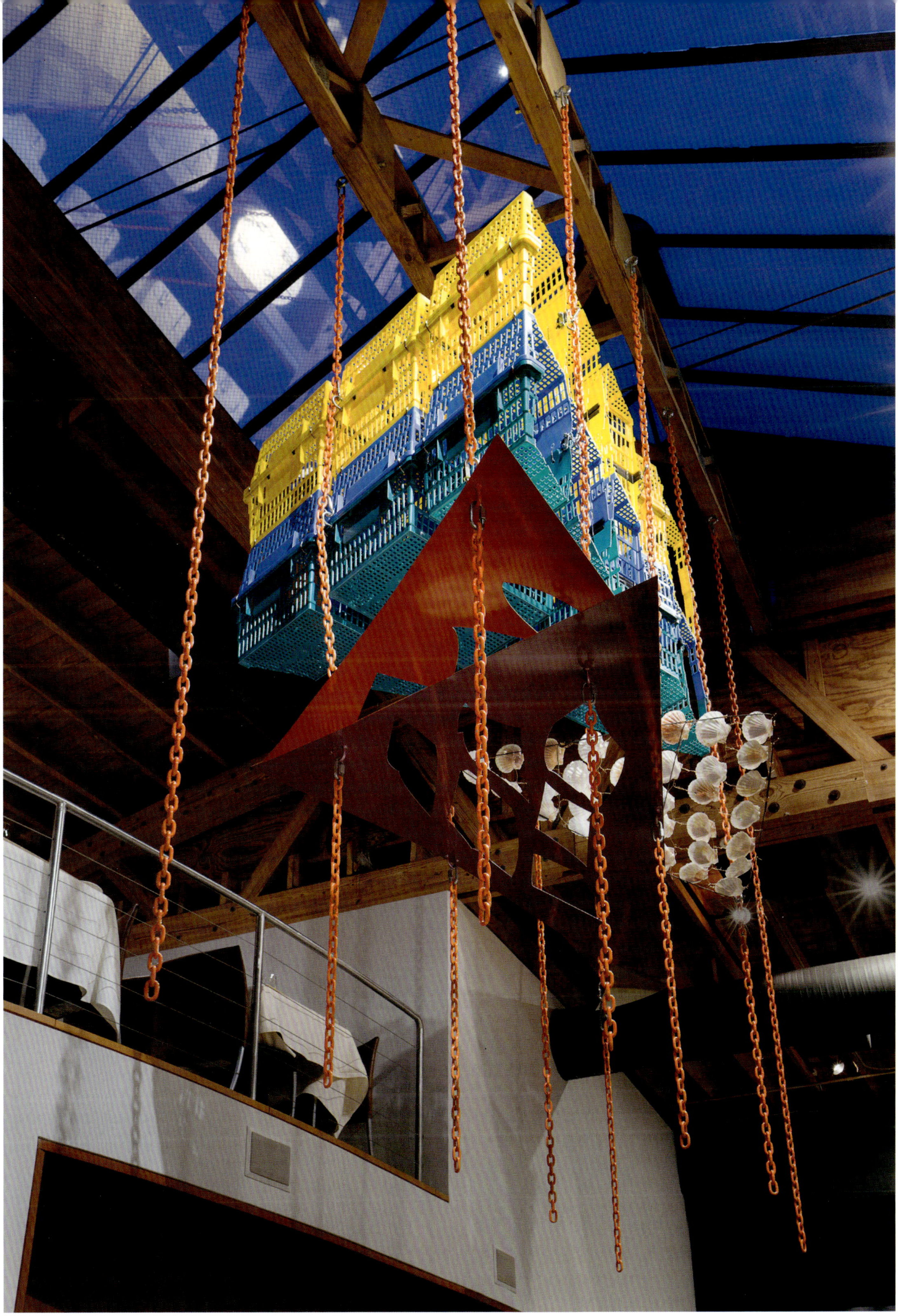

ANOTHER PIECE OF PIE, 2015
PLASTIC SHOPPING BASKETS, METAL PLATE, PAINT, ORANGE CHAINS, HARDWARE, METAL ROD, SCALLOP SHELLS

INSTALLATION VIEW AT MK RESTAURANT, CHICAGO, 2015

from left,
<u>SET EYES ON</u>, 2015
NINE TABLES, FOUR WOODEN STOOLS, FIVE DRIVEWAY MIRRORS, ACRYLIC AND OIL PAINT, HARDWARE, PLASTIC BINS FOR SHOPPING, STORAGE, AND LAUNDRY, CARPE SQUARES, FIVE HANGING LAMPS, CHAIN
VARIABLE HEIGHT (610 CM MINIMUM) X 518 X 244 CM

<u>INFORMAL GET TOGETHER</u>, 2014
ALUMINUM TUBE, YELLOW WEBBING, PINK PLASTIC AND FABRIC PARTS, BASKETS, 5 IKEA LAMPS, SMALL RUG, POWER BAR, ACRYLIC PAINT
VARIABLE HIGHT (244 CM MINIMUM) X 216 X 61 CM

<u>GROSS NATIONAL GROWTH</u>, 2014
DRIVE WAY MIRRORS, OIL PAINT, ACRYLIC PAINT, WOODEN STOOLS, SILICONE MOLD, LIGHT FIXTURE AND CORD, CLAMPS, BASKET BALL HOOP, PIE PAN RIM, CHAIN AND HARDWARE, SNAP TOGETHER DRIVEWAY TILES, BLACK RUBBER TILES, CARPET, PLASTIC PARTS, COPPER FOIL
VARIABLE HEIGHT (244 CM MINIMUM) X 227 X 160 CM

INSTALLATION VIEW AT GALERIE NATHALIE OBADIA, PARIS, 2015

next page,
<u>GROSS NATIONAL GROWTH</u>, 2014
DRIVE WAY MIRRORS, OIL PAINT, ACRYLIC PAINT, WOODEN STOOLS, SILICONE MOLD, LIGHT FIXTURE AND CORD, CLAMPS, BASKET BALL HOOP, PIE PAN RIM, CHAIN AND HARDWARE, SNAP TOGETHER DRIVEWAY TILES, BLACK RUBBER TILES, CARPET, PLASTIC PARTS, COPPER FOIL
VARIABLE HEIGHT (244 CM MINIMUM) X 227 X 160 CM

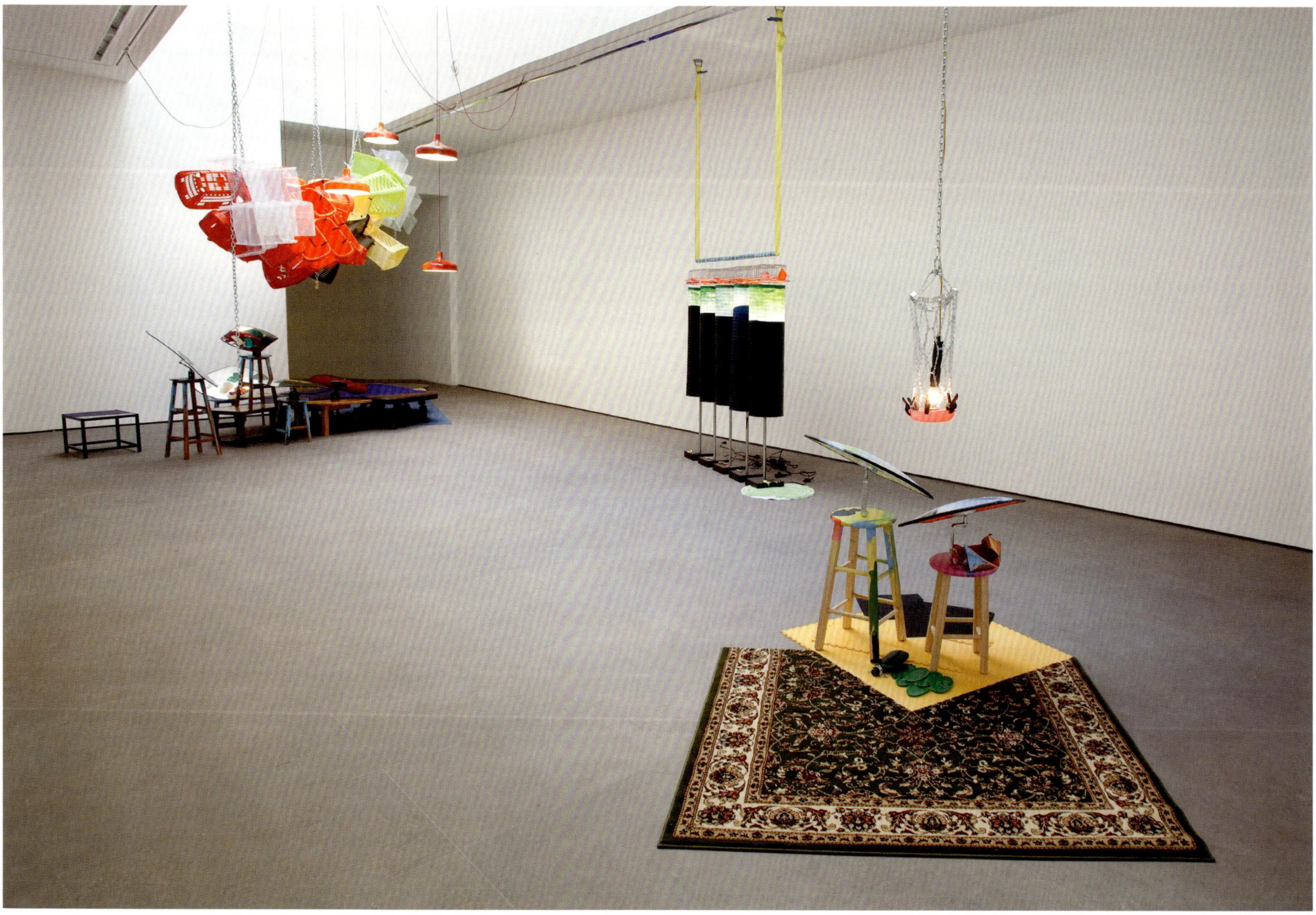

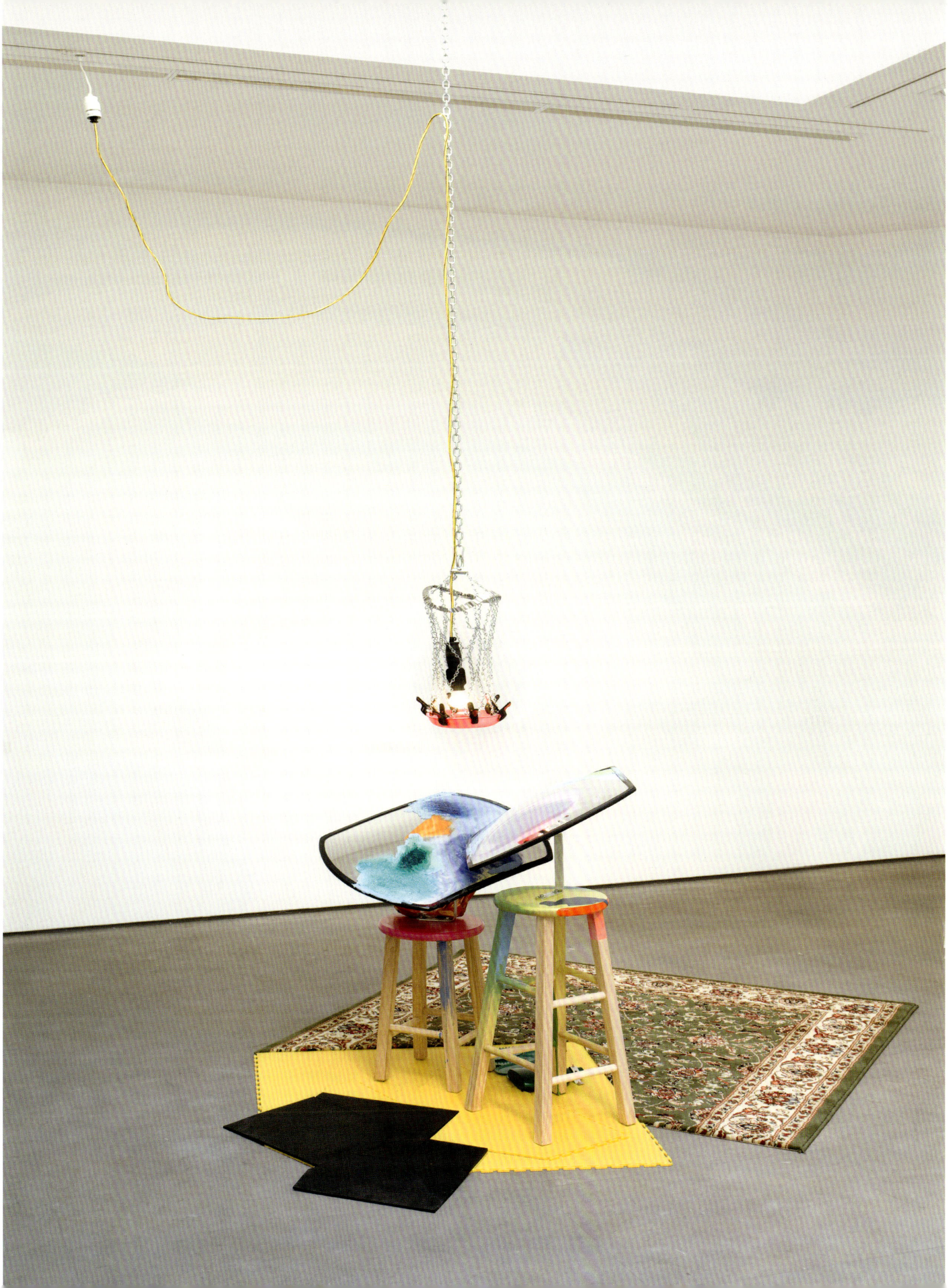

LIFT, 2013
SCISSORS LIFT, MARINE ROPE, ALUMINUM TUBING

INSTALLATION VIEW AT 1301PE, LOS ANGELES, 2013

or children who have not yet reached a sufficient degree of biological maturation are, considered strictly as such, given in nature, as are, with certainty or extreme probability, the attributes affecting them. The institution of society is always *obliged* to take into account this division of the collectivity considered as a set of heads) into two subsets, male and female. But they are taken into account in and through a transformation of the *natural fact* of being-male and being-female into an imaginary social *signification* of being-man and being-woman which refers to the magma of all the imaginary significations of the society considered. Neither this transformation itself nor the specific tenor of the signification in question can be deduced, produced or derived on the basis of the natural fact, which is always and everywhere the same. This natural fact puts stops or limits on the institution of society, but the consideration of these limits results in mere trivialities. When, as is the case, a certain archaic society compels the men, for weeks after the birth of a child, to mimic the woman in childbirth and to take her place, one may triumphantly point to the fact that men can never actually be obliged to give birth. But in order to know this, there is no need to study society, we could have simply looked at a herd of goats. What is important to us is, obviously, how and why a society obliges its men to mimic the situation of the other sex and what this signifies. In the same way, no society institutes men and women in such a way that they are, for one another, absolutely undesirable. But to say that a minimal heterosexual desire must be tolerated by the institution of society, under pain of the rapid extinction of the collectivity in question, still says nothing about the unending alchemy of desire that we observe in history – and this is what is important to us. Likewise, a natural fact can provide support or stimulus for a particular institution or signification, but an abyss separates this support or stimulus from a necessary and sufficient condition. Supports and stimuli are taken into account in one case, ignored in another, cancelled out or directed uphill in a third but, everywhere they are recovered, transformed, transubstantiated by their insertion in the network of imaginary social significations. We have only to think of what becomes, in different societies, of the natural facts of the human male's superior physical strength or of female menstruation.

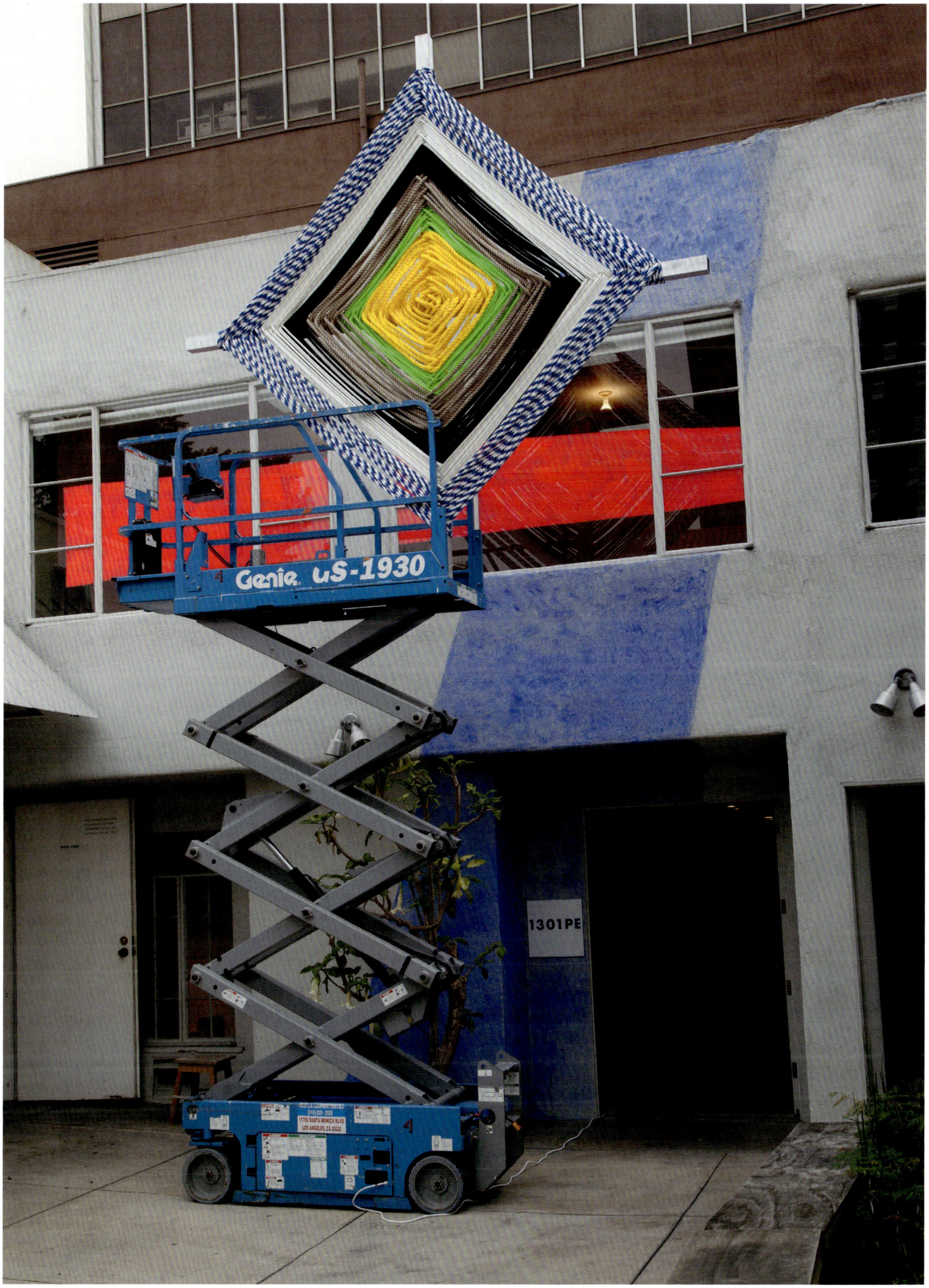
Genie uS-1930
1301PE

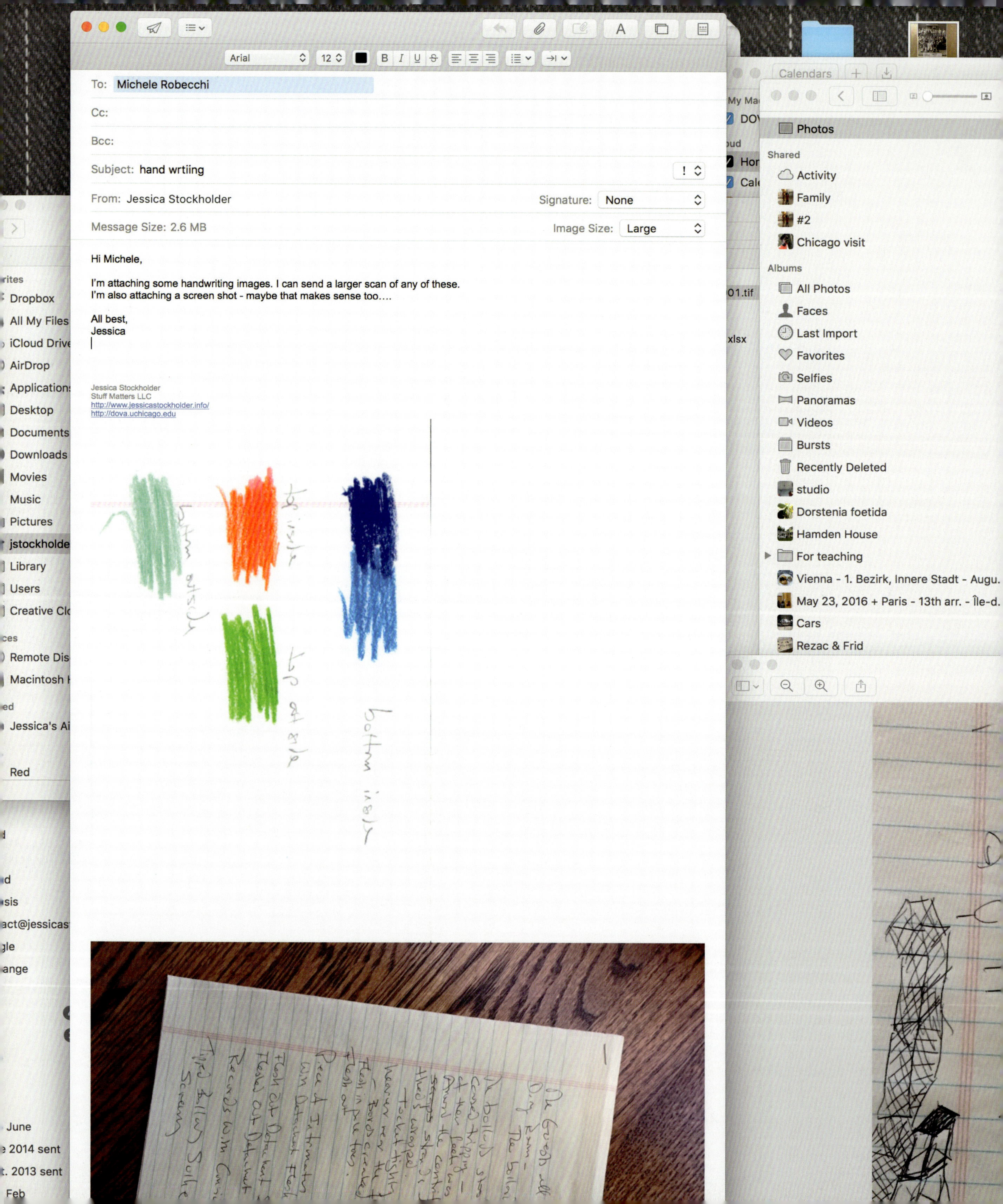
To: Michele Robecchi
Cc:
Bcc:
Subject: hand wrtiing
From: Jessica Stockholder
Signature: None
Message Size: 2.6 MB
Image Size: Large
Hi Michele,
I'm attaching some handwriting images. I can send a larger scan of any of these.
I'm also attaching a screen shot - maybe that makes sense too….
All best,
Jessica
Jessica Stockholder
Stuff Matters LLC
http://www.jessicastockholder.info/
http://dova.uchicago.edu
Photos
Shared
Activity
Family
#2
Chicago visit
Albums
All Photos
Faces
Last Import
Favorites
Selfies
Panoramas
Videos
Bursts
Recently Deleted
studio
Dorstenia foetida
Hamden House
For teaching
Vienna - 1. Bezirk, Innere Stadt - Augu.
May 23, 2016 + Paris - 13th arr. - Île-d.
Cars
Rezac & Frid
Calendars
Dropbox
All My Files
AirDrop
Desktop
Documents
Downloads
Movies
Music
Pictures
Library
Users
Red

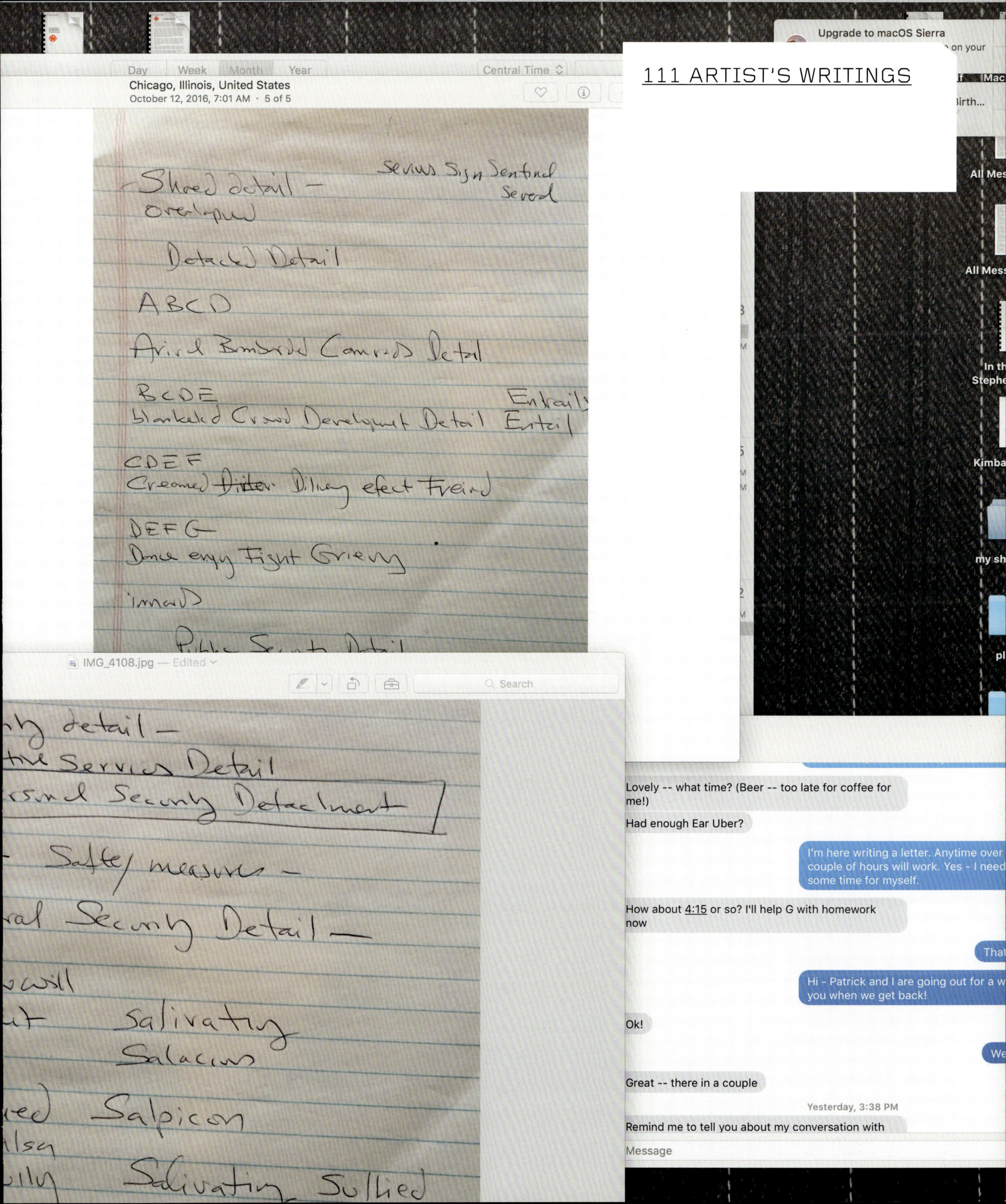
Upgrade to macOS Sierra
Day
Week
Month
Year
Central Time
Chicago, Illinois, United States
October 12, 2016, 7:01 AM · 5 of 5
Shred detail –
overlapped
Serious Sign Sentinel
Severed
Detached Detail
ABCD
Arrival Bombarded Canvassed Detail
BCDE
Blanketed Crowd Development Detail
Entrails
Entail
CDEF
Creamed Dilivery efect Freind
DEFG
Dance envy Fight Grievy
IMG_4108.jpg — Edited
Search
detail –
Services Detail
Personal Security Detachment
Safety measures –
Security Detail –
salivating
Salacious
Salpicon
Salivating Sullied
Lovely -- what time? (Beer -- too late for coffee for me!)
Had enough Ear Uber?
I'm here writing a letter. Anytime over couple of hours will work. Yes - I need some time for myself.
How about 4:15 or so? I'll help G with homework now
Hi - Patrick and I are going out for a w you when we get back!
Ok!
Great -- there in a couple
Yesterday, 3:38 PM
Remind me to tell you about my conversation with
Message

IT'S NOT OVER 'TIL THE FAT LADY SINGS, 1989
WOOD, SHEETROCK, PAINT, CARDBOARD, PAPER, CARPETS, PLASTER, CLOTHES, FURNITURE, PAPIER MACHÉ
SPACE: 816 M

INSTALLATION VIEW AT CONTEMPORARY ART GALLERY, VANCOUVER, 1987

It's Not Over 'til the Fat Lady Sings, 1987

My work has always grown from an attempt to gain a sense of control of, or at least comfort with, the material world. This discrepancy between the ease with which I can think of building something and the effort involved in actually building it is always a shock; even so, after finishing every piece I am awed at my own accomplishment.

This piece is the first in many years I have made in Vancouver, my home town. It is literally made of objects from my past, clothes and furniture taken from my parents' basements, and is titled by my grandmother. The work organizes this collection of history and objects, the very same history and objects that, having always eluded my control and understanding, have left me to this day trying to fit the pieces together into an ever-shifting whole. Together with my rather complicated network of family and friends, I can stand back from this work and match the present to the past. I am not sure how this bit of private information will inform the work for a wider public, but I hope that these bits of information will perhaps resonate with people's experience of the work.

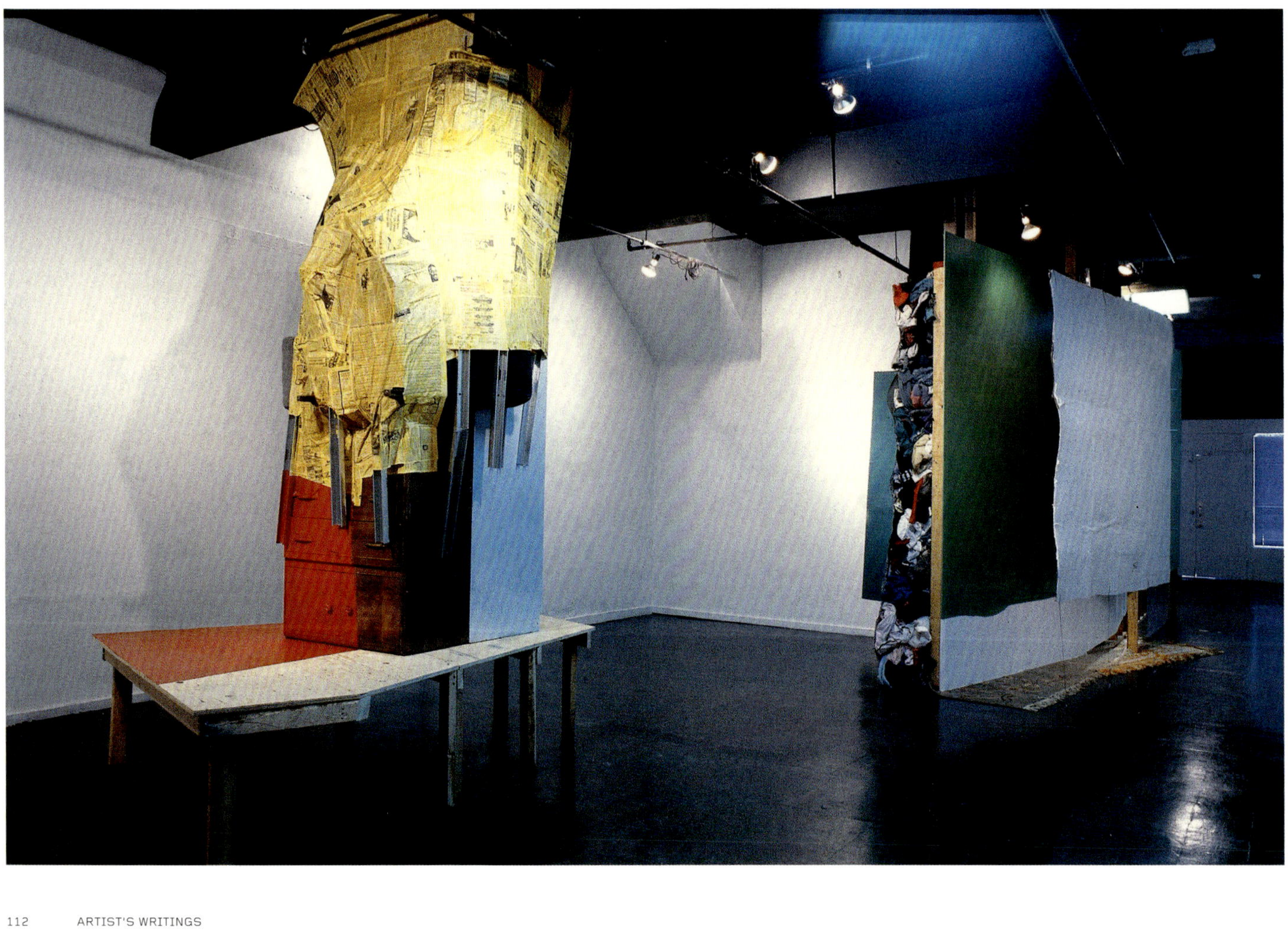

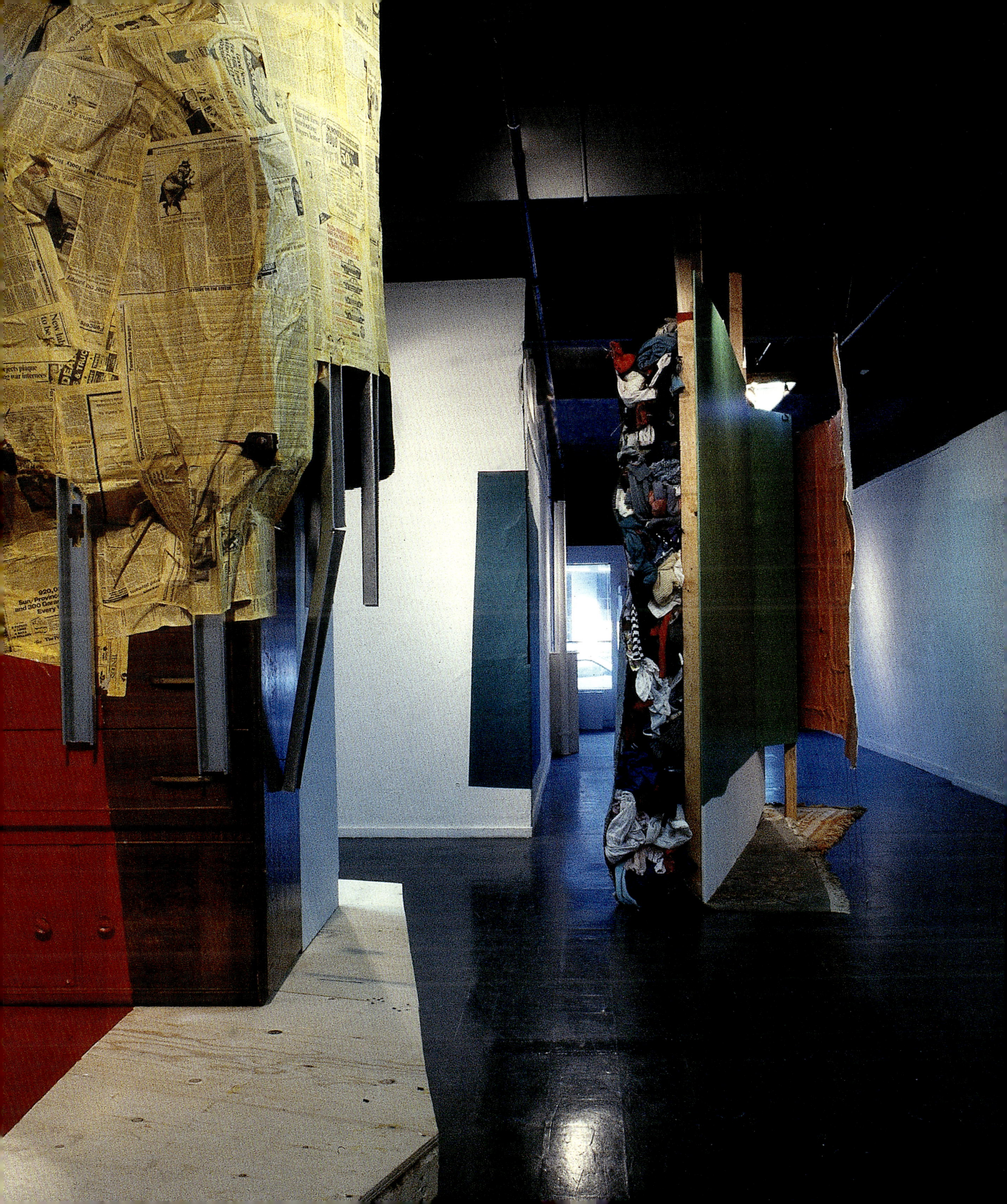

IT'S NOT OVER 'TIL THE FAT LADY SINGS, 1989
WOOD, SHEETROCK, PAINT, CARDBOARD, PAPER, CARPETS, PLASTER, CLOTHES, FURNITURE, PAPIER MACHÉ
SPACE: 816 M

However that may be, more available to a general audience is the experience of the things in the gallery; the clothes packed together forming a wall with Gyproc, 2x4s and carpets. The weight and solidity of these clothes and wall are pushed up against and compared to the weight and size of the flat painted colours on it and near it. As one walks through and around the gallery, the painted colours interact with each other and form an independent composition. At the same time these painted colours interact in a more subtle way with the objects on which they are painted or sit next to. The painted green stucco blends quietly into the unpainted colours of the clothes and carpets, even while it quickly reaches out to the painted turquoise patch across from it.

Clothes act as skins over our skins; carpets act as skins on our floors; walls are the skins of our rooms; we see the outside skin of the furniture; and the paint acts like a skin on all of these skins, including that of the gallery wall. All of these skins are intermingled and woven together. As one moves through the piece, all of the parts of life thus represented form a constantly shifting but balanced composition. They do not yield the impression of a unified work, separate from one's self, until one stands at the far corner of the gallery with one's back to the wall. The work is now seen against the opposite wall of the gallery. From this position it is seen and felt as a complete whole, other from the viewer. However, this experience is informed by the memory of having moved through the piece – by the memory of how it was revealed over time.

IT'S NOT OVER 'TIL THE FAT LADY SINGS, CONTEMPORARY ART GALLERY, VANCOUVER, 1987

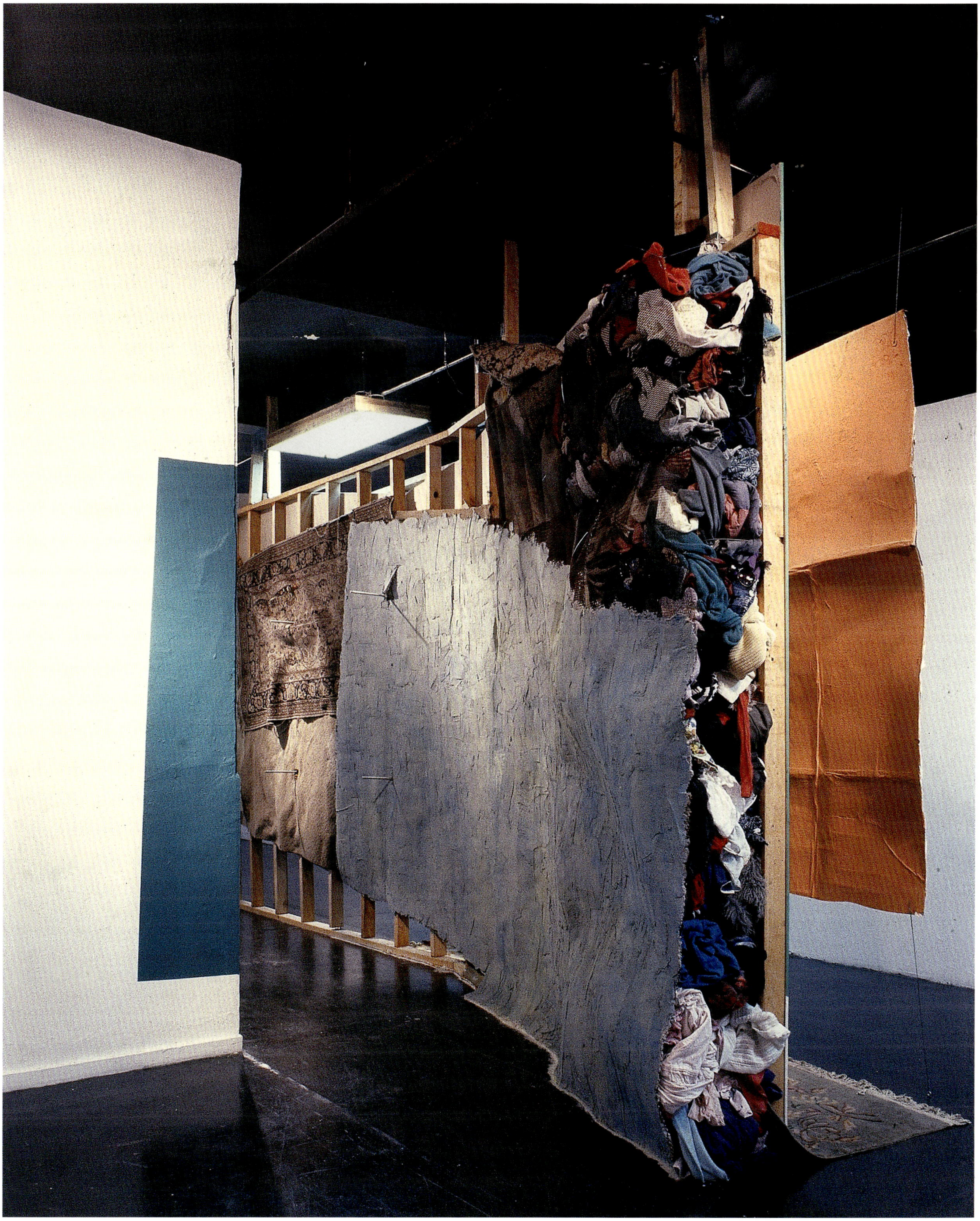

The State of Things: Questions to Three Object-Conscious Artists (extract), 1990

BOB NICKAS: *'The State of Things' applies to the way you work as well as to the work you produce. It applies to the object or objects both before and after the fact of being exhibited, presented as sculpture. In other words, these are objects that, having been brought into a studio or gallery, are not completely removed from the world from which they were taken. In your work, the original identity of the objects is preserved – even if they are radically combined with others.*

JESSICA STOCKHOLDER: 'My work makes use of the state of things. I make my work on top of what is already there. Of course the result is that the work is made of what is there. It is an interweaving of how I see things, how other people have seen things before me and how people see the work after I make it.
By mixing together elements that most people take for granted as being part of the 'real world' with elements that I make, elements which in some way express or represent emotional experience, my work calls the 'real' elements into question. Don't they too represent and express emotional experience? And it follows then that the elements I make may be as 'real' as the rest.

NICKAS: *In this sense, you don't seem to be solely involved with 'ideas about the thing, but the thing itself'.*

STOCKHOLDER: My starting point is with real stuff in the world, whether it be raw material or some kind of a functioning object. The particular qualities of these found materials give rise to the work. But the objects I choose are not precious; other objects might have served equally well. The final work is dependent on the narratives, evocations, and metaphors given rise to by the found materials, while at the same time existing as something other that might have attached itself to a different set of circumstances. The work is formal. Meaning is generated through the method of building and as a consequence of a knitting together of material elements.

NICKAS: *Can we talk about the world as yielding things as raw material?*

STOCKHOLDER: We certainly experience some materials as 'raw'. What that means is always in question; isn't 'raw' just another category of our making?

NICKAS: *Does this have any bearing on making some order of what we might call the chaos of the world? ... even one piece at a time?*

STOCKHOLDER: Life is a process of making order. My work brings the notion of chaos to the fore but all work, artwork and otherwise, makes order where there is little or none.

NICKAS: *Can we look at your work in terms of it being unfinished – not incomplete, but still within a 'life-cycle,' so to speak?*

STOCKHOLDER: I have a large interest in garbage (as we all do). I use a lot of garbage in my work because it brings with it a process that continues despite what I might do to it. The work will decay; it is not with us forever despite our desire that art might be. Garbage, on the other hand, is.
My work is complete when the questions and discontinuities within it become tied to one another and form a circular process of referencing that excludes any further struggle from me. I move on to the next. The work contains, or perhaps sit might be better to say, it elicits that same struggle that goes into the making of it. It is a struggle between stasis, or completeness and an ongoing continuation (...)

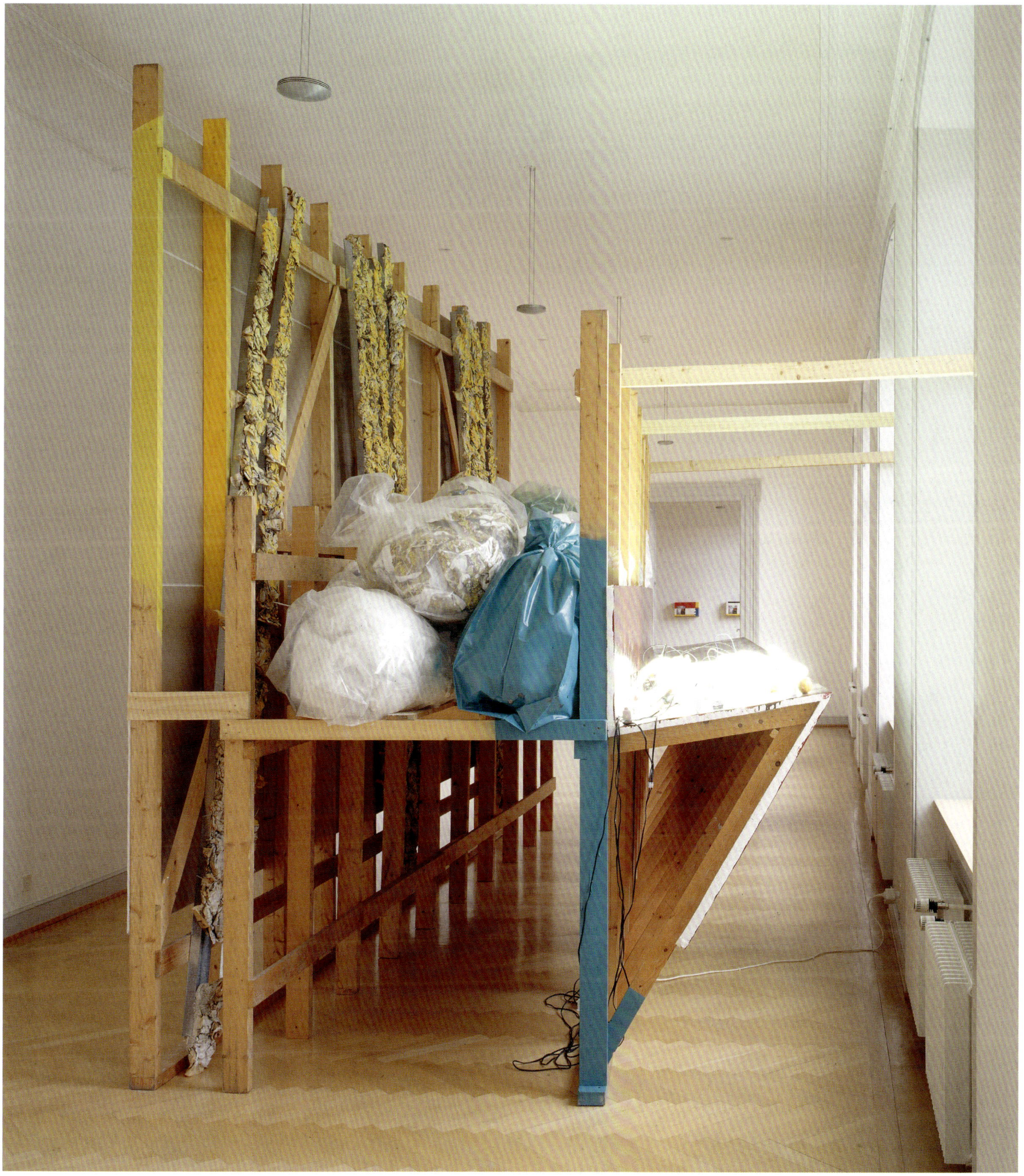

<u>MAKING A CLEAN EDGE</u>, 1989
CONSTRUCTION MATERIALS, GARBAGE, ORANGES, LIGHTS, PAINT
576 X 403 CM

INSTALLATION VIEW AT P.S.1 CONTEMPORARY ART CENTER, LONG ISLAND, NEW YORK, 1989

1989
CAR DOOR, SHEET ROCK, CLOTH, OIL, ACRYLIC AND LATEX PAINT, ORANGE LIGHT, YELLOW ELECTRICAL CORD, WOOD, HARDWARE
H. 130 CM

next page,
MAKING A CLEAN EDGE, 1989
CONSTRUCTION MATERIALS, GARBAGE, ORANGES, LIGHTS, PAINT
576 X 403 CM

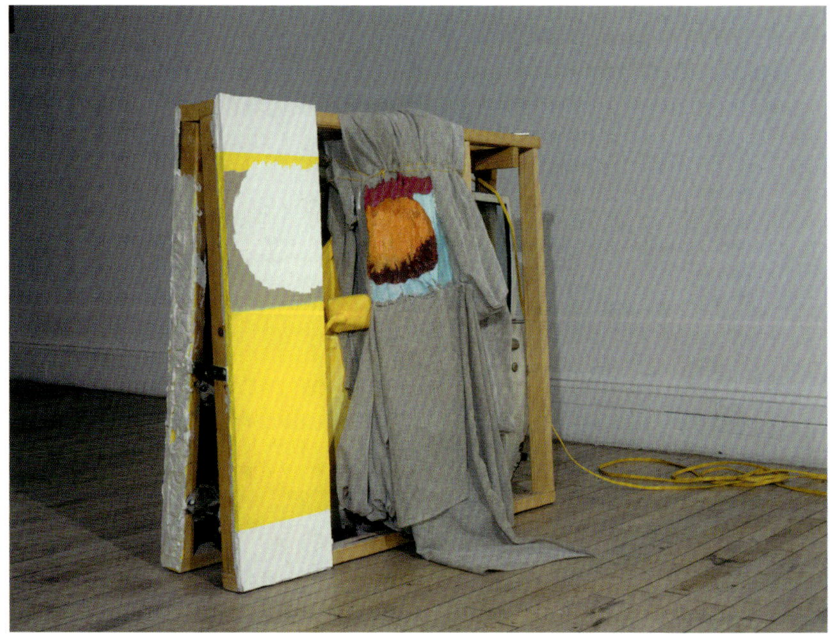

NICKAS: *Can we talk about your sculpture as* place*? And think about what goes on 'there'?*

STOCKHOLDER: When I make an installation, the place I'm working in is important but equally important is what I bring to the place; or perhaps it would be better to say that it is important to make clear that how that place is experienced is subject to wide variation dependent on how it has been treated, what I do to it and who's looking.

The idea of place is interesting in that while a place is a physical actuality it doesn't exist as such independently of how we treat it, how we view it or how we understand it. This quality of place has been recognized by Gaston Bachelard in his book *The Poetics of Space*. Every place is highly evocative.

NICKAS: *What of the place of the viewers – their reception of the work in terms of it being 'unfinished'?*

STOCKHOLDER: My hope is that the viewer will, like me, become engaged in a struggle between viewing a static fail accompli and feeling as if they are participating in a series of contradictions and narratives that come to no settling conclusion. I feel that my work provides both experiences and argues for the necessity of both. The narratives and evocations my work gives rise to are intended to be wide ranging. They are the result of my personal history, the culture I live in and the histories brought to the work by all whose who take an interest.

NICKAS: *Can we talk about behaviour as raw material?*

STOCKHOLDER: Behaviour as raw material. It's not how I would begin speaking of my work except to say that viewing the work is a process that takes place over time; it involves putting various pieces of information together and it takes an active human being to do that. I could also say that I would like it if my work forced recognition that that pleasant sensation of passive viewing is actually an active position.

NICKAS: *Having asked/said all this, how might the following apply to your work? 'It is always changing. It has order. It doesn't have a specific place. Its boundaries are not fixed. It affects other things. It may be accessible but go unnoticed. Part of it may also be part of something else. Some if it is familiar. Some of it is strange. Knowing of it changes it'. Robert Barry,* Art Work*, 1970.*

STOCKHOLDER: All these things could be said of my work but I would also say that I am concerned with how our perception of art being separate and eternal meshes with the facts stated in this paragraph.

FLASH ART, NO. 151, MARCH–APRIL 1980

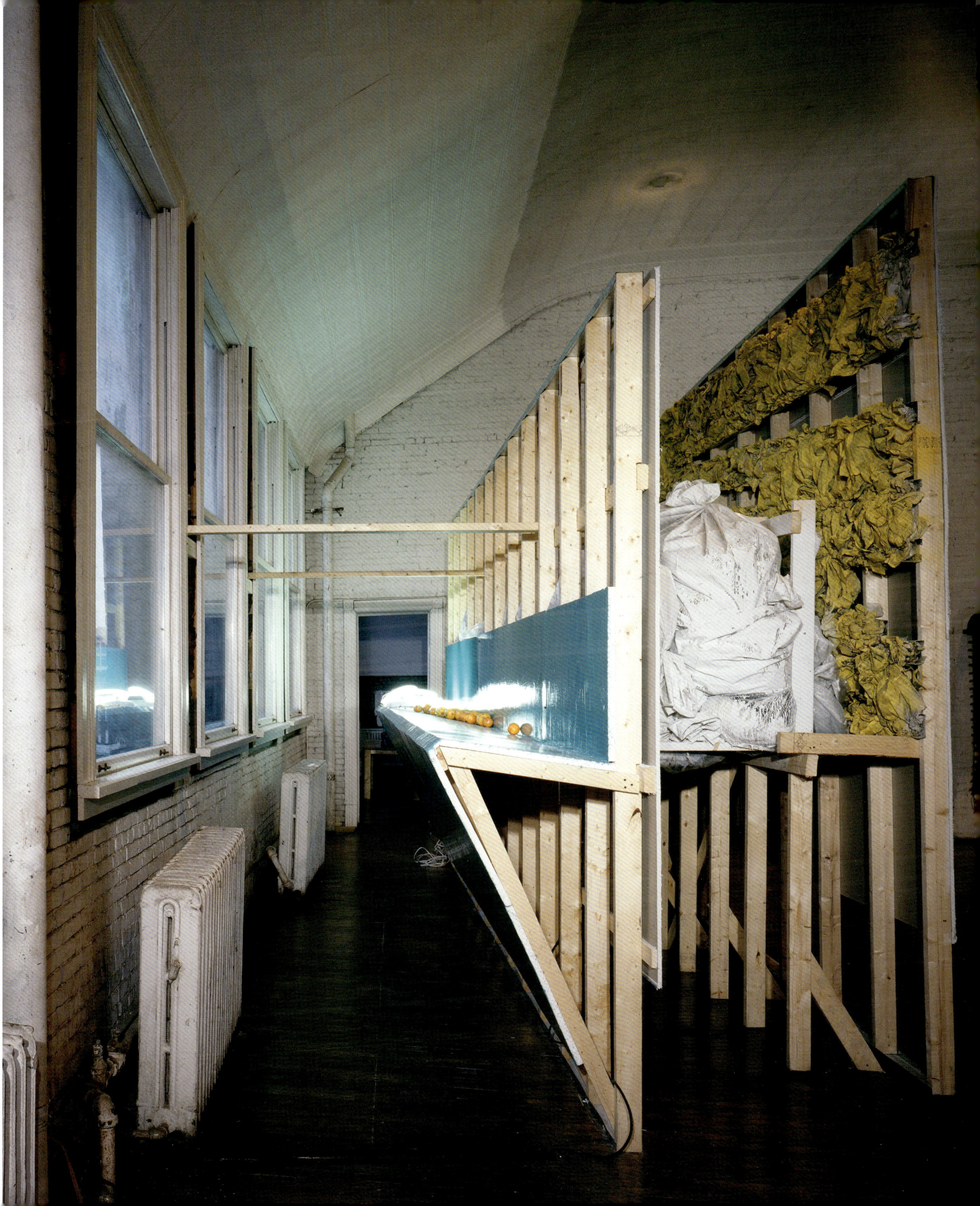

Interview with Klaus Ottmann, 1991

1989
CAR FENDER WITH STUFFED ANIMALS, STYROFOAM, NEWSPAPER, CLOTH, PLASTER, OIL PAINT
134X 67 X 29 CM

KLAUS OTTMANN: *What are the most important issues in your work?*

JESSICA STOCKHOLDER: My work developed through the process of making site-specific installations – site-specific sometimes in very specific ways but also just by virtue of being 'art' in a room; there's at least that much going on between the work and its context; after all, paintings don't hang on trees. In all the work I place something I make in relationship to what's already there. With installations it's the building, the architecture, or you might say, it's the place that I work on top of; with the smaller pieces I work on top of or in relation to stuff that I collect.

I don't see a dichotomy between formalism and something else. Form and formal relations are important because they mean something; their meaning grows out of our experience as physical mortal beings of a particular scale in relationship to the world as we find it and make it. I don't buy that formalism is meaningless.

OTTMANN: *Is there a particular aesthetic involved when you look for materials?*

STOCKHOLDER: It doesn't matter what I use. It can be anything. What's interesting is how what I'm doing meets with the stuff I use.

But then it's not entirely true to say that. I also choose things for particular reasons though not according to a particular aesthetic. More often I avoid the development of a cohesive look that will too powerfully direct the work in only one direction.

A lot of people have written about my work in terms of junk; that I sometimes use junk doesn't seem of central importance to me. I use all kinds of things, old and new. Much of the stuff I use could be found in your living room.

OTTMANN: *There is that danger of junk becoming 'art' by itself, without the artist addition meaning.*

STOCKHOLDER: I rely on that tendency to aestheticize as I do on chance and happenstance. What's exciting is how the more clearly structured, more formal, more pictorial side of the work meets the more chaotic – sometimes very clearly and logically, then bleeding off in all kinds of directions.

I see it as a mesh of Kaprow, Tinguely and the Surrealists on the one hand, using chaos and chance – making systems out of happenings; and on the other hand meshing that kind of thinking with formal painting and Minimalism.

John Cage's thinking also had a lot of influence.

OTTMANN: *Are there other influences that you would like to mention?*

STOCKHOLDER: I studied with Mowry Baden in Victoria. He's a sculptor with a large appreciation for painting; he addressed my work in both points of view. That's part of how I got where I am.

OTTMANN: *How did painting come to the work?*

STOCKHOLDER: I started as a painter and I never stopped making paintings. And still, part of what interests me is a pictorial way of looking at things. Viewing through pictures is part of our experience of the world, an experience which happens to be often associated with art.

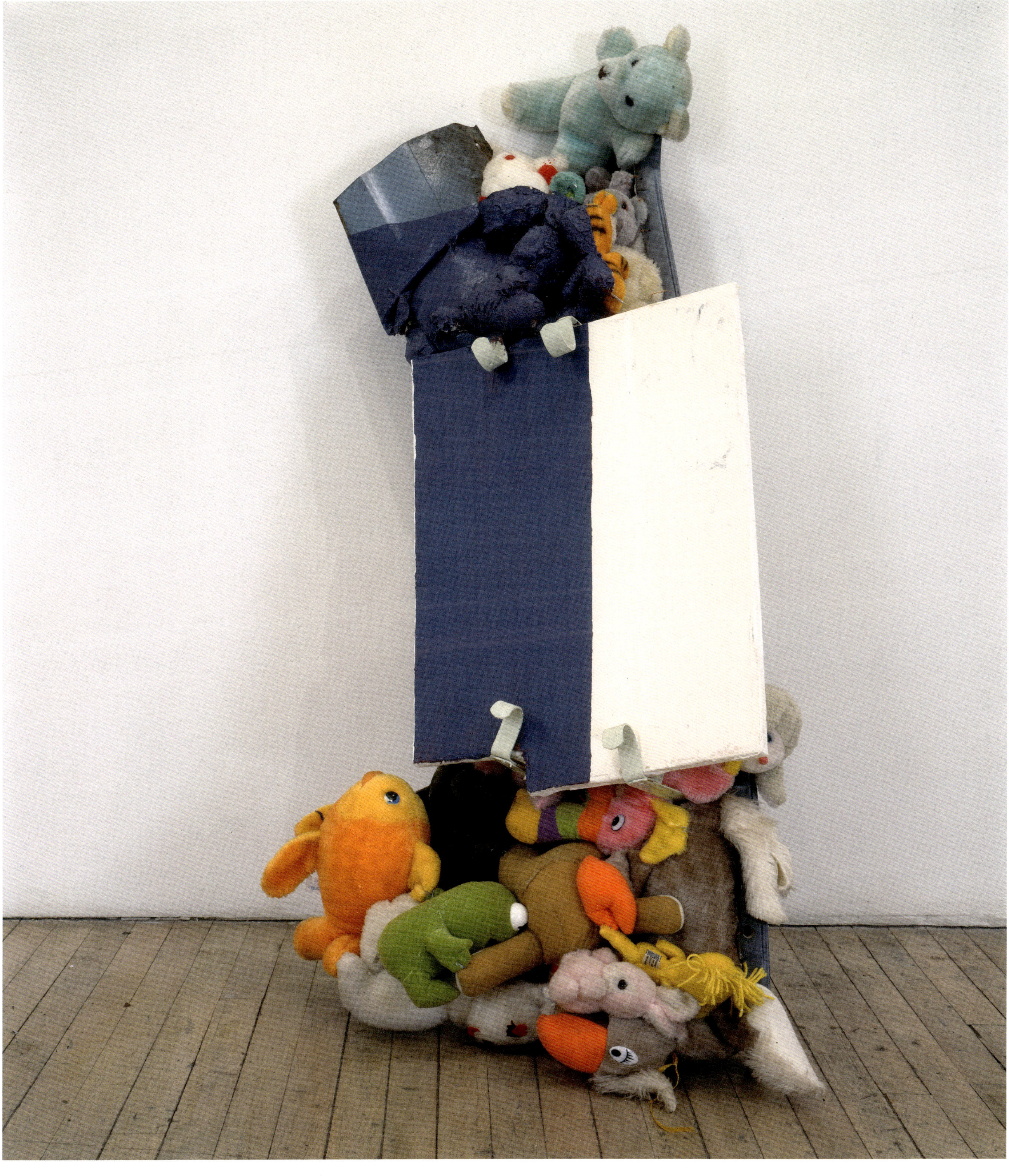

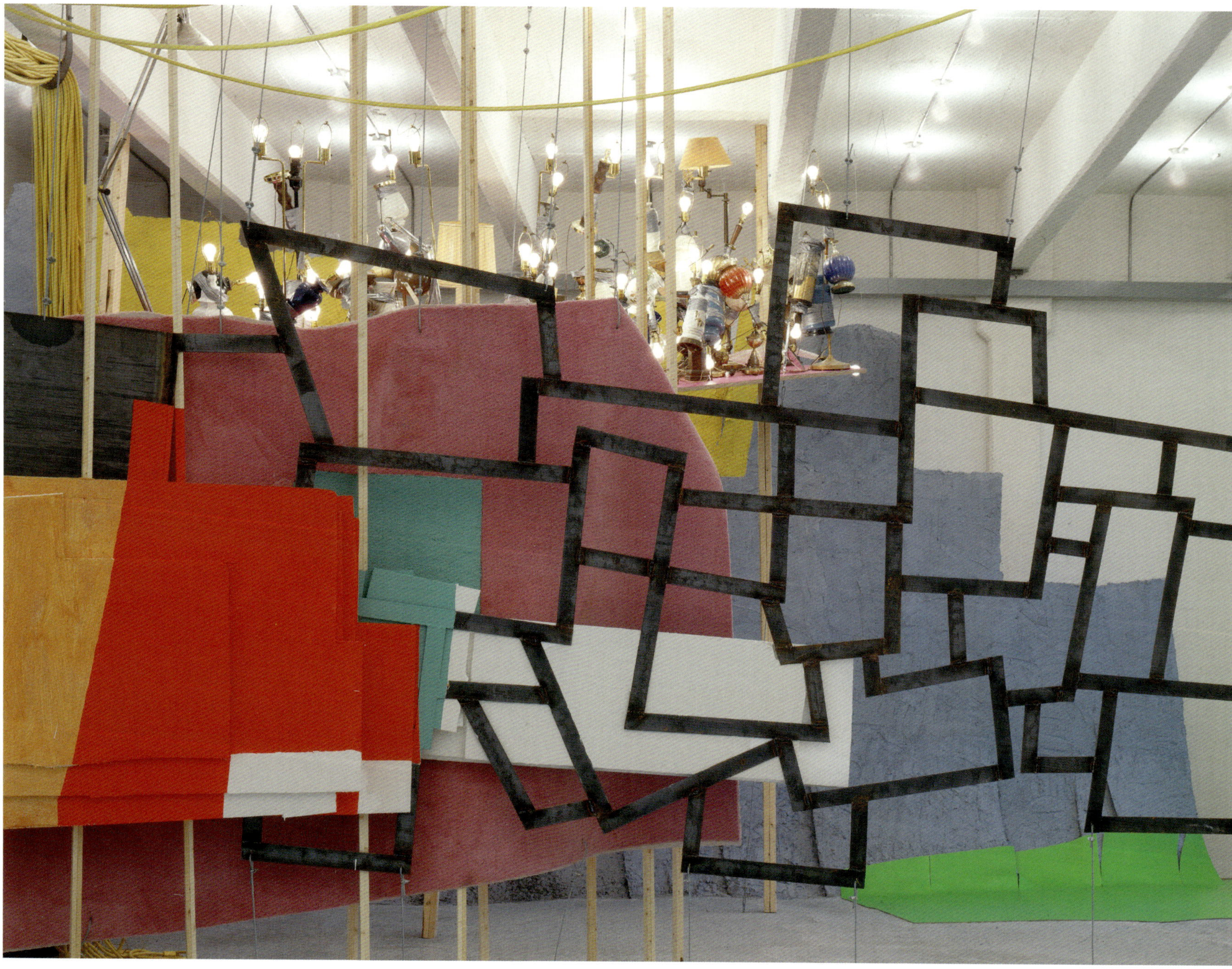

YOUR SKIN IN THIS WEATHER BOURNE EYE – THREADS & SWOLLEN PERFUME, 1995
PAINT, CONCRETE, STRUCTOLITE, BUILDING MATERIALS, CARPET, LAMPS, ELECTRICAL CORD, PURPLE PLASTIC STACKING CRATES, SWIMMING POOL LINER, WELDED STEEL, STUFFED SHIRTS PILLOWS, PAOER MACHÉ, BALLS
5 M X 1097 SQ

INSTALLATION VIEW AT DIA CENTER FOR THE ARTS, NEW YORK, 1995

Standing in front of one of my pieces, its size is important in relationship to your size, you feel how heavy it is or what the light is like in the room, and all that kind of information is seen in relation to the pictorial structure in the work. The thing cues you to measure one side against the other, trying to balance it as you would a picture, and for me, looking at things in a pictorial way includes a distancing where the thing that's pictured is far away and a little static, unchanging, without time. This distancing is exaggerated by the 'art' status of the work which brings with it a feeling of preciousness and the feeling that the work is somehow removed from or above human life. These qualities are deductive and they make me angry. So I place the pictorial in a context where it's always being poked at. The picture never stands, it's always getting the rug pulled out from under it.

I also love colour; and colour hasn't been dealt with much in sculpture.

OTTMANN: *Do you relate more closely to an American or a European painting tradition?*

STOCKHOLDER: I relate more to an American tradition, though probably to both. Matisse, Cézanne, and the Cubists certainly are important to me. I also feel a strong affinity to Clyfford Still, Frank Stella, the New York School hard-edge painting and Minimalism, as well as Richard Serra.

OTTMANN: *When did you decide to make smaller, site-independent objects?*

STOCKHOLDER: When I moved here I had no studio. I was working in my apartment. It didn't make sense to build installations there and I didn't want to have to find a show in order to be able to make my work. So I started to make objects. The first one I made had a light pointed at the wall making a circle of colour. The light uses electricity which is happening in time; although the work is static, a piece of art with this removed sense about it, the light gives it a sense of happening. Also, there's colour on the piece and colour on the wall from the light; the colour on the wall from the light is kind of ephemeral, and it's not physically attached to the piece, but the two things, the piece and the wall need each other to be a complete thing. So though I was making an object, it broke down a little bit. It wasn't isolated unto itself.

I also like that the smaller pieces are physically easier, more in my control. And I can work out ideas that I later use in installations.

OTTMANN: *Could you say something about how meaning is generated within your work?*

STOCKHOLDER: My work often arrives in the world like an idea arrives in your mind. You don't quite know where it came from or when it got put together, nevertheless it's possible to take it apart and see that it has an internal logic. I'm trying to get closer to thinking processes as they exist before the idea if fully formed. The various parts of my work are multivalent as are the various parts of dreams. At best there are many ways to put the pieces together.

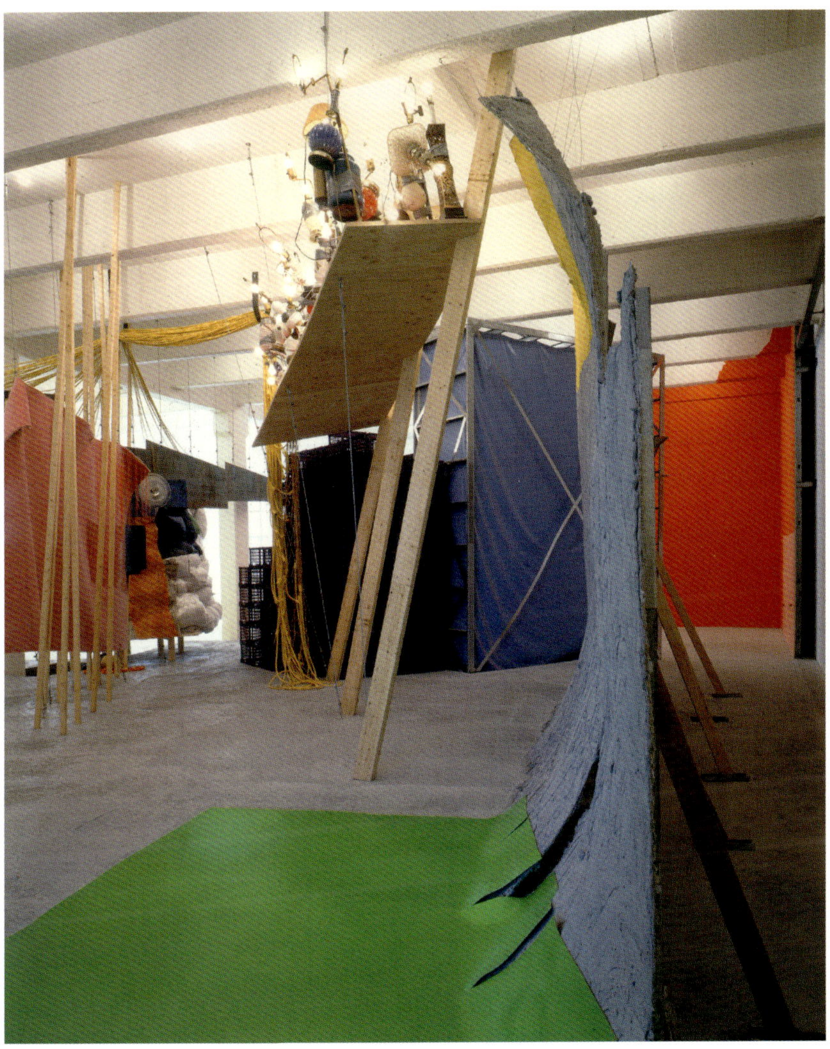

JESSICA STOCKHOLDER: THE BROKEN MIRROR (PART THREE), CENTER FOR THE ARTS, WESLEYAN UNIVERSITY, MIDDLETOWN, CONNECTICUT, 1991

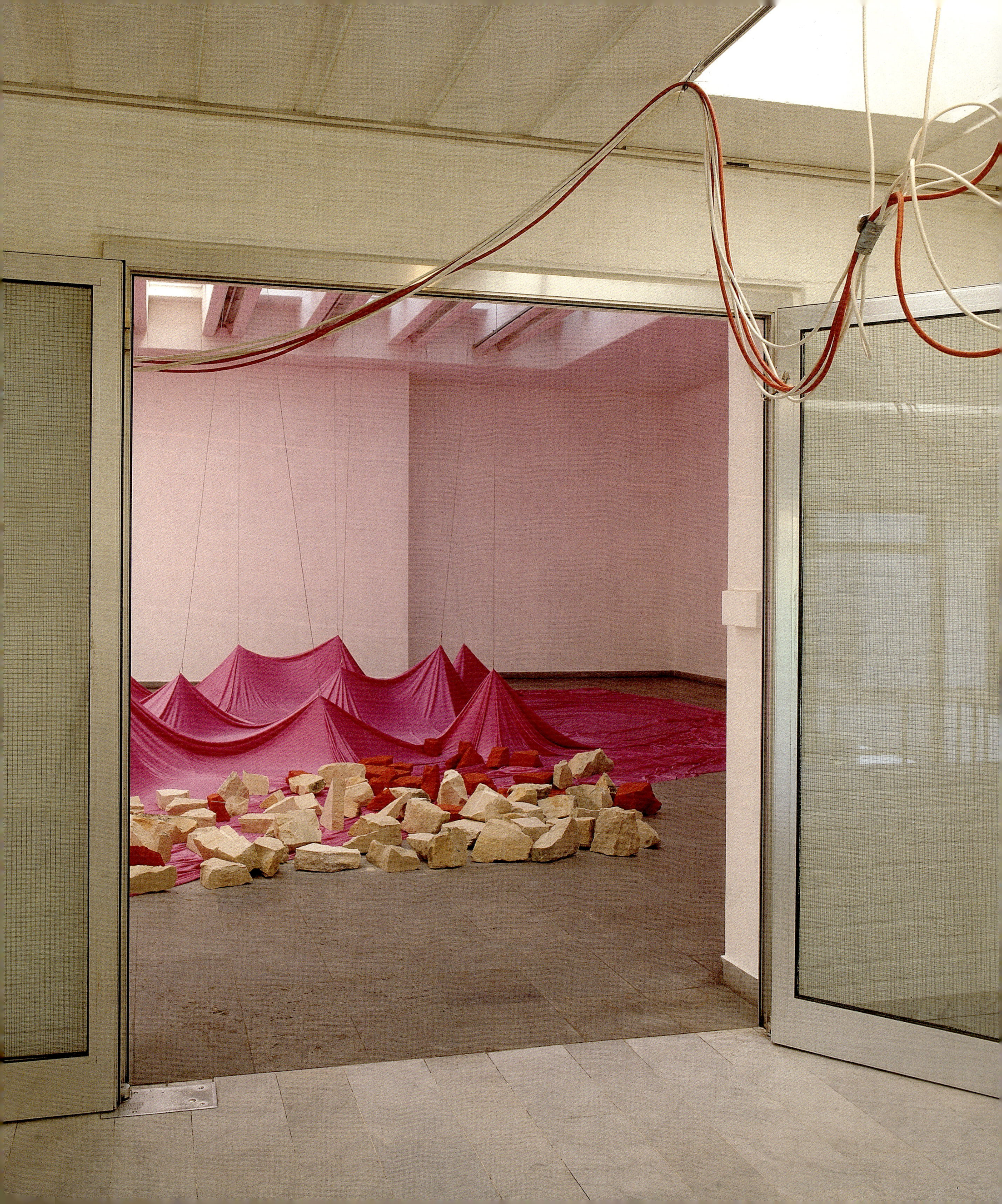

GROWING ROCK CANDY MOUNTAIN GRASSES IN CANNED SAND, 1992
VIOLET BATHING SUIT MATERIAL, SAND STONE NATIVE TO MUNSTER, GASEOUS CONCRETE BUILDING BLOCKS, PLASTER, BASKET MATERIAL, ELECTRICAL WIRING, THREE VERY SMALL LIGHTS, NEWSPAPER GLUED TO THE WALL, ACRYLIC PAINT, METAL, CABLES, STYROFOAM
ROOM: 2900 X 900 CM

INSTALLATION VIEW AT THE WESTFÄLISCHER KUNSTVEREIN, MÜNSTER, GERMANY, 1992

Interview with Stephen Westfall, 1992

STEPHEN WESTFALL: *It's funny that you express nervousness over the interview process because those stages that I've described, the transcription of the interview, and the restructuring of questions to establish a certain compacted continuity, find a corollary in your work process. You talk about the power of your own work coming from overlapping systems. The interview process is a literary version of that. It is part performance, on an intimate scale, for a projected audience. When you pull your work together in an installation the art audience has also yet to arrive.*

JESSICA STOCKHOLDER: Yeah, and the process of making it isn't observed. I mean, right away when you turned the tape recorded on there is another part of me watching that wasn't there before. Making an installation doesn't shift that much from being in my studio.

WESTFALL: *Even though you are manipulating, engaging and evoking feelings about yourself in the process of your work – an ongoing construction of identity. Do you think there is something very strange about the creative ego in art? There is a persona that I've become aware of in my own pile-up of work over the years.*

STOCKHOLDER: I've recently become aware of the pile-up of work as intrusive. When I made a decision about something I was going to do, it used to be very charged. Whatever I chose would become incredibly important because I chose this one way out of five. But now, with a history of having made similar choices, and knowing that I am going to do it again so many times, the weight on each decision is very different and that's a little unnerving.

WESTFALL: *Is it unnerving because there is an attachment to the idea of art being spoken from a sense of urgency or desperation?*

STOCKHOLDER: Perhaps, and there is also a comfort in thinking that the one choice you made was the right choice. Now I have this whole array of choices clearly possible from past experience and an imaginary future. It is clear that any one of those, or many of those choices could take one down an equally interesting path and be equally valid. I can't believe anymore that there is one right way to do things. I'm not sure that I ever did, but I think that I would have liked to.

WESTFALL: *Your work has an almost shocking sense of freedom of erasure and change, and uses that erasure or change as the connective tissue to a gestural extension.*

STOCKHOLDER: There is a covering up, a hiding of things and also an incredibly up-front quality. I don't often erase things, like make a mark and erase it the way you would on a drawing. I see it more as a covering up. It happens through a positive action rather than a negative one.

WESTFALL: *Oh, so it's obscuring by accretion rather than by attrition.*

STOCKHOLDER: Yes, exactly! I'm deciding not to show it.

WESTFALL: *What you did before is included in the passage of surface. Nothing is lost and yet, somehow something is inherently revoked by change.*

STOCKHOLDER: Well, I would agree with you but I think that it is irrevocable for my process, not for the finished product. Having noticed that I did something, that is irrevocable for my and my experience. It's not irrevocable in terms of what gets presented to the world. It is important to notice what it is you decided to do in the world.

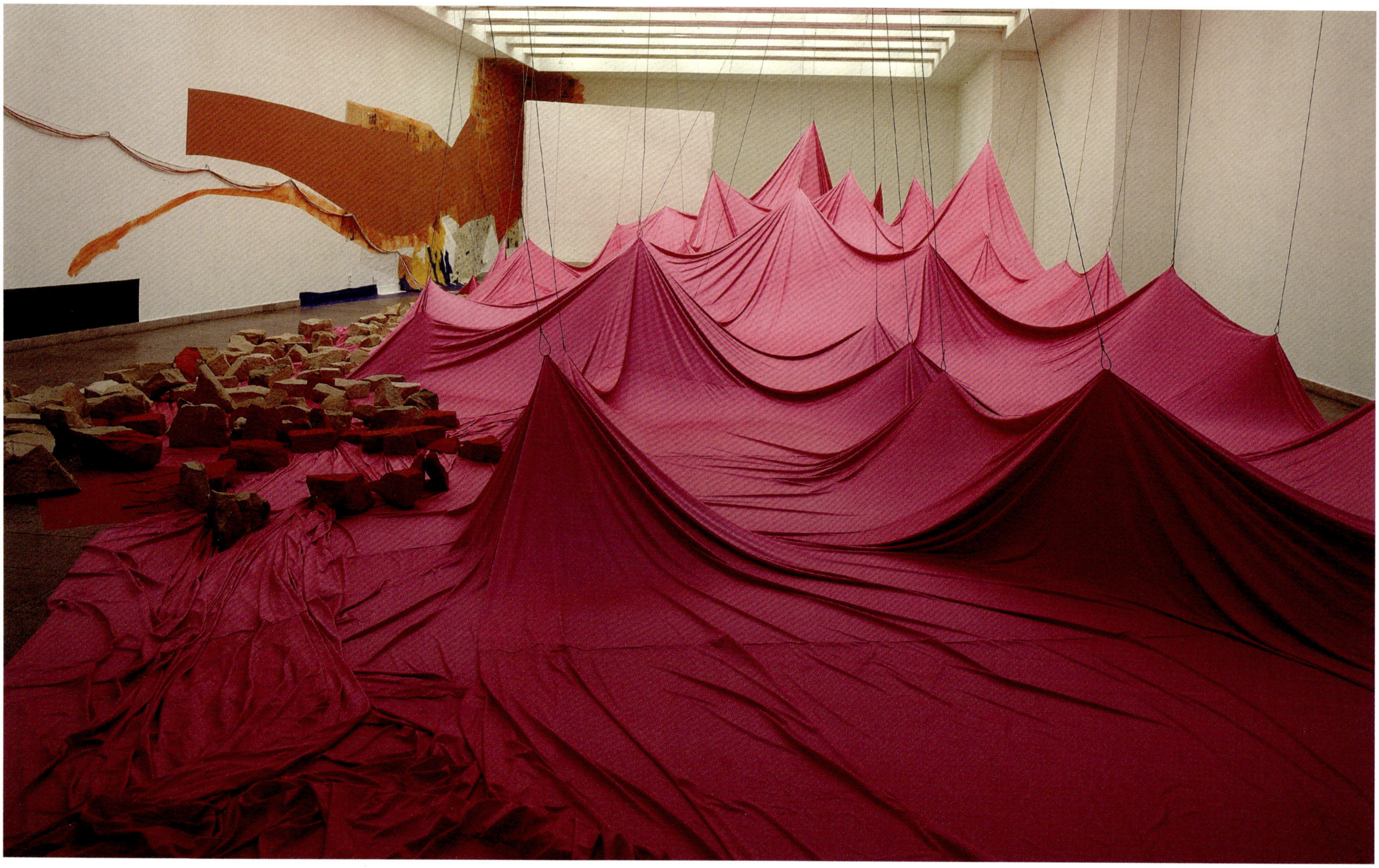

WESTFALL: *And your next action becomes a response to the consciousness of how you've just acted. In both our everyday lives and the presumably heightened consciousness of studio activity we have habitual actions. But to notice, in the way you are talking about, shakes us out of the conscious sleep of our habits. Does this happen in spite of the program established by your preparatory drawings?*

STOCKHOLDER: It does. They don't tell me exactly where in the space something will begin and end, or exactly how material will be there, or in many cases how it will be made, how something will be held together – all of which in the end is a large part of what the work is about. So the drawings for the installations are an outline that lets me decide to order some materials, and usually determines my thinking about how I am going to address the space. Sometimes I abandon them once I start to work, or at least I change a lot. They can get in my way a little bit. I try to leave things open enough so I don't have the feeling that I know what I am doing when I get there.

WESTFALL: *Colour becomes such an emotionally or psychologically directive element in your work and I notice that you often make basic colour decisions in your drawings. Have you ever found yourself deciding that a certain colour scheme is just not going to work in the middle of the action of the work?*

STOCKHOLDER: Yeah, sometimes I just change the colour, but sometimes I start to use the colour differently. Like the piece that I have just made in Vienna. Before I got there, I was thinking about the colour green creating a kind of atmosphere or charging the air in front of it, and green doesn't do that. Yellow and red do that.

GROWING ROCK CANDY MOUNTAIN GRASSES IN CANNED SAND, 1992
VIOLET BATHING SUIT MATERIAL, SAND STONE NATIVE TO MÜNSTER, GASEOUS CONCRETE BUILDING BLOCKS, PLASTER, BASKET MATERIAL, ELECTRICAL WIRING, THREE VERY SMALL LIGHTS, NEWSPAPER GLUED TO THE WALL, ACRYLIC PAINT, METAL, CABLES, STYROFOAM
ROOM: 29 X 9 M

WESTFALL: *At least certain types of green.*

STOCKHOLDER: Yeah, so the way in which the piece became cohesive was entirely different than how I thought about it in the drawings. The emphasis in the work changed to one of surface, because of the particular qualities of that gallery.

WESTFALL: *Did you keep the green?*

STOCKHOLDER: Yes, I kept the green.

WESTFALL: *And relinquished the idea of charging the atmosphere?*

STOCKHOLDER: Yeah.

WESTFALL: *And what did you gain when you let go of that original hope or intention?*

STOCKHOLDER: It has something to do with time restraints, energy and physical capability. To do the whole piece again might not have been possible. I tend to take advantage of what happens. I don't spend time getting upset if a piece of wood breaks, I figure out how to make use of the break. I would rather take what is available to me and run with it. I would rather do that than bang my head against the wall because I don't have what I need.

WESTFALL: *Are you aware that it is something you are capable of doing to yourself, a momentary depression in the face of contingencies?*

STOCKHOLDER: Yes, I don't thing I do it so much in terms of my work. Part of why I am an artist is that it's an arena where I am allowed to do whatever I want.

WESTFALL: *As opposed to the rest of life.*

STOCKHOLDER: Yeah, in the rest of my life I can spend a lot of time agonizing because I don't have exactly what I need. I have a script that says it should be thus and so, but for some reason I am able to abandon a script in making my art. And that's what I like about it so much. I like John Cage's and Allan Kaprow's thinking. I love that kind of philosophy, taking advantage of change. I read their writings and everything in me warms up to that kind of thinking. I do that, but there is more of a struggle in my work around those issues than in theirs. My work isn't about just that. There is clearly some kind of imposed order, some dependence on art history and aesthetics that overlays whatever chance and happenstance I let occur.

WESTFALL: *The whole notion of engaging chance in the creation of the work strikes me as truly outside of, or liberated from, a romantic sensibility, and yet there is so much about your work that I find romantic. I have actually made some notes here.*

STOCKHOLDER: Yes, say more about that.

WESTFALL: *Here is the question. I read a tremendous emotionality in your work. The titles such as* The Lion, the Witch and the Wardrobe, *and the pieces dedicated to your father and to the painter, Mary Heilmann, refer not only to the materials, but to the physical location of the work –* My Father's Backyard *– or shared aesthetic agendas with another artist who works in a more conventional traditional medium, but also to friendship, family ties and the imaginary life of childhood. These and other tendencies in your work, such as the often breathtaking scale of your installations, their gestural velocity and the recurring elegiac deployment of lumbering domestic furniture such as bureaus, refrigerators, mattresses which sometimes float along the floor like icebergs and which can also be set off like some heroic landscape feature – like a butte or mesa – all these tendencies strike me as* *a manifestation of romantic sensibility. I am really surprised, in the face of so much current discourse, to find it there so vividly. Are you disappointed by that reading or is that OK?*

STOCKHOLDER: Well no, I am not disappointed with it and I don't disagree with it but I don't know if I would have said it that way. I don't work in response to writing very much, you know, what the current critical talk is. When you talk about feelings and psychology and childhood it can become clichéd very quickly. When it becomes clichéd you have lost what it is you wanted. But my impulse to make a work begins with my feeling that emotional life isn't allowed room in the world. This feeling is personal to me and my history, but I think it is also a modern issue in that a lot of people share those worries and feelings. So my work becomes a place to make fantasy and emotional life as concrete and real and important as a refrigerator, or the room that you are in.

WESTFALL: *There's a monumentalization of gesture and memory in your work. One of the powerful, emotional reaches of romantic art has been this notion of extension of an imaginal terrain on a scale before which carefully held self-identity begins to break down.*

STOCKHOLDER: For you looking at it or for me creating it?

WESTFALL: *Art is a dialogue between the maker and the viewer. So I would say for both, and the risk, of course, for the maker is that self-identity is so much a part of the work. The cliché about the insane artist pretty much begins with romanticism but it also applies to the viewer. That is partly what is meant by the sublime. The poet, Gerard Manley Hopkins, first talked about an 'inscape' as opposed to a 'landscape'. In romantic art, a landscape, as vast as it may be, and as located as it may be – in Yosemite with Albert Bierstadt's paintings, or in the Amazon with Cole – there is a sense that something more is there. There is also a projection of the artist's inner life and the infinite extension implied that dwarfs the scale of our own body sense. It is perceived as a high wire act, a risky act by the audience and, presumably, is experienced as that by the artist. That is part of the audience's perception, at least. The process of the work tends to grind down habit or intentionality and something is formulated in that action as a fuller response to the pre-conceived idea.*

STOCKHOLDER: That's because it creates an experience, or creates the possibility for one. I put something in t he world and then I have an experience in relationship to it that I can't control, or at least I can't totally control. So there is room for things to grow. In terms of the work being romantic, or emotional or from childhood – all the ways it is rooted in my life – all of that information is important to other people only in so far as it provides a place for them to experience those things in their own life. In many ways people's experiences are very similar, in terms of what we are capable of experiencing and the range of emotions that we have available to us. The way in which those emotions are structured or ordered is more important than that they are there. What is important in the end is whether that emotional experience is given a new frame of reference or whether the piece provides a way to experience those feelings differently.

WESTFALL: *There is a classically modernist idea of opening up the process of the work to the viewer's imagination. That the image and the process become one in a way that it doesn't for an extended and total piece of music or a panoramic landscape painting, which are feats of technical virtuosity, is still very tied to notions of mastery that tend to exclude the audience. I look at your installations and I can hear the tape being pulled up when an edge is exposed on a plane of paint. I can hear the nails going in. I can feel the weight of things where they meet each other. In my bodily response to the work, I recreate the process of its coming together. It makes me feel that not only is it something I would want to do, but in fact I could do it. Part of the modernist agenda as I have always understood it has been that kind of democratization of the creative process. It says, 'Yes you can do it!' Someone says, 'Oh,*

GROWING ROCK CANDY MOUNTAIN GRASSES IN CANNED SAND, 1992
VIOLET BATHING SUIT MATERIAL, SAND STONE NATIVE TO MUNSTER, GASEOUS CONCRETE BUILDING BLOCKS, PLASTER, BASKET MATERIAL, ELECTRICAL WIRING, THREE VERY SMALL LIGHTS, NEWSPAPER GLUED TO THE WALL, ACRYLIC PAINT, METAL, CABLES, STYROFOAM
ROOM: 29 X 9 M

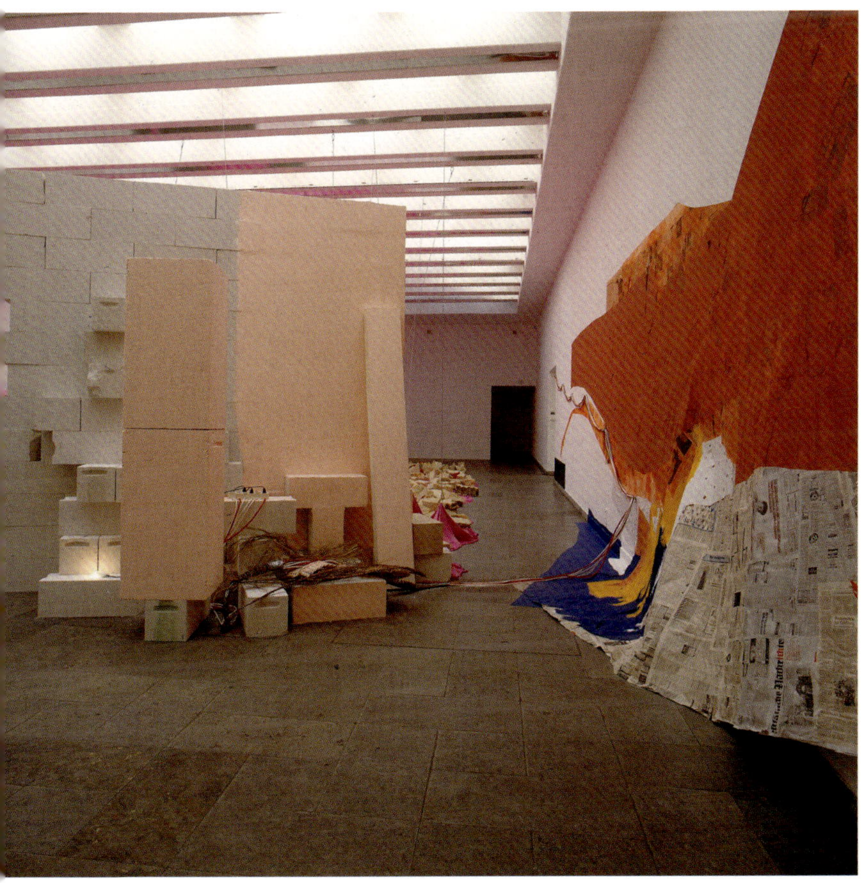

my three y ear old kid can do that', or, 'I can do that'. The modernist would respond 'Why don't you! Yes, you could, why don't you?' One of the great joys I find in your work is that sense of exciting the mind and the body to material, to all material. Rauschenberg used to say, 'My paintings are an invitation to look someplace else'. Your installations are an invitation to get into the flow.

STOCKHOLDER: That sounds nice. I do feel like there is a rarefication of art cultivated in the art market that I am not interested in and that I fight against. I do want my work to seem like somebody could do it. That it is not a work of genius, some rare object that nobody else could do.

WESTFALL: *Or a product of frontline technology.*

STOCKHOLDER: Yeah, it's not high tech. That is what has confused me about your statement. My focus isn't on keeping things available for people in terms of skill – I don't think that ends up being the truth. It is presenting the material world in a way that is understandable. I'm not interested in using a computer because you can't look at that and have a feeling about 'stuff'. I am interested in the quality of material, whether it is a chair or a piece of concrete: that you experience it over time, that it changes with the light, that you have a particular experience of it that is separate from talking about it, taking pictures of it, or writing about it. That's where the work grows for me, and the result of that is pretty low tech. There is also something that is very particular or specific that I struggle for in each piece that is in contrast to slap dash. But it's not about skill or technology either. It's about a structure of thinking. It's very formal. As the piece gets closer to being finished there are fewer decisions, fewer possibilities. Each decision becomes more important and has more weight in terms of how the whole thing fits together. I think it has to do with strings of references and a tension between the work being finished or not finished, complete or not complete. But in so far as I want things in the work not to have a fussed over quality, I want to provide a direct experience of things, I think that's true.

WESTFALL: *In the interaction of the elements in your work, I sense a celebration of ideas that we can only term aesthetic. This seems to be something that fell into disrepute, an idea or an admittance that has seemed more and more risky or nostalgic, especially to a lot of younger artists.*

STOCKHOLDER: It is important to say what you mean by aesthetic. I don't think aesthetics is just about pleasure. It's to allow pleasure and any other kind of experience that goes with it.

WESTFALL: *Pleasure and play. Play is highly communicative, interactive and a movement of the mind. It's also structural; it tends to build on itself.*

STOCKHOLDER: All of those things have meaning. When they don't have as much meaning, they become decorative, sometimes a little clichéd, all of that is part of our life. But when things are decorative or clichéd or less challenging they function to support a way of thinking. I think about taste in that way. Some people's notion of good taste reinforces a way of understanding the world that supports the world as they want it to be. Things that introduce a new way of thinking, challenge notions of taste are, for some people, wonderful. They like to have the world shook up a little, to have their thinking challenged. Other people don't want that, it offends them. That's the only way I can understand the difference between taste and beauty. For me, things that are beautiful are things that are awkward and shake things up, and stretch how I can understand things as complete. As I get to understand something a little better, it is less interesting and less beautiful.

WESTFALL: *There comes a point where if taste degrades enough it can be made use of again.*

STOCKHOLDER: Well, it becomes more defined. When you can isolate a certain taste then it means something for a certain time in history.

WESTFALL: *There is not a lot between the notion of abstractness as we understand it in the visual arts and a notion of the aesthetic that tends to degrade. The will to abstractness can also be read as a will to purity or a will to the aesthetic that tends to deny the psychological or the imaginistic.*

STOCKHOLDER: I don't follow what you are saying. For me, to the extent that the work is abstract and not literal or literary, it is freed up to say something. I feel trapped by the literary. I think I would feel my work more subject to degradation or emptying out if I were making a figurative work. Things that are abstract have the possibility to include different ways of thinking. I was at the Museum of Modern Art today looking at the way figures are presented. So often, people are trying to break the presentation of the figure. Lucas Samaras' portrait of a person holding a photograph of himself holding his own portrait in a jar breaks the believability of the body as a container – this body that we all have and we are all looking at that is being represented to us in painting or sculpture or photographs. Our modern dilemma seems to be a questioning of that containment. Questioning that the presentation of our bodies can in fact be us.

WESTFALL: *Or even the idea of the body as a boundary. The boundary to what? So much political discussion the last several years has been about the social boundaries of the body. But also, aesthetically, the body as a limit of action. There is nothing in your work which can't be done by a body, accomplished by a body. So much imagery has been about this question of where the body is. Our common sense tells us our bodies are right here and yet we are abstracted out of our notions of the limitations of the body. This happens in computer space and virtual reality. A non-sensate, purely visual space that can be 3D becomes a total mental construct, like a living memory with an attendant sense of vertigo.*

STOCKHOLDER: And also, bodies aren't like objects. In a painting, there's the body and there is the table, and they are somehow equal. But bodies are constantly changing, the shape is changing, how it appears when the light and you turn. Especially with babies, it's so amazing, they are changing in front of your eyes because they are growing so fast. There is something about the body as an event rather than an object that is a little disconcerting. It implies our death.

WESTFALL: *Oh, definitely, and in midlife there's secondary acceleration of change. When I see a grey hair in the mirror, I am so moved that something is happening that I don't have this vain response to just pluck it out. It is mythic in a way. I feel differently, however, when the hair starts growing out of my ears. But the idea of the body as an ongoing event is a powerful one.*

STOCKHOLDER: I think that in my work there is both a sense of time passing, that the work is temporal; and another feeling, that I'd say goes with art in this culture. Art is a little abstracted from the rest of our life and put in a separate building and made for those buildings, and thought of as separate from time. As a result, it is static, formal beautiful and has a quality of timelessness happing over and through this very temporal installation.

WESTFALL: *You refer to a certain calm, a serenity. There is all this furious action in your work and yet in the viewer's freedom to experience it at different times of day and walk through it, even if that occasion is itself temporal, there is a chance for it to unfold more slowly. Another action of the work becomes its unfolding to perception after it's done. Which must be very different from the energy that's expended in erecting it.*

STOCKHOLDER: Building the pieces is sometimes not much fun. There isn't the same pleasure that comes from looking at them. Building them is usually

UNTITLED SEEPAGE: SANDWASHED, SUNDRIED & SHRINKWRAPPED, 1991
LUMBER, SHEETROCK, PLYWOOD, CARPET, ELECTRICAL CORDS, ESCALATOR SLEEVE, BICYCLE, PAINT, MIRRORED TILES, PLASTER ON METAL LATH, WINE GLASSES IN PLASTER, NEWSPAPER MACHÉ HUNG ON CURTAIN RODS, FLUORESCENT LIGHTS, THEATRE LIGHT
SPACE: 576 X 144 CM
CEILING: H. 360

INSTALLATION VIEW AT EZRA AND CECILE ZILKHA GALLERY, WESLEYAN UNIVERSITY, MIDDLETOWN, CONNECTICUT, 1991

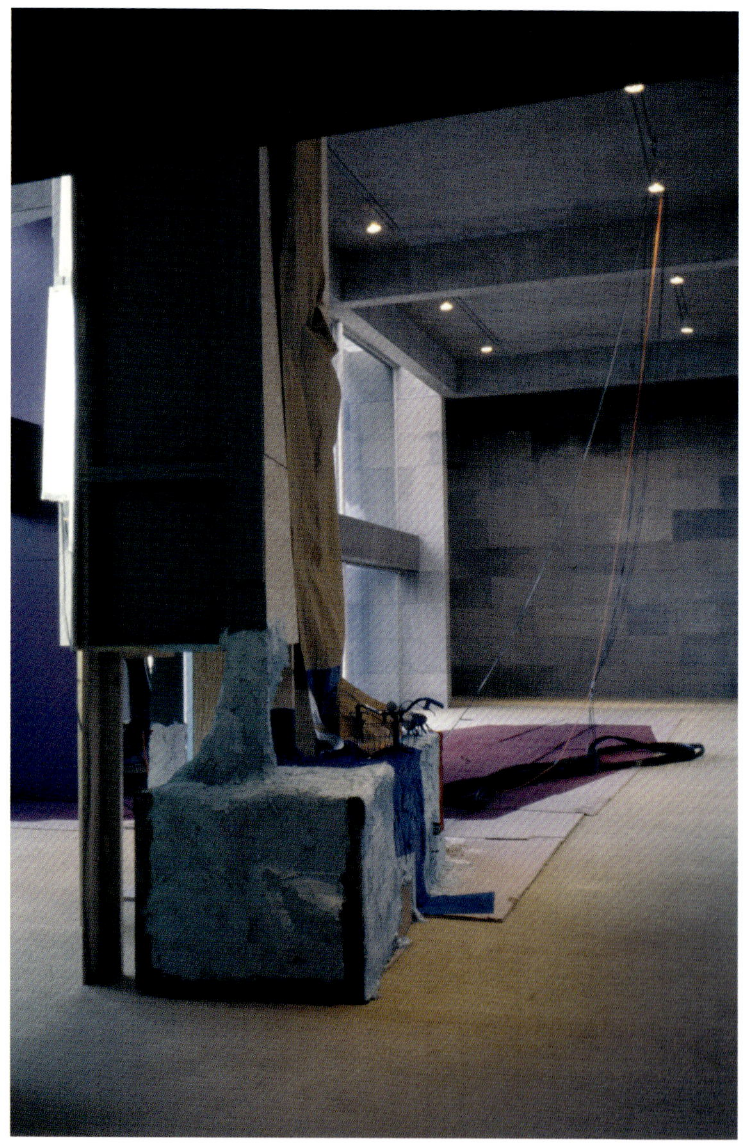

UNTITLED SEEPAGE: SANDWASHED, SUNDRIED & SHRINKWRAPPED, 1991
LUMBER, SHEETROCK, PLYWOOD, CARPET, ELECTRICAL CORDS, ESCALATOR SLEEVE, BICYCLE, PAINT, MIRRORED TILES, PLASTER ON METAL LATH, WINE GLASSES IN PLASTER, NEWSPAPER MACHÉ HUNG ON CURTAIN RODS, FLUORESCENT LIGHTS, THEATRE LIGHT
SPACE: 576 X 144 CM
CEILING: H. 360

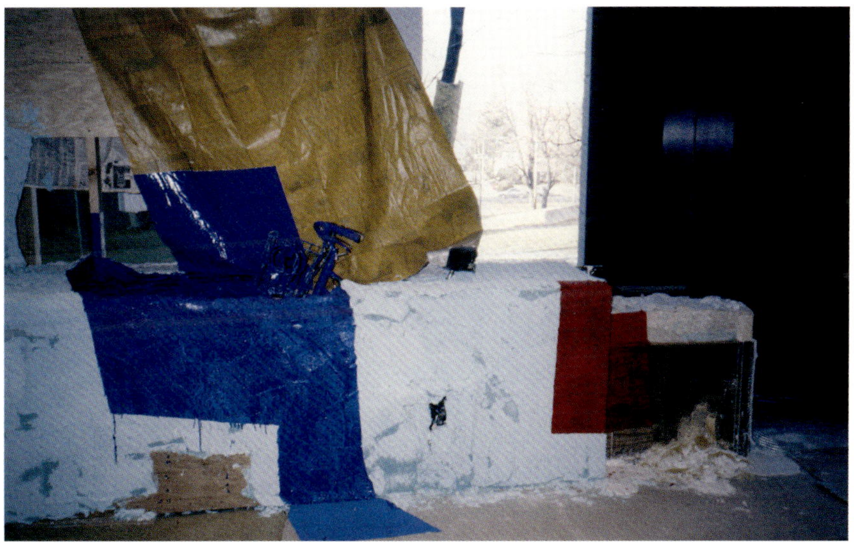

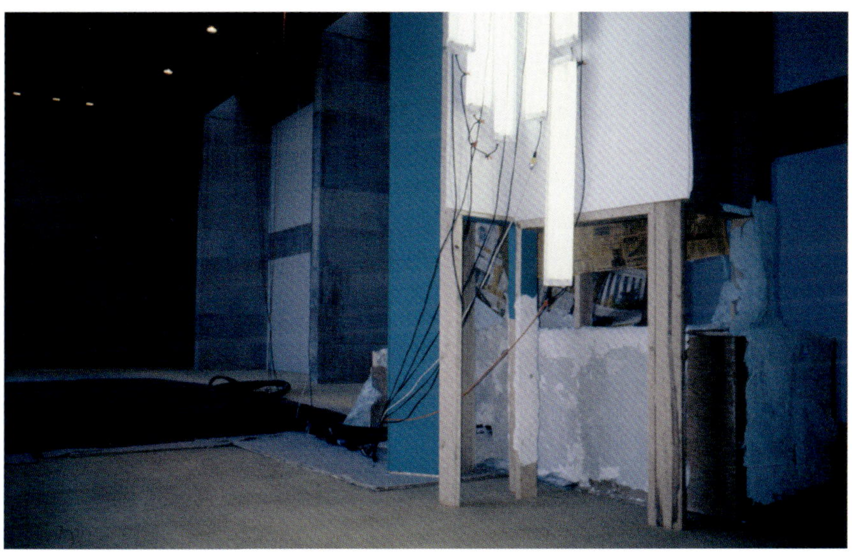

a struggle. I'm irritable, grumpy, upset and worried. It's difficult. Then looking at the piece afterward, there is still some of that, there are always difficult places in the work that make me uncomfortable. But, to the extent that the work is successful, I'm providing an experience that is not there while building it. It's an experience of being really wonderful or exciting. It keeps me moving just the right way; that is something that is very particular to its being finished. The static and timeless experience is in contrast to our own temporality. The static experience is an imaginary one and as such, full of possibility.

WESTFALL: *Harold Rosenberg talked about visual artwork as an action of the body suspended in material. This suspension strikes me as also referring to that calm or clarity, that reference to timelessness. The funny thing about the continuity of life in a body is that there are those moments of perceptual clarity which are often too few and far between. There is this sense that life is short, but it's not that short. We change, but we don't change radically enough that you are unrecognizable the next day or the next hour, or that I don't recognize myself in the mirror the next morning.*

STOCKHOLDER: Yeah, thank God. (Laughter)

WESTFALL: *George Steiner says that in art no new perception cancels out old perceptions, unlike science where a new perception invalidates an old perception. But in art that's not so.*

STOCKHOLDER: People try to make it so, the current conversation is always an attempt to try to invalidate what just happened. But that sounds good to me.

BOMB, FALL 1992

Parallel Parking, 1993

FOR MARY HEILMANN, 1990
WOOD, CONCRETE, STYROFOAM, PLASTER, BED SHEETS, DRIED FRUIT, OIL, ENAMEL, LATEX AND ACRYLIC PAINT, TOILET PAPER, LIGHTS, ROOFING TAR, MIRROR, PLASTIC SHEETING, NEWSPAPER
L: 461 CM

INSTALLATION VIEW AT GALERIE ISABELLA KACPRZAK, COLOGNE, 1990

In my work I am always concerned with the relationship between contradictory things, with the relationship between one part of the work to another, and the relationship of the work to the building it sits in.

It used to be that artists worked within shared conventions of iconography and style. Now each artist develops her/his own individual style or relationship to style as a concept; and each artist determines what the subject of their work will be. As a result, attention to context (the physical and social circumstances within which the work is viewed) is heightened as it has become one of few elements trying many divergent activities together as 'art'. Context, replete with meaning, has become a shared point of departure.

For me context as a point of focus became important as I noticed the padded, muffled feelings that accrue to the experience of an object as it becomes 'art' and is thus elevated, protected, cleaned and removed from my life. Responding to feelings of anger and frustration at the distance which develops between me and my work, and in an attempt to bring the work forward I tie it to particularities of physical circumstances.

In response to this aspect of 'art', and to a need to explore the nature of experience directly, my work is rooted in physical circumstances. It creates an experience, a time-bound experience happening to the body. Even so, it depends on its placement in the world as an art object, and on the history of art, to communicate at a level of intensity I relish.

The art objects of Western culture exist in an alienated space created by or framing of the work. Aside from literally framing the work or putting it on a pedestal, we frame it by placing it within the institution of the gallery; we then carry the institution with us, in mind, as the context or place for art. It becomes our 'frame' or reference; we use it to establish a 'point of view'. The resulting separation of the art object from normal time and space enables art to function as a metaphor for thinking processes. I love the level of abstraction and the freedom of action this makes possible.

My work doesn't have a frame, in the usual sense, nor a pedestal. But it often relies on its status as art to be a gestalt; it would otherwise not exist as a separate entity among everything else. Each piece relies on its context for definition and also on the idea of 'frame' that we all carry with us. We the viewers complete the work, or fill in the blanks, responding to cues in the work. There is an important contradiction here – the frame, though it is only an abstraction, functions to hold the work apart from real time and remove it to an elevated timelessness; but to the extend that the viewer participates in framing the work, the frame becomes part of real time, part of life.

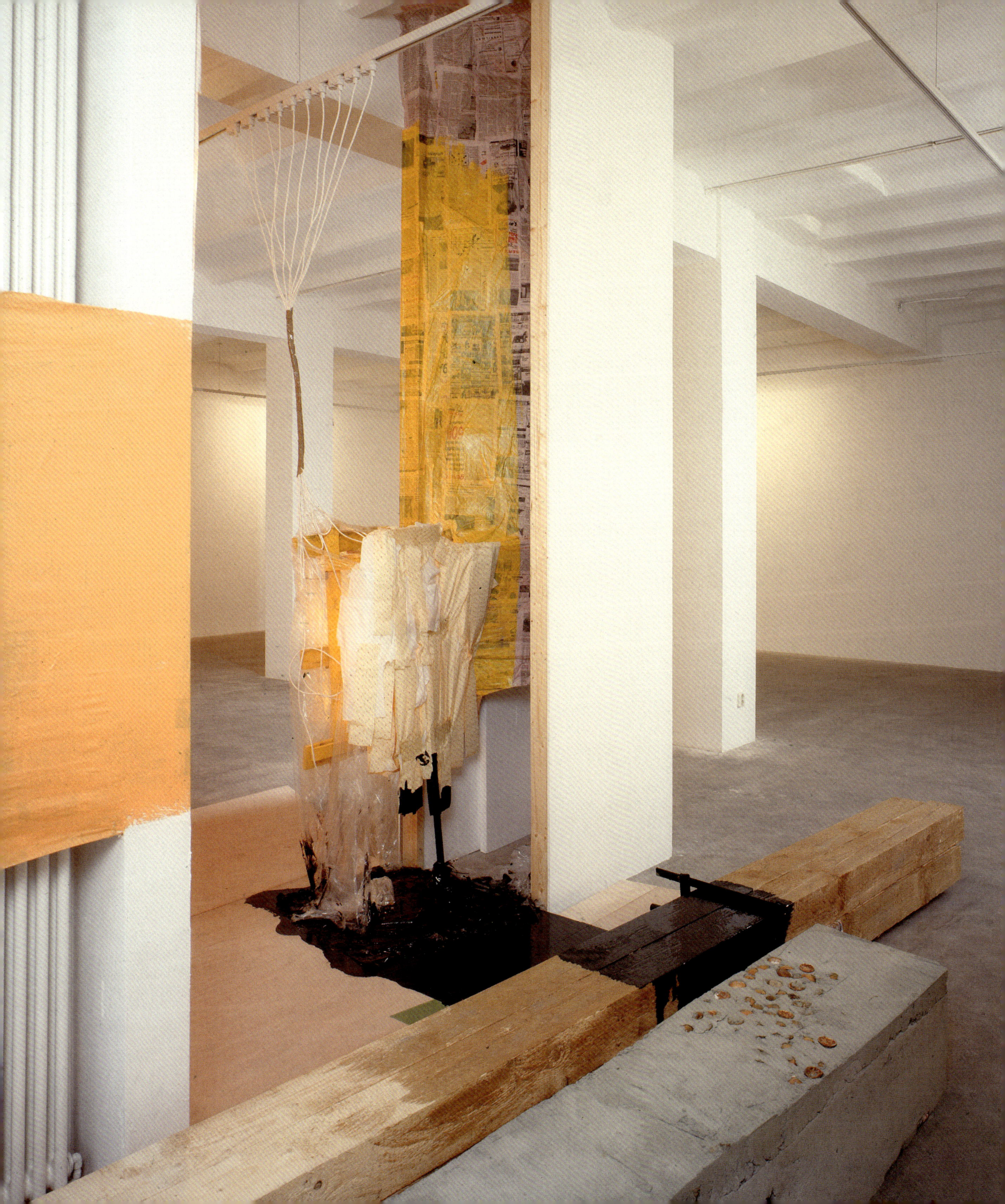

I structure the work so that experience of it engenders a struggle between these different ways of viewing. This struggle presents a process of questioning rather than a fait accompli. It contributes to the rise of a kind of blur, a confusion of boundary, and it questions the possibility of containing bodies of information or ideas. Perhaps the best systems for knowing do not involve a stable unchanging mode of operation.

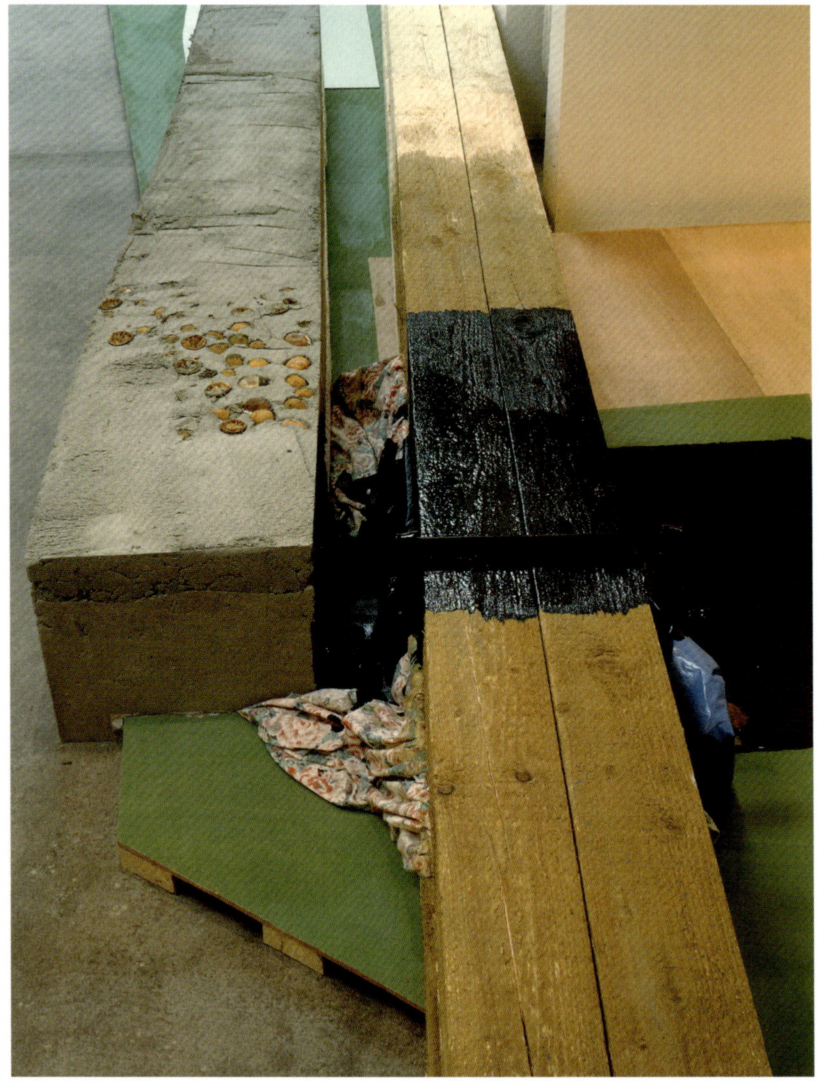

I engage in a constant process of pulling the rug out from under the ground on which my work rests. The stabs I make against this ground are doomed to fail because I am in love with what I am attacking. Nevertheless the holes or gaps created in the struggle are full of meaning. There is a feeling of fragmentation which can be aggressive, angry and uncomfortable; but it is also optimistic, hopeful and exciting in that space is left for the possibility of change and for the emergence of something new and fantastic.

My work grows through the process of making. It is an additive process where each piece is built from nothing to something clear to its foundation – by this I mean that there is no blank canvas from which to begin, no lump of stone; with each work its physical footing in the world must be invented. Instead of accepting a given physical parameter, I begin with a desire to engage in a struggle to alter what I know, or to make order and cohesion consistent with the heap of chaotic information in which we exist. The construction of such a heap within my work involves layering or overlapping many kinds of information. This process creates a conglomeration of elements which arise from absurd relationships between things, from chance occurrences, happenstance and from objects already laden with meaning; and last but not least, from painting. Within this deliberately shifting and tangles mass of overlapping strands there is enmeshed a clear, coherent form of order.

Painting functions in my work as a pictorial entity laden with history which, among other things, is inextricably bound to the history of the frame. More simply, the painting also draws attention to surface – to skins over objects and skins of objects. The surface is simultaneously rested on and poked into. It is treated as a flat weightless, almost abstract or not physical area; at the same time it is an extension of an object and is treated as such. The paint functions both to alter existing surfaces and as a very flat object in it sown right placed over or along side other objects. The surface of the object conceals the mass of the object from us; it is also the part of the object revealed to our sight, it is an area where we are vulnerable to deception and also a site poignantly ripe for the development of fiction. The surface becomes a tenuous site where fiction and reality struggle with notions of subjectivity and objectivity to find boundaries or to determine difference.

I hope that the finished object provides, if only for a brief moment, a site where myself and others can experience a confluence of inner life with concrete physical stuff. In this sense, and in other ways also, I think the work creates a static event. Visually not very much moves, except for the person viewing; but there are sparks flying through the air as electricity moves sight unseen through wires.

TURN OF THE CENTURY MAGAZINE, SPRING 1993

FOR MARY HEILMANN, 1990
WOOD, CONCRETE, STYROFOAM, PLASTER, BED SHEETS, DRIED FRUIT, OIL, ENAMEL, LATEX AND ACRYLIC PAINT, TOILET PAPER, LIGHTS, ROOFING TAR, MIRROR, PLASTIC SHEETING, NEWSPAPER
L. 461 CM

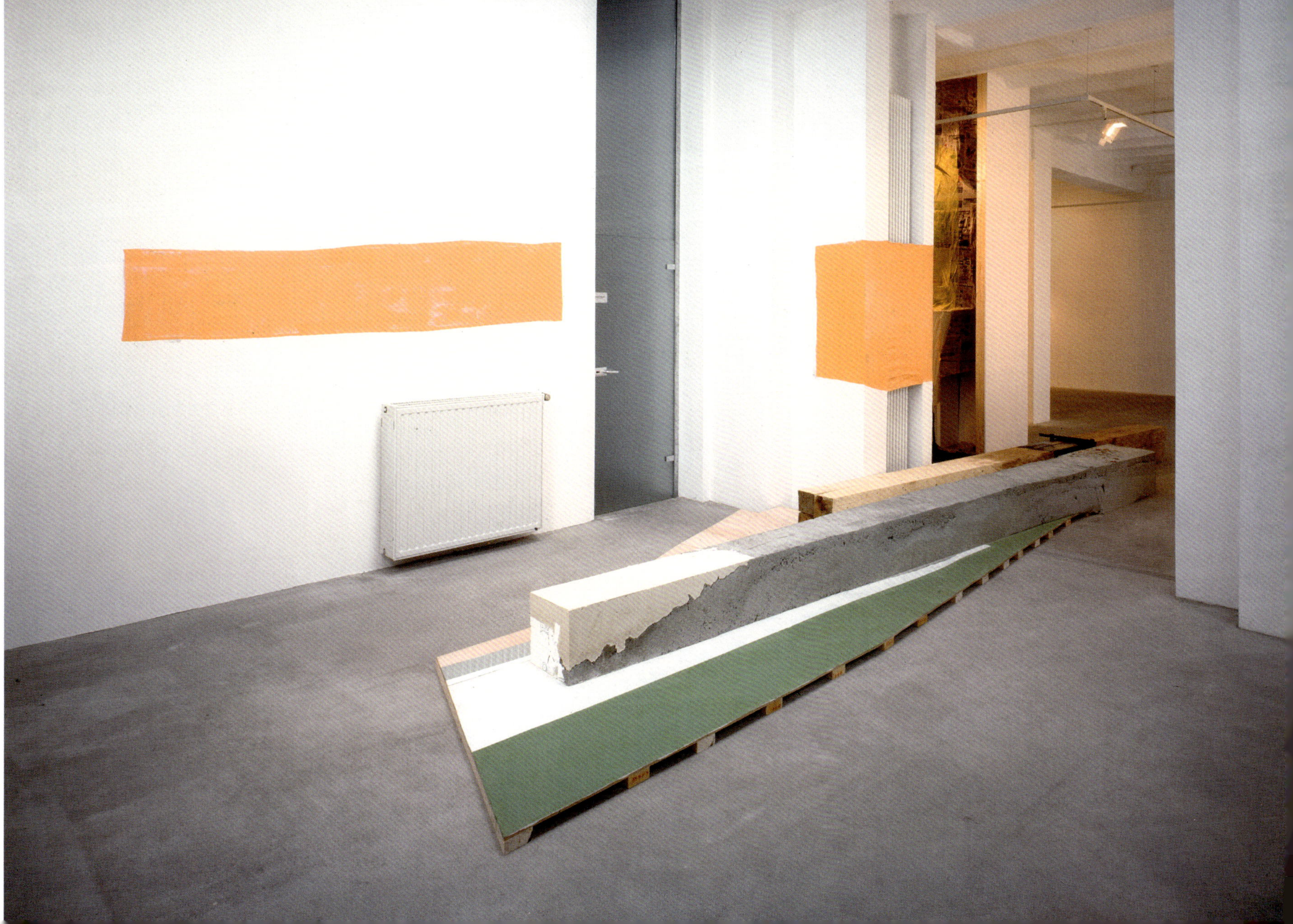

Figure Ground Relations, 1993

CATCHERS HOLLOW, 1993
BATHTUBS, LUMBER, SILICONE CAULKING, PAINT, LIGHTS AND WIRES, COLOURED FILTER, PAPER, TRANSPARENT TAPE OVER AND UNDER PAINT, YARN, A CABLE ANTENNA PAINTED GREEN OUTSIDE THE WINDOW TOGETHER WITH A QUARTZ LIGHT
312 X 588 X 173 CM

INSTALLATION VIEW AT WITTE DE WITH, ROTTERDAM, 1993

Part 1: 'Catchers Hollow', Alternate Title, 'Feeding Station Launching Pad'

The first view is of a wall; the wall is rectangular, flat and painted. There are three square holes in the wall through which a wooden structure breaks from the other side. While the wall acts as ground for the painting, it is also a sculptural element, or figure, in its relation to the wooden structure behind.

The three square holes through the wall become figures at play with the painted pieces on the wall. A painted grey shape is covered with transparent packing tape. The grey is very close to the colour of the floor. The tape runs onto the floor and forms a rectangle of shininess. The flat paint on the wall and the painted surface of the floor become ground to the shiny tape.

From here it is possible to see the green cable antenna fixed to the roof outside the window.

The wall stands in the centre of the room like an oversized column. Moving around to the other side of the column reveals the wooden structure. It spreads from the floor through the column, and back to one of the walls that forms the room. It is an object supported by, and attached to, the room, but nevertheless a figure in the room. It is also a grid which supports another grid, affixed to it made of pieces cut from nineteen bathtubs; the pieces sit together forming an awkward concave dish. As grid, this structure plays to the grids of the architecture seen through the windows, and as concave dish it plays to the green cable antenna that it faces.

Stuck onto the surface of the bathtubs is a white shape made of silicone caulking; over this is spread an orange painted shape spilling onto green. This green shape is papered and painted onto the floor and climbs up the column/wall. The green is a figure on the ground of the floor; it is also the ground or pedestal for the wooden structure/ bathtub figure, which acts, in turn, as ground for the white silicone and orange painted shapes that it throws into space.

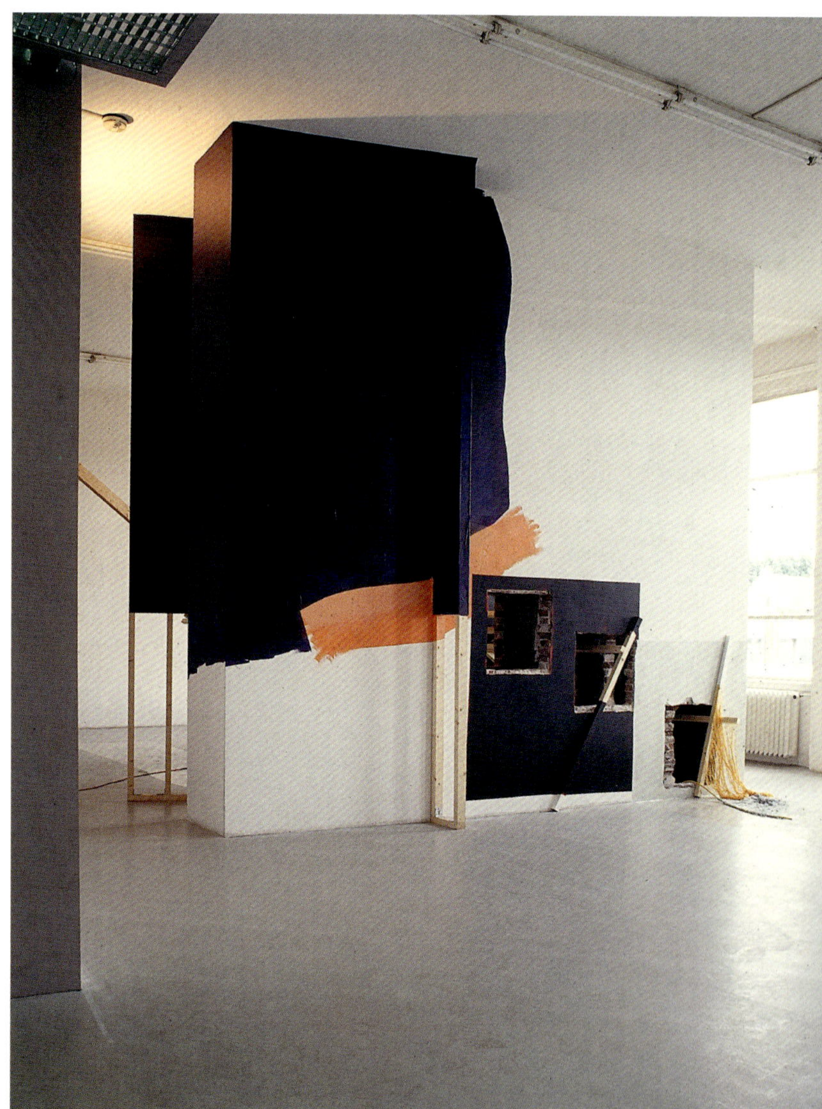

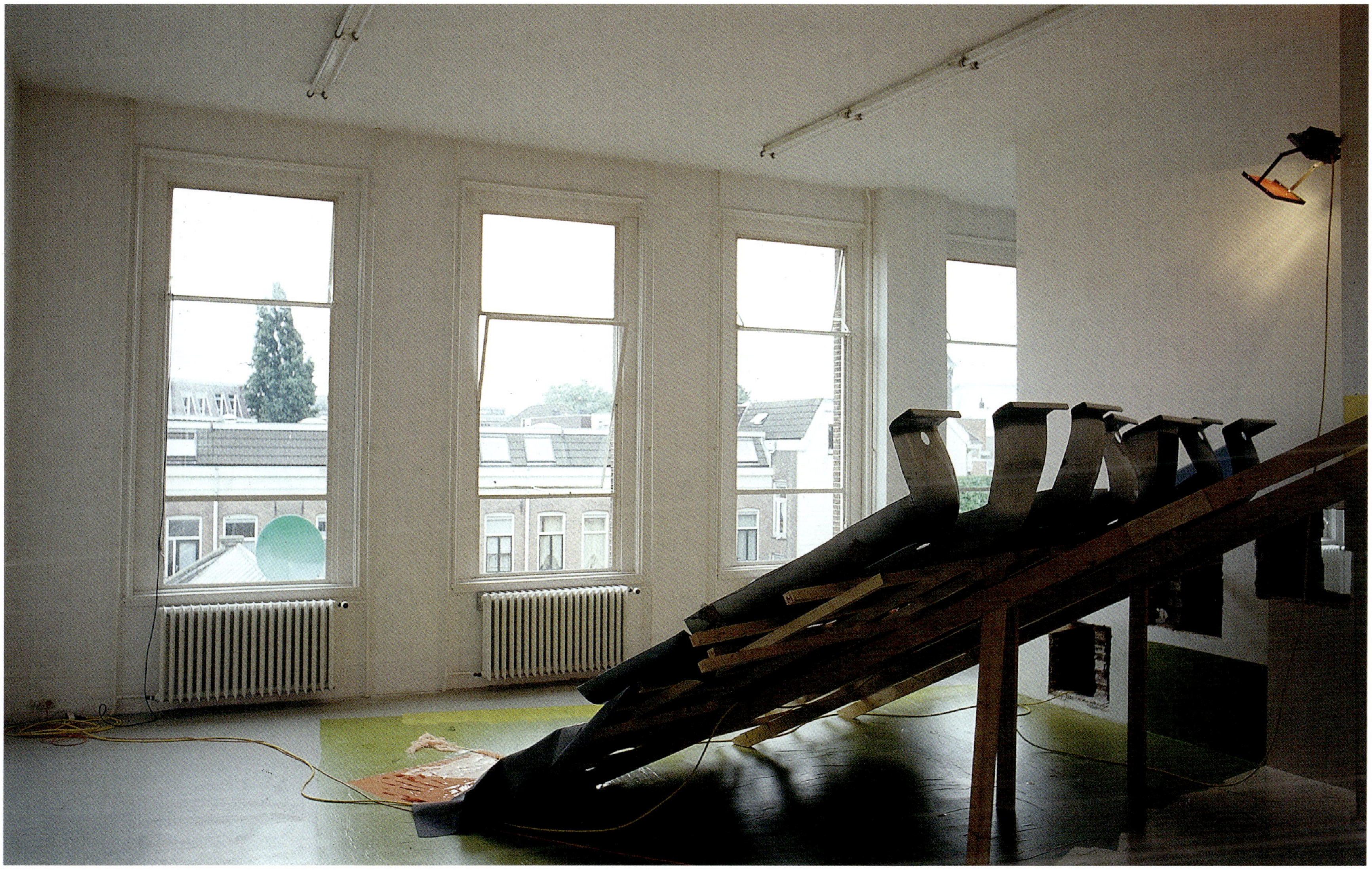

The two lights mounted on the wall enter into this play between figure and ground. They are objects while at the same time, the light they cast 'is' or makes the wall as we see it. The wires feeding them run across the space carrying colour and electricity. Their colour jumps to the other colour in the work. The electricity they carry comes from inside the walls of the building, the ground.

The viewer's place in the work changes as her/his perception moves between an understanding of the building alternately as container, ground and object. The viewer is at times a figure in the work and at times a consciousness quite separate from the site of the action. In the process of moving back and forth between these two positions, as experience of the work is combined with expectations of closure and notions of framing, the work begins to appear complete and as a static unity.

The wall with the mounted lights, the painted pieces, the holes in the walls, and the wooden/bathtub grid are all, at times, thrown forward as figures or objects in the room, performing an action that reaches into worlds of fiction and fantasy, even while they slip back in to the matter of fact building and place of Witte de With.

This is a description of *Catchers Hollow* made in Witte de With, Rotterdam, The Netherlands.

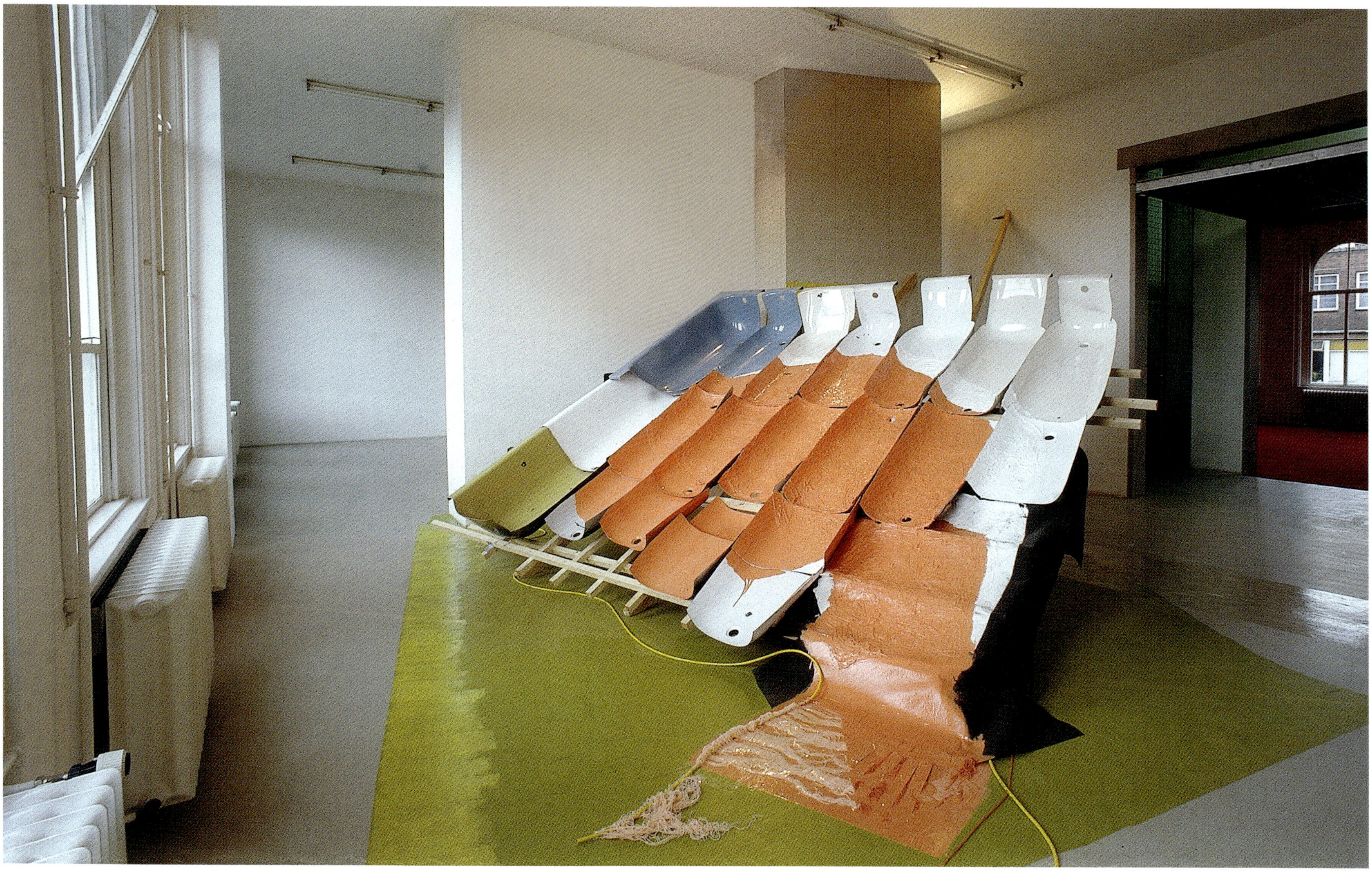

CATCHERS HOLLOW, 1993
BATHTUBS, LUMBER, SILICONE CAULKING, PAINT, LIGHTS AND WIRES, COLOURED FILTER, PAPER, TRANSPARENT TAPE OVER AND UNDER PAINT, YARN, A CABLE ANTENNA PAINTED GREEN OUTSIDE THE WINDOW TOGETHER WITH A QUARTZ LIGHT
312 X 588 X 173 CM

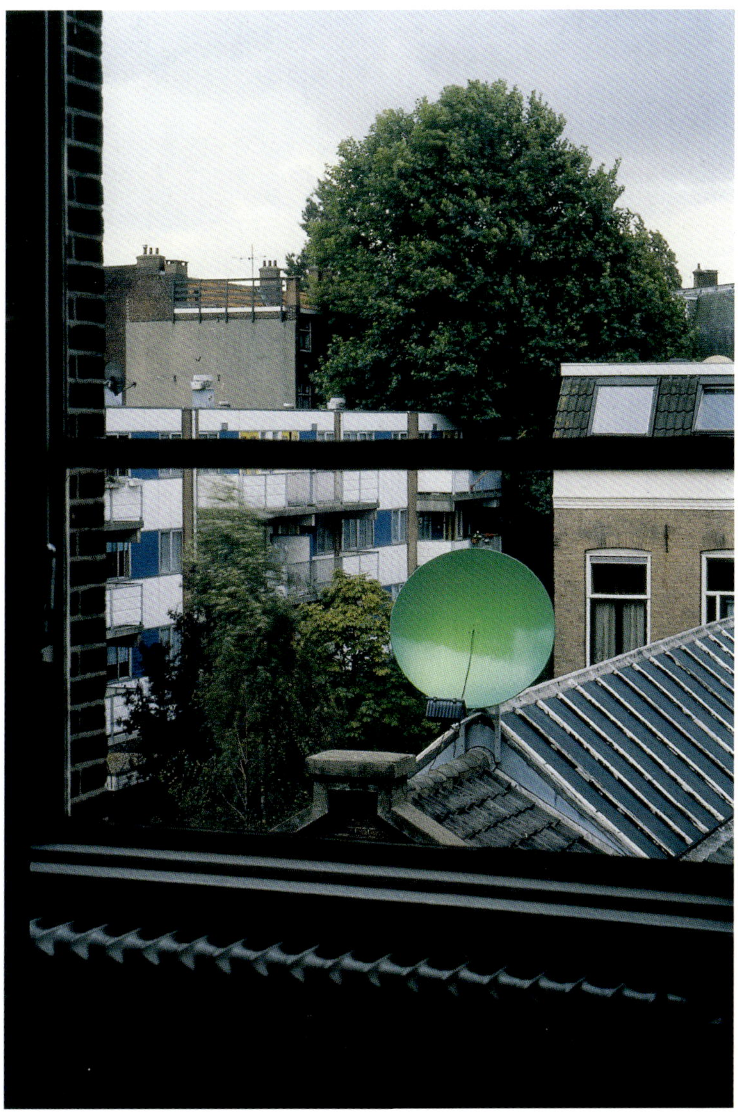

Part II: 'Self-Portrait'

The painting is rectangular; it hangs on the wall and the appropriate viewing distance seems to be about two and a half feet. The first information to come is that the painting is a portrait. There is a figure looking out from thick dark brown space. It seems that one can see consciousness and life in his face and eyes. The figure is looking at the viewer and one is reminded of oneself.

The figure seems to emerge from the depths of the painting; but the line between the clothes of the body and the dark space behind is very difficult to find, impossible to find, and then at times very clear. When the line can't be found, the whole painting seems to flatten and the figure becomes one with the dark background. For a time, the deep brown space disappears.

When seen as a flat thing, one's attention is drawn to the painting as an object, or figure on the wall, and again to oneself standing in front of the painting. It makes sense to move closer in order to look closely at the surface. Attention is drawn to the fact of the paint on the taut plane of the canvas. The surface of the paint is shiny and cohesive – a singular entity; but it is also clear that there are many layers of paint stacked and mingles, so that it is difficult to decipher how this occurred. Viewed from up close, these mingled layers of paint move back and forth – sometimes seeming to be flat physical entities and at others seeming to exist in a shallow space whose size is linked to the scale of the brush strokes.

With attention focused on the fact of the paint, the figure in the centre seems to be built of, or growing from, little dabs of lighter-coloured paint. These little dabs are often bumpier spots or objects on the surface of the painting. They are little objects on the canvas while at the same time they seem to be the incorporeal light which illuminates the figure. The figure is a thing lost in the background, perhaps one and the same with the background, even while emerging as figure. The little dabs that serve to illuminate the figure, which allow us to see it, are themselves figures on the flat surface of the painting.

The image of the figure looking out at us, the consciousness we imagine behind the eyes, and the light moving through the space of the painting are all dramas that dissolve into the skin of shiny paint made up of many sculptured strokes. All of this is stretched over the rectangular-canvas-covered object on the wall that is the painting. So much happens while one stands in front of this static painting that it comes as a shock to realize that one has only taken a few steps forward and back, and to realize the physical stillness of the past moments.

This is a description of Rembrandt's *Self-Portrait as the Apostle Paul* (1961), seen in the Rijksmuseum, Amsterdam, The Netherlands.

CAHIER 1, WITTE DE WITH, ROTTERDAM, 1993

Landscape Linoleum, 1998

I imagine the round earth, dark brown dirt and solid through. I am walking on the surface, the skin, shown to me.

This little patch, the park/garden in Middelheim has been resurfaced for generations. Each leaving their mark, their drawing; shaping the ground we walk/work on.

This canvas is not white.

I am walking over and in a fantasy garden – carefully mapped, orchestrated holding, framing, some nature. Full of life. Over this map I plan a few marks to converse.

We make our world. Each one of us too. A privilege for a moment to have such a large canvas. Marks so … to speak to.

Close Scrutiny

Under the magnifying glass.

Drawn in the sand. Drawing attention. Small details. Grass like paint, a surface, skin, place of illusion. The park contains, gives rise to illusion, or story telling, bracketing experience. Calm, tranquil, controlled nature.

More than a skin it seems a drawing. Like the children's story *Harold and the Purple Crayon*. Where Harold draws the world around him as he wishes it to be.

This work draws/carves into the work of the park, expands the dialogue or the story. It uses the 'real' material of the grass, trees, earth, 'sculpture', to support a further flight of fantasy/fancy.

Flying down the horizon line arriving at a human spine. The two things being one, they conflate. Microscopic and universal. Near and far.

LANDSCAPE LINOLEUM, 1998
POOLS, TWO HEAT LAMPS, TWO CIRCULAR CONCRETE SLABS, SCAFFOLDING, 17 CAR BODIES, BLUR ROPE, PAINTED GRASS AND TREES

INSTALLATION VIEW AT MIDDELHEIM SCULPTURE PARK, ANTWERP, 1998

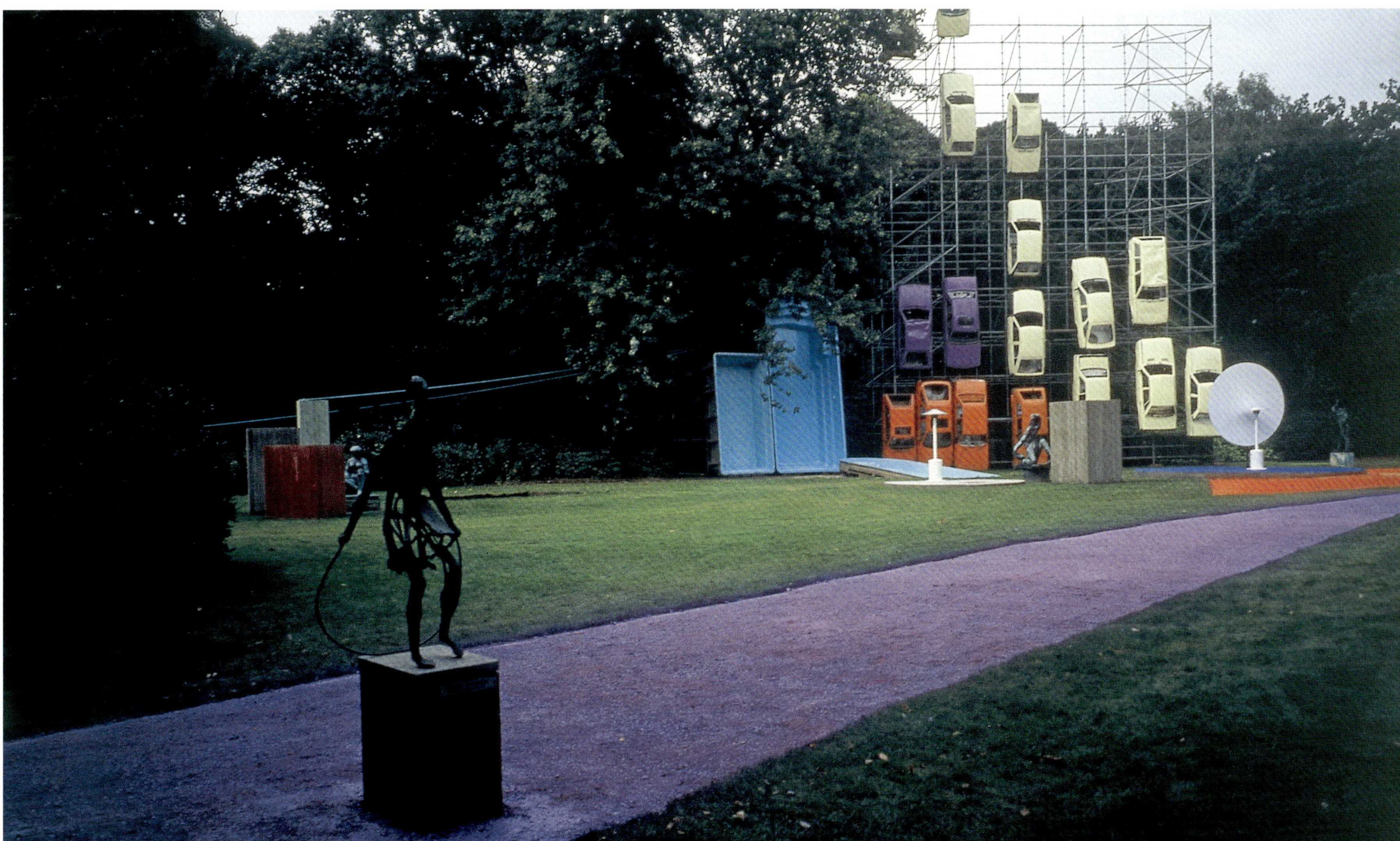

An ant wishing for an aerial view, slowly covering ground the human eye moves across like the wind.

The first moment a symphony orchestra begins to play, the violins tuning up, the sky full of stars opens up above.

A film cutting away from close intimate action to an aerial view of a plane flying.

Inserting ourselves in the landscape. An odd thing to do given that we are here a priori.

Points touching, lines drawn, outer and inner worlds, the earth covered, dark, stripped; pressed against the colours of the painting – plastered like a bandage. Peeling apart revealing interdependence.

The horizon line, drawn, where the lawn meets the edge of the trees. There is a flattening.

The lawn picks itself up and roles backwards to the feet of the eyes. A gash opens below the trees, a green cloud hovering over solid rock.

From this cut in the fabric of the scene there could arise trombone music and violins. Bass too. Sound filling the air floats to match the structured thought hovering over the park making it what it is. Forming it – bracketing it – framing. Music calls attention to times passage. Structured thought hovers as if timeless though it too is in flux. Ideas in the head forming reality do not include flux as part of the foreground.

JESSICA STOCKHOLDER: LANDSCAPE LINOLEUM, OPENLUCHTMUSEUM VOOR BEELDHOUWKUNST, MIDDELHEIM PARK, ANTWERP, 1997

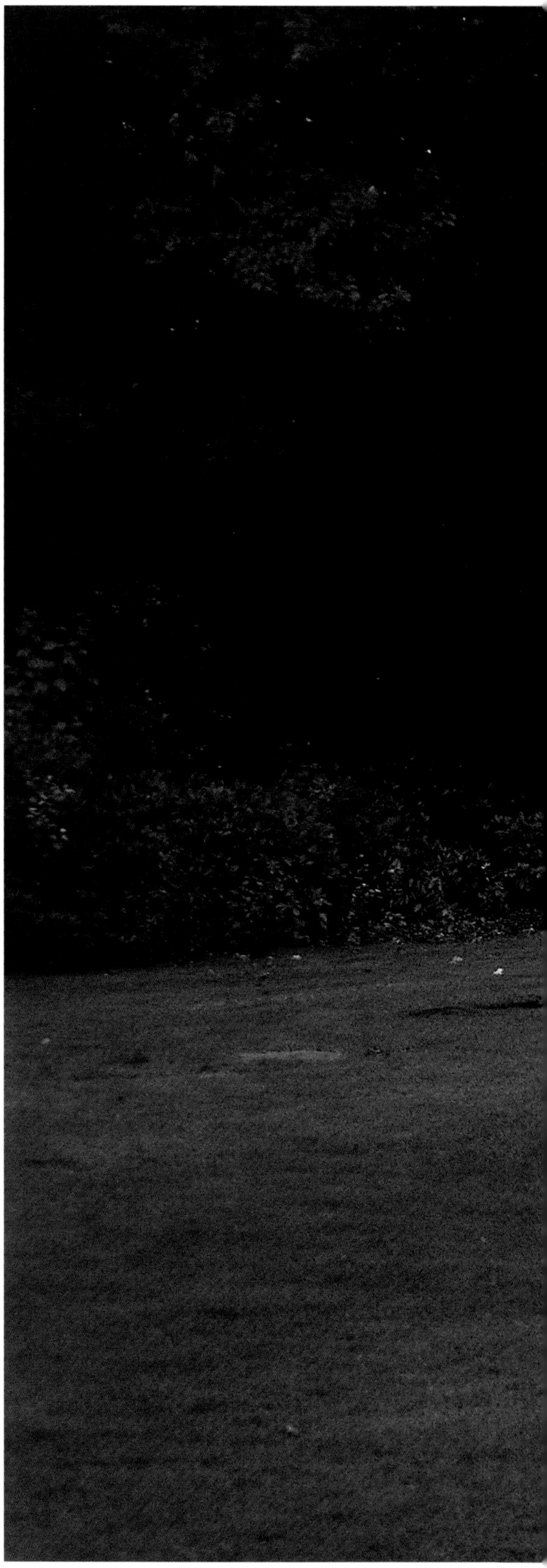

LANDSCAPE LINOLEUM, 1998
POOLS, TWO HEAT LAMPS, TWO CIRCULAR CONCRETE SLABS, SCAFFOLDING, 17 CAR BODIES, BLUR ROPE, PAINTED GRASS AND TREES

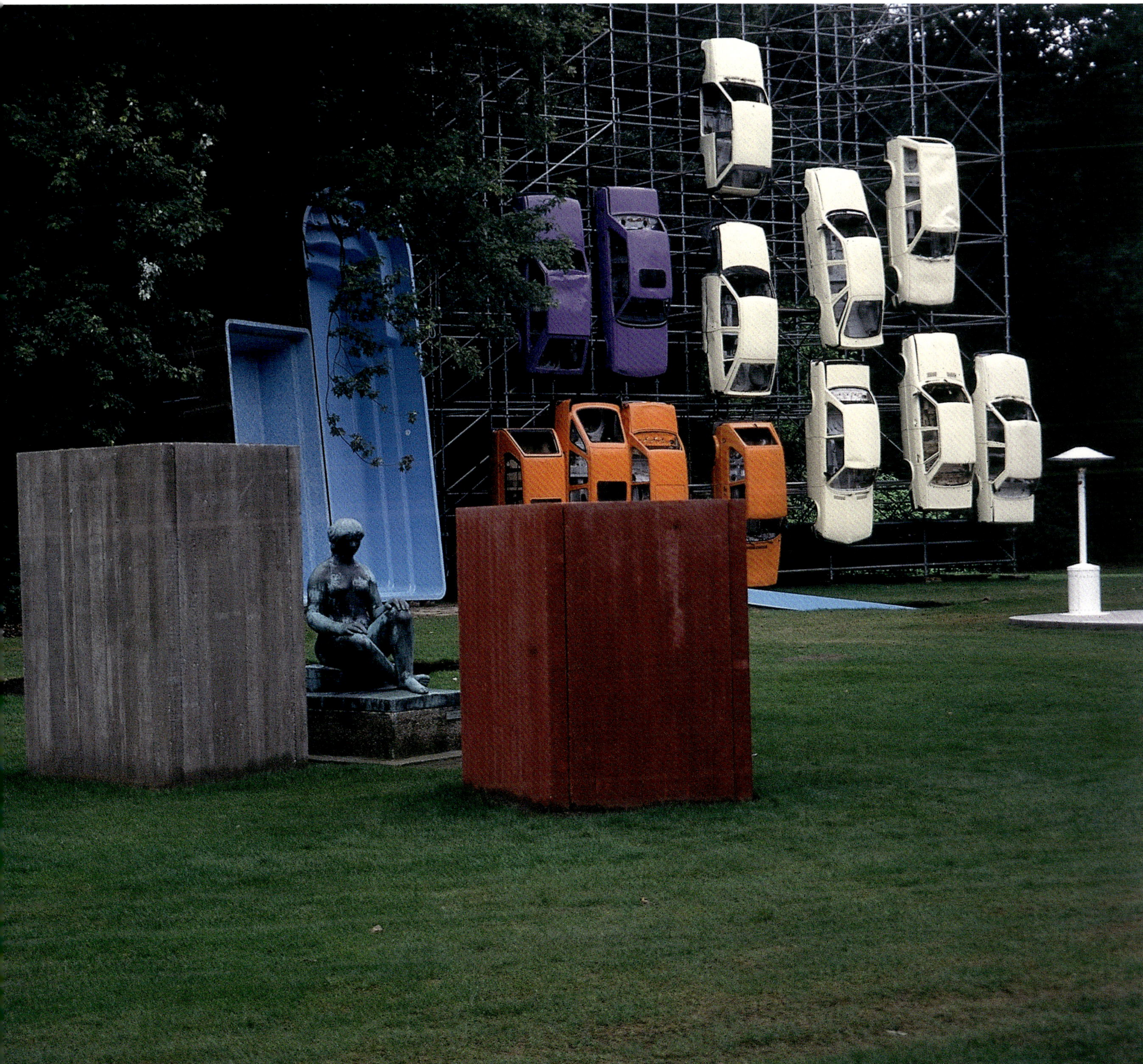

Art and Labour, 2004 (with Joe Scanlan)

JOE SCANLAN
MÖBEL (WHITE TRASH), 2011
CHROMED TIN, STRING,
FABRIC, CARBON FIBRE,
ALUMINIUM, GALVANIZED
STEEL, WOOD
200 X 300 X 250 CM

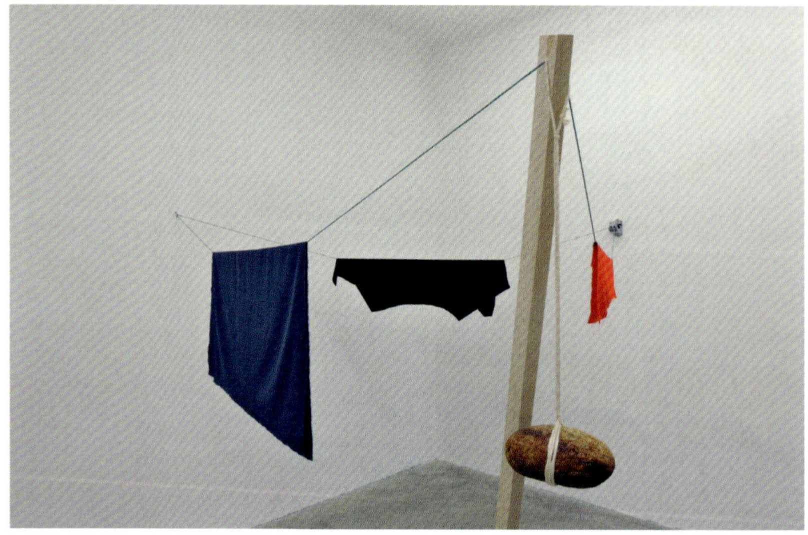

We have organized this daylong conference to explore the status of the art object in relation to how things are now produced. We are positing that labour is of central importance to art making. Labour can be explored as a popular and very juicy subject of art, and as the work of the artist and the many other labourers (artists assistants, curators, installers, writers, designers) that contribute to the manufacture of the object of art, or, in some cases, the moment of art. The act of making mediates between our inside and the outside, for each of us and for society as a whole. That we make things is driven by biology and necessity; like breathing and socializing it is part of being human. Each one of us grows into the history and culture of making that we are born into; our making is always transforming that culture even as it is determined by it.

We would like the conversations generated by this conference to contribute to the understanding of Art and Labour through various frames of reference. First, there is the labour it takes to make art; both the labour of the artist and/or the labour of others who produce the work. It is important to explore how this labour is valued or devalued. Labour and its value raise questions about the place of craft and skill in our valuing of art – if they have a place at all.

Second, we might also consider the labourers who work within the infrastructure of art: curators, art handlers, writers, dealers and museum directors. Thinking about the artist and the art object in relation to these people and the power structures they inhabit raises issues of class that are inextricably part of fine art's value and the labour relations that support it.

Third, the artist occupies a peculiar place in class structure. Working with our hands we are labourers. And yet, by expending a great amount of time and materials creating ostensibly useless objects, we are wastrels, dilettantes, connoisseurs. The artist functions at once as a *déclassé* labourer and as a decadent god. Either way the discomfort associated with mucking about in the dirt is pushed as far away as possible.

We often find ourselves in the position of a boss supervising labourers who are working for us. Unlike curators who rarely get their hands dirty rooting around in the physical world, artists often do. As we gain recognition, we artists often end up, by choice or necessity, keeping our hands clean as well. Historically, art making has been tied to working with materials. Working with materials involves intelligence and thoughts that are rich in ways quite different from the thoughts that are generated while seated at a desk. Desk thinking floats free from the resistance and logic of time and space in the material world; and yet desk thinking is no less fraught with the time and space of the material world. Freud has described thinking as the practicing of action. In fact, desk thinking is even more fraught than material thinking in that we are capable of expending much more time and materials by giving commands from our desk than we ever could if we had to execute those commands ourselves.

The two kinds of thinking need not be divorced from one. Our question is: why has the thinking that grows from physical labour been relegated to the lower status? What effect has this had on art, not only on the ways in which it gets made but also on the values that get ascribed to these various kinds of making?

We wonder, does art reflect our means of production? Artists used to be understood as craftspeople. Art was an object made by hand. Perhaps art was the repository of more eccentric impulses than those generated by the making of life's necessities – soap, toys, furniture, houses – all made by people locally and with available materials. Now we are aware of very little, if any, of the making of the things we need. It happens elsewhere, often overseas. We are able to have many things because they don't cost what they would if we ourselves were the makers. Where Marx worried about alienated labour – the effect of workers making things that they themselves could not afford to buy – today we experience the opposite (but no less alienating) phenomenon of being able to buy things that we could not afford to make. It is of course a great pleasure to have all these things and to be able to engage with such an enormous pool of significance and stimulation. But it is also painful and numbing to be so divorced from the making of things and from the people who make them for us.

Our art today reflects this distance. And so, a lot of art, on the face of it, seems to be not about making but about currating. To collect things and re-arrange them is a widely respected form of activity. Art mirrors our lack of production or, more precisely, it mirrors how acceptable modes of production – what we are willing or unwilling to do – have changed. Just as many of us are not willing to mend our clothes or clean our homes and are willing to pay other people to do those things for us, art conflates the luxury of choosing what we want to do with the menial tasks that make that luxury possible: painting, keyboarding, stitching, sanding, editing.

Art making has traditionally been the placeholder for the continuation of learning through making that we all engage in as children and which some of us continue to engage in as artists and tradesmen. Do we need this part of ourselves to be reflected in the culture we live in? Or are we happy to be rid of such reminders of the physical world together with its awkwardness, its frustrations, and its mortality?

YALE UNIVERSITY SCHOOL OF ART, NEW HAVEN, SEPTEMBER 2004

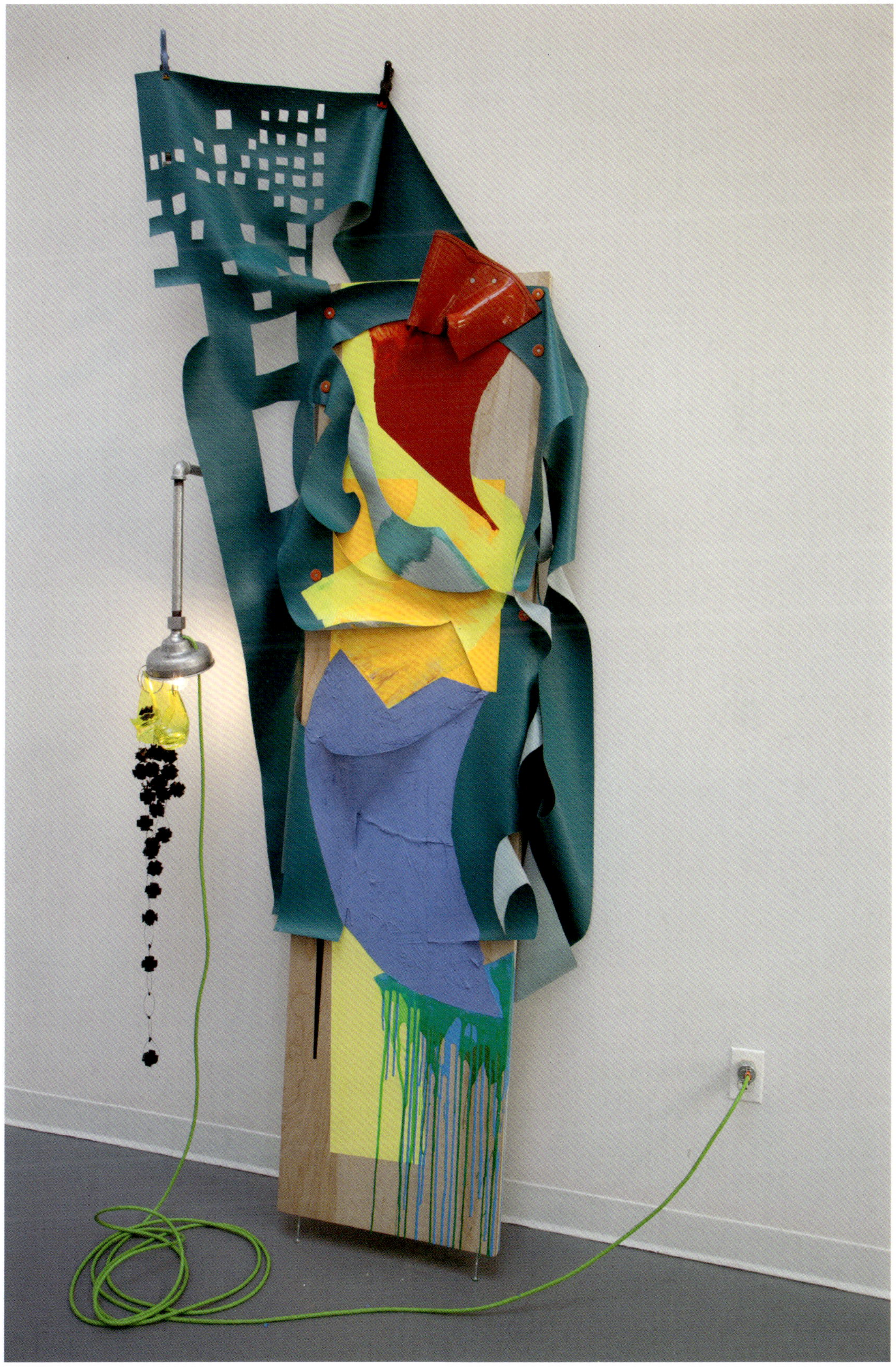

BOOT WEAVING, 2014
CUT VINYL, HOLLOW CORE DOOR, ACRYLIC PAINT, HARDWARE, BOOT RUBBER, HARDWARE, LED LIGHT AND FIXTURE, YELLOW PLASTIC CUPS, GREEN EXTENSION CORD, BLUE PLASTIC CLAMP, BLACK PLASTIC CLAMP
102 X 36 X 1.2 CM

BRIGHT LONGING AND SOGGY UP THE HILL, 2005
GREENHOUSES, THEATRE LIGHT, WOODEN RAMP, CORK, LINOLEUM, PAINT, CARPET

INSTALLATION VIEW AT KUNSTHALLEN BRANDTS, ODENSE, DENMARK, 2005

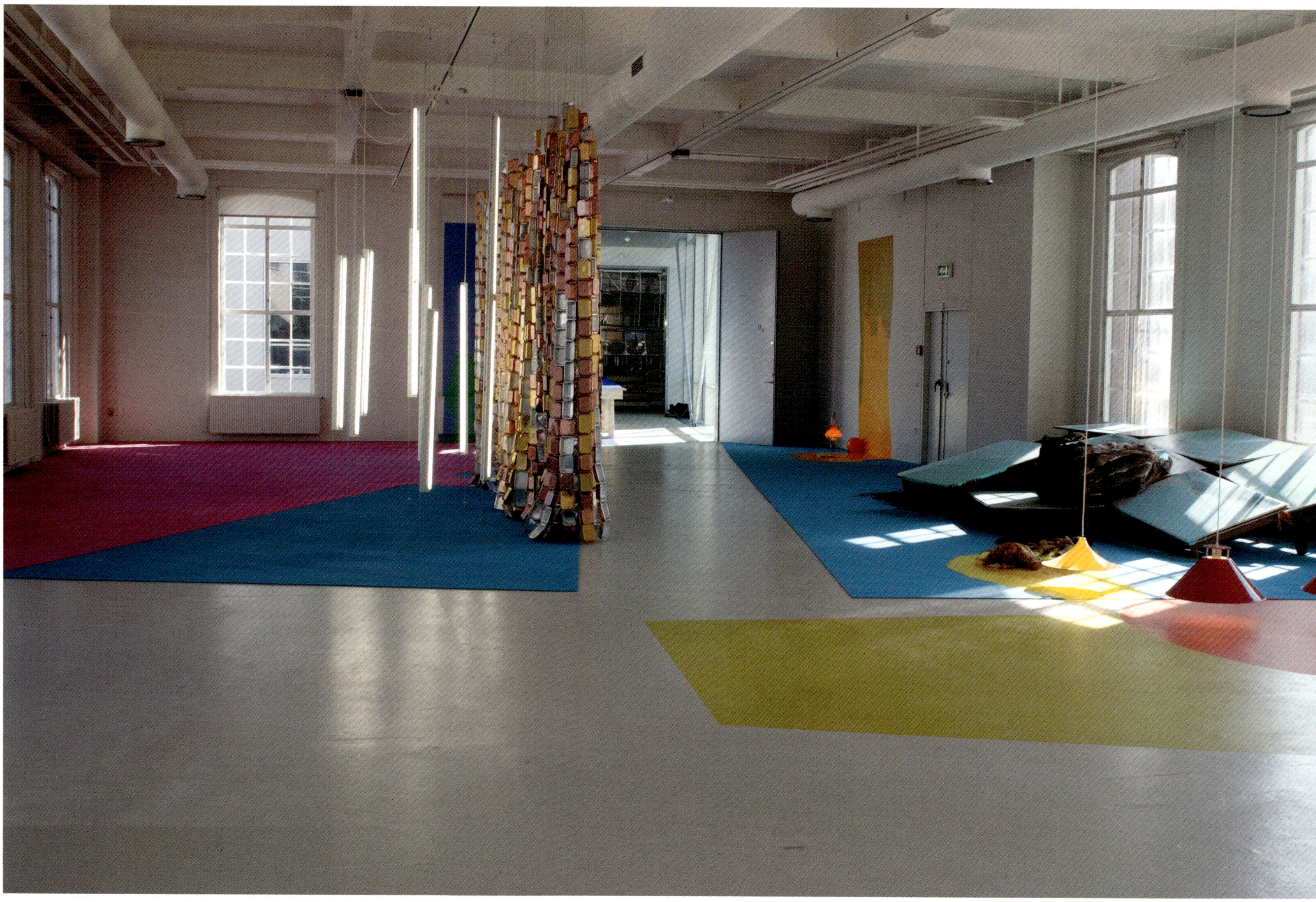

BRIGHT LONGING AND SOGGY UP THE HILL, 2005
GREENHOUSES, THEATRE LIGHT, WOODEN RAMP, CORK, LINOLEUM, PAINT, CARPET

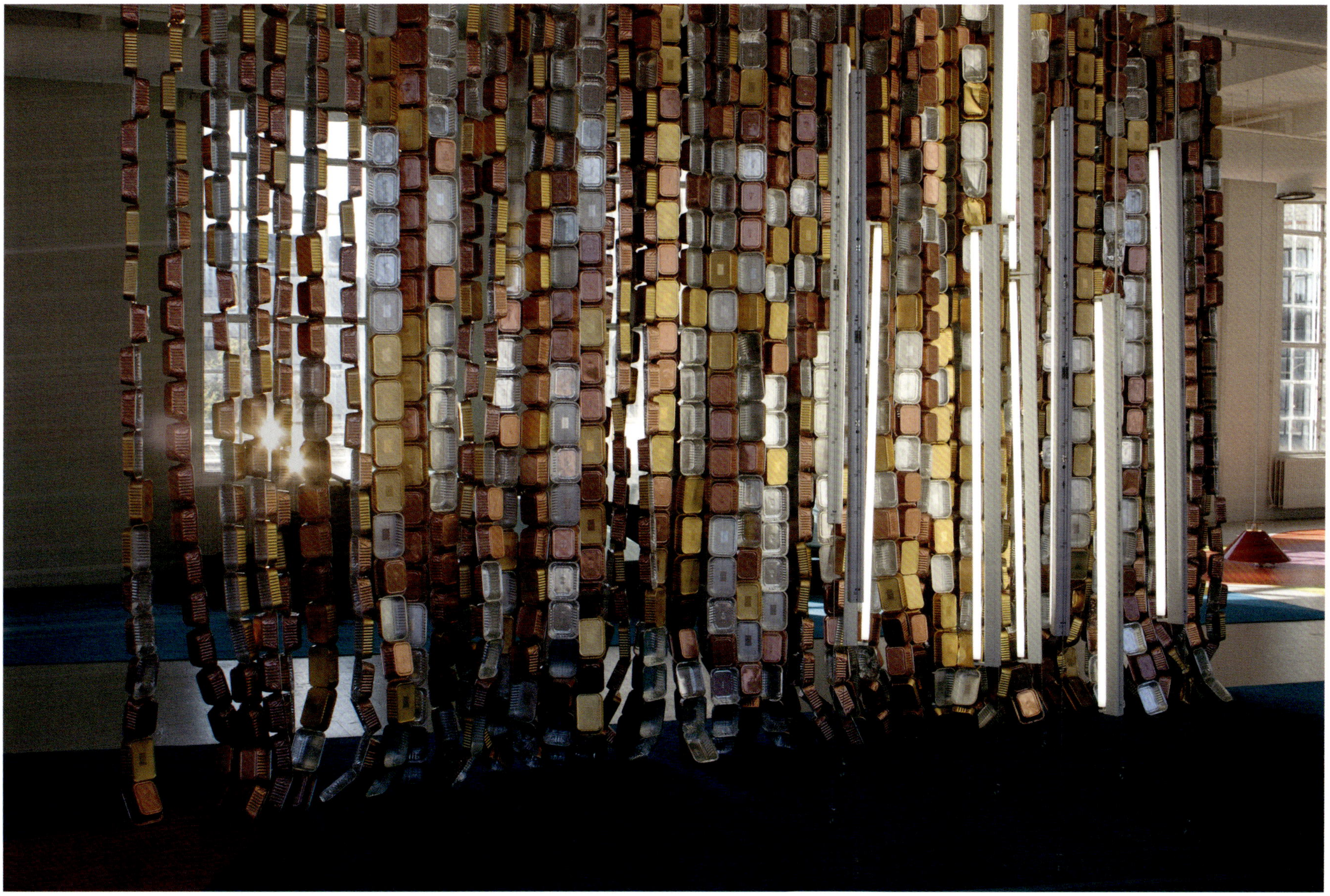

Sam Ran Over Sand or Sand Ran Over Sam: Rethinking Character, 2004

Materials and form have character and or give rise to character. This text aims to give voice to how and what might be a character in this work and what parts might be played by the various actors. The action takes place as the senses of the body meet the constructs of the mind.

The Cast of Characters

Three shadows wait to be. They wait for Sam to stand on three different occasions just there, in the future, out of sand. Three figures eclipsed; lost to the lights and slipped between the pages – the covers of a bed. They act – standing still on the stage. The event moves down the path, Life's middle road, the yellow brick road; mark-making as they go, teetering between artifice and good will.

Those three bend down, whispering to the lake flowing underground – their noses pressed to the floor – pressed some more – the nostrils squeezed tight so nothing can ooze. Backs bend, awkwardly. No robes flowing – no fabrics blowing in the wind. It is quiet.

The pots and pans clatter in the background. *The ongoing nature of daily life* in this case is sidelined. The stopped hush of snow falling is centred in the gallery. Projections – pictures – in the mind's eye and in the eye are patched together onto the wall and felt through a tunnel and in an empty space. They are in the middle of a page. The wind blows the leaves around their feet. Purple slime slips over their backs. Their noses are runny.

That eccentric branch at the door! Unsettled in isolation beckoning to the intruder with warm and enthusiastic invitation. So in love! Some wind slipping through the door and the energy and envy of the air moving is also a protagonist in the midst of the still staged artifice. The plateau of colours is still and yet more gushing, twisted and upsettingly alive than the plants at the door were last year. Here is a big heap of static event piled up like shards of broken plastic buckets.

The icebox is full of love metred out over time. Metring is a kind of control. Control is necessary to living, in concert with passion, breaking the bounds of predictability and ordered knowing. The cold of winter slows life processes. The cold of the icebox mimics winter. The cold of the gallery/white cube, like the icebox, is full of love and control.

Building – the verb and the noun – in all of its life process is a character in the event here orchestrated. The stuff – carpet, stone, hardware, wood, couch, freezer, lamps, cloths, shoes, and sheetrock – is in process as is the food cycling through our tubes – making passage.

Slow dancing mingles with the tinsel, the flashing lights of Christmas, the dance floor, and the cars on the highway at night passing through downtown. The dirt under the building is alive with worms, beetles, and mold. Being kept safe, but the surfaces are too clean and the walls have too much flex in them.
Plastic is so beautiful and so frightening.
The shiny thinness of experience.
Making holes in the veneer of the hard clear surface.

The line between two colours charged! It's impossible to separate one from the other, impossible to take that impossible place away and put it somewhere else. Try to put feet there. Dive into that place that is not there and point. Finger stretched out long and pointing like . . . and to the beach shore – the inter-tidal zone.

Carpet always stampes his feet – hard like there is mud on them. He doesn't like sand between his toes. She brushes her hair often. And she worries about the colour fading.

Green waterproof drywall rigidly embarks on a sea journey of mammoth proportions. The green sea seems to go on forever in all directions until you step back and see the edges. The size of experience changes so drastically! He is a little dry but then she likes to swim.

Wires with electricity mess up together with the air and dust specks and balls carried on breezes through coloured air.

Coloured air is thick and interrupted by body parts, bone, flesh, and blood flowing along channels. Channels, like the eye's point of view, flow through space and come into focus at the end, on the wall. Projected pictures overlay the rough and tumble of the current in all directions.

The Characters are orchestrated for the eye – riding on wheels – legs flapping in the wind. The eye screeches – along in the grooves laid out for it. like a train on its track. Meanwhile, experience and oceans of colour inform the action, figures, belly, dancing, and knitting.

Back to the wall, body and wall are screen; eyes painstakingly turned around character plots of stuff. The light tunnels weave together two kinds of mapping that lie side by side: the darting map the eye manufactures and the map of being as the body learns it.

The plot thickens.

SAM RAN OVER SAND OR SAND RAN OVER SAM, RICE GALLERY, HOUSTON, 2004

<u>SAM RAN OVER SAND OR SAND RAN OVER SAM</u>, 2004
CARPET, GREEN WATERPROOF SHEET ROCK, THEATRE LIGHTS, YELLOW AND WHITE ELECTRICAL CORDS, FURNITURE, LAMPS, STRYROFOAM, LUMBER, FREEZER, DIGITAL PROJECTOR, ACRYLIC PAINT, COOLERS, CHICKEN WIRE

INSTALLATION VIEW AT RICE UNIVERSITY GALLERY, HOUSTON, 2004

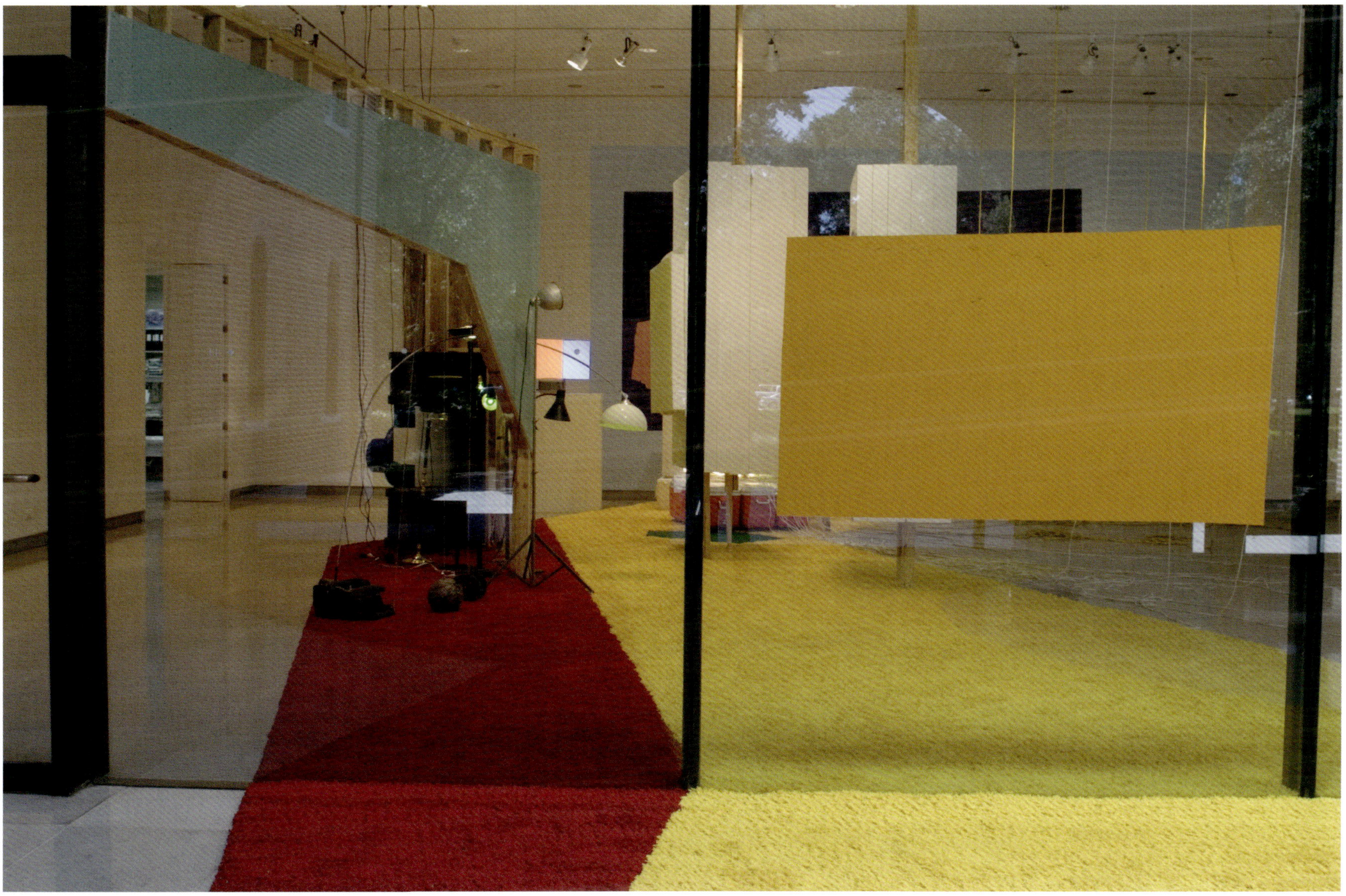

SAM RAN OVER SAND OR SAND RAN OVER SAM, 2004
CARPET, GREEN WATERPROOF SHEET ROCK, THEATRE LIGHTS, YELLOW AND WHITE ELECTRICAL CORDS, FURNITURE, LAMPS, STRYROFOAM, LUMBER, FREEZER, DIGITAL PROJECTOR, ACRYLIC PAINT, COOLERS, CHICKEN WIRE

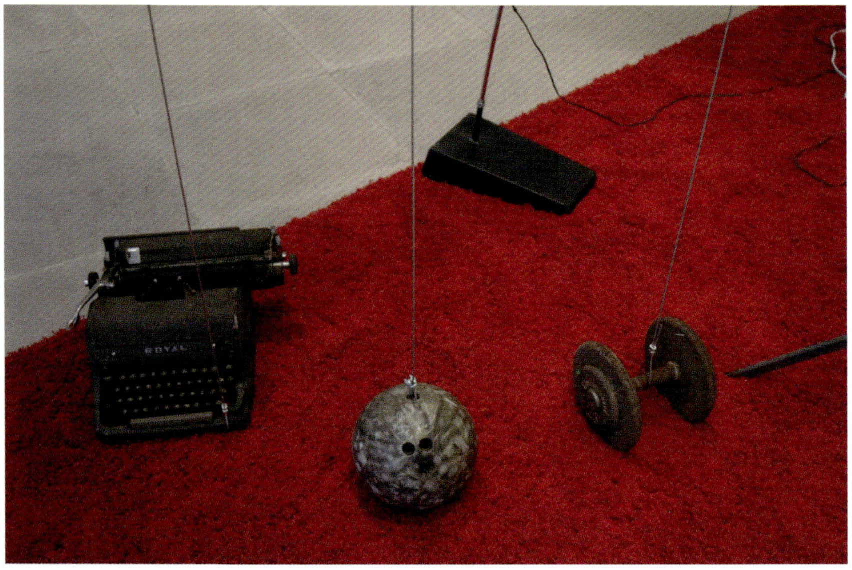

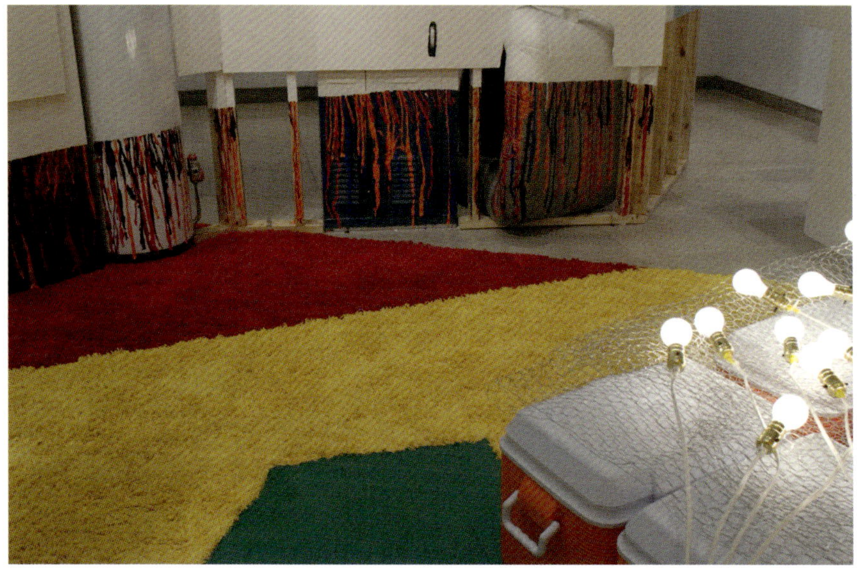

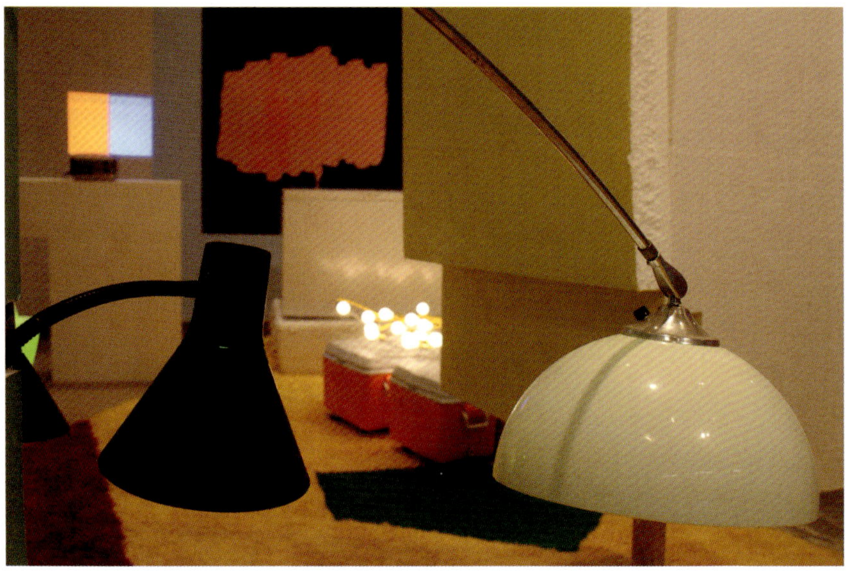

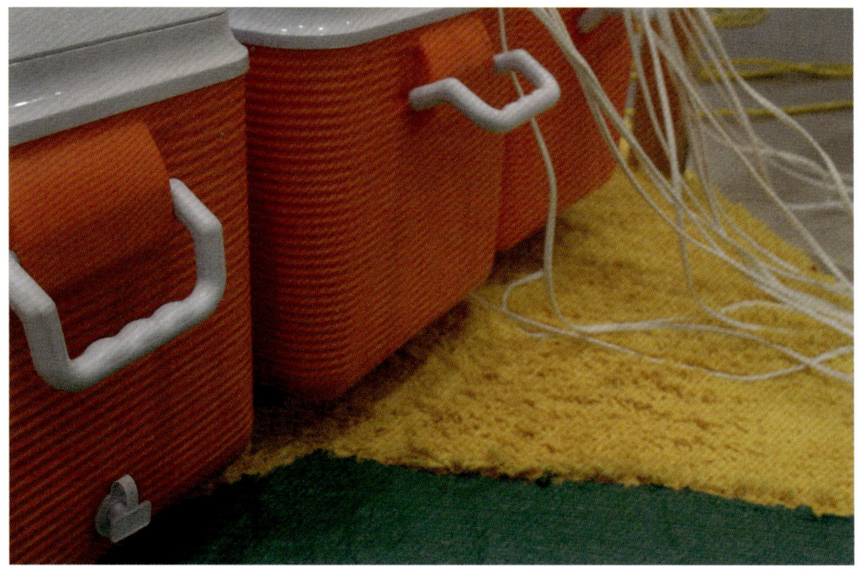

SAM RAN OVER SAND OR SAND RAN OVER SAM, 2004
CARPET, GREEN WATERPROOF SHEET ROCK, THEATRE LIGHTS, YELLOW AND WHITE ELECTRICAL CORDS, FURNITURE, LAMPS, STRYROFOAM, LUMBER, FREEZER, DIGITAL PROJECTOR, ACRYLIC PAINT, COOLERS, CHICKEN WIRE

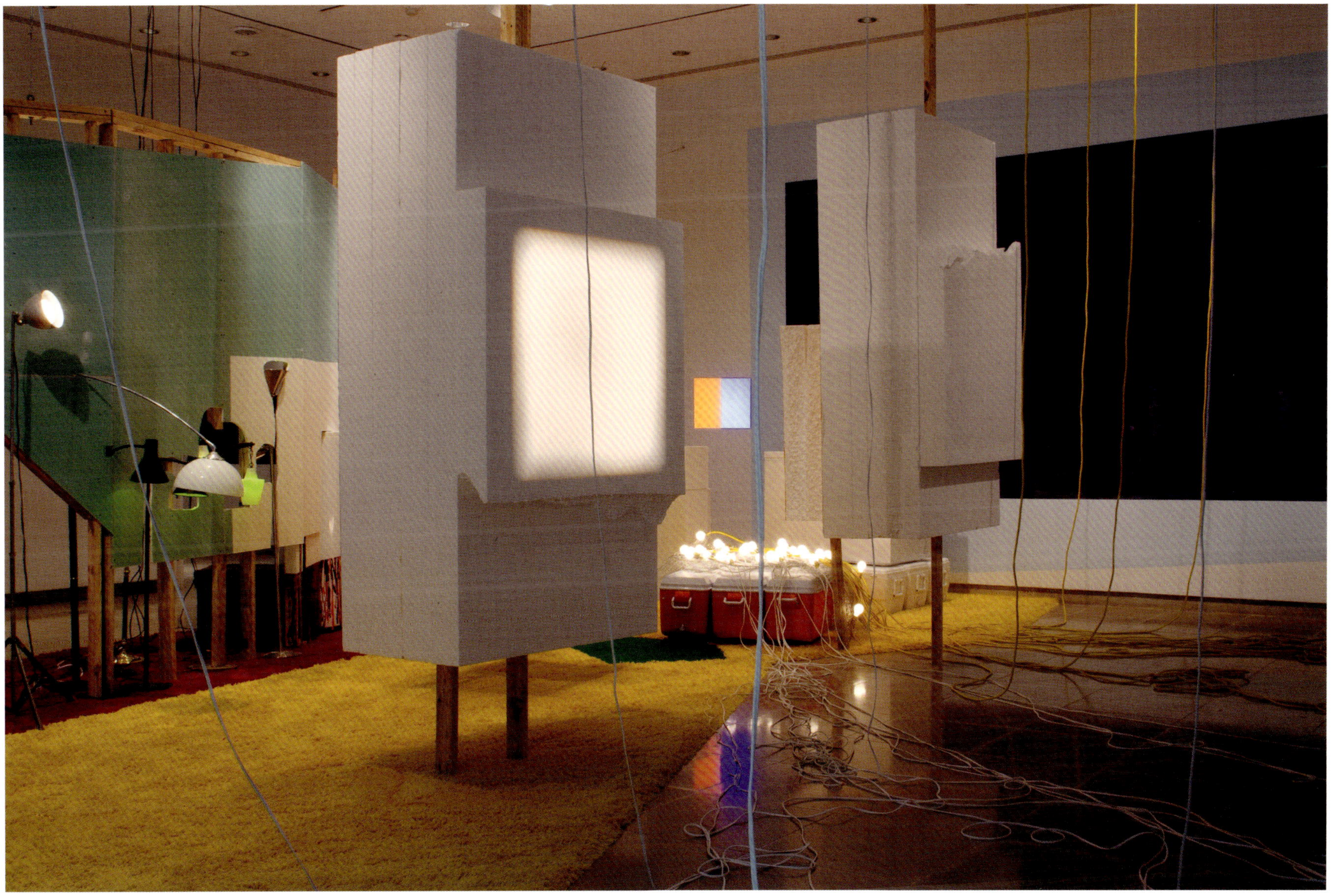

Powerful Art and Power, 2006

<u>OF STANDING FLOAT ROOTS IN THIN AIR</u>, 2006
PLASTIC BINS, ELECTRIC CORDS, FLUORESCENT LIGHTS, ONE INCANDESCENT LIGHT, ARM CHAIR, PLYWOOD AND 2X4S PLATFORM, PLYWOOD, FAKE FUR, ACRYLIC PAINT

INSTALLATION VIEW AT P.S.1 CONTEMPORARY ART CENTER, LONG ISLAND, NEW YORK, 2006

What follows is a meandering through some clouds of thought exploring how art can be understood as powerful, and how power can be the subject of art. I hope to open up some room for discussion and to be provocative.

Some of the more interesting contemporary art criticism has grown from Marxist thought where attempts to articulate art's meaning tie it to a discussion of production, economy, and sociopolitical power structure. Though this line of thinking is compelling, and strikes to the core of something essential to art making, it was also a shadow that I grew up under. It assumes that art's value lies in its challenge to the establishment, and that in this effort art is always co-opted by the reigning political and economic powers. This was, and is, a very glum vision of art's function placing it in a position of constant failure.

Raised as a red diaper baby my eyes are wide open to the serious flaws inherent in our capitalist structure. Our health, personal, economic and political, depends on maintaining room for the expression of dissension and eccentricity. I value the role that art plays creating friction, agitating, questioning and challenging the systems we live with. But, while it is true that art is always in the end complicit with the various powers that support its infrastructure, and that this complicity is part and parcel of it's meaning, I don't believe that it therefore fails. Good art has power before and after it is co-opted – both as a current lived activity and as history to be looked back at.

As so much art criticism has been tightly wrapped up with this Marxist view, it has become taboo to express desire for, intense interest in, and pleasure in power and its complex social expression. Power understood as 'bad'. is commonly assumed to be in the hands of the patrons and administrators of the art world, many of whom love and nurture what we as artists do. I am sure it is possible to find more complex ways to discuss the success and failure of art objects.

In addition to being ascribed to the different sides in an argument, or to opposing poles of political and economic controversy power is pervasive and essential to living. One has to execute power to stay alive and creative endeavors flow from that necessity.

All of the hustle and bustle, theatre, posturing, reporting, frenzied buying, socializing, and general exuberance attending art is testament to its dynamic and ever changing functioning!

In addition to unseating the powers that be in order to make successful art, it has also often been described as necessary for each artist to unseat his or her historical precedents. The narrative of art history describes success in terms of opposition and rejection. This way of valuing success is ironically in line with capitalist economy that demands constant change and newness. If we were to more highly value today's art, at this moment, as a vital part of the present, it might be possible to generate a richer dialogue around our relation to history.

I am speaking from a position of power. Teaching at Yale and having garnered some success, both I, and my work, are part and parcel of a power structure. It would not be difficult to dismiss my arguments for more space in the dialogue as a self-serving effort to make sense of my own place in the edifice. But my involvement in the convoluted, twisting and turning manifestations of the myriad different interests and powers that meet in and are represented here in the art world, in addition to raising questions and ire, is also fertile, invigorating, and constantly challenging.

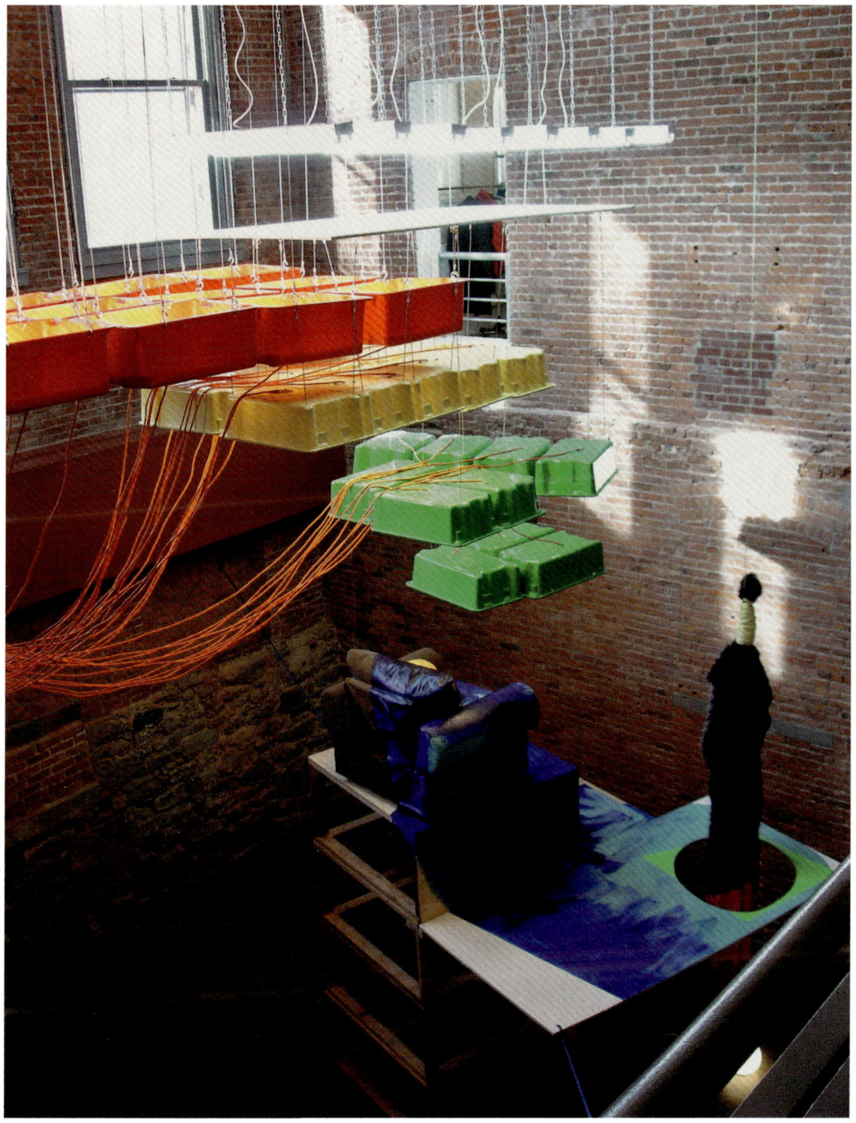

In my own work I provide circumstances for powerful private experience and for spectacle. I am obsessed with how the self alone, and the self understood as part of a group bump up against each other; and how both experiences of self can be empowering. At different moments my work can impress one with the power of the maker, the power of the institution exhibiting the work, or the power of the collective of viewers that contribute meaning to the event of exhibition.

That visual art often engenders pleasure is significant. I am sure that understanding the sources of, and reasons for pleasure are linked to power, and I am happy to revel in exploring how this might be so. I have found Dave Hicky and Carol Gilligan very useful as points of reference here.

I work with many students who as a result of their wish to be critical of, or unaligned with, the various power structures that support the art world make work that is itself without visual, formal or affective power. This seems a little painful to me though I can empathize. And I watch others who having discovered buttons for creating spectacle make work that is lapped up so quickly by the powers that grease the machine that they seem to be swept off their feet. The present intensity of focus on graduate student work can make it challenging to hold onto rich and varied expressions of value and power.

Power, itself neither good nor bad, can be used to various ends. It is not necessarily distributed fairly and it is not always earned. Perhaps given our democratic ideals and mythology it is difficult for us to tolerate the inequities inherent in the distribution of power, and it is consequently taboo to meander through the thicket of desire meeting power.

Nevertheless, that art objects can engender deep experience and affect, and are perhaps even effective in the world must have something to do with how they tap into the complexity of power relations of all sorts.

That we like artworks to have power over us and that it feels good to be overcome might be related to religious experience or to twelve step programs that urge us to accept and take comfort in our relative powerlessness. Some art insists that there is a greater power. And some insists that we have power over our circumstances.

The question of gender relations is laced with questions of power. It is relatively uncomplicated to assert that men and women make art; and many of us can agree that there are power inequities between men and women. The relative difference in the success of men and women in the art world is both an unfortunate fact and the subject of much art. It is more complicated to try and understand any single individuals relationship to these facts, and how we are all party to this power inequity. It is also important to say that there are, and have been, many powerful women, and that there are many women who make great and powerful art.

I would like to put my foot in it and explore this question a little in terms of form – I pose two sets of formal qualities:
The first: stiff, upright, hard, industrial, geometric and big.
The second: soft, round, flexible, organic, earth bound, and small.

It is easy to tie the first set of qualities to men and the second to women. That said, it is patently absurd to fix the meaning of any form to either gender. Efforts in this direction quickly disintegrate. There are, however, undeniable strands of meaning that weave through these facts of our experience. Our shared forms of communication, physical, visual, and verbal, use metaphor and grow from

OF STANDING FLOAT ROOTS IN THIN AIR, 2006
PLASTIC BINS, ELECTRIC CORDS, FLUORESCENT LIGHTS, ONE INCANDESCENT LIGHT, ARM CHAIR, PLYWOOD AND 2X4S PLATFORM, PLYWOOD, FAKE FUR, ACRYLIC PAINT

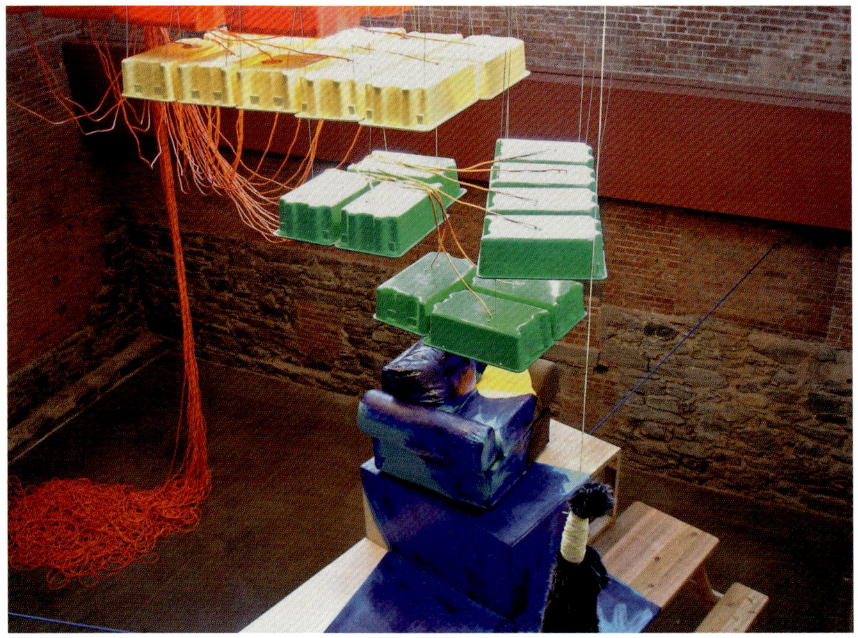

the facts of our bodies. How these forms are assigned status and power socially, economically, and politically is something that is constantly reinvented alongside life's givens. Art and design are party to this invention.

And there is the fact of war during which physical power is asserted over others and power is attained through force and subjugation. And economic power is achieved through increased means. Social power is informed by these physical realities but also by style, attitude, psychological maneuvering, knowledge, wisdom, and perhaps enlightenment. Art objects are situated within a power structure informed by all of this.

And power can arise from passivity (Ghandi) and the exposure of vulnerability. I'm thinking of Vito Acconci's work where he is both vulnerable and aggressive, waving a stick at his audience blindfolded. Masturbating under a floor, exposing his desire and his shame. And Lynda Benglis's work exposing its weakness in the face of gravity. And perhaps the work of Mary Heilmann whose geometry has 'expression' and 'character' having given up some of its hardness. And Hannah Wilkie, who presents her personal and mortal vulnerability up for our consideration.

Success accrues power to the successful. Most of us want our work and our persons to be successful. Money is power and most of us want and need money. How artworks are understood within the money economy intersects all these questions of power and presents an opportunity. As artists selling our works to people or institutions with money, we are at their service. We are in some respects in their power. On the other hand, we invent and decide what it is that we want to make and present the world with objects , ideas, and perhaps ideals to desire.

Information is power. How stories are told, how the facts of the world are represented with images support and help to uphold power structures. Map-making and history are often discussed from this point of view. Wallid Raad stirs this particular pot.

In order for our work to be part of the larger culture, for it to have an audience, it has to be inserted into existing power structures one way or another. The infrastructure of galleries, museums, and patrons, are powerful as is the work that we make.

I would like to end by asking: How do you understand and value power in art? What do you want from your work in terms of power? And, how do you negotiate the insertion of your work into existing structures of power?

ORIGINALLY PROPOSED FOR A PANEL AT YALE UNIVERSITY, NEW HEAVEN, 2006

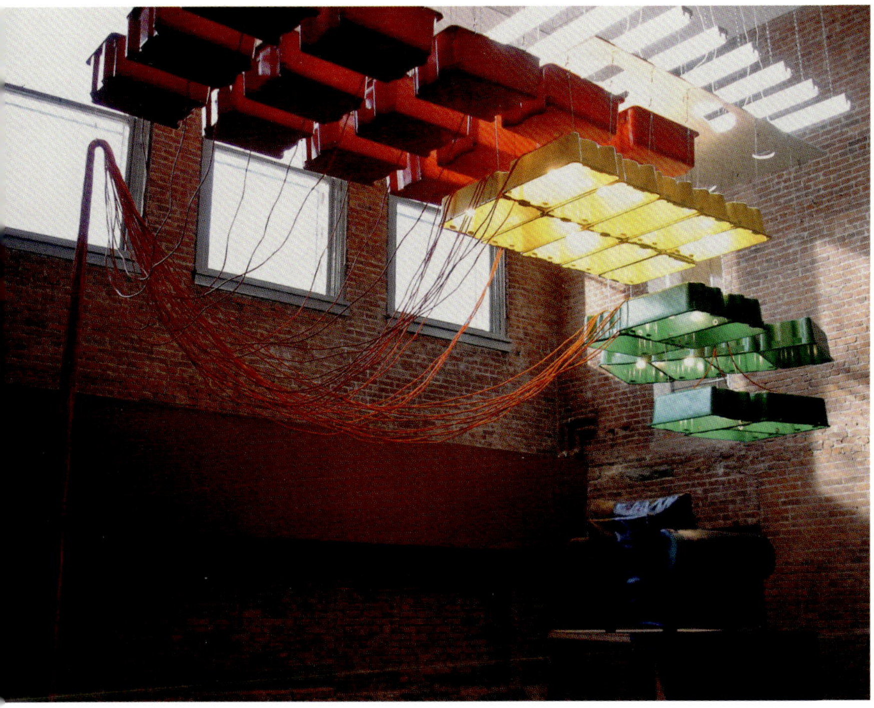

OF STANDING FLOAT ROOTS IN THIN AIR, 2006
PLASTIC BINS, ELECTRIC CORDS, FLUORESCENT LIGHTS, ONE INCANDESCENT LIGHT, ARM CHAIR, PLYWOOD AND 2X4S PLATFORM, PLYWOOD, FAKE FUR, ACRYLIC PAINT

OF STANDING FLOAT ROOTS IN THIN AIR, 2006
PLASTIC BINS, ELECTRIC CORDS, FLUORESCENT LIGHTS, ONE INCANDESCENT LIGHT, ARM CHAIR, PLYWOOD AND 2X4S PLATFORM, PLYWOOD, FAKE FUR, ACRYLIC PAINT

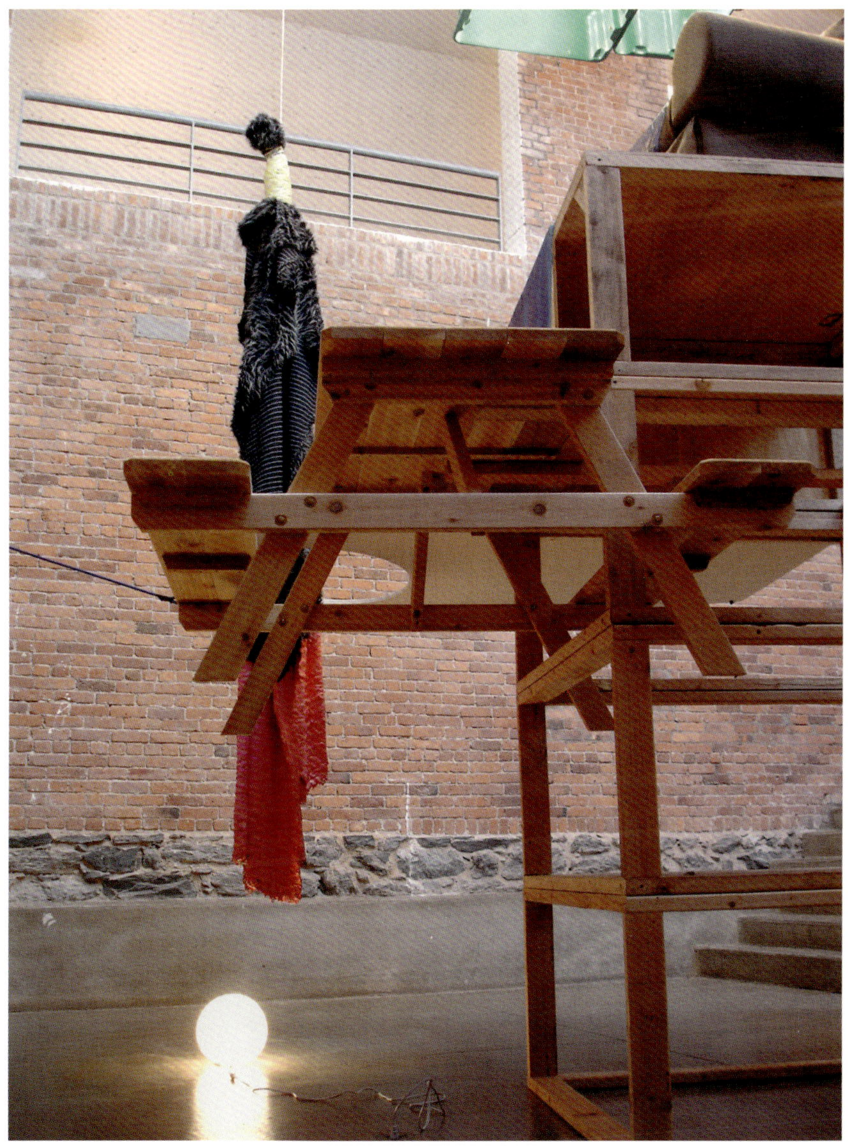

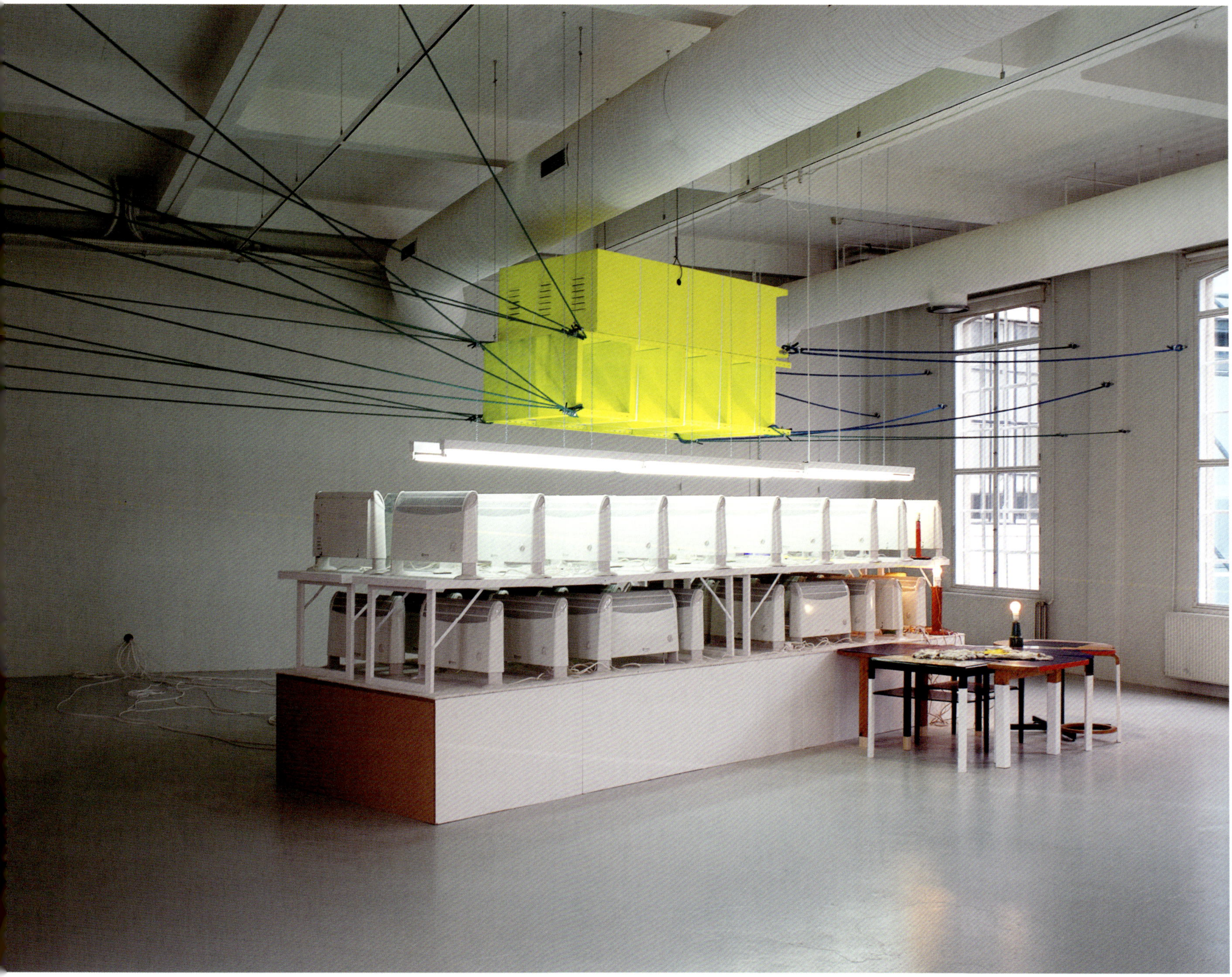

previous page,
WHITE LIGHT LAID FROZEN, 2005
METAL CABINETS, ROPE, ELECTRIC HEATERS, WOODEN PEDESTAL, WOODEN PAINTERS TABLES, SMALL PUZZLE OF TABLES, OIL PAINT, FUR, FLUORESCENT LIGHT FIXTURES
INSTALLATION HEIGHT 10 X 10 M

INSTALLATION VIEW AT KUNSTHALLEN BRANDTS, ODENSE, DENMARK, 2005

BLACK AND BLUE, 2007
BLUE PLASTIC SLED, BLACK HAND TRUCK, WOODEN LAMP BASE
264 X 218 X 193 CM

INSTALLATION VIEW AT GALERIE NACHST ST. STEPHAN ROSEMARIE SCHWARZWALDER, 2007

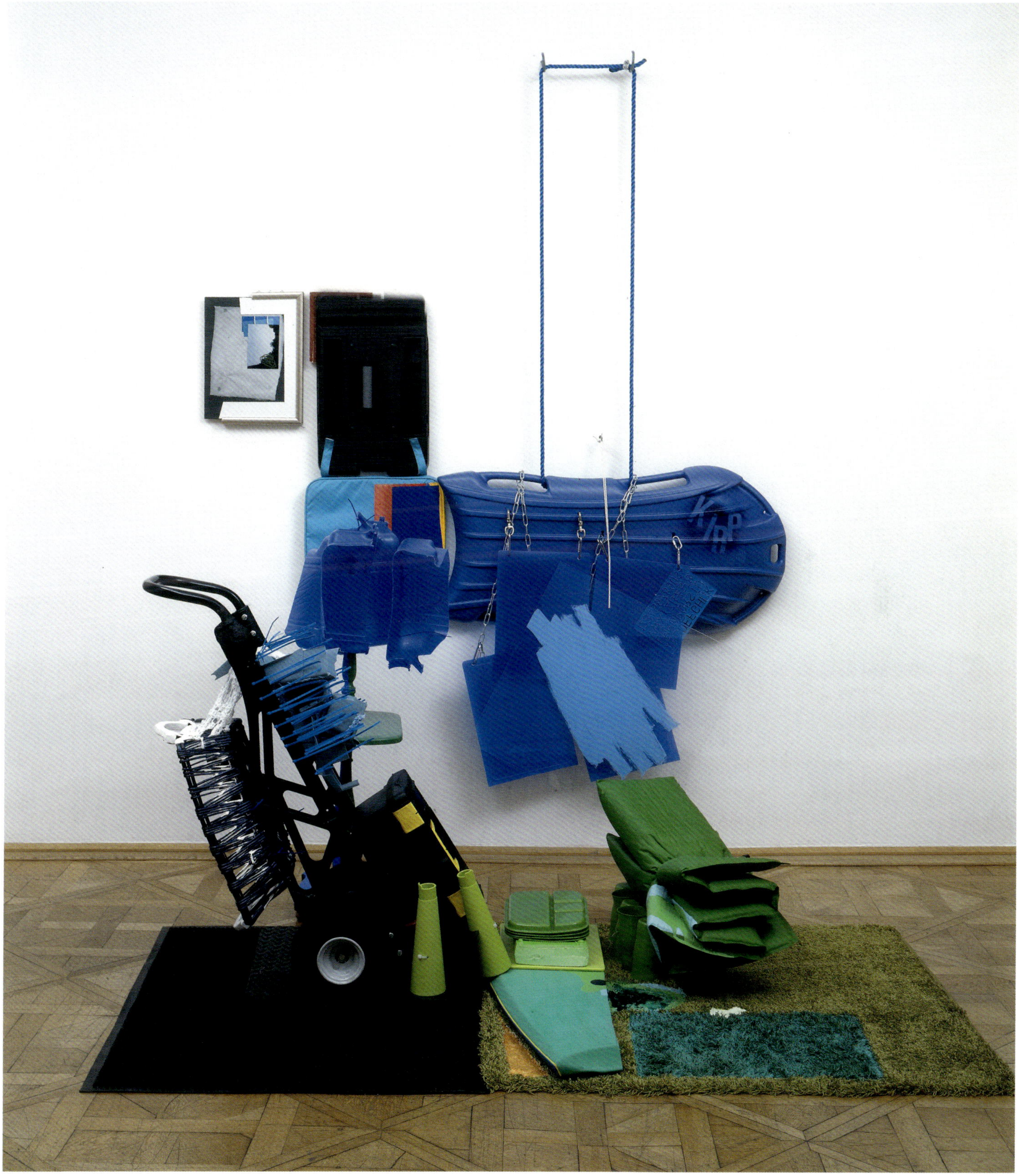

Swiss Cheese Field – And Sculpture Mingled, 2009

SWISS CHEESE FIELD 2, 2009
MONOPRINT WITH COLLAGE, FAKE FUR, SILKSCREEN, LASER CUTTING, MELTED STYROFOAM AND WOOD ENGRAVING WITH EMBOSSMENT
168 X 91 X 5 CM

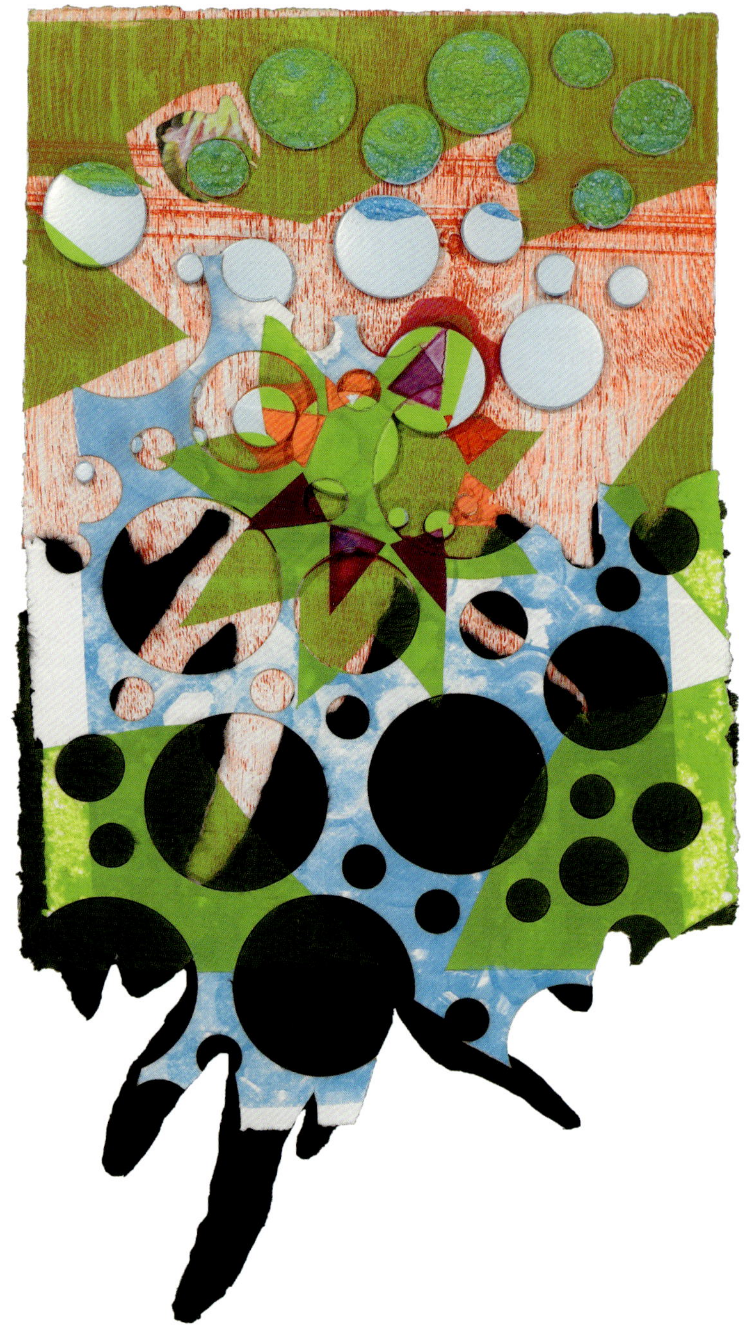

What is the field, and *what is* sculpture?

Rosalind Krauss invented the term *field* in an effort to articulate the wavering outline of sculpture that developed in the wake of Constantin Brancusi's pedestals, themselves objects running off into their locations, even while they served to delineate a line between the object they held aloft apart from the space around them.[1] The minimal works that Krauss points to in her essay – those of Mary Miss, Robert Morris, Bruce Nauman, and Richard Serra – demand that we create a new level of abstraction in our minds in order to understand such works as separate from their locations; at the same time, the term *field* has contributed to an increased appreciation for the particularity of viewing the intersection of each artwork with its place.

I do not know who invented the word *sculpture*. The word has become increasingly difficult to define, and there are now many other words being applied to the activity of filling up the field – *performance, installation, sound works, conceptual gestures.* I would like to hang on to that word *sculpture* and enjoy its expanded definition. The words we use in its place are no more meaningful.

The expanding field is both large and small. It can be engaged from the sky, from the edge with one's toe just touching, or from within the tumult of the game taking place on freshly mowed turf. The field is a net, a blanket, and a jungle of tall overgrown grasses. The field is used to put things (sculpture) in. It is used to describe the picture plane (Color Field painting). It is used as a backdrop, or as a stage for things we make that have no other place to be. It is used as backdrop or stage for actions that need to be bracketed from the flow of life (performance). And it is used as an abstract idea that we share in order to, in mind only, bracket particular moments of life that would otherwise be lost, unremarked upon, in the flow of life.

All of these quite diverse endeavors sitting under the art umbrella, share, as a point of departure, an effort to articulate some particularity that is the result of subjective observation or noticing. This noticing includes observation of the visual, or of how our eyes observe; observation of modes of production and economy, or of conflicts of interest inherent in the economic support structures of exhibition spaces; observation of events; and observation of how viewers absorb art.

Sculpture is not the field, but it does not exist without the field. Sometimes the sculpture sits in the field, and we gaze at the sculpture. Sometimes sculpture sits on a pedestal in the field. Sometimes the pedestal is organized so that its job as mediator between the sculpture and the field is what is at issue. At other times, the sculpture's *raison d'être* is to point at the field.

We need the field – an idea, a convention, an abstract place – where we *collectively carve out* and explore the intersection of the real with the symbolic, between the flow of life and the narrative of fiction. It is a place primed for our projection, a place that serves to reify the structures of our experience. The field is actual space in which we look at and walk around sculptures, and the field is a metaphoric description of the space, in mind and psyche, where the fictive dramas and emotive collages of our being must intersect our capacities and mechanisms for perceiving both the actual time and space and the shared fabrication we exist in.

SWISS CHEESE FIELD 14, 2009
MONOPRINT WITH COLLAGE, FAKE FUR, SILKSCREEN, LASER CUTTING, MELTED STYROFOAM AND WOOD ENGRAVING WITH EMBOSSMENT
175 X 91 CM

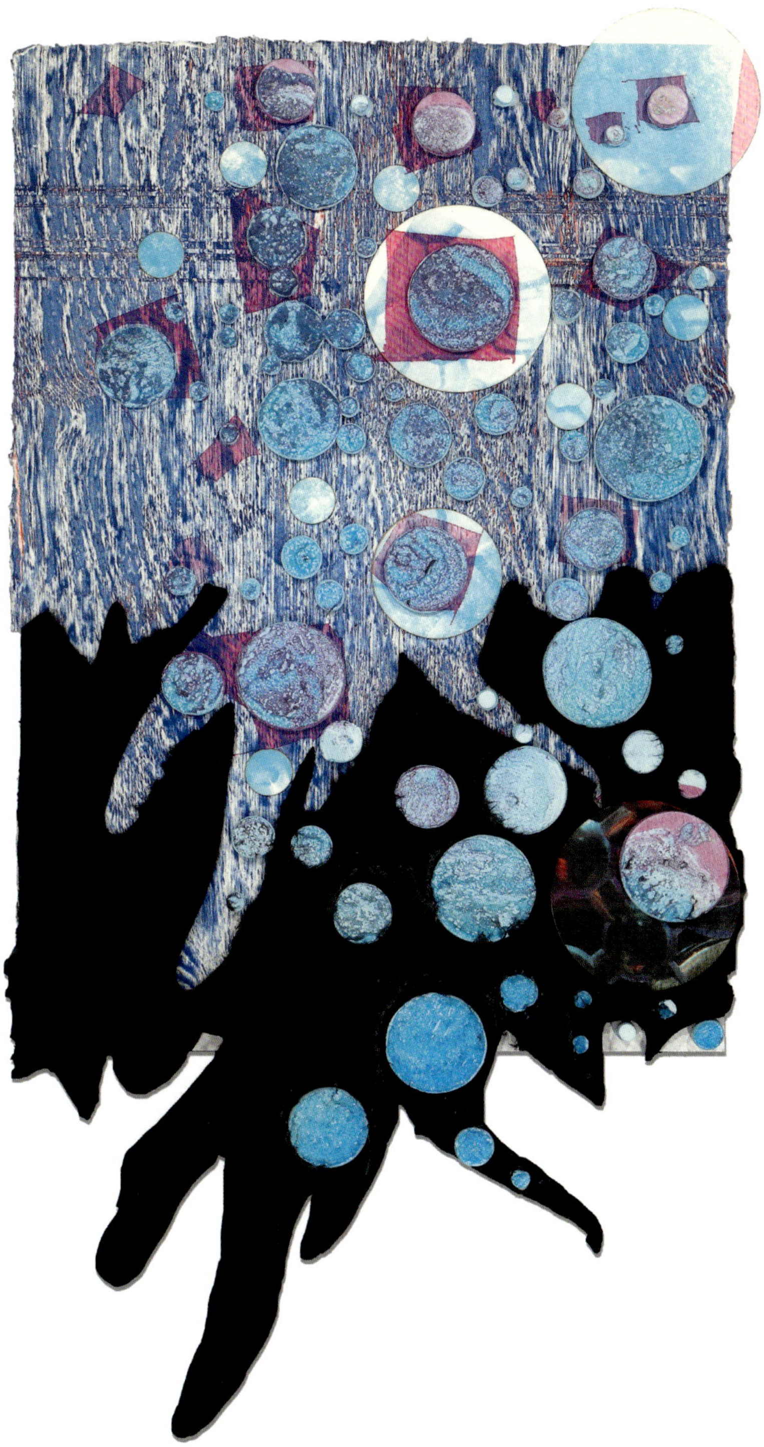

We make sense of this field differently, all of us, from different points of view in our different *fields* of study.

The field is not the frame. The frame, as it functions for painting and photography, superbly negotiates the relationship between the physicality of those images and the rest of the world they participate in. The frame establishes a dike that has been holding for centuries against the force of real life flowing on the other side. Both of these media, however, housed securely inside of their frames, do brush up against the flow of life, each in its own way. Photographs catch light and record events in the lives of real people. And the skin of the painting can be understood to be fluid with the skin of the wall in the real room of the buildings we stand in. The intensity of meaning in Color Field painting derives from its brush with the reality of the wall that its skin of illusion bleeds into. This brush with the flow of time and life in both painting and photography is, however, quite contained. The frame has persisted in its function as a compelling and firm bracket in contrast to the gaping holes that have been carefully honed in the conventions that bracket sculpture.

The range of what we can imagine on the field has expanded in response to what we know from physics, DNA studies, and chemistry. Our experience of time and space, two essential components of sculpture, has been altered as microwave ovens and cell phones have entered our lives and as entire movies fly through the air to our TV screens and into our living rooms. The space of the Internet – a very real space in our lives – nevertheless exists only as metaphor.

The white cube exhibition space and the field, full of not-architecture and notlandscape, have created a very exciting playing field with ever-shifting and permeable boundaries. Much of the gaming that takes place here includes the lassoing of small parts of life's flow to posit next to or as part of art. Perhaps religious ritual, football games, playing board games, and displaying good manners at the dinner table do this, too.

The word *sculpture,* now as difficult to define as the undulating field it sits in, encompasses carved lumps of wood and stone, plaster and poured bronze, any material one can think of perched on a pedestal or set within the white cube or field.

We can add to that any gesture that manipulates the space, mass, volume, void, or solids within the white cube and the field. The word *material* can include light waves, temperature, and sound waves. Johanna Burton describes this elaborated version of sculpture as 'Installation'. She defines *installation* as a 'work that creates a kind of triadic skin between itself, its viewers, and the space or place in which it . . . situates itself'.[2] I find the word *installation* now to be as loosely defined as the word *sculpture,* so instead of using the word *installation,* I prefer to use the term *sculpture,* and I prefer to think about the entire range of activities taking place within the field as sculpture. Those art objects concerned with picture making on a flat surface surrounded by a rectangular frame are something different, though they, too, exist in the field.

The pedestal sitting on the same floor we walk on, in the same space our bodies move through, provides a space above, elevated from the floor, that is proposed as separate from the flow of life. This space has not proved to be as charged and enduring as the space inside of the frame on the wall. Perhaps this has something to do with the relative levels of abstraction enabled by the two conventions. The framed space on the wall addresses the eyes that move separate from the body. The static image addressed by the eyes moves into the static 'space' of the mind where we imagine the experience separated from the flow of time. The space on top of the pedestal, however, requires the movement of the body through space, circling around the pedestal, in time to apprehend. The time taken to make the experience whole remains insistent as the memory or knowledge of the object takes shape 'in mind'.

Sculpture presents a series of images over time in space. Unlike film, we the viewers are left to choose sequencing and duration. The agency that is given to us in this process is not possible to document visually.

Though much is made of the difference between representational art and abstract art, I propose that it is the abstraction inherent in all art that makes it useful and powerful. Art posits form to describe something particular even as it is generalized in order to transcend the experience of an individual to be shared by many. Our ability to create whole abstract structures is the foundation of our capacity to think and to speak. The abstract nature of art enables it to share visions, thoughts, fantasies, and feelings over time and space. Any single artwork functions quite differently in this regard; some works reach farther over time and space, even transcending particular cultures, while others exist for only very small groups of people in particular moments.

Our capacity for abstraction is core to the internal workings of any single artwork and to the various shifting conventions, frame, pedestal, field, and white cube that outline each work. The structures of thought, of buildings, of language, of monument, of social interaction, of composition on picture planes, of the body, determine what the world is for us. We are not Spock of *Star Trek*'s USS Enterprise; our internal lives are large and volumetric, swimming with various levels of viscous emotions, dry strings of information housed in scientific method, time lines of our own life span, time lines abstract play with physical material, mirrors our sense of our thoughts as abstractions occurring in the space of our hearts and minds. Perhaps Melanie Klein's and Jacques Lacan's impulse to use diagrams to describe human subjective experience in the space of mind is convincing because it, too, uses physical tangibility or the diagram to mirror our subjectivity back to us.

The permeability of the field we have invented in some ways parallels the abstract space inside of the head of our physical body. We need that abstract space in our heads – our minds. The abstract structures we build posit a reality that is firmer than our swimming internal lives. The abstract structures we invent transcend the moment. The inventions of the frame, the pedestal, and the field create circumstances where we can make things that mirror this duality of our being back to us. A place is created where our realtime bound bodies can over time build virtual and physical abstractions that transcend our life span. Art achieves this mirroring by tending to the line between the thing made and the flow of the world it is made in.

Krauss, in her description of the site/nonsite polarity, describes an evolution of our capacity for abstraction. She writes that the loss of site produces 'the monument as abstraction'.[3] She seems to understand the of history, our crashing and banging desires, wishes, and creation stories. We need the playing field of art to gather the intelligence of this complexity of our beings and bring it to bear on life. The invention of the field to represent the abstract place our artworks occupy parallels the use of the figure in art. The figurative sculpture provides a site for us to imagine our own subjectivity mirrored back to us. The notion of a field, as the container for our development of this abstraction as a loss of place. Perhaps there is truth to this, but our capacity for abstraction allows us to think, enables us to transcend the particularity of who we are and to gather the experiences of our multiple subjectivities together. In the face of a shrinking, more global human world, and with an urge to address this largeness, art practice has furthered the selfconscious use of abstraction.

It became possible for the site of sculpture to be abstracted from the particularity of place. For it to refer to 'not-landscape' and 'not-architecture', as Krauss calls it, is to acknowledge the largeness of the world and our limitations as individuals as we attempt to speak past the smallness of our unique experience.

Thus, while we celebrate the field, the huge elaborate variation on frame or pedestal we have made for ourselves, we also feel that we have lost touch with the particularity of place and of audience. We feel the rug slide from under our feet. We are left wondering about the ground that we are not standing on. Wondering where the rug is that used to be by the fireplace that might now be an electrically powered image of a fire.

Perhaps the more stable pedestal of yore was not so different from the immaterial pedestal at work today. Now, as then, it serves to mark a difference between the actual and the represented, as Krauss points out. But now either we have developed more complicated ways to think about the intersection between these two realms or we have in fact morphed into another kind of being. Perhaps we are now beings whose survival depends on the many layers of plastic, air filtration, water treatment, molded foot beds in our shoes, curved metal boxes moving us through the landscape, myriad of pictures telling us what to do and why, and the specially engineered sweet plants and plump animals that we eat. We are anxious about where to draw this line between the 'actual' and the 'symbolic' as so many of our symbols turn up in the mundane passage of our daily lives.

Krauss proposes that through the loss of the base sculpture becomes siteless. I wonder if this is true. By expanding the bracket placed around objects to include the floor, the walls, duration, visitor participation, events in the world past the parameters of the object presented, there is an effort to bring the abstraction of the artwork closer to the actualities of lives lived in particular places or sites.

With the invention of the field as a bracket for art, together with its intense permeability and shifting edges, in addition to being able to call any thing art as Marcel Duchamp did by moving the urinal into the space of exhibition, we can also call any moment in the flow of life art. These are the facts of art practice now. These facts reflect a sophisticated cultural understanding about the flow between our fantasy lives, our dreams, and our feeling of, for, and about subjective spaces and how they do indeed flow with, and affect the materiality of, the earth we live on. We nevertheless struggle with where we should draw lines to preserve the privileged space that mirrors our subjectivity back to us. This space allows us to think, to feel, to experience, and even to re-create ourselves moving forward.

SWISS CHEESE FIELD 31, 2009
MONOPRINT WITH COLLAGE,
FABRIC, FAKE FUR, HANDPAINTING,
LASER CUTTING, SILKSCREEN,
MELTED STYROFOAM AND WOOD
ENGRAVING WITH EMBOSSMENT
119 X 92 CM

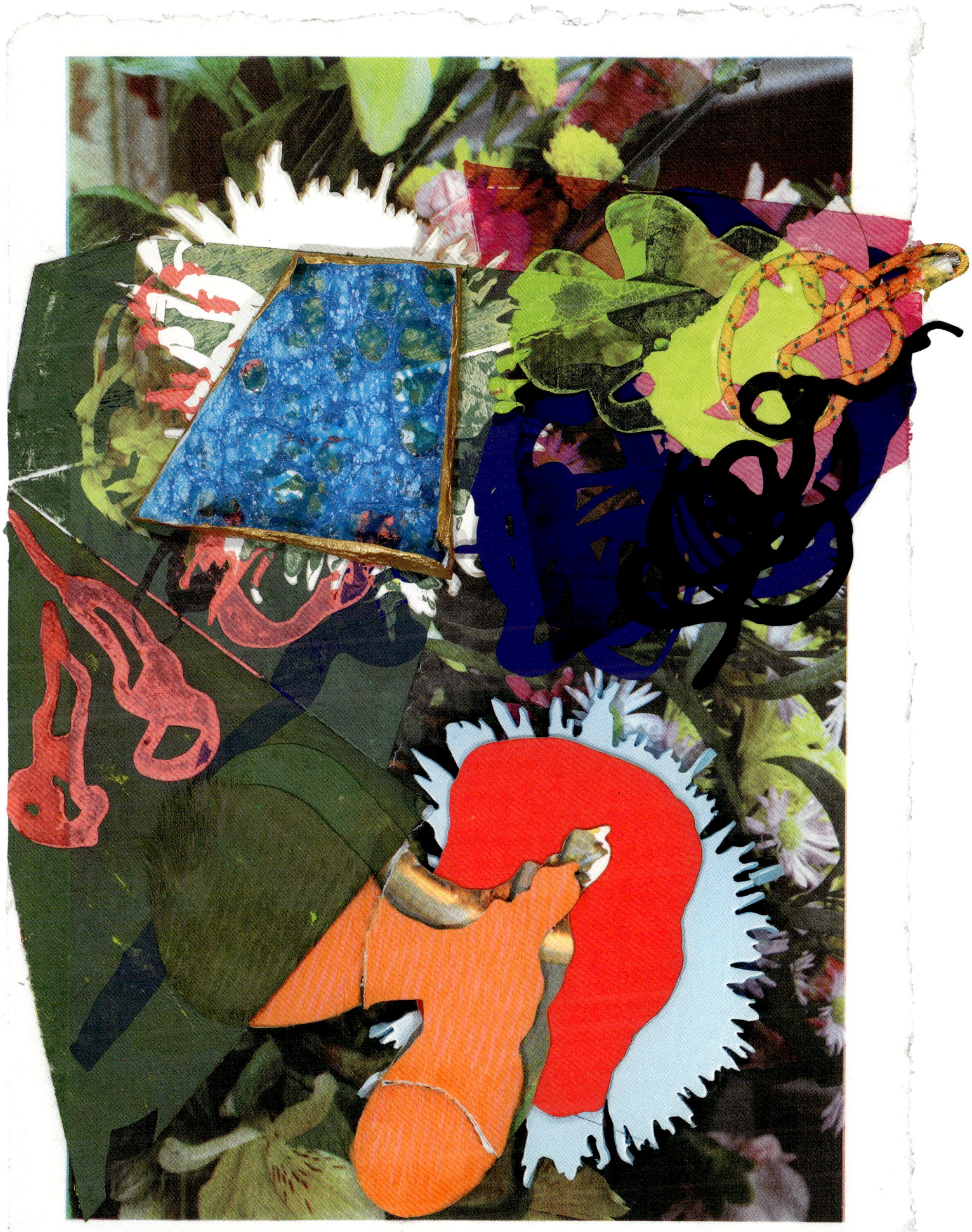

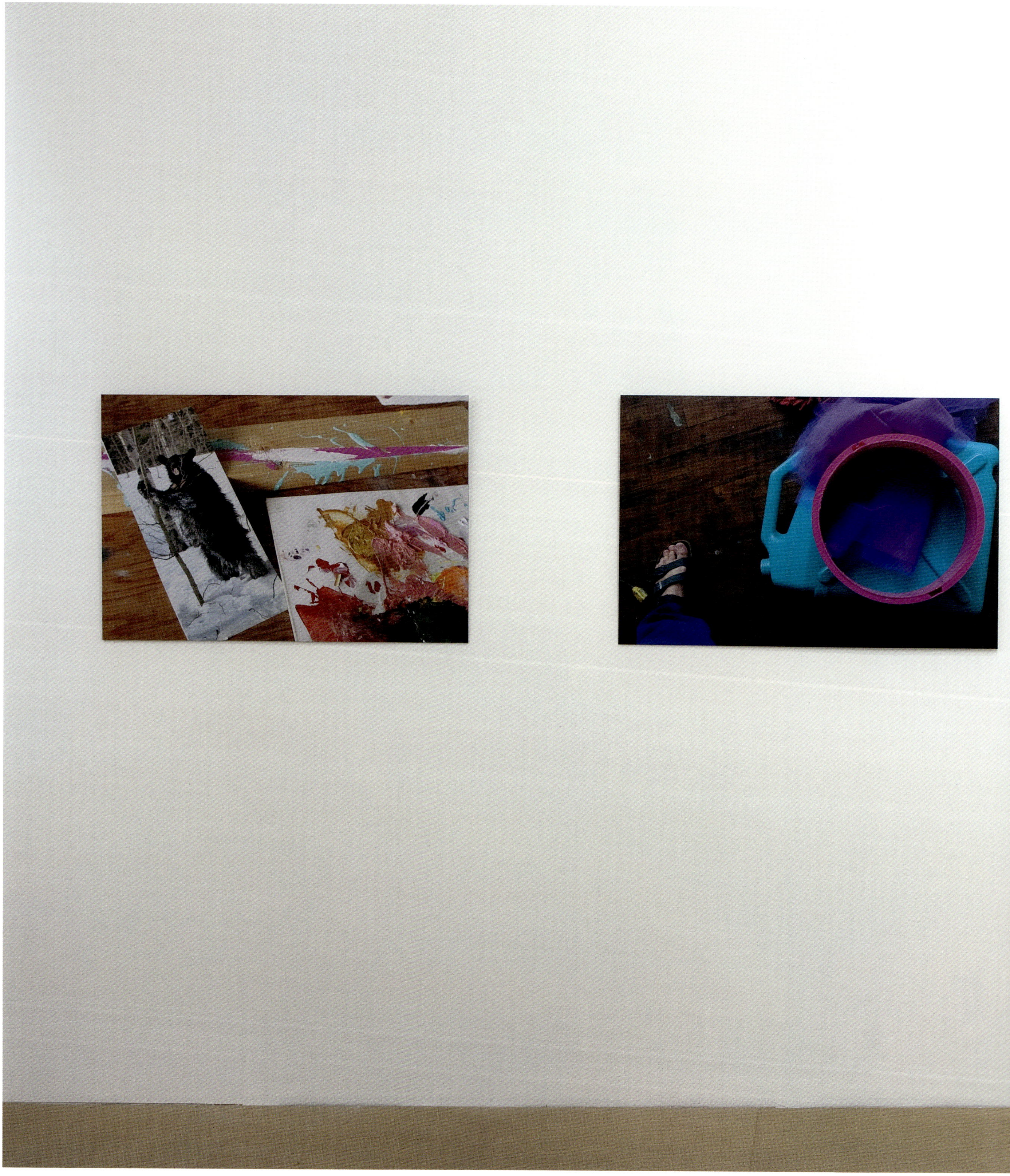

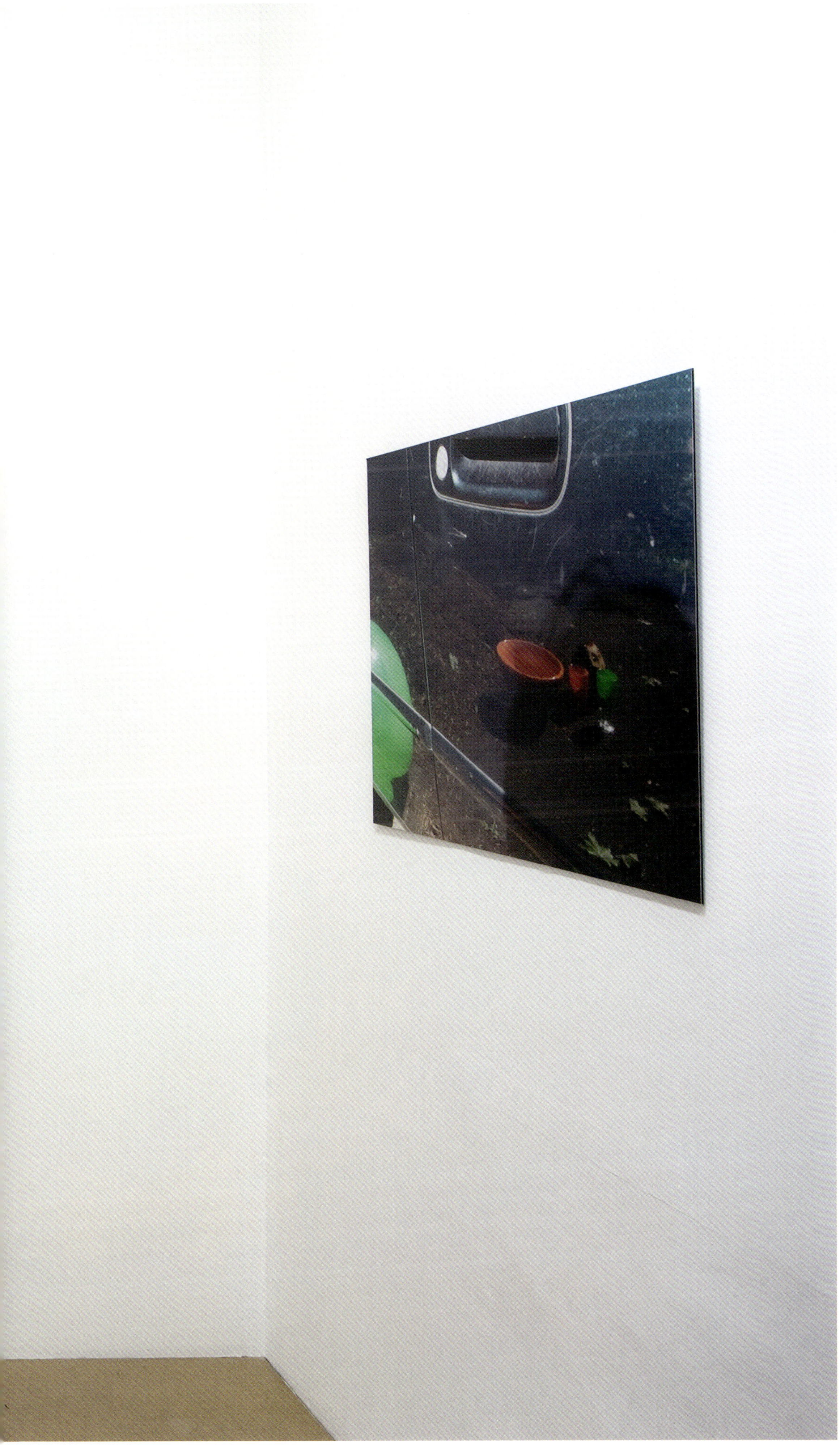

from left,
BEAR, 2008
DIGITAL PICTURE PRINTED ON LAMBDA PHOTO PAPER PASTED ON DIBON
65 X 98 CM

FOOT AND PINK PLASTIC CIRCLE ON GREEN PLASTIC, 2008
DIGITAL PICTURE PRINTED ON LAMBDA PHOTO PAPER PASTED ON DIBON
65 X 98 CM

GREEN AND ORANGE BOWL, 2008
DIGITAL PICTURE PRINTED ON LAMBDA PHOTO PAPER PASTED ON DIBON
65 X 98 CM

INSTALLATION VIEW AT GALERIE NATHALIE OBADIA, PARIS, 2009

The shifting boundaries we have invented between art activities and the performance of life are valuable to us and at the same time fraught. One function art provides is to allow for the expression of the parts of us that, unbounded, might hurt us and destroy the social fabric. This bounded site enables us to transgress safely. When the boundaries are vague or punctured, the content of our gestures brush more closely up against life, letting us understand and feel their relevance; but at the same time the transgression becomes part of life, giving rise to troubling ethical questions. Sometimes art is *used* to affect life, proposing that its practitioners, like social workers, give something to other people designed to direct the course of their living. The action of the sculpture is injected into the flow of life. This practice raises the same ethical problems that other 'helping' professions deal with regarding human dignity and individual choice. This work, depending on how the boundaries are drawn, risks losing the protected space of art.

How any single work negotiates its relationship to this line between itself and the flow of life is part of its content. Spectacle without transgression is about skillful personal achievement at its least interesting, and public or cultural achievement at its best. Spectacle laced with transgression crosses over the line between art and the flow of life, with tendrils of sculpture hanging off the playing field into life. If we ourselves do not transgress, then the voyeuristic consumption of someone else's transgression is hard to resist. Art absorbs, reflects, and embraces all the parts of our humanness – pleasant, uncomfortable, and horrific – providing a privileged space, place, or moment in time in which we can imagine, postulate, recast, notice, and remember, in order to enjoy, entertain, manage, structure, and make sense of our lives. Art is beautiful, luscious, mesmerizing, hypnotic, horrific, painful, shocking, cold, boring, dry, and romantic – eliciting the full range of human feeling and embracing all things. Though it is clear that we can, and do regularly, lasso real space and time with the abstract, siteless field like a big netted blanket – a sort of grid, thrown over bits and pieces of the world flowing outside the edges of the field – there are times when the lasso drags so much of the real into the protected arena of art that the safe zone allowing all things to be imagined is broken.

Because the formal conventions defining the place of the object or of sculpture in art are so full of holes, so permeable and elastic in space and time, there is an edgy quality to the practice of sculpture that is particular to it. Though it is essential that we protect the space of the field as separate from life, it is also pressing to recognize and allow actions on the field to be fully resonant with life's flow. The ragged edge where the fantasy lives of creative people crash into the order and protected agreements of civilization needs to be constantly tended.

YALE UNIVERSITY ART GALLERY BULLETIN, 2009

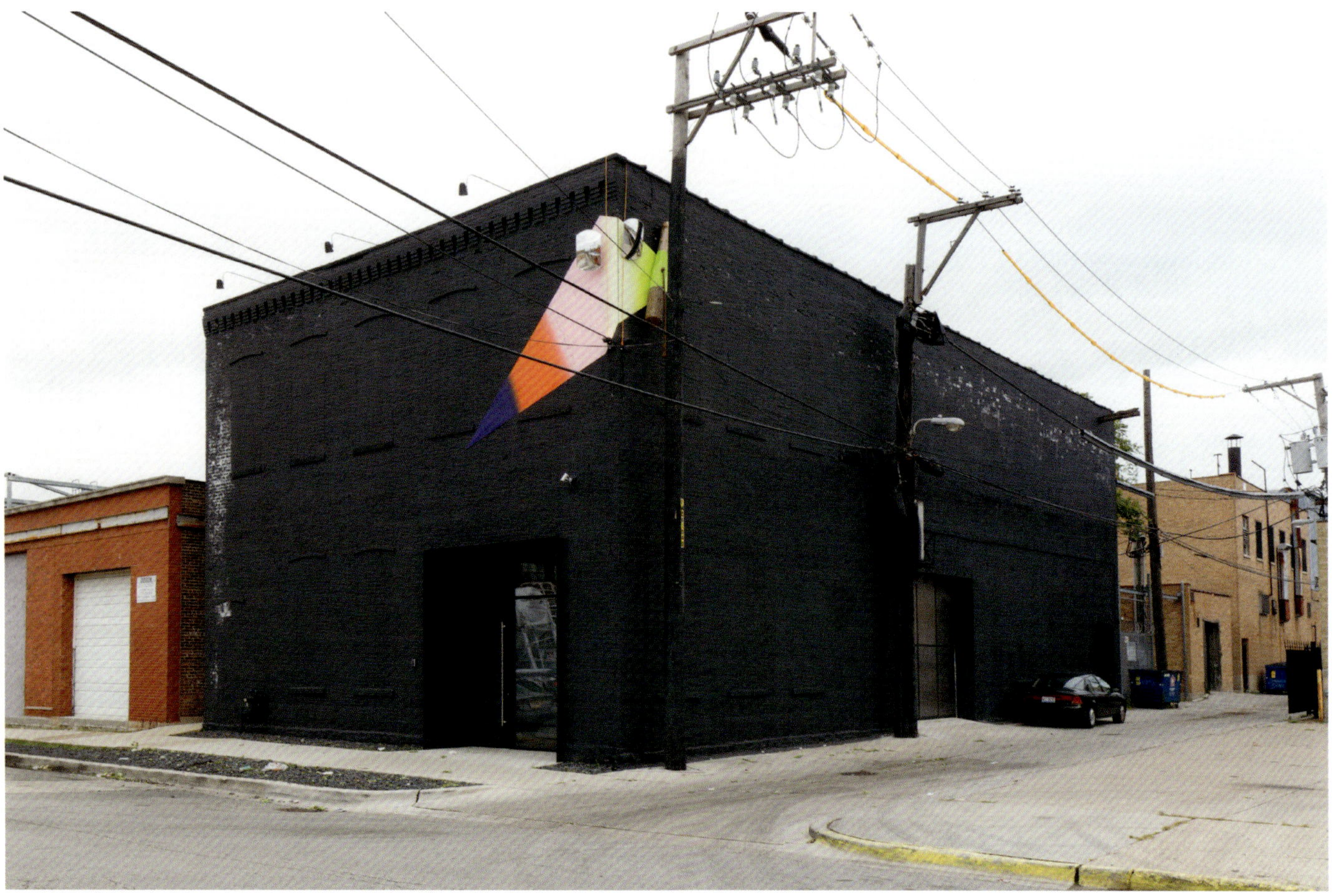

A LOG OR A FREEZER, 2016
PAINTED DIAMOND PLATE, TWO DRIVEWAY MIRRORS, TWO LIGHT FIXTURES, ONE PAINTED LOG, ROPE, LAMP POST, ROPE, PAINT, DRIVE WAY MIRRORS, WOODEN PLATFORM, FREEZER, BATH TUB

INSTALLATION VIEW AT KAVI GUPTA GALLERY, CHICAGO, 2016

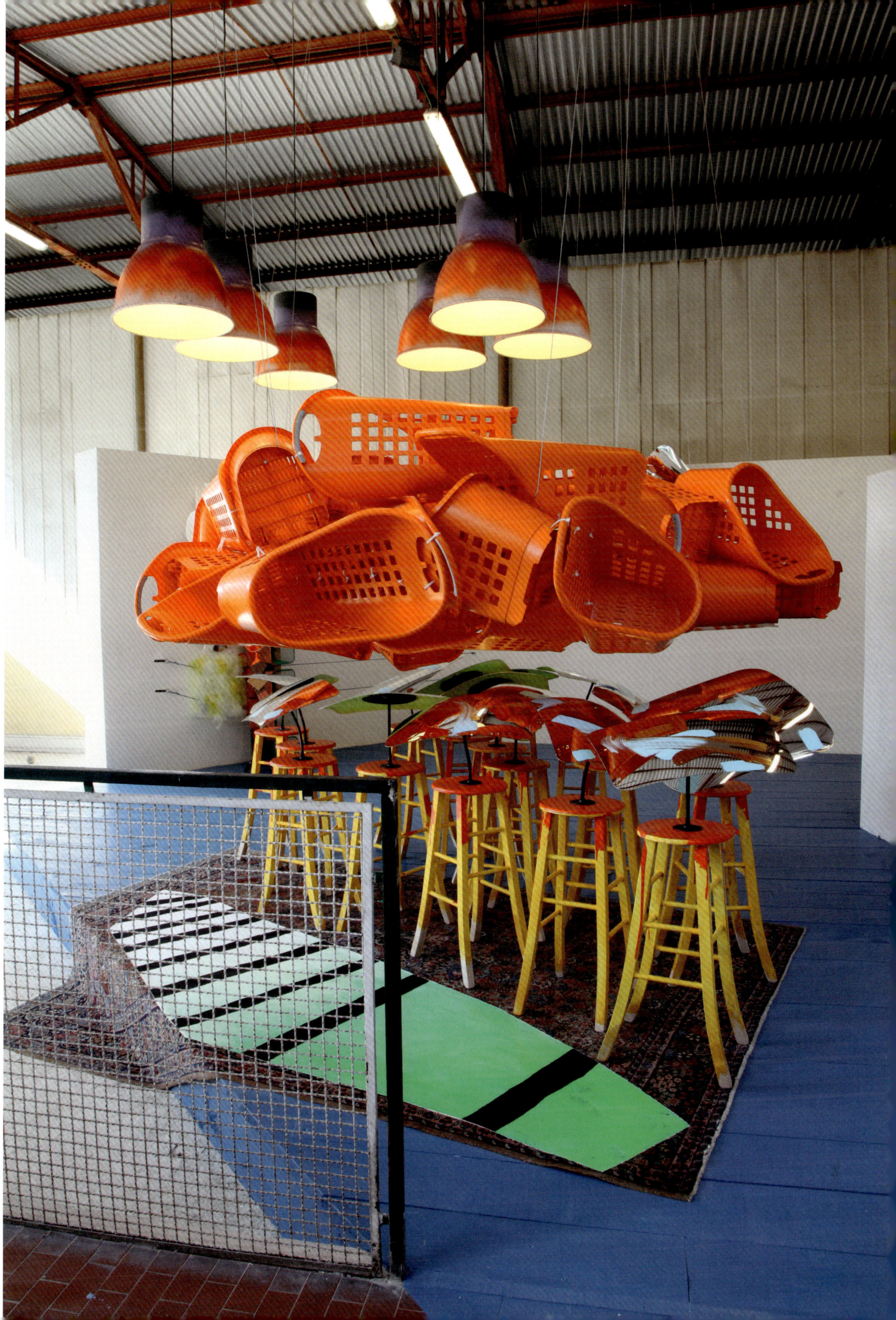

LAY OF THE LAND, 2014
ORANGE PLASTIC SHOPPING BASKETS, DRIVE WAY MIRRORS, ORIENTAL CARPET, WOODEN STOOLS, ACRYLIC PAINT, PENDANT LIGHTS AND BULBS, HARDWARE
275 X 345 X 350 CM

Rose's Inclination, 2015

<u>ROSE'S INCLINATION</u>, 2015–16
PAINT, CARPET, FRAGMENT OF JUDY LEDGERWOOD'S PAINTING, BRANCHES, ROPE, PLEXIGLAS, LIGHT FIXTURES, HARDWARE, EXTENSION CORD, MULCH, SMART MUSEUM FOYER, COURTYARD, SIDEWALKS, AND BEYOND

INSTALLATION VIEW AT THE SMART MUSEUM OF ART, CHICAGO, 2015

Rose's Inclination is to reach up and out. She slips under and over, and weaves into the landscape while flapping towards the sky.

She is painted on the walls, embodied by carpet on the floor, and her spirited entry into the world is carried by daylight streaming in through glass and by lamplight. Her essence is flapping in the wind as the doors are opened and closed.

Rose plays a part in the Smart Foyer. She includes visitors, tables, chairs, and coffee in her drama. She acknowledges and mirrors her surroundings; she is contained by the museum, and wears it like a close fitting jacket, though she is bursting through the seams. At times she is reminiscent of plant parts pushing through material so slowly that the eye can't detect the motion.

She is like the plant in the *Little Shop of Horrors* film growing bigger and bigger and more demanding. She is greedy and hungry. Her infiltration of the ground creates instability. The design of the building, the Smart courtyard, and by extension the sidewalks, and the grid of the city, could morph at any moment. The cumulous cloud of subjectivity that is each one of us – clattering words in mind and falling out of mouth – feelings in body, filling self-awareness and driving action –pass through her rosy glow.

<u>ROSE'S INCLINATION</u>, SMART MUSEUM, CHICAGO, 2015

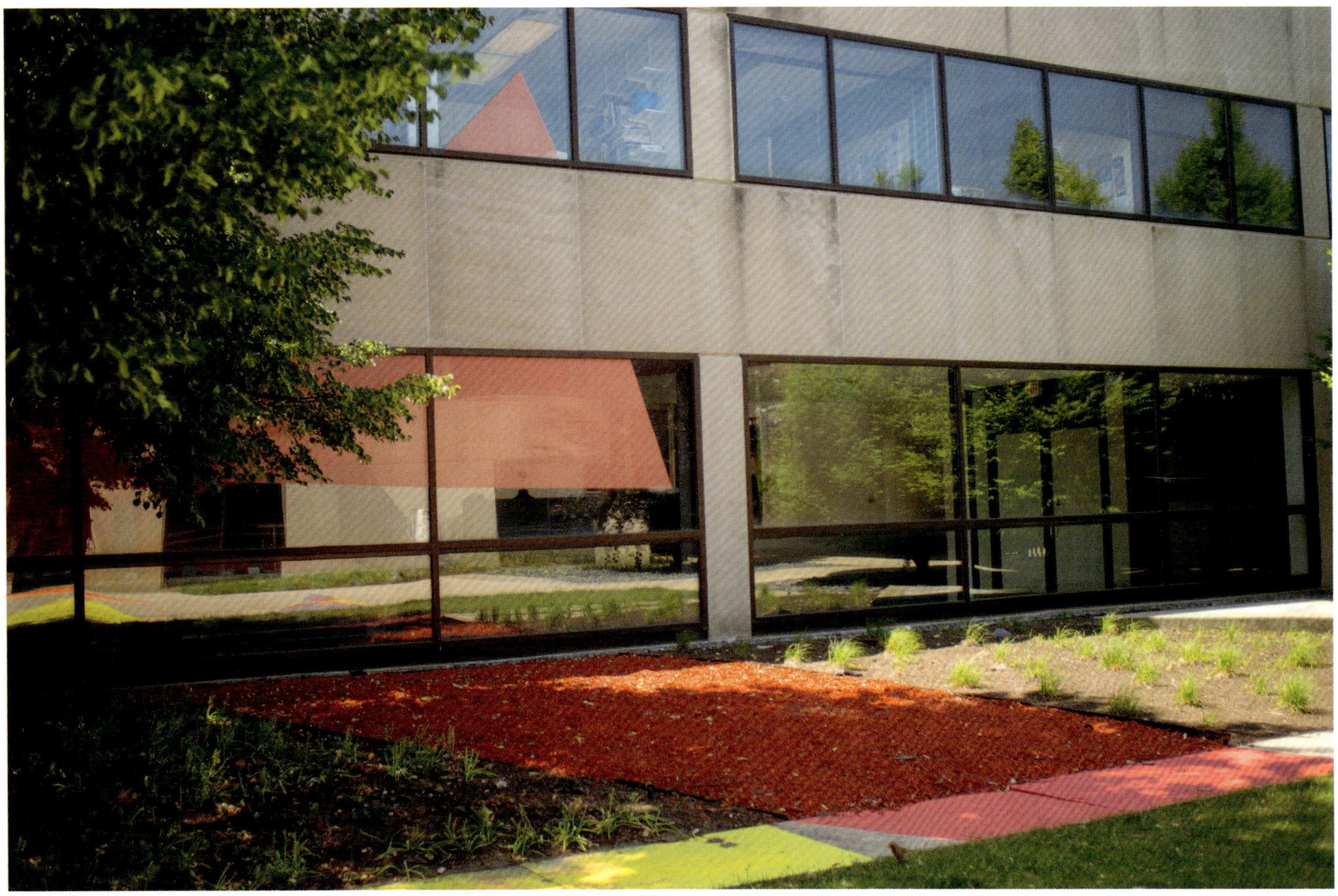

ROSE'S INCLINATION, 2015–16
PAINT, CARPET, FRAGMENT OF JUDY LEDGERWOOD'S PAINTING, BRANCHES, ROPE, PLEXIGLAS, LIGHT FIXTURES, HARDWARE, EXTENSION CORD, MULCH, SMART MUSEUM FOYER, COURTYARD, SIDEWALKS, AND BEYOND

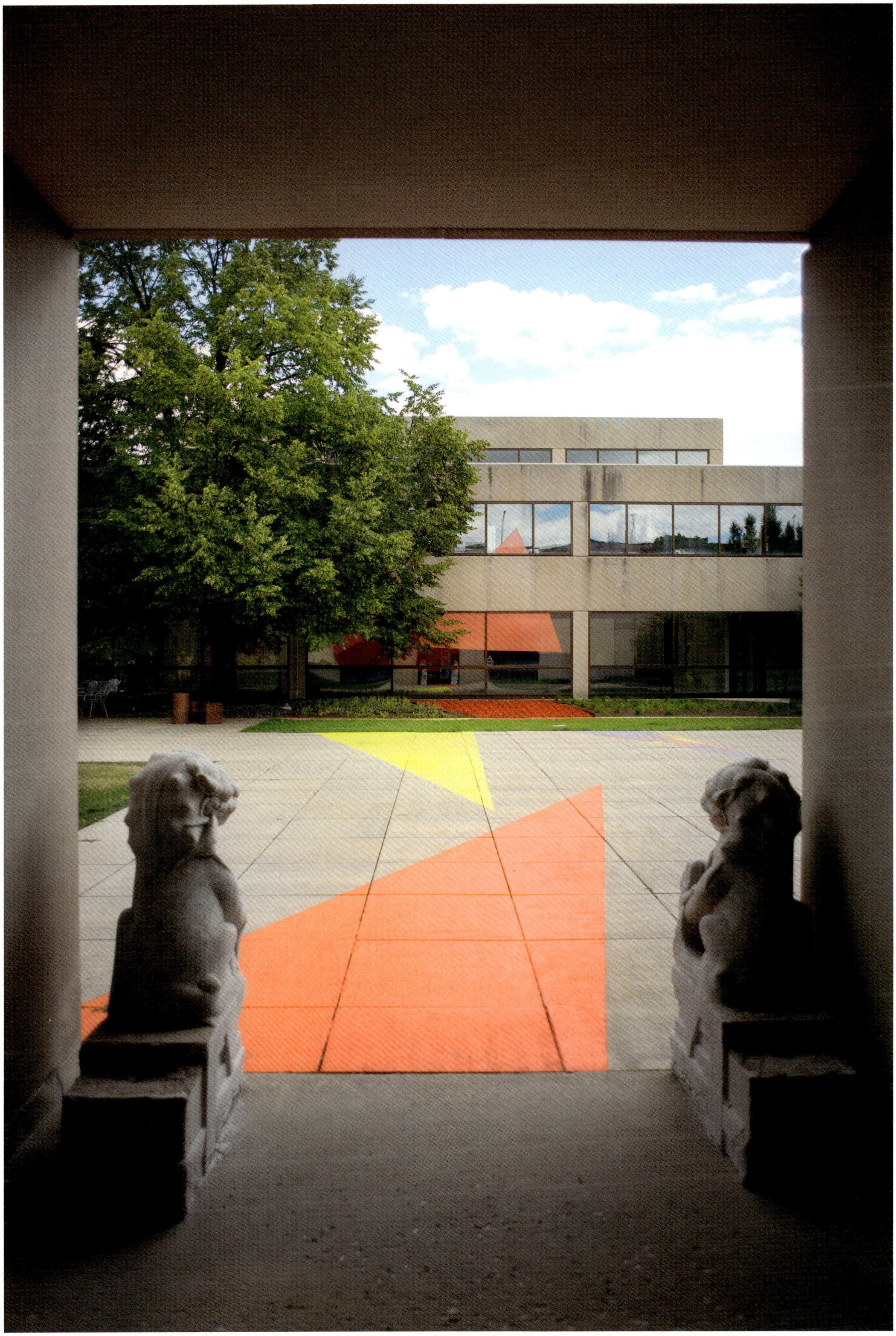

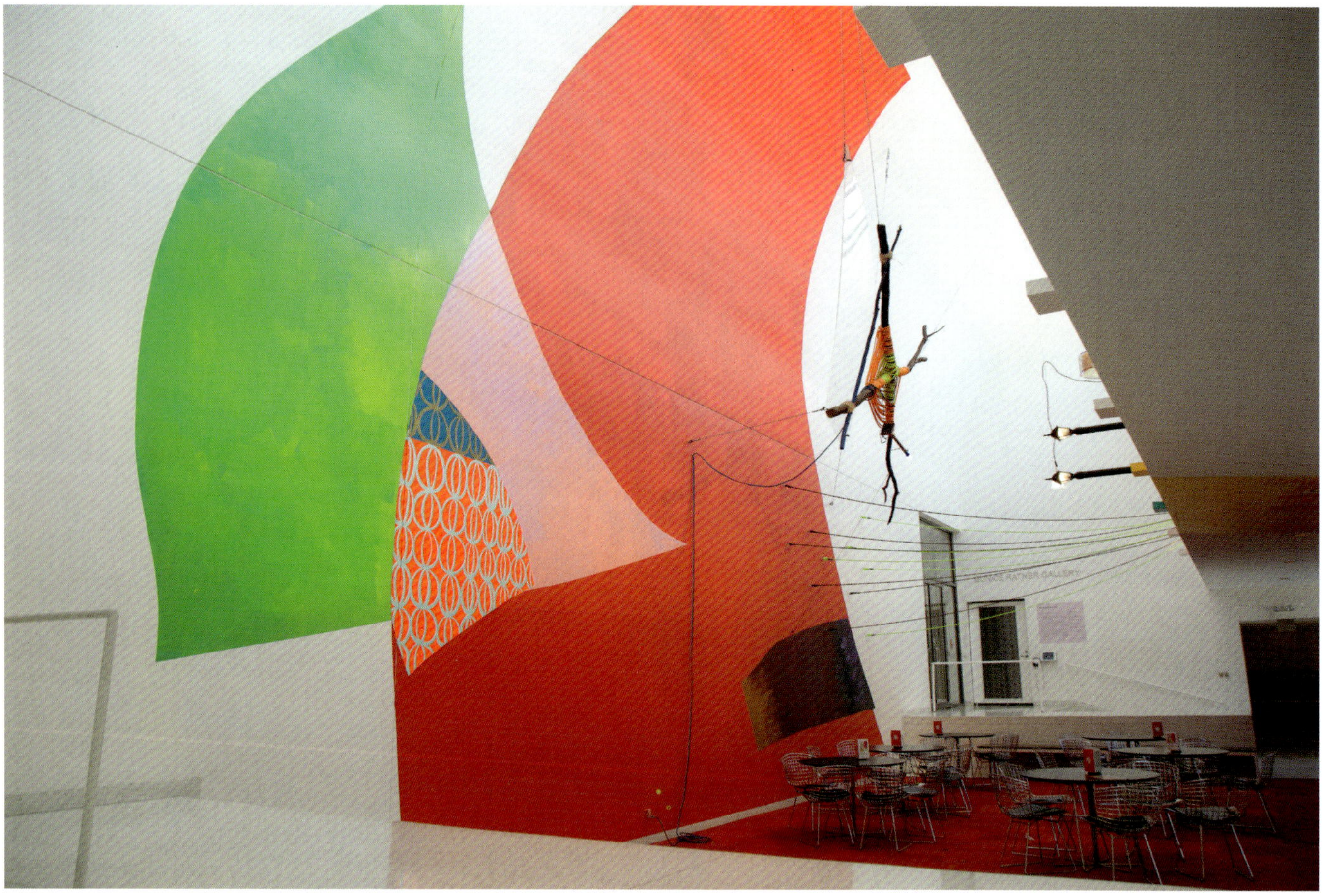

ROSE'S INCLINATION, 2015–16
PAINT, CARPET, FRAGMENT OF JUDY LEDGERWOOD'S PAINTING, BRANCHES, ROPE, PLEXIGLAS, LIGHT FIXTURES, HARDWARE, EXTENSION CORD, MULCH, SMART MUSEUM FOYER, COURTYARD, SIDEWALKS, AND BEYOND

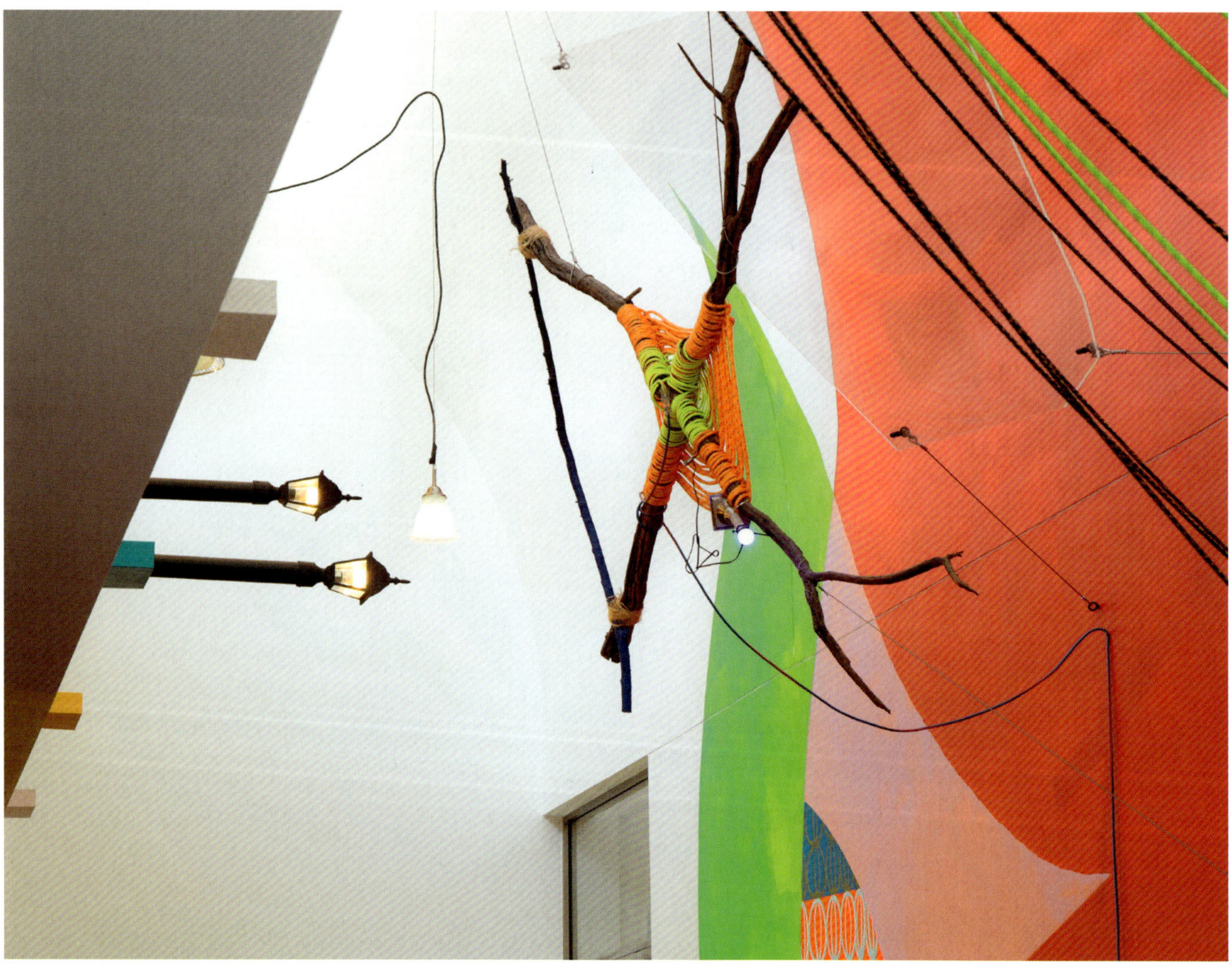

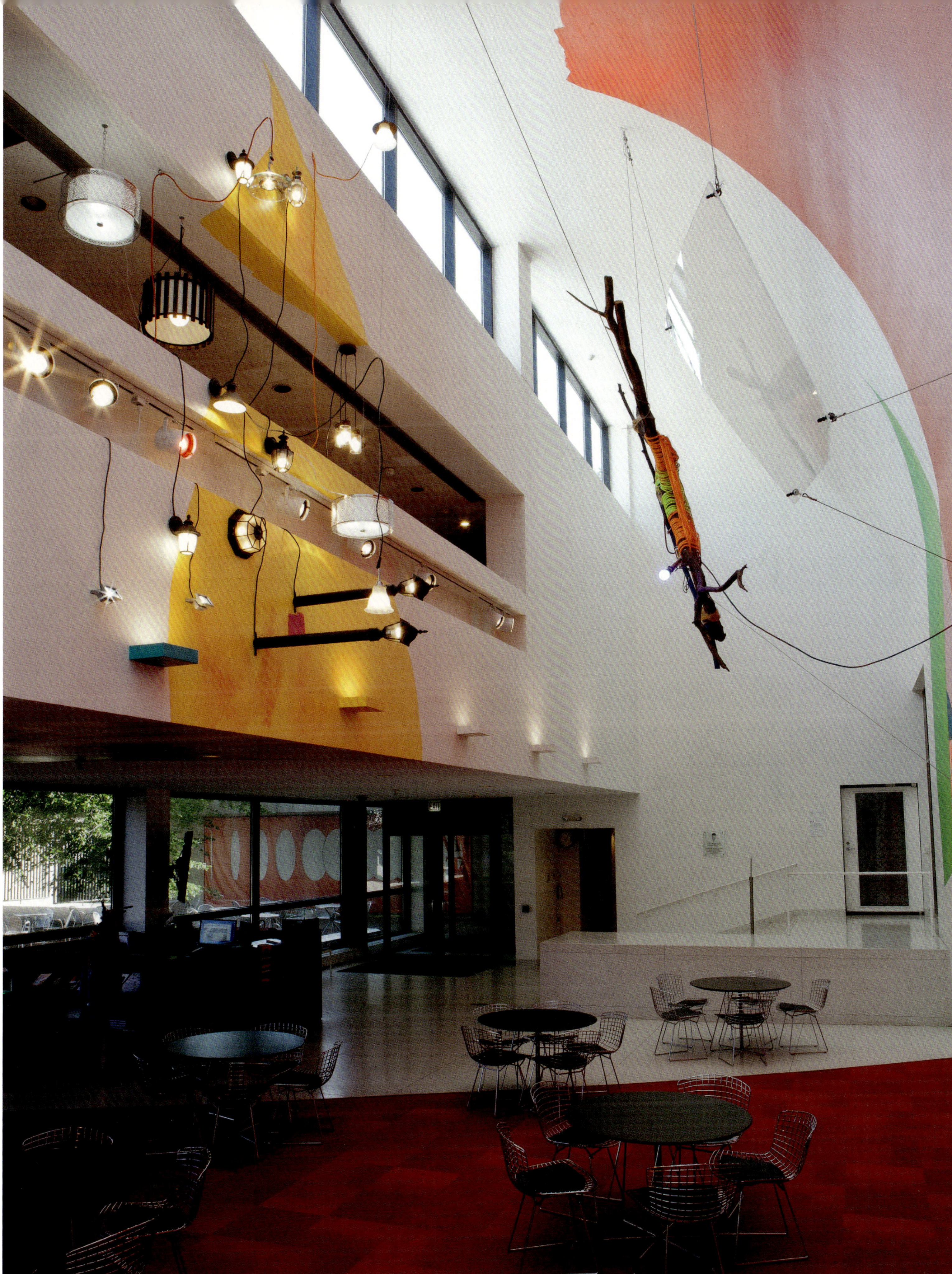

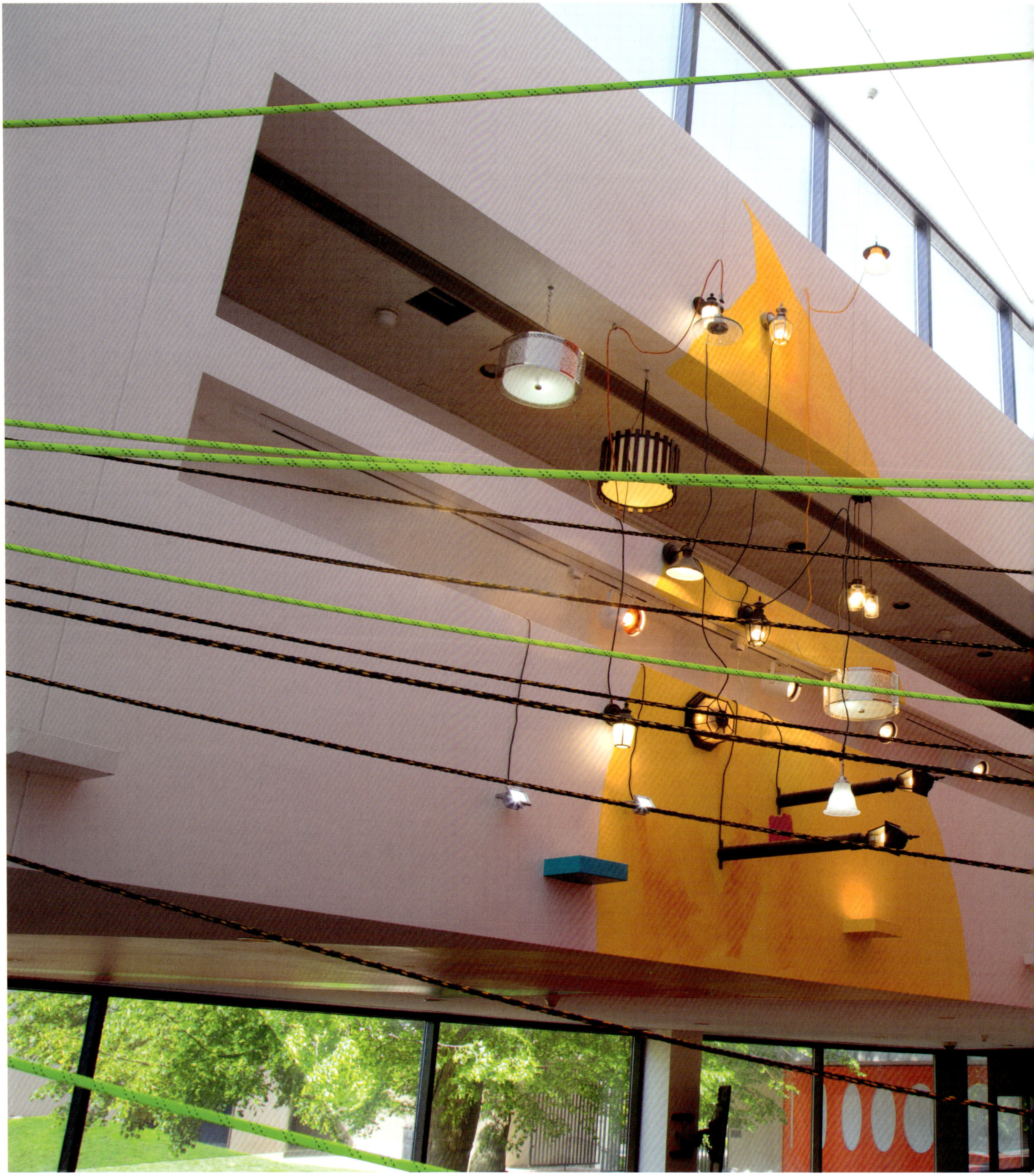

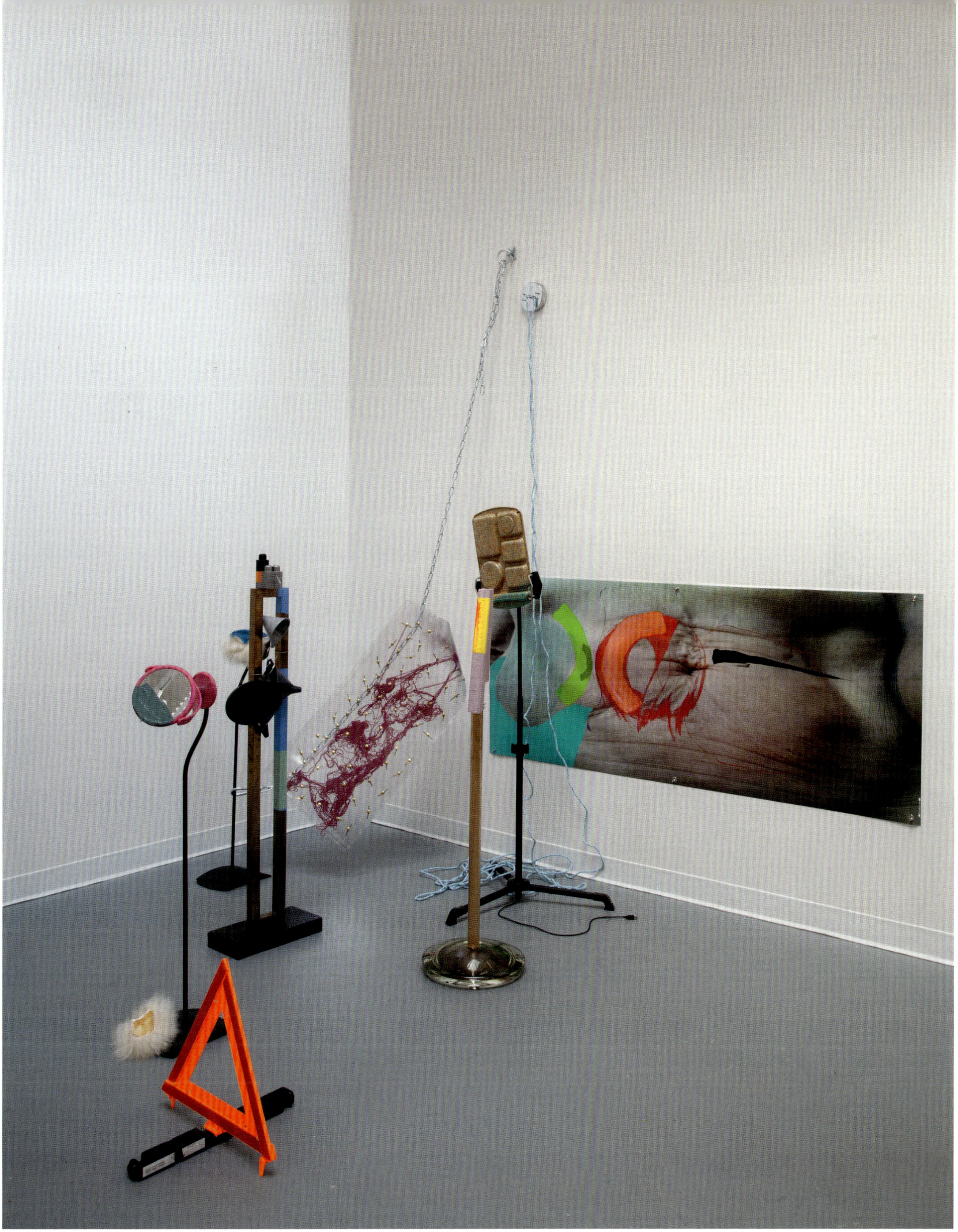

RUBBER MEETS THE ROAD, 2017
4 PLYWOOD COVERED PANELS,
ACRYLIC AND OIL PAINT, RUBBER
COATED WIRE HANDLES, HARDWARE
48 X 137 X 5 CM

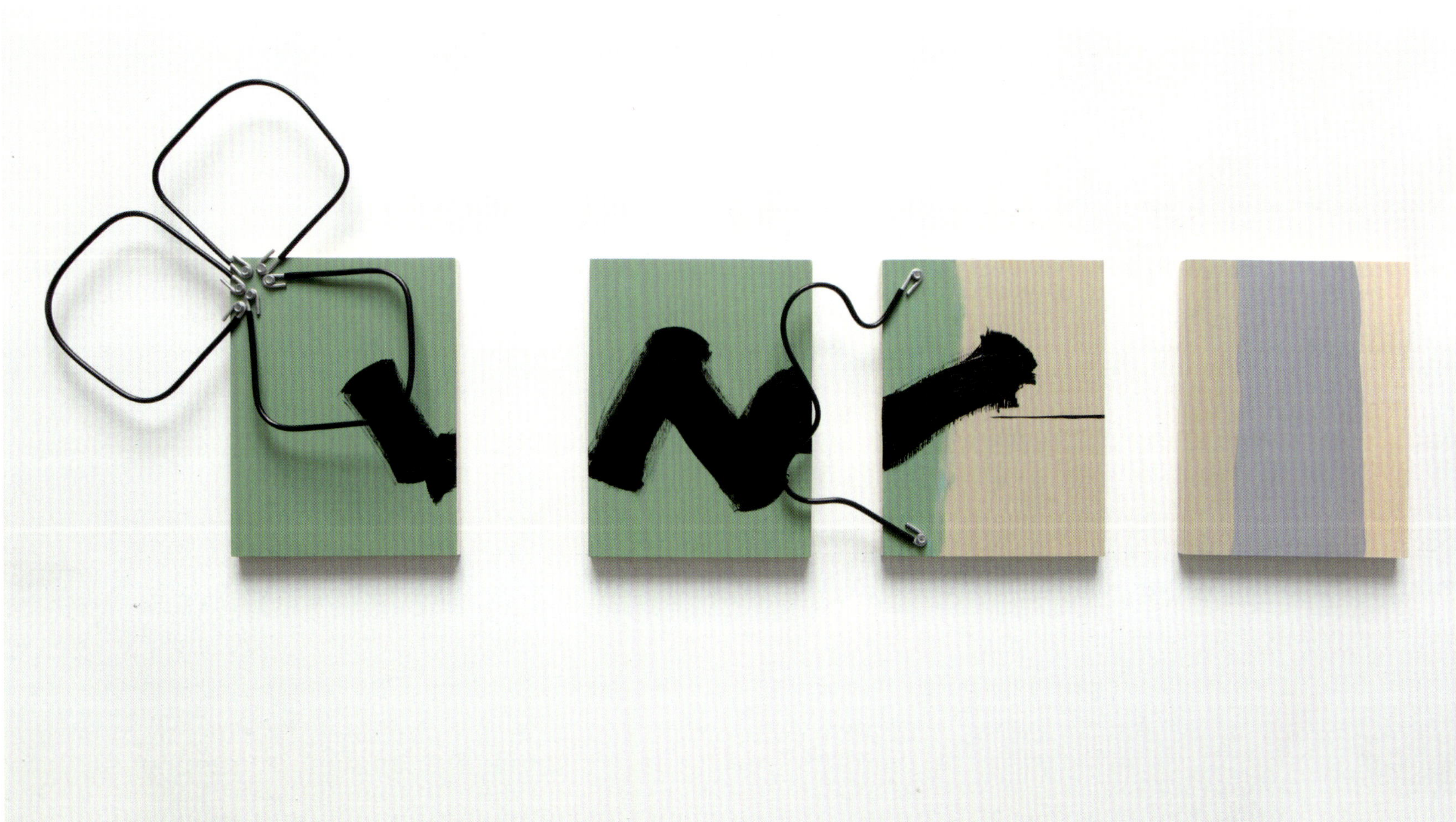

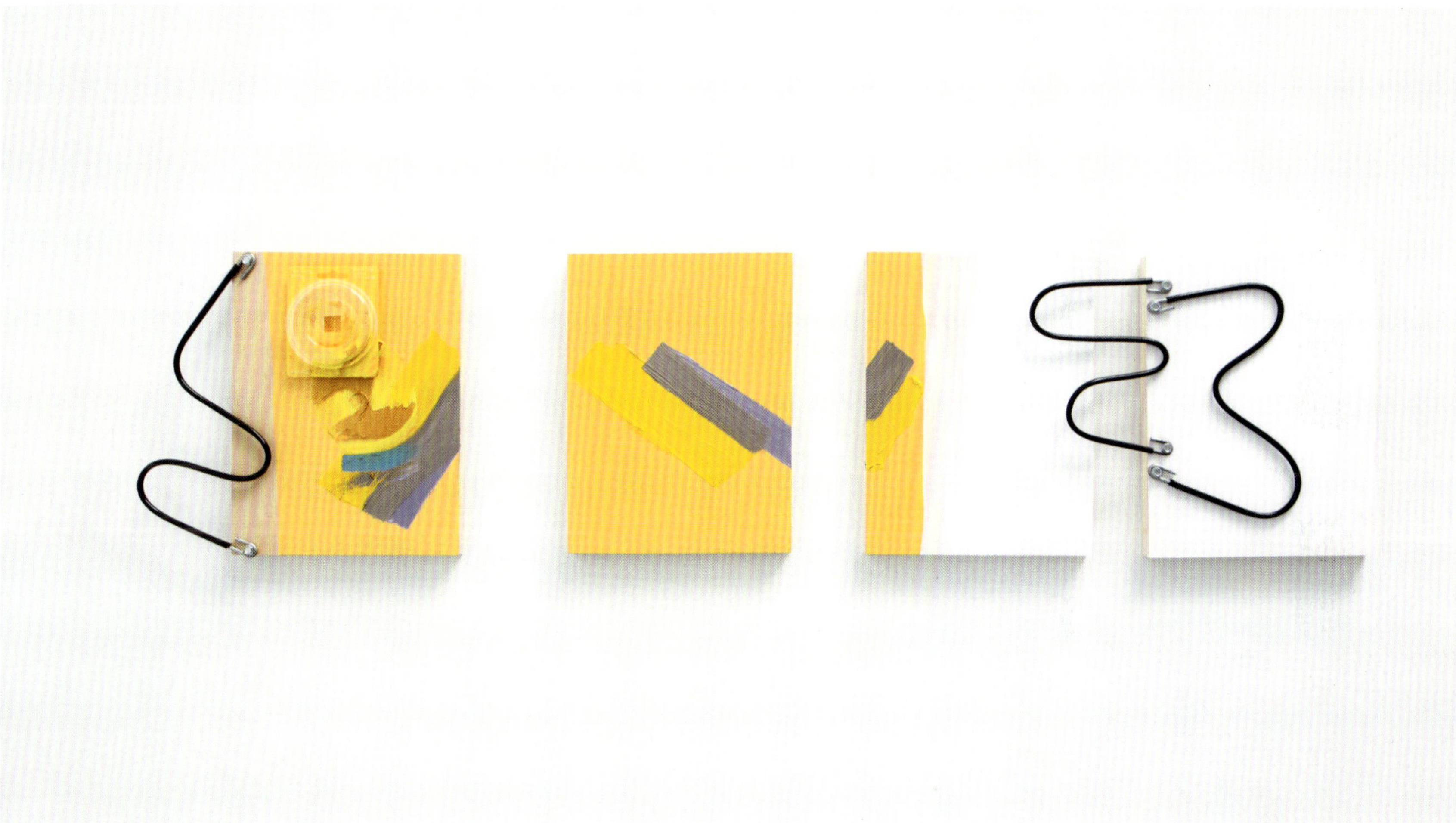

SUNBELT, 2017
4 PLYWOOD COVERED PANELS,
ACRYLIC AND OIL PAINT,
RUBBER COATED WIRE
HANDLES, HARDWARE,
PLASTIC PACKAGE
31 X 126 X 4 CM

The Goat's Knows, 2017

I saw pictures of his painting/sculpture *Monogram* very early on – I must have been in high school. I was riveted by the paint on the nose of the goat, and I still am – those vulnerable searching dabbing gestures of idiocentric world making on top of the world that was already there opened a door. Of course the world that was already there was a bit weird – a tire around the stuffed goat standing on a painting. I don't imagine that Rauschenberg stuffed the goat, but someone did, and that by itself is worth pondering. And the whole painting was treated as a pedestal for the 'sculpture' of the goat – the goat that is both 'real' and not real. The insistence that the painted world was both of our everyday world and apart – maybe a tug of war between the two – seemed just right to me. And of course that's the place I jumped into and have spent my time for many decades.

It comes as no surprise that I was invited to share my thoughts about Rauschenberg; his work has been raised as a precedent for mine time and again. And in response to the 'anxiety of influence;' I have of course been invested in articulating the differences between us. Though Rauschenberg (and Schwitters, Picasso and Braque's cubism, Judy Pfaff, and Frank Stella) did lay some groundwork for mine as he welcomed the increasing plethora of 'stuff' into the world of painting, fundamentally our projects are very different. Though his work embraces space, materiality and 'stuff' outside of the picture plane – the subject of the work is generally held inside of the frame. The goat sits in the middle of the painting without threatening to transgress the boundary of the work. Pictures often sit inside of pictures, but the edges of pictures and objects are rarely subjected to serious challenge; we are presented with distinct whole pictures and objects the edges of which are not called into question. And Rauschenberg makes use of the succinct 'whole' in a literary fashion – one can, and many do, put words to the objects or newspaper clippings he employs to tell a story.

I am more interested in asking questions about the edges of things and thought – so the objects I use are not initially the subjects of the work; they are its ground. Nevertheless the physical details of 'objects', 'material' or 'stuff' are replete with meaning that I care about more than their names. The shifting appraisal of where the edge is gives rise to many different 'pictures' emerging within a shifting set of frames that allow for myriad points of view within a single work. As clarity as to where the edge of the work might be is disallowed the work becomes enmeshed in its context, and figure ground relations are confused.

Focused attention necessarily has an edge but as focus changes the edge shifts.

The very formal, beautiful, composed order that I make with paint and colour is freighted by objects, but like leaves falling from a tree onto a lawnmower below the edges of this 'thing' has a certain serendipity.

ART IN AMERICA, JANUARY 2017

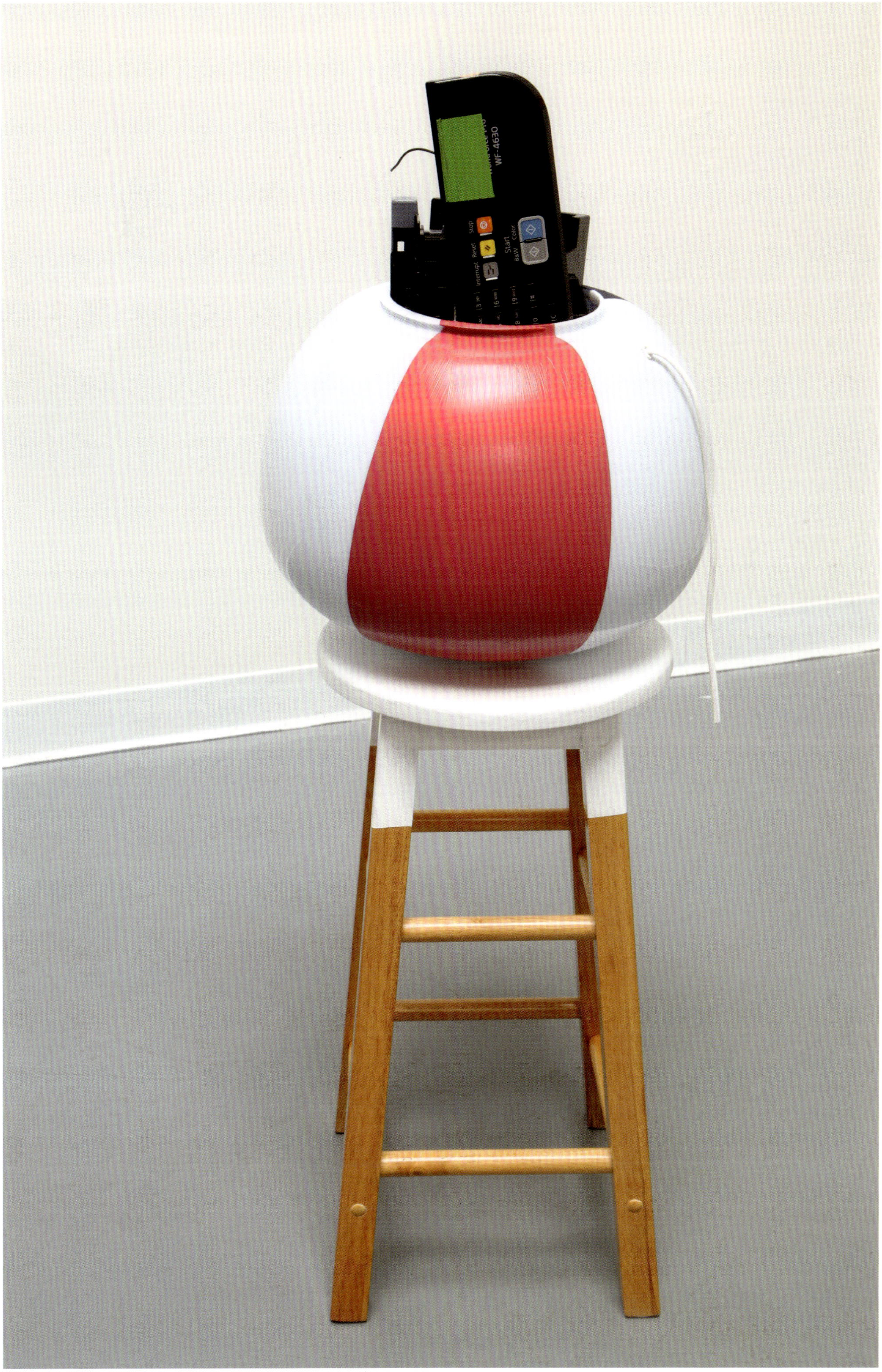

BOMB, 2017
STOOL, PLASTIC LAMP SHADE, COMPUTER PARTS, ACRYLIC AND OIL PAINT
STOOL: 61 X 30 X 30 CM
SHADE ELEMENT: 48 X 43 X 43 CM

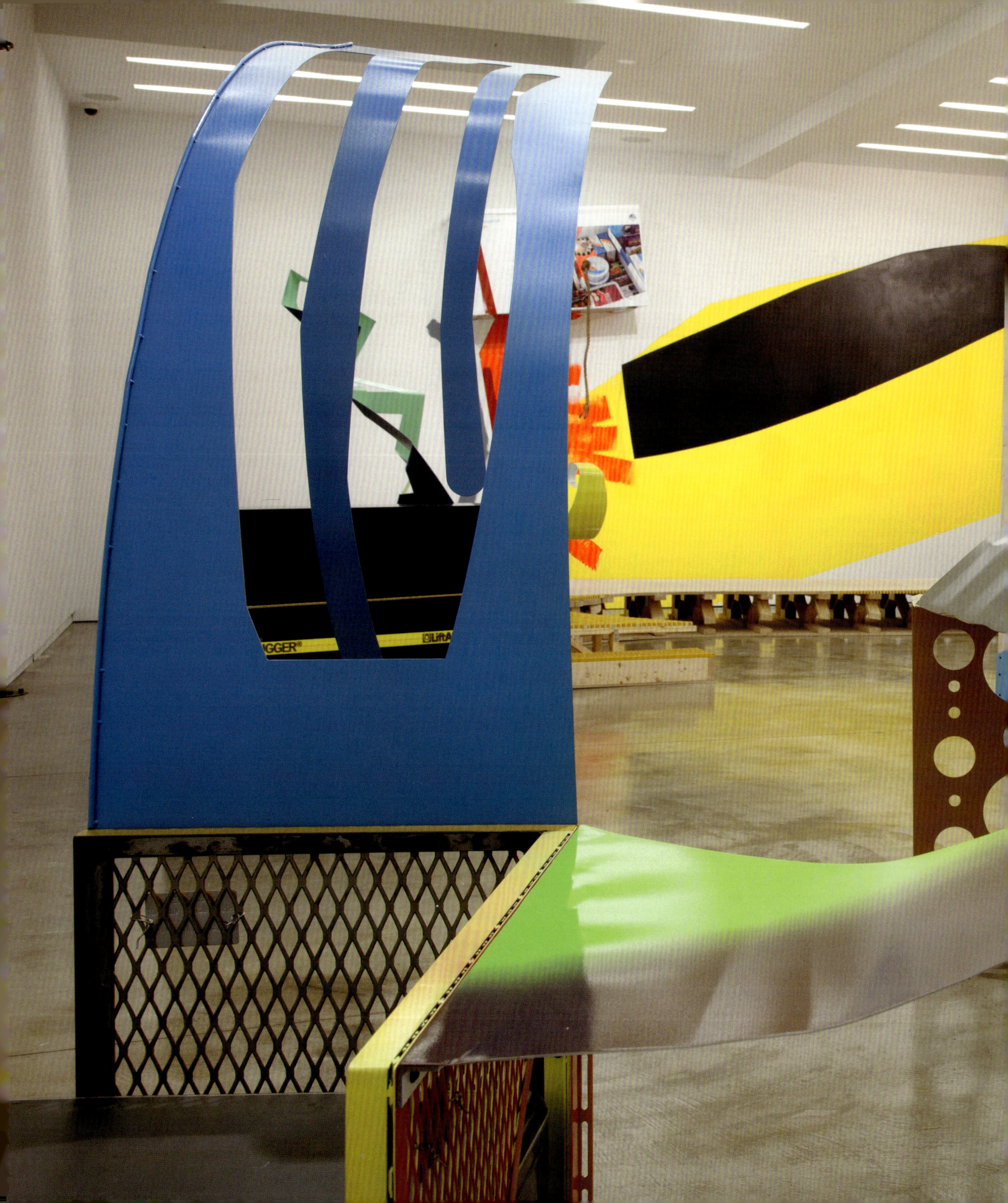

179 UPDATE

Installations in Symbiosis: Jessica Stockholder

Germano Celant

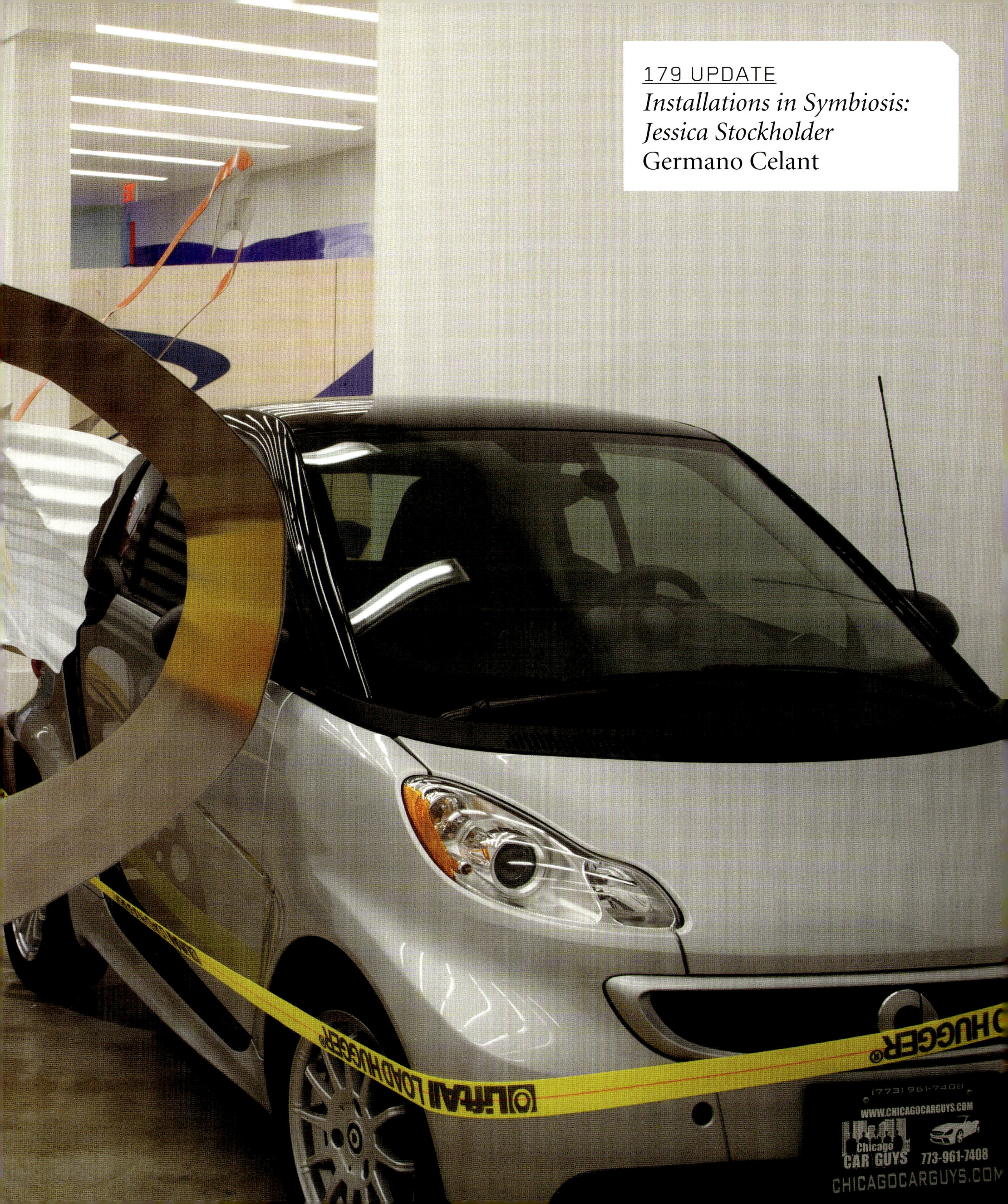

next page and previous pages,
EXHIBITION VIEW OF DOOR HINGES AT KAVI GUPTA GALLERY, CHICAGO, 2015

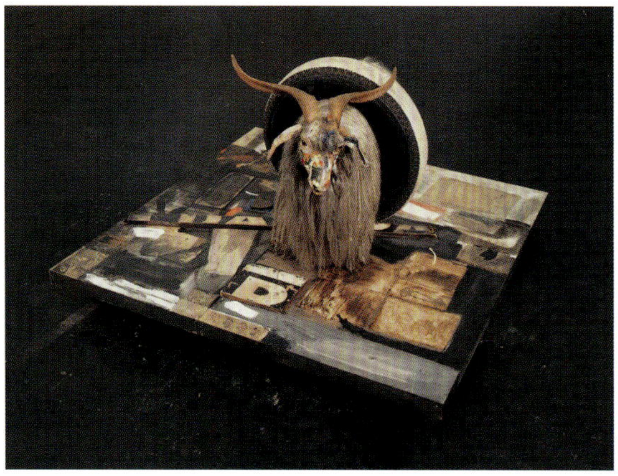

ROBERT RAUSCHENBERG
MONOGRAM, 1955–59
COMBINE: OIL, PAPER, FABRIC, PRINTED PAPER, PRINTED REPRODUCTIONS, METAL, WOOD, RUBBER SHOE HEEL, AND TENNIS BALL ON CANVAS WITH OIL AND RUBBER TIRE ON ANGORA GOAT ON WOOD PLATFORM MOUNTED ON 4 CASTERS
107 X 161 X 164 CM

The idea of establishing physical, corporeal relationships between artworks and the architectural context dates back over the centuries to a time when artists first thought about using the space as a 'vase' or 'recipient' for their visual interventions. The contextual arrangement of paintings and sculptures aroused a sense of reciprocity and mutuality, where art created an environment and the environment created art.

The desire for osmosis was reinforced in the twentieth century with the historical avant-garde movements, from Futurism to Suprematism and Dadaism, from Giacomo Balla to El Lissitzky and Kurt Schwitters. This coincided with an intention to break free from the object in order to allow viewers to enter an optical and plastic 'womb' that might envelop them, without limits, thus creating a 'totality'. Here, the environmental intervention distinguishes itself from the object/work in the sense that it refers to an intention to be, not autonomous and mobile, but relative and complementary, integrative and connective in a specific context. The arrival at a unique 'space', public or private, where the artwork is integrated with and configured into the site, entails the impact upon the site's dimensions and physical conditions. This practice is almost always manifested within the limited space of a room, defined by its six surfaces – ceiling, floor and four walls – a box that forms a 'topological field', where a relationship exists between the component and the whole.

However, a review of developments in art until the 1940s confirms that the expansion outward into the space largely evades intervention on the ground or floor. Exploration is focused on the aerial and parietal 'dome' that overhangs and surrounds the visitor, and does not go so far as to include the supporting surface. The reason could be that artists were thinking only in terms of the magical and sacred setting of the celestial vault and its horizons. Their intention was to establish a connection between heaven and earth, without actually inserting the physical and profane space. The ritual of decorating or illustrating the space, in fact, is connected to a reproduction of the *imago mundi*, which harbours the human being as ephemeral and temporary passenger, without securing his or her presence and function. Thus from prehistoric caves to Renaissance frescoes, from Baroque totalities to modernist structures, a symbolic universe has been represented through an immersive territory saturated with the transcendence of reality In the modern era, these include 'hypothetical' spaces of rational and social life, ranging from El Lissitzky's *Prounenraum* (1923) to Piet Mondrian's project for *Salon de Madame B* (Dresden, 1926), from Kurt Schwitters's *Merzbau* (Hannover, 1923–1943), to Lucio Fontana's *Ambiente spaziale a luce nera* (Milan, 1949). The realization of these types of all-encompassing spaces, however, does not take into consideration the surface on which people walk: the floor. This is where the passage into reality occurs. The floor embraces movements carried out in daily life. It underlies a body's entering into the space, its penetration of it. This inclusion would mark a radical leap into something that, until that point, had not existed: the Other that initiates a new life.

This initiate or neophyte, a human being who implements a rite of passage to achieve an ontological leap that becomes creative, can be seen in the person of Jackson Pollock. In 1950 Hans Namuth documented on film Pollock's intuition to seek solidarity between actor and art viewer, a complementary relationship that shatters the isolation of the artefact. This is always experienced from the front or side, even if carried out while circulating inside; it subtends a verticality that is now translated into an accessible horizontality. The actor-artist, as well as the viewer, is left outside. He does not tread upon the work's surface or material. He moves within the symbolic rather than the real. With Pollock, communication pushes to enter art in the same way that one enters the world, with its unknowns and downfalls, making the human being aware of a participation that moves from the corporeal to the spiritual.

A subsequent phase, where it is no longer the action but rather the object that is tied to the engaging surface of the territory of operation, within a space that can be walked upon and inhabited, occurs with Robert Rauschenberg's *Monogram* (1955–59). In this *Combine*, the artist puts together sculpture and painting, arranged on one of his canvases, placed horizontally on the floor,

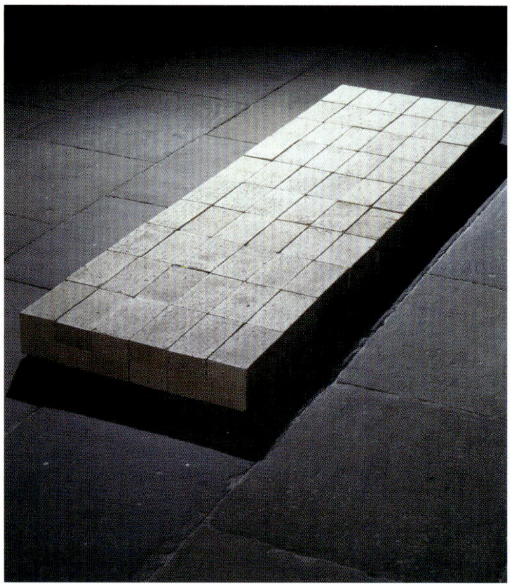

CARL ANDRE
EQUIVALENT VIII, 1966
FIREBRICKS
13 X 69 X 229 CM

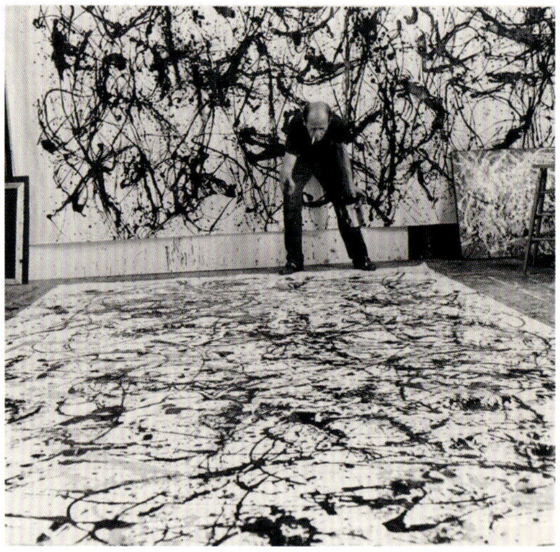

HANS NAMUTH
JACKSON POLLOCK IN THE ACT OF PAINTING, NEW YORK, 1950
BLACK AND WHITE PHOTOGRAPH

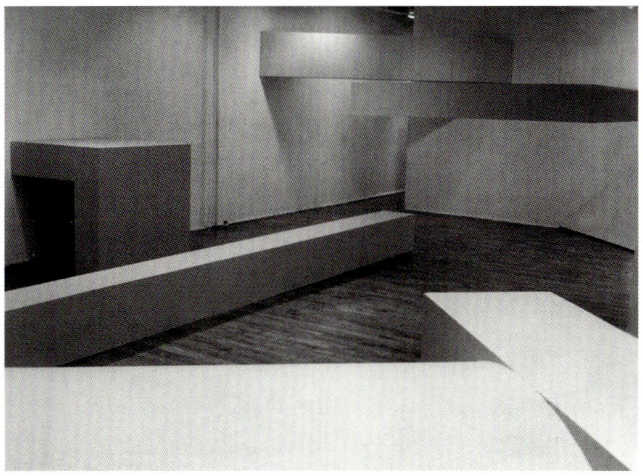

ROBERT MORRIS
INSTALLATION AT THE GREEN GALLERY, NEW YORK, 1964
WOOD POLYHEDRONS PAINTED GRAY

a stuffed angora goat, encircled by a rubber tyre. A work that was at first hung on the wall but in the end was placed horizontally, it symbolizes and signifies the found object's and the painting's extension into the world, to the point where it is 'glued' to the floor. It becomes an aggregate of things, mimicking Merce Cunningham's choreography or John Cage's environmental music, whose circularity suggest a continuous and multidirectional totality; *Monogram* invites immersion in the spectacle of life, without hierarchies, so that it is able to arrive at a cosmic and spherical vision of art making.

Putting art at the service of the public, as 'support' for that public's passage, finds definitive form in Carl Andre's *Equivalents* (1966), groupings of modular surfaces of metal, placed on the floor and meant to be walked on. Created in lead or steel, aluminium or zinc, they translate Pollock's field of intervention and drippings into sculpture. They further develop the transmutation of the classical sculptural object, where material is shaped to create another presence; counterposed vertically to the human being, they can thus be perceived by walking within them, in an accessible and traversable 'place'. It is an art that is no longer isolated, but can physically share and engage the viewer's participation. It presents a transition from object of worship to object of use, where the significance lies beneath our feet.

The work is transformed into a 'hosting' space. When walking on top of and inside the work, one is aware of the artifice and anxiety of traditional sculpture, a unified three-dimensional object, created in materials ranging from marble to Plexiglas, whose impracticability creates problems in terms of viewpoint. Other Minimalist investigations, from Robert Morris to Donald Judd, are connected to the space with voids and gaps, and not available as paths that involve being walked upon. In fact, Minimal art, like Pop art before it, typically reclaims a pure and untouchable idea of the image. It rejects the notion of being in reality, thus of being a stage and production of a vision that, in addition to being represented, can be shared. Andre's *Equivalents*, instead, move the work closer to reality and establish a fusion between the life of the place and its inhabitants. They do not reject contamination, but encourage it. They offer a present substance, a reactive diversity of minerals, to materialize and affirm the possible 'nonmetaphysical' existence of art. Beginning in 1968, this immersive evolution, where the components that participate in the aesthetic process are made available to all those who want to experience it, corresponds to an awareness that museums and galleries are 'non-sites' – territories of rapid and superficial consumption through which the works pass, depending on an exhibition's duration. They neither endure nor are integrated with the architecture, but need to revive the presence of the *situ*, the site, as

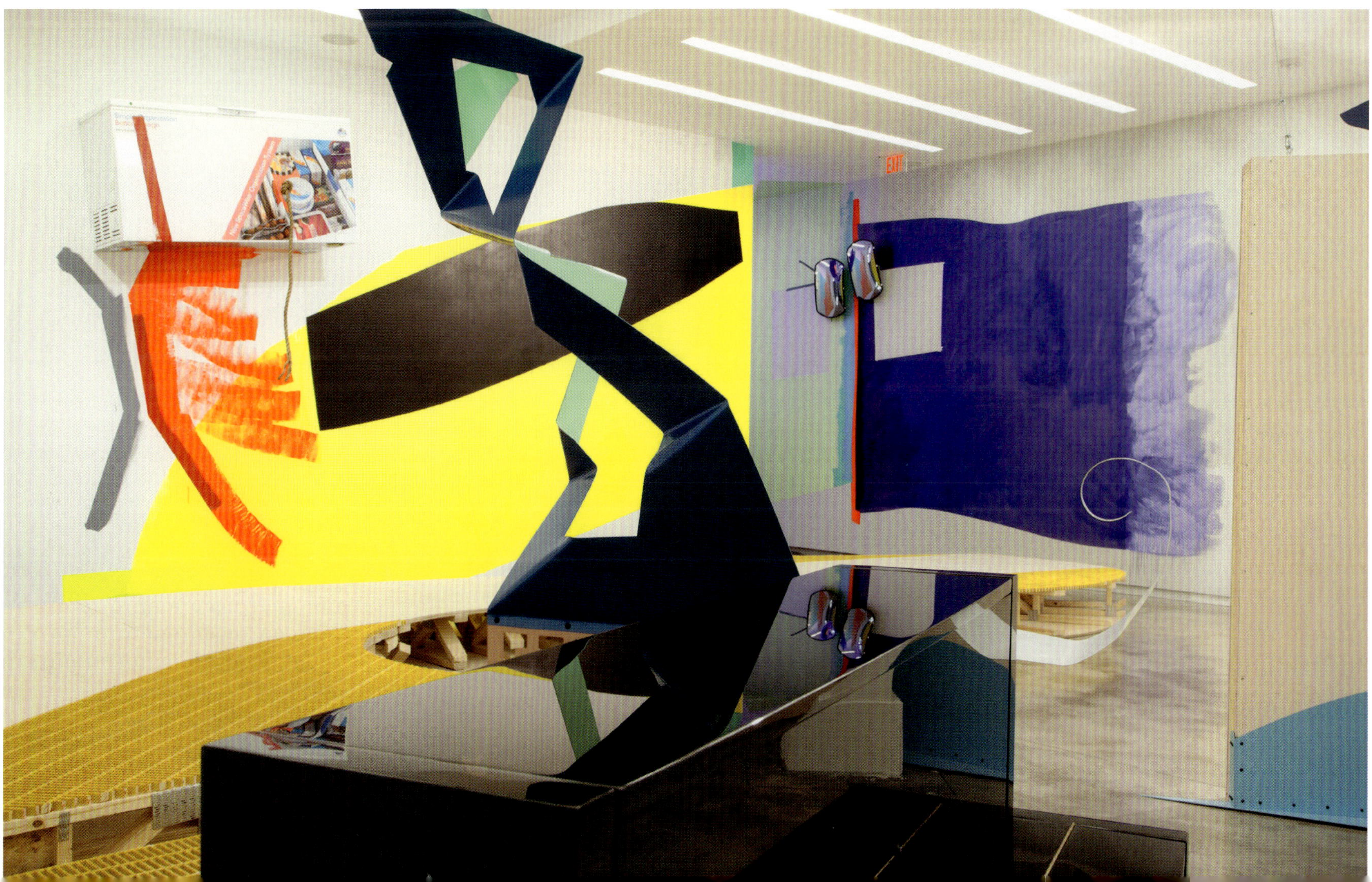

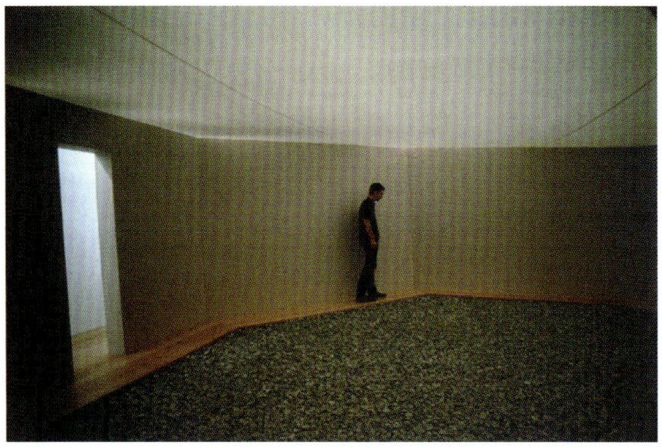

MOWRY BADEN
OTIS ROOM, 1975
WOOD, FABRIC, ROCK
914 X 914 X 304 CM

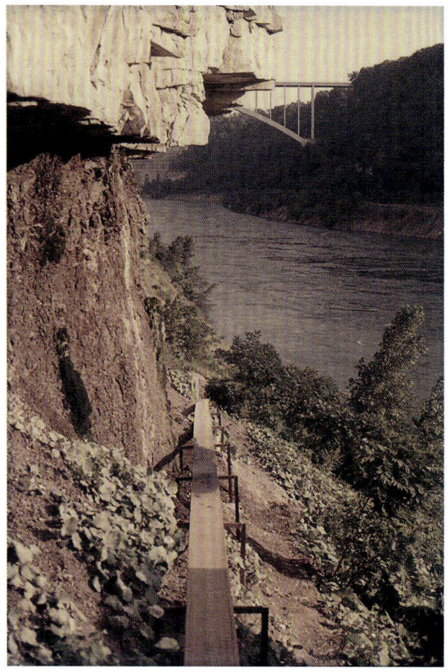

GEORGE TRAKAS
ROCK RIVER UNION, 1976
STEEL RAMP, CONCRETE
CASCADE STAIRS
RAMP: 97 M
STAIRS: 31 M

THE LION, THE WITCH AND THE WARDROBE, 1985
WOOD, PLYWOOD, CONCRETE, PLASTIC, PAINT, FLOOR PAINT, SAWDUST, ASPHALT, BEDSHEET, TOOLS, ELECTRIC LIGHT, NEWSPAPER, OIL PAINT, FLUORESCENT LIGHTS, INCANDESCENT LIGHTS
WORK SPANS TWO ROOMS
ROOM 1: 1008 X 374 CM
ROOM 2: 576 X 576 CM

INSTALLATION VIEW AT ARTIST'S SPACE, NEW YORK, 1985

seen in the macroscopic and permanent creations of Land art in deserts and plains by Michael Heizer, Walter De Maria and Robert Smithson.

From this perspective, artistic construction becomes an investigation of associations and relationships with social and natural conditions. It is presented as a circumstance for interaction with the public. It takes on the role of intermediary, through a focus on its contextual existence. Direct participatory enactment is reinforced, beginning in the 1970s, with the work of Mowry Baden and George Trakas. Their assemblages take the form of rooms or habitats that are meant to be traversed and occupied by people, who in turn are invited to participate. They encourage movement that, from 1976–77, is transformed into walkways and steps that interact with the natural landscape. Thus they are offered as tools for the perceptual mutation of the environmental context. Sculpture is no longer positioned at the centre of a room or a meadow, but becomes penetrable and accessible. People can walk inside, aware that they are in the midst of a journey that can lead to a discovery of new experiences. In the case of Baden, who was a very young Stockholder's teacher from 1972 to 1976, the sculptures become corridors or portals into which the viewer is invited to enter and participate, developing a free way of behaving. This is an invitation to utilize the entire sensory system, stimulated by obstacles or belts, sounds or barriers. It is something akin to a theatrical playground, but imbued with kinetic and optical motivations, calling into question Minimalist purism and formalism. In *Rock River Union* by Trakas, installed in Artpark in Lewiston, New York, the defined path traverses the various layers and levels of a riverbank, so that viewers find themselves immersed in an environment, subjected to changes in natural and atmospheric conditions.

It is during this period of territorial conquest, when art aspires to reappropriate its space through the control of the environmental conditions in which it is set, that Jessica Stockholder creates one of her first installations, in 1983. Using a coloured mattress, hung on the wall of a backyard garden, she seeks out a connection between object and architecture, interior and exterior, colour and material. She exploits the urban landscape, which occupies a territory between the personal and the collective, to invite a contemplation of art that fuses with everyday reality. She resorts to a grafting of diverse entities, nurtured by her first visual experiences and made with fragments of fabric, similar to Pattern Painting and its protagonists, from Robert Kushner to Joyce Kozloff. Her assemblages of fabric and other materials derive iconographically from her acrylic paintings, dating from 1978, which represent ties or magazine inserts. In 1981 her work progresses when portions of these assembled totalities, now in plywood, metal and carpet, visually 'explode' and are arranged

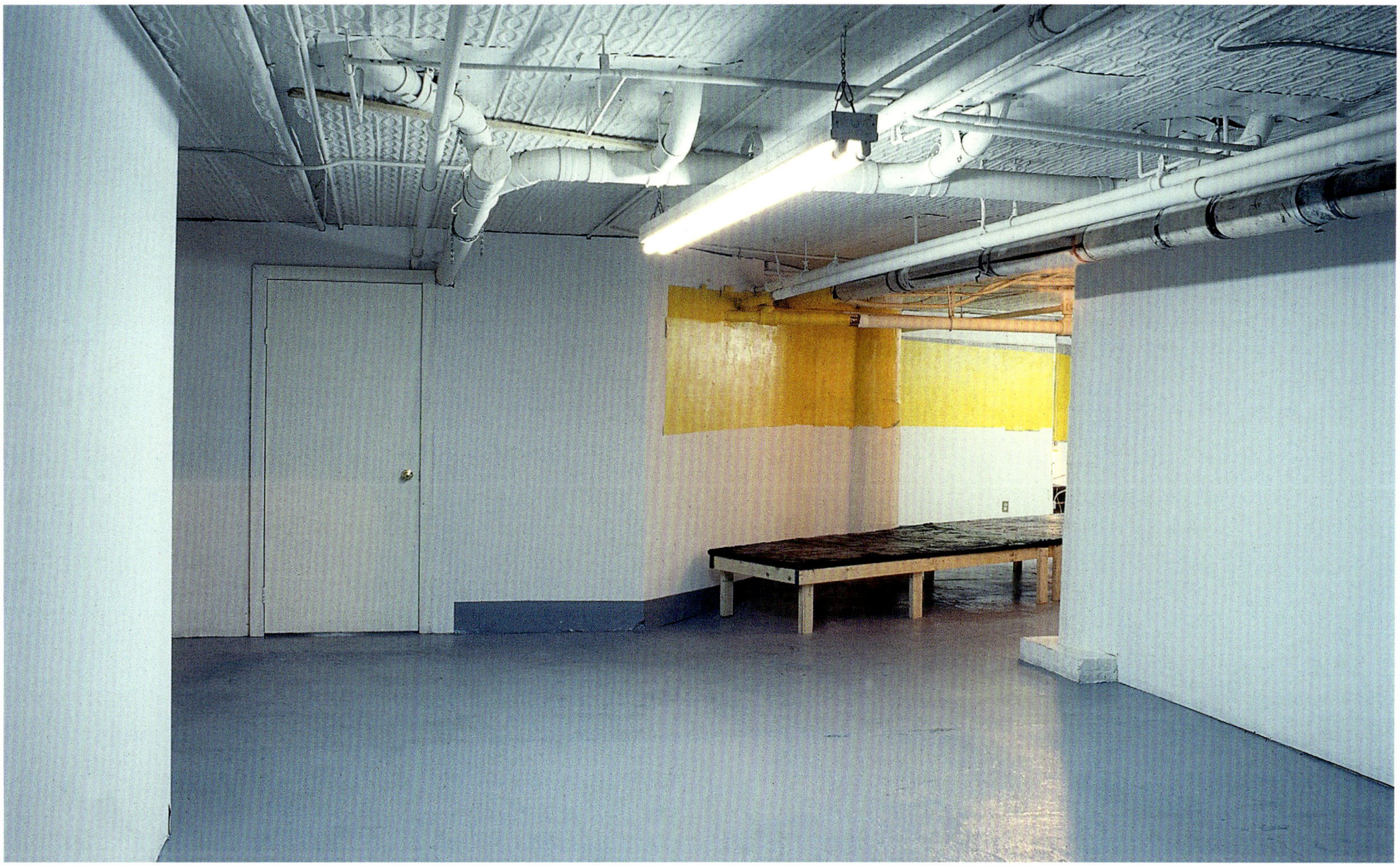

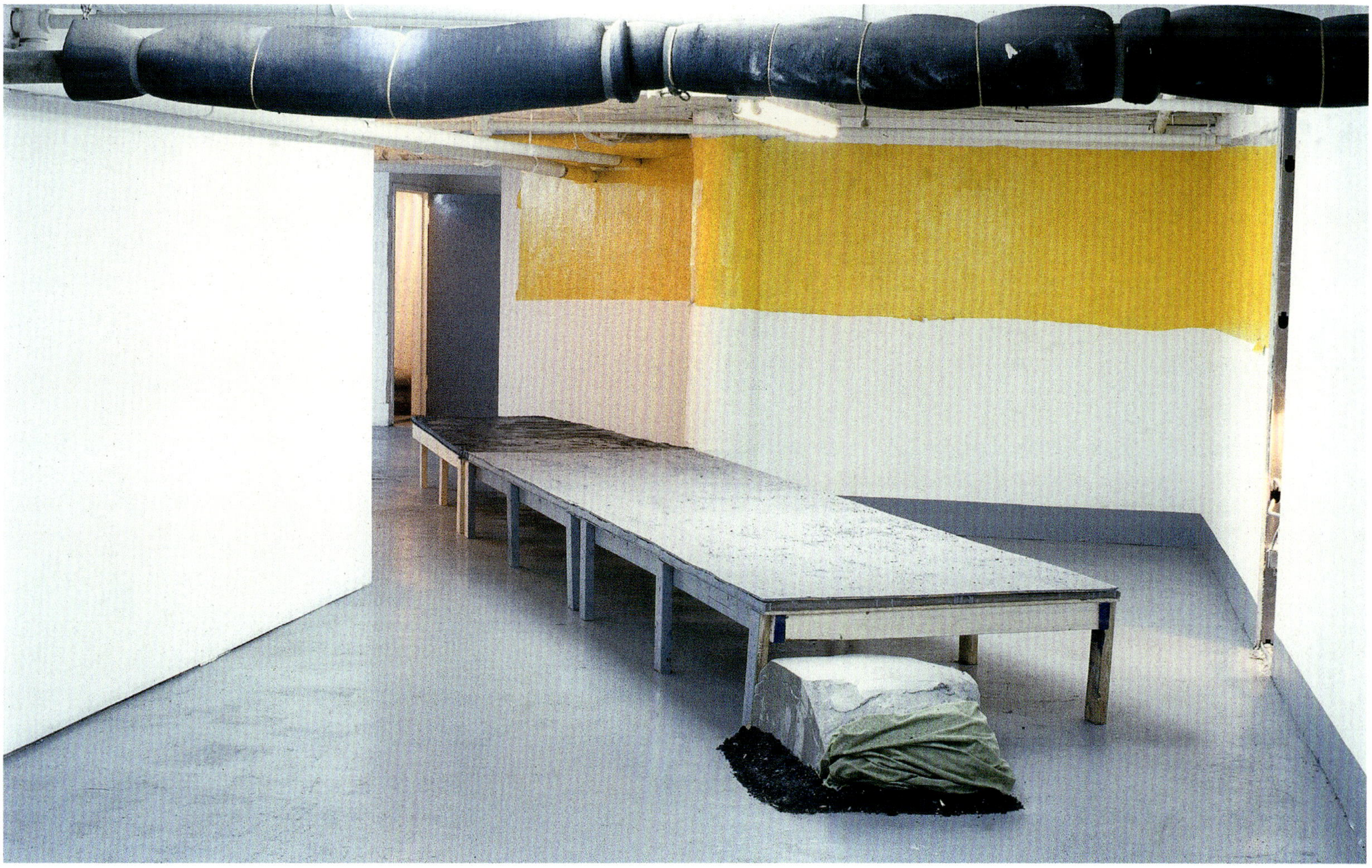

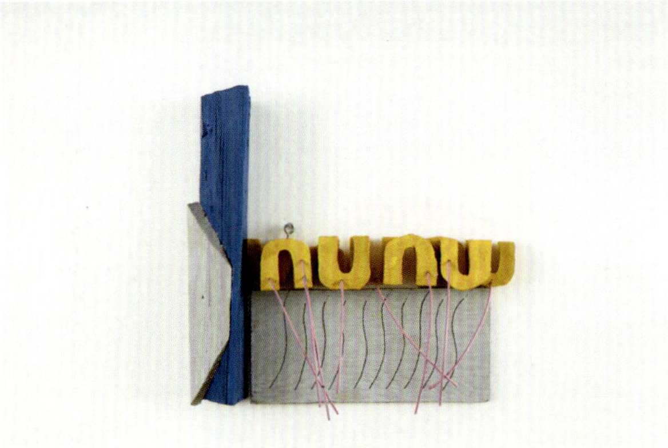

RICHARD TUTTLE
G 1, 1981
24 X 25 X 9 CM

freely on the wall, at the University of Victoria. The substantial portion that sustains the whole is transmuted into an 'environment' where, as in Minimal art, what matters is the breaks or intervals, but these now respond to a chance relationship between what is heard and what is seen: 'I like John Cage's and Alan Kaprow's thinking. I love that kind of philosophy, taking advantage of chance. I read their writings and everything in me warms up to that kind of thinking. I do that, but there is more of a struggle in my work around these issues than in theirs. My work isn't about just that. There is clearly some kind of imposed order, some dependence on art history and aesthetics that overlays whatever chance and happenstance I let occur.'[1]

These works, which oscillate, if microscopically, between Kushner and Richard Tuttle, attest to an expressive climate that, counterposing the immateriality of concepts against the monumentality of constructions and minimalist articulations, tends to revive expressive and communicative values through colour and figure. It is a rejection of metaphysical belief, in favour of the material, the abstract and the physical, in order to put the emphasis back on décor and on appearance, on sensory and emotional participation connected to the use of information embedded in the industrial project, using hard and sensual materials. It is a return to the real and to its representativeness, which tends to a relationship with things and with effigies. As a result, artists involved with movements ranging from European Neo-expressionism to American Bad Painting, from Anselm Kiefer to Sigmar Polke, from Enzo Cucchi to David Salle, revive the practice of visual storytelling. One line of narrative tendency, which proposes the fluid and flexible value of art, is carried out with recourse to fabrics and textiles. It thrusts open the space to 'superficiality', in the pictorial sense, which the artists themselves seek to mitigate, establishing a dialectic between painting and architecture, through a tie between objects and the painted surface. They connect the painting to the floor or ceiling, thereby documenting the intention to make painting emerge from its parietal isolation, establishing a connection and a concrete bond with the environmental context. Stockholder, from 1980 to 1982, during her university studies in Victoria, Canada, pursues similar goals, when she begins to confront the problem of the wall in relation to the space, appending elements that, in subsequent years, will descend from ceiling to floor, also looking at the work of Judy Pfaff and Frank Stella.

In 1983, with her *Installation in My Father's Backyard* (private residence, Vancouver), the artist begins to emphasize that her activity is linked to habitat. She establishes a direct relationship between art and building construction. This is the ritual 'cave' in which the painting or sculpture, the object or construction, is oriented. Thus it should be thought of as a new sort of habitat. It needs to be oriented, following entrances and portals, in order for it to correspond to the spirit of the place. And since the construction reflects the person who inhabits it, Stockholder installs a mattress, which can be equated with individuality, in such a way that her art, as a painter who uses colours but is integrated within a historical itinerary that also includes Minimal art, becomes a centre of life: 'I found this mattress in the garage and painted it red as complement to the grass. The backyard is more or less rectangular, so it's similar in shape to the mattress and garage. The lawn is brought into a dialogue with the mattress, and with the history of painting, because paintings are rectangular too. Here I'm making a painting – only it's also a back yard. The red of the mattress called to the colour of the berries in the tree, heightening colour that's already there. I painted the grass with a hard-edged form, kind of rectangular so it has a formal relationship to the door, and to the mattress.'[2]

foreground,
DRAFT, 2014
PLASTIC GARAGE FLOOR TILES, COPPER TUBING, FOIL, WOODEN PEPPER MILL PART, ACRYLIC PAINT, PLASTIC PARTS, ELECTRIC CORD, WOODEN BRANCH, RUBBER WASHERS, WIRE, SHELLS, GALVANIZED STEEL VENT PART, WHITE METAL BRACKET, ORANGE ROPE, WHITE ROPE, ZIP TIES, KEY CHAIN WIRES, ORANGE PING PONG BALLS, RUBBER, RIVETS. LIGHT FIXTURE: RECESSED LED CEILING FIXTURE
116 X 91 CM
HEIGHT VARIABLE

background,
2012
PRIMED MASONITE, ACRYLIC PAINT, CLOTH LEAVES, PLASTIC PARTS, RIBBON, HARDWARE, FAKE ROCK, LINOLEUM
102 X 76 X 19 CM

INSTALLATION VIEW AT GALLERIA RAFFAELLA CORTESE, MILAN, 2014

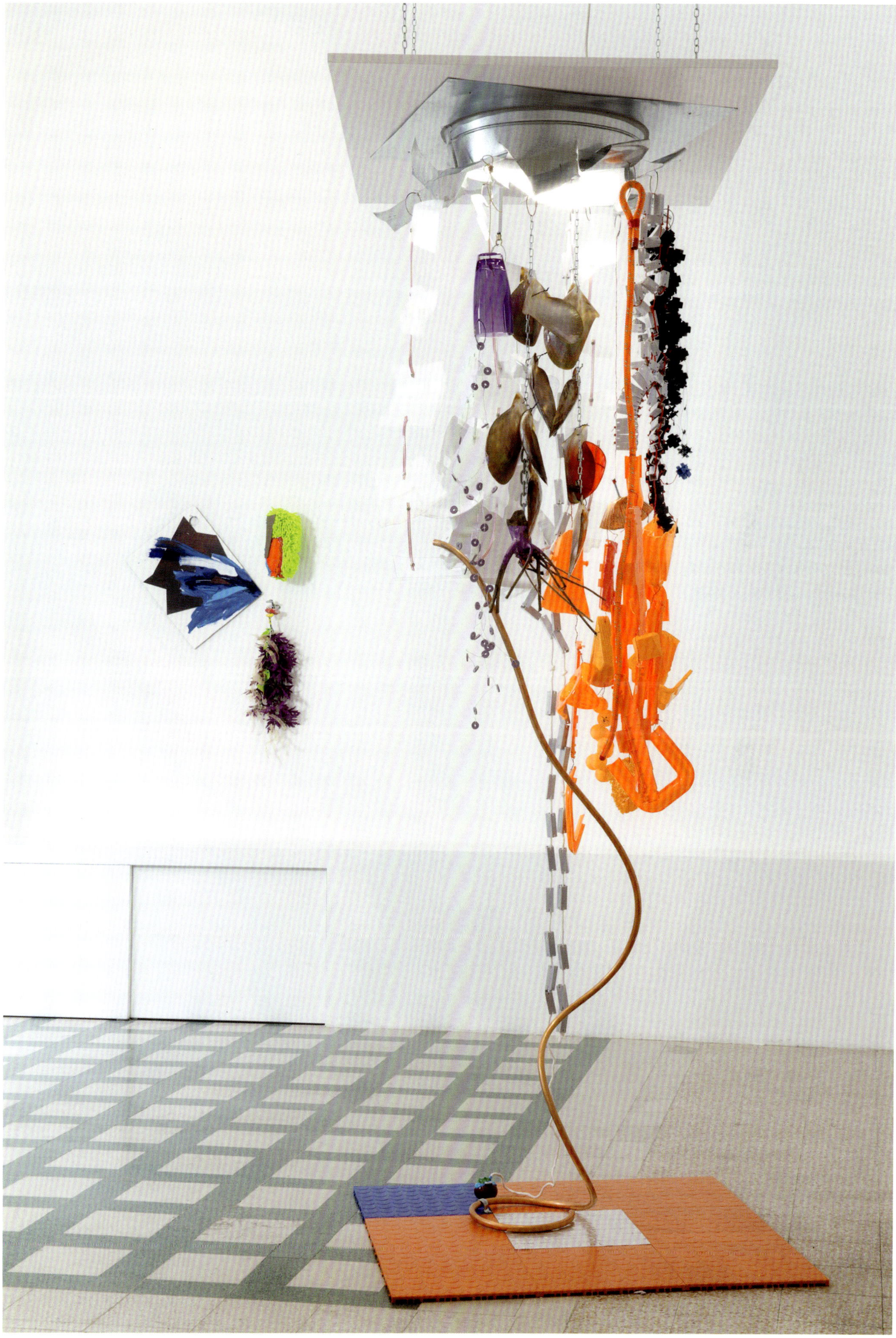

INDOOR LIGHTING FOR MY FATHER, 1988
NEWSPAPER, MEN'S AND WOMEN'S UNDERWEAR, CEMENT, STYROFOAM, ORANGES, HAY, LIGHTING
ROOM: 430 X 276 CM
CEILING: 134 CM

In *The Lion, the Witch and the Wardrobe* (Artists Space, New York, 1985), Stockholder constructed a path – made of walls, doors, wall paintings and inserted objects and signs – cutting a hole in the sheetrock wall in the basement gallery revealing the tool room behind. One ramp, half-painted and half-unpainted, recalled Trakas's works, including the way it connected the two large rooms that housed the exhibition. With this ambient but difficult-to-access connection, Stockholder proposes a trespassing and a vibration between sculpture and painting. She implements a transmission of energy throughout all the vital fibres of the space. She asserts its continuity and a related awareness of a mutating attempt, pertinent to the place and to the memory of all experienced places: 'I think it has something to do with providing a place to experience will. If you can actually be aware of a moment and aware of yourself existing immediately, separate from, or in addition to, your history or memory, and culture, and all that makes you you, then there's room for choice.'[3] She calls into question linguistic boundaries in order to launch a total occupation of the territory, whether interior or exterior architecture, to establish a relationship between image and situation, given or found, known or unknown. Similar to *Installation in My Father's Backyard*, here the artist aspires to an individual construction, between above and below, gallery and basement. She turns the art installation into a 'divided' complex of materials and forms, colours and things, which the public is free to perceive, depending on their sensitivity to the elements and the movements.

With this work, she aspires to a summation of the attitudes that had governed her earlier investigations, from Minimal art to Arte Povera, and, in contrast to their centralization of the artefact, she proposes a liberating synthesis. Here, all possible aesthetic identities converge, animated by intense colours, fluid and rigid materials, from wood to paper and fabric, from the grafting of natural and industrial elements, from plants to lights: a plurality of entities that produces a diversity of opposing responses and behaviours, but within a single system. In this way Stockholder's research has analogies with the idea of the 'fractal', a term and related theory coined in 1975 by Benoît Mandelbrot. The situations created by the artist appear chaotic, but in fact they define dynamic systems with complex articulations. Thus her work since 1983 has no longer been solely 'autonomous' and does not function as a compact 'otherness' so much as it accepts within itself the complementarity of the habitat and its visitor: a self-similarity that unites all the parts into a whole. She adapts her forms and materials, her graftings and montages as a response to a dialectic, based on a congruent number of interactions and multiple influences.

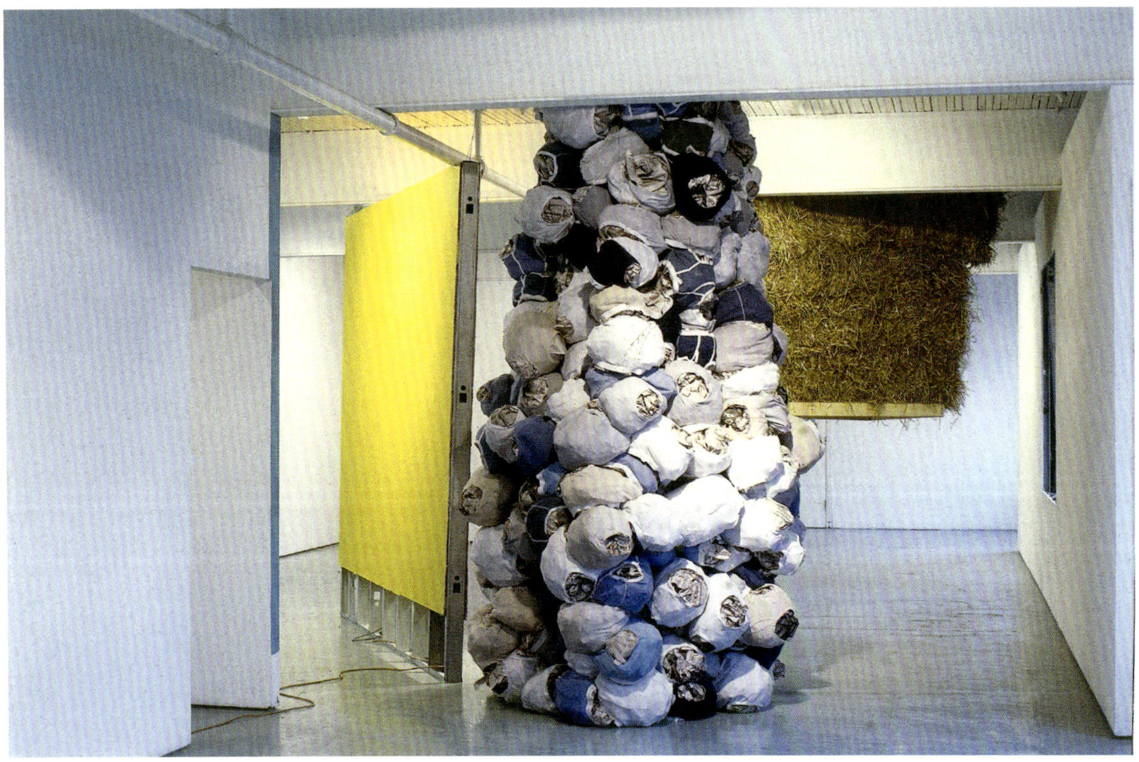

<u>KISSING THE WALL #1</u>, 1988
SMALL PIECE OF FURNITURE,
ENAMEL, INCANDESCENT
LIGHT, NEWSPAPER, GLUE
H. 76 CM

<u>KISSING THE WALL #5</u>, 1990
METAL STRAPPING, SPOOLS OF
THREAD AND WOOD, CHAIR, OIL
AND LATEX AND ACRYLIC PAINT,
FLUORESCENT LIGHT, PAPER,
GLUE
72 X 86 X 130 CM

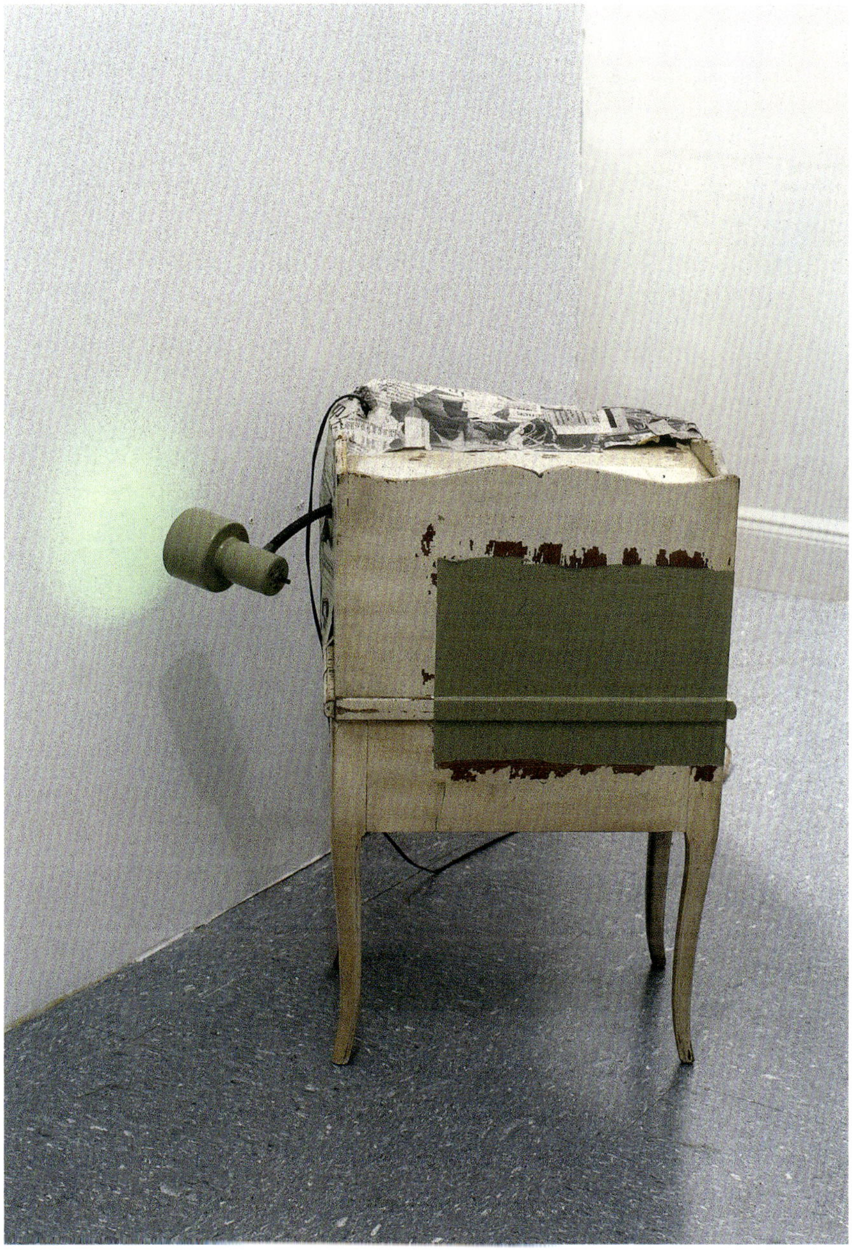

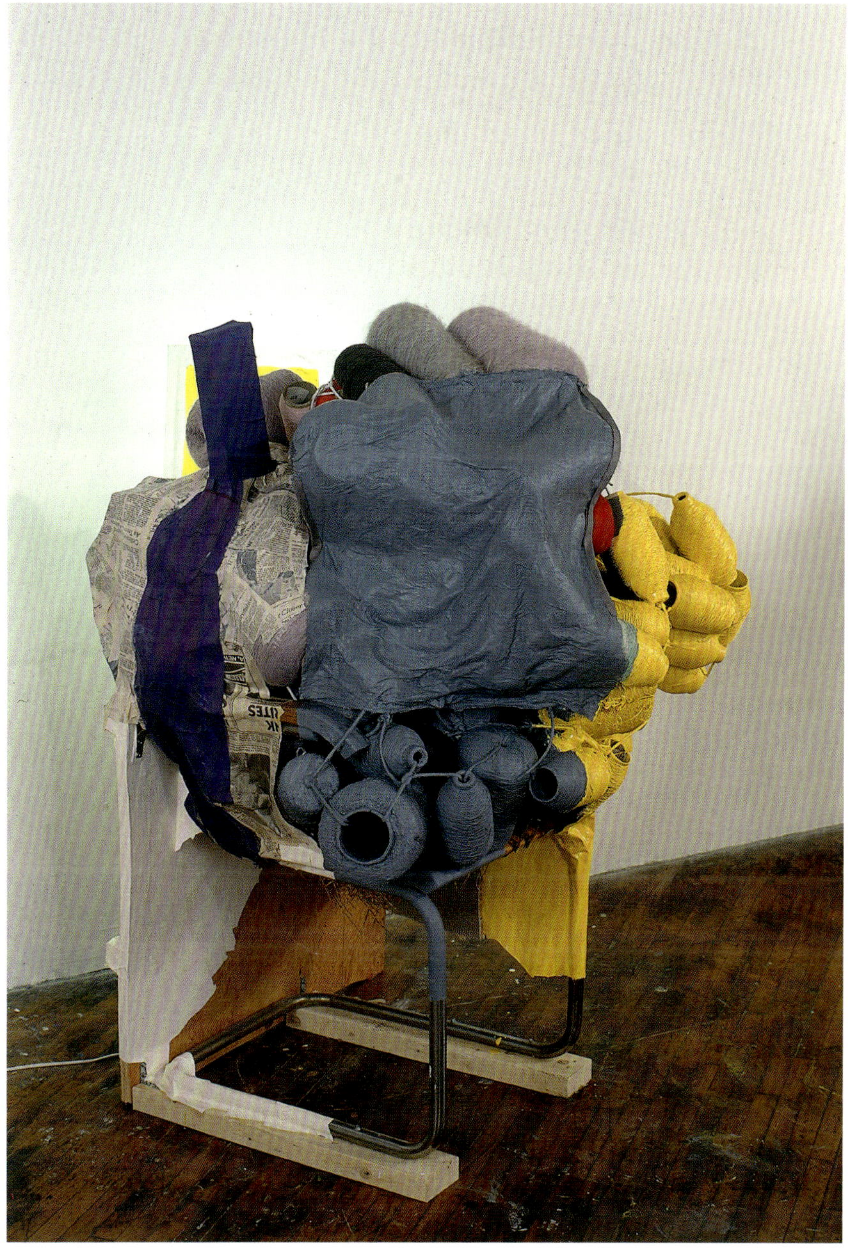

FLOORED, 2015
SNAP TOGETHER DANCE FLOOR, ACRYLIC PAINT, BROKEN PLASTIC BASKETS, STICKS, WIRE, CHAIN, BUNGEE CORD, VACUUM CLEANER HANDLE
191 X 262 X 175 CM

INSTALLATION VIEW AT ROSEMARIE SCHWARZWALDER GALERIE NACHST ST. STEPHAN, VIENNA, 2015

next page,
TWO FRAMES, 2007
PINK PLASTIC, PINK CHILDREN'S CHAIR, FAKE FUR, MISCELLANEOUS PLASTIC PARTS, VINYL, HALOGEN LIGHT AND FIXTURE, WEIGHT, BRACKET, CABLE, EXTENSION CORD, BLACK GARBAGE BAG, YARN, BEADS, ACRYLIC AND OIL PAINT, WOODEN DRAWER, METAL FRAME
236 X 130 X 56 CM

INSTALLATION VIEW AT 1301PE, LOS ANGELES, 2007

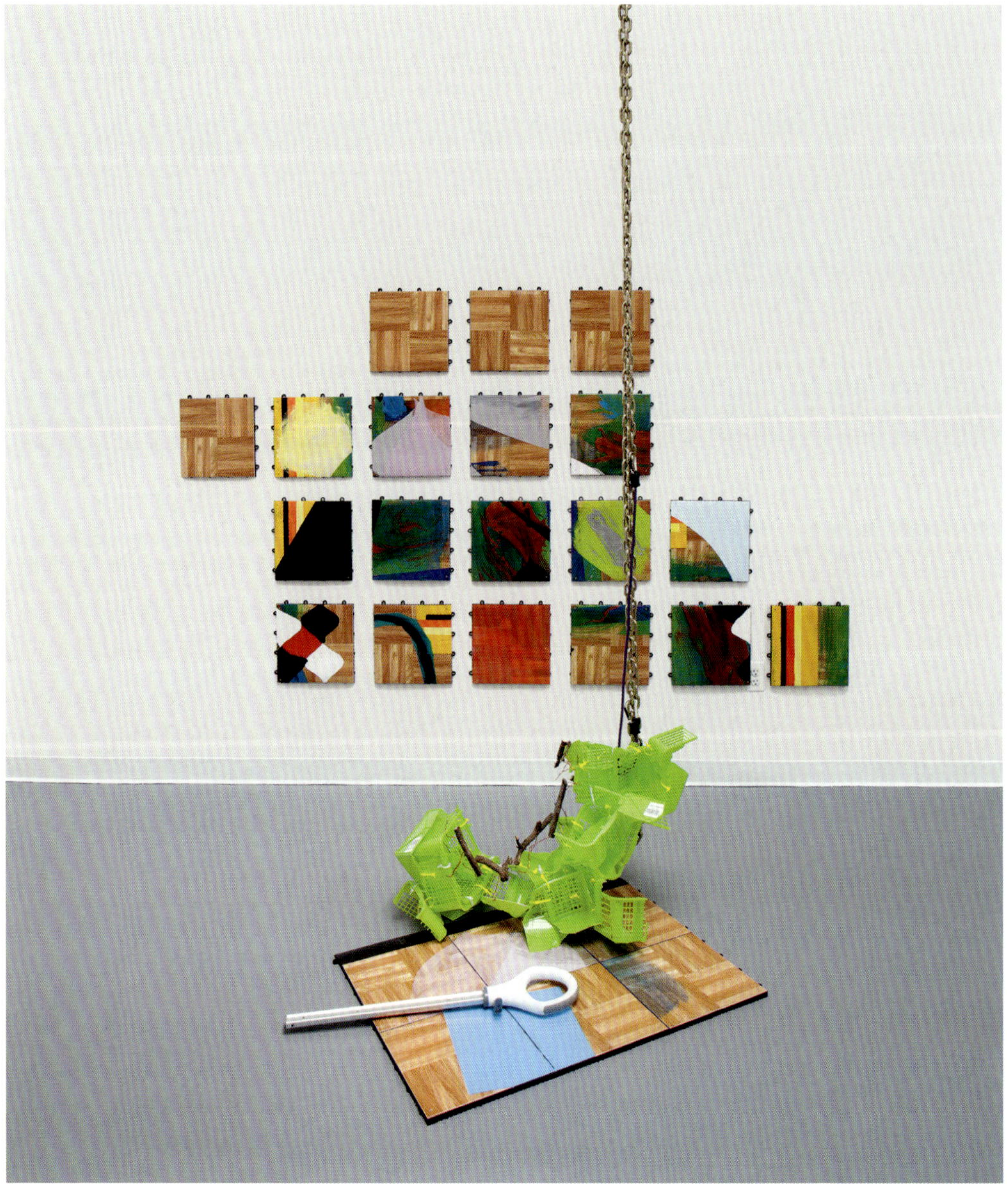

This is highlighted by sculptures that share wall and floor, that are fed by electrical connections and by chromatic passages, as in the series *Kissing the Wall*, and that are positioned in a corner, as in *Indoor Lighting for My Father* (Mercer Union, Toronto, 1988). The assemblage of materials, from cement to Styrofoam, from hay to glass, from paper to underwear, stages something between subordination and the independence of artistic conduct, oscillating between project and improvisation, between interior environment and urban environment. Here the construction of a place of contemplation, located at the back of the gallery, is conjoined with the act of being a viewer with a sensitive and intelligent perception, reflecting, however, an approach from the context of the city to the context of art. A 'chaotic' dialectic arises, between rigid and soft, heavy and light, resulting in the formation of a sculptural composition: 'I think that my work is in fact highly composed, even classical in this respect. I don't know how to articulate why composition matters so much … What can we say in words to approximate what tensions in composition evoke? But I do think that composition like timing in film or in music is highly evocative in my work. I try to make sense of chaos, happenstance and disorder within composition. The very formal, very beautiful, static composition is somehow knit into the chaos that is also always present.'[4] The title *Kissing the Wall* is indicative of Stockholder's spherical vision, where the pictorial identity is entrusted to a soft contact between object and wall.

Her sculptures do not exploit and occupy the wall, but graze it, through a slight connection that runs from the electrical socket to a light bulb, from a coloured square to a luminous projection, from *Kissing the Wall #1* to *Kissing the Wall #5* (1988). This exchange of energy can also take place between ceiling and assembled object, implemented in *Edge of Hothouse Glass* (1992) through a white fluorescent tube so that it forms a circular entity. These sculptures establish a 'short circuit' between the architectural components and the installation of the materials. They can range from their insertion into a space or the studio to flying in space, from *St. Clementines* (1988) to *Two Frames* (2007).

The sculpture's radiation out in different directions, so that it functions as a hinge between high and low, becomes a metaphor for a tension that causes the work

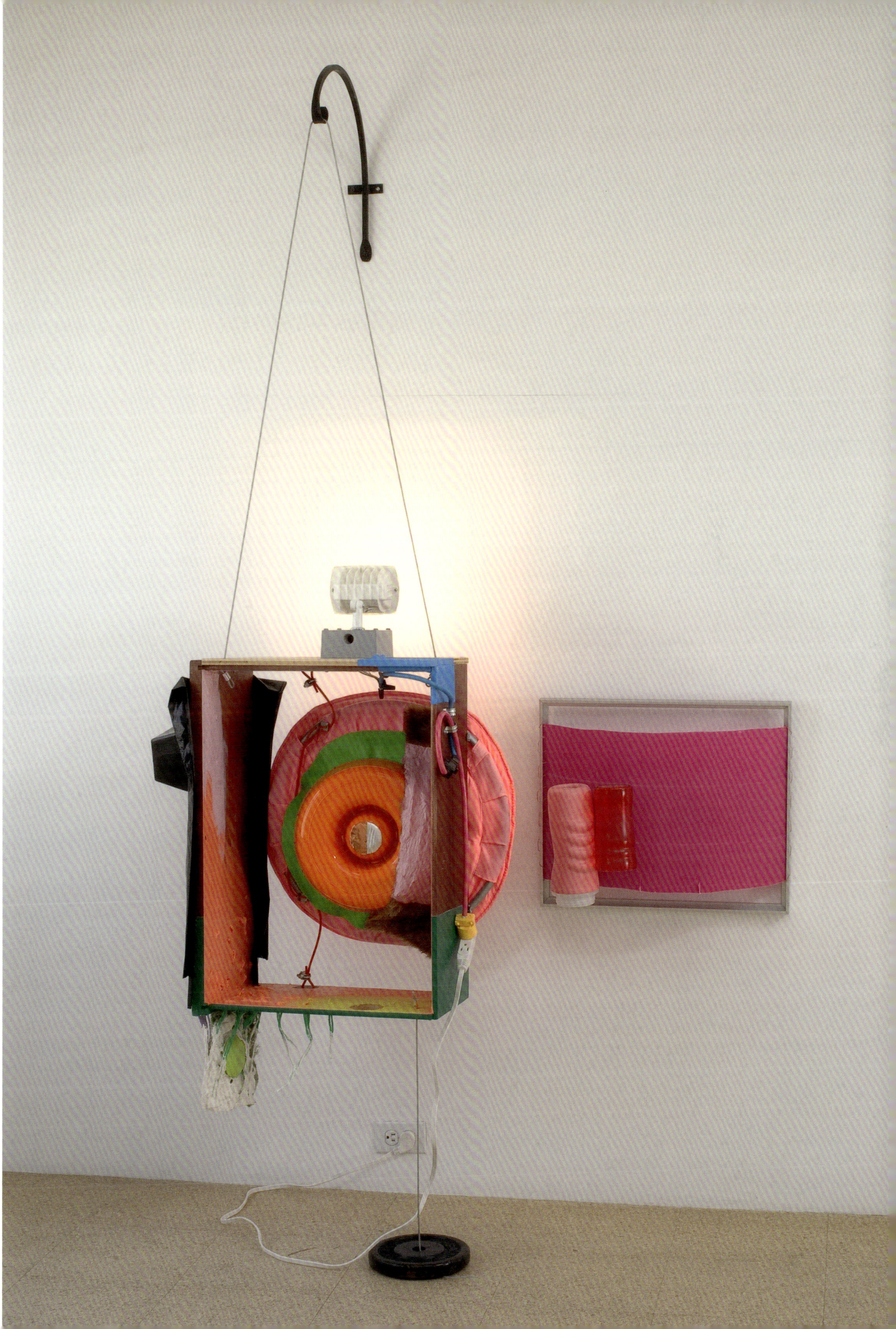

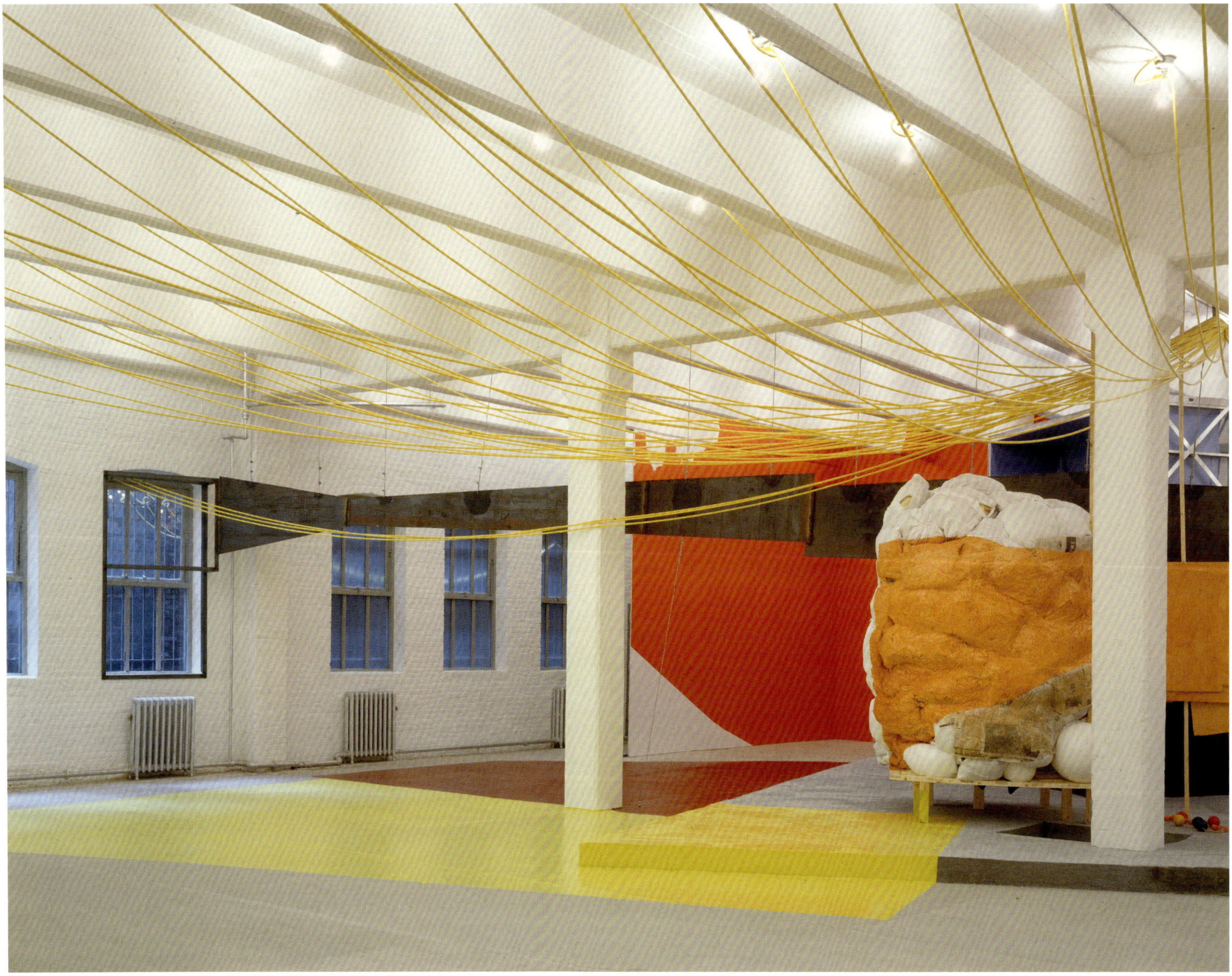

YOUR SKIN IN THIS WEATHER BOURNE EYE – THREADS AND SWOLLEN PERFUME, 1995
PAINT, CONCRETE, STRUCTOLITE, MISC. BUILDING MATERIAL, CARPET LAMPS, ELECTRICAL CORD, PURPLE PLASTIC STACKING CRATES, SWIMMING POOL LINER, WELDED STEEL, STUFFED SHIRTS PILLOWS, PAPIER MÂCHÉ AND BALLS
5.48 X 2788 SQM

INSTALLATION VIEW AT DIA CENTER FOR THE ARTS, NEW YORK, 1995

to breathe, like a plant mass. The artist, mixing materials and colours, environments and paintings, agitates forms and spaces, creating a labyrinth, a geography of the unformed and the larval, which offers viewers the possibility of entering a cave in which they can get lost, almost harbouring a second experiential birth. These are architectures that refer to Stockholder's visions and fixations, but also accommodate projective procedures that are yet to come, secret germinations of persons and places: 'My hope is that the viewer will, like me, become engaged in a struggle between viewing a static *fait accompli* and feeling as if they are participating in a series of contradictions and narratives that come to no settling conclusion. I feel that my work provides both experiences and argues for the necessity of both. The narratives and evocations my work gives rise to are intended to be wide ranging. They are the result of my personal history, the culture I live and the histories brought to the work by all those who take an interest.'[5]

There is an additional osmosis: the collapse of the distinction between real object and imaginary object. Stockholder goes about investigating and researching the elements that will come to constitute her final work in shops and warehouses of the city where her intervention takes place. Thus she ends up affirming that reality itself can become an awe-inspiring and surprising event, where parts merge and become confused, colour becomes object and vice versa: 'I never stopped using paint. I use paint as an object. I started to use objects as equivalents to paint. A painted surface and a coloured object both have weight. Sometimes it is an illusion of weight, sometimes it is real weight, mass and scale. And the colour seems to me always to be something insubstantial. It floats off the surface or changes the surface. So the action of the colour is atmospheric, analogous to fantasy and fiction and story telling.'[6]

She exceeds the conditions of life and, scandalously, as in surrealist territories, she changes their identity. She sets up a relationship between the functional efficacy of furniture and fittings, but transmutes them into 'unreality': from *Where it Happened* (1990) to *Your Skin in this Weather Bourne Eye – Threads & Swollen Perfume* (DIA Center for the Arts, New York, 1995). The former, an installation in the gallery space of American Fine Arts, Co. in New York, made an immediate impact on viewers as soon as they crossed

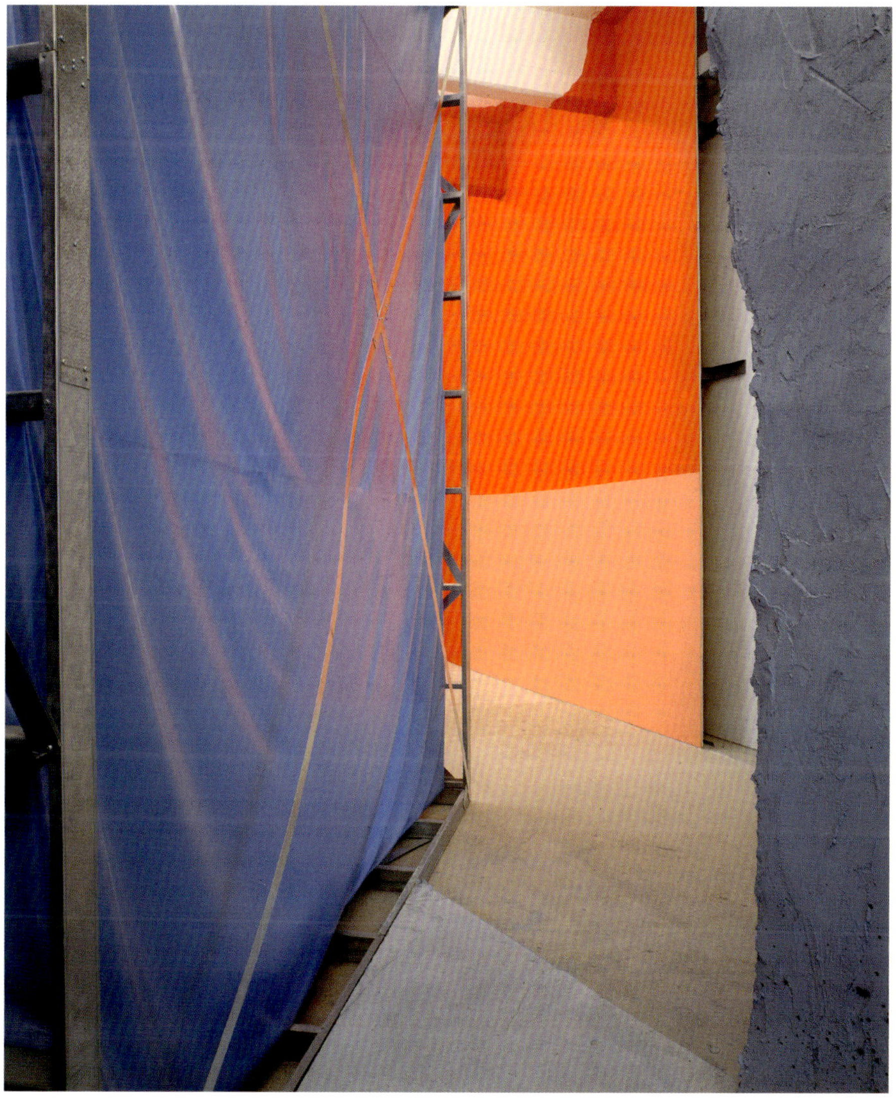

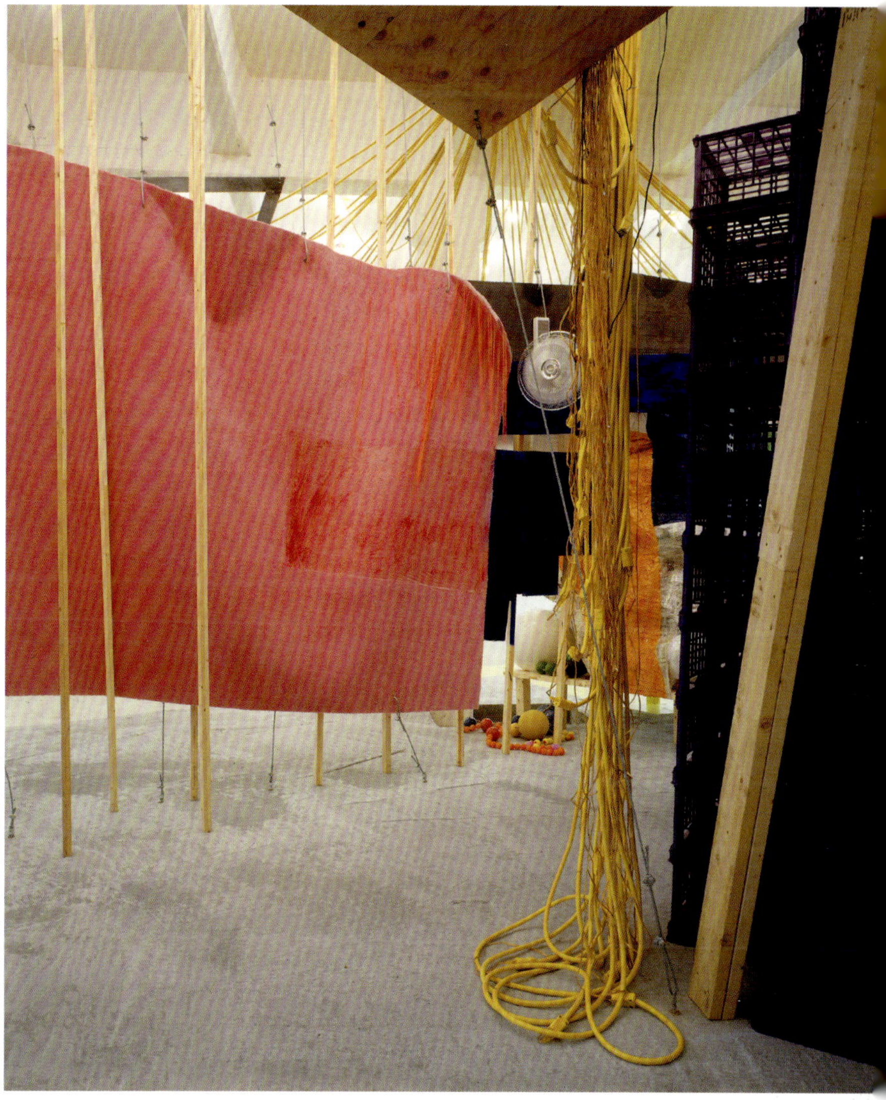

PEER OUT TO SEE, 2010
PLASTIC TUBS, PLATFORM, PAINT, DUCK WEED POND, ORANGE PIGMENT, BURNT WOOD AND WHEELCHAIR RAMP

INSTALLATION VIEW AT PALACIO DE CRISTAL REINA SOFÍA, MADRID, 2010

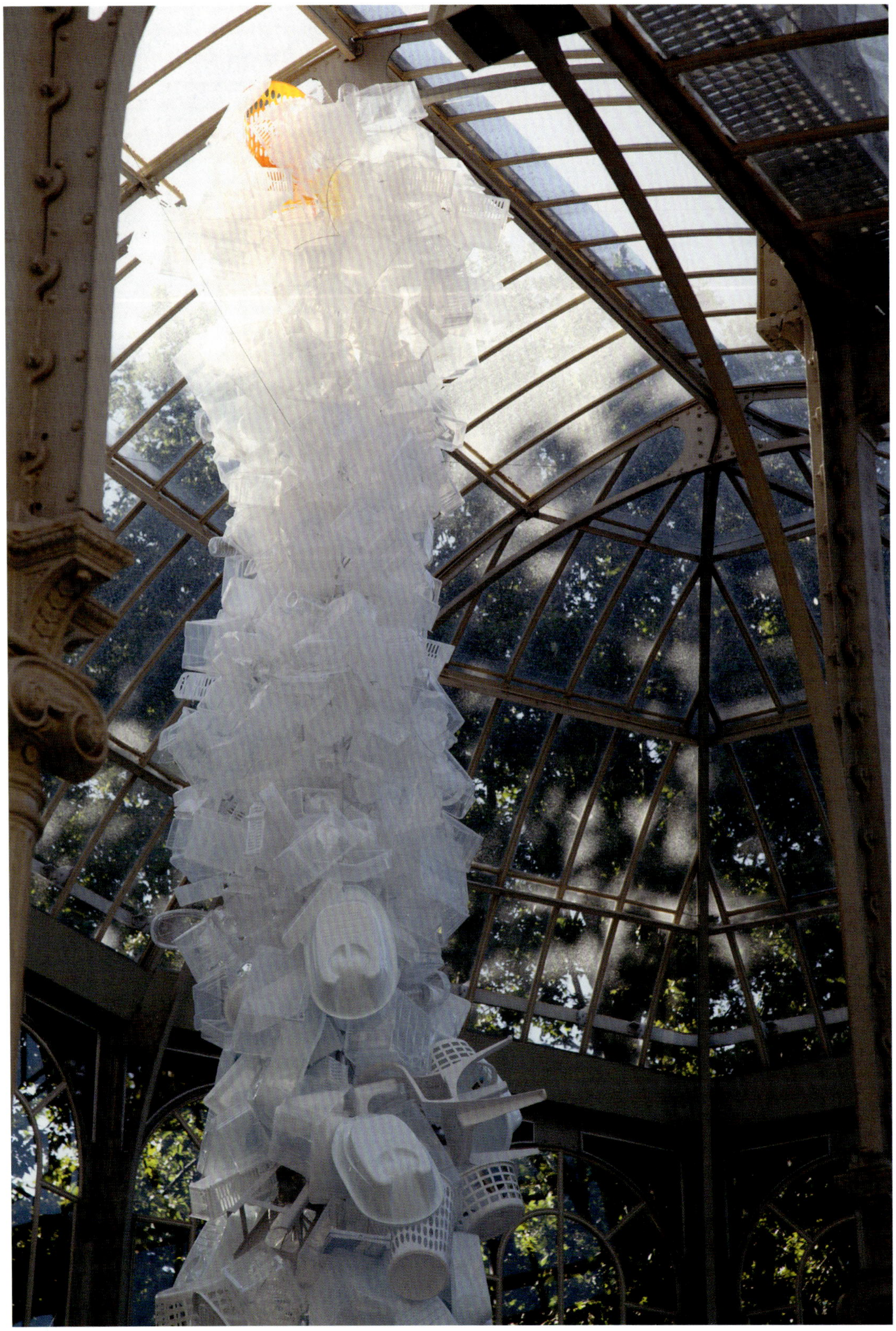

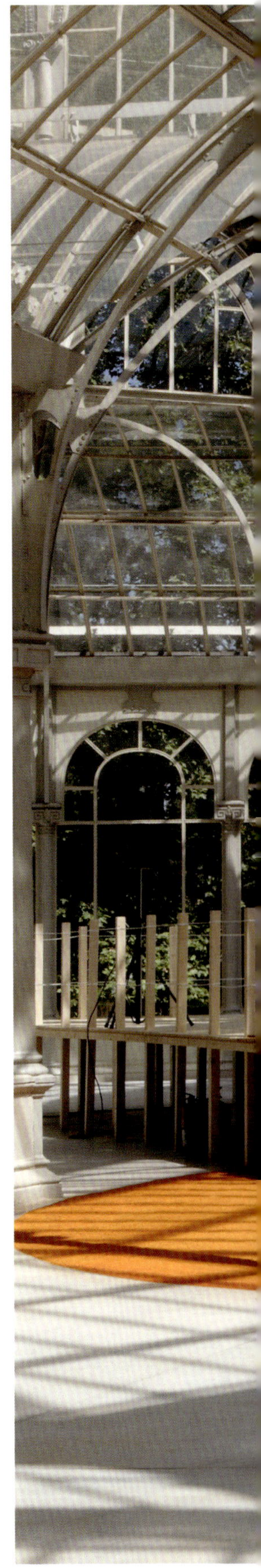

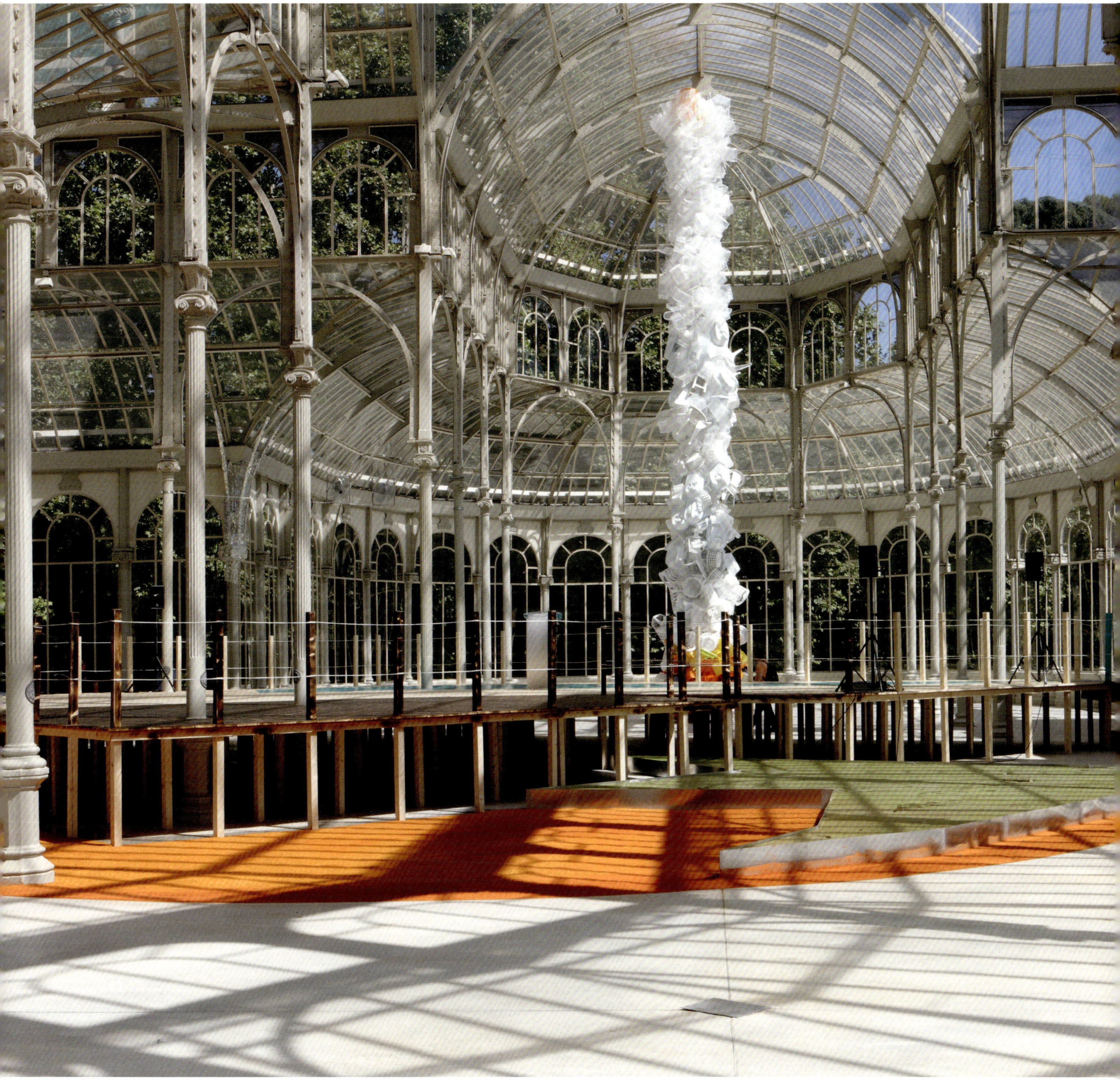

TV TIPPED TOE NAILS & THE GREEN SALAMI, 2003
CARPET, LINOLEUM, HEATER, WHITE APPLIANCES, LIGHTS, BLEACHERS, WOODEN PLATFORM, BRICKS, PAINT, WOOD

INSTALLATION VIEW AT CAPC, MUSÉE D'ART CONTEMPORAIN DE BORDEAUX, 2003

the threshold. It consisted of an assemblage of furniture, one piece on top of another, positioned in relation to a concrete and pictorial parietal intervention – almost an interdisciplinary grafting of art, painting, architecture and design. The latter project, composed of a stratification of materials and elements, lights and objects, responds to a poetry where the public merges with the installation. Visitors are invited into an almost initiatory 'maze'. 'I hope that the finished object provides, if only for a brief moment, a site where myself and others can experience a confluence of inner life with concrete physical stuff. In this sense, and in other ways also, I think the work creates a static event. Visually not very much moves, except for the person viewing; but there are sparks flying through the air as electricity moves sight unseen through wires.'[7]

Another salient element in Stockholder's work is her determination to favour the experience of art over the product. It is a form of communication that happens live, with the visitor, and is experienced: 'providing a place to experience will'. Her art advances towards 'psychosculpture', with open-ended effects, whether the visitor is aware of them or not – effects that are induced and perceived, directly implemented depending on the behaviour of individuals. Stockholder works on a unified vision of the habitat, proposing certain forms for it that, in addition to having a function, reveal her attention to play and pleasure, which implies an existential component, as in *House Beautiful* (Dijon, 1994). The perceptual and mental productivity that is encouraged by having people pass through 'membranes' of walls or fabric, lights or colours – enacting Stockholder's desire to shatter and overturn solids into voids, pictorial surfaces into architectural structures – produces a continuous vibration: from *It's Not Over 'Till The Fat Lady Sings* (Vancouver, 1988) to *Growing Rock Candy Mountain Grasses in Canned Sand* (Münster, 1992), from *Sam Ran Over Sand or Sand Ran Over Sam* (Toronto, 2004) to *Peer Out to See* (Madrid, 2010). Entering these works, visitors perceive a continuous flow of materials and spaces, a fluid force connoted by all-consuming qualities. The feeling is similar to

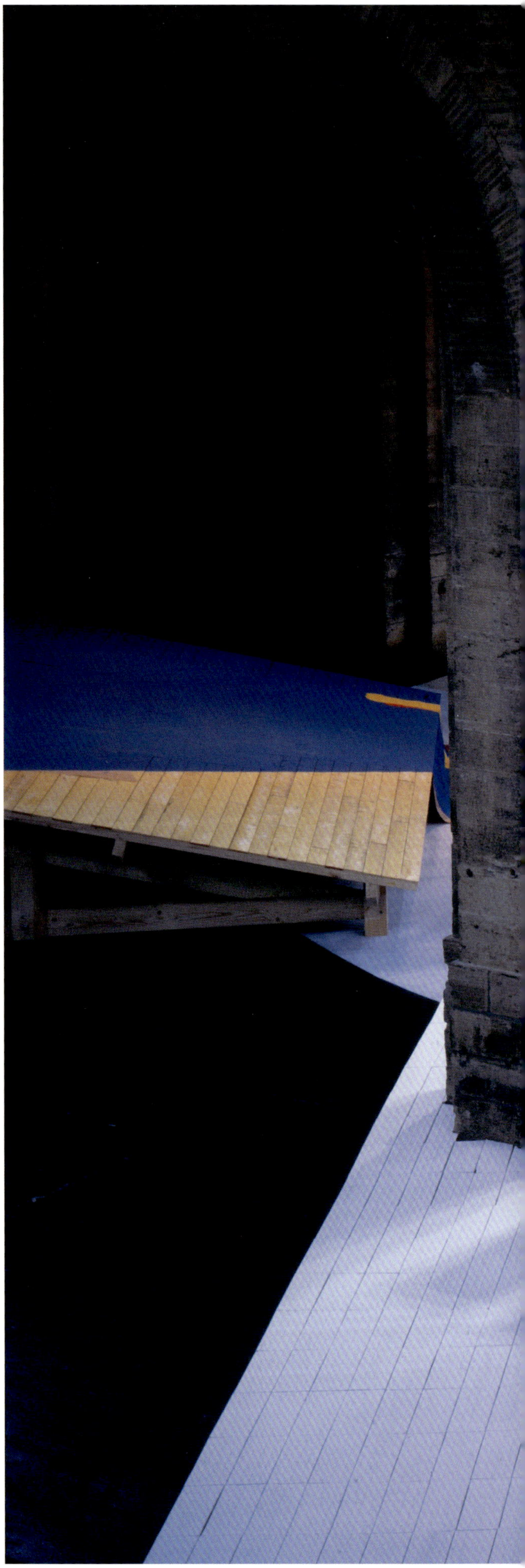

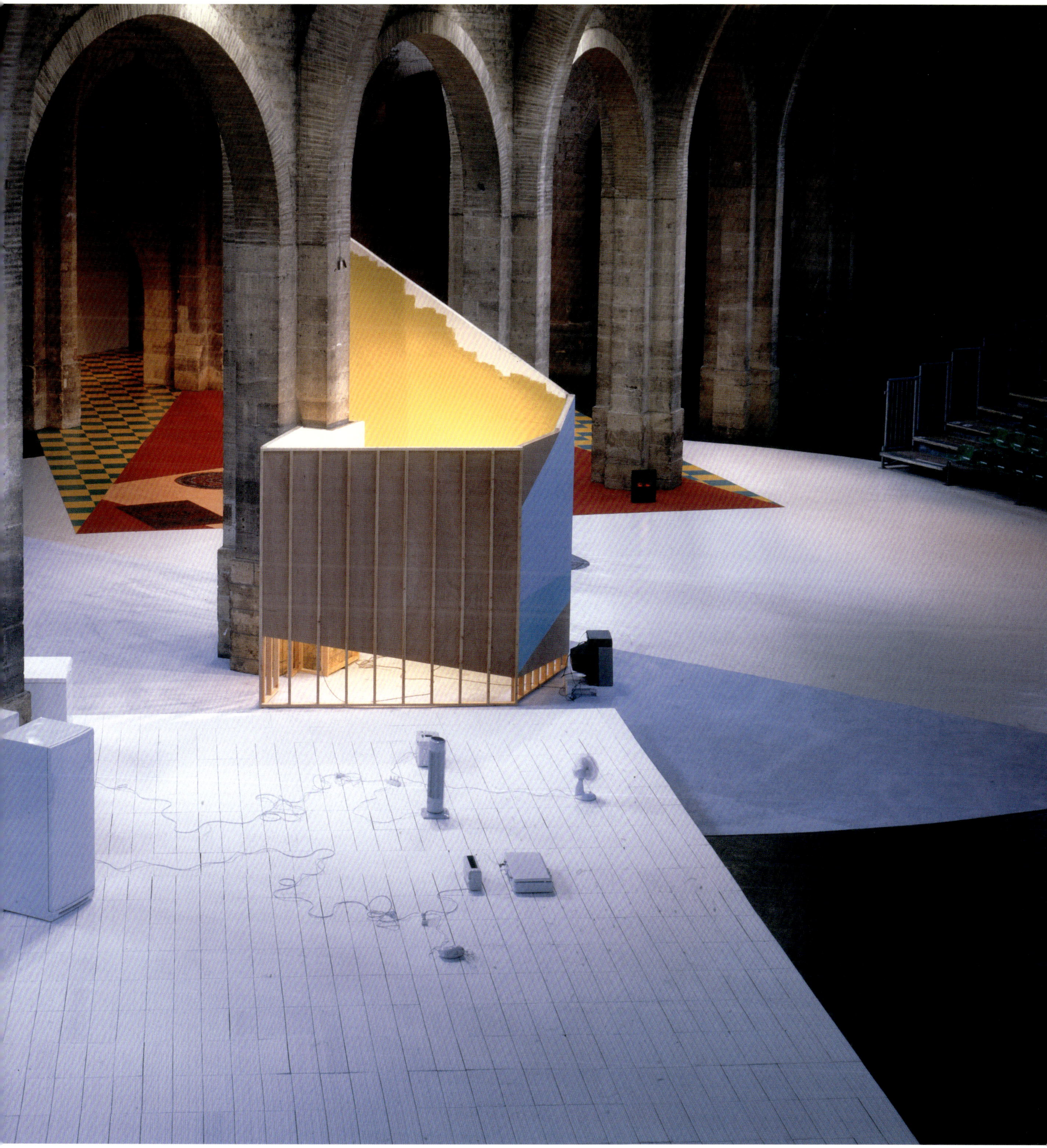

venturing into a convulsive and erratic forest, a 'where' impregnated by natural and fantastical analogies, which almost becomes a hive or matrix, gradually pushing for its own behaviour to be taken into consideration and scrutinized – an inner and outer regression, primary and elementary: 'Behaviour as raw material. It's not how I would begin speaking of my work except to say that viewing the work is a process that takes place over time; it involves putting various pieces of information together and it takes an active human being to do that. I could also say that I would like it if my work forced recognition that that pleasant sensation of passive viewing is actually an active position.'[8]

The situations Stockholder sets up are offered as plays of circumstances and references. They feed off individual improvisation and the constructed development that she derives from the architectural and urban-technical territory from which she has extracted the materials. Forming a totality, these end up losing their original and pre-existing significance; they are removed from their destination and placed in an aesthetically and functionally different context.

FLOWER BED, 2004
COBBLESTONES, FIVE TABLES, TWO BENCHES, ONE QUARTZ LIGHT, ONE STREET LAMP, WOODEN BED STRUCTURE, ALUMINIUM, LINOLEUM CIRCLE, ENAMEL OIL BASED PAINT, ARTIST OIL PAINT, LIGHTS AND ELECTRICAL CORDS
COBBLESTONE PLATFORM
420 X 300 CM

INSTALLATION VIEW AT PALAIS RAMEAU, LILLE, FRANCE, 2004

next page,
FLOWER BED, 2004
COBBLESTONES, FIVE TABLES, TWO BENCHES, ONE QUARTZ LIGHT, ONE STREET LAMP, WOODEN BED STRUCTURE, ALUMINIUM, LINOLEUM CIRCLE, ENAMEL OIL BASED PAINT, ARTIST OIL PAINT, LIGHTS AND ELECTRICAL CORDS
COBBLESTONE PLATFORM
420 X 300 CM

INSTALLATION VIEW AT ÉCOLE SUPERIEURE DES BEAUX-ARTS DU MANS, LILLE, FRANCE, 2004

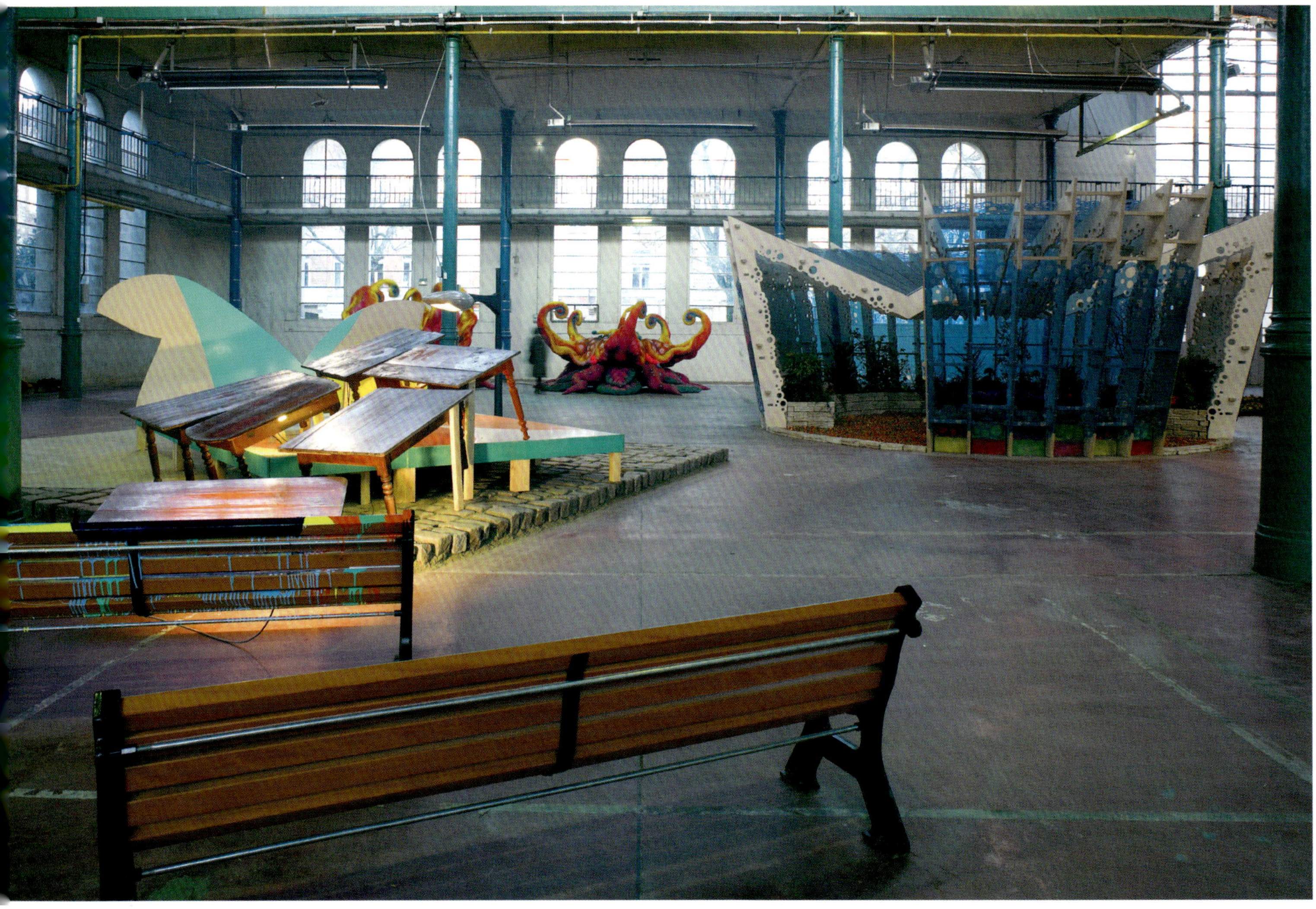

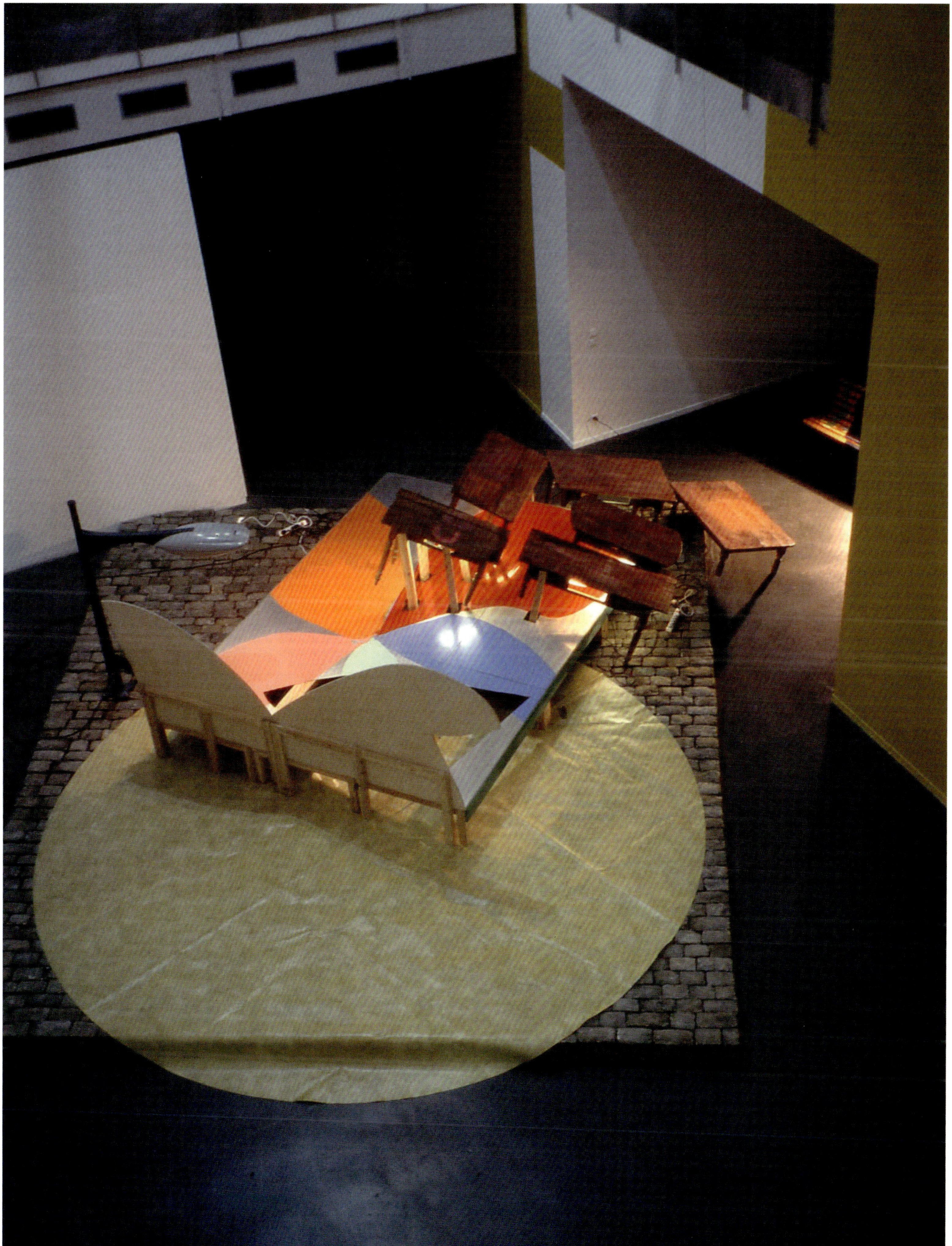

HOLLOW PLACES COURT IN ASH-TREE WOOD, 2011
AMERICAN ASH WOOD, PAINT, PLYWOOD
173 X 280 X 58 CM

INSTALLATION AT THE ALDRICH CONTEMPORARY ART MUSEUM, 2011

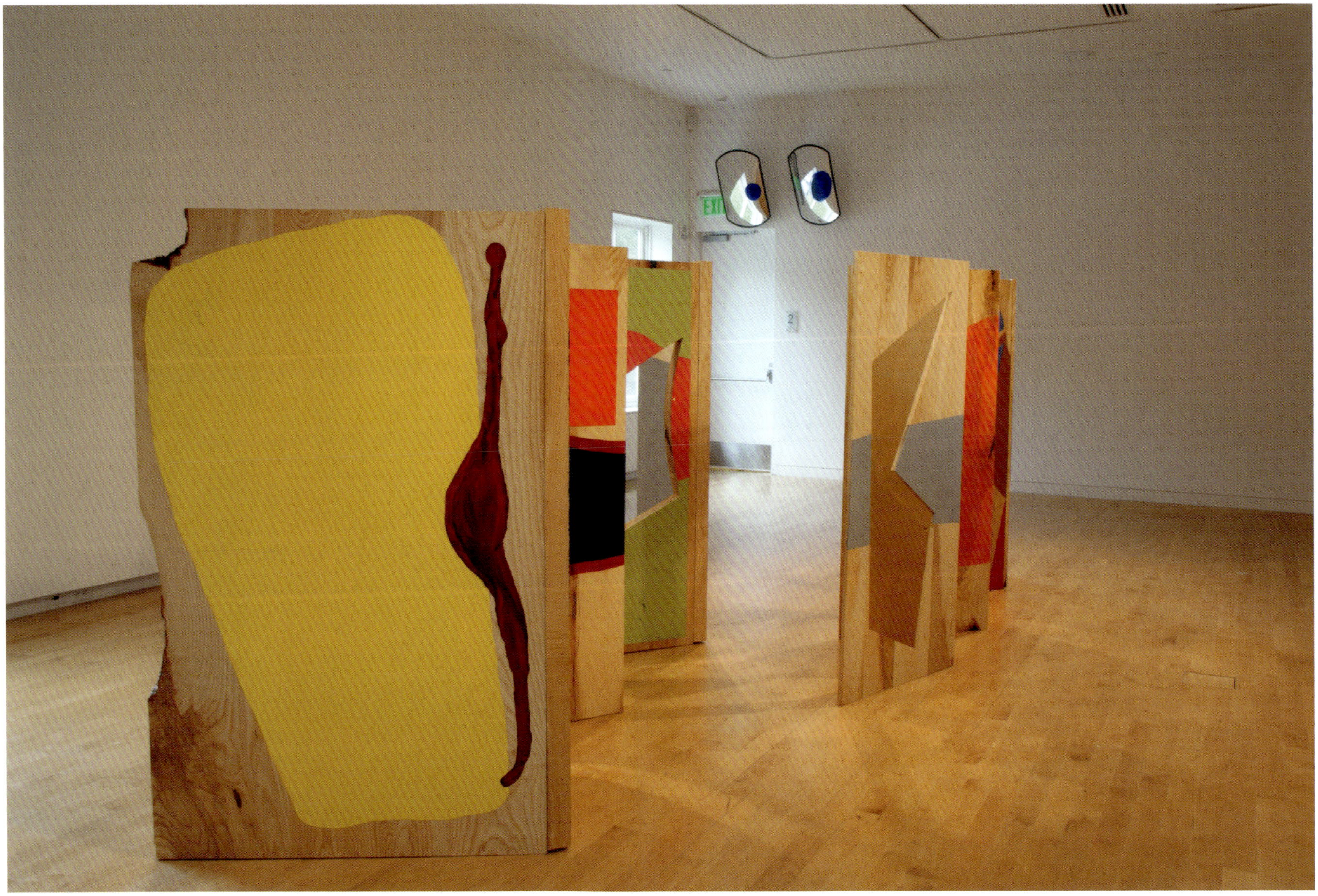

<u>HOLLOW PLACES COURT IN ASH-TREE WOOD</u>, 2011
SCREENPRINTING INKS ON 48 PLANKS EACH MARKED WITH A LETTER A–H

INSTALLATION AT THE ALDRICH CONTEMPORARY ART MUSEUM, 2011

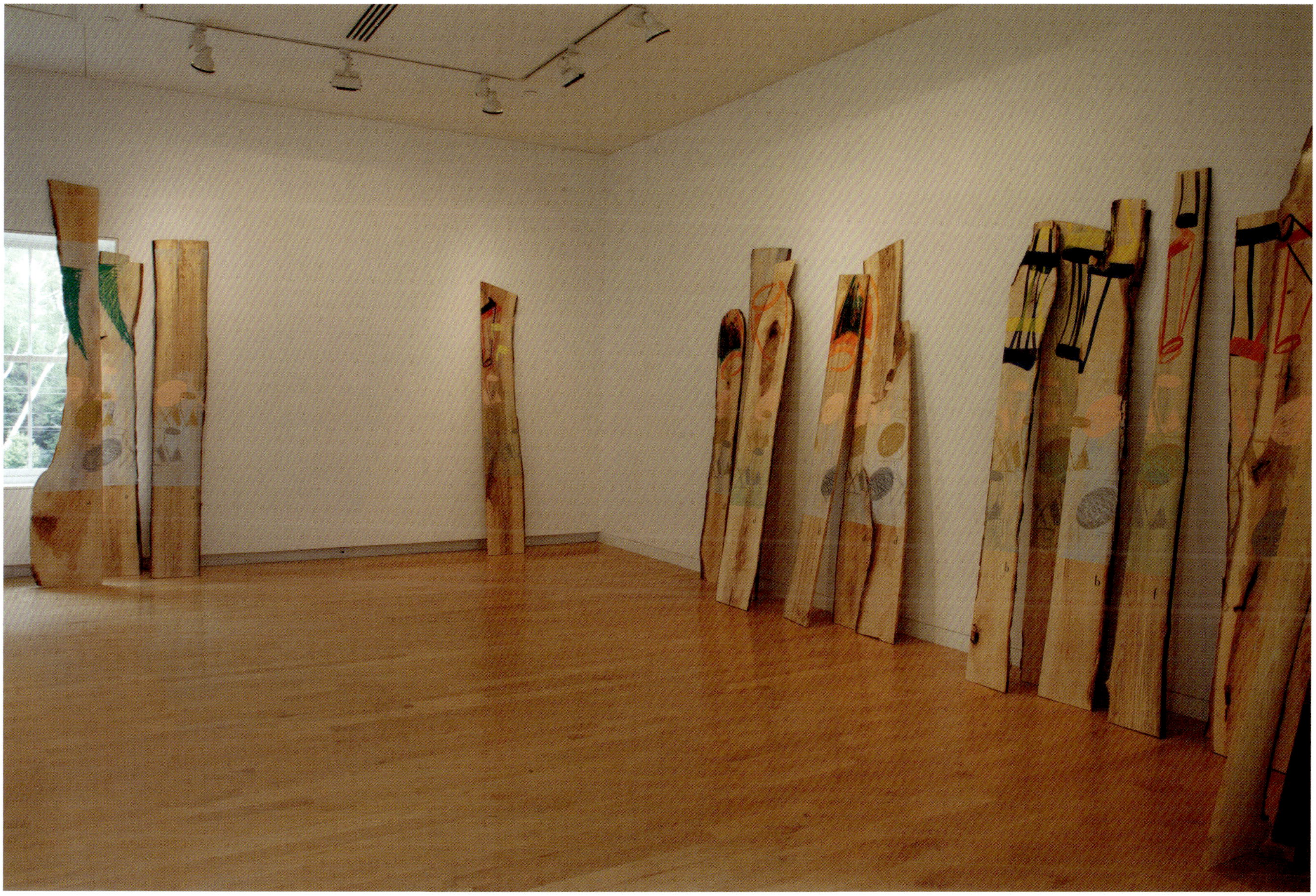

ON THE SPENDING MONEY TENDERLY, 2002
CARPET, SCAFFOLDING, PAINT, LINOLEUM, LIGHTS, 4 COUCHES, TENT, PLASTIC FRUIT, REAL ORANGES AND LEMONS, CHRISTMAS BAUBLES, BALLS, BOXES, TABLES, BUILDING MATERIALS

INSTALLATION VIEW AT K20 KUNSTSAMMLUNG NORDRHEIN-WESTFALEN, DÜSSELDORF, 2002

They operate like portions of a Native American totem pole that represents, in abstract language, the relationship between controlled structure and animal/human form. She attains this goal in an exemplary fashion in a project for occupation, implemented in the CAPC Musée d'Art Contemporain in Bordeaux: *TV Tipped Toe Nails & the Green Salami* (2003). Here much of the ground surface of the ancient *bâtiment*, a warehouse for goods and spices arriving by sea, is occupied so that it forms a pattern of colours, from blue to red to yellow, and materials, from wood to carpets and linoleum, on which objects and architectural fragments rest, such as large bleachers and inclined planes. An environmental envelope that contains other things, like carpets and televisions, alongside, even more, a large array of white appliances sitting on a rectangular platform of white painted bricks – all plugged in so that the viewer could hear the hum of their motors – it succeeds in manifesting the 'stratification' that accompanies the exhibition site. In fact, it is a critique of the museum accumulation, a journey that, in itself, has distinct meaning: a historical and formal becoming that renders all the elements of the site equivalent to one another. '*TV Tipped Toe Nails and the Green Salami* intercepts this … 19th century coffee, vanilla and spice storage facility. The stuff of fairy tales. And the Green Salami [is] the protagonist. Great big, slightly offensive, out of place, obscene, and also inanimate, the Green Salami is as a dream and as a metaphor. Of course the *Green Salami* has no body. It might not taste good but the words are fine.'[9]

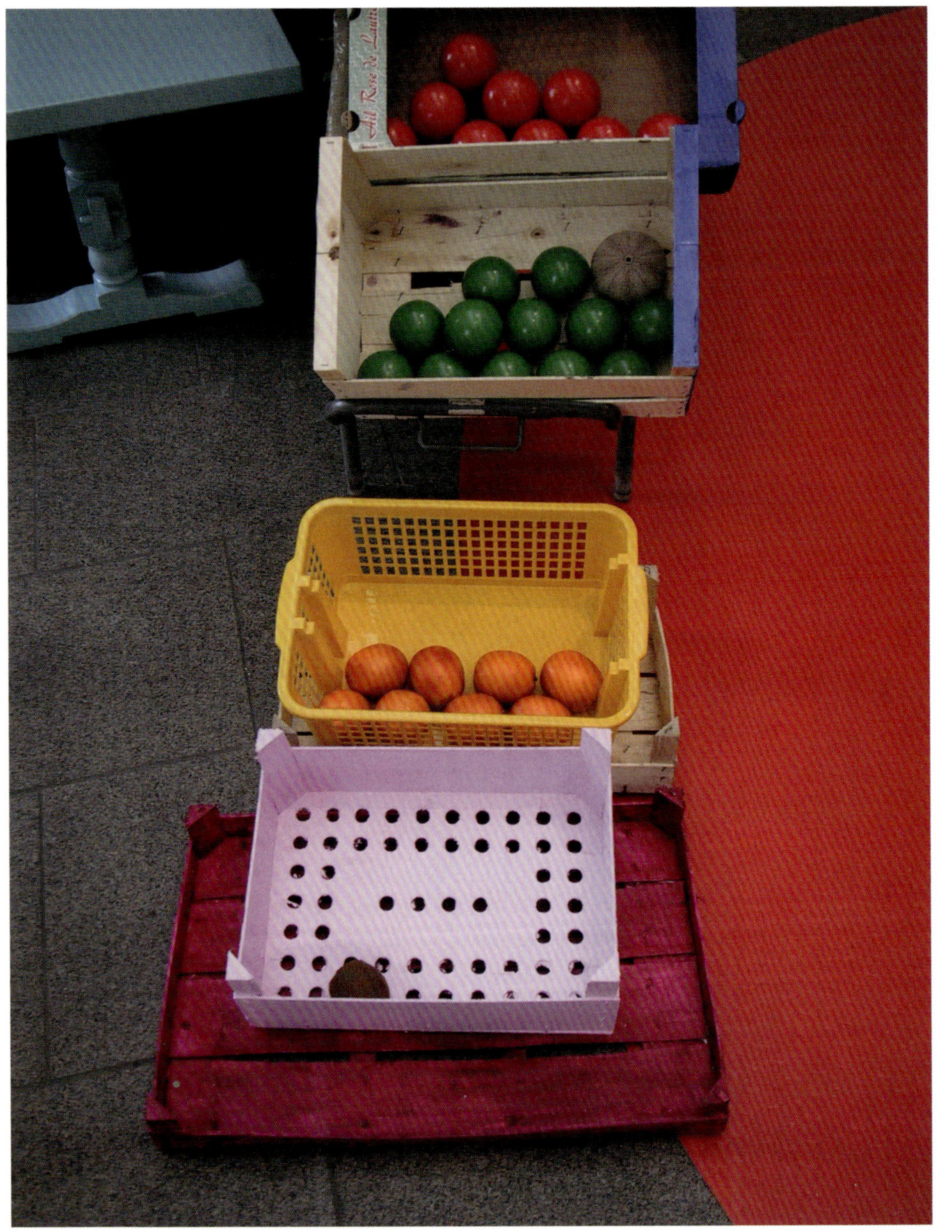

In other situations, such as *Flower Bed* (Lille, 2004), the materials include coloured benches and sectioned tables, while in *On the Spending Money Tenderly* (Düsseldorf, 2002), the collection of elements range from scaffolding to crates of fruit, lamps and sofas, everyday items

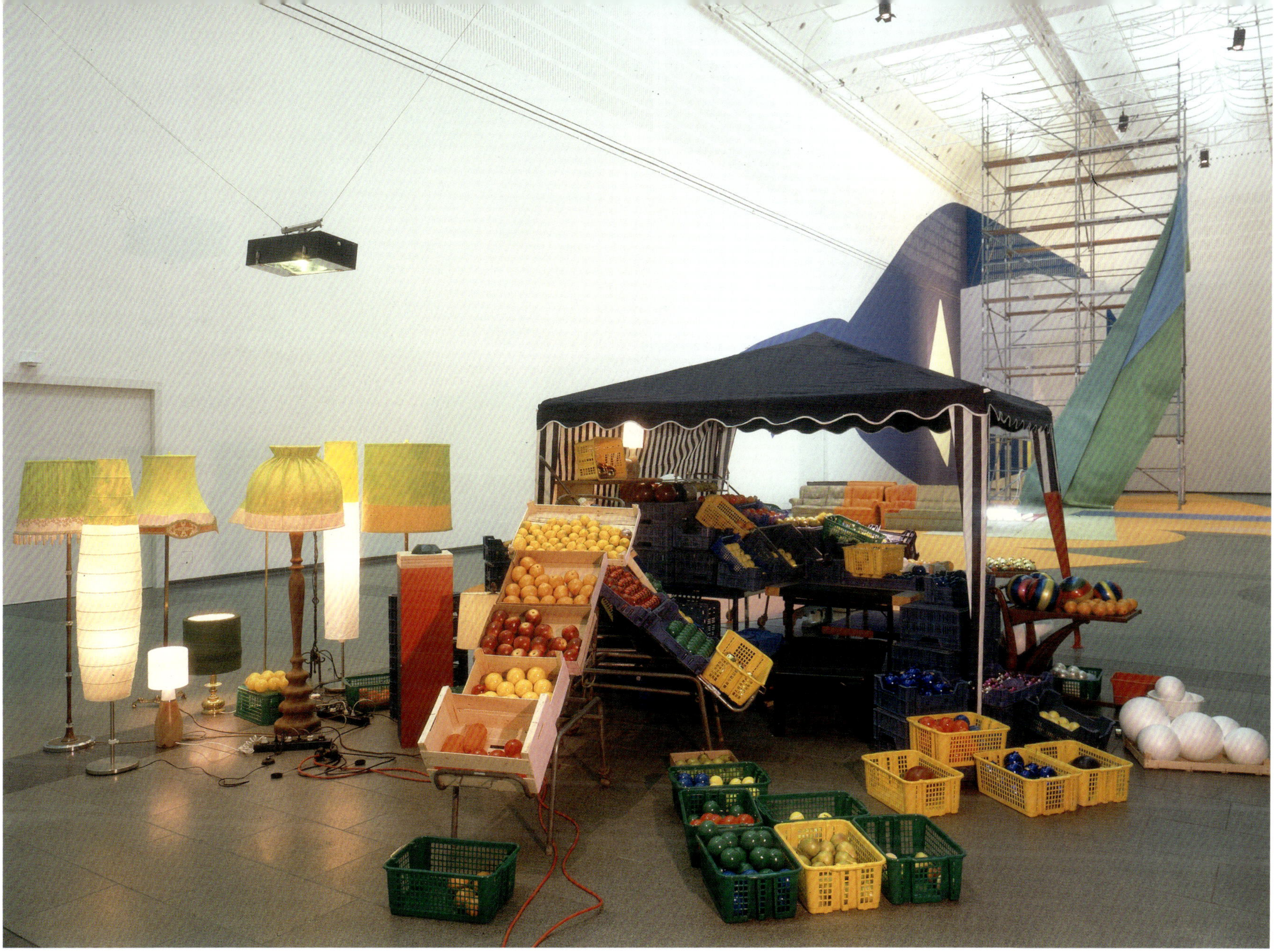

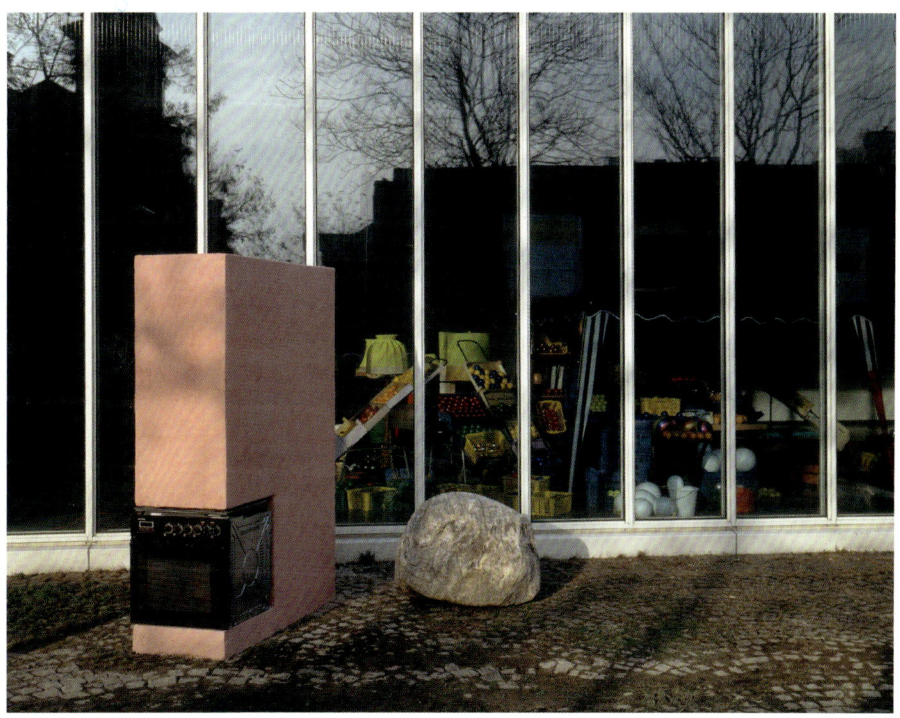

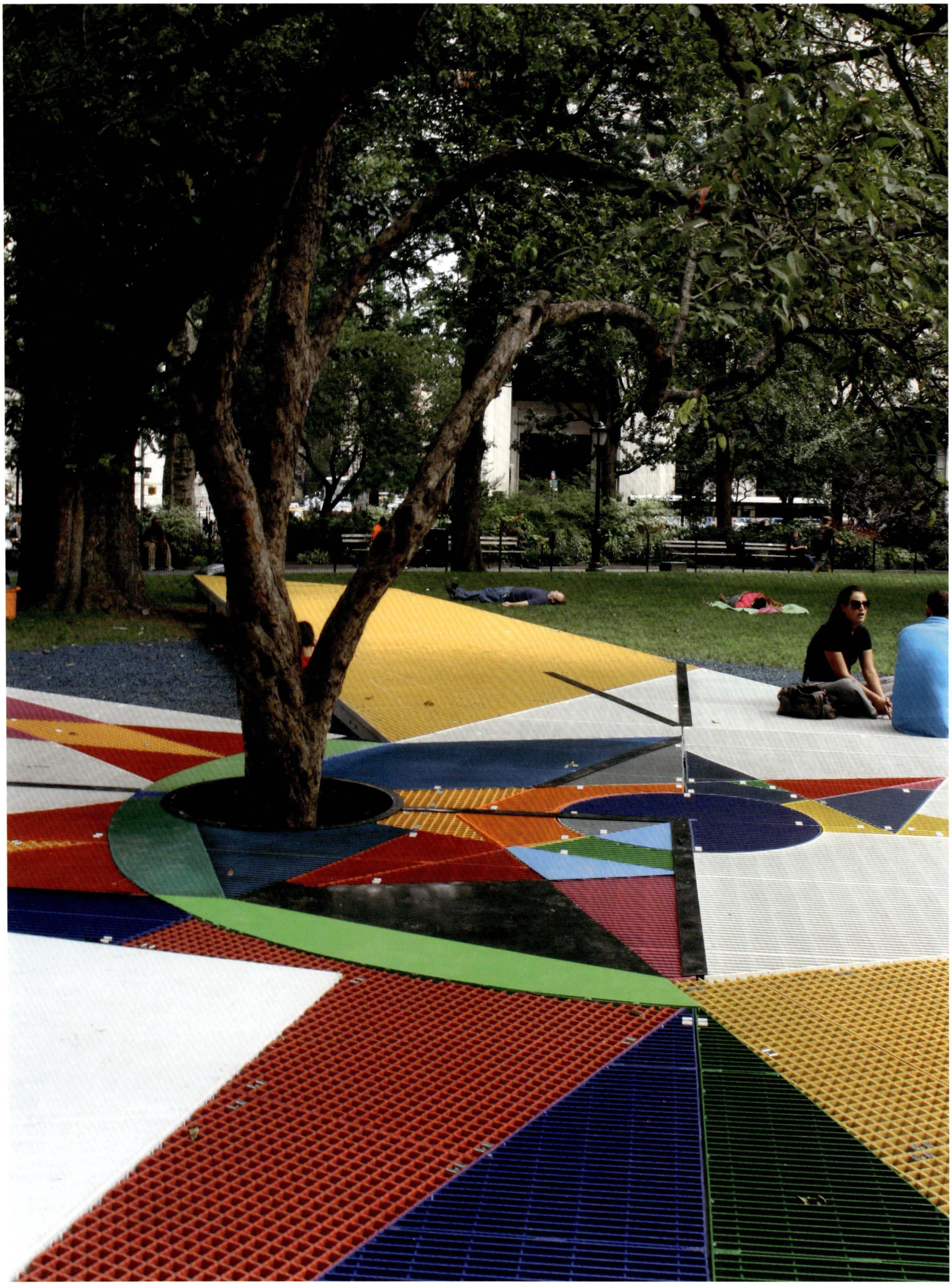

FLOODED CHAMBERS MAID, 2009
INDUSTRIAL STEEL AND MOLDED FIBREGLASS GRATING PLATFORM
2438 X 1171 X 2286 CM

INSTALLATION VIEW AT MADISON SQUARE PARK, NEW YORK, 2009, AND LAUMEIER SCULPTURE PARK, SUNSET HILLS, MISSOURI, 2009

that allow additional human relationships. This interweaving of things, which represents time lived, further accentuates the artist's disinterest in 'elitist' and exclusive art, in favour of the 'banality' and simplicity of the real world. These things are removed from that world, but for Stockholder, they remain a statement of the true possibilities of existence: a declaration of solidarity with ordinary life. For the artist, constructing is a real operation on which the viewer's perception focuses. Thus she emphasizes the operative and effective quality assigned to the event of installing. It is not only a question of employing an illusionistic and representative strategy to create the conditions for a superficial optical immersion, but also an implementation of the real and felt recognition of art on the part of the visitor's unconscious: a decantation for regenerative ends.

In Victoria 1982, it was already possible to intuit the importance of the deconstructive matrix that impregnates Stockholder's early works, where she sections the whole and arrives at fragments positioned

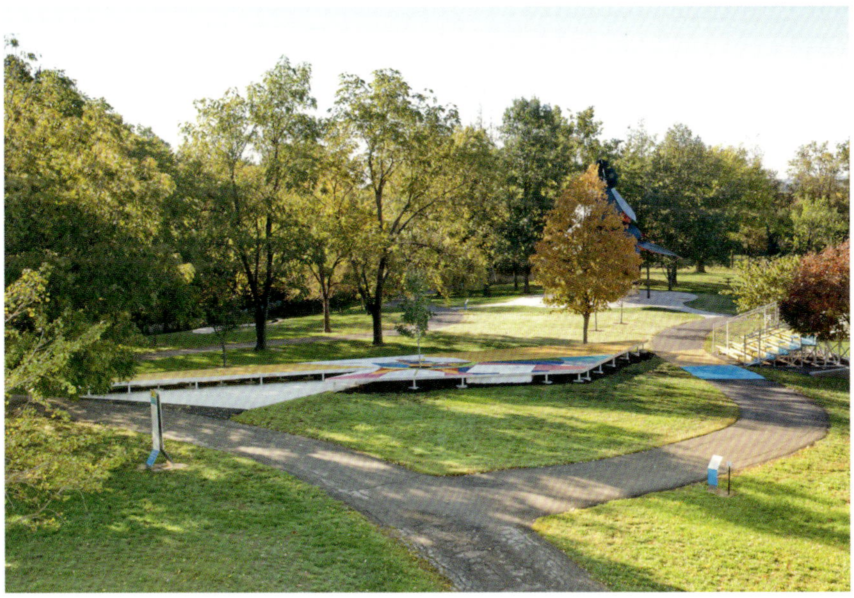

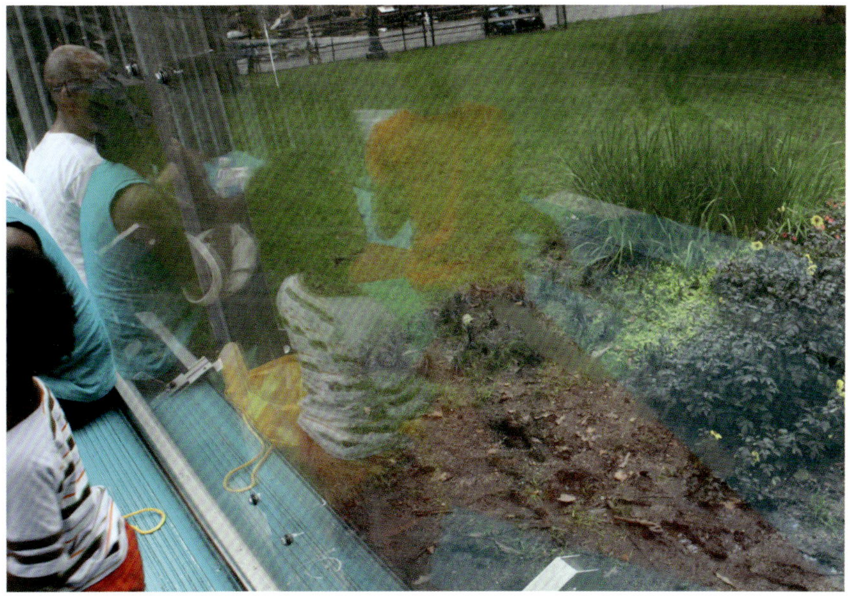

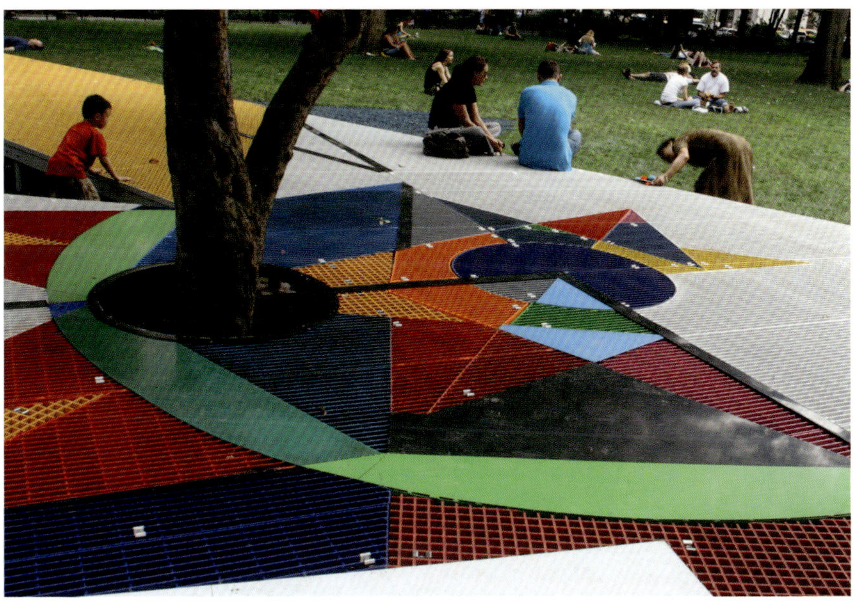

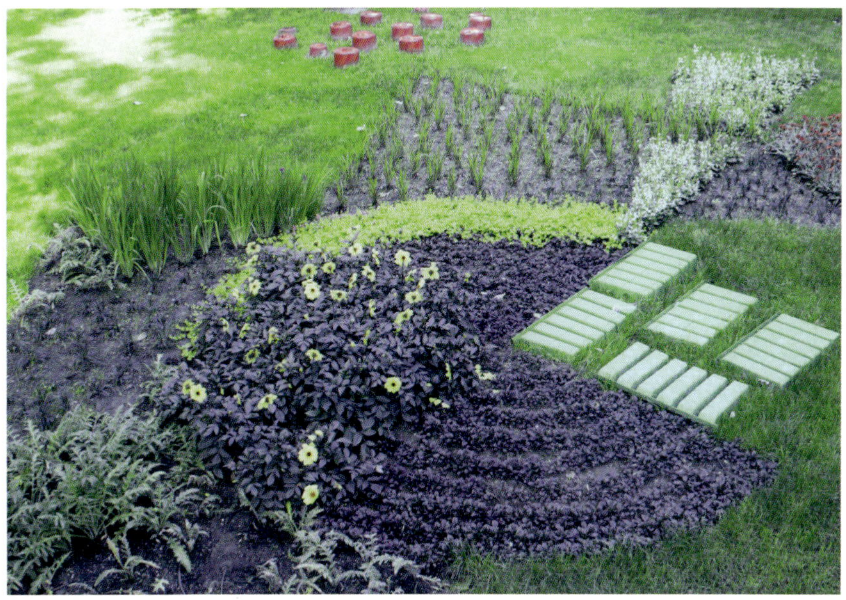

COLOR JAM HOUSTON, 2012–16
ADHESIVE VINYL, VINYL SCRIM

INSTALLATION VIEW AT THE THE INTERSECTION OF MCKINNEY AND MAIN STREETS, HOUSTON, 2016

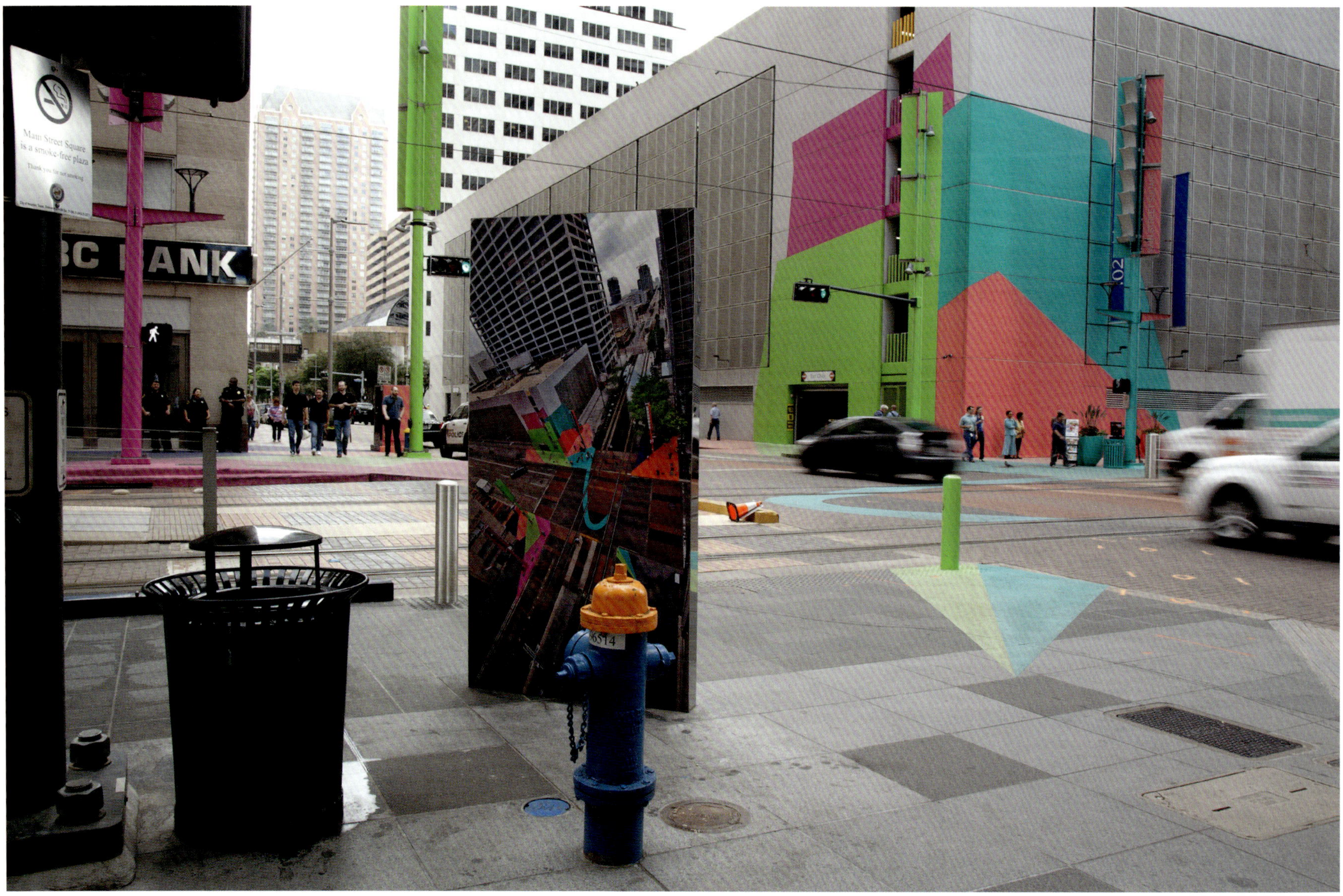

COLOR JAM HOUSTON, 2012–16
ADHESIVE VINYL, VINYL SCRIM

on the wall. This surgical dissecting pushes her to rediscover a continuum of limited individualities, with the intention of a new life. She performs a vivisection in order to effect a transformation, so that the inexistent emerges from its lethargy. She corrodes the immovable, which dominated art until the 1980s, to liberate the 'volatile' – the power of life enclosed in the habitat and in its components. She moves away from fragmentation, displacing it with something of another nature, connected to the complete fullness of the energy of things and environments.

From 2004 to the present, Stockholder has created situations, both pictorial and sculptural, marked by a disorienting fullness that delineates clear external and internal spaces, from *Flooded Chambers Maid* (Madison Square Park, New York, 2009) to *Door Hinges* (Chicago, 2015). The process of installing a sculptural or environmental entity in a place refers to the concept of 'connection' that, in art from the 1960s, replaced the idea of division and the autonomy of the work. It is a new paradigm, nurtured by aggregation and setting up a network, in order to share resources

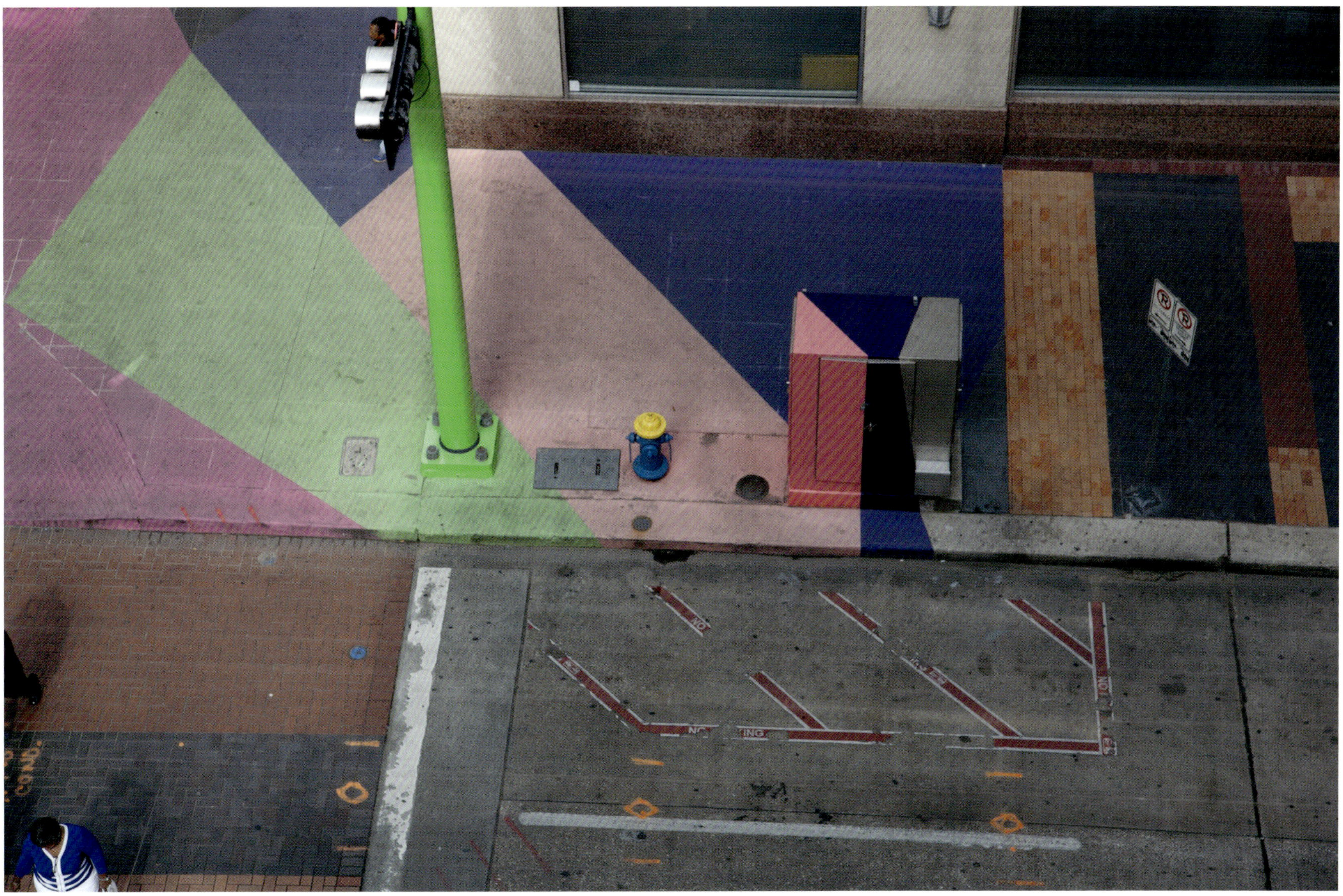

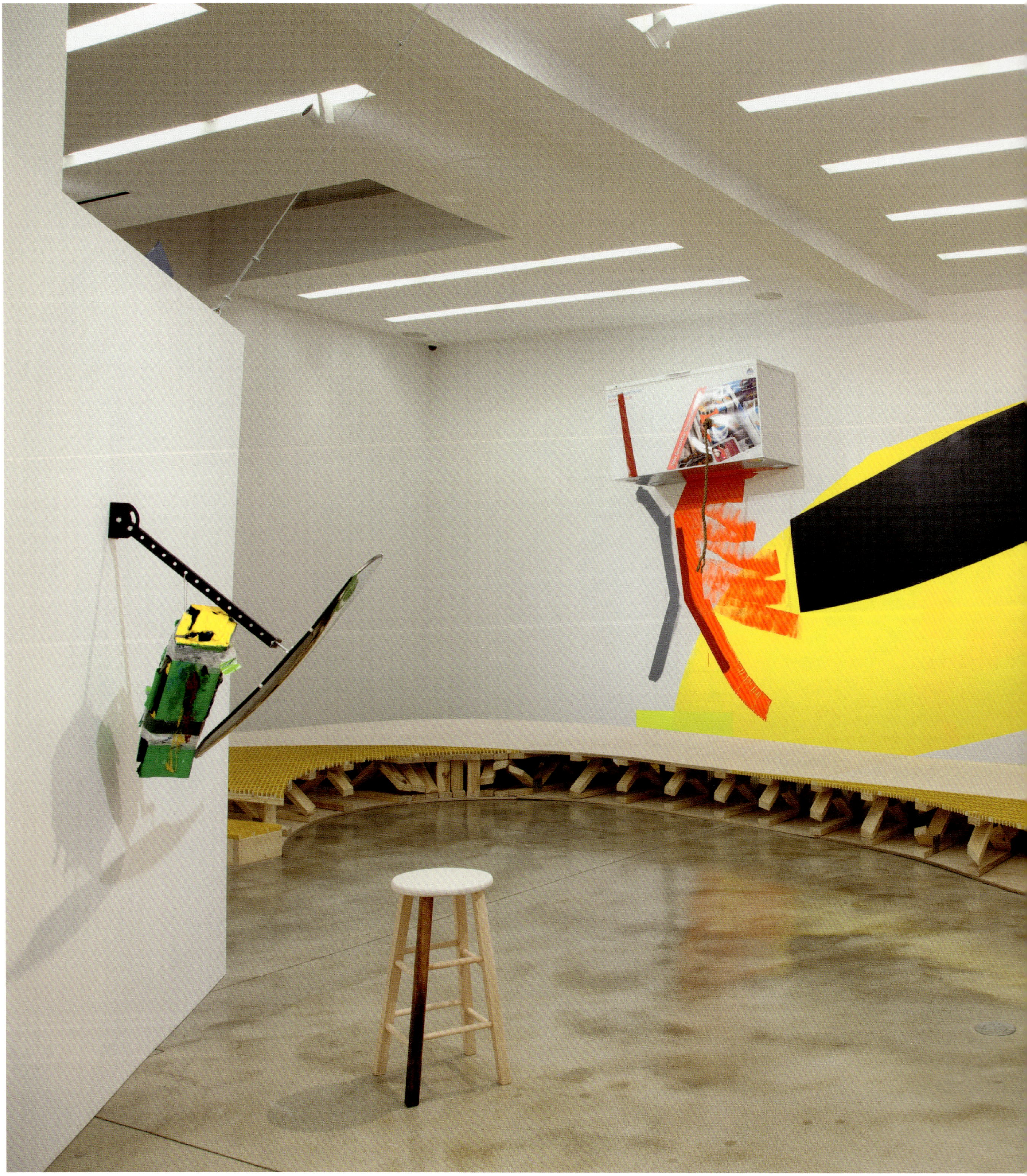

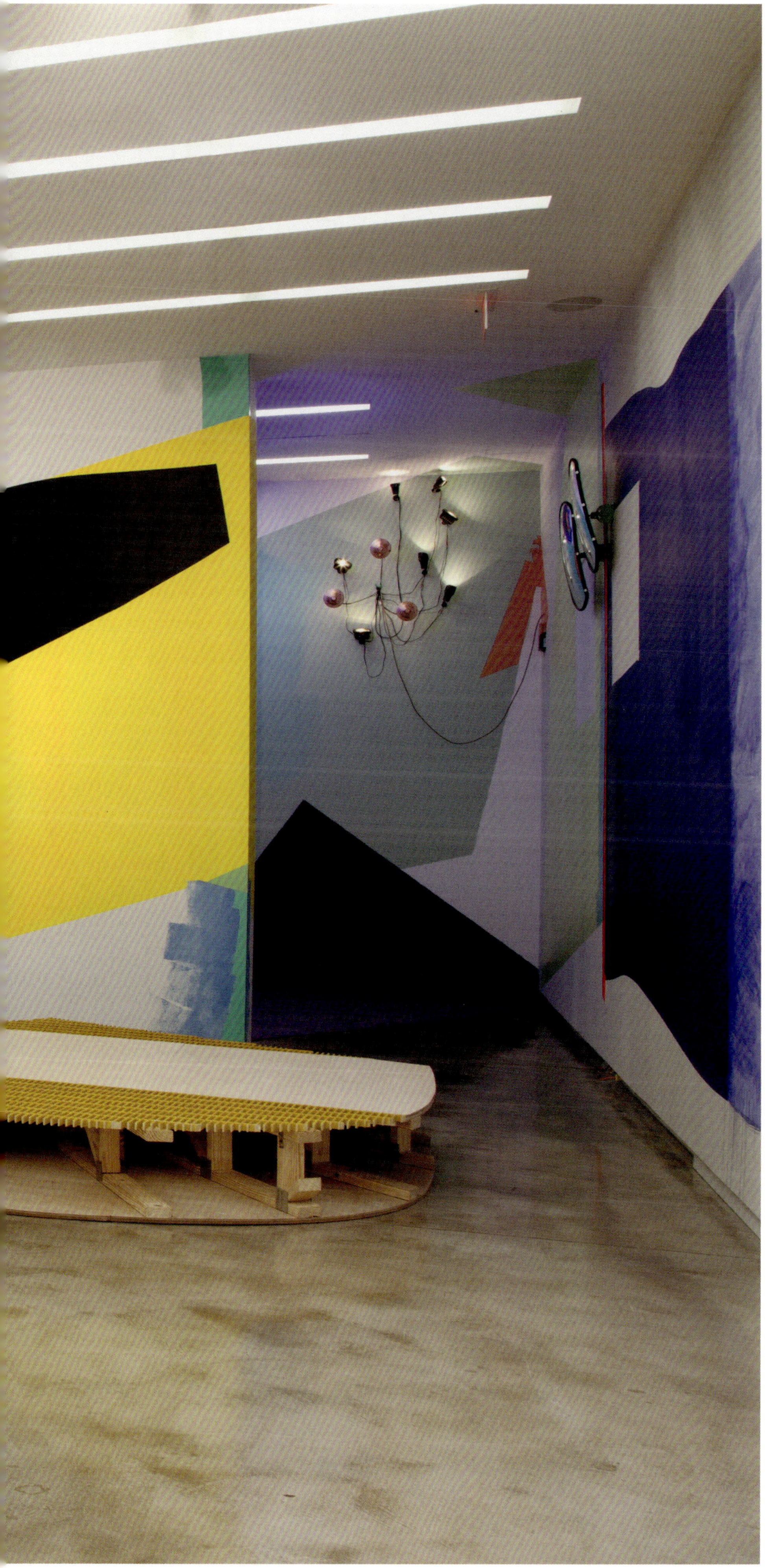

EXHIBITION VIEWS OF DOOR HINGES AT KAVI GUPTA GALLERY, CHICAGO, 2015

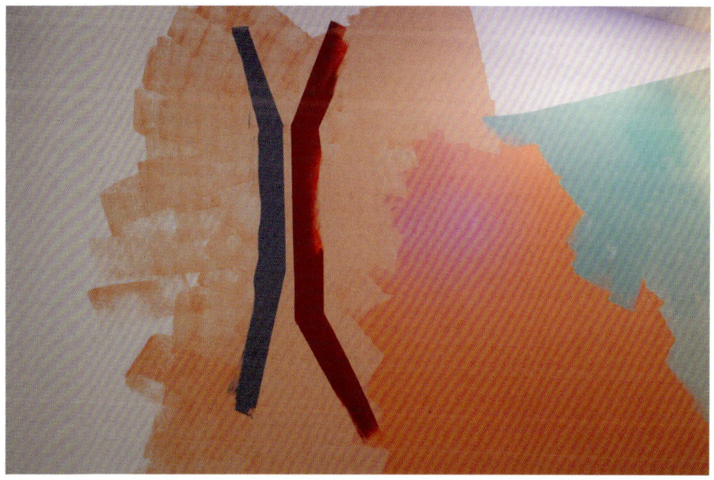

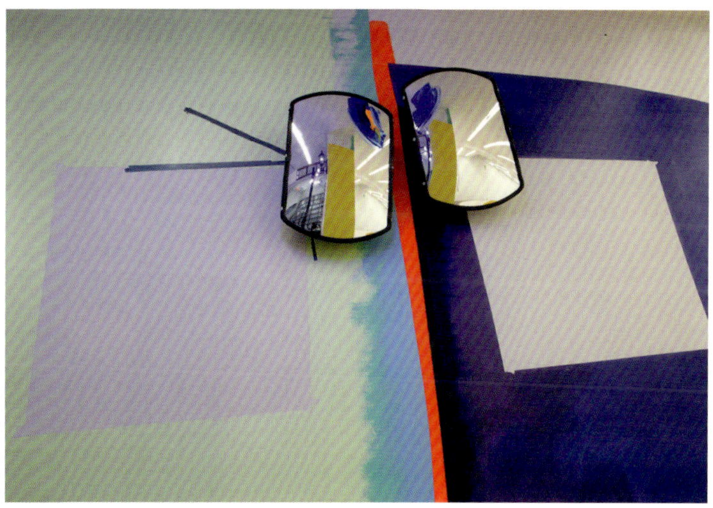

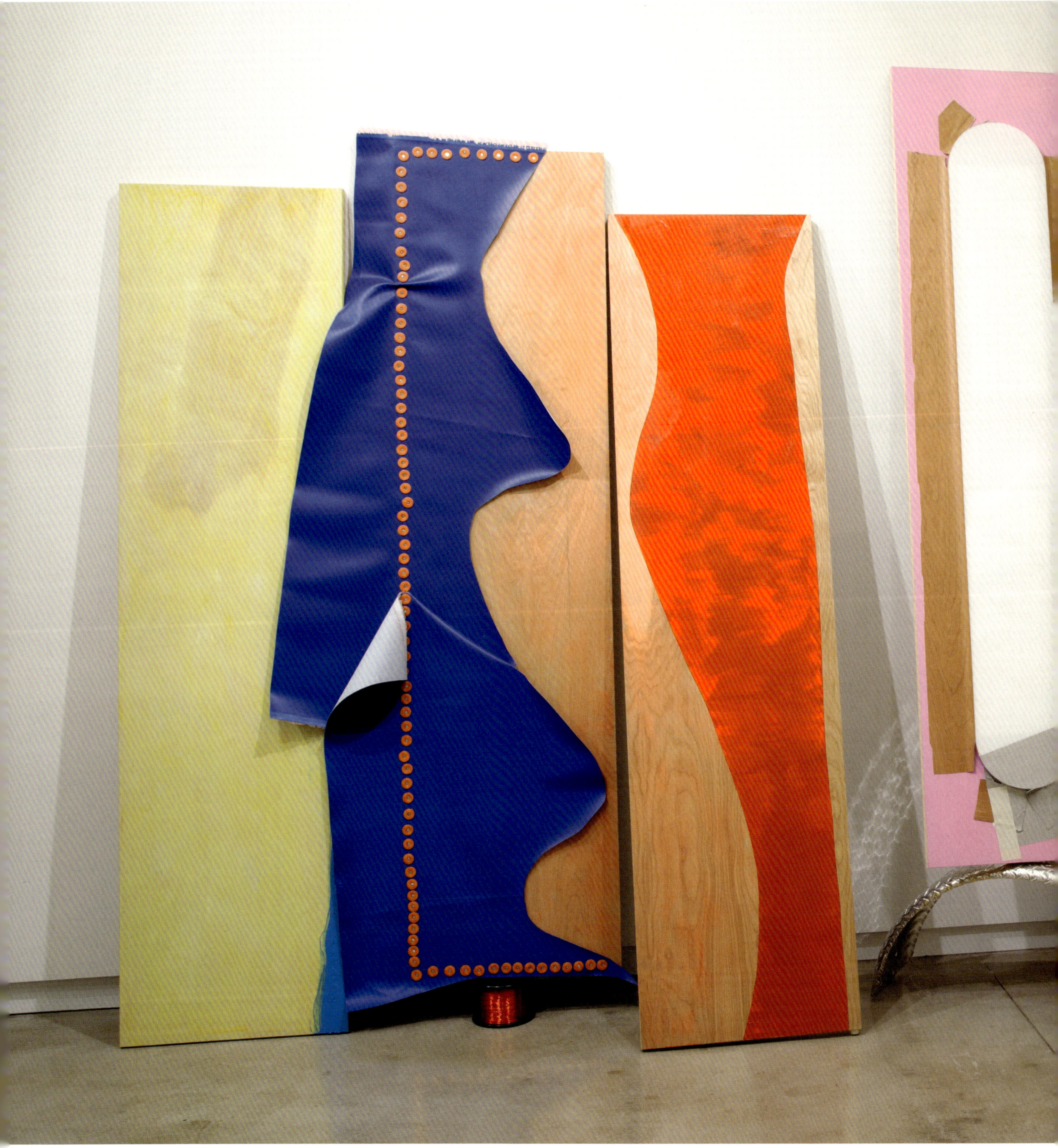

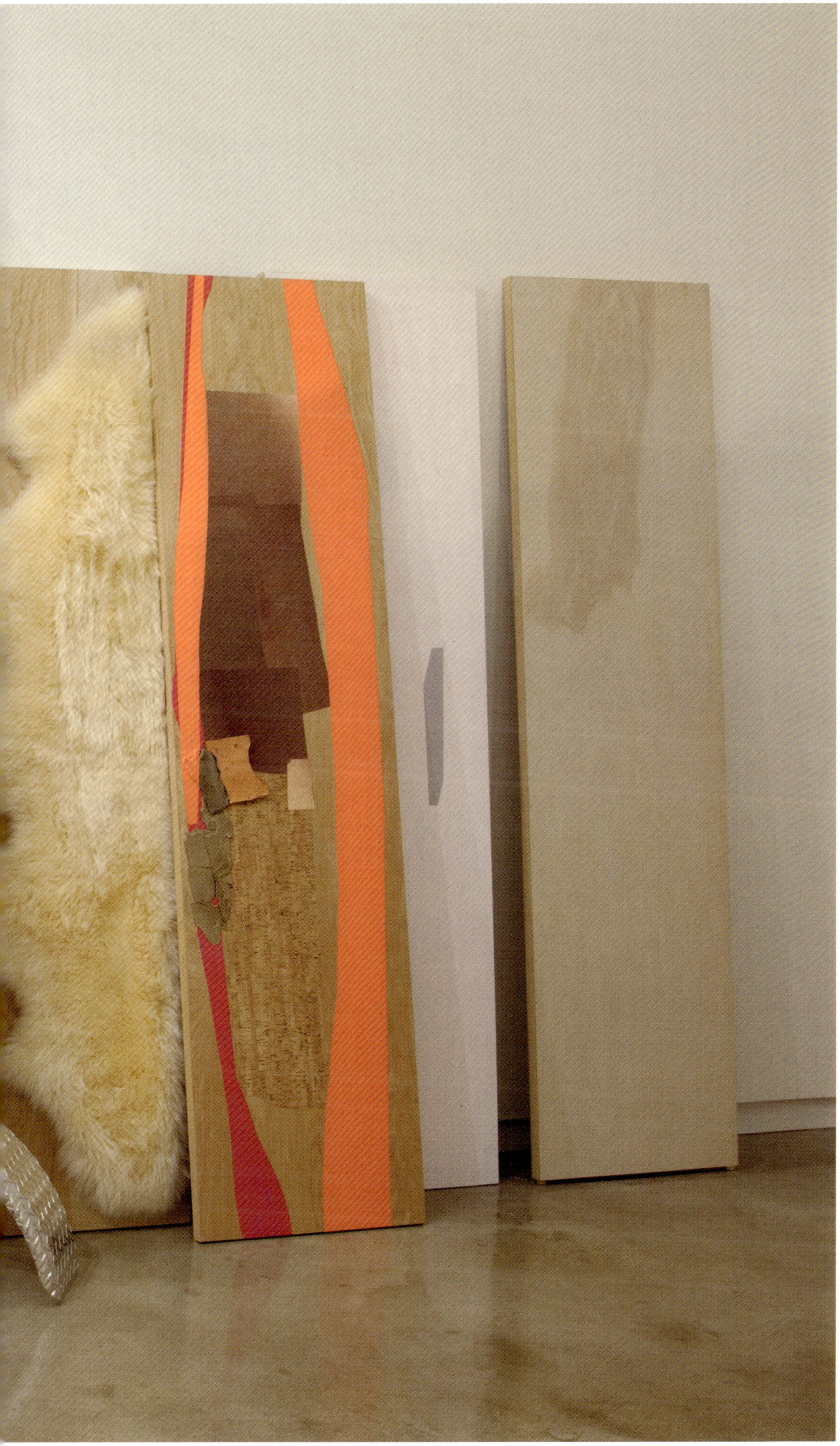

DECALS ROAM TO MOVE, 2015
8 HOLLOW CORE DOOR PANELS, VINYL, HARDWARE, TREE BARK, COPPER FLASHING, CORK VENEER, PHOTOGRAPH, ACRYLIC PAINT, SHEEPSKIN, SPOOL OF WIRE, GALVANIZED CAR PART, PLEXIGLAS AND WOOD VENEER
422 X 138 X 62 CM

and energies. This connectivity was the driving force that marked the artist's interventions in the landscape and in architecture, so as to merge the art with *in situ* conditions. Stockholder's works can also be interpreted as a structural grid that rejects boundaries – material and chromatic, rigid and soft, artisanal and industrial – but, instead, feeds off their free geography, because it is based on the passage from one to the other. Moreover the insertion of elements is strategic for their survival. Being interwove, they support each other, do not compete among themselves, but form a strong entity, capable of welcoming other entities, from the human being to the objective context. This flexibility also allows mutation, because the boundaries become elastic, keeping up-to-date with the given situation. This is why Stockholder's assemblages continually depict the reality of the 'terrain'. They are nomad figures that feed off the proximities and connections. They are 'amoebas' of wood, fabric, plastic, bricks… that have the ability to sense the atmosphere and adapt to it. They insert themselves and penetrate a situation and comprehend its connotations and characteristics. However this condition renders them solitary and dependent, always nailed down to a physical and concrete 'elsewhere' that is neither secure nor stable. For this reason in certain cases, the artist states: 'take note, this structure will not stand on its own'. In search of an uncertain and promised land, the work thus is destined to follow an infinite path, for it has no home, no family. It is never rejected, but has need of 'assistance' in order to survive. Thus the *Assists,* a body of work begun in 2015, has two types of behaviour: 'The *Assists* need to be strapped to something else – a freestanding object – in order to stand up. They do not have a prescribed relationship to the wall or to se conditions reflect a non-belonging to any place, as figures in motion in time and space, but some works, coming to rest, set in motion a 'hosting' mechanism; they become territories of welcome, collaborating with other autonomous situations: a solitude that hosts solitude.

ASSIST #3: A CHORD, 2015
PAINTED METAL, RATCHET
CLAMP WITH YELLOW WEBBING
AND FELT SHOWN ON THESE
TWO PAGES STRAPPED TO
FOUR DIFFERENT PROPS
130 X 114 X 223 CM

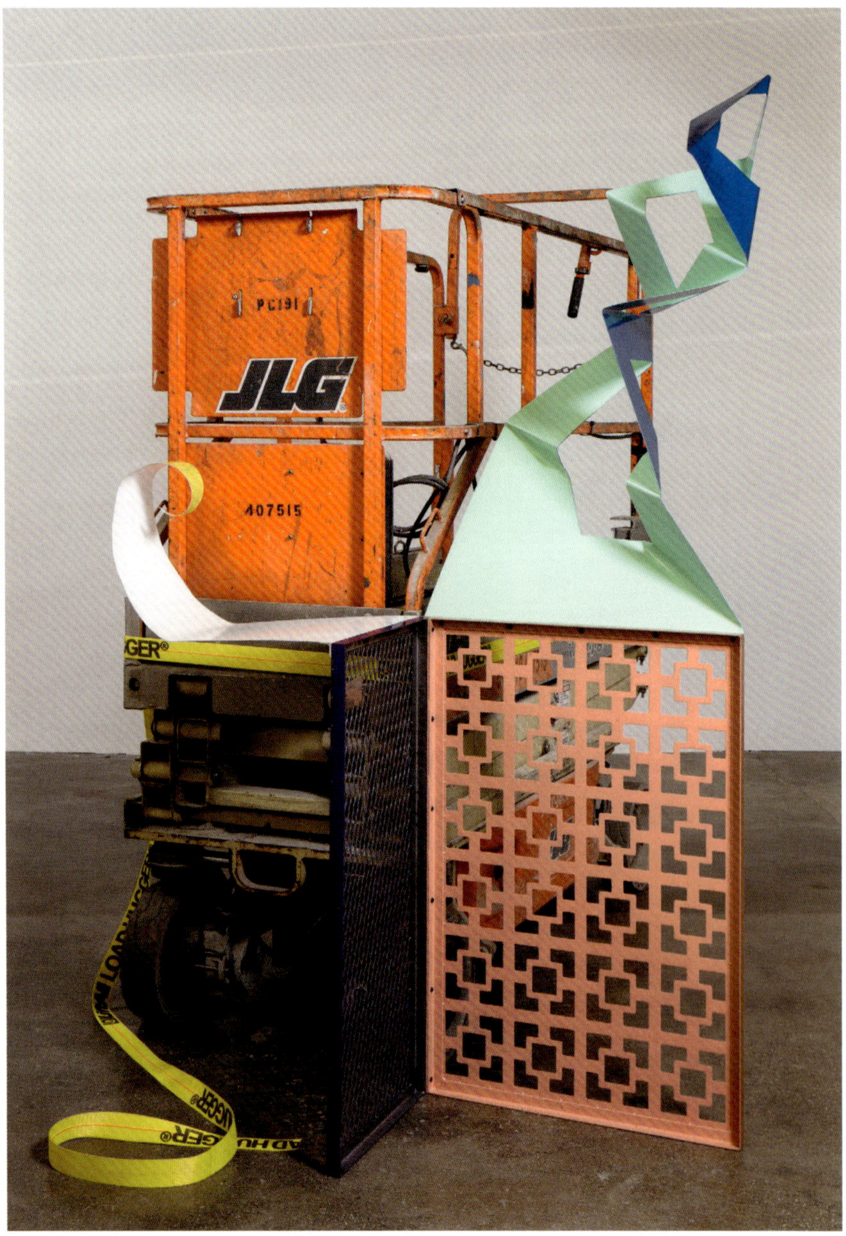

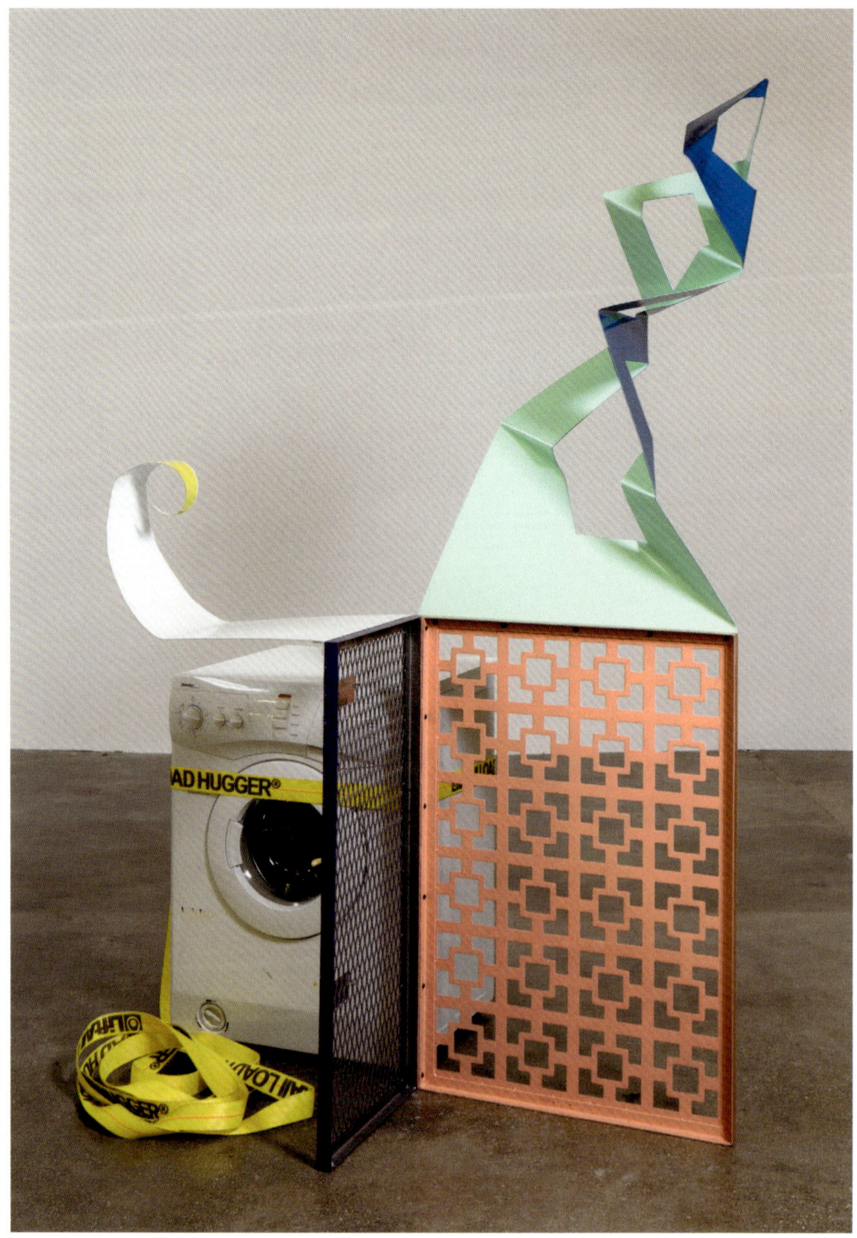

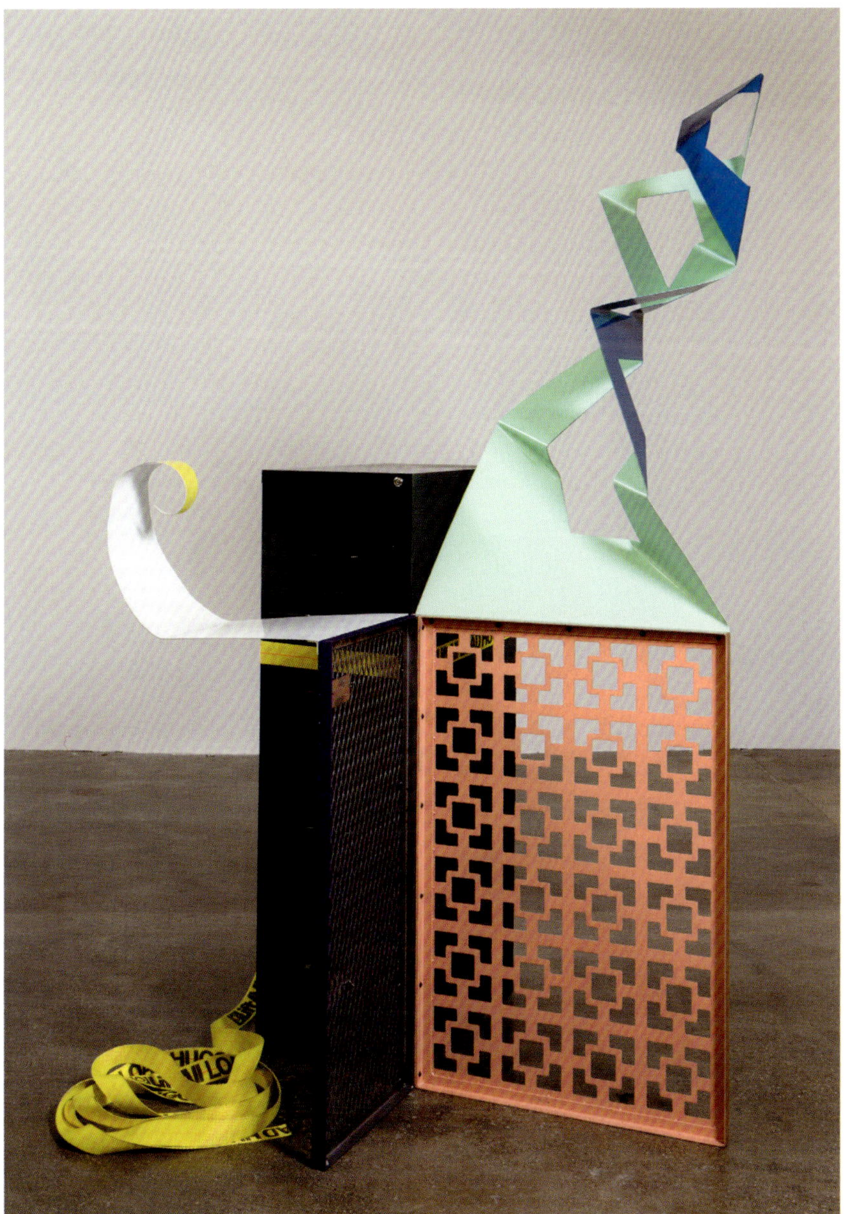

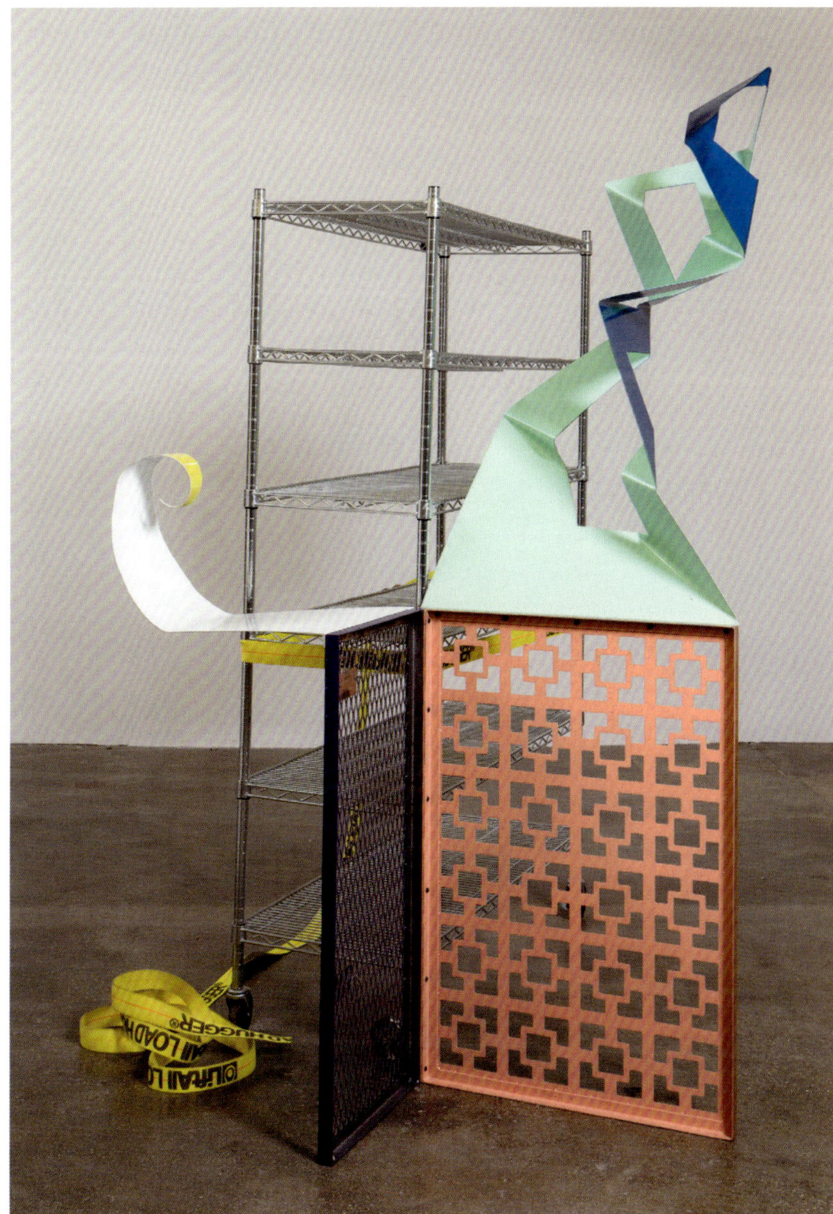

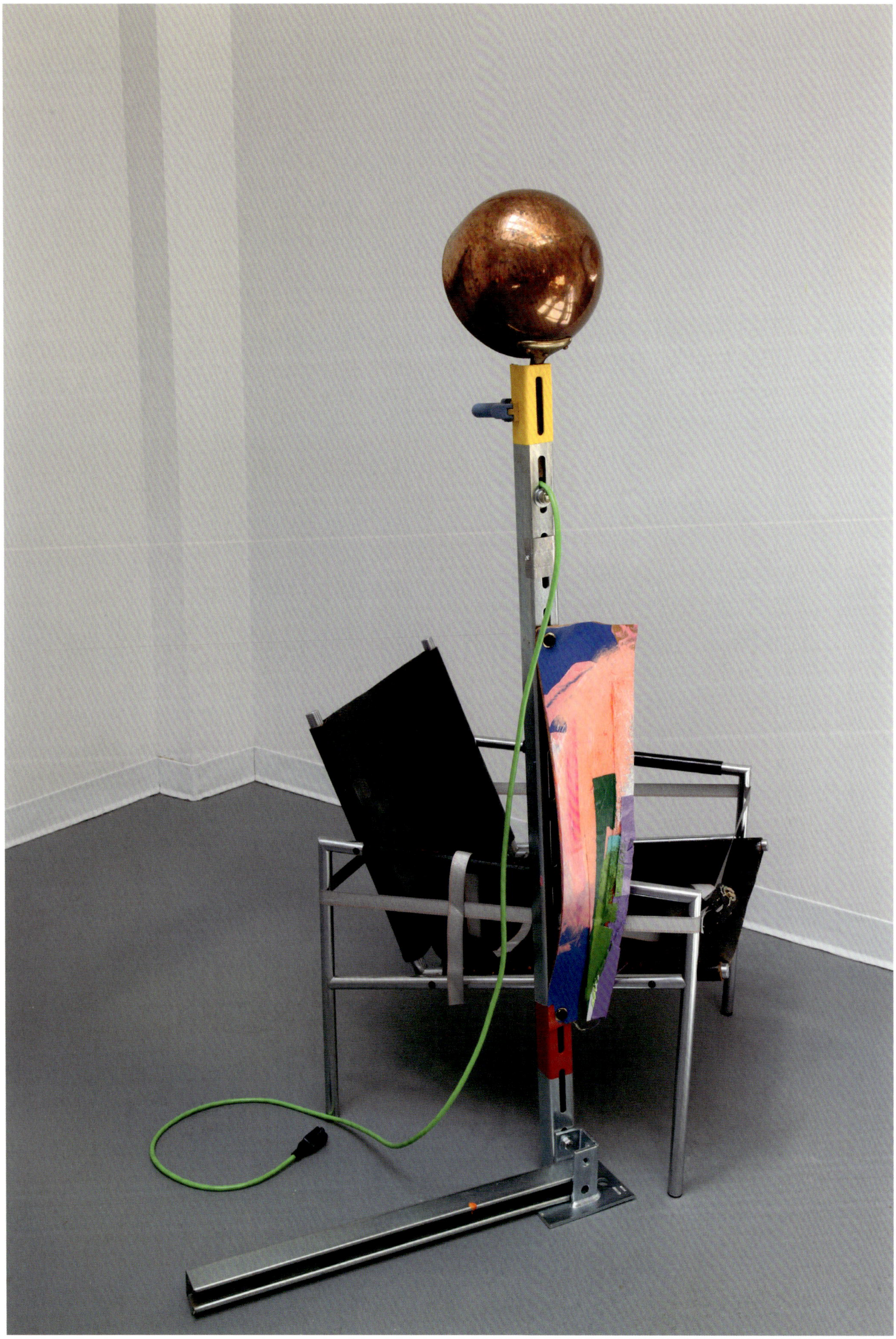

this and previous page,
ASSIST SIDLED, 2016
UNISTRUT, COPPER BOWL,
PLASTIC CLAMP, GREEN
EXTENSION CORD, LEATHER,
VINYL, ACRYLIC PAINT, PAPER,
STRING, GLUE, RATCHET CLAMP
AND TIE DOWN WEBBING
SHOWN ON THESE TWO
PAGES STRAPPED TO TWO
DIFFERENT PROPS
144 X 18 X 67 CM

next pages,
THE GUESTS ALL CROWDED
INTO THE DINING ROOM, 2016
PLATFORM, DECK, RAMP,
RAILING, WIRE CABLE
PLATFORM: 442 X 965 X 36 CM
DECK: 264 X 915 X 131 CM
(227 CM WITH RAILING)

INSTALLATION VIEW AT
MITCHELL-INNES & NASH,
NEW YORK

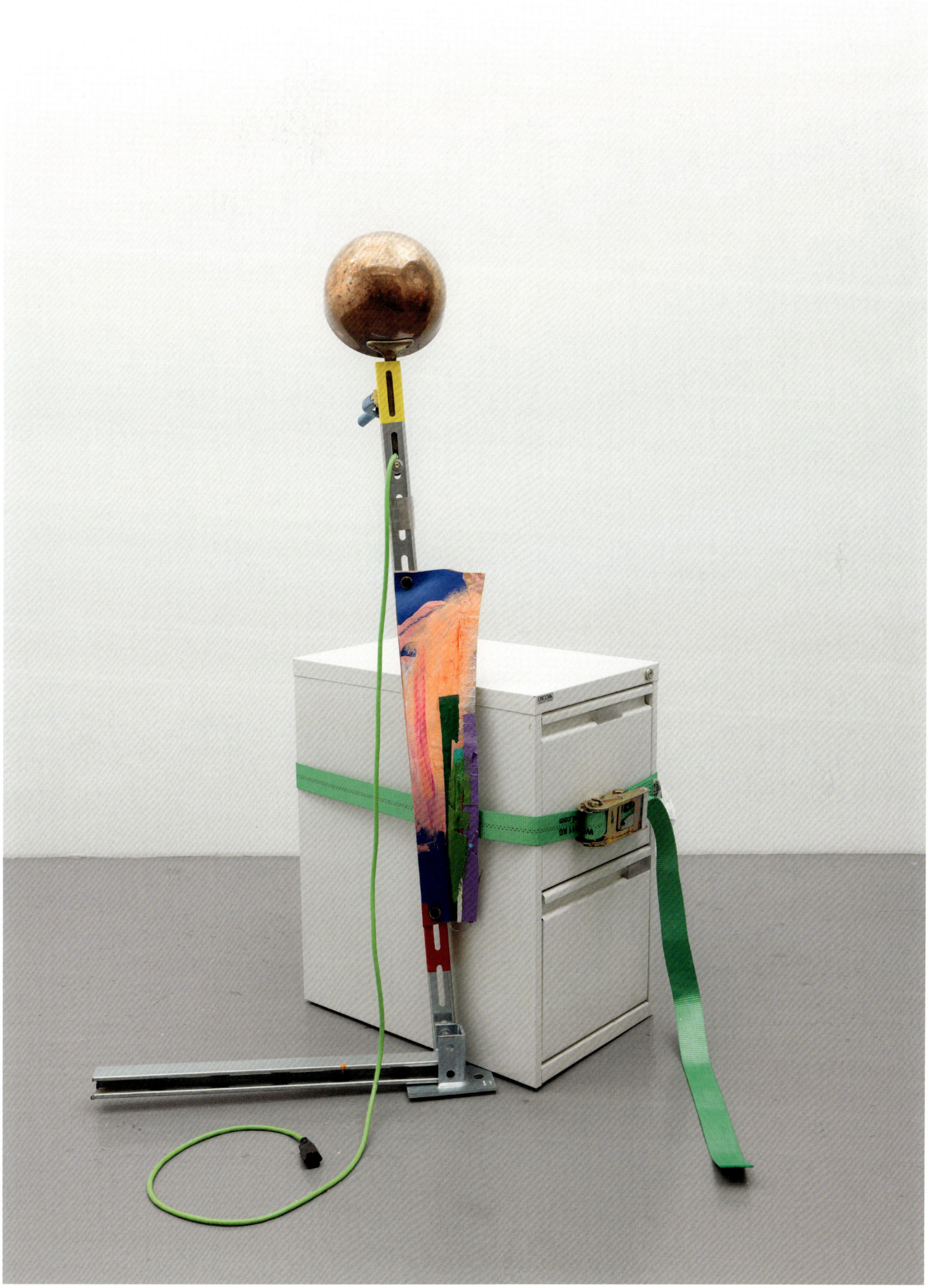

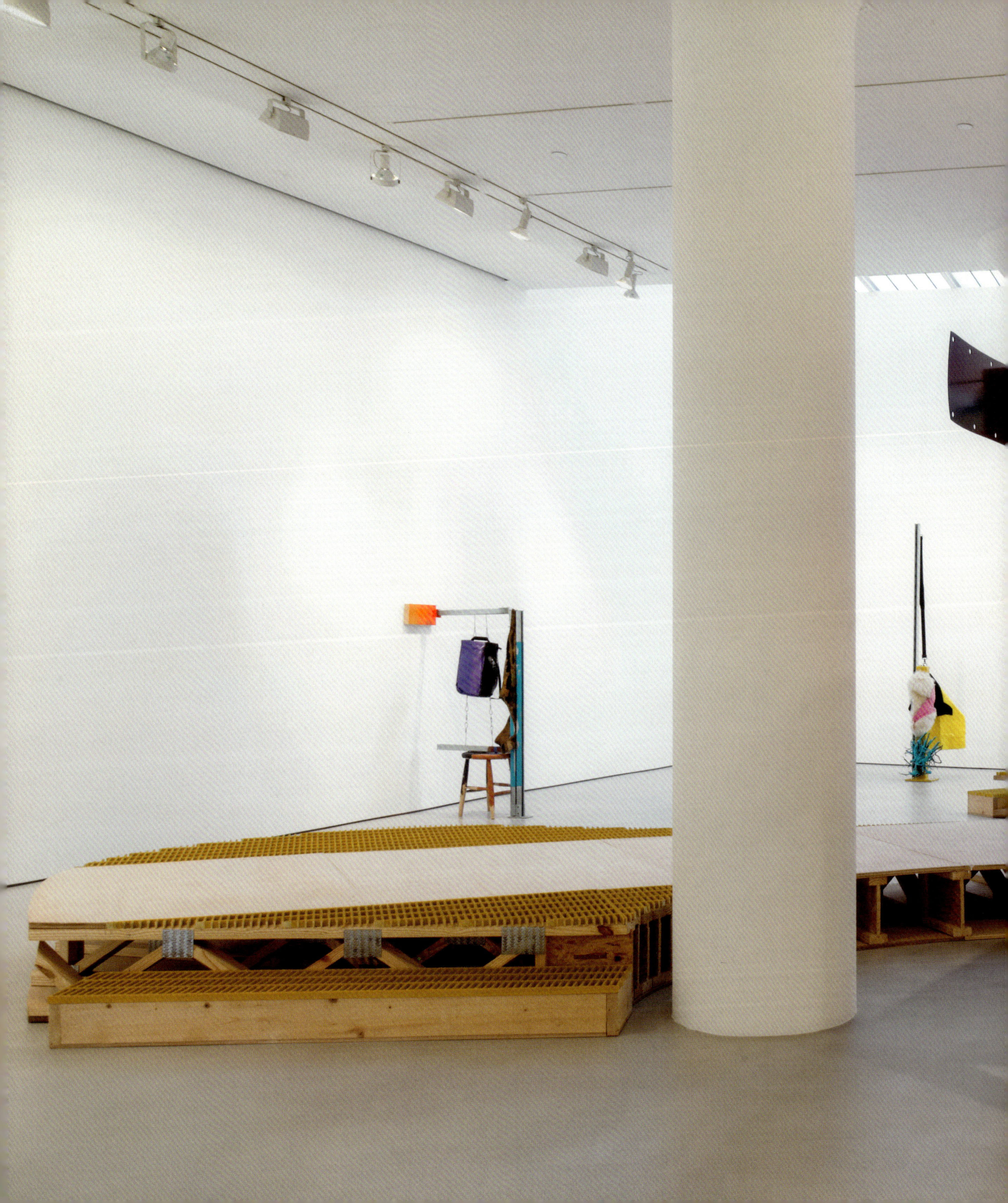

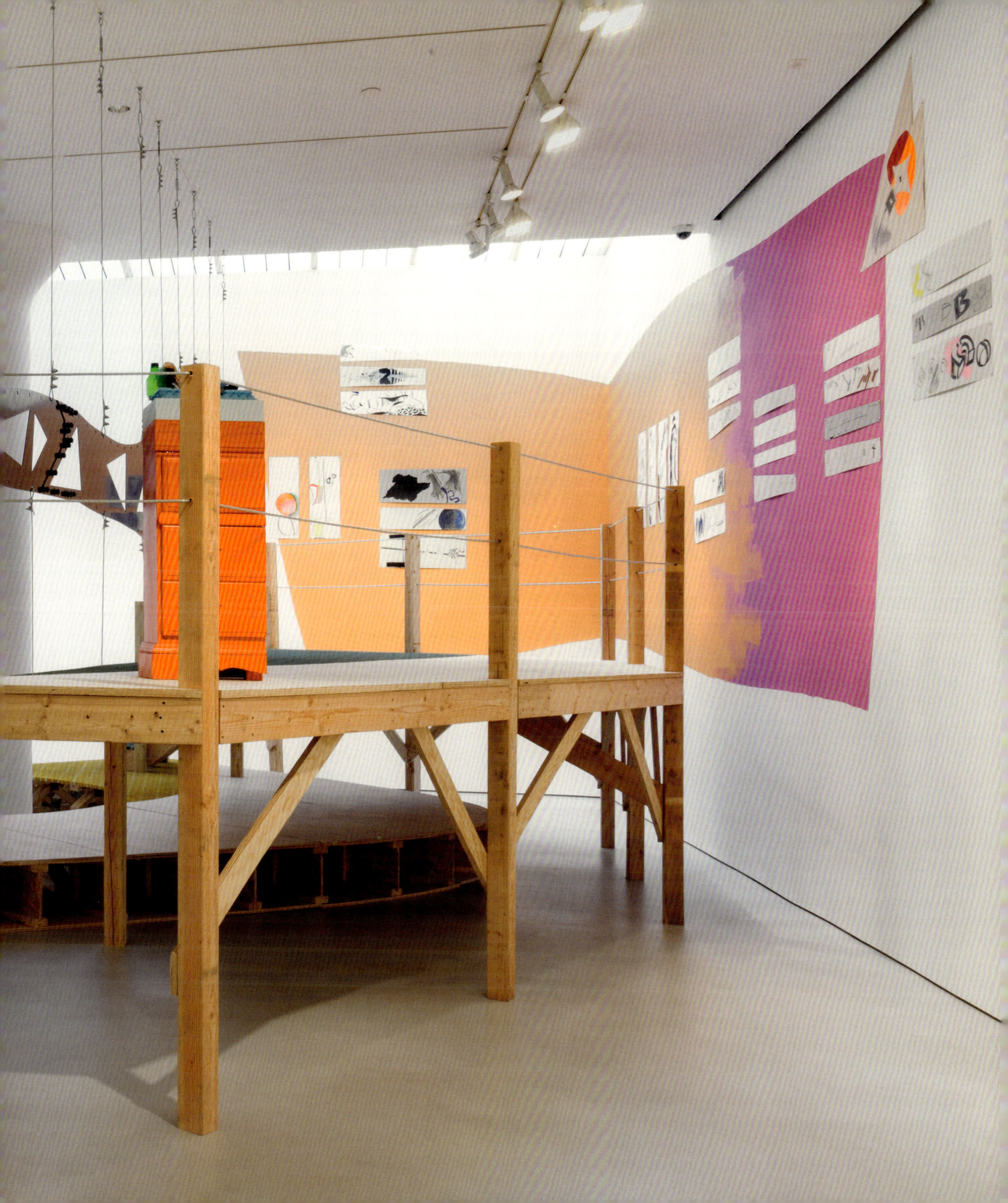

left column,
VACUUM SERIES FITTED, 2015
DRAWING ON PAPER
79 X 28 CM

VACUUM SERIES PARTS, 2015
DRAWING ON PAPER
79 X 23 CM

VACUUM SERIES TUBBED, 2015
DRAWING ON PAPER
79 X 28 CM

VACUUM SERIES NIPPLED, 2015
DRAWING ON PAPER
79 X 27 CM

SPREAD MOVES, 2014
DRAWING ON PAPER
17 X 76 CM

SHOULDER JOINT, 2014
DRAWING ON PAPER
15 X 76 CM

ROUND GRID + COLLAGE, 2014
DRAWING ON PAPER
16 X 76 CM

LEFTFOOT, 2014
DRAWING ON PAPER
14 X 76 CM

WHY, 2014
DRAWING ON PAPER
15 X 76 CM

AFLOAT, 2014
DRAWING ON PAPER
12 X 76 CM

L H T, 2014
DRAWING ON PAPER
14 X 76 CM

right column,
bbB, 2014
DRAWING ON PAPER
33 X 75 CM

TRACKS, 2014
DRAWING ON PAPER
20 X 76 CM

I, 2014
DRAWING ON PAPER
32 X 76 CM

STOMACH LINE EXPLOSIONS, 2014
DRAWING ON PAPER
18 X 75 CM

SLIP, 2014
DRAWING ON PAPER
23 X 76 CM

BRACKETS & THREAD, 2014
DRAWING ON PAPER
17 X 76 CM

BBBBB, 2014
DRAWING ON PAPER
13 X 75 CM

VOLUME, 2014
DRAWING ON PAPER
22 X 76 CM

next page,
DETACHED DETAIL, 2016
INDUSTRIAL METAL FENCING, DANCE FLOOR TILE, LEATHER, VINYL, ROPE HARDWARE, FLOOR TILE, FLOOR MAT, MASONRY SQUARE TILE, BENT METAL ROD, ACRYLIC AND OIL PAINT
146 X 118 X 152 CM

INSTALLATION VIEW AT MITCHELL-INNES & NASH, NEW YORK, 2016

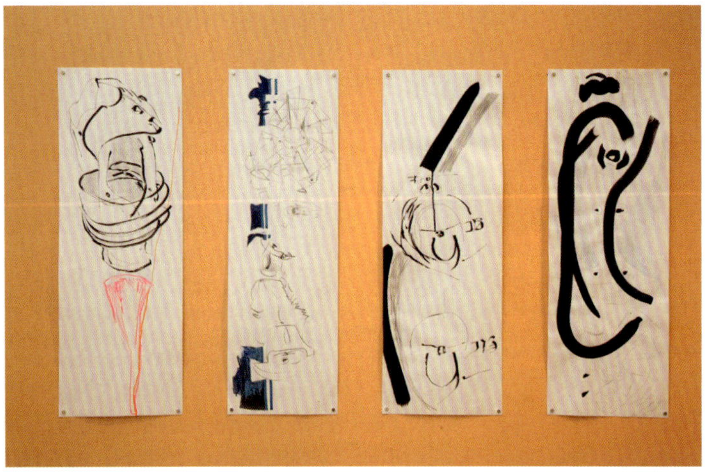

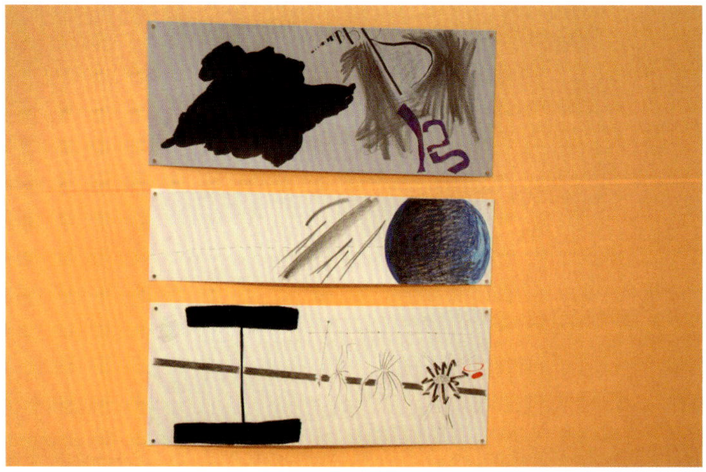

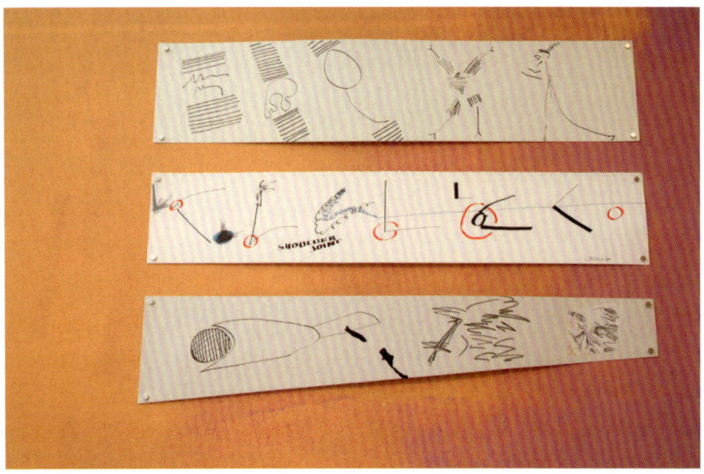

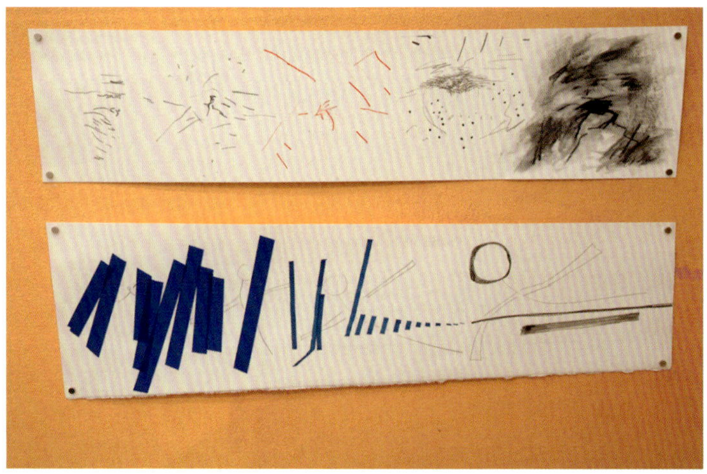

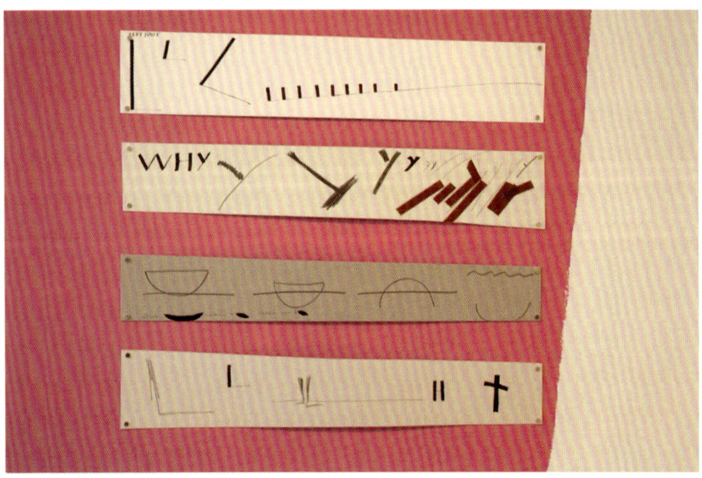

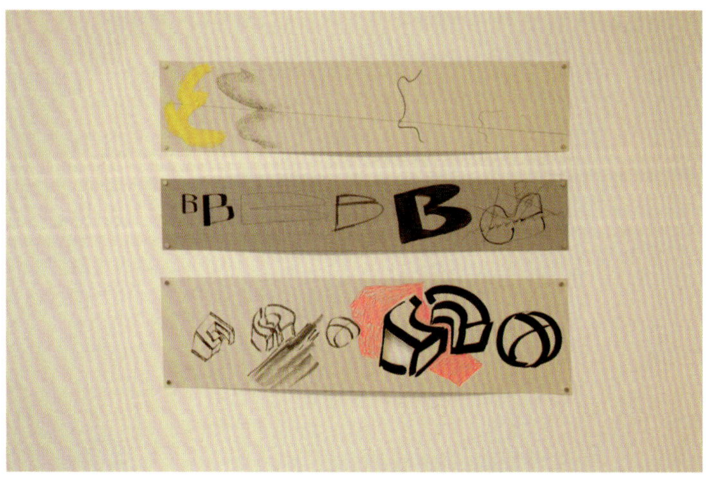

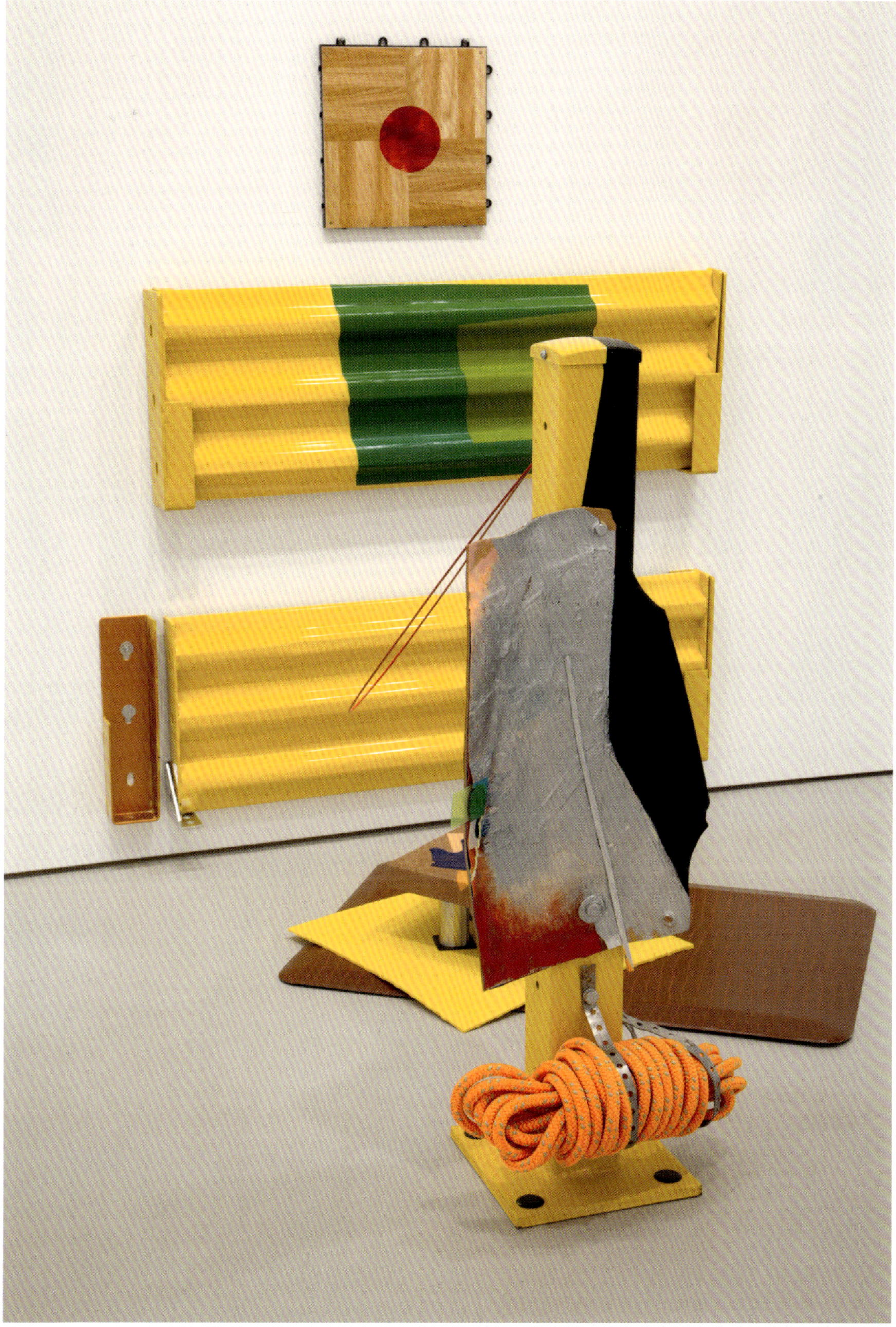

The latter project, *The Guests All Crowded Into the Dining Room* (New York, 2016) – where the grafting of materials in the individual sculptures is now transformed into a grafting between intervals and assembled objects, expanding the completely inclusive territory – finally, results in a story: the story of the artist's life and the places she has passed through. It is interwoven with an impalpable plot, the leading character of which is the material, but also its installation in a specific territory, namely where the materials she uses and the spaces the work occupies can be found. This translates into a mix between action and narration that is connoted by its unrepeatability: a multi-perspective tale made up of digressions and suspensions, difficult to translate into words: 'I don't think that words exist to describe properly my relationship to stories. I don't choose materials to tell stories, but inevitably stories are told. It is impossible to put materials together and not have a story arise. I choose material to disrupt those stories, so that there is no one story that comes to the fore. Materials come with histories and narratives that sit next to the abstract things that I am doing. I am really glad for that.'[11]

Stockholder's research, producing something that is narratable, if autonomous and spontaneous, provokes all viewers or visitors to live their own story, through the materials, without being able to distinguish the narrating 'I' from what is narrated. Thus a circular story is established, which affirms its uniqueness in the sense that each person reflects in it the product of his or her own memory and experience. In this way, the process of expansion and stabilization grows. The situation is now composed of visual and plastic molecules, known and unknown, reflections and non-reflections of existence, which freely circulate in the space. Architecture and aesthetic tools mix with corporeal forms and psychic references. They enter into symbiosis, break apart every instance of isolation, eliminate specificity and specialty. They construct a capillary universe of individual spaces to actualize a global process. It is a questioning of the fragmentation of awareness and perspectives, in favour of an all-encompassing vision, devoid of hierarchies and boundaries.

TRANSLATED FROM ITALIAN BY MARGUERITE SHORE

SURVEY: PAGES 047–075

1 Harold Rosenberg, 'On Art Movements', in *The Anxious Object: Art Today and Its Audience*, University of Chicago Press, 1982, pp. 237–38.
2 Fredrich Meschede, 'Images After a Journey', in Fredrich Meschede, Eva Schmidt and Antje von Graevenitz, *Jessica Stockholder*, Westfälischer Kunstverein, Münster, and Kunsthalle Zürich, 1992, p. 27.
3 Bill Jones, 'False Documents: A Conversation with Jeff Wall', *Arts Magazine*, May 1990, p. 54.
4 Jo-Anne Birnie Danzker, 'Vancouver: Land-and Culture-Scape', in Lorna Farrell-Ward (ed.), *Vancouver: Art and Artists 1931–1983*, Vancouver Art Gallery, 1983, p. 216.
5 Interview with Klaus Ottmann, in *Jessica Stockholder: The Broken Mirror: Part Three*, exhibition brochure, Ezra and Cecile Zilkha Gallery, Wesleyan University, Middletown, Connecticut, 1991.
6 Clement Greenberg, 'Cézanne', in *Art and Culture: Critical Essays*, Beacon Press, Boston, 1961, p. 55.
7 Scott Watson, 'The Generic City and Its Discontents: Vancouver Accounts for Itself', *Arts Magazine*, February 1991, p. 62. The comparison between Stockholder and Rauschenberg is most fully developed by Jack Bankowsky, 'The Obligatory Bed Piece', *Artforum*, October 1990, pp. 141–45 and a year later is already treated as conventional by David Pagel, 'Jessica Stockholder', *Arts Magazine*, October 1991, p. 89. An important essay, discussing a number of the aspects of Rauschenberg's work which will be relevant to Stockholder's as well, is James Leggio, 'Robert Rauschenberg's Bed and the Symbolism of the Body', in John Elderfield (ed.), *Studies in Modern Art 2: Essays on Assemblage*, The Museum of Modern Art and Harry N Abrams, New York, 1992, pp. 79–117.
8 Donald Judd, 'Specific Objects', *Arts Yearbook*, no. 8, 1965, reprinted in his *Complete Writings 1959–1975*, The Press of the Nova Scotia College of Art and Design, Halifax, 1975.
9 Michael Fried, 'Art and Objecthood', 1967, in Gregory Battcock (ed.), *Minimal Art: A Critical Anthology*, Dutton, New York, 1968, p. 142.
10 Although John Miller writes that for Stockholder 'the gallery space serves as an expanded canvas, not as a minimalist-derived "theatre"', ('Formalism and its other', in John Miller, Chris Dercon and Suzanne Ghez, *Jessica Stockholder*, Witte de With Centre for Contemporary Art, Rotterdam, and The Renaissance Society at the University of Chicago, 1991, p. 38), it is impossible to make the distinction hold.
11 Jerry Saltz, 'Mis-appropriation: Jessica Stockholder's Sculpture with No Name', *Arts Magazine*, April 1990, p. 21; Jeanne Siegel, 'Jessica Stockholder', *Arts Magazine*, June 1990, p. 77.
12 Susan Sontag, 'Happenings: An Art of Radical Juxtaposition' (1962), in *Against Interpretation and Other Essays*, Farrar, Straus & Giroux, New York, 1966, pp. 263–74.
13 Roland Barthes, 'The Wisdom of Art', 1979, in *The Responsibility of Forms: Critical Essays on Music, Art and Representation*, Hill & Wang, New York, 1985, p. 177; 'Cy Twombly: Works on Paper', 1979, ibid., p. 174.
14 Bankowsky, *Artforum*, 1990, op. cit., p. 141.
15 *Jessica Stockholder*, Witte de With, Rotterdam, and The Renaissance Society at the University of Chicago, 1991, op. cit., p. 29.
16 Bankowsky, *Artforum*, 1990, op. cit., p. 142.
17 *Jessica Stockholder*, Westfälischer Kunstverein, and Kunsthalle Zürich, op. cit., p. 22.
18 Robert Morris, 'Notes on Sculpture, Part 1', in *Continuous Project Altered Daily: The Writings of Robert Morris*, MIT Press, Cambridge, Massachusetts, 1993, p. 3; originally published in *Artforum*, February 1966.
19 Mowry Baden, *Maquettes & Other Preparatory Work 1967–1980*, Art Gallery of Greater Victoria, British Columbia, 1985, pp. 5–6 (See also Mowry Baden and Liane Davison, *Mowry Baden: Sculpture*, Alberta College of Art Gallery, Calgary, 1989).
20 *Jessica Stockholder*, Witte de With, Rotterdam, and The Renaissance Society at the University of Chicago, 1991, op. cit., p. 19.
21 Eva Schmidt, 'Interview with Jessica Stockholder', in *Jessica Stockholder*, Westfälischer Kunstverein, Münster, and Kunsthalle Zürich, op. cit., p. 42.
22 Frederick Jameson, 'The Cultural Logic of Late Capitalism' (1984), in *Postmodernism, or, The Cultural Logic of Late Capitalism*, Duke University Press, Durham, North Carolina, 1991, pp. 33–34.
23 Elizabeth Wilson, 'The Rhetoric of Urban Space', *New Left Review*, no. 209, January–February 1995, pp. 146–60. This essay extends analyses begun in Wilson's book *The Sphinx in the City: Urban Life, the Control of Disorder, and Women*, Virago Press, London, 1991.
24 Dan Graham, 'Homes for America' (1966), in *Rock My Religion: Writings and Art Projects 1965–1990*, MIT Press, Cambridge, Massachusetts, 1993, pp. 14–23.
25 *Jessica Stockholder*, Witte de With, Rotterdam, and The Renaissance Society at the University of Chicago, 1991, op. cit., p. 19.
26 Bankowsky, *Artforum*, 1990, op. cit., p. 145.

FOCUS: PAGES 077–085

1 Andrew Marvell, 'Bermudas', in Richard Rodney Bennett (ed.), *The Bermudas: Poem by Andrew Marvell*, Universal Edition, Vienna, 1975.
2 This dual property of pertaining to colour and object seems particular to certain citrus fruit, notably lemons, which Stockholder has also used in an installation, limes and tangerines.
3 Bankowsky, *Artforum*, 1990, op. cit., p. 142.
4 Jessica Stockholder, 'Interview with Klaus Ottmann', in *Journal of Contemporary Art*, Spring–Summer 1991. Reprinted in this book, pp. 120–123.
5 David Pagel, 'Jessica Stockholder', *Arts Magazine*, 1991, op. cit., p. 89.
6 Stockholder quoted in *Jessica Stockholder*, Witte de With, Rotterdam, and The Renaissance Society at the University of Chicago, 1991, op. cit., p. 17.
7 The exhibition was held at the Sala Montcada de la Fundació La Caixa, Barcelona, 18 January–16 February 1995.
8 See Michael Baxandall, *Patterns of Intention: On the Historical Explanation of Pictures*, Yale University Press, New Haven, 1985, p. 45.
9 Quoted in Bob Nickas, 'The State of Things: Questions to Three Object Conscious Artists', *Flash Art*, no. 151, March–April 1990, pp. 132. Reprinted in this book, p. 116–119.
10 'Interview with Klaus Ottmann', *Journal of Contemporary Art*, 1991, op. cit., see pp. 120–123.

ARTIST'S WRITINGS: PAGES 111–177

1 Rosalind Krauss, 'Sculpture in the Expanded Field', *October*, Spring, 1979, pp. 30–44.
2 Johanna Burton, 'Sculpture: Not-Not-Not (or, Pretty Air)', in Anne Ellegood and Johanna Burton, *The Uncertainty of Objects and Ideas: Recent Sculpture*, Hirshhorn Museum and Sculpture Garden, Washington, D.C., 2006, p. 14.
3 Rosalind Krauss, *October*, 1979, op. cit., p. 34.

UPDATE: PAGES 179–219

1 Stephen Westfall, 'Interview with Jessica Stockholder', *Bomb*, September 1992 (reprinted in this book on pp. 125–131).
2 See Lynne Tillman, p. 30.
3 Ibid., p. 34.
4 'Composition is everywhere. A Conversation between Jessica Stockholder and Jean-Pierre Criqui', in Miwon Kwon, Maurice Fréchuret and Jean-Pierre Criqui, *Jessica Stockholder: TV Tipped Toenails and the Green Salami*, CAPC Musée d'Art Contemporain, Bordeaux, 2003, pp. 69–70.
5 Bob Nickas, 'The State of Things: Questions to Three Object Conscious Artists', *Flash Art*, 1990, op. cit., p. 132.
6 'More than Young and Beautiful: Gerard Mack in conversation with Jessica Stockholder', in Konrad Bitterli, Gerhard Mack and Roland Wäspe, *Jessica Stockholder: Vortex in the Play of Theater with Real Passion*, Kunstmuseum St. Gallen, Switzerland, and Verlag für Modern Kunst, Nuremberg, Germany, 2001, p. 31.
7 Jessica Stockholder, 'Parallel Parking', typescript of statement published in *Turn of the Century Magazine*, New York, Spring 1993.
8 Jessica Stockholder, in 'The State of Things', op. cit.
9 Jessica Stockholder, in *TV Tipped Toe Nails*, CAPC Musée d'Art Contemporain, Bordeaux, 2003, op. cit., p. 58.
10 Jessica Stockholder, email to the author, February 2017.
11 Gerard Mack and Jessica Stockholder, in 'More than Young and Beautiful', Kunstmuseum St. Gallen, Switzerland, and Verlag für Modern Kunst, Nuremberg, Germany, 2001, op. cit., p. 31.

ASSIST #4: CARVED SPACES, 2016
PAINTED STEEL STRAPPED TO A PROP
(ARM CHAIR)
222 X 155 X 163 CM

INSTALLATION VIEW AT MITCHELL-INNES & NASH, NEW YORK, 2016

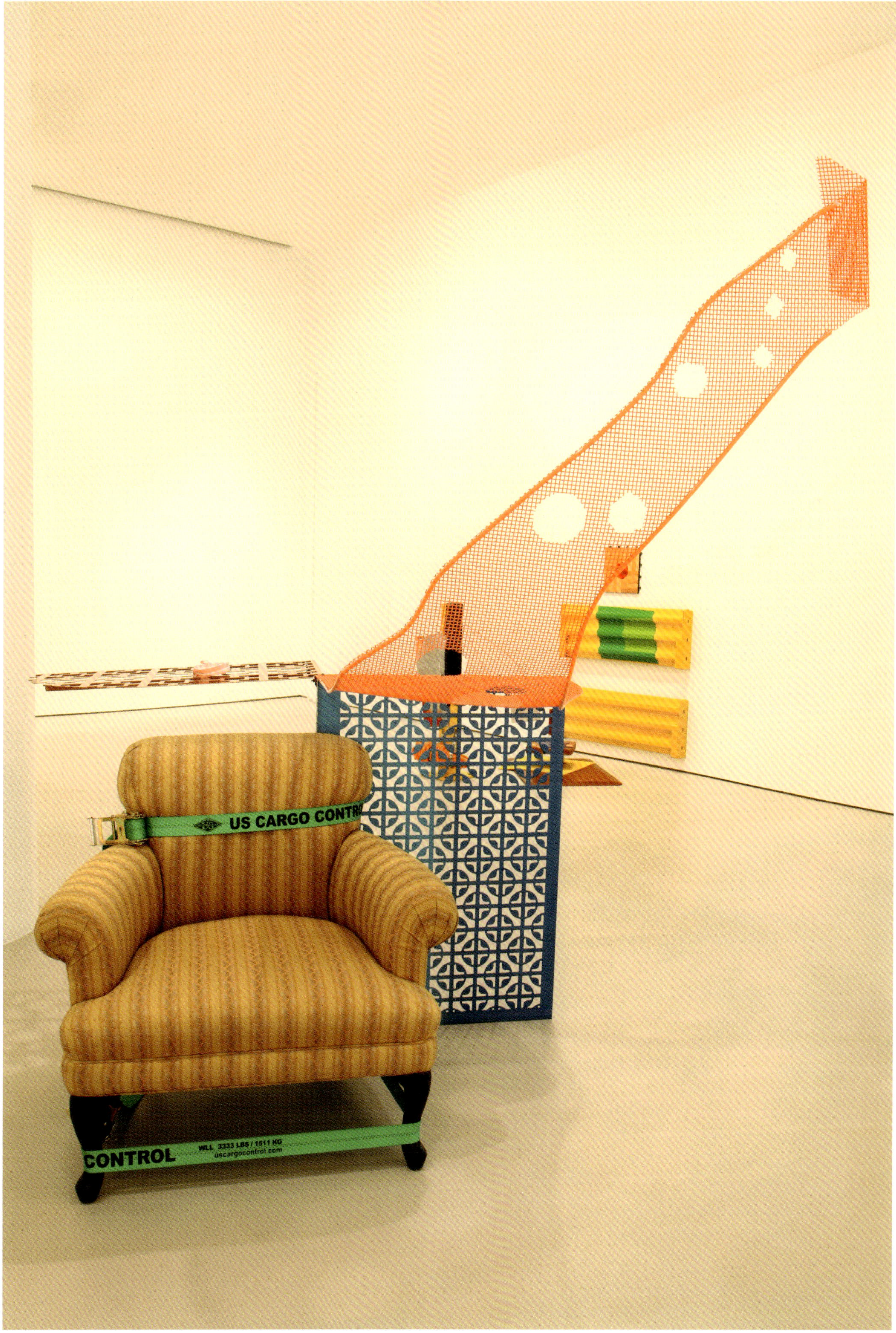

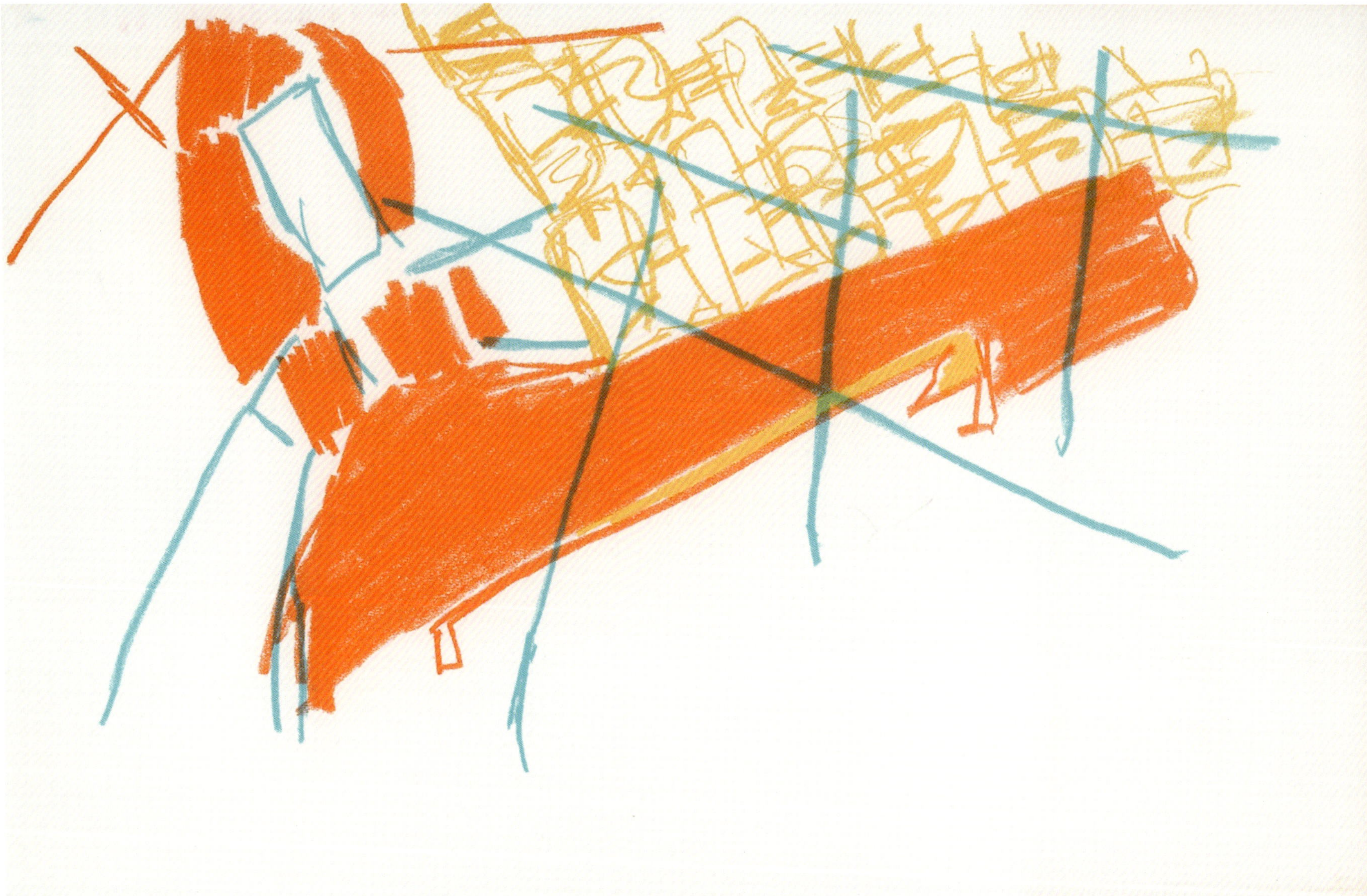

SKIN TONED GARDEN MAPPING, 1991
INVITATION CARD FOR EXHIBITION AT
THE RENAISSANCE SOCIETY AT THE
UNIVERSITY OF CHICAGO
15 X 23 CM

CHRONOLOGY: Jessica Stockholder, born 1959 in Seattle. Lives and works in Chicago.

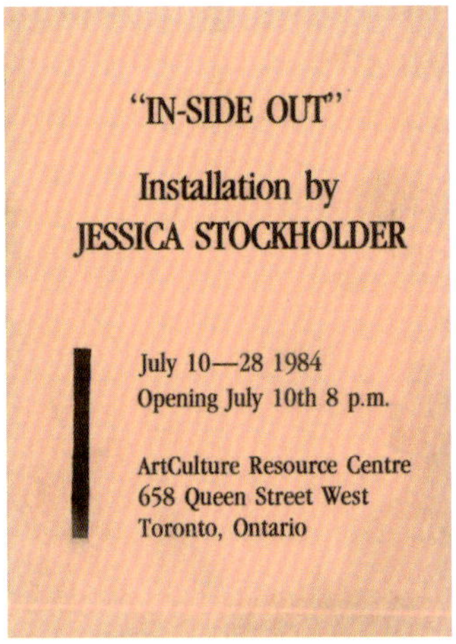

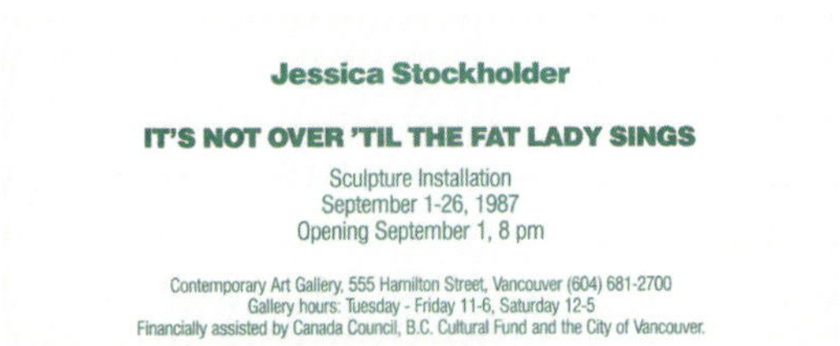

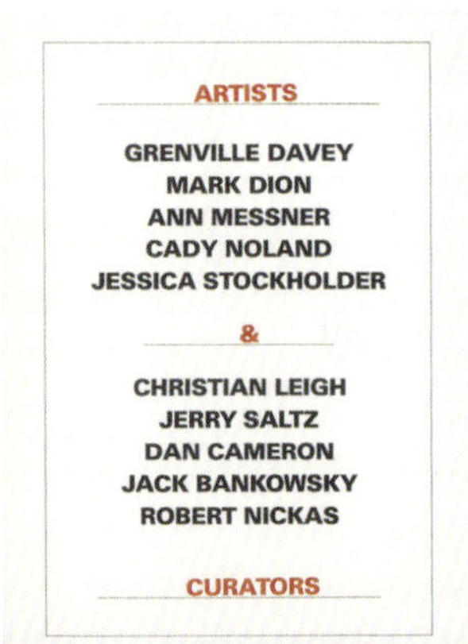

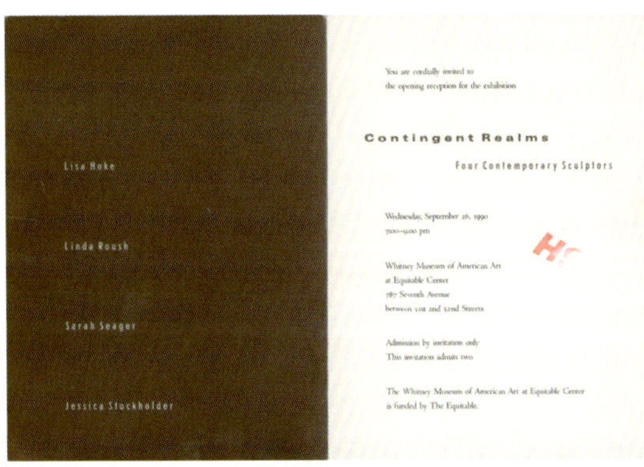

SELECTED EXHIBITIONS AND PROJECTS 1977–90	SELECTED ARTICLES AND INTERVIEWS 1977–90
1977–1980 Attends the University of British Columbia, Vancouver	
1980–82 Attends the University of Victoria, British Columbia	
1982 'Graduation Exhibition', McPHERSON LIBRARY GALLERY at UNIVERSITY OF VICTORIA, British Columbia (group)	1982 Burnham, Clint, and Katy Chan, 'Honest Material, Simple Methods', The Marlet, 28 September
1983–1985 Attends Yale University in New Haven, Connecticut	
1984 'In-Side Out', ART CULTURE RESOURCE CENTER, Toronto (solo)	
1985 'Wall Sandwich', MELINDA WYATT GALLERY, New York (solo) Receives the Susan H. Whedon Award at Yale University, New Haven	
1987 'It's not over til the fat lady sings', CONTEMPORARY ART GALLERY, Vancouver (solo)	1987 Perry, Art, 'Appreciating Creative Fun', The Province, 11 September
1988 'Indoor Lighting for My Father', MERCER UNION, Toronto (solo) 'Artists and Curators', JOHN GIBSON GALLERY, New York (group) Invited as visiting artist to the Brock University in Toronto	
1989 'Mixing Food with the Bed', THE MATTRESS FACTORY, Pittsburgh (solo) 'A Climate of Site', BARBARA FARBER GALLERY, Amsterdam (group) 'Berkshire Art Association Exhibition of Painting and Sculpture', BERKSHIRE MUSEUM, Pittsfield, Massachusetts (group)	1989 Homisak, Bill, 'At 1414 Monterey, Art Moves Off the Wall', Tribune Review, 20 October Lowry, Patricia, 'Exhibits Range from Restrained to Stimulating', Pittsburgh Press, 11 November Miller, Donald, 'Victor Grauer, Kathleen Montgomery, Cady Noland, Jessica Stockholder', Pittsburgh Post Gazette, 21 October
1990 'Where it Happened', AMERICAN FINE ARTS, CO., New York (solo) 'Mary Heilmann and Jessica Stockholder: For Mary Heilmann', GALERIE ISABELLA KACPRZAK, Cologne (solo) TERRAIN: INFORMATION, San Francisco (group) 'Stendhal Syndrome: The Cure', ANDREA ROSEN GALLERY, New York (group) 'Contingent Realms', WHITNEY MUSEUM OF AMERICAN ART, New York (group)	1990 Nickas, Bob, 'The State of Things: Questions to Three Object-Conscious Artists', Flash Art, no. 151, March–April Saltz, Jerry, 'Notes on Sculpture. Mis-appropriation: Jessica Stockholder's Sculpture with No Name', Arts Magazine, April Siegel, Jeanne, 'Jessica Stockholder', Arts Magazine, June Spector, Nancy, 'Jessica Stockholder', Contemporanea, June Avgikos, Jan, 'Jessica Stockholder', Artscribe, Summer Dupont, Valérie, 'Le choix des femmes', Art en Bourgogne, Summer

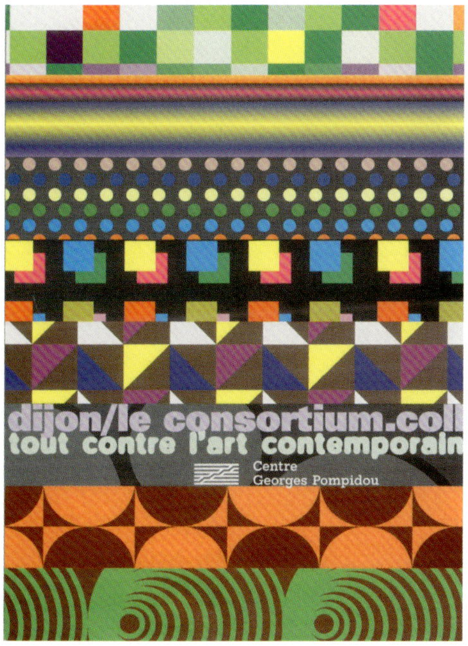

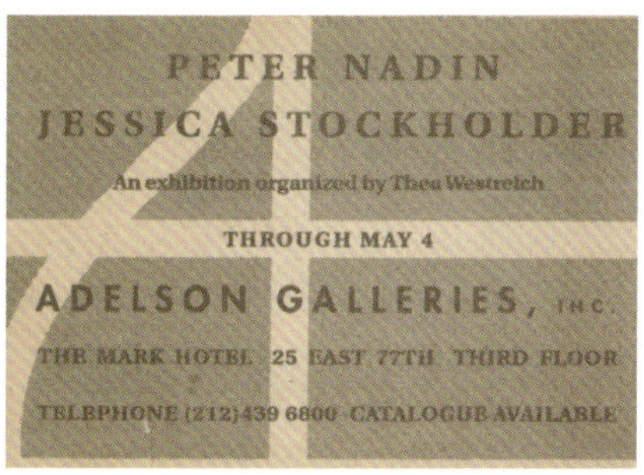

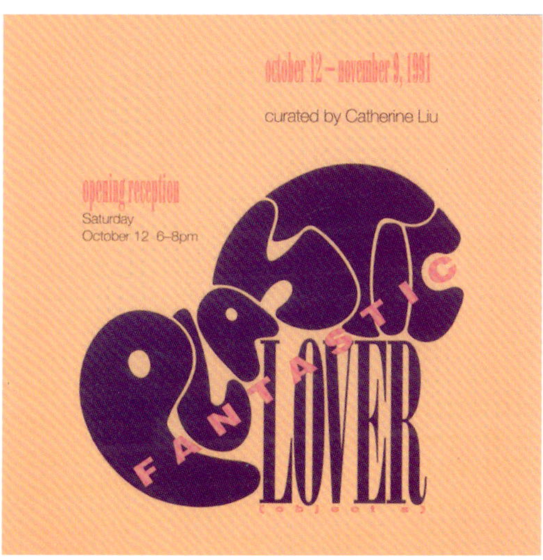

SELECTED EXHIBITIONS AND PROJECTS
1990–92

SELECTED ARTICLES AND INTERVIEWS
1990–92

1990 (cont.)
'The Technological Muse',
KATONAH MUSEUM OF ART, New York (group)

'Le choix des femmes',
LE CONSORTIUM, FONDS RÉGIONAL D'ART CONTEMPORAIN (FRAC) BOURGOGNE and L'USINE, Dijon, France (group)

1990 (cont.)
Schaffner, Ingrid, 'Jessica Stockholder', Sculpture Magazine, July–August

Bankowsky, Jack, 'The Obligatory Bed Piece', Artforum, October

Fernel, Héléne, 'Le choix des femmes', Les Depêches, 25 November

Mahoney, Robert, 'Jessica Stockholder: Where It Happened', Sculpture Magazine, November–December

1991
'Untitled Seepage: Sandwashed, Sundried & Shrinkwrapped',
EZRA AND CECILE ZILKHA GALLERY at WESLEYAN UNIVERSITY CENTER FOR ARTS, Middletown, Connecticut (solo)

'Studio Works',
DANIEL WEINBERG GALLERY, Santa Monica (solo)

'Near Weather Wall and Making a Clean Edge II',
WITTE DE WITH, Rotterdam (solo)

'Peter Nadin and Jessica Stockholder',
WARREN ADELSON GALLERY, New York (solo)

'Skin Toned Garden Mapping',
THE RENAISSANCE SOCIETY, Chicago (solo)

'Jürgen Meyer, Jessica Stockholder, Franz West',
CHRISTINE BURGIN GALLERY, New York (group)

'Physicality: An Exhibition on Color Dimensionality in Painting',
THE GALLERY, New York (group)

'Outside America: Going into the 1990s',
FAY GOLD GALLERY, Atlanta (group)

'The Museum of Natural History',
BARBARA FARBER GALLERY, Amsterdam (group)

'Awards in the Visual Arts 10',
TOLEDO MUSEUM OF ART, Ohio, toured to SOUTHEASTERN CENTER FOR CONTEMPORARY ART, Winston-Salem, North Carolina; HIRSHHORN MUSEUM AND SCULPTURE GARDEN, Washington, D.C.; ALBUQUERQUE MUSEUM, New Mexico (group)

'Plastic Fantastic Lover (Object A)',
BLUM HELMAN WAREHOUSE, New York (group)

'American Artists of the 1980s',
MUSEO D'ARTE TRENTO (MART) (group)

WHITNEY BIENNIAL OF AMERICAN ART, New York (group)

1991
Sichel, Berta, 'Undomesticated Still Lifes: The Order and Disorder of Jessica Stockholder', Balcon, no. 7, January

Schimidt, Eva, 'Mary Heilmann, Jessica Stockholder', Kunstforum International, no. 111, January–February

Mahoney, Robert, 'Jessica Stockholder', Tema Celeste, no. 30, March–April

Smith, Roberta, 'Peter Nadin and Jessica Stockholder', The New York Times, 2 March

Ottmann, Klaus, 'Interview with Jessica Stockholder', The Journal of Contemporary Art, Spring–Summer

Decter, Joshua, 'Jessica Stockholder', Arts Magazine, May

Curtis, Cathy, 'Jessica Stockholder', Los Angeles Times, 17 May

Johnson, Ken, 'Generational Saga', Art in America, June

Peeters, Mark, 'Stockholder bouwt pozie uit rotzooi van de nieuwewereld', NRC, 24 June

Von Graevenitz, Antje, 'Jessica Stockholder: Making A Clean Edge', Archis, July

Berbudeau, Eric, 'Le Consortium s'expose', Nouvelle République, 26 August

Lambrecht, Luk, 'Jessica Stockholder'; Eric Berbudeau, 'Whitney Biennale', Forum International, September

Pagel, David, 'Jessica Stockholder', Arts Magazine, October

Gillespie, Mary, 'Arts Get Their Day at University of Chicago', Chicago Sun Times, 4 October

Artner, Alan G., 'Smart Choices in the University of Chicago Centennial Shows', Chicago Tribune, 25 October

Glatt, Cara, 'Installation Finds Meaning in Everyday Objects', The Herald, 30 October

Van den Broogerd, Dominic, 'Jessica Stockholder', Artefactum, November–December

1992
'Growing Rock Candy Mountain: Grasses in Canned Sand',
WESTFÄLISCHER KUNSTVEREIN, Münster, Germany (solo)

'Flower Dusted Prosies',
AMERICAN FINE ARTS, CO., New York (solo)

'SpICE BOXed Project(ion)',
GALERIE METROPOL, Vienna (solo)

1992
Hixson, Kathryn, 'Jessica Stockholder', Arts Magazine, January

Obrist, Hans Ulrich, 'The Installation is Coming Through the Backdoor', Meta 1 Die Kunst und Ihr Oht, January

Faust, Gretchen,'Jessica Stockholder', Arts Magazine, March

Horst, Michael, 'Ein lila Gebirge aus Stoff und Sandstein', Westfälische Nachrichten, 10 April

SELECTED EXHIBITIONS AND PROJECTS
1992–1994

1992 (cont.)
'Sea Floor Movement to Rise of Fire Place Stripping',
KUNSTHALLE ZÜRICH (solo)

'Mary Heilmann, Jack Pierson, Jessica Stockholder',
PAT HEARN GALLERY, New York (group)

'Women Artists Not Included in Documenta 9',
KUNSTLERHAUS STUTTGART, Germany (group)

'Transgressions in the White Cube: Territorial Mappings',
SUZANNE LEMBERG USDAN GALLERY at BENNINGTON COLLEGE, Vermont (group)

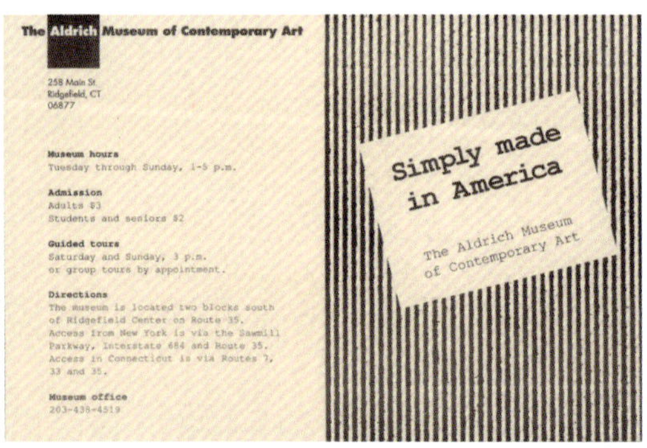

1993
'Edge of Hothouse Glass',
MUSÉE D'ART CONTEMPORAIN DE NÎMES, France (solo)

GALERIE LUDWIG, Krefeld, Germany (solo)

'Mettlesome & Meddlesome: Selections from the Collection of Robert J. Schiller',
CONTEMPORARY ARTS CENTER, Cincinnati (group)

'Simply Made in America',
ALDRICH MUSEUM OF CONTEMPORARY ART, Ridgefield, Connecticut (group)

'Ordnung und Zerstorung',
LOTHRINGER STRASSE 13, Munich (group)

'Jours Tranquilles a Clichy',
40 RUE DE ROCHECHOUART, Paris, toured to TENNISPORT ARTS, New York (group)

'As Long as It Lasts',
WITTE DE WITH, Rotterdam (group)

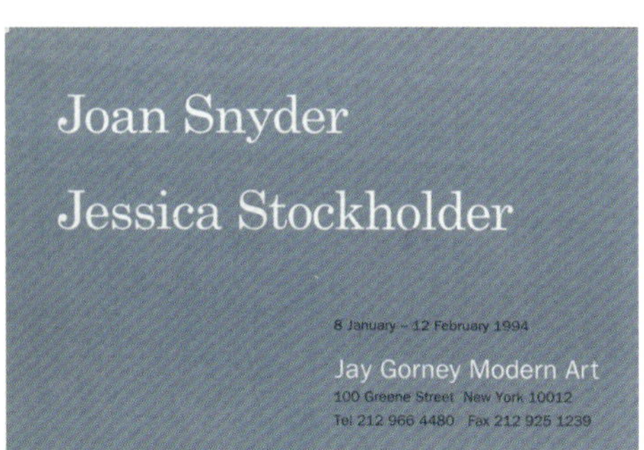

1994
'Joan Snyder and Jessica Stockholder',
JAY GORNEY MODERN ART, New York (solo)

'Pink Lady',
WEATHERSPOON ART GALLERY at THE UNIVERSITY OF NORTH CAROLINA, Greensboro (solo)

SELECTED ARTICLES AND INTERVIEWS
1992–1994

1992 (cont.)
Weitkamp, Andreas, 'Ein Lob der Farbe Lila', Münstersche Zeitung, 10 April

Jaeckel, Claudia, 'Jessica Stockholder', Art, May

Westfall, Stephen, 'Interview with Jessica Stockholder', Bomb, September

Tanger, Alisa, 'The Question of Gender in Art', Tema Celeste, no. 42–3, Autumn

S., K., 'Vakuum und Weiblichkeit, Ausgestellt: Höfer, Spero, Stockholder', Die Presse, 24 September

Myers, Terry R., 'Heilmann, Pierson, Stockholder', Flash Art, no. 167, November–December

Frehner, Matthias, 'Liebesspiel zwischen Object und Raum', Neue Zürcher Zeitung, 6 November

Polzer, Brita, 'Zürich: Stockholder in der Kunsthalle', Kunst Bulletin, December

Schmidt, Sabine M, 'Portrait: Jessica Stockholder, Eine Amerikanerin in Münster', Stadtblatt, no. 12

1993
Kravagna, Christian, 'Jessica Stockholder: Galerie Metropol', Artforum, January

Troncy, Éric, 'Painting from All Over to All Round: Lauren Szold and Jessica Stockholder Start Gigging'; Daniel Kurjakovic, 'Jessica Stockholder', Flash Art, no. 168, January–February

Liebman, Lisa, 'Junk Cultured', Frieze, no. 9, March–April

Stockholder, Jessica, 'Parallel Parking', Turn of the Century Magazine, no. 1, Spring

Van den Boogerd, Dominic, 'As Long As It Lasts', Metropolis M, August

'Jessica Stockholder, création pour un lieu donné', Marseillaise, 6 August

Butler, Connie, 'Terrible Beauty and the Enormity of Space', Art & Text, no. 46, September

R., M. A., 'Jessica Stockholder: Graffitis Dreidimensional', Rheinische Post, 29 September

Krajewski, Michael, 'Krefeld: Galerienrundschau', Kunst Bulletin, October

Chamberlain, Patrick, 'On an Antidote', Witte de With Cahier, no. 1, October

Richter, Horst, 'Art Cologne 93', Weltkunst, November

Donegan, Cheryl, 'One Portrayal, Four Portraits', Tema Celeste, no. 39, Winter

1994
Hess, Elizabeth, 'Fem Fatale', The Village Voice, 25 January

Bouisset, Maïten, 'Le Consortium: Deux Collections... l'Université', Art Press, February

Levin, Kim, 'Voice Choice: Joan Snyder and Jessica Stockholder', The Village Voice, 1 February

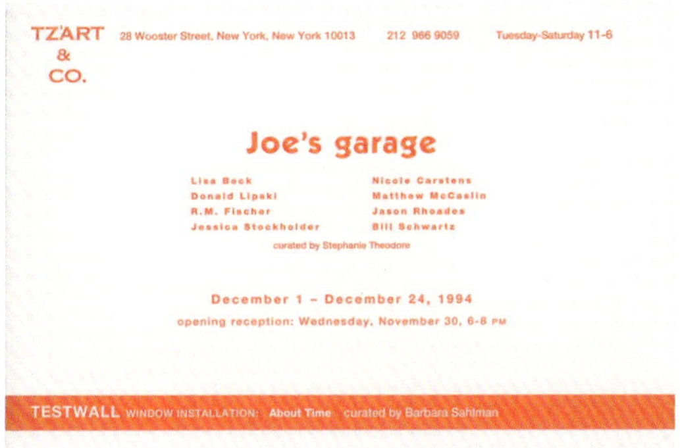

SELECTED EXHIBITIONS AND PROJECTS
1994–95

1994 (cont.)
'Possible Things: A Drawing Show',
BARDAMU GALLERY, New York (group)

'The Beauty Show',
FOUR WALLS, New York (group)

'Don't Look Now',
THREAD WAXING SPACE, New York (group)

'Unbound: Possibilities in Painting',
HAYWARD GALLERY, London (group)

'Information Service',
GOETHE HOUSE, New York (group)

'Country Sculpture',
LE CONSORTIUM, Dijon (group)

'Ethernal Materialism',
APEX ART, New York (group)

'Joe's Garage',
TZ'ART & CO., New York (group)

SELECTED ARTICLES AND INTERVIEWS
1994–95

1994 (cont.)
Kimmelman, Michael, 'Joan Snyder and Jessica Stockholder', The New York Times, 4 February

Smith, Roberta, 'Group Shows of Every Kind', The New York Times, 25 February

Hilton, Tim, 'Every Which Way But Forwards', The Independent, 6 March

Cork, Richard, 'Painting is Back in the Picture', Times, 7 March

Lillington, David, 'Zeitgeist', Time Out New York, 9 March

Norman, Geraldine, 'Exhibition Highlights: New Wave of Painting "Unbound" for Success'; Andrew Graham-Dixon, 'Sort of, Almost, In a Way, Nearly', The Independent, 14 March

Jonaes, Abe, 'Sculptor's Work Explores the Material World', News & Record Sunday, 27 March

Morley, Simon, 'Unbound: Possibilities in Painting', Art Monthly, April

Harris, Susan, 'Joan Snyder and Jessica Stockholder', Art Press, April

Gayford, Martin, '"Nerdism" Could Become the Movement of the 1990s', Telegraph, 6 April

Slatin, Peter, 'Joan Snyder and Jessica Stockholder', ARTnews, May

Maloney, Martin, 'Unbound: Possibilities in Painting', The Burlington Magazine, no. 1094, May

Bachelor, David, 'Behind a Painted Smile: ..."Unbound""...', Frieze, no. 16, May

Patterson, Tom, 'Jessica Stockholder's Works Hold Attention, Test the Mind', Winston-Salem Journal Sunday, 1 May

Dannatt, Adrian, 'London by Numbers: Three Painting Shows', Flash Art, no. 176, July–September

Myerson, Clifford, 'On Painting 1', Art Monthly, September

Hess, Elizabeth, 'Garage Sale', The Village Voice, December

Birnbaum, Daniel, 'Rîhet och mîngfald', Dagens Nyheter, 9 December

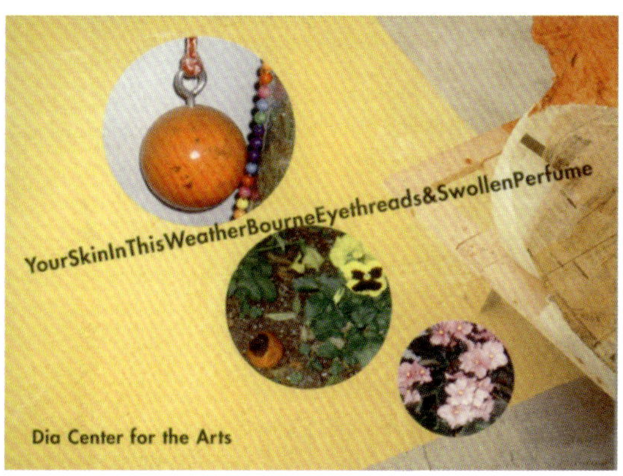

1995
'Sweet for Three Oranges',
FUNDACIÓ LA CAIXA, Barcelona (solo)

S. L. SIMPSON GALLERY, Toronto (solo)

JAY GORNEY MODERN ART, New York (solo)

GALERIE NATHALIE OBADIA, Paris (solo)

'Your Skin in this Weather Bourne Eye-Threads & Swollen Perfume',
DIA CENTER FOR THE ARTS, New York (solo)

'Pittura-Immedia: Malerei in den 90er Jahren',
NEUE GALERIE AM LANDESMUSEUM JOANNEUM, Graz, Austria (group)

1995
S., C, 'Una instalación de la artista estadounidense Jessica Stockholder transforma el espacio de la sala Montcada', El País, 18 January

Spiegel, Olga, 'La Norteamericana Jessica Stockholder abre temporada en la sala Montcada', La Vanguardia, 21 January

'"Sweet for Three Oranges"' de Jessica Stockholder, primera exposició', Panorama, February

Juncosa, Enrique, 'Abetos y naranjas', El País, 4 February

Taylor, Kate, 'Of Green Shower Curtains and Lavender Fuzzy Fur', The Globe and Mail, 11 February

Levin, Kim, 'The Joy of Curating', The Village Voice, 29 February

ELENA SISTO

LISA HOKE

JESSICA STOCKHOLDER

OCTOBER 28 – DECEMBER 2, 1995
Opening October 28, 6-8

DRU ARSTARK GALLERY
568 Broadway #403 NYC 10012
Tel/Fax 212-431-7334
darstark@inch.com
www.inch.com/~darstark/art/gall.html

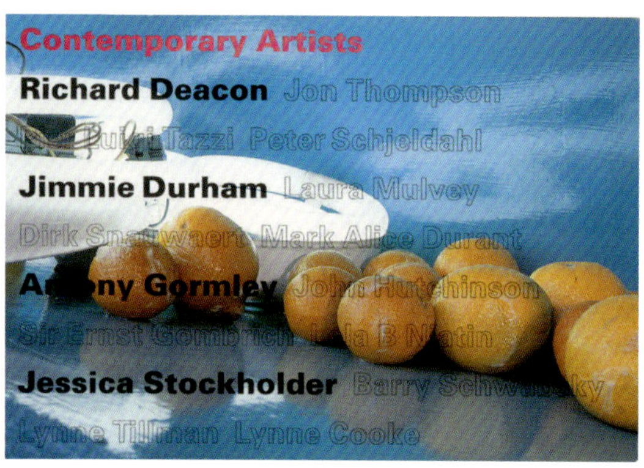

SELECTED EXHIBITIONS AND PROJECTS
1995–96

1995 (cont.)
'New York: Positionen Aktueller Malerei',
STUDIOGALERIE DER KUNSTVEREIN SCHLOß MORSBROICH, Leverkusen, Germany (group)

'1995 Collectie Presentatie Moderne Kunst',
CENTRAAL MUSEUM UTRECHT, The Netherlands (group)

'Color in Space: Pictorialism in Contemporary sculpture',
DAVID WINSTON BELL GALLERY at BROWN UNIVERSITY LIST ART CENTER, Providence, Rhode Island (group)

'Elena Sisto, Lisa Hoke, Jessica Stockholder',
DRU ARSTARK GALLERY, New York (group)

SELECTED ARTICLES AND INTERVIEWS
1995–96

1995 (cont.)
Klein, Monike, 'Sieben New Yorker Maler stellen in der Studiogalerie aus', Rheinische Post, 21 March

Servetar, Stuart, 'Jessica Stockholder', N. Y. Press, 30 March

Servin, James, 'Abstract Artist Brings Home the Familiar', Associated Press, 14 April

Smith, Roberta, 'Jessica Stockholder', The New York Times, 14 April

Rubenstein, Rafael, 'Full Circle', Art in America, May

Myers, Terry R, 'Jessica Stockholder', New Art Examiner, June

Birnbaum, Daniel, 'Jessica Stockholder', Dagens Nyhter, 16 July

Jaeger, Jack, 'Jessica Stockholder at Dia Art Foundation', Zapp Magazine, no. 8

Feinstein, Roni, 'Jessica Stockholder: Chaos Theory', Canadian Art, September

Kimmelman, Michael, 'At Dia, Fresh Wounds and a Fresh Start', The New York Times, 15 September

Schwabsky, Barry, 'Jessica Stockholder', Art Press, Autumn

Princenthal, Nancy, 'Jessica Stockholder: Reinventing the Real', Art+Text, no. 52, October

Kimmelman, Michael, 'Exhuberantly Operatic, In Scale and Emotion', The New York Times, 6 October

Newhall, Edith, 'Insider Art', New York Magazine, 16 October

Schjeldahl, Peter, 'Out of Nothing', The Village Voice, 24 October–1 November

Perrée, Rob, 'Jessica Stockholder in New York: De Schoonheid Achter Het Lelijke Gezicht', Kunstbeeld, November

Smith, Roberta, 'Making the Abstract Light, Sunny and Personal', The New York Times, 3 November

Budney, Jean, 'Jessica Stockholder at Dia', Flash Art, no. 185, November–December

Lind, Maria, 'Som att hitta ett outforskat sinnligt n''jesfält', Svenska Dagbladet, 29 November

Levin, Kim, 'Art Short List', The Village Voice, 31 November

Buchloh, Benjamin H.D, and Lisa Liebmann, 'Best & Worst, 1995, excerpt: End Of the Line', Artforum, December

Jover, Manuel, 'Le Bricolage Existentiel de Jessica Stockholder', Beaux Arts, December

Perl, Jed, 'The Third Degree', The New Republic, 11 December

Milani, Joanne, 'Gallery Glimpses: Re: Fab...', The Tampa Tribune, 15 December

Lewis, JoAnn, 'Painting Outside the Lines', The Washington Post, 23 December

Shaw-Eagle, Joanna, 'Painting Beyond Traditional Limits', The Washington Times, 24 December

Kimmelman, Michael, 'A Wrapped Reichstag: That's the Spirit', The New York Times, 31 December

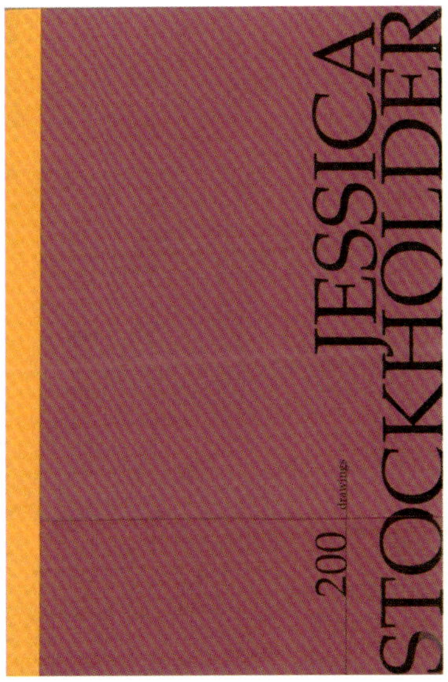

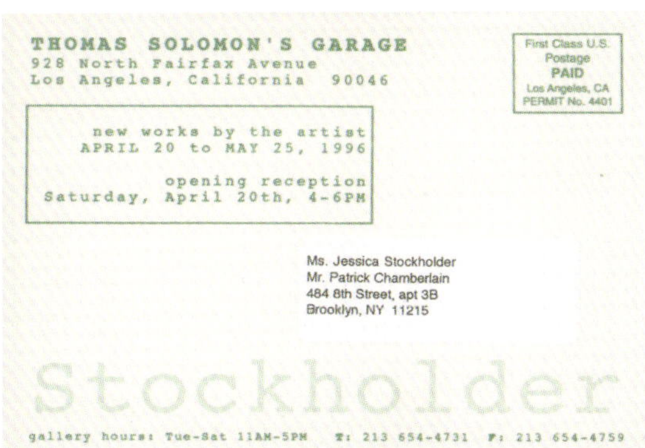

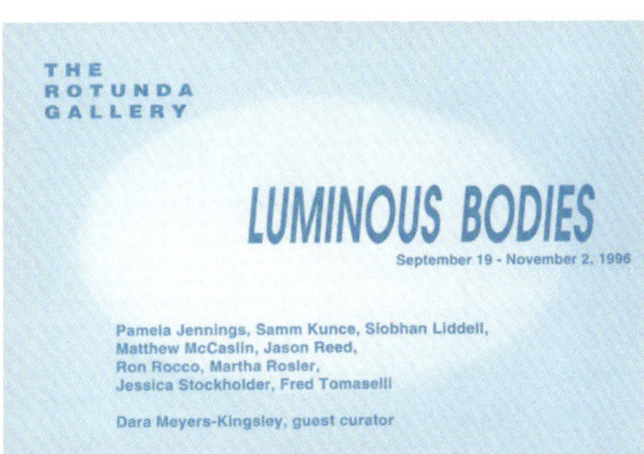

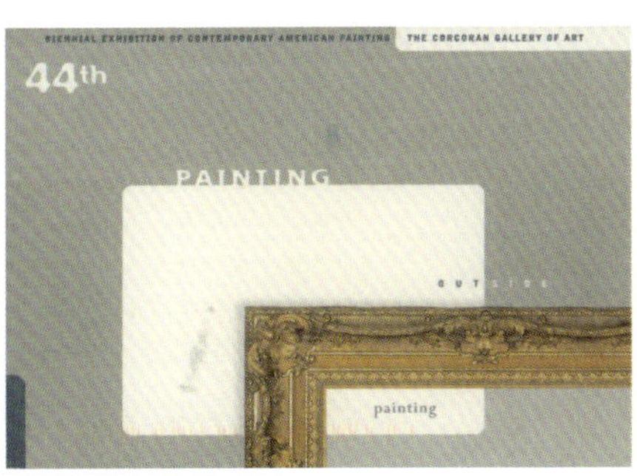

<u>SELECTED EXHIBITIONS AND PROJECTS</u>
1996

1996
STUDIO LA CITTÀ, Verona, Italy (solo)

'Bowtied In the Middle',
TOM SOLOMON'S GARAGE, Los Angeles (solo)

'Jessica Stockholder: 200 Drawings',
BAXTER GALLERY at MAINE COLLEGE OF ART, Portland, Oregon (solo)

'Painting: The Extended Field',
ROOSEUM, Malmö, toured to MAGASIN 3, Stockholm (group)

'Elena Sisto, Lisa Hoke, Jessica Stockholder',
DRU ARSTARK GALLERY, New York (group)

'Re:Fab: Painting Abstracted, Fabricated',
FLEMING MUSEUM at UNIVERSITY OF VERMONT, Burlington (group)

'Millennium Eve Dress ',
THE FABRIC WORKSHOP AND MUSEUM, Philadelphia (group)

'Unconditionally Abstraction',
SCHMIDT CONTEMPORARY ART, St. Louis (group)

'Patterns of Excess',
BEAVER COLLEGE ART GALLERY, Glenside, Pennsylvania (group)

'Luminous Bodies',
ROTUNDA GALLERY, New York (group)

'What I Did On My Summer Vacation',
WHITE COLUMNS, New York (group)

'Square Bubbles',
NOTT MEMORIAL ART MUSEUM, Schenectady, New York (group)

44th BIENNIAL EXHIBITION OF CONTEMPORARY PAINTING,
Washington, D.C. (group)

'Painting in an Expanding Field',
USDAN GALLERY at BENNINGTON COLLEGE, Vermont (group)

<u>SELECTED ARTICLES AND INTERVIEWS</u>
1996

1996
Volk, Gregory, 'Jessica Stockholder at Dia Center for the Arts', <u>ARTnews</u>, January

Wallis, Stephen, 'Sketchbook: Shows Not to Miss', <u>Art & Antiques</u>, January

Dagen, Phillippe, 'Jessica Stockholder', <u>Le Monde</u>, 15 January

Plagens, Peter, 'Peeling Paint: A Wash. Museum Asks: What's in a Picture?', <u>Newsweek</u>, 15 January

'Wham: Jessica Stockholder', <u>Interview</u>, February

Berkman, Robert, 'Pulling Matisse Off the Wall', <u>Linewaiters' Gazette</u>, 1 February

Smith, Roberta, 'Art in Review', <u>The New York Times</u>, 3 February

Meneghelli, Luigi, 'Gli oggetti di Jessica', <u>L'Arena</u>, 22 February

Gardner, Paul, 'Studio Visits: Pleasure, Pain & Protocol', <u>ARTnews</u>, March

McDonough, Thomas F., 'Your Skin... Jessica Stockholder im Dia Center for the Arts', <u>Texte zur Kunst</u>, March

Ostrow, Saul, 'History is Now', <u>The New Art Examiner</u>, March

'Self-Portrait by Jessica Stockholder', <u>The New Yorker</u>, 4 March

Aukeman, Anastasia, 'Jessica Stockholder at Dia', <u>C Magazine</u>, Spring

Spada, Sabina, 'Jessica Stockholder', <u>Tema Celeste</u>, no. 56, Spring

Van den Boogerd, Dominic, 'Ontbonden schilderkunst: Picturale ensceneringen van Rob Birza, Avery Preesman en Jessica Stockholder', <u>Metropolis M</u>, April

Iannacci, Anthony, 'Jessica Stockholder im Dia Center for the Arts', <u>Kunst Bulletin</u>, April

Pagel, David, 'Having and Using...', <u>Los Angeles Times</u>, 25 April

Castle, Frederick Ted, 'A Day at Chelsea's Dia Center for the Arts', <u>Review</u>, May

Molesworth, Helen, 'Jessica Stockholder at Dia Art Foundation', <u>Frieze</u>, no. 28, May

Frank, Peter, 'Art Picks of the Week: Jessica Stockholder, Joyce Lightbody', <u>L. A. Weekly</u>, 3–9 May

Mumford, Steve, 'Art and Objecthood Redux: Jessica Stockholder at Dia', <u>Review</u>, June

Wachtmeister, Marika, 'Konst P Grüansen Till Kaos', <u>Femina</u>, June

Knight, Christopher, 'Jessica Stockholder at Tom Solomon's Garage', <u>Art Issues</u>, September–October

Halley, Peter, 'Icy Silence', <u>Tema Celeste</u>, no. 58, Autumn

Wilson, Malin, 'Coming to Our Senses', <u>Art Issues</u>, November–December

Tomlinson, Jessica, 'Target Art Opening Invited Participation', <u>Portland Press Herald</u>, 7 November

Van de Walle, Mark, '1996: Best & Worst of the Year. Exhibitions: Party Flavor', <u>Artforum</u>, December

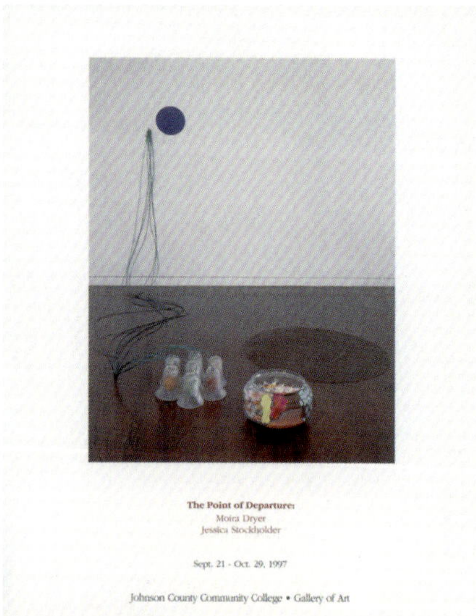

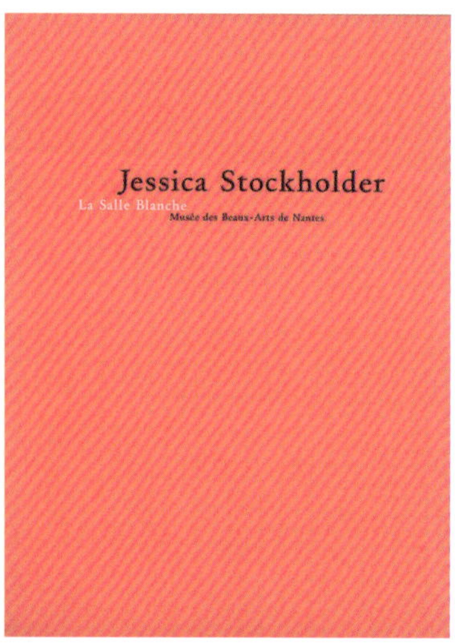

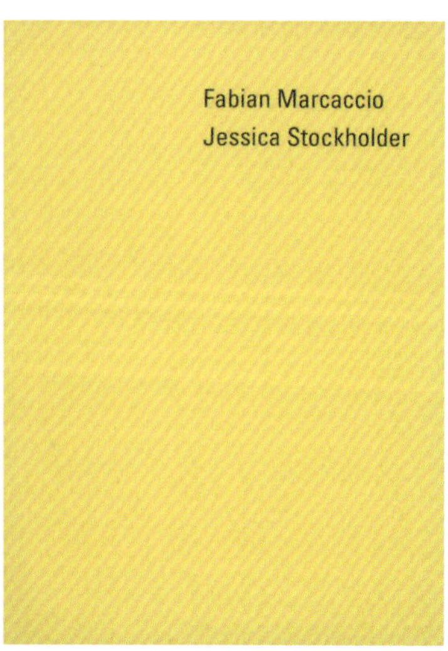

SELECTED EXHIBITIONS AND PROJECTS
1997–98

1997
JAY GORNEY MODERN ART, New York (solo)

CONTEMPORARY FINE ARTS, Berlin (solo)

DEUTSCHER AKADEMISCHER AUSTAUSCHDIENST (DAAD), Berlin (solo)

'The Point of Departure: Moira Dryer & Jessica Stockholder', GALLERY OF ART AT JOHNSON COUNTY COMMUNITY COLLEGE, Overland Park, Kansas (solo)

'Jessica Stockholder: 200 Drawings', OTIS COLLEGE OF ART & DESIGN, Los Angeles (solo)

'Slab of Skinned Water, Cubed Chicken & White Sauce', KUNSTNERNES HUS, Oslo (solo)

47th VENICE BIENNALE (group)

4th LYON BIENNALE (group)

'Heart, Mind, Body, Soul: American Art in the 1990s', WHITNEY MUSEUM OF AMERICAN ART, New York (group)

'New York: Divergent Models', NASSAUISCHEN KUNSTVEREIN, Wiesbaden, Germany (group)

'Colorflex', APEX ART, New York (group)

'Across Lines' ROSENBERG GALLERY at HOFSTRA UNIVERSITY, Hempstead, New York (group)

1998
'Nit Picking Trumpets of Iced Blue Vagueries', MUSÉE DES BEAUX-ARTS DE NANTES, France (solo)

'Torque, Jelly Role, and Goose', MUSÉE PICASSO D'ANTIBES, France (solo)

'Coupling', WHITE CUBE, London (solo)

'Turning Paper', BETSY SENIOR GALLERY, New York (solo)

'Landscape Linoleum', OPENLUCHTMUSEUM VOOR BEELDHOUWKUNST MIDDELHEIM, Antwerp (solo)

'Fabian Marcaccio & Jessica Stockholder', SAMMLUNG GOETZ, Munich, and WORKS ON PAPER, Los Angeles (solo)

'Turning Paper', GALERIE NATHALIE OBADIA, Paris (solo)

CATRIONA JEFFRIES GALLERY, Vancouver (solo)

'The Prophecy of Pop', CONTEMPORARY ARTS CENTER, New Orleans (group)

'Coming Off the Wall', SUSQUEHANNA ART MUSEUM, Harrisburg, Pennsylvania (group)

SELECTED ARTICLES AND INTERVIEWS
1997–98

1997
Birnbaum, Daniel, 'Painting: The Extended Field', Artforum, February

Wiensowski, Ingeborg, 'Kunst: Jessica Stockholder', Spiegel Extra, May

Arning, Bill, 'Jessica Stockholder', Time Out New York, 1–8 May

Tietenberg, Annette, 'Wenn Jessica Stockholder Kombiniert', Frankfurter Allgemeine Zeitung, 10 May

'Stockholder bei D.A.A.D. und Contemporary Fine Arts', Die Tageszeitung, 17 May

Panzera, Mauro, 'Spotlight: Jessica Stockholder', Flash Art, no. 199, Summer

Bouglé, Frédéric, 'Le tableau mis en scène ou l'illusion du tableau', Zéro deux, October

Thorson, Alice, 'Coping with the Cutting Edge: Stockholder show is razor-sharp', The Kansas City Star, 5 October

Wilson, William, 'Sketches Whet Appetite for Stockholder's Final Product', Los Angeles Times, 7 October

Harbo, John, 'Kunstnerisk dugnad i Oslo', Aftenposten, 24 October

Storr, Robert', 'Just Exquisite? The Art of Richard Tuttle', Artforum, November

Rubinstein, Raphael, 'Abstraction Out of Bounds', Art in America, November

Hedberg, Hans, 'Stockholder kommunicerar med världen', Svenska Dagbladet, 8 November

1998
Foucher, Eliane, 'Jessica Stockholder', Nantes Poche, January

Tigoe, Yasmine, 'Une installation de Jessica Stockholder', Ouest, 13 January

Régnier, Philippe, 'Stockholder, l'après Calder', Le Journal des Arts, 16 January

Lindgaard, Jade, 'Objets trouvés là', Les Inrockuptibles, 21–27 January

'L'art jubilatoire et coloré de Jessica Stockholder', Nice Matin, 23 January

Lebovici, Élisabeth, 'Ouverture sur la mer à Antibes'; Hervé Gauville, 'Stockholder vue en double exposition', Libération, 27 January

'Jessica Stockholder', Le Monde, 27 January

Ernoult-Gandouet, Marielle, 'Stockholder ou le chaos', L'Oeil, February

Arkhipoff, Elisabeth, 'Artiste du Mois: Stockholder', Beaux-Arts, March

'Jessica Stockholder', Art Press, March

'Jessica Stockholder', Cahiers de la peinture, March

Restoff, Jörg, 'Seherlebnis: St. Gallen: Jessica Stockholder', Kunstzeitung, March

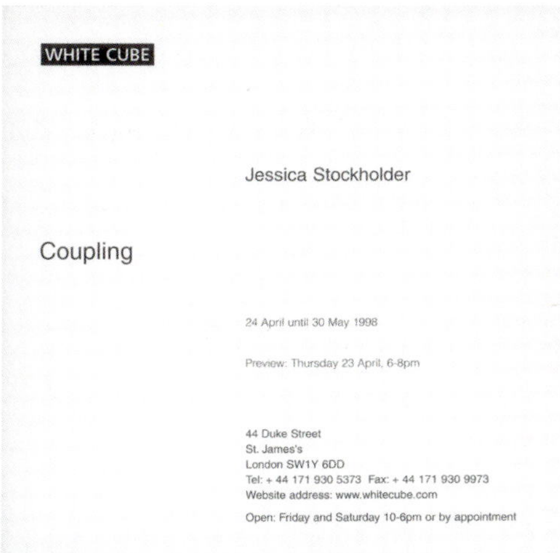

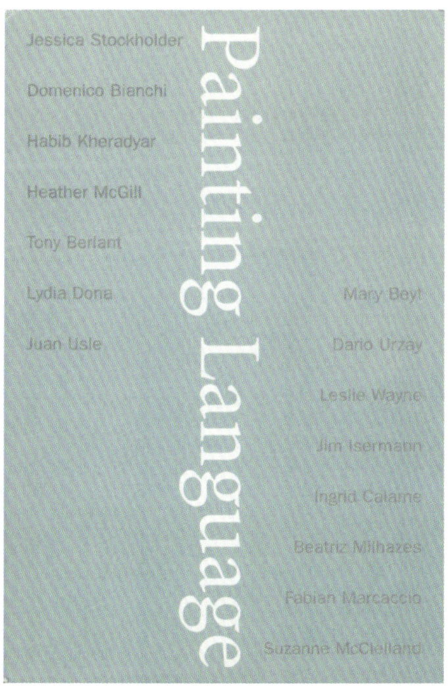

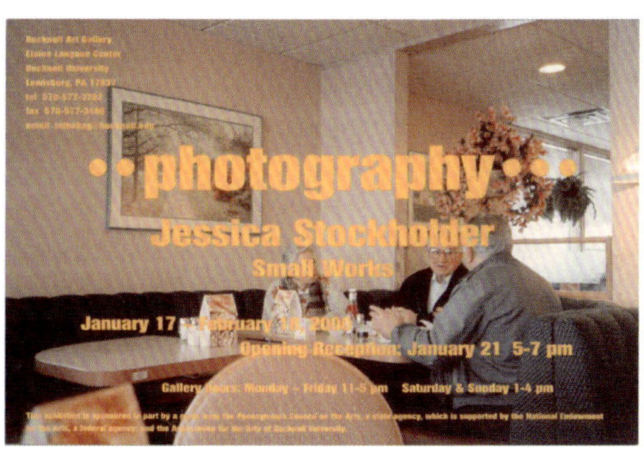

SELECTED EXHIBITIONS AND PROJECTS
1998–2000

1998 (cont.)
'I Love New York: Crossover der aktuellen Kunst',
MUSEUM LUDWIG, Cologne (group)

'Auf der Spur: Kunst der 90er Jahre im Spiegel von Schweizer Sammlungen',
KUNSTHALLE ZÜRICH (group)

'Young Americans 2',
SAATCHI GALLERY, London (group)

'Interpreting',
THE ROTUNDA GALLERY, New York (group)

'Chromaform: Color In',
SANTA BARBARA CONTEMPORARY ARTS FORUM, toured to NEW MEXICO STATE UNIVERSITY ART GALLERY, Las Cruces; UNIVERSITY OF TEXAS ART GALLERY, San Antonio (group)

'Painting Language',
LA LOUVER GALLERY, Los Angeles (group)

'Now and Later',
YALE UNIVERSITY ART GALLERY, New Haven (group)

'Pop/Abstraction',
MUSEUM OF AMERICAN ART at PENNSYLVANIA ACADEMY OF THE FINE ARTS, Philadelphia (group)

'Alternative Measures ',
CASTLE GALLERY at COLLEGE OF NEW ROCHELLE, New York (group)

'Le Consortium Dijon Collection',
CENTRE POMPIDOU, Paris (group)

1999
'With Wanton Heed and Giddy Cunning, Heding Red and That's Not Funny',
CENTER FOR VISUAL ARTS, Cardiff (solo)

GALERIE ROLF RICKE, Cologne (solo)

'First Cousin Once Removed or Cinema of Brushing Skin',
THE POWER PLANT, Toronto (solo)

'Geez Louise!: Art After Louise Nevelson',
EDUCATIONAL ALLIANCE GALLERY, New York (group)

'Think Twice: International Sculpture Show',
GALERIA OMR, Mexico City (group)

'Drawing in the Present',
PARSON SCHOOL OF DESIGN, New York (group)

'Special Offer: Eine Ausstellung des Kölner Galeristen Rolf Ricke',
KASSELER KUNSTVEREIN, Kassel, Germany (group)

Appointed Director of the Sculpture Department at the Yale School of Art, New Haven

2000
'Jessica Stockholder: Photography',
BUCKNELL UNIVERSITY ART GALLERY, Lewisburg, Pennsylvania (solo)

'Vortex in the Play of Theater with Real Passion (for Kay Stockholder)',
KUNSTMUSEUM ST. GALLEN, Switzerland (solo)

SELECTED ARTICLES AND INTERVIEWS
1998–2000

1998 (cont.)
Budney, Jean, 'Jessica Stockholder', Flash Art, no. 187, March–April

Zimmer, William, 'Show of Work Resembling Items at Hand', The New York Times, 15 March

'Jessica Stockholder', Critique d'Art, Spring

Hirsch, Faye, 'Working Proof: Turning Paper', On Paper, May–June

Packer, William, 'Not so Sweet Nothings from America', Financial Times, 2–3 May

Kent, Sarah, 'Wrappers' Delight: Young Americans Flex their Grunge Muscle', Time Out London, 6–13 May

Jobey, Liz, 'Young Americans', The New Statesman, 8 May

KeFeaver, William, 'Jumble Fever', The Observer, 17 May

Cotter, Holland, 'Humble County', The New York Times, 10 July

Roelandt, Els, 'Jessica Stockholder in Middelheim', De Financieel-Economische Tijd, 14–15 August

Pagel, David, 'Abstract Views', Los Angeles Times, 28 August

Demeester, Ann, 'Douches, matrassen en tapijten in een nieuwe context', De Morgen, 5 September

Vanbelleghem, Kurt, 'Jessica Stockholder', The Bulletin, 8 October

Ostrow, Saul, 'Piecing the Pieces Together Again: Phenomenal Objects, Pictorial Events', Sculpture: Contemporary Form and Theory, no. 55

1999
Milroy, Sarah, 'Jessica Stockholder's Material World', The Globe and Mail Visual Arts, 2 January

Feaver, William, 'The Century's 25 Most Influential Artists', ARTnews, May

Baker, Kenneth, 'Rauschenberg Coup at SFMoMA', San Francisco Chronicle, 8 May

Whyte, Murray, 'In an Era Obsessed with Meaning, a Pure Abstraction', National Post, 25 June

Solomon, Deborah, 'Domesticity is Bliss: Jessica Stockholder's deeply cultured installation art offers a zany, profound view of history as decor', Time, 12 July

2000
Anderson, Cecilia, 'Artists for Hire: Houses X Artists', NU, May

Eakin, Hugh, 'Dia's New Direction', ARTnews, June

Restorff, Jorg, 'Prinzip Collage', Kunstzeitung, August

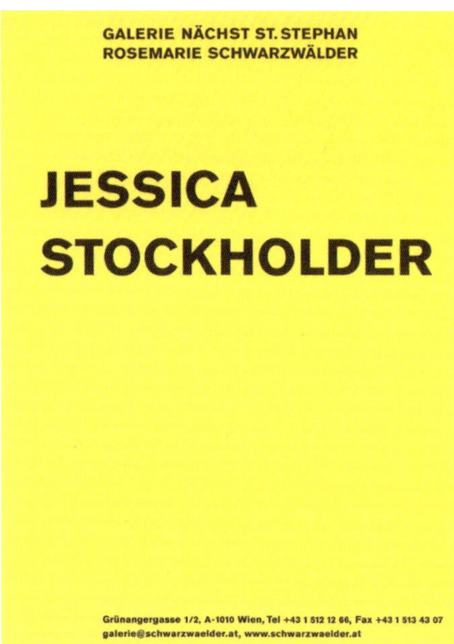

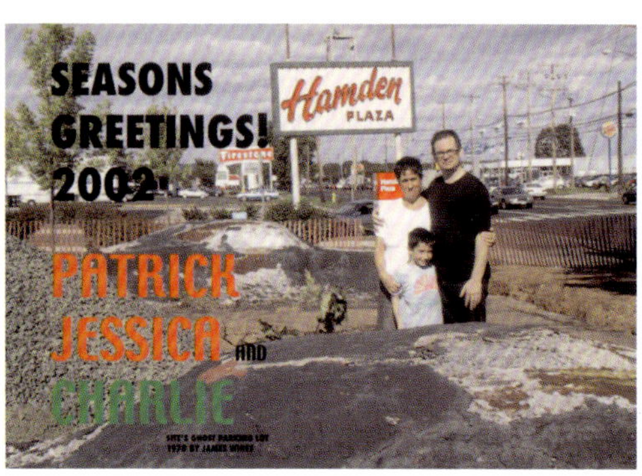

SELECTED EXHIBITIONS AND PROJECTS
2000–02

SELECTED ARTICLES AND INTERVIEWS
2000–02

2000 (cont.)

'In the Beginning was Merz: From Kurt Schwitters to the Present Day',
SPRENGEL MUSEUM, Hannover, toured to HAUS DER KUNST, Munich (group)

'Skulptur 2000',
KUNSTHALLE WILHELMSHAVEN, Germany (group)

'Beyond the Press: Innovations in Print',
HAND WORKSHOP ART CENTER, Richmond, Virginia (group)

'Spilled Edge/Soft Corner',
BLACKWOOD GALLERY at UNIVERSITY OF TORONTO AT MISSISSAUGA, Ontario (group)

2000 (cont.)

Glanz, Alexandra, 'Das Sommergeschwitter', Hannoversche Allgemeine Zeitung, 4 August

Glanz, Alexandra, 'Die Dinge der Welt', Hannoversche Allgemeine Zeitung, 19–20 August

Stockmann, Jochen, 'Müll war sein Motiv', Focus, 21 August

Müller, Dorothee, 'Kurt Schwitters: Kein Fall fur den Abfall', Süddeutsche Zeitung, 28 August

Bosetti, Petra, 'Auf die Besucher wird geschlossen', Art, September

Möckinghoff, Heidi, 'Mit Pop-Vater in die Abfallkunst', Münster Zeitung, 12 September

Lütgens, Annelie, 'Schnittemenge Schwitters', Der Tagesspiegel, 17–18 October

Berg, Roland, 'Die Dienstleister', Der Tagesspiegel, 2 December

2001

GALERIE NATHALIE OBADIA, Paris (solo)

GORNEY BRAVIN + LEE, New York (solo)

GALERIE NÄCHST ST. STEPHAN ROSEMARIE SCHWARZWÄLDER, Vienna (solo)

'Beau Monde: Toward a Redeemed Cosmopolitanism',
SITE SANTA FE, New Mexico (group)

'On Collecting: Pictures, Patents, Monkeys and More...',
JOHN MICHAEL KOHLER ARTS CENTER, Sheboygan, Wisconsin, toured to SOUTH BEND REGIONAL MUSEUM, Indiana; INSTITUTE OF CONTEMPORARY ART, Philadelphia; WESTERN WASHINGTON UNIVERSITY, Bellingham; AKRON ART MUSEUM, Ohio; FULLER MUSEUM OF ART, Brockton, Massachusetts; PITTSBURGH CENTER FOR THE ARTS (group)

'Objective Color',
YALE UNIVERSITY ART GALLERY, New Haven (group)

'American Art from Sammlung Goetz',
RUDOLFINUM, Prague (group)

2001

Ryan, David, 'Jessica Stockholder: The Theater of the Inferred', Contemporary, no. 32

Levin, Kim, 'Voice Choices: Jessica Stockholder', The Village Voice, 27 February

'Working Proof: Jessica Stockholder', Art on Paper, March–April

Cotter, Holland, 'Review: Jessica Stockholder', The New York Times, 2 March

'Galleries Downtown: Jessica Stockholder', The New Yorker, 12 March

Chambers, Christopher, 'Jessica Stockholder at Gorney Bravin + Lee', Flash Art, no. 118, May–June

Pollack, Barbara, 'Reviews: Jessica Stockholder at Gorney Bravin + Lee', ARTnews, Summer

Smith, Roberta, 'Quick as A Shutter, Group Shows Shatter Conventional Wisdom', The New York Times, 6 July

Rush, Michael, 'In Santa Fe, Searching for the Meaning of Beauty', The New York Times, 8 July

Schjeldahl, Peter, 'Desert Songs: A Maverick Biennial in Santa Fe', The New Yorker, 13 August

D'Souza, Aruna, 'Reviews: Jessica Stockholder at Gorney Bravin + Lee', Art in America, October

Mitchell, Charles Dee, 'Making the Case for Pleasure', Art in America, November

2002

GALLERIA RAFFAELLA CORTESE, Milan (solo)

'Quiet Stops Rattling Thin Air',
BALTIC ART CENTER, Visby, Sweden (solo)

'Art Downtown: New Photography',
WALL STREET RISING, New York (group)

'Beyond the Pale: Material Possibilities',
NEUBERGER MUSEUM OF ART, Purchase, New York (group)

2002

Beatrice, Luca, 'Stockholder: alla ricerca della casualità', Arte, February

Moratto, Rossella, 'Le Costruzioni di Jessica Stockholder', Art & Job Magazine, 27 February

Perra, Daniele, 'Jessica Stockholder at Galleria Raffaella Cortese', Tema Celeste, no. 90, March–April

Cotter, Holland, 'Review: Jessica Stockholder', The New York Times, 2 March

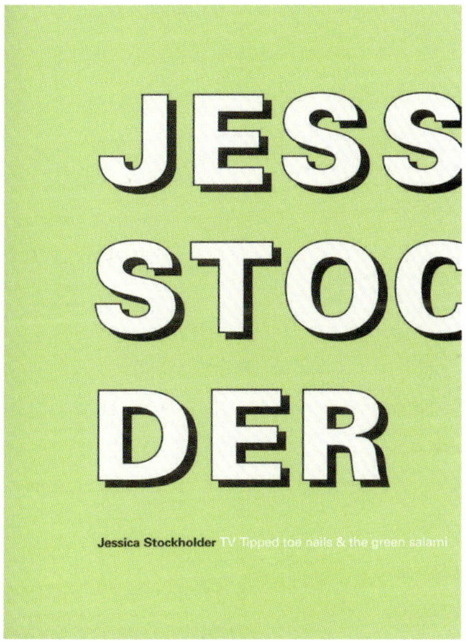

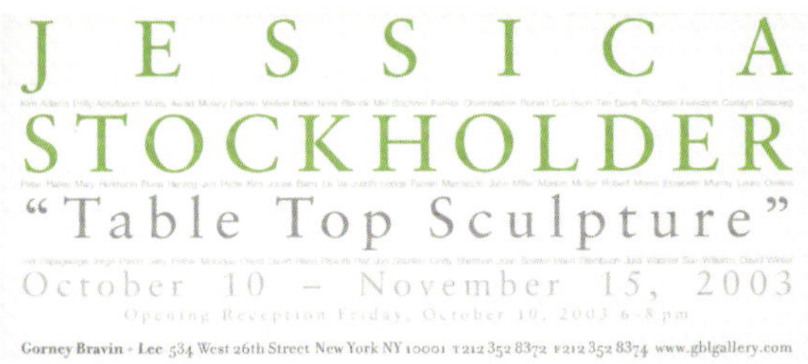

SELECTED EXHIBITIONS AND PROJECTS
2002–04

2002 (cont.)
'Under Pressure: Prints from Two Palms Press',
UNIVERSITY OF MASSACHUSETTS GALLERY, Amherst (group)

'SiteLines: Art on Main',
ADDISON GALLERY OF AMERICAN ART at PHILLIPS ACADEMY, Andover, Massachusetts (group)

'Trespassing: Houses x Artists',
PALM SPRINGS DESERT MUSEUM, California, toured to BLAFFER GALLERY, Houston; UNIVERSITY OF SOUTH FLORIDA CONTEMPORARY ART MUSEUM, Tampa; MAK CENTER FOR ART AND ART HISTORY, Los Angeles; BELLEVUE ART MUSEUM, Washington (group)

2003
STIFTUNG WILHELM LEHMBRUCK MUSEUM, Duisburg, Germany (solo)

MAK CENTER FOR ART AND ART HISTORY, Los Angeles (group)

UNIVERSITY OF SOUTH FLORIDA CONTEMPORARY ART MUSEUM, Tampa (solo)

BLAFFER GALLERY, Houston (solo)

PALM SPRINGS DESERT MUSEUM, California (solo)

'On The Spending Money Tenderly',
KUNSTSAMMLUNG NORDRHEIN-WESTFALEN, Düsseldorf (solo)

'Jessica Stockholder',
GALERIE ROLF RICKE, Cologne (solo)

'Jessica Stockholder: Prints',
CHELSEA ART MUSEUM, New York (solo)

'Jessica Stockholder: TV Tipped Toe Nail & the Green Salami',
CAPC MUSÉE D'ART CONTEMPORAIN DE BORDEAUX (solo)

'Table Top Sculpture',
GORNEY BRAVIN + LEE, New York (solo)

'Under Pressure: Prints from Two Palms Press',
THE COOPER UNION SCHOOL OF ART, New York (group)

2004
SABLE-CASTELLI GALLERY, Toronto (solo)

'Sam Ran Over Sand or Sand Ran Over Sam',
RICE UNIVERSITY ART GALLERY, Houston (solo)

'Jessica Stockholder: Kissing the Wall – Works 1988–2003',
WEATHERSPOON ART GALLERY at UNIVERSITY OF HOUSTON (solo)

'Peintures Migrantes'
ÉCOLE SUPERIEURE DES BEAUX ARTS DU MANS, Lille (group)

'Flower Power',
PALAIS RAMEAU, Lille (group)

'Transformer',
KUNSTVEREIN LUDWIGSBURG, Germany (group)

'179th Annual: An Invitational Exhibition of Contemporary American Art',
NATIONAL ACADEMY MUSEUM, New York (group)

WHITNEY BIENNIAL OF AMERICAN ART, New York (group)

SELECTED ARTICLES AND INTERVIEWS
2002–04

2002 (cont.)
Pollack, Barbara, 'Jessica Stockholder at Gorney Bravin + Lee', ARTnews, Summer

Strati, Maria Cristina, 'Stockholder at Galleria Raffaella Cortese', Arte & Critica, no. 30–31

Leinz, Gottlieb, 'Jessica Stockholder: Jenseits der Malerei, Deiburg'; Pia Müller-Tamm, 'Jessica Stockholder: On the Spending Money Tenderly, Eine Installation in K20 Kunstsammlung Nordrhein/Westfalen', Vernissage, Winter

2003
'The 1980s: Part Two', Artforum, April

MacMahon, Carrie, 'Studio Visits', Art on Paper, April

Yablonsky, Linda, 'Even the Kitchen Sink', ARTnews, May

Roug, Louise, 'Home as Art, and Vice Versa', Los Angeles Times, 15 May

Tumlir, Jan, 'Trespassing: Houses X Artists', Frieze, no. 76, Summer

Dannatt, Adrian, 'Contemporary Commercial Galleries: Jessica Stockholder's Table Top Sculpture', The Art Newspaper, no. 140, October

Yablonsky, Linda, 'Art Reviews: Jessica Stockholder', Time Out New York, 23–30 October

Smith, Roberta, 'Review: Jessica Stockholder', The New York Times, 31 October

'Reviews: Jessica Stockholder', The New Yorker, 3 November

Cohen, David, 'Arts & Letters: Gallery-Going', The New York Sun, 5 November

Levin, Kim, 'When a "Tender Collision" becomes an Artist's "Situation",' The Village Voice, 5–11 November

2004
Verdier, Evence, 'Jessica Stockholder', Art Press, February

Princethal, Nancy, 'Jessica Stockholder at Gorney Bravin + Lee', Art in America, March

Johnson, Ken, 'The 179th Annual', The New York Times, 14 May

Cheetham, Mark, 'Visual Arts: Jessica Stockholder', Border Crossings, no. 91

Kwon, Miwon, 'Promiscuity of Space: Some Thoughts on Jessica Stockholder's Scenographic Compositions', Grey Room, no. 18 Winter

SELECTED EXHIBITIONS AND PROJECTS
2005–07

2005
'Skolem, Choc de blocs & chiffres au vent',
INSTITUT DES HAUTES ETUDES SCIENTIFIQUES, Bures-sur-Yvette, France (solo)

PALAZZO MASSARI, Ferrara, Italy (solo)

'Rawhide Harangue of Aching Indices as Told by Light',
MUSEUM OF FINE ARTS, Boston (solo)

'Sculpture and Prints',
GALLERIA CIVICA D'ARTE MODERNA, Turin (solo)

KUNSTHALLEN BRANDTS KLAEDEFABRIK, Odense, Denmark (solo)

'Four Gummed-Up Bits of a Crepe Sole Balled Up Together with the Grimy Dirt on the Sidewalk and Stuck Dangling, but Firm, to the Bottom of the Shoe that Hangs on the Toe of the Foot under the Diving Board',
MARIO DIACONO GALLERY, Boston (solo)

'Material Matters',
CORNELL UNIVERSITY JOHNSON MUSEUM OF ART, Ithaca, New York (group)

2006
'Space Between',
GALERIE NATHALIE OBADIA, Paris (solo)

'Of Standing Float Roots in Thin Air',
P.S.1 CONTEMPORARY ART CENTER, New York (solo)

'Jessica Stockholder',
GALLERIA RAFFAELLA CORTESE, Milan (solo)

'Jessica Stockholder',
MITCHELL-INNES & NASH, New York (solo)

MEGA VOTT, Multiple venues, Hafnarfjörður, Iceland (group)

'Paint',
VANCOUVER ART GALLERY (group)

'Transitional Objects: Contemporary Still Life',
NEUBERGER MUSEUM OF ART, New York (group)

'Il diavolo del focolare',
PALAZZO DELLA TRIENNALE, Milan (group)

2007
GALERIE THOMAS SCHULTE, Berlin (solo)

'Hanging',
GALERIE NÄCHST ST. STEPHAN , Vienna (solo)

1301PE, Los Angeles (solo)

'Lust for Life: The Ricke Collection',
KUNSTMUSEUM LIECHTENSTEIN, Vaduz (group)

'Like Color in Pictures',
ASPEN ART MUSEUM, Colorado (group)

'Connecticut Contemporary',
WADSWORTH ATHENEUM MUSEUM OF ART, Hartford (group)

'Paragons: New Abstraction',
ALBRIGHT-KNOX GALLERY, Buffalo, New York, toured to DORIS McCARTHY GALLERY at UNIVERSITY OF TORONTO, Scarborough (group)

SELECTED ARTICLES AND INTERVIEWS
2005–07

2005
Schwabsky, Barry, 'Jessica Stockholder', MAP, no. 5, January

Colpitt, Frances, 'Jessica Stockholder: A Merging of Mediums', Art in America, February

Halperen, Max, 'Jessica Stockholder at the Weatherspoon Art Museum', Art Papers, July–August

Scanlan, Joe, and Jessica Stockholder, 'Art and Labor: Some Introductory Ideas', Art Journal, Winter

Bucci McCoy, Mary, 'Jessica Stockholder: Rawhide Harangue of Aching Indices as Told by Light', Art New England, December–January

2006
Schambelan, Elizabeth, '1000 Words: Jessica Stockholder', Artforum, January

Johnson, Ken, 'Constrasts in Sculpture, in Theme and in Medium', The New York Times, February 21

Lowenstein, Kate, 'Jessica Stockholder: Of Standing Float Roots in Thin Air', Time Out New York,

Kraft, Jessica, 'New York: Jessica Stockholder at Mitchell-Innes & Nash', Contemporary, no. 88

Schwendener, Martha, 'Jessica Stockholder at Mitchell-Innes & Nash', The New York Times, 29 September

Schjeldahl, Peter, 'Art Stockpiled: Jessica Stockholder', The New Yorker, 2 October

Buhmann Mitchell, Stephanie, 'ArtSeen: Jessica Stockholder', The Brooklyn Rail, November

Nadelman, Cynthia, 'Jessica Stockholder', ARTnews, December

2007
Vogel, Carol, 'A Passage for the Master of Heavy Metal', The New York Times, 25 July

Cotter, Holland, 'Quirks and Attitude to Burn', The New York Times, 8 June

Banai, Nuit, 'In Defense of Ardor', Time Out New York, 21–27 June

Schwendener, Martha, 'Galleries: Chelsea, 'In Defense of Ardor'', The New Yorker, 25 June

McElheny, Josiah, 'Readymade Resistance: Art and the Forms of Industrial Production', Artforum, 2 October

Taft, Catherine, 'Jessica Stockholder: Sex in the Office', Art Review, December

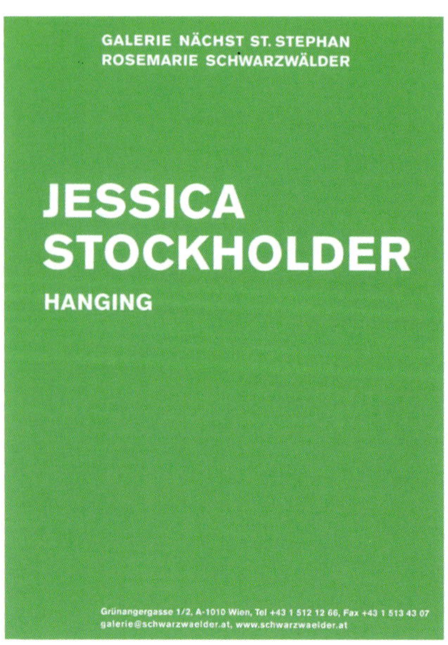

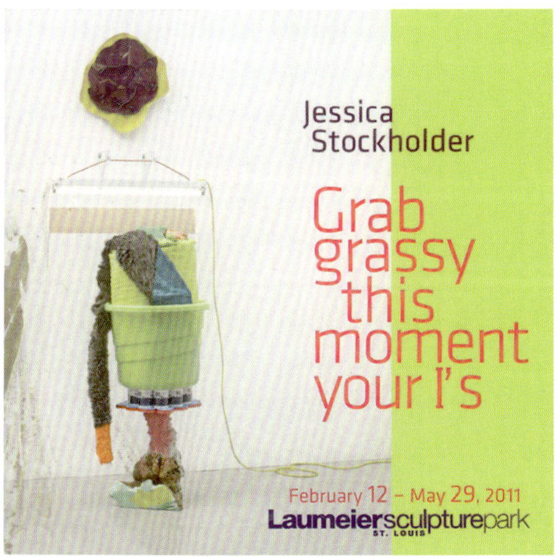

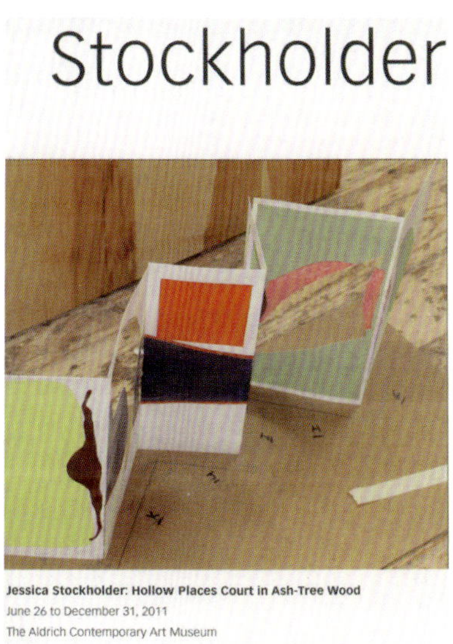

SELECTED EXHIBITIONS AND PROJECTS
2007–11

SELECTED ARTICLES AND INTERVIEWS
2007–11

2007 (cont.)
Receives the Lucelia Artist Award at the Smithsonian American Art Museum, Washington, D.C.

Receives the Award for the Best Installation or Single Work of Art in a Boston Museum at the New England Chapter of the Association Internationale des Critiques d'Art (AICA)

2008
'Jessica Stockholder: Lumps Bumps & Windy Figures Too',
GALERIE ART & ESSAI, Rennes, France (solo)

'Color in 3D',
WESTPORT ART CENTER, Westport, Connecticut (group)

'Not Printed on Paper',
CENTER FOR CONTEMPORARY PRINTMAKING, Norwalk, Connecticut (group)

2008
Genocchio, Benjamin, 'Drawings Set Apart in a World of Lines', The New York Times, 9 March

Elliott, Patrick, 'Sculpture Today', The Burlington Magazine, no. 1266, September

---

2009
'Coating',
GALERIE NATHALIE OBADIA, Paris (solo)

ROBISCHON GALLERY, Denver (solo)

'Swiss Cheese Field'
SENIOR AND SHOPMAKER GALLERY, New York (solo)

'Flooded Chambers Maid',
MADISON SQUARE PARK, New York (solo)

'Sailcloth Tears',
MITCHELL-INNES & NASH, New York (solo)

'Embrace!',
DENVER ART MUSEUM (group)

'Painting and its Environs',
PALACIO DE SESTÁGO, Zaragoza, Spain (group)

'Transitions: Painting at the (Other) End of Art',
COLLEZIONE MARAMOTTI, Reggio Emilia, Italy (group)

2009
Johnson, Paddy, 'Two Great Shows in Chelsea', The L Magazine, 22 May

Mataraga, Francesco, 'Expanded Painting in the Work of Helio Oiticica and Jessica Stockholder', The International Journal of the Arts in Society, no. 4

Kino, Carol, 'Go Ahead, Play With (And On) the Art ',The New York Times, Arts and Leisure, 14 June

Katz, Vincent, 'Image/Word', Tate Etc., no. 16, Summer

Kerr, Merrily, 'Jessica Stockholder at Mitchell-Innes & Nash and Madison Square Park, New York', Flash Art, no. 268, October

Sears, Rebecca, 'Postal Projects: Wish You Were Here', Art on Paper, September–October

---

2010
'Air Padded Table Haunches, and...',
CARRERAS MUGICA, Bilbao (solo)

BARBARA EDWARDS CONTEMPORARY, Toronto (solo)

'Peer Out to See',
MUSEO DE ARTE REINA SOFÍA, Madrid (solo)

'Prints and Sculpture',
USDAN GALLERY, Bennington College, Vermont (solo)

'The Jewel Thief' (selected by Jessica Stockholder),
TANG TEACHING MUSEUM at SKIDMORE COLLEGE, Saratoga Springs, New York (group)

Receives an Honorary Doctor of Fine Arts degree from the Emily Carr College of Art, Vancouver

2010
Smith, Roberta, 'Self-Fulfilling Prophecies', The New York Times, 16 April

Marshall, Tara, 'Jessica Stockholder', Border Crossings, December

---

2011
'Grab grassy this moment your I's,'
LAUMEIER SCULPTURE PARK, St. Louis (solo)

'Hollow Places Court in Ash-Tree Wood',
ALDRICH CONTEMPORARY ART MUSEUM, Ridgefield, Connecticut (solo)

2011
Princenthal, Nancy, 'The Jewel Thief', Art in America, January

Cotter, Holland, 'New Sparkle for an Abstract Ensemble', The New York Times, 6 January

Baran, Jessica, 'Jessica Stockholder', Art Papers, May–June

SELECTED EXHIBITIONS AND PROJECTS
2011–13

SELECTED ARTICLES AND INTERVIEWS
2011–13

2011 (cont.)
'Schnitte im Raum: Skulpturale Collagen',
MUSEUM MORSBROICH, Leverkusen, Germany (group)

'Circa 1986: The 1980s from Six Important New York Art Collections',
HUDSON VALLEY CENTER FOR CONTEMPORARY ART, Peekskill, New York (group)

Appointed Raymond W. & Martha Hilpert Gruner Distinguished Service Professor and Chair of the Department of Visual Arts at the University of Chicago

2011
Scanlan, Joe, 'Free Time: An Introduction', Art Journal, Summer

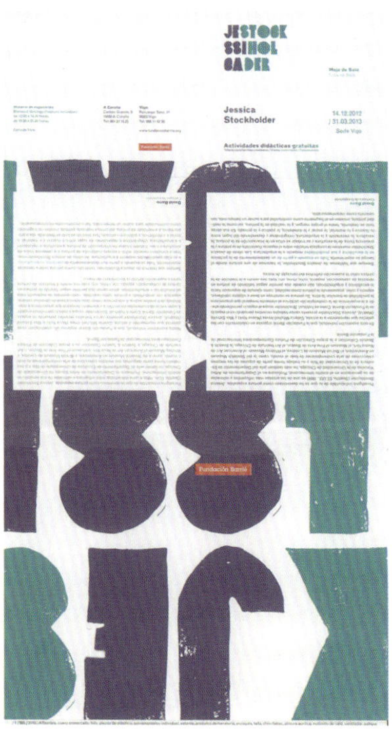

2012
'Jessica Stockholder',
MAX ESTRELLA GALLERY, Madrid (solo)

'Wide Eyes Smeared Here Dear',
MUSÉE D'ART MODERNE, Saint-Etienne, France (solo)

'Hollow Places Court in Ash-Tree Wood',
FONDS RÉGIONAL D'ART CONTEMPORAIN (FRAC) DES PAYS DE LA LOIRE, Nantes (solo)

FUNDACIÓN BARRIÉ DE LA MAZA, Vigo, Spain (solo)

'Greetings from Los Angeles',
STARKWHITE, Auckland (group)

'Everyday Things: Contemporary works from the Collection',
RHODE ISLAND SCHOOL OF DESIGN MUSEUM OF ART (group)

2012
Milioulis, Chiara, 'Color the Loop', Today's Chicago Woman, May

Krc, Matt, 'New Public Art Piece Largest, Trippiest in Chicago's History', AV Club Chicago, 25 May

Coleman, Victoria, 'Color Jam Aims to Brighten Up the Loop', NBC Chicago, 30 May

Esposito, Stefano, 'Splash of Color for Loop', Chicago Sun Times, 30 May

Weinberg, Lauren, 'Jessica Stockholder Completes Color Jam in the Loop', Time Out Chicago, 31 May–7 June

Metcalf, John, 'Chicago's Downtown Goes All 1980s with Immense, Fluorescent Art', The Atlantic, 1 June

Caro, Mark, '"Color Jam" Lights up the Loop', Chicago Tribune, 4 June

Baird, Daniel, 'Stand Up Performance', Canada Art Magazine, Winter

Blair, Gwenda, 'At a Busy Intersection, Going Beyond Red', The New York Times, 6 June

Ryan, Paul, 'Potential Images', Art Papers, September–October

Foumberg, Jason, 'Chicago: Burn the Pedestal', Sculpture, October

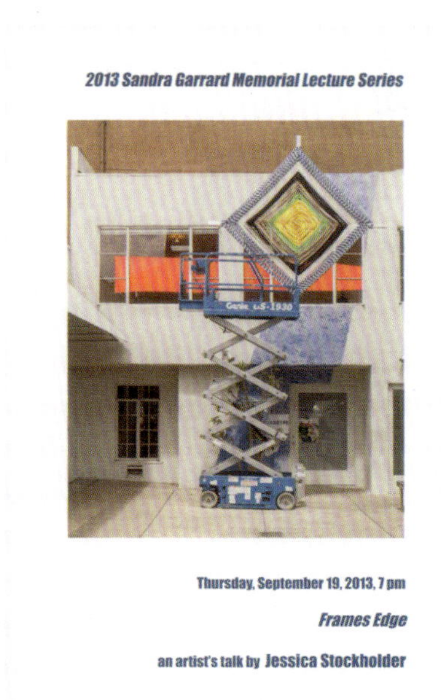

2013
'Lift',
1301PE, Los Angeles (solo)

BARBARA EDWARDS CONTEMPORARY, Calgary (solo)

'Painting in the Expanded Field',
MARY S. BYRD GALLERY OF ART at GEORGIA REGENTS UNIVERSITY (group)

'Impulse and Connoisseurship: Selections from the Forde Collection',
WESTMONT RIDLEY-TREE MUSEUM OF ART, California (group)

'Paint Things',
DECORDOVA MUSEUM AND SCULPTURE PARK, Lincoln, Massachusetts (group)

'On the Art of Abstraction',
ROSE ART MUSEUM at BRANDEIS UNIVERSITY, Waltham, Massachusetts (group)

Receives an Honorary Doctor of Fine Arts degree from Columbia College in Chicago

2013
Ambler, Charlie, 'Tired Thinking: Sculpting in the City of Angels', Modern Painters, July–August

Enright, Robert, 'Taking Notice: An Interview with Jessica Stockholder', Border Crossings, no. 127

Picard, Caroline, 'Jessica Stockholder'; George Melrod, 'Editor's Note', Art Ltd, September–October

Kogod, Lauren, and Michael Osman, 'Girding the Grid: Abstraction and Figuration at Ground Zero', Grey Room, no. 13, Autumn

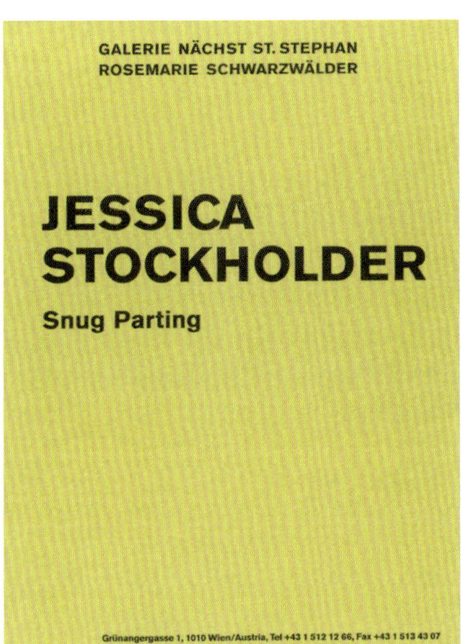

SELECTED EXHIBITIONS AND PROJECTS
2014–17

SELECTED ARTICLES AND INTERVIEWS
2014–17

2014

'Glimpse: Jessica Stockholder and Karla Black',
GALLERIA RAFFAELLA CORTESE, Milan (solo)

'Erstwhile & Notwithstanding',
CONTEMPORARY ART AND DESIGN (CARD), Pianello Val Tidone, Italy (solo)

GARY LICHTENSTEIN EDITIONS AT MANA CONTEMPORARY, Jersey City (solo)

'Ladies First! Künstlerinnen aus der Sammlung Schaufler',
SCHAUWERK SINDELFINGEN, Germany (group)

'OK Great Thanks This is so Ridiculous',
DCKT, New York, and ACME Gallery, Los Angeles (group)

'In Future: A Potential',
MAGAZIN 4 BREGENZER KUNSTVEREIN, Bregenz, Austria (group)

'Painting Made Different',
SALINA ART CENTER, Kansas (group)

'2014 Invitational Exhibition of Visual Arts',
ACADEMY OF ARTS & LETTERS, New York (group)

2014

Scoccimarro, Antonio, 'Jessica Stockholder and Karla Black', Mousse, no. 44, Summer

---

2015

'Palpable Glyphic Rapture',
GALERIE NATHALIE OBADIA, Paris (solo)

'Door Hinges',
KAVI GUPTA GALLERY, Chicago (solo)

'Rose's Inclination',
SMART MUSEUM, Chicago (solo)

'SITE 20 Years/20 Shows SPRING',
SITE SANTA FE, New Mexico (group)

2015

MacMillan, Kyle, 'Jessica Stockholder', Art in America, November

Waxman, Lori, 'Bathtub or Mattress, It's All Art to Jessica Stockholder', Chicago Tribune, 28 October

Cristello, Stephanie, 'Jessica Stockholder: Door Hinges', Art Review, December

---

2016

'Jessica Stockholder: Works on Paper from the 1980s',
CLEOPATRA'S, New York (solo)

'Snag Parting',
GALERIE NÄCHST ST. STEPHAN ROSEMARIE SCHWARZWÄLDER (solo)

'Jessica Stockholder: The Guests All Crowded into the Dining Room',
MITCHELL-INNES & NASH, New York (solo)

'Contemporary Highlights from the Collection',
THE NATIONAL ACADEMY MUSEUM, New York (group)

'Revolution in the Making: Abstract Sculpture by Women 1994–2016',
HAUSER & WIRTH, Los Angeles (group)

'Assisted' (selected by Jessica Stockholder),
KAVI GUPTA GALLERY, Chicago (group)

2016

Stockholder, Jessica, 'Degrees of Separation', Tate Etc., no. 36, Spring

Laster, Paul, 'Interview with artist Jessica Stockholder', The New York Times, 30 August

Mendelsohn, Meredith, '8 Can't Miss Fall Art Shows in New York', 1stDibs, September

Wilk, Deborah, 'Mutable Feast', Art + Auction, November

Frankel, David, 'Jessica Stockholder', Artforum, December

2017

'The Idea in a Sign',
CENTRO DE ARTE ALCOBENDAS, Madrid (group)

SCULPTURE MILWAUKEE (group)

'99 Cents or Less',
MUSEUM OF CONTEMPORARY ART DETROIT (group)

2017

Linnert, Nicolas, 'Jessica Stockholder', Artforum, February

Tarasoff, Sabrina, 'Staging Affect', Mousse, no. 57, February–March

BIBLIOGRAPHY

MONOGRAPHS AND ARTIST'S BOOKS

Stockholder, Jessica, and Mark Holmes, Jessica Stockholder: It's not Over till the Fat Lady Sings, Contemporary Art Gallery, Vancouver, 1987

Westreich, Thea, Peter Nadin and Jessica Stockholder, Warren Adelson Gallery, New York, 1991

Ottmann, Klaus, Jessica Stockholder: The Broken Mirror, Wesleyan University, Middletown, Connecticut, 1991

Miller, John, Chris Dercon and Suzanne Ghez, Jessica Stockholder, Witte de With, Rotterdam, and University of Chicago Press, 1992

Meschede, Friedrich, Eva Schmidt and Antje von Graevenitz, Jessica Stockholder, Westfälischer Kunstverein, Münster, and Kunsthalle Zürich, 1992

Avgikos, Jan, and Olivier Mosset, Jessica Stockholder: Edge of Hot House Glass, Musée d'Art Contemporain de Nîmes, France, 1993

Richardson, Trevor, Jessica Stockholder: Pink Lady, University of North Carolina Press, Greenboro, 1993

Swartz, Jeffrey, Jessica Stockholder: Sweet for Three Oranges, Fundació la Caixa, Barcelona, 1995

Cooke, Lynne, Ann Lauterbach, Michael Govan and Lynne Tillman, Jessica Stockholder: Your Skin In This Weather Bourne Eye-Threads & Swollen Perfume, Dia Center for the Arts, New York, 1995

Tillman, Lynne, Barry Schwabsky and Lynne Cooke, Jessica Stockholder, Phaidon, London, 1995

Gross, Jennifer, Jessica Stockholder: 200 Drawings, Maine College of Art Press, Portland, Maine, 1996

Ostrow, Saul, The Point of Departure: Moira Dryer, Jessica Stockholder, Johnson County Community Collge Press, Overland, Kansas, 1996

Iannacci, Anthony, Jessica Stockholder, Studio La Città, Verona, 1996

Thorkildsen, Åsmund, Ståle Vold and Jamie Parslow, Jessica Stockholder: Slab of Skinned Water, Cubed Chicken & White Sauce, Kunstnernes Hus, Oslo, 1997

Jessica Stockholder: 9 Installations, Edition du Centre d'Art imprimé, Paris, 1997

Hilty, Greg, and Menno Meewis, Jessica Stockholder: Landscape Linoleum, Openluchtmuseum voor Beeldhouwkunst, Middelheim, Antwerp, 1997

Criqui, Jean-Pierre, and Thierry Davila, Jessica Stockholder, Musée Picasso, Antibes, France, 1997

Pélenc, Arielle, Jessica Stockholder: Nit Picking Trumpets of Iced Blue Vagueries, Musée des Beaux-Arts de Nantes, France, 1998

Meschede, Friedrich, Christiane Meyer-Stoll, David Ryan, Eva Schmidt and Gregory Volk, Jessica Stockholder/Fabian Marcaccio, Kunstverlag Ingvild Goetz, Hamburg, 1998

Higgie, Jennifer, Alex Farquharson and Sally Medlyn, Jessica Stockholder: With Wanton Heed and Giddy Cunning Hedging Red and That's Not Funny, Centre for Visual Arts, Cardiff, 1999

Mayer, Marc, Jessica Stockholder: First Cousin Once Removed or Cinema of Brushing Skin, Power Plant, Toronto, 2000

Bitterli, Konrad, Gerhard Mack and Roland Wäspe, Jessica Stockholder: Vortex in the Play of Theater with Real Passion, Verlag Fur Moderne Kunst, Nürnberg, and Kunstmuseum, St. Gallen, 2001

Brockhaus, Christoph, John Yau, Armin Zweite, Gottlieb Leinz and Pia Muller-Tamm, Jessica Stockholder, Kunstsammlung Nordrhein-Westfalen, Düsseldorf, and Stiftung Wilhelm Lehmbruck Museum, Duisburg, 2002

Kwon, Miwon, Maurice Fréchuret and Jean-Pierre Criqui, Jessica Stockholder: TV Tipped Toe Nails & the Green Salami, CAPC Musé d'Art Contemporain de Bourdeaux, 2003

Carruthers, Elspeth, and Miwon Kwon, Jessica Stockholder: Kissing The Wall, Works 1988–2003, Marquand Books, Seattle, and Weatherspoon Art Museum, Greenboro, North Carolina 2003

Davenport, Kimberly, Jessica Stockholder: Sam Ran Over Sand or Sand Ran Over Sam, Rice Gallery, Houston, 2004

Burkard, Lene, and Birte Westing, Jessica Stockholder: White Light Laid Frozen & Bright Longing and Soggy up the Hill, Kunsthallen Brandts, Odense, Denmark, 2005

Gauthier, Michel, and Giorgio Verzotti, Jessica Stockholder, Gallleria Civica d'Arte Moderna and Hopefulmonster, Turin, 2005

Weinberg, Adam, Jessica Stockholder: Flooded Chambers Maid, Madison Square Park Conservancy, New York, 2009

Stockholder, Jessica, Coating, Les Compagnons du Sagittaire, Rennes, France, 2009

Jessica Stockholder: ABC Taste: The Perfect Guest, Captures Éditions, Valence, France, 2010

Knode, Marilu, Jessica Stockholder Crab Grassy This Moment Your I'S, Laumeier Sculpture Park, Saint Louis, 2011

Madoff, Steven Henry, and Pascal Pique, Jessica Stockholder: Wide Eyes Smeared Here Dear, Musée d'Art Moderne Saint-Etienne, France, 2012

Barro, David, and Álvaro Negro, Jessica Stockholder, Fundación Barrié, Vigo, Spain, 2013

Berry, Ian, and Jessica Stockholder, The Jewel Thief, Skidmore College, Saratoga Springs, New York, 2014

Stockholder, Jessica, and Katherine Harvath, Door Hinges & Assisted, Kavi Gupta Gallery, Chicago, 2015

Tillman, Lynne, Barry Schwabsky, Lynne Cooke, Germano Celant and Michele Robecchi (ed.), Jessica Stockholder, Phaidon, London, 2017

EXHIBITION CATALOGUES AND SURVEYS

Aeneas, Bastian, and Harriet Häußler, From an Artist's Perspective: 13 Questions, 51 Interviews, Bielefeld, Germany, 2011

Altshuler, Bruce (ed.), et al, Biennials and Beyond: Exhibitions that Made Art History, Phaidon, London, 2013

Armstrong, Richard, John G. Hanhardt, Richard Marshall and Lisa Phillips, Withney Biennial 1991, Whitney Museum, New York, 1991

Ball, Philip, Mark Clarke and Carinna Parraman, Colour in the Making: From Old Wisdom to New Brilliance, Black Dog Publishing, London, 2013

Barnes, Rachel, Martin Coomer, Carl Freedman, Tony Godfrey, Simon Grant, Melissa Larner, Simon Morley and Gilda Williams, The 20th Art Century Art Book, Phaidon, London, 1996

Batchelor, David (ed.), Documents of Contemporary Art: Colour, Whitechapel Art Gallery, London, 2006

Baudson, Michel, Peter Lodermeyer and Kitty Zijlmans, Personal Structures: Time, Space, Existence, DuMont, Cologne, 2010

Bergmann, Barbara, Ladies First! Künstlerinnen aus der Sammlung Schaufler, Schaufler Foundation, Sindelfingen, Germany 2015

Blackman, Susan (ed.), Mattress Factory: Installation and Performance 1982–89, Mattress Factory, Pittsburgh, 1989

Brooks, Adams, and Lisa Liebmann, Young Americans 2, Saatchi Gallery, London, 1998

Buchloh, Benjamin H. D., Jean-Francois Chevrier, Chris Dercon, Ludger Gerdes and Hermann Pitz, Witte De With Cahier #1, Richter and Witte de With, Rotterdam, 1999

Canning, Susan, Alternative Measures, College of New Rochelle, New Rochelle, New York, 1998

Celant, Germano (ed.), Past, Present, Future, Venice Biennale and Electa Mondadori, Milan, 1997

Chamberlain, Patrick, Eric de Bruy, Benjamin H.D. Buchloh, Jean-François Chevrier, Chris Dercon, Victor Erice, Rosalind Krauss, Hermann Pitz, Camiel van Winkel, et al., As Long as It Lasts, Witte de With, Rotterdam, 1993

Colliard, Eric, René Denizot, Xavier Douroux, Franck Gautherot, Bernard Marcadé, Le Choix Des Femmes, Le Presses du Réel, Dijon, France, 1990

Collins, Judith, Sculpture Today, Phaidon, London, 2007

Collins, Tricia, and Richard Milazzo, Outside America: Going into the 1990s, Fay Gold Gallery, Atlanta, 1991

Collins, Tricia, and Richard Milazzo (eds), 99: Turn of the Century, Collins & Milazzo,New York, 1993

Le Consortium Collectionne, Château d'Oiron, France, 1991

Cooke, Lynne (ed.), Robert Lehman Lectures On Contemporary Art No. 2, Dia Art Foundation, New York, 2004

Decter, Joshua, Transgressions in the White Cube: Territorial Mappings, Bennington College Press, Vermont, 1992

Decter, Joshua, Don't Look Now, Thread Waxing space, New York, 1990

Elgar, Dietmar, and Isabel Ewig, In the Beginning Was Merz: From Kurt Schwitters to the Present Day, Hatje Cantz, Ostfildern, Germany, 2000

Fillin-Yeh, Susan, The Technological Muse, Katonah Museum of Art, New York, 1990

Gaßner, Hubertus, L.D. Riehle and Stephanie Rosenthal, Trespassing: Houses X Artists, Hatje Cantz, Odtfildern, Germany, 2003

Heartney, Eleanor, Art & Today, Phaidon, London, 2008

Heinrich, Christoph, Embrace!, Denver Art Museum, 2009

Hickey, David, and Louis Grachos, Beau Monde: Toward a Redeemed Cosmopolitanism, SITE Santa Fe, New Mexico, 2001

Hixson, Kathryn, Awards in the Visual Arts 10, Southeastern Center for the Arts, Winston Salem, North Carolina, 1991

Hoffmann, George, Physicality: An Exhibition on Color Dimensionality in Painting, University of New York Press, 1991

Hoffmann, George, Color in Space: Pictorialism in Contemporary Sculpture, Brown University, Providence, Rhode Island, 1995

Hoffmann, Jens (ed.), 99 Cents or Less, Museum of Contemporary Art Detroit and Karma, New York, 2017

Hunter, Sam, and John Jacobus, Modern Art: Painting, Sculpture, Architecture, Henry N. Abrams, New York, 2000

King, Elaine, Jan Riley, Robert Schiffler and Marcia Tucker, Mettlesome and Meddlesome: Selections from the Collection of Robert J. Schiffler, Contemporary Arts Center, Cincinnati, 1993

Kob, Edelbert, Rainer Fuchs and Gabriel Hubmann, Painting: Process and Expansion, Walther König, Cologne, 2011

Krivitsky, Kristy, Clyde McGeary and Jonathan VanDyke, Coming Off the Wall, Susquehanna Art Museum, Harrisburg, Pennsylvania, 1999

Inselmann, Andrea, Material Matters, Cornell University Press, Ithaca, New York, 2005

Laclotte, Michelet, and Jean-Pierre Cuzin, Dictionnaire de la peinture, Larousse, Paris, 2003

Larson, Kay, Selections from the Artists File, Artists Space, New York, 1986

Lieberman, Rhonda, Catherine Liu and Lawrence Rickels, Stendhal Syndrome: The Cure, Andrea Rosen Gallery, New York, 1990

Liu, Catherine, Plastic Fantastic Lover (Object A), Blum Helman Warehouse, New York, 1991

Ludwig, Georg, New York: Positionen Aktueller Malerei, Studiogalerie Schloβ Morsbroich, Leverkusen, Germany, 1995

Material, Mitchell-Innes & Nash, New York, 2007

Meyer-Stoll, Christiane (ed.), Rolf Ricke Collection: Ein Zeitdokument/A Document Of The Times, Kunstmuseum Liechtenstein, Vaduz, and Hatje Cantz, Ostfildern, 2016

Milroy, Sarah, Ian Dejardin, Matthew Teitelbaum, Corrine Hunt, James Hart, Jessica Stockholder, Robert Storrie, Gerta Moray, Charles Hill, Marianne Nicolson, Ian Thom, Peter Doig, Karen Duffek and Kathryn Bridge, From the Forest to the Sea: Emily Carr in British Columbia, Goose Lane Editions, Fredericton, New Brunswick, 2015

Moos, David, Art in Embassies Program: Contemporary American Art, United States Embassy, Prague, United States Department of State, Washington, D.C., 2004

Muniz, Vik, Possible Things: A Drawing Show, Barmadu Gallery Publishing, New York, 1994

Myers, Terry (ed.), Documents of Contemporary Art: Painting, Whitechapel Art Gallery, London, 2011

Neuman, David, and Bo Nilsson, Painting: The Extended Field, Magasin 3 and Rooseum, Stockholm, 1996

Nickas, Bob, A Climate of Site, Barbara Farber Gallery, Amsterdam, 1989

Nickas, Bob, The Museum of Natural History, Barbara Farber Gallery, Amsterdam, 1991

Olch Richards, Judith (ed.), Inside the Studio: Two Decades of Talks with Artists in New York, Independent Curators International, New York, 2004

Pagel, David, and Terrie Sultan, Painting Outside Painting: 44th Exhibition of Contemporary American Painting, The Corcoran Gallery of Art, Washington, D.C., 1994

Phillips, Lisa, Berkshire Art Association 1989 Exhibition of Painting and Sculpture, Berkshire Museum, Pittsfield, Massachusetts, 1989

Poetter, Jochen, Karsten Schmidt and Jan Avgikos, I Love New York: Crossover der aktuellen Kunst, Museum Ludwig and Dumont, Cologne, 1998

Porgeirsdóttir, Sigríður, Mega Vott, Syning, Hafnarfjörður and Reykjavik, 2006

Riemschneider, Burkhard, and Uta Grosenick (eds), Art at the Turn of the Millennium, Taschen, Cologne, 1999

Ricke, Rolf, Elke Grützmacher, Bernhard Balkenhol and Silke Hartenstein, Special Offer, Kasseler Kunstverein, Kassel, Germany, 1999

Riese, Ute (ed.), Skulptur 2000: Stefan Kern, Andrea Ostermeyer, Manfred Pernice, Thomas Rentmeister, Jessica Stockholder, Vincent Tavenne, Kunsthalle Wilhelmshaven and Kerber, Bielefeld, Germany, 2000

Rodriguez Fominaya, Alvaro, Tony Godfrey, Anatxu Zabalbeascoa, Miroslaw Balka, Marjetica Potrć, Jessica Stockholder, Cristina Iglesiasand Maria José Balcells, Antoni Tapies: From Object to Sculpture 1964–2009, Guggenheim Bilbao, 2013

Rosenberg, Barry, The World as We Find It, Aldrich Museum of Contemporary Art, Ridgefield, Connecticut, 1991

Rosenberg, Barry, Simply Made in America, Aldrich Museum of Contemporary Art, Ridgefield, Connecticut, 1993

Rubenstein, Raphael, Colorflex, Apex Art, New York, 1997

Ryan, David, Talking Painting: Dialogues with Twelve Contemporary Abstract Artists, Routledge, Oxon, England, 2002

Saltz, Jerry, American Artists of the 1980s, Museo d'Arte di Trento e Rovereto, Italy, 1991

Schaffner, Ingrid, and Werner Muensterberger, On Collecting: Pictures, Patents, Monkeys and More..., Independent Curators Incorporated, New York, 2001

Schimmel, Paul, Jenni Sorkin, Elizabeth Smith and Anne Wagner, Revolution in the Making: Abstract Sculpture by Women 1947–2016, Hauser & Wirth & Schimmel, Los Angeles, 2016

Schwabsky, Barry, The Perpetual Guest: Art in the Unfinished Present, Verso Books, New York, 2016

Searle, Adrian, and Linda Schofield, Unbound: Possibilities in Painting, Hayward Gallery, London, 1994

Settembrini, Luigi, Claudia Gian Ferrari, Francesca Sorace, Consuelo Ciscar Casabán, Rosario Messina and Davide Rampello, Il diavolo del focolare, Triennale and Electa Mondadori, Milan, 2006

Smolik, Noemi, American Art: From the Goetz Collection, Munich, Galerie Rudolfinum, Prague, 2002

Sollins, Susan, and Marybeth Sollins, Art in the Twenty-first Century, Harry N. Abrams, New York, 2005

Stockholder, Jessica, and Charles Wilson, Edward Weston: Nudes, Aperture, New York, 2005

Szeemann, Harald (ed.), Thierry Raspail, Thierry Prat, Hannes Böhringer, Cecilia Liveriero Lavelli and Olivier Kaeppelin, The Other, Lyon Biennale and Les Presses du Réel, Dijon, 1997

Tapié, Alain, Franck Gautherot, Seung-Duk Kim, Xavier Douroux, Éric Troncy and Lio Lionni, Flower Power, Lille 2004 and Les Presses du Réel, Dijon, 2004

Till, Jeremy (ed.), Sarah Wigglesworth, Åsmund Thorkildsen et al, The Everyday and Architecture, John Wiley & Sons, Hoboken, New Jersey, 1998

Tillman, Lynne, This is Not It, Distributed Art Publishers, New York, 2002

Tillman, Lynne, Gilda Williams (ed.), et al., Press Play, Phaidon, London, 2005

Weibel, Peter, and Thomas Dreher, Pittura–Immedia: Malerei in den 90er Jahren, Neue Galerie am Landesmuseum Joanneum, Graz, Austria, 1995

Weinberg, Adam, Contingent Realms: Four Contemporary Sculptors, Whitney Museum of American Art, New York, 1990

Yau, John, The Passionate Spectator: Essays on Art and Poetry, University of Michigan Press, Ann Arbor, 2006

Zuckerman Jacobson, Heidi, Rhonda Lieberman and James Welling, Like Color in Pictures, Aspen Art Press, 2007

PUBLIC COLLECTIONS

ADDISON GALLERY OF AMERICAN ART, PHILLIPS ACADEMY, Andover, MA

ALBRIGHT-KNOX ART GALLERY, Buffalo

ART INSTITUTE OF CHICAGO

AUCKLAND ART GALLERY, New Zealand

BIRMINGHAM MUSEUM OF ART, Alabama

BRITISH MUSEUM, London

CAPC MUSÉE D'ART CONTEMPORAIN DE BORDEAUX

CENTRAAL MUSEUM, Utrecht, The Netherlands

CENTRE POMPIDOU, Paris

LE CONSORTIUM, Dijon

CORCORAN GALLERY OF ART, Washington, D.C.

FONDS RÉGIONAL D'ART CONTEMPORAIN (FRAC) LIMOUSIN, Limoges, France

FONDS RÉGIONAL D'ART CONTEMPORAIN (FRAC) PROVENCE-ALPES-CÔTE D'AZUR, Marseille

GALLERIA D'ARTE MODERNA, Turin

INDIANAPOLIS MUSEUM OF ART

KUNSTMUSEUM ST. GALLEN, Switzerland

LAUMEIER SCULPTURE PARK, Sunset Hills, Missouri

LEHMBRUCK MUSEUM, Duisburg, Germany

LOS ANGELES COUNTY MUSEUM OF ART

MUSÉE D'ART CONTEMPORAIN DE NÎMES, France

MUSÉE D'ART MODERNE, ST. ETIENNE, FRANCE

MUSÉE PICASSO D'ANTIBES, France

MUSEUM OF FINE ARTS, Boston

MUSEUM OF MODERN ART, New York

MUSEUM MODERNER KUNST STIFTUNG LUDWIG, Vienna

NATIONAL GALLERY OF AUSTRALIA, Canberra

NEUBERGER MUSEUM OF ART, Purchase, New York

OPENLUCHTMUSEUM VOOR BEELDHOUWKUNST MIDDELHEIM, Antwerp

ORANGE COUNTY MUSEUM OF ART, Newport Beach, California

SAN FRANCISCO MUSEUM OF MODERN ART

STAEDEL MUSEUM, Frankfurt

STEDELIJK MUSEUM, Amsterdam

ULRICH MUSEUM AT WICHITA STATE UNIVERSITY, Kansas

VANCOUVER ART GALLERY

WEATHERSPOON ART GALLERY AT THE UNIVERSITY OF NORTH CAROLINA, Greensboro

WESTFÄLISCHER KUNSTVEREIN, Münster, Germany

WESTMOND RIDLEY-TREE MUSEUM, Santa Barbara

WHITNEY MUSEUM OF AMERICAN ART, New York

YALE UNIVERSITY ART GALLERY, New Haven

ILLUSTRATED WORKS

COMPARATIVE IMAGES

PHAIDON PRESS LTD.
REGENT'S WHARF
ALL SAINTS STREET
LONDON N1 9PA

PHAIDON PRESS INC.
65 BLEECKER STREET
NEW YORK, NY 10014

PHAIDON.COM

First published 1995
Second edition, revised and expanded, 2018

ISBN:
978-0-7148-7207-0

A CIP catalogue record of this book is available from the British Library and the Library of Congress.

Commissioning Editor
Michele Robecchi

Production Controller
Sarah Kramer

Design
Melanie Mues, Mues Design, London

Printed in Hong Kong

PUBLISHER'S ACKNOWLEDGEMENTS

Special thanks to Josephine Nash, Isabelle Hogenkamp and Elizabeth DiSabatino at Mitchell-Innes & Natch, New York; Kavi Gupta and Jessica Campbell at Kavi Gupta Gallery, Chicago; Rosemarie Schwarzwälder and Elisabeth Madlener at Galerie Nächst St. Stephan Rosemarie Schwarzwälder, Vienna; Raffaella Cortese and Daniela Legotta at Galleria Raffaella Cortese, Milan; Brian Butler at 1301PE, Los Angeles; Nathalie Obadia and Camille Comas at Galerie Nathalie Obadia, Paris; Elisa Bottinelli, Laura Conconi and Marcella Ferrari at Studio Celant, Milan; Nanaho Kamei at the Noguchi Museum, New York; Tom Smith at Two Palms, New York; The Robert Rauschenberg Foundation, New York; The Hans Namuth Estate/Center for Creative Photography, Tucson; National Portrait Gallery, Washington, D.C.; Clyfford Still Museum, Denver; PACE Gallery, New York; Galerie Martin Janda, Vienna; Artists Rights Society (ARS), New York; Design and Artists Copyright Society (DACS), London; VAGA, New York; Carl Andre, Mowry Baden, Emma Barton, Bridget Finn, Catalina Imizcoz, Leonie Kellman, Melissa Larner, Robert Morris, Bob Nickas, Klaus Ottmann, Beatrix Ruf, Joe Scanlan, Frank Stella, George Trakas, Stephen Westfall.

Photographers: Philip Amdal, Rudolph Burkardt, Cathy Carver, Geoffrey Clements, Ken Cohen, Angela Cumberbirch, Colin De Land, Frédéric Delpech, Charles Erickson, Serge Gal, Paul Hester/Hester+Hardaway, Ken Heyman, Elisabeth Hogeman, Bertrand Huet/Tutti Image, Evan Jenkins, Tim Johnson, Jochen Littkemann, David Lubarsky, Peter McCallum, J. Mud, Jordi Nieva, Lorenzo Palmieri, Eric Pollitzer, Franz Schachinger, Jessica Stockholder, Alexander Troehler, Tom Van Eynde, Stephen White.

ARTIST'S ACKNOWLEDGEMENTS

I would like to thank Michele Robecchi for his invitation to reissue and expand this volume, and for shepherding it to publication; Iwona Blazwick for her original invitation to produce the book; and Lynne Cooke, Lynne Tillman, Barry Schwabsky and Germano Celant for their contributions.

I have great appreciation of the following galleries and their staff, all of whom have provided support over many years: Mitchell-Innes & Nash, New York; Kavi Gupta Gallery, Chicago; 1301PE, Los Angeles; Galerie Nächst St. Stephan Rosemarie Schwarzwälder, Vienna; Galerie Nathalie Obadia, Paris; Galleria Raffaella Cortese, Milan; American Fine Arts, Co., New York; and Jay Gorney.

I am also deeply appreciative for the support I have received from Yale University, New Haven, and The University of Chicago; and for the opportunity to learn from my colleagues in both institutions, including Joe Scanlan, Daphne Fitzpatrick, Laura Letinsky, William Pope.L, Jason Salavon, David Schutter, Matthew Jackson, Catherine Sullivan, Geof Oppenheimer and Theaster Gates.

For thirty years my husband Patrick Chamberlain has been my closest friend, an admired colleague, and offered constant support of my work. I continue to learn from my son Charles Chamberlain, and from Fred Stockholder, Kay Stockholder, Maia Stockholder, Peter Stockholder, Max Stockholder, Louise Mandell, Macy Awad, Elana Herzog, Elspeth Carruthers and many many others too numerous to mention here. None of us stands alone.

CONTEMPORARY ARTISTS:

Contemporary Artists is a series of authoritative and extensively illustrated studies of today's most important artists. Each title offers a comprehensive survey of an individual artist's work and a range of art writing contributed by an international spectrum of authors, all leading figures in their fields, from art history and criticism to philosophy, cultural theory and fiction. Each study provides incisive analysis and multiple perspectives on contemporary art and its inspiration. These are essential source books for everyone concerned with art today.

MARINA ABRAMOVIĆ KLAUS BIESENBACH, KRISTINE STILES, CHRISSIE ILES / VITO ACCONCI FRAZER WARD, MARK C. TAYLOR, JENNIFER BLOOMER / AI WEIWEI HANS ULRICH OBRIST, KAREN SMITH, BERNARD FIBICHER / DOUG AITKEN DANIEL BIRNBAUM, AMANDA SHARP, JÖRG HEISER / PAWEŁ ALTHAMER ADAM SZYMCZYK, ROMAN KURZMEYER, SUZANNE COTTER / FRANCIS ALŸS CUAUHTÉMOC MEDINA, RUSSELL FERGUSON, JEAN FISHER / UTA BARTH PAMELA M. LEE, MATTHEW HIGGS, JEREMY GILBERT-ROLFE / CHRISTIAN BOLTANSKI DIDIER SEMIN, TAMAR GARB, DONALD KUSPIT / MONICA BONVICINI ALEXANDER ALBERRO, JANET KRAYNAK, JULIANE REBENTISCH / LOUISE BOURGEOIS PAULO HERKENHOFF (WITH THYRZA GOODEVE), ROBERT STORR, ALLAN SCHWARTZMAN / MARK BRADFORD ANITA HILL, SEBASTIAN SMEE, CONNIE BUTLER / CAI GUO-QIANG DANA FRIIS-HANSEN, OCTAVIO ZAYA, TAKASHI SERIZAWA / MAURIZIO CATTELAN NANCY SPECTOR, FRANCESCO BONAMI, BARBARA VANDERLINDEN, MASSIMILIANO GIONI / VIJA CELMINS ROBERT GOBER, LANE RELYEA, BRIONY FER / NIGEL COOKE DARIAN LEADER, TONY GODFREY, MARIE DARRIEUSSECQ / RICHARD DEACON PIER LUIGI TAZZI, JON THOMPSON, PETER SCHJELDAHL, PENELOPE CURTIS / TACITA DEAN JEAN-CHRISTOPHE ROYOUX, MARINA WARNER, GERMAINE GREER / MARK DION LISA GRAZIOSE CORRIN, MIWON KWON, NORMAN BRYSON / PETER DOIG ADRIAN SEARLE, KITTY SCOTT, CATHERINE GRENIER / STAN DOUGLAS SCOTT WATSON, DIANA THATER, CAROL J. CLOVER / MARLENE DUMAS DOMINIC VAN DEN BOOGERD, BARBARA BLOOM, MARIUCCIA CASADIO, ILARIA BONACOSSA / JIMMIE DURHAM LAURA MULVEY, DIRK SNAUWAERT, MARK ALICE DURANT, KATE NESIN / OLAFUR ELIASSON MADELEINE GRYNSZTEJN, DANIEL BIRNBAUM, MICHAEL SPEAKS / PETER FISCHLI AND DAVID WEISS ROBERT FLECK, BEATE SÖNTGEN, ARTHUR C. DANTO / TOM FRIEDMAN DENNIS COOPER, BRUCE HAINLEY, ADRIAN SEARLE / THEASTER GATES CAROL BECKER, LISA YUN LEE, ACHIM BORCHARDT-HUME / ISA GENZKEN ALEX FARQUHARSON, DIEDRICH DIEDERICHSEN, SABINE BREITWIESER / ANTONY GORMLEY ERNST GOMBRICH, JOHN HUTCHINSON, LELA B. NJATIN, W. J. T. MITCHELL DAN GRAHAM BIRGIT PELZER, MARK FRANCIS, BEATRIZ COLOMINA / PAUL GRAHAM ANDREW WILSON, GILLIAN WEARING, CAROL SQUIERS / HANS HAACKE WALTER GRASSKAMP, MOLLY NESBIT, JON BIRD / MONA HATOUM GUY BRETT, MICHAEL ARCHER, CATHERINE DE ZEGHER, NANCY SPECTOR / THOMAS HIRSCHHORN BENJAMIN H. D. BUCHLOH, ALISON M. GINGERAS, CARLOS BASUALDO / JENNY HOLZER DAVID JOSELIT, JOAN SIMON, RENATA SALECL / RONI HORN LOUISE NERI, LYNNE COOKE, THIERRY DE DUVE / CHRIS JOHANSON CORRINA PEIPON, BOB NICKAS, JULIE DEAMER / ILYA KABAKOV BORIS GROYS, DAVID A. ROSS, IWONA BLAZWICK / ALEX KATZ ROBERT STORR, CARTER RATCLIFF, IWONA BLAZWICK, BARRY SCHWABSKY / ON KAWARA 'TRIBUTE', JONATHAN WATKINS, RENÉ DENIZOT / MIKE KELLEY ISABELLE GRAW, JOHN C. WELCHMAN, ANTHONY VIDLER / MARY KELLY MARGARET IVERSEN, DOUGLAS CRIMP, HOMI K. BHABHA / WILLIAM KENTRIDGE CAROLYN CHRISTOV-BAKARGIEV, DAN CAMERON, J. M. COETZEE / YAYOI KUSAMA AKIRA TATEHATA, LAURA HOPTMAN, UDO KULTERMANN, CHATERINE TAFT / CHRISTIAN MARCLAY JENNIFER GONZALEZ, KIM GORDON, MATTHEW HIGGS / KERRY JAMES MARSHALL CHARLES GAINES, GREG TATE, LAURENCE RASSEL / PAUL McCARTHY KRISTINE STILES, RALPH RUGOFF, MASSIMILIANO GIONI, ROBERT STORR / CILDO MEIRELES PAULO HERKENHOFF, GERARDO MOSQUERA, DAN CAMERON / LUCY ORTA ROBERTO PINTO, NICOLAS BOURRIAUD, MAIA DAMIANOVIC / TREVOR PAGLEN LAUREN CORNELL, JULIA BRYAN-WILSON, OMAR KHOLEIF / JORGE PARDO CHRISTINE VÉGH, LANE RELYEA, CHRIS KRAUS / RAYMOND PETTIBON DENNIS COOPER, ROBERT STORR, ULRICH LOOCK / RICHARD PRINCE ROSETTA BROOKS, JEFF RIAN, LUC SANTE / PIPILOTTI RIST HANS ULRICH OBRIST, PEGGY PHELAN, ELIZABETH BRONFEN / STERLING RUBY KATE FOWLE, FRANKLIN SIRMANS, JESSICA MORGAN ANRI SALA HANS ULRICH OBRIST, MARK GODFREY, LIAM GILLICK / DORIS SALCEDO NANCY PRINCENTHAL, CARLOS BASUALDO, ANDREAS HUYSSEN / WILHELM SASNAL ANDRZEJ PRZYWARA, DOMINIC EICHLER, JÖRG HEISER / THOMAS SCHÜTTE JULIAN HEYNEN, JAMES LINGWOOD, ANGELA VETTESE / STEPHEN SHORE MICHAEL FRIED, CHRISTY LANGE, JOEL STERNFELD / ROMAN SIGNER PAULA VAN DEN BOSCH, GERHARD MACK, JEREMY MILLAR / LORNA SIMPSON KELLIE JONES, THELMA GOLDEN, CHRISSIE ILES / NANCY SPERO JON BIRD, JO ANNA ISAAK, SYLVÈRE LOTRINGER / SIMON STARLING FRANCESCO MANACORDA, DIETER ROELSTRAETE, JANET HARBORD / FRANK STELLA ANDRIANNA CAMPBELL, KATE NESIN, LUCAS BLALOCK /JESSICA STOCKHOLDER BARRY SCHWABSKY, LYNNE TILLMAN, LYNNE COOKE, GERMANO CELANT / SARAH SZE OKWUI ENWEZOR, BENJAMIN H. D. BUCHLOH, LAURA HOPTMAN / WOLFGANG TILLMANS PETER HALLEY, JAN VERWOERT, MIDORI MATSUI, JOHANNA BURTON / LUC TUYMANS ULRICH LOOCK, JUAN VICENTE ALIAGA, NANCY SPECTOR, HANS RUDOLF REUST / JEFF WALL THIERRY DE DUVE, ARIELLE PÉLENC, BORIS GROYS, JEAN-FRANÇOIS CHEVRIER, MARK LEWIS / GILLIAN WEARING RUSSELL FERGUSON, DONNA DE SALVO, JOHN SLYCE LAWRENCE WEINER BENJAMIN H. D. BUCHLOH, ALEXANDER ALBERRO AND ALICE ZIMMERMAN, DAVID BATCHELOR / FRANZ WEST ROBERT FLECK, BICE CURIGER, NEAL BENEZRA / YIN XIUZHEN HOU HANRU, WU HUNG, STEPHANIE ROSENTHAL / ZHANG HUAN ROSELEE GOLDBERG, YILMAZ DZIEWOR, ROBERT STORR